MULTI-TIER APPROACHES TO THE RESOLUTION OF INTERNATIONAL DISPUTES

Multi-tier dispute resolution (MDR) entails an early attempt at mediation followed by arbitration or litigation if mediation is unsuccessful. Seemingly, everyone acknowledges MDR's attractiveness as a means of resolving disputes due to its combination of the flexibility and informality of mediation with the rigour and formality of arbitration or litigation. Yet, except in China and some Asian jurisdictions, MDR is not resorted to around the world and MDR clauses in commercial contracts remain relatively uncommon; why is that? This book responds to that question by (1) surveying global regulatory frameworks for MDR, (2) comparing MDR trends in Asia and the wider world, (3) identifying MDR's strengths and weaknesses and (4) prescribing ways to address MDR's challenges (the enforceability of MDR clauses, the difficulties arising when the same person acts as both mediator and decision-maker in the same dispute, and enforcement of mediated settlement agreements resulting from MDR).

ANSELMO REYES is an International Judge of the Singapore International Commercial Court. He was Professor of Legal Practice at the University of Hong Kong from 2012 to 2018 and is a visiting professor at Doshisha University in Kyoto. He was a judge of the Hong Kong High Court from 2003 to 2012.

WEIXIA GU is an Associate Professor at the University of Hong Kong Faculty of Law, a Co-Chair of the American Society of International Law (ASIL) Asia-Pacific Interest Group (2018–21) and a governing council member of the China Society of Private International Law, where she specialises in arbitration, dispute resolution and private international law.

MULTI-TIER APPROACHES TO THE RESOLUTION OF INTERNATIONAL DISPUTES

A Global and Comparative Study

Edited by

ANSELMO REYES
Doshisha University
Singapore International Commercial Court

WEIXIA GU
The University of Hong Kong

CAMBRIDGE
UNIVERSITY PRESS

University Printing House, Cambridge CB2 8BS, United Kingdom

One Liberty Plaza, 20th Floor, New York, NY 10006, USA

477 Williamstown Road, Port Melbourne, VIC 3207, Australia

314–321, 3rd Floor, Plot 3, Splendor Forum, Jasola District Centre,
New Delhi – 110025, India

103 Penang Road, #05-06/07, Visioncrest Commercial, Singapore 238467

Cambridge University Press is part of the University of Cambridge.

It furthers the University's mission by disseminating knowledge in the pursuit of education, learning, and research at the highest international levels of excellence.

www.cambridge.org
Information on this title: www.cambridge.org/9781108490603
DOI: 10.1017/9781108854306

© Cambridge University Press 2022

This publication is in copyright. Subject to statutory exception and to the provisions of relevant collective licensing agreements, no reproduction of any part may take place without the written permission of Cambridge University Press.

First published 2022

A catalogue record for this publication is available from the British Library.

ISBN 978-1-108-49060-3 Hardback
ISBN 978-1-108-79605-7 Paperback

Cambridge University Press has no responsibility for the persistence or accuracy of URLs for external or third-party internet websites referred to in this publication and does not guarantee that any content on such websites is, or will remain, accurate or appropriate.

CONTENTS

List of Figures page viii
List of Tables ix
List of Contributors x
Acknowledgements xiii
Table of Cases xv
Table of Statutes and Instruments xxiii
Table of Rules, Codes and Guidelines xli
List of Abbreviations xlvi

PART I **A Global Overview of Multi-tier Dispute Resolution: Main Themes** 1

1 Mapping and Assessing the Rise of Multi-tiered Approaches to the Resolution of International Disputes across the Globe: An Introduction 3
WEIXIA GU

2 A Snapshot of National Legislation on Same Neutral Med-arb and Arb-med around the Globe 25
HIRO N ARAGAKI

PART II **Multi-tier Dispute Resolution in Asia** 67

A **General Trends** 67

3 Combinations of Mediation and Arbitration: The Case of China 69
WEIXIA GU

4 The Resolution of International Commercial and Financial Disputes: Hybrid Dispute Resolution in Hong Kong 92
JULIEN CHAISSE AND CARRIE SHU SHANG

v

CONTENTS

5 Multi-tier Dispute Resolution: Present Situation and Future Developments in Taiwan 110
KUAN-LING SHEN

6 Perspectives and Challenges of Multi-tier Dispute Resolution in Japan 142
YUKO NISHITANI

7 Might There Be a Future for Multi-tiered Dispute Resolution in Korea? Challenges and Prospects 161
JOONGI KIM

8 Combinations of Mediation and Arbitration: The Singapore Perspective 182
MAN YIP

B **Specific Cases** 203

9 HKIAC's Experience of the Use of Multi-tier Dispute Resolution Clauses 205
SARAH GRIMMER

10 The Use of Conciliation and Litigation by the Hong Kong Equal Opportunities Commission (EOC) 232
ANSELMO REYES AND WILSON LUI

PART III **Multi-tier Dispute Resolution in the Wider World** 269

11 Multi-tier Commercial Dispute Resolution Processes in the United States 271
THOMAS J STIPANOWICH

12 Multi-tiered Dispute Resolution Clauses: An English Perspective 294
EVA LEIN

13 Multi-tier and Mixed-Method Dispute Resolution in Canada: From Obscurity to Prominence in a Single Generation 315
JOSHUA KARTON AND MICHELLE DE HAAS

14 Multi-tier Dispute Resolution in Australia: A Tale of 'Escalating' Acceptance 343
RICHARD GARNETT

15 Praised, but Not Practised: The EU's Paradoxes of Hybrid
   Dispute Resolution   363
   JULIEN CHAISSE

16 Multi-tier Dispute Resolution in Russia   384
   ALEXANDER MOLOTNIKOV

17 Multi-tier Dispute Resolution under OHADA
   Law   397
   JUSTIN MONSENEPWO

   PART IV **Conclusion**   415

18 Making Multi-tier Dispute Resolution Work   417
   ANSELMO REYES

   Bibliography   443
   Index   476

FIGURES

2.1 Regulation of same neutral med-arb   *page* 37
2.2 Regulation of same neutral arb-med   43
2.3 Regulation of same neutral hybrid processes by region and legal tradition   51
2.4 Timeline of permissive same neutral arb-med legislative enactments (1969–2004)   55
2.5 Regulation of same neutral hybrid processes by income level   60
5.1 In-court resolution of labour disputes   126
7.1 Civil litigation in leading civil law countries (2014–18) (cases per 100 persons)   164
7.2 Civil litigation in leading civil law countries (2014–18) (cases per GDP USD million)   166

TABLES

2.1 Countries excluded from the database   *page* 35
4.1 FDRC cases (2012–18)   106
5.1 Number of cases resolved through mediation: Chinese Arbitration Association (CAA) versus district courts   111
5.2 Number of different types of cases handled by the CAA   112
7.1 Civil litigation in leading civil law countries (2014–18) (cases per 100 persons)   163
7.2 Civil litigation in leading civil law countries (2014–18) (cases per GDP USD million)   165
7.3 Number of attorneys in Korea (1990–2018)   168
7.4 KCAB arbitration cases (2010–19)   169
7.5 KCAB and SBA court-annexed mediation cases (2010–19)   171
7.6 KCAB 'private' mediation cases (2010–19)   173
7.7 Korea's ADR survey   177
15.1 Enforcement of the Mediation Directive by countries   374

CONTRIBUTORS

HIRO N ARAGAKI FCIArb is an international arbitrator and mediator at JAMS, a tenured professor of law at Loyola Law School (Los Angeles) and a professorial research associate at SOAS School of Law (London).

JULIEN CHAISSE is a professor of law at City University of Hong Kong and serves as an advisory board member of the Academy of International Dispute Resolution & Professional Negotiation (AIDRN).

MICHELLE DE HAAS is a final-year JD student at the Queen's University Faculty of Law. In 2021–22, she will serve as a law clerk to justices of the British Columbia Court of Appeal.

RICHARD GARNETT is a professor of private international law at the University of Melbourne and a consultant to Corrs Chambers Westgarth. He regularly advises on cross-border litigation and arbitration matters and has written extensively in these fields, with his work cited by leading courts.

SARAH GRIMMER is Secretary-General of the Hong Kong International Arbitration Centre.

WEIXIA GU is an associate professor of law at the University of Hong Kong, a co-chair of the American Society of International Law (ASIL) Asia-Pacific Interest Group and a governing council member of the China Society of Private International Law, where she specialises in arbitration, dispute resolution and private international law.

JOSHUA KARTON is an associate professor and Associate Dean for Graduate Studies and Research at the Queen's University Faculty of Law, as well as the managing editor of the *Canadian Journal of Commercial Arbitration*.

LIST OF CONTRIBUTORS

JOONGI KIM is a professor of law at Yonsei Law School. His research focuses on international dispute resolution, international trade and investment, corporate governance and good governance.

EVA LEIN is a professor of comparative law and private international law at the University of Lausanne in Switzerland and Director of the Centre for Comparative Law at the British Institute of International and Comparative Law (BIICL) in London.

WILSON LUI is an independent researcher in law and a former chief editor of the *Hong Kong Journal of Legal Studies*. He is a chartered linguist, a member of the Chartered Institute of Linguists and an associate of the Chartered Institute of Arbitrators. He is pursuing an MPhil at the University of Oxford and holds an LLM from the University of Cambridge.

ALEXANDER MOLOTNIKOV is an associate professor at the Law Faculty of Lomonosov Moscow State University, where he is Executive Director of the Scientific-Educational Centre (Law and Business MSU) and Executive Manager of the Centre for Asian Legal Studies. He is also a member of the International Academy of Commercial and Consumer Law (IACCL).

JUSTIN MONSENEPWO is a doctoral candidate at the University of Würzburg, a research associate at the University of Johannesburg, a guest lecturer in OHADA law and a member of the 'China, Law and Development' Project (University of Oxford).

YUKO NISHITANI is a professor at the Kyoto University Graduate School of Law in Japan and a member of the Curatorium of the Hague Academy of International Law. She holds a PhD from the University of Heidelberg in Germany.

ANSELMO REYES is an International Judge of the Singapore International Commercial Court. He was Professor of Legal Practice at the University of Hong Kong from 2012 to 2018 and is a visiting professor at Doshisha University in Kyoto. He was a judge of the Hong Kong High Court from 2003 to 2012.

CARRIE SHU SHANG is an assistant professor of business law at California State Polytechnic University, Pomona, and a practising mediator. Before joining academia, she was the acting chief representative of HKIAC Shanghai (2017–18).

KUAN-LING SHEN is a distinguished professor at National Taiwan University, specialising in civil procedure law, family proceedings, ADR and comparative legal studies.

THOMAS J STIPANOWICH holds the William H. Webster Chair as a professor of law at Caruso School of Law, Pepperdine University, where for fourteen years he led the Straus Institute for Dispute Resolution. He is an arbitrator and mediator, now with JAMS, in Los Angeles.

MAN YIP is an associate professor of law at Singapore Management University (SMU) and Director of the SMU Centre for Commercial Law in Asia. She researches in private law and private international law.

ACKNOWLEDGEMENTS

The help of many persons and institutions in putting this book together needs to be acknowledged.

We are above all grateful for the support of the Law Faculty of the University of Hong Kong. That support has enabled us to carry out research on innovations in dispute resolution, including multi-tiered dispute resolution (MDR). Special thanks go to Dean Hualing Fu, Associate Dean for Research Simon Young and Department of Law Head Yun Zhao for their encouragement throughout the organisation and writing of this book.

We acknowledge the financial support of the General Research Fund (GRF) Scheme of the Hong Kong Government Research Grants Council for research on comparative dispute resolution and MDR in the context of China's global dispute resolution engagements in the Greater Bay Area, the Belt and Road Initiative and beyond (Project Codes: 17617416, 17602218 and 17609419). The funding enabled us to invite the contributors of this book to a conference at the University of Hong Kong in September 2018 to discuss their early ideas and draft chapters. The Centre for Chinese Law at the University of Hong Kong kindly provided administrative backing for the conference. We thank Michael Palmer, professor of law at the University of London School of Oriental and African Studies and Senior Research Fellow at the Institute of Advanced Legal Studies, for chairing conference sessions and commenting on draft chapters. We thank the Hong Kong International Arbitration Centre (HKIAC), the China International Economic and Trade Arbitration Commission Hong Kong Arbitration Center (CIETAC Hong Kong), the Japan International Mediation Center (JIMC) and the Chartered Institute of Arbitrators East Asia Branch (CIArb East Asia) for the help in co-organising the conference. Sarah Grimmer (HKIAC's Secretary-General), Wenying Wang (CIETAC Hong Kong's Secretary-General), Professor Naoshi Takasugi (JIMC's deputy chief director) and Mary Thomson (CIArb East Asia's then chair) all took time out of their busy schedules to participate in the conference and offer their views on MDR.

We are enormously indebted to the contributors to this book, all of whom are leading academics or practitioners in the dispute resolution field. Without their time and commitment, this book would simply not have been possible. There have also been many other scholars of comparative dispute resolution, international civil procedure and private international law who have shared their insights into MDR and dispute resolution innovation trends in China, Asia and elsewhere. Unfortunately, space does not permit us to list all of them here by name.

We thank Pongyu Wai for producing an original artwork (Mediation I – Study in Ballpoint Pen, Alcohol & Bleach) for this book's cover. He comments on the work: 'The wavy line of messy dots can be regarded as "disputes" which disrupt a more or less orderly flow of cyclical lines (that is, our daily lives). The artist attempts to "resolve" the disputes through the use of ink, water, alcohol and bleach (to lighten the blue hue of the pen). The references in the title to pen, alcohol and bleach further echo our shared experience of being compelled to work at home during the COVID-19 pandemic. We work at home with pens and other instruments, but we sometimes resort to "alcohol" to relieve our tensions and "bleach" to cleanse our immediate surroundings. The title thus connotes the never-ending mediation between our interior lives and the exterior world.'

We thank our research assistants, Wilson Lui and Herman Wan, for undertaking the time-consuming task of editing this book for publication and ensuring consistency and accuracy throughout.

Finally, we thank Joe Ng and Gemma Smith of Cambridge University Press for their advice on navigating through the process of getting a manuscript ready for publication. This has been no mean feat in the days of COVID-19.

TABLE OF CASES

3-J Hospitality LLC v Big Time Design Inc 09–61077-CIV-MARRA/JOHNSON, 2009 US Dist LEXIS 100601 (SD Fl, 27 October 2009)
3289444 Nova Scotia Ltd v RW Armstrong & Associates Inc 2016 NSSC 330
407 ETR Concession Co v Day 2016 ONCA 709
Adjustrite Systems Inc v GAB Business Services Inc 145 F 3d 543 (2d Cir 1998)
Advanced Bodycare Solutions LLC v Thione International Inc 524 F 3d 1235 (11th Cir 2008)
Advanced Construction Techniques Ltd v OHL Construction Canada 2013 ONSC 7505
Aiton Australia Pty Ltd v Transfield Pty Ltd [1999] NSWSC 996, (1999) 153 FLR 236
Alberici Western Constructors Ltd v Saskatchewan Power Corp 2015 SKQB 74
Alliation Property Inc v Sirpi Alustel Construction et Société Elf Serepca [1998] TPI Douala, Ordonnance de référé no 40, (1999) 4 Revue Camerounaise de l'Arbitrage 13
Anderson Group Co Inc v MC Hotels LLC 0:17-cv-1564-TLW, 2017 WL 7513223 (DSC, 16 October 2017)
Aradia Fitness Canada Inc v Dawn M Hinze Consulting 2008 BCSC 839
Arctic Glacier USA Inc v Principal Life Insurance Co PX 16–3555, 2017 US Dist LEXIS 93822 (D Md, 19 June 2017)
B&O Manufacturing Inc v Home Depot USA Inc C 07–02864 JSW, 2007 US Dist LEXIS 83998 (ND Cal, 1 November 2007)
Bank of America NA v SFR Investments Pool 1 LLC No 2:15-cv-0693-GMN-VCF, 2016 US Dist LEXIS 11526 (D Nev, 31 January 2016)
Benner & Associates Ltd v Northern Lights Distribution Inc [1995] OJ No 626
BG Group plc v Republic of Argentina 572 US 25 (2014)
Bombardier Corp v National Railroad Passenger Corp 298 F Supp 2d 1 (DDC 2002)
Brandao v Jan-Pro Franchising International Inc 17-P-636, 2018 Mass App Unpub LEXIS 263 (22 March 2018)
Brosnan v Dry Cleaning Station Inc C-08–02028 EDL, 2008 US Dist LEXIS 44678 (ND Cal, 6 June 2008)
Buffalo Point First Nation v Cottage Owners Association 2020 MBQB 20
Bundesgericht, 6 June 2007 (4A_18/2007) (Switzerland)
Bundesgericht, 16 May 2011 (4A_46/2011) (Switzerland)
Bundesgerichtshof, 4 July 1977, NJW 1977, 2263 (Germany)
Bundesgerichtshof, 23 November 1983, NJW 1984, 669 (Germany)
Bundesgerichtshof, 18 November 1998, NJW 1999, 647 (Germany)
C v D [2021] HKCFI 1474

C Y Foundation Group Ltd v Leonara Yung [2012] 2 HKC 448
Cable & Wireless plc v IBM United Kingdom Ltd [2002] EWHC 2059 (Comm), [2002] 2 All ER (Comm) 1041
Cafarelli v Colon-Collazo CV055000279S, 2006 Conn Super LEXIS 1833 (20 June 2006)
Calyniuk Restaurants Inc v DC Holdings Ltd 2012 SKQB 160
Canada (Attorney General) v Marineserve MG Inc 2002 NSSC 147
Canada (Minister of Citizenship and Immigration) v Vavilov 2019 SCC 65
Canadian Ground Water Association v Canadian Geoexchange Coalition 2010 QCCS 2597
Cecrop Co v Kinetics Sciences Inc 2001 BCSC 532
Centaur Corp v ON Semiconductor Components Industries LLC 09 CV 2041 JM (BLM), 2010 US Dist LEXIS 8495 (SD Cal, 2 February 2010)
Chase v Great Lakes Altus Motor Yacht Sales 2010 ONSC 6365
Chorley Enters v Dickey's Barbecue Restaurants Inc 807 F 3d 553 (4th Cir 2015)
Chorley Enters v Dickey's Barbecue Restaurants Inc 136 S Ct 1656 (2016)
Cioffi v Modelevich et al 2018 ONSC 7084
Cityscape Richmond Corp v Vanbots Construction Corp [2001] OJ No 638, 8 CLR (3d) 196
Clinique du Golfe v Le Gall, Cour de cassation, 6 May 2003, Semaine Juridique, G, 11 February 2004, II 10021, no 01–01291
Collins & Aikman Products Co v Building Systems Inc 58 F 3d 16 (2d Cir 1995)
Colt Industries Operating Corporation v Republic of Korea (ICSID Case No ARB/84/2)
Commercial Bank of Cameroon (CBC) v Kenmogne [2006] Tribunal de Grande Instance of Mifi, Judgment no 79/civ, Ohadata J-07-70
Compass Group UK v Mid Essex Hospital Services NHS Trust [2013] EWCA Civ 200, [2013] BLR 265
Computershare Ltd v Perpetual Registrars Ltd (No 2) [2000] VSC 233
Conmac Enterprises Ltd v 0928818 BC Ltd 2018 BCSC 360
Consolidated Contractors Group SAL (Offshore) v Ambatovy Minerals SA 2017 ONCA 939
Construction Co v UXB International Inc No 7:13-CV-340, 2015 WL 926036 (WD Va, 4 March 2015)
Contec Corp v Remote Solution Co 398 F 3d 205 (2d Cir 2005)
Contrast Constructions Pty Ltd v Allen [2020] QCAT 194
County of Rockland v Primiano Construction Co 51 NY 2d 1, 8–9 (1980)
Cour de cassation, 14 February 2003, no 00–19.423, 00–19.424
Cour de cassation, 28 April 2011, comments by M Billiau, Semaine Juridique, G, 26 September 2011, doctr 1030
Courtney & Fairbairn Ltd v Tolaini Brothers (Hotels) Ltd [1975] 1 WLR 297
Cove Contracting Ltd v Condominium Corp No 012 5598 (Ravine Park) 2020 ABQB 106
CPC Group Ltd v Qatari Diar Real Estate Investment Co [2010] EWHC 1535 (Ch)
Cricket Canada v Syed 2017 ONSC 3301
Cumberland & York Distributors v Coors Brewing Co 01–244-P-H, 2002 US Dist LEXIS 1962 (D Me, 7 February 2002)

David L Threlkeld & Co v Metallgesellschaft Ltd 923 F 2d 245 (2d Cir 1991)
Davidson v Richman 2003 CarswellOnt 509, [2003] OJ No 519
Delameter v Anytime Fitness Inc 722 F Supp 2d 1168 (ED Cal 2010)
Dell Computer Corp v Union des consommateurs 2007 SCC 34
Desouza v Secom Australia Pty Ltd [2013] FCCA 659
DeValk Lincoln Mercury Inc v Ford Motor Co 811 F 2d 326 (7th Cir 1987)
Dialysis Access Center LLC v RMS Lifeline Inc 638 F 3d 367 (1st Cir 2011)
Dimattina Holdings LLC v Steri-Clean Inc 195 F Supp 3d 1285 (SD Fla 2016)
Director of Proceedings v Brooks (Application for Final Non-Publication Orders) [2019] NZHRRT 33
Downer EDI Mining Pty Ltd v Wambo Coal Pty Ltd [2012] QSC 290
Dustex Corp v Board of Trustees of the Municipal Electric Utility of Cedar Falls 13-CV-2087-LRR, 2014 US Dist LEXIS 82842 (ND Iowa, 18 June 2014)
El Dorado School of District No 15 v Continental Casualty Co 247 F 3d 843 (8th Cir 2001)
Elizabeth Bay Developments Pty Ltd v Boral Building Services Pty Ltd (1995) 36 NSWLR 709
Elizabeth Chong Pty Ltd v Brown [2011] FMCA 565
Emerald Green Grp LLC v Norco Construction Inc 155336/2014, 2014 WL 3107904 (NY Sup Ct, 1 July 2014)
Emirates Trading Agency LLC v Prime Mineral Exports Private Ltd [2014] EWHC 2104 (Comm), [2015] 1 WLR 1145
Empress Towers Ltd v Bank of Nova Scotia 1990 CanLII 2207 (BCCA)
Enka Insaat Ve Sanayi AS v OOO Insurance Company Chubb [2020] UKSC 38, [2020] 1 WLR 4117
Erceg v Erceg [2016] NZSC 135, [2017] 1 NZLR 310
Ervin v Nashville Peace & Justice Center 673 F Supp 2d 592 (MD Tenn 2009)
Estrada v CleanNet USA Inc No C 14–01785 JSW, 2015 WL 833701 (ND Cal, 24 February 2015)
Ex parte Industrial Technologies 707 So 2d 234 (Ala 1997)
Fiona Trust & Holding Corp v Privalov [2007] UKHL 40, [2007] 4 All ER 951
Fisher v GE Medical Systems 276 F Supp 2d 891 (MD Tenn 2003)
FKA v HAM [2006] CCJA, 1st chamber, Decision no 9, Ohadata J-07–23
Fluor Enterprises Inc v Solutia Inc 147 F Supp 2d 648 (SD Tex 2001)
Foley v Classique Coaches Ltd [1934] 2 KB 1 (CA)
Footprint Power Salem Harbor Development LP v Iberdrola Energy Products Inc 651963/2018, 2018 NY Slip Op 30794(U) 3 (NY Sup Ct, 1 May 2018)
Frei v Davey 124 Cal App 4th 1506 (2004)
Gao Haiyan v Keeneye Holdings Ltd [2011] 3 HKC 157
Gao Haiyan v Keeneye Holdings Ltd [2012] 1 HKLRD 627
Gate Precast Co v Kenwood Towne Place LLC No 1:09-CV-00113, 2009 WL 3614931 (SD Ohio, 28 October 2009)
Getchell v Suntrust Bank No 6:15-cv-1702-Orl-TBS, 2016 US Dist LEXIS 23238 (MD Fla 25 February 2016)

Glencot Development & Design Co Ltd v Ben Barrett & Son (Contractors) Ltd [2001] All ER (D) 384
Goel v Dhaliwal 2015 BCSC 2305
Government of Saskatchewan v Capitol Steel Corp 2017 SKQB 302
Green Tree Financial Corp v Bazzle 539 US 444 (2003)
Greenclose Ltd v National Westminster Bank plc [2014] EWHC 1156 (Ch), [2014] WLR (D) 173
Grigor-Scott v Jones (2008) 168 FCR 450
Grossner Jens v Raffles Holdings Ltd [2004] 1 SLR(R) 202
Hak Tung Alfred Tang v Bloomberg LP (unreported, HCA 198/2010, 16 July 2010)
Halsey v Milton Keynes General NHS Trust [2004] EWCA Civ 576
Halter Marine Inc v OK Shipping Ltd No Civ A 98–3184, 1998 US Dist LEXIS 18771 (ED La, 25 November 1998)
Hanocal Holding BV and IPIC International BV v Republic of Korea (ICSID Case No ARB/15/17)
Harrison v Nissan Motor Corp 111 F 3d 343 (3d Cir 1997)
Heartonics Corporation v EPI Life Pte Ltd [2017] SGHCR 17
Hebei Import & Export Corp v Polytek Engineering Co Ltd [1998] 1 HKLRD 287
Henry Schein Inc v Archer and White Sales Inc 139 S Ct 524, 526 (2019)
Heston v GB Capital LLC No 16cv912-WQH-RBB, 2016 US Dist LEXIS 113355 (SD Cal, 23 August 2016)
Heston v GB Capital LLC No 16cv912-WQH-AGS, 2018 US Dist LEXIS 3210 (SD Cal, 5 January 2018)
HIM Portland LLC v DeVito Builders Inc 317 F 3d 41 (1st Cir 2003)
Hobbs Padgett & Co (Reinsurance) Ltd v JC Kirkland Ltd [1969] 2 Lloyd's Rep 547
Holloway v Chancery Mead Ltd [2007] EWHC 2495 (TCC), [2008] 1 All ER (Comm) 653
Hooper Bailie Associated Ltd v Natcon Group Pty Ltd (1992) 28 NSWLR 194
Howsam v Dean Witter Reynolds Inc 537 US 79 (2002)
Hryniak v Mauldin 2014 SCC 7
HSBC Institutional Trust Services (Singapore) Ltd v Toshin Development Singapore Pte Ltd [2012] 4 SLR 738
Hubbard Construction Co v Jacobs Civil Inc 969 So 2d 1069 (Fla Dist Ct App 2007)
Hui v Esposito Holdings Pty Ltd [2017] FCA 648
Hyundai Engineering & Construction Co Ltd v Vigour Ltd [2004] 3 HKLRD 1
Hyundai Engineering & Construction Co Ltd v Vigour Ltd [2005] 3 HKLRD 723
ICC Case No 4230
ICC Case No 9984
ICC Case No 10256
In re Lakeland Fire District v East Area General Contractors Inc 16 AD 3d 417 (NY App Div 2005)
In re Pisces Foods LLC 228 SW 3d 349 (Tex App 2007)
In re R & R Personal Specialists of Tyler Inc 146 SW 3d 699 (Tex App 2004)
Inghams Enterprises Pty Ltd v Hannigan [2020] NSWCA 82

Interfoto Picture Library Ltd v Stiletto Visual Programmes Ltd [1989] QB 433
International Research Corp plc v Lufthansa Systems Asia Pacific Pte Ltd [2013] 1 SLR 973
International Research Corp plc v Lufthansa Systems Asia Pacific Pte Ltd [2014] 1 SLR 130
IWK Health Center Northfield Glass Group Ltd 2016 NSSC 281
Jakobsen v Wear Vision Capital Inc 2005 BCCA 147
Jesuit Fathers of Upper Canada v Guardian Insurance Co of Canada [2006] 1 SCR 744
John Wiley & Sons Inc v Livingston 376 US 543 (1964)
JPD Inc v Chronimed Holdings Inc 539 F 3d 388 (6th Cir 2008)
Kabou Henriette (BTM) v Société Sahel Compagnie (SOSACO) [2008] Court of Appeal of Ouagadougou, civil and commercial chamber, Judgment no 116 of 19 May 2006, Ohadata-J-09-25
Kemiron Atlantic Inc v Aguakem International Inc 290 F 3d 1287 (11th Cir 2002)
Kernahan v Home Warranty Administrator of Florida Inc 199 A 3d 766 (2019)
Knappe Composites v Art Métal, 3rd civil section of the *Cour de cassation*, 29 January 2014, no 13-10833
Kneider v Benson Percival Brown 2000 CarswellOnt 990, 95 ACWS (3d) 1049
Ku-ring-gai Council v Ichor Constructions Pty Ltd [2018] NSWSC 610
Ku-ring-gai Council v Ichor Constructions Pty Ltd [2019] NSWCA 2
L-3 Communications SPAR Aerospace Ltd v CAE Inc 2010 ONSC 7133
Lange v Schilling 163 Cal App 4th 1412 (2008)
Latstiwka v Bray 2006 ABQB 935
Lawton v Lawson [2002] FMCA 68
Leamon v Krajkiewcz 107 Cal App 4th 424 (2003)
Leeds Standard Condominium Corp No 41 v Fuller 2019 ONSC 3900
Ling Kong Henry v Tanglin Club [2018] SGHC 153
Lumbermens Mutual Casualty Co v Broadspire Management Services 623 F 3d 476 (7th Cir 2010)
Maiocchi v Royal Australian and New Zealand College of Psychiatrists [2014] FCA 301
Maldives Airports Co Ltd v GMR Malé International Airport Pte Ltd [2013] 2 SLR 449
Mann v Elphick 2015 BCSC 1853
Matsqui First Nation v Canada (Attorney General) 2015 BCSC 1409
May & Butcher Ltd v The King [1934] 2 KB 17 (HL)
MB America Inc v Alaska Pac Leasing Co 367 P 3d 1286 (Nev 2016)
MCC Development Corp v Perla 81 AD 3d 474, 916 NYS 2d 102 (NY App Div 2011)
McParland & Partners Ltd v Whitehead [2020] EWHC 298 (Ch), [2020] Bus LR 699
Medissimo v Logica, decision no 12-27.004, 20 April 2014 (France)
Metzler Contracting Co LLC v Stephens 774 F Supp 2d 1073 (D Haw 2011)
Mortimer v First Mount Vernon Industrial Loan Association No Civ AMD 03-1051, 2003 US Dist LEXIS 24698 (D Md, 19 May 2003)
Moses H Cone Memorial Hospital v Mercury Construction Corp 460 US 1 (1983)
N-Tron Corp v Rockwell Automation Inc No 09-0733-WS-C, 2010 US Dist LEXIS 14130 (SD Ala, 18 February 2010)

NetSys Technology Group AB v Open Text Corp [1999] CanLII 14937 (ONSC)
Noble China Inc v Lei (1998) 42 OR (3d) 69
Nordion Inc v Life Technologies Inc 2015 ONSC 99
Northland Utilities (NWT) Ltd v Hay River (Town of) 2021 NWTCA 1
Ohpen Operations UK Ltd v Invesco Fund Managers Ltd [2019] EWHC 2246 (TCC), [2020] 1 All ER (Comm) 786
Ontario First Nations (2008) Limited Partnership v Ontario Lottery and Gaming Corporation 2020 ONSC 1516
Onslow Salt Pty Ltd v Buurabalayji Thalanyji Aboriginal Corp [2018] FCAFC 118
Passlow v Butmac Pty Ltd [2012] NSWSC 225
Petromec Inc v Petroleo Brasileiro SA Petrobras [2005] EWCA Civ 891, [2006] 1 Lloyd's Rep 121
Philips v Australian Girls' Choir Pty Ltd [2001] FMCA 109
Placoplâtre v SA Eiffage TP, 1st civil session of the *Cour de cassation*, 6 February 2007, comments by J Béguin, Semaine Juridique, E&A, 30 August 2007, no 05–17573
PMT Partners Pty Ltd (in liq) v Australian National Parks and Wildlife Service (1995) 184 CLR 301
PQ Licensing SA v LPQ Central Canada Inc 2018 ONCA 331
Primov v Serco Inc 296 Va 59, 817 SE 2d 811 (Va 2018)
PT Selecta Bestama v Sin Huat Huat Marine Transportation Pte Ltd [2015] SGHCR 16
Resource Development Ltd v Swanbridge Ltd (unreported, HCA 1873/2009, 31 May 2010)
Roberts v Morphett Constructions Pty Ltd [2018] NSWCATAP 33
Rogacki v Belz 2003 CarswellOnt 3717, [2003] OJ No 3809
Rudd v Trossacs Investments Inc 2006 CarswellOnt 1417, [2006] OJ No 922
Ruling of 10th *arbitrazh* Court of Appeal, 27 March 2018, Ruling No 10АП-2025/2018, Case No A41-87102/17 (Russia)
Ruling of *arbitrazh* court of Central district, 25 December 2015, Case No A35-11066/2014 (Russia)
Ruling of *arbitrazh* court of Far Eastern district, 22 January 2016, Case No A73-6268/2015 (Russia)
Ruling of *arbitrazh* court of Northwest district, 14 December 2006, Case No A56-17842/2006 (Russia)
Ruling of *arbitrazh* court of Penzinskaya region, 16 November 2016, Case No A49-9323/2016 (Russia)
Ruling of *arbitrazh* court of Penzinskaya region, 26 January 2017, Case No A49-15015/2016 (Russia)
Ruling of *arbitrazh* court of Udmurtskaya region, 3 May 2017, Case No A71-1815/2017 (Russia)
Ruling of *arbitrazh* court of Volgo-Vyatka district, 27 October 2016, Case No A43-15711/2016 (Russia)
Ruling of International Commercial Arbitration Court of the Chamber of Commerce and Industry of the Russian Federation (ICAC), 30 September 2013, Case No 108/2011 (Russia)

TABLE OF CASES   xxi

Ruling of Moscow city court, 14 August 2017, Case No 33–30776/2017 (Russia)
Ruling of Moscow city court, 30 May 2017, Case No 33–14571/2017 (Russia)
Ruling of Russian Supreme Court, 23 July 2015, Case No A55-12366/2012 (Russia)
Ruling of Russian Supreme Court, 26 April 2017, Case No A56-7889/2016 (Russia)
Ruling of Supreme Arbitration Court, 13 November 2009, Ruling No SAC-14616/09 (Russia)
Santos Ltd v Fluor Australia Pty Ltd [2016] QSC 129
Sattva Capital Corp v Creston Moly Corp [2014] 2 SCR 633
Secala v Moore 982 F Supp 609 (ND Illinois 1997)
Seidel v Telus Communications Inc 2011 SCC 15
Skills Tiling v Trio Construct (Civil) [2014] VMC 4
Skvaridlo v Cross Country Saskatchewan Assn Inc 2015 SKQB 356
Slater v Amendola 1999 CarswellOnt 3049, [1999] OJ No 3787
Société de Manufacture de Côte d'Ivoire dit MACABI v May Jean-Pierre [2005] CCJA, 1st chamber, Ohadata J-05–357
Société Wanson v Société d'Etudes et de réalisation pour l'industrie caféière et cacaoyère (SERIC) [1997] Court of Appeal of Abidjan, civil and commercial chamber, Decision no 484, (1998) 1 Revue Camerounaise de l'Arbitrage 10
SOR Technology LLC v MWR Life LLC No 3:18-CV-2358 JLS (NLS), 2019 US Dist LEXIS 146817 (SD Cal, 28 August 2019)
Space Tech Development Corp v Boeing Co 209 F App'x 236 (4th Cir 2006)
Stone & Webster Inc v Georgia Power Co 968 F Supp 2d 1 (DDC 2013)
Sulamerica CIA Nacional de Seguros SA v Enesa Engenharia SA [2012] EWCA Civ 638, [2013] 1 WLR 102
Suncor Energy Products Inc v Howe-Baker Engineers Ltd 2010 ABQB 310
Sundercan Ltd v Salzman Anthony David [2010] SGHC 92
Supreme Court Civil Judgment Tai-shang-tzu 671 (2003) (Taiwan)
Supreme Court Civil Judgment Tai-shang-tzu 992 (2004) (Taiwan)
Supreme Court Civil Judgment Tai-shang-tzu 1183 (2012) (Taiwan)
Supreme Court Civil Ruling Tai-kang-tzu 1080 (2014) (Taiwan)
Supreme Court Civil Ruling Tai-shang-tzu 1634 (2012) (Taiwan)
Swartz v Westminster Services Inc No 8:10-cv-1722-T-30AEP, 2010 US Dist LEXIS 93107 (MD Fla, 8 September 2010)
Tattoo Art Inc v TAT International LLC 711 F Supp 2d 645 (ED Va 2010)
Teal Cedar Products Ltd v British Columbia 2017 SCC 32
Tekmen & Co v S Builders Inc 04C-03–007 RFS, 2005 Del Super LEXIS 181 (25 May 2005)
Templeton Development Corp v Superior Court 144 Cal App 4th 1073 (2006)
Termguard Pty Ltd v Statewide Pest Control Pty Ltd [2016] WASC 359
The Hua Tian Long (No 2) [2010] 3 HKLRD 611
The United Mexican States v Burr 2020 ONSC 2376
The United Mexican States v Cargill Inc 2011 ONCA 622
Tillman Park LLC v Dabbs-Williams General Contractors LLC 679 SE 2d 67 (Ga Ct App 2009)

Timmins Nickel Inc v Marshall Minerals Corp 2001 CarswellOnt 1762, [2001] OTC 369
TNB Fuel Services Sdn Bhd v China National Coal Group Corp [2017] 3 HKC 588
Tokyo District Court, 8 December 2010, 2116 Hanrei Jiho, 68, Westlaw Japan No 2010WLJPCA12088010 (Japan)
Tokyo High Court, 22 June 2011, 2116 Hanrei Jiho 64 (Japan)
Trujillo v Gomez No 14cv2483 BTM (BGS), 2015 US Dist LEXIS 51068 (SD Cal, 17 April 2015)
Ts'Kw'Aylaxw First Nation v Graymont Western Canada Inc 2018 BCSC 2101
TSA v Promoto [1997] Supreme Court of Ivory Coast, Decision no 317/197, (1999) 5 Revue Camerounaise de l'Arbitrage 16
Uber Technologies v Heller 2020 SCC 16
Ungava Techs v Innerspec Techs 6:17-cv-6, 2017 US Dist LEXIS 83392 (WD Va, 31 May 2017)
United Artists Singapore Theatre Pte Ltd v Parkway Properties Pte Ltd [2003] 1 SLR (R) 202
United Group Rail Services Ltd v Rail Corp of New South Wales [2009] NSWCA 177; (2009) 74 NSWLR 618
Upplan Co Ltd v Li Ho Ming [2010] 6 HKC 457
Vigour Ltd v Hyundai Engineering and Construction Co Ltd (unreported, FAMV 4/2006, 22 May 2006)
Vinmar Overseas (Singapore) Pte Ltd v PTT International Trading Pte Ltd [2018] 2 SLR 1271
Wah (aka Alan Tang) v Grant Thornton International Ltd [2012] EWHC 3198 (Ch), [2013] 1 All ER (Comm) 1226
Wales (t/a Selective Investment Services) v CBRE Managed Services Ltd [2020] EWHC 1050 (Comm), [2020] Costs LR 603
Walford v Miles [1992] 1 AC 128
Wastech Services Ltd v Greater Vancouver Sewerage and Drainage District 2021 SCC 7
Waxman v Pal (Application for Non-Publication Orders) [2017] NZHRRT 4
Welborn Clinic v Medquist Inc 301 F 3d 634 (7th Cir 2002)
Welldone Plumbing, Heating & Air Conditioning (1990) v Total Comfort Systems 2002 SKQB 475
Willis Corroon Corp of Utah v United Capital Insurance Co 97–2208 MHP, 1998 US Dist LEXIS 23226 (ND Cal, 5 January 1998)
WN Hillas & Co Ltd v Arcos Ltd (1932) 147 LT 503 (HL) (UK)
WTE Co-Generation v RCR Energy Pty Ltd [2013] VSC 314
Yam Seng Pte Ltd v International Trade Corporation Ltd [2013] EWHC 111 (QB), [2013] 1 All ER (Comm) 1321
Yashwant Bajaj v Toru Ueda [2018] SGHC 229 (Singapore)
Yukon Energy Corp v Chant Construction Co 2007 YKSC 22
Zoological Board of Victoria v Australian Liquor, Hospitality and Miscellaneous Workers Union (1993) 49 IR 41

TABLE OF STATUTES AND INSTRUMENTS

International Instruments

1958 United Nations Convention on the Recognition and Enforcement of Foreign Arbitral Awards
 art I(1)
 art V(1)
 art V(2)
1961 Hague Convention Abolishing the Requirement of Legalisation for Foreign Public Documents
 art 1(d)
1965 Convention on the Settlement of Investment Disputes between States and Nationals of Other States
2005 Hague Convention on Choice of Court Agreements
2019 Hague Convention on the Recognition and Enforcement of Foreign Judgments in Civil or Commercial Matters
2019 United Nations Convention on International Settlement Agreements Resulting from Mediation
 art 1
 art 1(1)
 art 1(3)
 art 2(3)
 art 3(3)
 art 4
 art 4(1)(b)(ii)
 art 4(1)(b)(iii)
 art 5
 art 5(1)(d)
 art 5(1)(e)
 art 8
 art 8(1)(a)
 art 8(1)(b)

Bilateral Agreements

Closer Economic Partnership Arrangement Investment Agreement (Hong Kong SAR-China)

art 19
art 20
Korea–Central America FTA
Korea–Colombia FTA
　art 8.17(2)
Korea–Dominica BIT
　art 8(1)
Korea–El Salvador BIT
　art 9(1)
Korea–Peru FTA
　art 9.16(2)

Domestic Legislation

Afghanistan

Commercial Arbitration Law 2007

Australia

Australian Human Rights Commission Act 1986 (Cth)
　s 11(1)(aa)
　s 11(1)(o)
　s 14
　s 21
　s 29(2)
　s 35(2)
　s 46P
　s 46PD
　s 46PF(1)(c)
　s 46PI
　s 46PJ
　s 46PJ(5)
　s 46PJ(6)
　s 46PJ(7)
　s 46PK(1)
　s 46PK(2)
　s 46PKA
　s 46PM
　s 46PM(3)
　s 46PO
　s 46PO(3)
　s 46PO(3A)
　s 46PO(4)
　s 46PR

s 46PS
s 46PS(2)
s 46PSA
s 46PT
s 46PU
s 46PU(2)
s 46PV
Commercial Arbitration Act 1984 (Vic)
Commercial Arbitration Act 1985 (NT)
Commercial Arbitration Act 1985 (WA)
Commercial Arbitration Act 1986 (ACT)
Commercial Arbitration Act 1986 (Tas)
Commercial Arbitration Act 1990 (Qld)
Commercial Arbitration Act 2010 (NSW)
   s 1C(1)
   s 4
   s 9
   s 12
   s 14
   s 14(1)
   s 14(2)
   s 14(3)
   s 15
   s 16
   s 17J
   s 18
   s 27D
   s 27D(1)
   s 27D(2)
   s 27D(3)
   s 27D(4)
   s 27D(5)
   s 27D(6)
   s 27D(7)
   s 27D(8)
   s 34
Commercial Arbitration Act 2017 (ACT)
   s 2D(7)
Commercial Arbitration and Industrial Referral Agreements Act 1986 (SA)
Conciliation and Arbitration Act 1904 (Cth)
   s 23(2)
Conciliation and Arbitration Amendment Act 1984 (Cth)
Equal Opportunity Act 1984 (SA)
   s 95C
Equal Opportunity Act 1984 (WA)
   s 93A(1)

International Arbitration Act 1974 (as amended in 2010) (Cth)
Land and Environment Act 1979 (NSW)
  s 34
Model Commercial Arbitration Act 2010 (Cth)
  s 27D
  s 27D(4)

Austria

Law on Mediation in Civil Law Matters 2003
  s 16(1)

Belgium

Judicial Code
  art 1724
  art 1725
  art 1737

Bermuda

Arbitration Act 1986
  s 3(2)
International Conciliation and Arbitration Act 1993
  s 14(1)

Brazil

Law No 13140 (2005)
  s 7
  s 42
Law No 9.307 (1996)
  s 21(4)

British Virgin Islands

Arbitration Act 2013
  s 30
  s 31(4)
  s 31(5)

Brunei Darussalam

Arbitration Order 2009
  s 62
  s 63(3)
  s 63(4)

Cambodia

Commercial Arbitration Law
  s 38

Canada

Arbitration Act (Alberta)
  s 35
  s 35(1)
  s 35(2)
Arbitration Act (British Columbia)
  s 47(1)
Arbitration Act (Manitoba)
  s 35
Arbitration Act (New Brunswick)
  s 35
Arbitration Act (Ontario)
  s 3
  s 35
Arbitration Act (Saskatchewan)
  s 36
British Columbia Notice to Mediate (General) Regulation
  s 3
  s 5
Code of Civil Procedure (Québec)
  art 1
  art 620
Commercial Arbitration Act (Nova Scotia)
  s 38
Federal Commercial Arbitration Act
International Commercial Arbitration Act (Alberta)
  s 5
International Commercial Arbitration Act (British Columbia)
  s 30
  s 30(1)
International Commercial Arbitration Act (Manitoba)
  s 5
  s 6
International Commercial Arbitration Act (New Brunswick)
  s 6
International Commercial Arbitration Act (Nova Scotia)
  s 6
International Commercial Arbitration Act (Ontario)
  sch 5

International Commercial Arbitration Act (Saskatchewan)
  s 4
Limitations Act (Alberta)
Limitations Act (Ontario)
  s 5(1)(a)(iv)
Mediation Rules of the Provincial Court – Civil Division (Alberta)
  s 2(1)
Notice to Mediate (General) Regulation (British Columbia)
  s 3
  s 5
Provincial Court Act (Alberta)
  s 65
  s 66
Queen's Bench Act (Saskatchewan)
  s 42(1.1)
  s 42(3)
  s 42(4)
  s 42(5)
Rules of Civil Procedure (Ontario)
  r 24.1
Rules of Court (Alberta)
  r 4.16
  r 4.16(1)
Rules of the Newfoundland and Labrador Supreme Court
  r 37A
Supreme Court Civil Rules (British Columbia)
  r 5-3(1)(o)
Uniform Arbitration Act 2016
  s 42
  s 42(2)
Uniform International Commercial Arbitration Act 1986
  s 6
Uniform International Commercial Arbitration Act 2014
Uniform International Commercial Mediation Act 2005
  s 9

China

Faguan Fa (法官法) [Judges' Law] (promulgated by the National People's Congress Standing Committee, 23 April 2019, effective 1 October 2019)
Laodong zhengyi tiaojie zhongcai Fa (劳动争议调解仲裁法) [Labour Dispute Mediation and Arbitration Law] (promulgated by the National People's Congress Standing Committee, 29 December 2007, effective 1 May 2008)
Minshi Susong Fa (民事訴訟法) [Civil Procedure Law] (promulgated by the National People's Congress Standing Committee, 9 April 1991, effective 9 April 1991)

Minshi Susong Fa (民事訴訟法) [Civil Procedure Law] (promulgated by the National People's Congress Standing Committee, 28 October 2007, effective 1 April 2008)
Minshi Susong Fa (民事訴訟法) [Civil Procedure Law] (promulgated by the National People's Congress Standing Committee, 27 June 2017, effective 1 July 2017)
   art 34
Renmin tiaojie Fa (人民调解法) [People's Mediation Law] (promulgated by the National People's Congress Standing Committee, 28 August 2010, effective 1 January 2011)
Supreme People's Court, 'Zuigao renmin fayuan guanyu renmin fayuan jinyibu shenhua duoyuanhua jiufen jiejue jizhi gaige de yijian' [Supreme People's Court Opinion on the People's Courts Further Deepening the Reform of the Diversified Dispute Resolution Mechanism] [2016] Fa Fa 14
Supreme People's Court, 'Zuigao renmin fayuan guanyu sheli guoji shangshi fating ruogan wenti de guiding' [Provisions of the Supreme People's Court on Several Issues Regarding the Establishment of the International Commercial Court] [2018] Fa Shi 11
   art 1
   art 2
   art 3
   art 4
   art 11
   art 12
   art 13
   art 14
Supreme People's Court, 'Zuigao renmin fayuan guanyu zhongcai sifa shencha anjian baohe wenti de youguan guiding' [Relevant Provisions of the Supreme People's Court on Issues concerning Applications for Verification of Arbitration Cases under Judicial Review] [2017] Fa Shi 21
   art 2(2)
   art 3(2)
Zhongcai Fa (仲裁法) [Arbitration Law] (promulgated by the National People's Congress Standing Committee, 1 September 2017, effective 1 January 2018)
   art 50
   art 51
   art 51(1)

Colombia

Estatuto de Arbitraje Nacional e Internacional 2012
   s 24

Czech Republic

Arbitral Proceedings and Enforcement of Arbitral Awards (Act No 216/1994)
   s 24(1)
Mediation Act (Act No 202/2012 Coll)

European Union

Council Regulation (EC) No 44/2001 of 22 December 2000 on Jurisdiction and the Recognition and Enforcement of Judgments in Civil and Commercial Matters [2002] OJ L12/1
Directive 2008/52/EC of the European Parliament and of the Council of 21 May 2008 on Certain Aspects of Mediation in Civil and Commercial Matters [2008] OJ L136/3
   art 1(1)
   art 1(2)
Directive 2013/11/EU of the European Parliament and of the Council of 21 May 2013 on Alternative Dispute Resolution for Consumer Disputes and Amending Regulation (EC) No 2006/2004 and Directive 2009/22/EC [2013] OJ L165/53
European Parliament Resolution of 12 September 2017 on the Implementation of Directive 2008/52/EC of the European Parliament and of the Council of 21 May 2008 on Certain Aspects of Mediation in Civil and Commercial Matters (2016/2066(INI)) [2018] OJ C337/2
European Parliament Resolution of 12 March 2019 on Building EU Capacity on Conflict Prevention and Mediation (2018/2159(INI))
Regulation (EU) No 1215/2012 of the European Parliament and of the Council of 12 December 2012 on Jurisdiction and the Recognition and Enforcement of Judgments in Civil and Commercial Matters [2012] OJ L351/1
Treaty on the Functioning of the European Union [2012] OJ C326/47
   art 81
   art 114
   art 114(3)

Estonia

Code of Civil Procedure 2006
   s 3(3)
   s 144
Conciliation Act 2010

Germany

Arbeitsgerichtsgesetz [Labour Courts Act] (1979, as amended)
Einführungsgesetz zum Bürgerlichen Gesetzbuche [Introductory Act to the Civil Code] (1994, as amended)
   art 240
Mediationsgesetz [Mediation Act] (2012, as amended)
Zivilprozessordnung [Code of Civil Procedure] (2005, as amended)
   art 1053

TABLE OF STATUTES AND INSTRUMENTS xxxi

Hong Kong

Arbitration Ordinance (Cap 341)
    s 2A(2)
    s 2A(2)(a)
Arbitration Ordinance (Cap 609)
    s 23
    s 24
    s 32
    s 32(3)
    s 33
    s 33(1)
    s 33(4)
    s 33(5)
Disability Discrimination (Investigation and Conciliation) Rules (Cap 487B)
    r 5
Disability Discrimination Ordinance (Cap 487)
District Court Ordinance (Cap 336)
    s 73B(3)
    s 73B(5)
    s 73C(3)
    s 73C(5)
    s 73D(3)
    s 73D(5)
    s 73E(3)
    s 73E(5)
Family Status Discrimination (Investigation and Conciliation) Rules (Cap 527A)
    r 5
Family Status Discrimination Ordinance (Cap 527)
Mediation Ordinance (Cap 620)
    s 8
Race Discrimination (Investigation and Conciliation) Rules (Cap 602B)
    r 5
Race Discrimination Ordinance (Cap 602)
Rules of the High Court (Cap 4A)
Sex Discrimination (Investigation and Conciliation) Rules (Cap 480B)
    r 5
    r 6
    r 8
Sex Discrimination Ordinance (Cap 480)
    s 5
    s 64(1)(d)
    s 84(3)(a)
    s 84(3)(b)

xxxii TABLE OF STATUTES AND INSTRUMENTS

   s 84(4)
   s 84(6)
   s 85(1)
   s 85(2)
   s 85(2)(b)
   s 85(3)(d)

India

Arbitration and Conciliation Act 1996
   s 30

Italy

Code of Civil Procedure
   art 185
   art 420
Civil Code
   art 1341

Ivory Coast

Act on Mediation (20 June 2014)

Japan

Act on Promotion of Use of Alternative Dispute Resolution (Act No 151 of 2004)
   art 1
   art 26(1)
Act on Securing etc of Equal Opportunity and Treatment between Men and Women in Employment (Law No 113 of 1 July 1972)
   art 25(1)
Act on Special Measures concerning the Handling of Legal Services by Foreign Lawyers (Law No 66 of 23 May 1986; amended by Law No 33 of 29 May 2020)
Arbitration Act (Law No 138 of 2003)
   art 38
   art 38(1)
Civil Conciliation Act (Law No 222 of 9 June 1951)
   art 5
   art 20(1)
Civil Execution Act (Law No 4 of 30 March 1979)
   art 22
Code of Civil Procedure (Law No 109 of 26 June 1996)
   art 118

TABLE OF STATUTES AND INSTRUMENTS   xxxiii

  art 267
  art 275(1)
Constitution of Japan (promulgated on 3 November 1946; entered into force on 3 May
    1947)
  art 32
Construction Business Act (Law No 100 of 24 May 1949)
  art 25-17
Domestic Relations Case Procedure Act (Law No 52 of 25 May 2011)
  art 274(1)
  art 275(1)
Labour Relations Adjustment Act (Act No 25 of 27 September 1946)

Korea

Family Litigation Act
Framework Act on the Construction Industry
Judicial Conciliation of Civil Disputes Act
  art 7
  art 23

Laos

Decree of the President of the Lao People's Democratic Republic on the Promulgation
    of the Law on Resolution of Economic Disputes 2005

Liechtenstein

Civil Law Mediation Act 2005
  s 12(1)

Mauritius

Supreme Court (Mediation) Rules 2010

New Zealand

Human Rights Act 1993
  s 5(2)(h)
  s 20(3)
  s 21
  s 61
  s 62
  s 63
  s 64

s 65
s 66
s 67
s 68
s 69
s 76(1)
s 77
s 78
s 80
s 80(4)
s 81
s 85
s 86
s 91(2)
s 92
s 92A(1)(b)
s 92D
s 92E
s 92H
s 92I(3)
s 92R
s 92S
s 92T
s 92U
s 107

Nigeria

Arbitration and Conciliation Act 1988
    ss 37–42
Arbitration and Conciliation Act Cap A18 LFN 2004 (Repeal and Re-enactment) Bill 2018 (SB 427)
    s 75
    s 77

OHADA

Treaty on the Harmonisation of Business Law in Africa
    art 1
    art 2
    art 4
    art 6
    art 7
    art 7(1)
    art 7(3)
    art 7(4)
    art 8

TABLE OF STATUTES AND INSTRUMENTS xxxv

   art 9
   art 14(1)
   art 14(3)
   art 20
   arts 21–26
   art 27(1)
   arts 27(2)–30
   arts 31((1), (2), (3))–32
   art 40
   art 40(1)
   art 40(2)
   art 40(3)
   art 41
   art 41(1)
   art 41(4)
Uniform Act on Arbitration
   art 3-1(4)
   art 8-1
   art 8-1(2)
   art 13(4)
   arts 30–34
Uniform Act on Contracts for the Carriage of Goods by Road
Uniform Act on Cooperatives
Uniform Act on Mediation
   art 3
   art 4(3)
   art 12(1)
   art 12(1)(a)
   art 12(1)(b)
   art 12(1)(c)
   art 12(1)(d)
   art 12(1)(e)
   art 12(2)
   art 14(1)
   art 14(2)
   art 15
   art 15(1)
   art 15(2)
   art 16(8)
Uniform Act on the Harmonisation of the Accounts of Enterprises
Uniform Act Organising Collective Proceedings for Clearing of Debts
Uniform Act Organising Securities
Uniform Act Organising Simplified Recovery Procedures and Enforcement Measures
Uniform Act Relating to Commercial Companies and Economic Interest Groups
Uniform Act Relating to General Commercial Law

xxxvi   TABLE OF STATUTES AND INSTRUMENTS

Oman

Royal Decree No 98-2005 for the Issuance of the Mediation and Reconciliation Act 2005

Philippines

Alternative Dispute Resolution Act 2004
   s 18
Implementing Rules and Regulations of the Alternative Dispute Resolution Act 2004
   S 7.8(c)
   s 17.4

Poland

Code of Civil Procedure 2005

Romania

Law 192/2006

Russia

Civil Code 1996
   art 165
Civil Code 2002
   art 797
Civil Procedure Code 2002
   art 132
   art 135
   art 169
   art 222
Commercial Procedure Code 2002
   art 4
   art 125
   art 126
   art 133
   art 148
Federal Law on Alternative Procedure for Dispute Resolution with Participation of a Mediator (Mediation Procedure) 2010
   art 3
   art 4
   art 7

Law on the Judicial System 1996
   art 4
Resolution of the Plenum of the Supreme Court of the Russian Federation, No 25, 23 June 2015, 'On the Application by the Courts of Certain Provisions of Section I of Part One of the Civil Code of the Russian Federation', 'Rossiyskaya gazeta', No 140, 30 June 2015
   clause 63
   clause 64
   clause 65
   clause 66
   clause 67

Senegal

Decree no 2014-1653 of 24 December 2014 on Mediation and Conciliation

Singapore

Arbitration Act 2001
   s 3
   s 6
   s 30
   s 37
   s 62(1)
   s 62(3)
   s 62(4)
   s 63(3)
   s 63(2)(a)
   s 63(2)(b)
   s 63(3)
   s 63(4)
International Arbitration Act 1994
   s 16(3)
   s 17(3)
   s 17(4)
International Arbitration Act 2002
   s 5
   s 6
   ss 12(1)(c)–12(1)(i)
   s 12A
   s 12A(1)(b)
   s 12A(3)
   s 12A(4)
   s 12A(5)
   s 12A(6)

xxxviii TABLE OF STATUTES AND INSTRUMENTS

    s 16(1)
    s 16(3)
    s 16(4)
    s 16(5)
    s 17(2)(a)
    s 17(2)(b)
    s 17(3)
    s 18
Mediation Act 2017
    s 4
    s 6
    s 8
    s 9
    s 10
    s 12
    s 17

Slovenia

Mediation in Civil and Commercial Matters Act 2008

Spain

Commercial Mediation Bill 2010

Switzerland

Schweizerische Zivilprozessordnung [Swiss Code of Civil Procedure] (19 December 2008), SR 272
    art 214

Taiwan

Arbitration Act
    art 4(1)
    art 36
    art 44(1)
    art 53
Code of Civil Procedure
    art 278
    art 380
    art 403
    art 414
    art 415-1
    art 415-3
    art 416
    art 417
    art 418

Commercial Disputes Act
  arts 20–32
Family Proceedings Act
  art 33
  art 33(1)
  art 35(1)
  art 36
Financial Consumer Protection Act
  art 13(2)
  art 23(2)
  art 25(1)
  art 29(1)
  art 30
Government Procurement Act
  art 85-1
  art 85-1(1)
  art 85-1(2)
  art 85-1(3)
  art 85-3
  art 85-4
Labour Incident Act
  art 16
  art 20
  art 21
  art 24
  art 24(3)
  art 25
  art 27
  art 28
  art 29
  art 30(1)
  art 30(2)
  art 34
Notary Act
  art 13(1)
Township and County-Administered City Mediation Act

United Kingdom

Arbitration Act 1996
  s 1(b)
Civil Procedure Rules
  r 1.4
  r 26.4

Enterprise and Regulatory Reform Act 2013
  s 64
  s 64(1)(b)
Equality Act 2006
  s 3
  s 8
  s 9
  s 11
  s 13
  s 14
  s 16
  s 20
  s 21(4)
  s 21(7)
  s 23
  s 27
  s 28
  s 30
Northern Ireland Act 1998
Rules of the Supreme Court
Scottish Commission for Human Rights Act 2006

United States

Alternative Dispute Resolution Act
Equal Pay Act
Federal Arbitration Act
Federal Rules of Civil Procedure
  art 16
Federal Rules of Evidence
  art 408
Genetic Information Non-Discrimination Act
Uniform Mediation Act
US Code
  Title 42
    para 2000e-5

Vietnam

Decree on Commercial Mediation 2017

TABLE OF RULES, CODES AND GUIDELINES

ADR Institute of Canada Arbitration Rules (2014)
    s 4.27.1
ADR Institute of Canada Med-Arb Rules (2020)
Arbitration Institute of the Stockholm Chamber of Commerce Mediation Rules (2014)
    art 7(2)
Beijing Arbitration Commission Arbitration Rules (2015)
    art 42(5)
    art 43
    art 43(2)
    art 67
    art 67(2)
Centre d'Arbitrage du Congo Rules of Arbitration (2003)
    art 20
Centre d'Arbitrage du Groupement Interpatronal du Cameroun Rules of Arbitration (2019)
    art 34
Chambre de Commerce, d'Industrie et d'Agriculture de Dakar Arbitration, Mediation, and Conciliation Rules (1998)
    art 39(1)
China International Commercial Court Procedural Rules (2018)
    art 8(1)
    art 17(3)
    art 24
    art 26
China International Economic and Trade Arbitration Commission Arbitration Rules (2005)
China International Economic and Trade Arbitration Commission Arbitration Rules (2012)
China International Economic and Trade Arbitration Commission Arbitration Rules (2015)
    art 4(3)
    art 47
    art 47(2)
    art 47(8)

Chinese Arbitration Association International Arbitration Rules (2001)
Chinese Arbitration Association International Arbitration Rules (2017)
  art 34
  art 35(1)
Chinese Arbitration Association Mediation Rules (2009)
  art 25
  art 26
  art 27(1)
  art 27(4)
  art 28(4)
Chinese Arbitration Association Rules of the Construction Dispute Adjudication Board (2016)
  art 16
  art 17(3)
Chinese Arbitration Association Rules of the Construction Dispute Review Board (2016)
  art 15–1
  art 16
Chinese Arbitration Association Rules on Arbitration for Financial Disputes (2011)
  arts 34–35
Chinese Arbitration Association Rules on Pre-arbitration Mediation for Simplified Procedure (2017)
  r 2
  r 8(1)
Common Court of Justice and Arbitration Arbitration Rules (2017)
Common Court of Justice and Arbitration Arbitration Rules of Procedure (1996)
  art 20
Common Court of Justice and Arbitration Arbitration Rules of Procedure (2014)
  art 5(e)
  art 6(b)
  art 6(c)
  art 6(d)
  art 20
  art 21
  art 21-1
  art 21-1-1
  art 21-1-2
  art 25
  arts 30–31
Cour d'Arbitrage de la Côte d'Ivoire Arbitration Rules of Procedure (2019)
  art 32.5
Cour d'Arbitrage de la Côte d'Ivoire Mediation Rules of Procedure (2018)
  art 11

art 15
Financial Dispute Resolution Scheme Mediation and Arbitration Rules (2018)
    r 2.1
    r 2.3
    r 2.4
    r 2.5
    r 3.2
    r 3.4
    r 3.12
Financial Regulations of the OHADA Institutions
Hong Kong International Arbitration Centre Administered Arbitration Rules (2018)
    art 13.8
    sch 4 para 1
    sch 4 para 21
International Bar Association Rules of Ethics for International Arbitrators (1987)
    r 5.3
International Bar Association Rules on the Taking of Evidence in International Arbitration (2010)
International Chamber of Commerce Mediation Rules (2014)
    art 10(3)
Japan Commercial Arbitration Association Commercial Arbitration Rules (2019)
    art 58
    art 59
Japan Commercial Arbitration Association Commercial Arbitration Rules (2020)
Japan Commercial Arbitration Association Interactive Arbitration Rules (2019)
    art 48
Korean Commercial Arbitration Board Domestic Arbitration Rules (2016)
    art 38
Korean Commercial Arbitration Board Mediation Rules (2012)
OHADA Staff Regulations
Opinion of the European Economic and Social Committee on the Proposal for a Directive of the European Parliament and of the Council on Certain Aspects of Mediation in Civil and Commercial Matters (COM(2004) 718 final – 2004/0251 (COD)) [2005] OJ C286/1
Practice Direction 31 (Hong Kong) (2014)
Prague Rules on the Efficient Conduct of Proceedings in International Arbitration (2018)
    art 9
Public Construction Commission Official Notice No 09700479460 (Taiwan) (2008)
Shanghai International Economic and Trade Arbitration Commission Arbitration Rules (2015)
Shenzhen Court of International Arbitration Guidelines for the Administration of Arbitration under the UNCITRAL Arbitration Rules (2019)

art 7(3)
Shenzhen Court of International Arbitration Rules (2016)
　art 3(4)
　art 45
SIMC-SIAC Arb-Med-Arb Protocol (2014)
　clauses 4–5
　clause 5
　clause 7
Singapore International Arbitration Centre Investment Arbitration Rules (2017)
Singapore International Arbitration Centre Rules (2016)
　art 32.10
Swiss Rules of Mediation (2019)
　art 16(5)
UNCITRAL Arbitration Rules (2013)
　art 12(1)
　art 13(4)
UNCITRAL Conciliation Rules (1980)
　art 16
　art 19
UNCITRAL Model Law on International Commercial Arbitration (1985)
　art 30
UNCITRAL Model Law on International Commercial Arbitration (2006)
　art 2A
　art 4
　art 9
　art 14
　art 14(3)
　art 17J
　art 18
　art 19
　art 28
　art 30
　art 30(1)
UNCITRAL Model Law on International Commercial Conciliation (2002)
　art 1
UNCITRAL Model Law on International Commercial Mediation and International Settlement Agreements Resulting from Mediation (2018)
　art 1(3)
　art 5(2)
　art 7(2)
　art 7(3)
　art 11
　art 11(3)

art 13
art 14
United Nations General Assembly A/CN.9/460 (6 April 1999)
United Nations General Assembly A/CN.9/468 (10 April 2000)
United Nations General Assembly A/CN.9/485 (20 December 2000)

ABBREVIATIONS

2006 Model Law	UNCITRAL Model Law on International Commercial Arbitration 2006
2018 Model Law	UNCITRAL Model Law on International Commercial Mediation and International Settlement Agreements Resulting from Mediation 2018
ACDC	Australian Commercial Disputes Centre
ADR	alternative dispute resolution
ADRIC	Alternative Dispute Resolution Institute of Canada
AFC	Administration and Finance Committee, EOC
AHRC	Australian Human Rights Commission
AHRCA	Australian Human Rights Commission Act 1986
AMA Protocol	SIMC–SIAC Arb-Med-Arb Protocol
ANCOM	Andean Common Market
AO	Arbitration Ordinance (Cap 609)
APEC	Asia-Pacific Economic Cooperation
arb-med	arbitration-mediation
ASEAN	Association of Southeast Asian Nations
BAC	Beijing Arbitration Commission
BCICAC	British Columbia International Commercial Arbitration Centre
BRI	Belt and Road Initiative
BRTN	Balanced Relationship Target Number
BVI	British Virgin Islands
CAA	Chinese Arbitration Association
CAA	Commercial Arbitration Act 2010
CAA Construction DAB Rules	Rules of the Construction Dispute Adjudication Board, Chinese Arbitration Association
CAA Construction DRB Rules	Rules of the Construction Dispute Review Board, Chinese Arbitration Association
CAAI	Chinese Arbitration Association International
CAC	*Centre d'Arbitrage du Congo*
CACI	*Cour d'Arbitrage de la Côte d'Ivoire*

xlvi

CCIAD	*Chambre de Commerce, d'Industrie et d'Agriculture de Dakar*
CCJA	*Cour Commune de Justice et d'Arbitrage*
CCP	Code of Civil Procedure
CDD	Corporate Communications Division, EOC
CEDR	Centre for Effective Dispute Resolution
CEOO	chief equal opportunities officer, EOC
CEPA	Closer Economic Partnership Arrangement
CICC	China International Commercial Court
CIETAC	China International Economic and Trade Arbitration Commission
CJR	civil justice reform
COO	chief operating officer, EOC
CPPC	Community, Participation and Publicity Committee, EOC
CPR	Civil Procedure Rules
CPR	International Institute for Conflict Prevention and Resolution
COMESA	Common Market for Eastern and Southern Africa
COVID-19	Coronavirus disease 2019
CPSD	Corporate Planning and Services Division, EOC
CRGBP	Complaint Review Board for Government Procurement
CSD	Complaint Services Division, EOC
DDO	Disability Discrimination Ordinance (Cap 487)
DHDR	diversified harmonious dispute resolution
DRAM	dynamic random access memory
DRCPA	Domestic Relations Case Procedure Act
eBRAM	electronic business related arbitration and mediation
ECOWAS	Economic Community of West African States
EEOC	US Equal Employment Opportunity Commission
EOC	Hong Kong Equal Opportunities Commission
EOO	equal opportunities officer, EOC
ERSUMA	*Ecole Régionale Supérieure de la Magistrature*
EU	European Union
FAA	Federal Arbitration Act
FDRC	Financial Dispute Resolution Centre
FDRS	Financial Dispute Resolution Scheme
FIDIC	*Fédération Internationale Des Ingénieurs-Conseils*
FOS	Financial Ombudsman Service
FSDO	Family Status Discrimination Ordinance (Cap 527)

FTA	free trade agreement
GICAM	*Centre d'Arbitrage du Groupement Interpatronal du Cameroun*
HKIAC	Hong Kong International Arbitration Centre
HKIAC-HKMC	HKIAC Mediation Council
HKMA	Hong Kong Monetary Authority
HKMAAL	Hong Kong Mediation Accreditation Association Limited
HPC	High People's Court
HRA	Human Rights Act 1993
HRRT	Human Rights Review Tribunal
IAR	2019 Interactive Arbitration Rules
IBA	International Bar Association
ICAC	International Commercial Arbitration Court of the Chamber of Commerce and Industry of the Russian Federation
ICC	International Chamber of Commerce
ICE	international commercial expert
ICEC	International Commercial Expert Committee
ICSID	International Centre for Settlement of Investment Disputes
IIA	international investment agreement
IOP Manual	Internal Operating Procedures Manual
ISDS	investor–state dispute settlement
JCAA	Japan Commercial Arbitration Association
JCCDA	Judicial Conciliation of Civil Disputes Act
JDC	Jeju Free International City Development Center
KCAB	Korean Commercial Arbitration Board
LAIA	Latin American Integration Association
LCC	Legal and Complaints Committee, EOC
LSD	Legal Services Division, EOC
MDR	multi-tier dispute resolution
med-arb	mediation-arbitration
med-arb-med	mediation-arbitration-mediation
MSMEs	micro-, small and medium-sized enterprises
neg-arb	negotiation-arbitration
New York Convention	1958 United Nations Convention on the Recognition and Enforcement of Foreign Arbitral Awards
OECD	Organisation for Economic Co-operation and Development
OHADA	*Organisation pour l'Harmonisation en Afrique du Droit des Affaires*

OHRP	Office of Human Rights Proceedings
OPEC	Organization of the Petroleum Exporting Countries
Prague Rules	Prague Rules on the Efficient Conduct of Proceedings in International Arbitration
PRIME Finance	Panel of Recognised International Market Experts in Finance
PRTC	Policy, Research and Training Committee, EOC
QMUL	Queen Mary University of London
RDO	Race Discrimination Ordinance (Cap 602)
PARLe	Platform to Assist in the Resolution of Litigation Electronically
REIO	regional economic integration organisation
RHC	Rules of the High Court
RMB	renminbi
RSC	Rules of the Supreme Court
SAR	Special Administrative Region
SBA	Seoul Bar Association
SCIA	Shenzhen Court of International Arbitration
SDO	Sex Discrimination Ordinance (Cap 480)
SEOO	senior equal opportunities officer, EOC
SFC	Securities and Futures Commission
SHIAC	Shanghai International Arbitration Center
SIAC	Singapore International Arbitration Centre
SII	self-initiated investigation
SIMC	Singapore International Mediation Centre
SIMI	Singapore International Mediation Institute
Singapore Convention	2019 United Nations Convention on International Settlement Agreements Resulting from Mediation
SPC	Supreme People's Court
TFEU	Treaty on the Functioning of the European Union
UAA	Uniform Arbitration Act 2016
UAE	United Arab Emirates
UAM	universal agreement to mediate
UCR	UNCITRAL Conciliation Rules
UICMA	Uniform International Commercial Mediation Act 2005
UK	United Kingdom
ULCC	Uniform Law Conference of Canada
UMA	Uniform Mediation Act 2001
UN	United Nations
UNCITRAL	United Nations Commission on International Trade Law

LIST OF ABBREVIATIONS

US	United States
USD	US dollar
VanIAC	Vancouver International Arbitration Centre
WAC	Wuhan Arbitration Commission
XAC	Xi'an Arbitration Commission

PART I

A Global Overview of Multi-tier Dispute Resolution: Main Themes

1

Mapping and Assessing the Rise of Multi-tiered Approaches to the Resolution of International Disputes across the Globe

An Introduction

WEIXIA GU*

1.1 Introduction

There are many ways in which disputes can arise in the commercial world and there are just as many ways in which they can be resolved. Much as different modes of alternative dispute resolution (ADR) have gained in popularity around the world, there has been growing interest in the combined use of such modes.

The Queen Mary University of London and White & Case LLP 2018 International Arbitration Survey observes that 'there has been a significant increase in the combination of arbitration with ADR'.[1] Nearly half of the participants[2] in the 2018 survey preferred a hybrid approach, as compared to just 35 per cent in the 2015 survey.[3] This is unsurprising in view of the benefits of mediation as a prerequisite to arbitration.[4] An initial mediation allows for a 'cooling off' between the parties, thereby avoiding an escalation of their dispute.[5] It also has a filtering effect. It enables the parties to assess

---

* This chapter benefits from the financial support of the Hong Kong Research Grants Council General Research Fund (HKU 17617416, 17602218 and 17609419).
[1] Queen Mary University of London and White & Case LLP, '2018 International Arbitration Survey: The Evolution of International Arbitration' <www.arbitration.qmul.ac.uk/media/arbitration/docs/2018-International-Arbitration-Survey-report.pdf> accessed 2 February 2020, 5.
[2] Of the respondents to the survey, 25 per cent were from the Asia Pacific region: see ibid 41.
[3] ibid 5.
[4] Constance Castres Saint-Martin, 'Arb-Med-Arb Service in Singapore International Mediation Centre: A Hotfix to the Pitfalls of Multi-tiered Clauses' [2015] Asian Journal of Mediation 35, 37.
[5] Craig Tevendale, Hannah Ambrose and Vanessa Naish, 'Multi-tier Dispute Resolution Clauses and Arbitration' (2015) 1 Turkish Commercial Law Review 31, 33.

the relative strengths of their respective cases. Even if only partly successful in resolving a dispute, it should result in only the truly contentious issues proceeding to arbitration, while everything else is resolved with the assistance of a skilled mediator.[6] The 2018 survey indicates that, generally, commercial parties would rather avoid disputes and preserve established relationships. For instance, within the in-house counsel sub-group of participants to the 2018 survey, there was a 'clear preference' for combining arbitration with other forms of ADR (60 per cent).[7] Mediation as a precondition to arbitration or even litigation thus offers a prospect of parties' maintaining an amicable commercial relationship.

The 2018 Pound Conference Report further confirms that there is now a global interest in hybrid modes of dispute resolution.[8] These typically require mediation, arbitration and possibly other modes of ADR (for example, neutral evaluation) to be attempted in an agreed sequence. Such processes are referred to as 'multi-tier dispute resolution' (MDR). Despite its widespread popularity, MDR, in its development, has followed different trajectories in different jurisdictions. This introductory chapter will therefore provide a survey of MDR and its many pathways around the world. Section 1.2 will discuss concepts and procedures underlying MDR. Section 1.3 will explore how MDR has developed from a regulatory perspective in different countries. Section 1.4 will examine specific situations in a few prominent jurisdictions in both the East and the West. Section 1.5 will conclude with some comparative insights into MDR global trends.

1.2 Dispute Resolution Innovation

1.2.1 Concept

MDR refers to a hybrid form of dispute resolution that combines an initial non-adjudicative approach (such as mediation or neutral evaluation) with a subsequent adjudicative approach (such as arbitration or litigation) in the event that the initial non-adjudicative process is unsuccessful in resolving all or part of the parties' differences. This innovative approach accordingly combines two seemingly contrary methods of

---

[6] ibid.
[7] Queen Mary University of London and White & Case LLP (n 1) 5.
[8] Herbert Smith Freehills and PricewaterhouseCoopers, *Global Pound Conference Series: Global Data Trends and Regional Differences* (2018) <www.imimediation.org/download/909/reports/35507/global-data-trends-and-regional-differences.pdf> accessed 2 April 2021, 3.

dispute resolution: one adversarial, the other non-adversarial or at least less so. The first stage of an MDR will typically entail a mediation, that is, a 'person-oriented' process that takes place within an informal and conciliatory atmosphere. If the mediation proves abortive, the second stage will often mandate the parties to go through an arbitration, that is, an 'act-oriented' process that places a premium on formal legal argument, accurate fact-finding and strict observance of due process.[9] Consequently, MDR has the benefit of providing a pre-planned customised framework for the resolution of the parties' differences. The parties are contractually bound to attempt mediation in good faith for a specified number of days before they can pursue arbitration or start an action in court. However, in interposing an initial non-adversarial tier, MDR also gives the parties the flexibility to reach a 'deal' early on. That deal may not reflect the strict legal merits of the parties' respective contentions, but it can more satisfactorily address their real needs and concerns, which will often be of a non-legal nature (for example, preserving reputation, maintaining cash flow or supply lines, or saving 'face'). MDR's promotion of non-adversarial means for settling disputes gives the parties the freedom to fashion creative solutions for resolving their differences. Constrained as they are by rules and precedents, an arbitral tribunal or court would simply not be able to order such solutions.[10] As Stipanowich has commented, MDR is particularly suited for contractual relationships, as parties maintain control over the resolution of their disputes from the outset by reason of the flexibility afforded by the contractually mandated initial non-adversarial tier.[11]

Modes of MDR are often referred to as hyphenated phrases, employing the abbreviations 'arb' and 'med' in varying permutations (for example, 'med-arb', 'arb-med', 'arb-med-arb', etc). But the use of these terms is not consistent and can become a source of confusion. This is because these terms imply a sequence in which different stages of a dispute resolution process are supposed to be carried out. It is submitted that, while these double-barrelled or triple-barrelled terms can be used to refer to specific

---

[9] Weixia Gu, 'Looking at Arbitration through a Comparative Lens' (2018) 13(2) Journal of Comparative Law 164, 181.

[10] Tribunals and courts are normally limited to ordering damages, specific performance or injunctions to resolve a dispute. They can also make declarations as to a party's rights in a matter. But they would not be able to order that one party apologise to the other or give that other party more business under some contract in return for the latter agreeing to drop its complaints.

[11] Chapter 11 in this volume.

modes of MDR, they should not be used as umbrella terms covering the entire range of MDR.[12] In this chapter, the term 'MDR' will be used to denote the concept of multi-tier dispute resolution as a whole, while expressions such as 'med-arb' and 'arb-med' will be used to refer to specific MDR processes.

1.2.2 Procedure

The sequence of mediation and arbitration in MDR can vary. One can have med-arb, arb-med-arb, and arb-med. In med-arb, the parties start with mediation. If that is unsuccessful, they may commence arbitration. Despite the simplicity of the concept, as Nottage and Garnett point out, when a mediation is successful, there is logically no further dispute capable of triggering an arbitration to generate an enforceable arbitral award.[13] Thus, it may be preferable for parties to engage in arb-med-arb. Parties begin with an arbitration and, during the arbitration, attempt to settle some or all of their differences through mediation. At this point, the arbitration is stayed. If the mediation is successful and a settlement is reached, the mediated settlement agreement can be incorporated into an award by the arbitral tribunal.[14] On the other hand, if the mediation is unsuccessful, the arbitration simply continues until the tribunal makes an award. As for arb-med, such process presumes that the parties will voluntarily carry out their mediated settlement agreement once reached. Otherwise, the arbitration will need to be resumed and the tribunal requested to incorporate the mediated settlement into an enforceable award. If parties opt to arbitrate from the outset, it is unlikely that they will be satisfied with a mediated settlement agreement and they will probably request the arbitral tribunal to convert the settlement into an enforceable arbitral award instead.[15] This situation may change after the coming into effect of the 2019 United Nations Convention on International Settlement Agreements Resulting from Mediation (the 'Singapore Convention') in September 2020. The Singapore Convention enables mediated settlement agreements to be

---

[12] Weixia Gu, 'Hybrid Dispute Resolution beyond the Belt and Road: Toward a New Design of Chinese Arb-med(-arb) and Its Global Implications' (2019) 29(1) Washington International Law Journal 117, 121–22.

[13] Luke Nottage and Richard Garnett, 'The Top 20 Things to Change in or around Australia's International Arbitration Act' in Luke Nottage and Richard Garnett (eds), *International Arbitration in Australia* (The Federation Press 2010) 149, 179.

[14] See, for instance, article 30 (Settlement) of the 2006 UNCITRAL Model Law on International Commercial Arbitration (the '2006 Model Law').

[15] Gu (n 12) 122.

enforced in contracting states.[16] However, to date, only 3 countries have acceded to the Singapore Convention, in contrast to the 163 states that are parties to the 1958 United Nations Convention on the Recognition and Enforcement of Foreign Arbitral Awards (the 'New York Convention'). It is hoped that, in the near future, more countries will become parties to the Singapore Convention and mediated settlement agreements can be as easily and widely enforced across borders as arbitration awards.[17]

A particular concern associated with MDR relates to the multiple roles assumed by the same neutral. Throughout the MDR process, the same neutral may take up the roles of arbitrator and mediator. This leads to worries as to the confidentiality of information imparted to the neutral by a party in the course of mediation and the possibility that, when acting as an arbitrator, the neutral may be influenced by what one party or the other has said during the mediation stage. This problem is one that regulatory frameworks around the world have sought to address. How a jurisdiction deals with this issue can affect the trajectory of MDR in that jurisdiction. This is a matter that will be further discussed in Sections 1.3–1.5.

1.3 Regulatory Regimes Generally

MDR has been regulated in different ways in different jurisdictions. Regulatory provisions may be found in a jurisdiction's civil procedure code or in bespoke mediation or arbitration statutes. But, as Aragaki points out, med-arb and arb-med are often regulated separately.[18] There is no holistic legislation for MDR in most countries. Guidelines for med-arb on an international stage can be found in the UNCITRAL Model Law on International Commercial Mediation and International Settlement

---

[16] Chapter 8 in this volume.
[17] The problem of enforcing a mediated settlement agreement across borders should not, however, be exaggerated. Presumably the parties reach a settlement agreement because they are prepared to abide by it. Some 90 per cent of arbitral awards are in fact honoured by losing parties without need for recourse to the New York Convention. See, for instance, Queen Mary University of London and PricewaterhouseCoopers, 'International Arbitration: Corporate Attitudes and Practices' (2008) <www.pwc.co.uk/assets/pdf/pwc-international-arbitration-2008.pdf> accessed 24 September 2020, 8. It is likely that a similar (if not higher) percentage of mediated settlement agreements will be adhered to without need for a court order. In practice, it will only be in a small proportion of cases (10 per cent or less) that the mechanisms of the Singapore Convention will be required.
[18] Chapter 2 in this volume.

Agreements Resulting from Mediation 2018 (the '2018 Model Law').[19] While the UNCITRAL Conciliation Rules 1980 prohibited a mediator from later acting as arbitrator in the same dispute, the 2018 Model Law revised that position by providing in article 13 that the prohibition can be overridden by the parties' agreement. On the other hand, UNCITRAL has apparently adopted a different approach for arb-med. Unlike the 2018 Model Law, the UNCITRAL Model Law on International Commercial Arbitration 2006 (the '2006 Model Law') does not explicitly address MDR.[20] Instead, article 19 of the 2006 Model Law merely states that the parties may agree on the procedure to be followed by the arbitral tribunal in conducting the arbitration proceedings. It is submitted that the language is broad enough to allow a tribunal to direct that there be an attempt at mediation, conducted by the tribunal or one of its members, at some point within arbitration proceedings.

Aragaki's survey of MDR in 129 jurisdictions shows that most countries have laws regulating arbitration and mediation.[21] In particular, all jurisdictions surveyed have arbitration laws, while 67 per cent have mediation laws. However, only 38 per cent regulate med-arb. Among these, 90 per cent do so through their mediation law or by their arbitration law, and 76 per cent permit med-arb with the consent of the parties while the rest prohibit med-arb outright. On the other hand, 17 per cent of the jurisdictions regulate arb-med. Among them, 64 per cent authorise arbitrators to act as mediators with the parties' consent, while roughly 32 per cent allow arbitrators to do so at their discretion. Only Serbia prohibits arb-med. Notably, only 7 per cent of the jurisdictions surveyed regulate med-arb and arb-med.[22] These few jurisdictions are primarily in Australasia, followed by the Americas and Africa. None of the jurisdictions in Europe or the Middle East have done so. Meanwhile, among states that regulate at least one form of MDR, there are three times more common law (as opposed to civil law) jurisdictions.[23] Based on these findings, Aragaki has argued that MDR should not simply be regulated piecemeal, with different statutes applying to mediation and arbitration respectively. He suggests instead that there should be a unified approach to MDR, with a single statute regulating arbitration, mediation and their hybrids.

---

[19] UN Doc A/73/17 (2018).
[20] UN Doc A/40/17 (2006).
[21] Chapter 2 in this volume.
[22] ibid.
[23] ibid.

From Aragaki's survey results, it can also be observed that the regulatory frameworks for MDR differ not only across jurisdictions but also among different geographical areas and legal systems. The impact of geography and legal system on MDR will be discussed in Sections 1.4 and 1.5.

1.4 Regulatory Regimes in Different Jurisdictions

1.4.1 MDR in Asia

1.4.1.1 Common Law Asia

MDR has developed rapidly in Hong Kong and Singapore. As both jurisdictions aspire to become Asia's leading dispute resolution hub, MDR is being actively promoted in both.

Singapore's open attitude towards MDR is manifest from its judicial decisions and legislation. MDR is expressly allowed by Singapore's Arbitration Act (Cap 10) and its International Arbitration Act (Cap 143A), both of which permit the same person to act as mediator and arbitrator in a dispute.[24] The Singaporean judiciary's recognition of MDR can be seen in the seminal decision of *International Research Corp plc v Lufthansa Systems Asia Pacific Pte Ltd*,[25] in which the Court of Appeal held that MDR contractual clauses were enforceable. Commentators have characterised the court's approach as 'commercially sensible' as guidance on the requirement of certainty in MDR clauses.[26] In coming to its conclusion, the court emphasised the principle of party autonomy, stating that 'where the parties have clearly contracted for a specific set of dispute resolution procedures as preconditions for arbitration, those preconditions must be fulfilled'.[27]

On top of legislative and judicial support for MDR, the Singapore International Arbitration Centre (SIAC) and the Singapore International Mediation Centre (SIMC) jointly launched the SIMC–SIAC Arb-Med-Arb Protocol (the 'AMA Protocol') in 2014. The AMA Protocol is in effect a unified MDR framework. If parties choose to adopt the AMA Protocol, their SIAC arbitration will be stayed for a maximum of eight weeks pending

---

[24] Singapore Arbitration Act, ss 37, 62(4); Singapore International Arbitration Act, ss 16(3), 18.
[25] *International Research Corp plc v Lufthansa Systems Asia Pacific Pte Ltd* [2014] 1 SLR 130 (Singapore).
[26] Seng Onn Loong and Deborah Koh, 'Enforceability of Dispute Resolution Clauses in Singapore' [2016] Asian Journal of Mediation 51, 59.
[27] *Lufthansa* (n 25) [62].

mediation at the SIMC. If the mediation succeeds, the resulting settlement agreement can be incorporated into an SIAC award which would then be enforceable under the New York Convention. On the other hand, if the mediation is unsuccessful, the SIAC arbitration will resume. Yip points out that the AMA Protocol has the advantages of specific procedures, enforceability on a par with an arbitral award, and access to a large pool of independent, impartial and experienced mediators and arbitrators.[28] However, Yip notes that the AMA Protocol may have a negative impact on party autonomy and procedural flexibility, two important features of MDR. This is because it is unclear whether parties can modify the steps and timelines stipulated by the AMA Protocol.[29] While the AMA Protocol is a relatively new feature of MDR in Singapore, a survey indicates that, since its launch in 2014, approximately a fifth of more than fifty SIMC administered mediations have utilised the AMA Protocol.[30]

Hong Kong is a special administrative region of China which enjoys a separate legal system under the 'One Country, Two Systems' arrangement. Accordingly, Hong Kong boasts an established common law system with an independent judiciary that is distinct from the socialist civil law system in place in Mainland China. Like Singapore, Hong Kong has long aimed to become a leading regional dispute resolution hub. Consequently, it, too, has a legislative framework and judiciary supportive of MDR. The Arbitration Ordinance (Cap 609) in Hong Kong allows arbitrators to act as mediators before or following an arbitration with the parties' consent.[31] In a similar vein, various dispute resolution centres in Hong Kong encourage MDR through their rules. For instance, the Hong Kong International Arbitration Centre (HKIAC) revised its Arbitration Rules in 2018 to allow for the suspension of an arbitration to enable parties to pursue other means of settlement (including mediation) in the interim.[32] According to Grimmer, there are also plans to introduce similar amendments to the mediation rules in Hong Kong as well.[33] The Hong Kong Court of Appeal endorsed MDR in *Gao Haiyan v Keeneye Holdings Ltd*[34]

---

[28] Chapter 8 in this volume.
[29] ibid.
[30] Aziah Hussin, Claudia Kück and Nadja Alexander, 'SIAC-SIMC's Arb-Med-Arb Protocol' (2018) 11 New York Dispute Resolution Lawyer 85.
[31] Arbitration Ordinance (Cap 609) (Hong Kong), s 33.
[32] Hong Kong International Arbitration Centre, *2018 Administered Arbitration Rules* <www.hkiac.org/arbitration/rules-practice-notes/hkiac-administered-2018> accessed 26 February 2020, art 13.8.
[33] Chapter 9 in this volume.
[34] *Gao Haiyan v Keeneye Holdings Ltd* [2012] 1 HKLRD 627 (Hong Kong).

by enforcing an award made after an abortive mediation in which one of the arbitrators had taken part. The Court of Appeal overruled the first instance decision, which had held that the arb-med-arb process employed had been tainted by apparent bias.[35] Nevertheless, despite the many features favouring its use in Hong Kong, the popularity of MDR there remains limited.

The effectiveness of Hong Kong's efforts in promoting MDR can be gleaned from a survey of all cases administered by the HKIAC between 2014 and 2018. According to the HKIAC survey, almost all cases brought to the HKIAC involved dispute resolution clauses, most of which were well crafted with specific steps and timelines. But only 17 per cent of the cases concerned dispute resolution clauses that referred to different modes of dispute resolution and only 2 per cent of the relevant clauses provided for med-arb.[36] The agreements surveyed mostly came from the construction sector and typically adopted a four-tier dispute resolution process of (1) an engineer's decision, (2) mediation, (3) adjudication and (4) arbitration.[37] While the survey excluded cases not submitted to the HKIAC, it evidences a limited resort to MDR in Hong Kong overall.

1.4.1.2 Civil Law Asia

Much as their common law counterparts, civil law jurisdictions in Asia have endeavoured to promote MDR. In Japan, parties tend to be litigation-averse and, as a matter of Japanese culture, there seems to be a preference for the amicable settlement of disputes. As a result, mediation plays a significant role whenever arbitration is used. In family law cases, it is not unusual for the judge hearing a matter to supervise a mediation between the relevant parties.[38] A family law mediation is typically conducted by a third-party mediator who meets in caucus with each party. The mediator, however, reports all communications made to him or her by a party in the course of a caucus to the supervising judge. The mediations are usually successful, albeit conducted over a long time span, due to the parties' respect for the authority of the supervising judge.

---

[35] *Gao Haiyan v Keeneye Holdings Ltd* [2011] 3 HKC 157 (Hong Kong).
[36] Chapter 9 in this volume.
[37] Keyao Li and Sai On Cheung, 'The Potential of Bias in Multi-tier Construction Dispute Resolution Processes' in Paul W Chan and Christopher J Neilson (eds), *Proceedings of the 32nd Annual ARCOM Conference* (ARCOM 2016).
[38] Harald Baum, 'Mediation in Japan: Development, Forms, Regulation and Practice of Out-of-Court Dispute Resolution' in Klaus J Hopt and Felix Steffek (eds), *Mediation: Principles and Regulation in Comparative Perspectives* (Oxford University Press 2012) 1011–94.

Under Japan's Arbitration Law, an arbitrator may conduct mediation with the parties' written consents, which can be withdrawn at any stage.[39] This is known as the 'double-consent' mechanism. Japan's Arbitration Law does not elaborate on how a neutral should conduct him- or herself when acting as mediator and arbitrator in a dispute. This is instead governed by institutional rules such as those of the Japan Commercial Arbitration Association (JCAA) which require (among other matters) that a neutral disclose at each instance that an *ex parte* communication has occurred.[40] According to a study by the JCAA, the parties in 40 per cent of its arbitration cases between 1999 and 2008 attempted mediation. Of these, 52 per cent concluded with a settlement.[41] This indicates that MDR is becoming increasingly popular in Japan, notwithstanding the lack of a vibrant arbitration market in the jurisdiction.

In Mainland China,[42] MDR such as med-arb is popular for both domestic and cross-border disputes. Arbitrators actively promote mediation to disputing parties. In a survey, 50 per cent of the respondents had recommended mediation to the parties in more than 90 per cent of the cases in which the respondents were acting as arbitrators.[43] Thus, MDR in China is promoted not only by legislation and judicial decisions but also by arbitral institutions. Meanwhile, China's Arbitration Law (recently revised in 2017) requires that arbitral institutions have procedures in place for MDR.[44] The result is that each arbitral institution has its own set of MDR rules. Since there are more than 250 such institutions, this has led to a plethora of MDR procedures in China.

A major criticism against MDR in China concerns the potential conflict of interest that arises when a neutral acts as mediator and arbitrator in the same dispute. While China's legislation is silent on whether parties can request a third party to act as a mediator in the middle of an arbitration, it is assumed as a matter of practice that arbitrators can act as mediators in the

---

[39] Arbitration Act (Law No 138 of 2003) (Japan), art 38(1).
[40] 'Commercial Arbitration Rules (2019)' (*Japan Commercial Arbitration Association*) <www.jcaa.or.jp/en/arbitration/rules.html> accessed 14 November 2020 (the '2019 JCAA Rules'), art 59(2).
[41] Tatsuya Nakamura, 'Brief Empirical Study on Arb-med in the JCAA Arbitration' <www.jcaa.or.jp/e/arbitration/docs/news22.pdf> accessed 24 September 2020.
[42] In this chapter, China refers to 'Mainland China', excluding Hong Kong, Macau and Taiwan.
[43] Kun Fan, 'An Empirical Study of Arbitrators Acting as Mediators in China' (2014) 15(3) Cardozo Journal of Conflict Resolution 777, 791.
[44] Zhongcai Fa (仲裁法) [Arbitration Law] (promulgated by the National People's Congress Standing Committee, 1 September 2017, effective 1 January 2018) (China), art 51(1).

same dispute. This is reflected in the rules of major Chinese arbitral institutions, including those of the China International Economic and Trade Arbitration Commission (CIETAC) and the Beijing Arbitration Commission (BAC). Another issue with MDR as practised in China is confidentiality. As a mediator meeting with a party in caucus, a neutral will almost certainly receive sensitive confidential information which is not meant to be communicated to the other side and which would not in the normal course of an arbitration be communicated to the tribunal. If the mediation is unsuccessful, such information may consciously or subconsciously influence the neutral's mind when determining the case as arbitrator. This will be despite the other side being unaware of the nature of the information and therefore not having an opportunity to rebut any adverse impression that the information may have conveyed to the neutral's mind. This issue was highlighted in the Hong Kong decision of *Gao Haiyan v Keeneye Holdings Ltd* mentioned earlier.[45] There, a Chinese arbitration tribunal in Xi'an suggested that the parties attempt mediation. The tribunal appointed the Xi'an Arbitration Commission's Secretary-General and one of its members to act as mediators. The mediators urged a friend of a party (party A)[46] to accept their proposed settlement in the course of dinner at a Xi'an hotel. After the proposal was rejected by party A (who had previously stated that it was not interested in attempting any mediation), the tribunal made an award in favour of the other party. The award was challenged but upheld by the Xi'an Intermediate People's Court, which found that nothing exceptional about the mediation had taken place. The enforcement of the award was then challenged in Hong Kong. The Court of First Instance refused enforcement due to the apparent bias arising from what happened at the Xi'an dinner. This decision was reversed on appeal on the ground that the Hong Kong court should defer to the decision of the Xi'an court, as the court of the arbitral seat. While it is unclear whether the Hong Kong court's approach will be followed internationally, *Keeneye* demonstrates the problems that can arise from a lack of due process safeguards in China's MDR rules. The upshot is that foreign parties are likely to be suspicious of the procedural fairness of the MDR process in China.

More recently, China has introduced the Belt and Road Initiative (BRI), an ambitious plan to connect China with different countries across the Eurasia region. To facilitate the development of the BRI, the Chinese International

---

[45] *Keeneye* (n 34); *Keeneye* (n 35).
[46] The friend attended the mediation at the mediators' request. Party A was not asked to attend the mediation and may not even have been aware that it was taking place.

Commercial Courts (CICC) was set up in 2018. The CICC exists as a permanent body within the Supreme People's Court (SPC) and is staffed by senior judges familiar with international laws.[47] Two courts have been set up under the CICC, one in Shenzhen (Guangdong Province) focusing on the BRI's Maritime Silk-Road and another in Xi'an (Shaanxi Province) focusing on the BRI's land-based Silk Road Economic Belt. While the CICC's primary function is to adjudicate international commercial cases, it has innovatively incorporated elements of MDR to provide a 'one-stop-shop' service. The service essentially combines litigation and mediation, although it may also allow for parts of a dispute to be resolved through arbitration. An International Commercial Expert Committee (ICEC) consisting of Chinese and foreign judges, mediators and arbitrators has been set up.[48] If parties to a dispute before the CICC reach a settlement of all or part of their dispute through a member of the ICEC, the CICC will issue a judgment incorporating the settlement agreement.[49] As of December 2018, the CICC has designated five Chinese arbitration institutions and two mediation institutions as part of this platform. This suggests that MDR under the CICC mechanism does not require different stages of dispute resolution to be conducted by the same persons or even institution. Instead, the CICC's platform allows for different persons to provide different dispute resolution services as necessary or appropriate. While details on precisely how this platform is to operate have yet to be worked out, its flexibility and convenience may well attract BRI-related cases to the CICC by addressing parties' likely concerns relative to avoiding conflicts of interest and maintaining confidentiality.[50]

1.4.2 *MDR Elsewhere*

1.4.2.1 Common Law Jurisdictions

The United Kingdom and the United States have been cautious about MDR in the situation where the same person acts as mediator and arbitrator in a dispute. Both jurisdictions are wary of the due process issues in such situation. That is in contrast with China and, at least insofar as family law matters are concerned, Japan.

---

[47] Supreme People's Court, '*Zuigao renmin fayuan guanyu sheli guoji shangshi fating ruogan wenti de guiding*' [Provisions of the Supreme People's Court on Several Issues Regarding the Establishment of the International Commercial Court] [2018] Fa Shi 11, art 1.
[48] ibid, art 11.
[49] ibid, arts 12, 13.
[50] Gu (n 12).

The 1996 English Arbitration Act does not address MDR. In *Glencot Development & Design v Ben Barrett & Son*,[51] an arb-med-arb was conducted in which the same neutral acted as adjudicator, then as mediator, and again as adjudicator in the same dispute. When the plaintiff sought to enforce the final award, the defendant resisted the claim on the ground of bias. The court agreed with the defendant, holding that one should consider whether the 'circumstances would lead a fair-minded and informed observer to conclude that there was a real possibility, or a real danger ... that the tribunal was biased'.[52] At the end, it was found that the neutral's award was tainted by apparent bias. In the premises, it can be said that the current state of UK law does not support the MDR mode where the same person acts as mediator and adjudicator. The UK situation is further exemplified by *Sulamerica CIA Nacional de Seguros SA v Enesa Engenharia SA*.[53] The court held that MDR clauses may be enforceable insofar as the processes that the parties are required to undertake pursuant to such clauses can be defined with a reasonable degree of certainty.[54]

In the USA, legislation and judicial decisions have similarly been ambivalent in relation to MDR. Bühring-Uhle and others comment that legislation in the USA has not kept up with the growth in MDR's popularity.[55] In *Advanced Bodycare Solutions v Thione International*,[56] the Court of Appeal of the 11th Circuit ruled that a contractual provision requiring parties to institute mediation or non-binding arbitration was not enforceable under the Federal Arbitration Act (FAA). This was because, to be enforceable under the FAA, an agreement has to provide for a dispute resolution process that will 'result in an "award" declaring the rights and duties of the parties'. Insofar as mediation under the relevant clause was concerned, the difficulty was that

> [m]ediation does not resolve a dispute; it merely helps the parties do so. In contrast, the FAA presumes that the arbitration process itself will produce a resolution independent of the parties' acquiescence of an award which

---

[51] *Glencot Development & Design v Ben Barrett & Son* [2001] All ER (D) 384 (United Kingdom).
[52] ibid [86].
[53] *Sulamerica CIA Nacional de Seguros SA v Enesa Engenharia SA* [2012] EWCA Civ 638, [2013] 1 WLR 102 (United Kingdom).
[54] Although restrictive in the sense of holding that only certain MDR clauses are enforceable, the case evidences a more liberal attitude to the enforceability of mediation clauses than that shown by the Hong Kong court. See further n 58.
[55] Christian Bühring-Uhle, Lars Kirchhoff and Gabriele Scherer, *Arbitration and Mediation in International Business* (2nd edn, Kluwer Law International 2006) 122.
[56] *Advanced Bodycare Solutions v Thione International* 524 F 3d 1235, 1238 (11th Cir 2008) (United States).

declares the parties' rights and which may be confirmed with the force of a judgment. That a typical mediation produces no award is highly probative evidence that an agreement to mediate a dispute is not 'an agreement to settle by arbitration a controversy'. 9 USC §2. Parties to a mediation contract have not 'agreed to submit a dispute for decision by a third party', *AMF Inc [v Brunswick Corp]*, 621 F Supp at 460, because the third party makes no decision.[57]

The court continued:

Further, a dispute resolution clause that may be satisfied by arbitration or mediation, at the aggrieved party's option, is not 'an agreement to settle by arbitration a controversy' and thus is not enforceable under the FAA either. Because we decide the case on this basis, we reserve for another day whether non-binding arbitration is within the scope of the FAA.

Nonetheless, insofar as MDR was concerned, the court helpfully stated at the end of its judgment:

We emphasise the limited nature of our ruling. This opinion should not be read as denigrating mediation-quite the contrary. We encourage parties to make liberal use of it, and we encourage district courts to liberally employ any authority they have under local rules to order mediation *sua sponte* when doing so may expedite the resolution of a case. Nor do we hold that agreements to mediate are per se unenforceable. They might be specifically enforceable in contract or under other law; that issue is not before us. Finally, we emphasise that we do not hold that stays in aid of mediation are per se impermissible. To the contrary, district courts have inherent, discretionary authority to issue stays in many circumstances, and granting a stay to permit mediation (or to require it) will often be appropriate. We merely hold that the mandatory remedies of the FAA may not be invoked to compel mediation.

This dictum is in fact more liberal than the position in some of the Asian common law jurisdictions such as Hong Kong today.[58] As we have seen, Singapore is more liberal than Hong Kong and has gone further than *Advanced Bodycare*.[59]

[57] ibid 1240.
[58] See *Hyundai Engineering & Construction Co Ltd v Vigour Ltd* [2005] 3 HKLRD 723 where the Hong Kong Court of Appeal overruled the first instance decision (at [2004] 3 HKLRD 1) which had held that some mediation agreements can be enforced. The Court of Appeal instead took the view that mediation agreements are merely 'agreements to agree' and so are unenforceable as a matter of common law. The Hong Kong Court of Final Appeal refused leave to appeal against the Court of Appeal's decision, which therefore remains the position in Hong Kong today: *Vigour Ltd v Hyundai Engineering & Construction Co Ltd* (unreported, FAMV 4/2006, 22 May 2006).
[59] See *Lufthansa* (n 25).

Another issue arises from how US courts address non-compliance with valid MDR agreements. Some courts stay judicial proceedings to compel parties to comply with an agreed dispute resolution process. In *Swartz v Westminster Services Inc*,[60] the court held that 'when confronted with an objection that a plaintiff has initiated litigation without satisfying arbitration or mediation requirements, courts routinely stay rather than dismiss the proceedings to allow for implementation of the agreed-upon dispute resolution mechanism'.[61] However, other courts may dismiss the action altogether by treating MDR as a condition precedent to judicial adjudication. In *Tattoo Art Inc v TAT International LLC*,[62] the court held: 'The plain language of the mediation provision unambiguously shows that the parties elected not to be subject to this Court's jurisdiction, at least with respect to any dispute stemming from the Licensing Agreement, until one of the parties either requests mediation and that request is denied or mediation commences and fails.'[63] Some courts may even dismiss the action and enter a judgment against the party that has failed to comply with the obligation, as in the case of *Primov v Serco*.[64] Despite the inconsistent approaches of different courts, MDR has attracted increased attention from commercial parties in the USA. In a survey of Fortune 1000 companies, 40 per cent of respondents in 1997 reported recent use of MDR. The number rose to 51 per cent in 2011.[65] As noted by Stipanowich, the tendency of arbitration in the USA to take on the trappings of litigation, including increasingly sophisticated procedures with associated cost increases, has led parties to be more willing to settle their disputes through mediation in the course of arbitration proceedings.[66]

In Australia, judicial decisions have played a significant role in shaping the MDR landscape. Prior to the 1990s, MDR clauses involving mediation were treated as agreements to agree and so were unenforceable.

---

[60] *Swartz v Westminster Services Inc* No 8:10-cv-1722-T-30AEP, 2010 US Dist LEXIS 93107 (MD Fla, 8 September 2010) (United States).
[61] ibid 3.
[62] *Tattoo Art Inc v TAT International LLC* 711 F Supp 2d 645, 651 (ED Va 2010) (United States).
[63] ibid 650.
[64] *Primov v Serco Inc* 296 Va 59, 817 SE 2d 811 (Va 2018) (United States).
[65] Thomas J Stipanowich and J Ryan Lamare, 'Living with ADR: Evolving Perceptions and Use of Mediation, Arbitration and Conflict Management in Fortune 1,000 Corporations' (2014) 19 Harvard Negotiation Law Review 1, 36, 41 chart F.
[66] Chapter 11 in this volume.

This changed with *Hooper Bailie Associated Ltd v Natcon Group Pty Ltd*,[67] in which the court ruled that some mediation clauses can be enforced if sufficiently certain. Later cases have built on this foundation. In *Aiton Australia Pty Ltd v Transfield Pty Ltd*,[68] the court held that an enforceable MDR clause would be one which (1) did not require a party's consent to the initiation of any given stage of the MDR process; (2) stipulated the procedure for the appointment of any mediator; and (3) set out defined procedures or identified rules for the conduct of any mediation. More recent decisions have relaxed requirement (1) in *Aiton*.[69] Further, *Ku-ring-Gai Council v Ichor Constructions Pty Ltd*[70] has made it difficult to appeal against a court's decision with regard to MDR agreements, thereby enhancing the finality of such arrangements. The Australian courts may thus be seen to have been actively promoting and encouraging MDR.

Australian legislation has also contributed to the development of MDR. Since 2010, uniform legislation has been promulgated across Australia in respect of domestic arbitration. Australian states have sought to mirror international practice in their MDR-related legislation. The 2010 New South Wales Commercial Arbitration Act is closely based on the arbitration statutes of Singapore and Hong Kong.[71] The Australian Capital Territory's Commercial Arbitration Act 2017 permits an arbitrator to act as mediator in the same dispute with the parties' written consent. The parties' written consent is also required for the mediator to resume an arbitration.[72] However, despite supportive legislative initiatives in various states, international disputes are governed by the Australian International Arbitration Act 1974 (last amended in 2018), which does not deal with MDR.[73] This omission has been the subject of criticism.[74]

1.4.2.2 Continental Europe

As a jurisdiction comprising member states, the European Union (EU) has a legal framework different from that of other countries. Consequently, the

---

[67] *Hooper Bailie Associated Ltd v Natcon Group Pty Ltd* (1992) 28 NSWLR 194 (Australia).
[68] *Aiton Australia Pty Ltd v Transfield Pty Ltd* [1999] NSWSC 996 (Australia).
[69] Chapter 14 in this volume.
[70] *Ku-ring-gai Council v Ichor Constructions Pty Ltd* [2018] NSWSC 610 (Australia).
[71] Chapter 14 in this volume.
[72] Commercial Arbitration Act 2010 (NSW), s 27D.
[73] Richard Garnett, 'Australia's International and Domestic Arbitration Framework' in Gabriël Moens and Philip Evans (eds), *Arbitration and Dispute Resolution in the Resources Sector: An Australian Perspective* (Springer 2015) 7, 21.
[74] Chapter 14 in this volume.

development of MDR in the EU has not been achieved through national legislations or statutes but through directives and resolutions of the European Parliament. A directive requires member states to achieve a result without specifying how the outcome is to be achieved.[75] A resolution is a statement providing guidance which has no binding legal effect.[76] A key EU instrument on MDR has been Directive 2008/52/EC on Certain Aspects of Mediation in Civil and Commercial Matters (the 'Mediation Directive'), which took effect in 2008. The Mediation Directive's objective is to 'facilitate access to alternative dispute resolution and to promote the amicable settlement of disputes by encouraging the use of mediation and by ensuring a balanced relationship between mediation and judicial proceedings'.[77] The scope of the Mediation Directive is wide, covering both civil and commercial matters in cross-border disputes. But it does not apply to specified matters.[78] Apart from the Directive, the EU adopted the European Parliament Resolution on the EU Mediation Directive in 2017 (the 'Resolution') to continue the promotion of MDR.[79] The Resolution recognises the steps taken by member states and provides further recommendations, such as the development of EU-wide standards for dispute resolution. Although the Resolution is not binding, it demonstrates the EU's commitment to the development of different modes of dispute resolution.

Given the EU's legal framework, it is necessary to consider whether each member state has taken steps to implement the Directive through local legislation. Chaisse conducted a survey of the Directive's implementation in member states, noting an uneven development of mediation across the EU.[80] He concludes: 'While mediation has flourished in countries such as the UK and the Netherlands, basic problems exist in countries such as Estonia and the Czech Republic as a result of national legislation that inadequately differentiates between mediation and

---

[75] Chapter 15 in this volume.
[76] ibid.
[77] Directive 2008/52/EC of the European Parliament and of the Council of 21 May 2008 on Certain Aspects of Mediation in Civil and Commercial Matters [2008] OJ L136/3 (European Union), art 1(1).
[78] ibid, art 1(2).
[79] European Parliament Resolution of 12 September 2017 on the Implementation of Directive 2008/52/EC of the European Parliament and of the Council of 21 May 2008 on Certain Aspects of Mediation in Civil and Commercial Matters (the 'Mediation Directive') (2016/2066(INI)) [2018] OJ C337/2 (European Union).
[80] Chapter 15 in this volume.

conciliation.'[81] According to Bühring-Uhle and others, even in jurisdictions like France and Switzerland where MDR is popular, the civil procedure legislations still tend to address mediation during litigation only.[82] Although the French Code of Civil Procedure does not prevent arbitrators from acting as mediators, this is rarely done in practice.[83] On the other hand, Germany's Code of Civil Procedure makes reference to MDR as a means for parties to settle their dispute in the course of an arbitration.[84] If parties agree to settle their dispute during an arbitration, a tribunal may record the settlement in the form of an award. Interestingly, most MDR cases in Germany are conducted by the same neutral acting as arbitrator and mediator. This mirrors the practice in German courts, where judges may act as mediators in a case before them. This pre-existing practice may have helped German parties to adapt more readily to the dual role of neutrals in MDR proceedings.[85] As Bühring-Uhle and others' survey reveals, only a minority of respondents find it inappropriate for an arbitrator to act as mediator in the same proceedings.[86] Thus, it can be said that different jurisdictions within the EU have pursued different strategies towards MDR.

The development of MDR in Russia can be described as a work in progress. While the country has been promoting MDR to reduce the courts' caseload, development is hampered by the lack of clear procedural laws. A particular feature of Russian law is the mandatory pre-trial settlement procedure. For some types of disputes (such as carriage of goods cases), parties are required to attempt a settlement before court proceedings begin.[87] As a result, some Russian lawyers treat settlement negotiations as merely a step towards launching a litigation.[88] The lack of sincere attempts towards settlement is complicated by the fact that intended defendants may use the time gap between the filing of a claim and the commencement of court proceedings to avoid liability. A major source of confusion lies in the lack of clear standards of evidence to prove that a settlement has been attempted. As Molotnikov points out, the requirement can be satisfied by the plaintiff sending the claim to the

---

[81] ibid.
[82] *Schweizerische Zivilprozessordnung* [Swiss Code of Civil Procedure] (19 December 2008), SR 272 (Switzerland), art 214; Bühring-Uhle, Kirchhoff and Scherer (n 55) 122.
[83] Bühring-Uhle, Kirchhoff and Scherer (n 55) 122.
[84] *Zivilprozessordnung* [Code of Civil Procedure] (2005, as amended) (Germany), art 1053.
[85] Gu (n 12) 157.
[86] Bühring-Uhle, Kirchhoff and Scherer (n 55) 122.
[87] Civil Code of Russian Federation 2002 (Russia), art 797.
[88] Chapter 16 in this volume.

defendant via specified means that, however, do not require proof that the defendant has actually received the claim.[89] This is but one example showing that Russian procedure law is still in the making. While there are some helpful court cases, there remain significant areas of controversy.

1.5 Comparative Studies

1.5.1 Common Law vs Civil Law

In common law jurisdictions, the judiciary has played a major role in the development of MDR. Among the common law jurisdictions discussed already, a more widespread acceptance of MDR has usually been prompted by a landmark decision. In Australia, *Hooper Baillie Associated Ltd v Natcon Group Pty Ltd*[90] first recognised the validity of MDR clauses. In Singapore, *International Research Corp PLC v Lufthansa Systems Asia Pacific Pte Ltd*[91] demonstrated the court's positive attitude towards MDR. In Hong Kong, the judiciary has promoted mediation in Hong Kong through Practice Direction 31. In the meantime, the development of MDR in Hong Kong is influenced by *Gao Haiyan v Keeneye Holdings Ltd*,[92] which has even had repercussions for MDR in Mainland China. Without such decisions, parties will not have incentives to adopt MDR for fear of MDR clauses not being enforceable as mere agreements to agree. Regulatory schemes by governments or dispute resolution protocols from arbitral institutions tend to emerge after judicial affirmation.[93] Their role is complementary as compared to judicial decisions in terms of developing MDR. While this mode of development has the advantage of being flexible, it may also have the drawback of being sporadic and unpredictable. This is because it depends on when a case involving MDR finds its way to the courts and how it is decided. Consequently, to promote MDR, a common law jurisdiction may have to consider passing relevant legislation in advance of judicial decision.

On the other hand, in civil law jurisdictions, legislation plays an important role in developing MDR. Where a weak regulatory framework exists, as in Russia and certain Eastern European states, MDR is generally

---

[89] ibid.
[90] *Hooper* (n 67).
[91] *Lufthansa* (n 25).
[92] *Keeneye* (n 35).
[93] Governments can regulate MDR even without judicial decisions, precisely in order to avoid doubt as to the enforceability of MDR clauses.

less developed. Conversely, where countries have a detailed legislative framework for MDR, development is generally more advanced. This is so even if the legislative framework is not comprehensive. For instance, French and Swiss laws address only mediation during litigation, but MDR remains popular in these countries. Similarly, the development of MDR in Germany has been facilitated by legislation and pre-existing judicial practice. The same is true for China. Despite the lack of regulation there addressing due process concerns, MDR remains vibrant in China, thanks to the nudge given by the China Arbitration Law and numerous Chinese arbitration institutions filling the gap of regulations by developing their own rules in-house.[94]

Another facet of the difference between common law and civil law jurisdictions in terms of the development of MDR relates to procedural safeguards. Common law jurisdictions usually have more procedural requirements than their civil law counterparts. For instance, Hong Kong and Singapore expressly require parties' written consent for a neutral to take on the roles of arbitrator and mediator in a dispute. Furthermore, legislation in Hong Kong and Singapore imposes an obligation on arbitrators to disclose all confidential information obtained during mediation that may be relevant to an arbitration. The same requirement is not present in civil law jurisdictions in Asia such as Mainland China and Japan.[95]

1.5.2 Dispute Resolution Tradition and Culture

Given the differences in the state of development of MDR among different jurisdictions, one might speculate that there is a cultural aspect underlying how MDR is perceived in different parts of the world. Among the states surveyed in this book, jurisdictions in Asia have been more willing to countenance the use of MDR, especially where the same person acts as both mediator and arbitrator. While European and American jurisdictions are still developing a comprehensive legal framework for MDR, China and Singapore have been experimenting with innovative mechanisms. This difference might conceivably be attributable to Confucian culture. Chinese scholarship has often linked the success of MDR to a Confucian tradition of harmony, which stresses the preserving of social relationships over adversarial confrontation. An

---

[94] Most arbitral institutions (even in common law jurisdictions) have their own mediation rules. Even if they do not, nothing stops parties from adopting the mediation or MDR rules of (say) the ICC or similar bodies.
[95] Gu (n 9) 183–84.

'Eastern' culture of collectivism and harmony is typically characterised by commentators as inclining Asian parties to resolving disputes through conciliatory mechanisms, thereby preserving 'face'.[96] It has been repeatedly asserted, for instance, that the Japanese society regards disputes as culturally unacceptable.[97] As pointed out by Shen, as another face of the Chinese society, in Taiwan, litigation is generally viewed as a perilous undertaking, while mediation is preferred due to classical Confucian teachings such as 'there must not be any litigation' and 'peace is best'.[98] But such cultural explanations and stereotypes must be regarded with extreme caution. For example, the 'Confucian' thesis does not seem to hold true for the jurisdiction of Korea, which may be considered an archetypal Confucian society. The Choson dynasty ruled there for some 600 years. It maintained its hegemony by emphasising Confucian teaching and virtues, especially obedience to the state. However, paradoxically, contrary to what one might expect from an application of the Confucian thesis, according to Kim, mediation and MDR today are under-developed and under-utilised in South Korea; the most popular modes of dispute resolution are instead adversarial in nature (litigation and arbitration).[99] At the end of the day, it is submitted that there is no easy correlation between the 'East' and the 'West' and the use or non-use of MDR. It is risky to link a particular culture to the development of MDR in a jurisdiction. Numerous factors are at play and it is doubtful that a facile cultural dichotomy contrasting 'Western individualism' with 'Eastern social harmony' will be of any real utility as a tool for analysing trends and trajectories of MDR.

1.6 Conclusion

The development of MDR around the world has been diverse. Without a standardised global framework, different jurisdictions have followed different paths to develop their own versions of MDR procedure and rules. But due process concerns arise where the same neutral acts as both the mediator and the adjudicator. MDR, however, covers more than just that one situation. Some jurisdictions have remained more sceptical towards MDR, while others have been more active in devising rules and

---

[96] ibid 181–82.
[97] M Scott Donahey, 'Seeking Harmony: Is the Asian Concept of the Conciliator/Arbitrator Applicable in the West?' (1995) 50 Dispute Resolution Journal 74, 75.
[98] Chapter 5 in this volume.
[99] Chapter 7 in this volume.

procedures to govern MDR. Furthermore, there are jurisdictions which have embraced the concept of MDR and designed innovative ways to promote it without compromising due process. The way in which MDR is developed may depend on many factors, including a jurisdiction's legal system, its traditions, and its multi-faceted and variegated cultural aspects, as subsequent chapters in this book demonstrate.

2

A Snapshot of National Legislation on Same Neutral Med-arb and Arb-med around the Globe

HIRO N ARAGAKI[*]

2.1 Introduction

Med-arb and arb-med represent innovative combinations of two distinct processes of alternative dispute resolution (ADR) with shared but also different value orientations: arbitration and mediation. Arbitration is an adjudicative process that generally results in a binding award, whereas mediation is a facilitative process that may result in a voluntary settlement.

There are many reasons to favour med-arb and arb-med, which I refer to collectively as 'hybrid processes'. They are a testament to the essential insight of Frank Sander's 1976 address to the Pound Conference that there is no one way to resolve a dispute and that the challenge of procedural law reform is to find ways to 'fit the forum to the fuss'.[1] They also promote values such as efficiency and private ordering. For example, arb-med enables parties to short-circuit a potentially lengthy arbitral process by having the arbitrator act instead as a settlement facilitator. Med-arb enables parties to instruct their mediator to issue a binding award if a settlement appears out of their grasp.

But the hybridity achieved by mixing arbitration and mediation also creates problems, especially when the same neutral presides over both processes. From the standpoint of arbitration values, the problem arises

---

[*] For extremely helpful feedback and guidance, I am grateful to Weixia Gu, Anselmo Reyes and participants at the Conference on Multi-tier Approaches to the Resolution of International Disputes held at the University of Hong Kong, and to Lydia Nussbaum, Jennifer Reynolds and participants at the Experimental ADR Conference held at the University of Oregon. I also thank Gabriella Assmar, Eleni Charalambidou, Constantin-Adi Gavrila, Joongi Kim, Blažo Nedić and Emilia Onyema for country-specific input, and Alberto Gomez, Carlo Nardone and Laura Rodi for excellent research assistance.

[1] See Frank EA Sander, 'Varieties of Dispute Processing' (1976) 70 Federal Rules Decision 111, 130–31; Frank EA Sander and Stephen B Goldberg, 'Fitting the Forum to the Fuss: A User-Friendly Guide to Selecting an ADR Procedure' (1994) 10 Negotiation Journal 49.

when the mediator-to-be-arbitrator holds separate caucuses – effectively *ex parte* communications – during the mediation phase. Such communications threaten fundamental norms of due process and equal treatment in adjudication, norms whose violation could potentially result in a final award being set aside or refused enforcement.[2] From the perspective of mediation values, there are concerns regardless of whether separate caucuses are held. For example, parties might feel pressure to settle or to keep things close to the vest if they fear that something they do or say could be held against them after the mediator becomes the arbitrator.[3] Alternatively, they might use the mediation phase only instrumentally, as an opportunity to prime a future decision-maker rather than to explore settlement in good faith. And the mediator might feel emboldened to take a more directive or even coercive approach if he or she will ultimately be in a position to bind the parties absent a settlement. As we shall soon see, these arbitration and mediation values are implicated regardless of whether the hybrid process begins in mediation ('med-arb') or in arbitration ('arb-med').

In this chapter, I provide a broad overview of how jurisdictions around the world have attempted to address these issues through national law. I focus almost exclusively on same neutral processes (even though mediation and arbitration are very often combined using different neutrals) because the need for regulation is most acute in this context. I begin by surveying how the principal model laws and legislative precedents on mediation and arbitration regulate same neutral med-arb and arb-med, respectively. I then provide a descriptive account of the main regulatory approaches on the subject taken in national mediation and arbitration laws of 195 jurisdictions around the world. Finally, I conclude by eliciting broad regulatory patterns. Many patterns, when broken down by region and legal tradition, are difficult to explain in light of literature about the receptivity of Asian or civil law European countries towards same neutral hybrid processes.

---

[2] Harold I Abramson, 'Protocols for International Arbitrators Who Dare to Settle Cases' (1999) 10 American Review of International Arbitration 1, 4; KP Berger, 'Integration of Mediation Elements into Arbitration: "Hybrid" Procedures and "Intuitive" Mediation by International Arbitrators' (2003) 19 Arbitration International 387, 391–92; Gabrielle Kaufmann-Kohler, 'When Arbitrators Facilitate Settlement: Towards a Transnational Standard' (*Clayton UTZ*, 2007) <www.claytonutz.com/internal/archive/ialecture/content/previous/2007/speech_2007> accessed 14 January 2018.

[3] Henry J Brown and Arthur L Marriot, *ADR Principles and Practice* (2nd edn, Sweet & Maxwell 1999) para 7–110; Alan Redfern and Martin Hunter, *Law and Practice of International Commercial Arbitration* (3rd edn, Sweet & Maxwell 1999) para 1–60.

As far as I am aware, this is the first comprehensive, comparative study of the subject devoted to national laws.[4] Attempting such a study comes with its own set of perils. For example, because I am not an expert in the domestic laws of all countries surveyed, I will not capture all the ways in which the law on the books may be interpreted differently in action. The English translations of statutes on which I rely may also obscure important nuances. My goal is therefore modest by necessity: To paint a high-level overview of legislative trends in this area by surveying as many jurisdictions as possible, and to draw out some key implications for existing literature on the subject.

Before proceeding, let me be clear about certain concepts and terms used throughout this chapter.

Conciliation and mediation. Depending on the jurisdiction, there are sometimes salient differences in practice between conciliation and mediation. Nonetheless, for the purposes of this chapter, I treat the two as interchangeable as long as both refer to a voluntary, non-binding process in which the neutral has no power to impose a solution or decide an outcome. Thus, national legislation that regulates such a process but refers to it as 'conciliation' will be considered to be mediation legislation.

Med-arb and arb-med. By 'med-arb', I mean a process in which the resolution of a given dispute originates in mediation and is followed by arbitration. The same is true, *mutatis mutandis*, for 'arb-med'. This is the only criterion. Thus, although some commentators would limit arb-med to a process where the arbitrator drafts and seals the final award prior to commencing mediation, I impose no such limitations beyond the requirement of the process originating in arbitration. If an arbitration law addresses a situation where the parties agree to mediate prior to commencing arbitration (for example, pursuant to a 'stepped' arbitration clause), as is the case in Hong Kong, Singapore and a handful of other jurisdictions, I consider the law to regulate med-arb rather than arb-med. The same is true if an arbitration law contemplates mediation after the appointment of the tribunal but 'prior to [the] commencement of formal arbitration proceedings'.[5] In both cases, the rationale is that even though administrative acts such as filing a claim or appointing the arbitrators may have taken place beforehand, the actual work of resolving the dispute began during a mediation phase.

---

[4] Numerous books and articles have examined selected national laws on the subject, however. See Pieter Sanders, *Quo Vadis Arbitration? Sixty Years of Arbitration Practice: A Comparative Study* (Kluwer Law International 1999).

[5] See eg Commercial Arbitration Law of the Kingdom of Cambodia 2006, s 38.

Region. Throughout this chapter, I adopt the United Nations' M49 standard, also known as the UN 'geoscheme', which classifies countries and political entities into five main regions: Africa, the Americas, Asia, Europe and Oceania.[6] Each region is divided into sub-regions. For example, Africa is divided into Northern, Southern, Eastern, Western and Middle Africa. Notably, there is no Middle East region; instead, the Caucasus, the Levant and the Gulf Region all fall within Asia – specifically, the 'Western Asia' sub-region. Although Taiwan is not included in the geoscheme, I have included it nonetheless and classified it within the East Asia sub-region.

Legal tradition. With minor changes, I adopted a simplified version of the classification of political entities and legal systems compiled by JuriGlobe, a research group based at the Faculty of Law of the University of Ottawa.[7] As used in this chapter, the category 'common law' includes pure common law jurisdictions such as Australia, mixed common/Muslim law jurisdictions such as Bangladesh and mixed common/customary law jurisdictions such as Ghana. The category 'civil law' includes pure civil law jurisdictions such as France, mixed civil/Muslim law jurisdictions such as Egypt and mixed civil/customary jurisdictions such as Ethiopia. The category 'mixed common law/civil law' denotes a jurisdiction such as Cameroon or Sri Lanka, which has elements of both common and civil law traditions. The remaining categories are pure Muslim law jurisdictions (for example, Saudi Arabia), customary law jurisdictions (for example, Andorra) and mixed Muslim/customary law jurisdictions (for example, UAE).

2.2 Commonly Used Precedents

Hybrid processes are generally regulated, if at all, in stand-alone mediation acts, arbitration acts or combined ADR acts. Many of these acts are based on or influenced by internationally recognised model laws, such as the UNCITRAL Model Law on International Commercial Arbitration (the 'Model Arbitration Law'), and international legal instruments that have the force of positive law, such as the EU Directive 2008/52/EC on Certain Aspects of Mediation in Civil and Commercial Matters (the 'EU Directive'). This section provides a brief overview of how these models

---

[6] United Nations Secretariat Statistical Division, Standard Country or Area Codes for Statistical Use, Series M no 49 <https://unstats.un.org/unsd/methodology/m49/> accessed 14 August 2020.

[7] See 'Alphabetical Index of the Political Entities and Corresponding Legal Systems' (University of Ottawa) <www.juriglobe.ca/eng/sys-juri/index-alpha.php> accessed 14 August 2020.

and legal instruments, which I refer to collectively as 'precedents', address med-arb and arb-med.

Several observations about these precedents deserve mention. First, with the possible exception of restrictions on the disclosure or admissibility of mediation communications in a subsequent arbitration proceeding,[8] none specifically regulates *different* neutral med-arb or arb-med – for example, by encouraging or requiring an arbitral tribunal to refer the dispute to a third party mediator, and if so at what stage of the proceedings. To the extent that the precedents regulate hybrid processes at all, the focus is on processes where the same neutral serves as the arbitrator and the mediator. This is understandable because using a different neutral avoids the problems with med-arb and arb-med identified in Section 2.1, thereby largely obviating the need for legislation.[9]

Second, there is no precedent that seeks to harmonise the regulation of hybrid processes regardless of whether the process originated in mediation or arbitration – that is, no precedent seeks to ensure that med-arb and arb-med are regulated consistently. Nor is there any precedent dedicated exclusively to hybrid processes. Instead, the regulation of hybrid processes is siloed: Med-arb is treated only in mediation law precedents (for example, the UNCITRAL Model Law on International Commercial Mediation and International Settlement Agreements Resulting from Mediation 2018), and arb-med is treated only in arbitration law precedents (for example, the Canadian Uniform Arbitration Act 2016).

Third, the nature and the scope of regulation tend to be limited solely to the question of whether the same neutral may or may not serve in both roles. How the precedents each regulate this limited issue will be surveyed in Sections 2.2.1 and 2.2.2. The upshot is that none of the precedents delves into any other details of same neutral hybrid processes – for example, whether a final award issued by an arbitrator who also served as a mediator in the same dispute is enforceable even if he or she received *ex parte* information during caucuses, or whether any additional procedural protections are warranted before the mediator may assume or resume the arbitrator role.

---

[8] Most mediation law precedents provide that evidence of mediation communications may not be introduced in subsequent judicial or arbitral proceedings involving the same dispute. See eg UNCITRAL Model Law on International Commercial Mediation and International Settlement Agreements Resulting from Mediation 2018, s 11(3).
[9] Although different neutral hybrid process regulation could also benefit from regulation designed to promote it or improve its efficiency, for the most part the precedents have not been concerned with this type of reform. Perhaps private rule-making is considered a better vehicle for this purpose than national legislation.

2.2.1 Approaches to Same Neutral Med-arb

The UNCITRAL Conciliation Rules (UCR), published in 1980, were originally intended to serve as a set of rules that private parties could use to govern their conciliation process. But until UNCITRAL published the first version of its model mediation law in 2002 (and occasionally even thereafter) the UCR was sometimes used as a template for national conciliation legislation.

Article 19 of the UCR provides: 'The parties and the conciliator undertake that the conciliator will not act as an arbitrator or as a representative or counsel of a party in any arbitral or judicial proceedings in respect of a dispute that is the subject of the conciliation proceedings.' Read in its proper context, this provision does not necessarily imply a policy judgement that mediators should *never* act as arbitrators in the same dispute. The reason is that the UCR is a set of default rules that the parties may alter by mutual consent. That said, when a provision such as Article 19 comes to be incorporated verbatim into national legislation, it rather conveys the sense of a mandatory rule around which the parties are not entitled to contract. Wittingly or not, therefore, states that have adopted Article 19 have effectively prohibited med-arb outright unless a contrary interpretation is followed.

The UCR would eventually serve as a blueprint for the UNCITRAL Model Law on International Commercial Conciliation 2002, which was recently revised and renamed in 2018 (the 'Model Mediation Law').[10] Article 13 of the 2018 Model Mediation Law addresses the problem by explicitly providing for party consent to override the default prohibition against mediators acting as arbitrators: '*Unless otherwise agreed by the parties*, the mediator shall not act as an arbitrator in respect of a dispute that was or is the subject of the mediation proceedings or in respect of another dispute that has arisen from the same contract or legal relationship or any related contract or legal relationship.'[11]

Canada's Uniform International Commercial Mediation Act 2005 (UICMA), which was designed to be used for either international or domestic mediation, contains a substantially similar provision.[12] By contrast, not one of the US Uniform Mediation Act 2001 (UMA), the EU Directive or the 2019 United Nations Convention on International

---

[10] UNCITRAL Model Law on International Commercial Mediation and International Settlement Agreements Resulting from Mediation 2018, which supersedes the UNCITRAL Model Law on International Commercial Conciliation 2002.
[11] Model Mediation Law, s 13 (emphasis added).
[12] Uniform International Commercial Mediation Act 2005 (Canada), s 9.

Settlement Agreements Resulting from Mediation (the 'Singapore Mediation Convention') addresses med-arb.

2.2.2 Approaches to Same Neutral Arb-med

The principal model for arbitration legislation worldwide is the UNCITRAL Model Law on International Commercial Arbitration 2006 (the 'Model Arbitration Law'). But unlike its mediation counterpart, the Model Arbitration Law does not specifically address hybrid processes, regardless of whether the same or a different neutral is used.

For example, Article 30(1) provides only that '[i]f, during arbitral proceedings, the parties settle the dispute, the arbitral tribunal shall terminate the proceedings and, if requested by the parties and not objected to by the arbitral tribunal, record the settlement in the form of an arbitral award on agreed terms'. It does not contemplate that the arbitrators will themselves facilitate settlement, nor does it necessarily contemplate combining arbitration specifically with mediation (as opposed to bilateral negotiation).

Article 19 provides that 'the parties are free to agree on the procedure to be followed by the arbitral tribunal in conducting the proceedings', and Article 28 allows the tribunal to decide *ex aequo et bono* or as *amiable compositeurs*, but 'only if the parties have expressly authorized it to do so'. It is an open question as to whether these provisions can be taken to authorise same neutral arb-med. On the one hand, Article 19 of the Model Arbitration Law is almost identical to section 1(b) of the English Arbitration Act 1996, which some commentators have interpreted as permitting parties to agree to have the arbitrator act as a mediator.[13] On the other hand, it could be argued that Articles 19 and 28 address only the manner in which the tribunal may *adjudicate* disputes, and thus do not speak to the issue of whether the arbitrators may mediate. Regardless of how these questions are ultimately resolved, the point remains that the text of the Model Arbitration Law is fundamentally agnostic about same neutral arb-med. Thus, any state that has adopted the Model Arbitration Law wholesale has, just by virtue of doing so, likewise ostensibly refrained from taking a particular stance on the issue.

---

[13] See Jens M Scherpe and Bevan Marten, 'Mediation in England and Wales: Regulation and Practice' in Klaus J Hopt and Felix Steffek (eds), *Mediation: Principles and Regulation in Comparative Perspective* (Oxford University Press 2013) 375.

The 1958 United Nations Convention on the Recognition and Enforcement of Foreign Arbitral Awards (the 'New York Convention') is likewise silent on arb-med. By contrast, the Australian Model Commercial Arbitration Act 2010 and the Canadian Uniform Arbitration Act 2016 (UAA), both of which govern domestic arbitration, allow same neutral arb-med with party consent.[14]

2.3 National Laws

In this section, I report findings from a database of national mediation and arbitration laws that I am currently in the process of compiling and translating. Some caveats are in order before I begin.

First, my database focuses on law-making at the national level and excludes any subnational regulation, such as at the level of the individual US states. The exception is for self-governing territories that are recognised by the UN geoscheme, such as Hong Kong (a special administrative region of China) or the British Virgin Islands (BVI, a UK overseas territory). The loss of subnational data was the price I was willing to pay in order to capture each country's overall approach to the regulation of hybrid processes. In the case of a federation of states such as Australia, Canada or the United States, where possible, I populated my national law database with uniform acts (for example, the US Revised Uniform Arbitration Act) rather than federal enactments (for example, the US Federal Arbitration Act). My rationale is that the former are likely to provide a better proxy for nationwide regulatory trends, whereas the latter are sometimes limited in scope to addressing a narrow range of issues that fall within federal jurisdiction.

My use of uniform acts means that sometimes a country will be classified as following a particular approach based on its current uniform law even though a majority of subnational territories may have very different laws on the books. This is particularly likely to be the case for Canada, whose new Uniform International Commercial Arbitration Act 2014 has removed a provision permitting same neutral arb-med – a provision that remains in force in many provinces and territories that still follow the older uniform law.

Second, the database focuses principally on legislation in the form of arbitration, mediation or ADR acts, some of which are codified in civil

---

[14] Model Commercial Arbitration Act 2010 (Cth) (Australia), s 27D; Uniform Arbitration Act 2016 (Canada), s 42.

2 SNAPSHOT OF NATIONAL LEGISLATION ON SAME NEUTRAL   33

procedure codes. Rules of private arbitral institutions, case law and rules of court have been excluded. Only if a state or political entity had no mediation legislation did I turn to other proxies – specifically, ministerial decrees and rules of court that apply at the *national* level (for example, the mediation rules issued by a Supreme Court).[15] In this chapter, I use terms such as 'legislation' and 'regulate' loosely, to refer to any of these sources of law.

Third, I have included arbitration or mediation laws regardless of whether they applied to international disputes, domestic disputes or both. For example, even though the UK has no domestic mediation legislation, it is included in the database because it has enacted cross-border mediation legislation to comply with the EU Directive.

Fourth, with respect to subject matter, I have included only commercial or omnibus mediation, arbitration and ADR laws; subject-specific ADR legislation, such as labour arbitration laws and family mediation laws, has been excluded.

Fifth, because the database focuses on top-down, centralised law-making, my findings have little to say about the actual practice or institutions of hybrid processes on the ground – for example, how often they are used, the attitudes of lawyers and end-users towards them, and whether the realities of hybrid processes conform to the normative ideals embodied in national law.

2.3.1 Representativeness of the Database

There are currently 195 jurisdictions represented in the database, out of a total of 245 world jurisdictions accounted for by the UN geoscheme (including Taiwan). Asia is the region best represented in the database, with only one country (Turkmenistan) missing. Oceania is the least

---

[15] For example, in Laos, Oman and Vietnam, mediation is regulated at the national level in the form of ministerial decree rather than legislation. See Decree of the President of the Lao People's Democratic Republic on the Promulgation of the Law on Resolution of Economic Disputes 2005 (Laos); Royal Decree No 98-2005 for the Issuance of the Mediation and Reconciliation Act 2005 (Oman); Decree on Commercial Mediation 2017 (Vietnam).
  Many countries have established successful court mediation programmes, complete with their own mediation rules. To be clear, these were included only if there was no national mediation legislation or ministerial decree, and then only if they had nationwide applicability (rather than just within a local or state court programme). For example, in the case of Mauritius, I referred to the Supreme Court (Mediation) Rules 2010 because, as at the time of writing, there is no other national legislation or decree governing mediation.

represented region, with only 42.9 per cent of jurisdictions reflected in the database. These lacunae raise a threshold question about the extent to which the database is broadly representative of the world. I submit that it is, for the following reasons.

First, the database captures 100 per cent of countries in Western Europe, Southern Europe, Eastern Europe, Eastern Asia, Southeastern Asia, Southern Asia, Western Asia, Central America, Middle Africa and Southern Africa. It also reflects 100 per cent of the member states of the Andean Common Market (ANCOM), the Asia-Pacific Economic Cooperation (APEC), the Association of Southeast Asian Nations (ASEAN), the Common Market for Eastern and Southern Africa (COMESA), the Economic Community of West African States (ECOWAS), the European Union (EU), the Latin American Integration Association (LAIA), the Organisation for Economic Co-operation and Development (OECD), the Organization of the Petroleum Exporting Countries (OPEC) and the Organisation pour l'Harmonisation en Afrique du Droit des Affaires (OHADA).

Second, the 50 jurisdictions not thus far included in the database all fall into one of the following categories: (1) small island nations or territories in Oceania, the Caribbean, Northern Europe, Southern America and Western Africa; (2) sparsely populated territories (for example, Greenland); or (3) Least Developed Countries as defined by the UN (for example, Burundi). These jurisdictions are unlikely to regulate same neutral med-arb or arb-med. They are set forth in Table 2.1.

Third, the database is broadly representative of civil and common law traditions even though the former is slightly overrepresented. The database captures 87.0 per cent of civil law jurisdictions, as compared with 75.8 per cent of common law, 76.2 per cent of mixed common law/civil law and 33.3 per cent of customary law jurisdictions.[16]

The incompleteness of the database may, however, skew some conclusions about the rate at which certain regions regulate same neutral hybrid processes. For example, my data show that Oceania regulates them at the lowest rate, but this may just be because the small sample of Oceania jurisdictions in the database is not representative of Oceania as a whole.

In Sections 2.3.2 and 2.3.3, I provide a broad overview of the various approaches to same neutral med-arb and arb-med, respectively, taken by jurisdictions in the database.

---

[16] It also captures 100.0 per cent of pure Muslim law and mixed Muslim/customary law jurisdictions.

Table 2.1 *Countries excluded from the database*

Country	Region	Sub-region	Legal tradition
Åland Islands	Europe	Northern Europe	Unknown
American Samoa	Oceania	Polynesia	Common law
Anguilla	Americas	Caribbean	Common law
Aruba	Americas	Caribbean	Civil law
Bonaire, Sint Eustatius and Saba	Americas	Caribbean	Civil law
Burundi	Africa	Eastern Africa	Mixed civil/ customary
Cayman Islands	Americas	Caribbean	Common law
Christmas Island	Oceania	Australia and New Zealand	Unknown
Cocos (Keeling) Islands	Oceania	Australia and New Zealand	Unknown
Curaçao	Americas	Caribbean	Civil law
Falkland Islands (Malvinas)	Americas	Southern America	Common law
Faroe Islands	Europe	Northern Europe	Civil law
French Guiana	Americas	Southern America	Civil law
French Polynesia	Oceania	Polynesia	Civil law
Greenland	Americas	Northern America	Civil law
Guadeloupe	Americas	Caribbean	Civil law
Guam	Oceania	Micronesia	Common law
Guernsey	Europe	Northern Europe	Customary
Heard Island and McDonald Islands	Oceania	Australia and New Zealand	Unknown
Isle of Man	Europe	Northern Europe	Common law
Jersey	Europe	Northern Europe	Customary
Martinique	Americas	Caribbean	Civil law
Mayotte	Africa	Eastern Africa	Civil law
Micronesia (Federated States of)	Oceania	Micronesia	Mixed common/ customary
Montserrat	Americas	Caribbean	Common law
Nauru	Oceania	Micronesia	Common law
New Caledonia	Oceania	Melanesia	Civil law

Table 2.1 (cont.)

Country	Region	Sub-region	Legal tradition
Niue	Oceania	Polynesia	Common law
Norfolk Island	Oceania	Australia and New Zealand	Common law
Northern Mariana Islands	Oceania	Micronesia	Unknown
Palau	Oceania	Micronesia	Common law
Pitcairn	Oceania	Polynesia	Common law
Puerto Rico	Americas	Caribbean	Mixed common/civil
Réunion	Africa	Eastern Africa	Civil law
Saint Barthélemy	Americas	Caribbean	Civil law
Saint Helena, Ascension and Tristan da Cunha	Africa	Western Africa	Common law
Saint Kitts and Nevis	Americas	Caribbean	Common law
Saint Martin	Americas	Caribbean	Civil law
Saint Pierre and Miquelon	Americas	Northern America	Civil law
Sark	Europe	Northern Europe	Unknown
Sierra Leone	Africa	Western Africa	Mixed common/customary
Sint Maarten	Americas	Caribbean	Civil law
South Georgia and the South Sandwich Islands	Americas	Southern America	Common law
Svalbard and Jan Mayen	Europe	Northern Europe	Unknown
Tokelau	Oceania	Polynesia	Unknown
Turkmenistan	Asia	Central Asia	Civil law
Turks and Caicos Islands	Americas	Caribbean	Common law
Virgin Islands (US)	Americas	Caribbean	Common law
Wallis and Futuna	Oceania	Polynesia	Civil law
Western Sahara	Africa	Northern Africa	Unknown

2.3.2 Approaches to Med-arb

Of the 195 jurisdictions in the database, 59 (or 30.3 per cent) address situations where the proceeding starts off as a mediation and the mediator switches hats to become the arbitrator. They are represented in yellow and red in Figure 2.1(a) below. Jurisdictions falling into the yellow category permit same neutral med-arb with the consent of the parties, while those falling into the red category prohibit the practice outright. The remaining jurisdictions, represented in grey, have no legislation regarding same neutral med-arb.

Within the set of jurisdictions that either permit or prohibit same neutral med-arb – those represented in yellow and red in Figure 2.1(a) – by far the best represented region is Africa. Figure 2.1(b) shows that 42.3 per cent of African states regulate same neutral med-arb, as compared with 30.6 per cent of jurisdictions in the Americas, 26.7 per cent in Europe, 26.0 per cent in Asia and 8.3 per cent in Oceania. The sub-regions with the greatest concentration of states that regulate same neutral med-arb are Western and Middle Africa (80.0 per cent and 77.8 per cent of states,

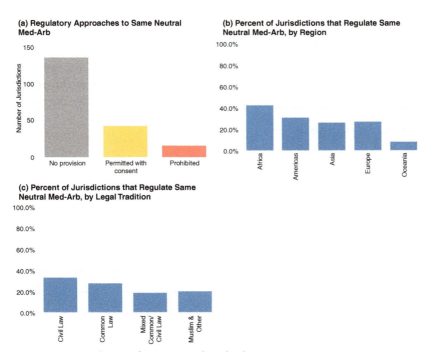

Figure 2.1 Regulation of same neutral med-arb

respectively), and those with the smallest are Northern Europe and Eastern Asia (10.0 per cent and 12.5 per cent of states, respectively). Northern and Southern Africa and Central Asia do not appear to regulate the practice at all.

The dominance of Western and Middle African jurisdictions in this cohort is explained almost entirely by the OHADA Uniform Act on Mediation, which has the force of positive law in all 17 OHADA states. The OHADA Uniform Act on Mediation adopts the Model Mediation Law provision on med-arb almost verbatim.[17] If the OHADA states are excluded, African jurisdictions as a whole regulate same neutral med-arb at the second lowest rate (14.3 per cent).

The low numbers in Northern Europe are consistent with the fact that very few European states have legislated around same neutral med-arb. This is so even though 88.9 per cent of European jurisdictions have a mediation law – by far the highest rate of mediation law reception of any other region in the world. Figure 2.1(c) shows that a higher percentage of civil law jurisdictions regulate same neutral med-arb than do common law jurisdictions (33.1 per cent versus 27.7 per cent).

Sections 2.3.2.1–2.3.2.3 will describe the approaches to same neutral med-arb illustrated in Figure 2.1(a).

2.3.2.1 Permitted with Party Consent

In 43 of the 59 states that have chosen to regulate med-arb, the mediator is permitted to act as an arbitrator in the same dispute if the parties provide their consent. These jurisdictions are represented by the yellow bar in Figure 2.1(a).

Africa (21 jurisdictions) is the best represented region in this cohort, followed by Asia and Europe (8 jurisdictions each), the Americas (5 jurisdictions) and Oceania (1 jurisdiction). There are 29 civil law and 10 common law jurisdictions falling within this category.[18]

In general, permissive same neutral med-arb provisions do not specify *when* consent to med-arb must be given by the parties. There are two possibilities. Parties might agree in advance, thus committing themselves to a same neutral hybrid process from the outset. Or they might initially agree only to mediation (with or without any idea of switching to

---

[17] See Acte uniforme relatif à la médiation 2017 [Uniform Act on Mediation] (OHADA), art 14.
[18] These numbers may be deceptive because civil law jurisdictions already outnumber common law jurisdictions in the database by a factor of 2.7 to 1. As a percentage, civil law and common law states permit same neutral med-arb at roughly equal rates (22.8 per cent and 21.3 per cent, respectively).

arbitration using the same neutral at a later point) and, during the course of mediation, agree to arbitration. I refer to the former type of consent as *ex ante* consent' and the latter as *ex post* consent'.

If *ex ante* consent is sufficient, it might paint a much more med-arb -'friendly' picture than if *ex post* consent were required because it would allow parties to plan for a same neutral med-arb process in advance, such as by binding themselves to it pre-dispute. But to say that *ex ante* consent is sufficient is also to say that no further consent is strictly speaking necessary in order for the mediator to switch hats and assume an adjudicative role after the mediation fails. This raises a bigger issue, which is whether the parties have thereby agreed to anything that resembles 'mediation' in the first place. If the mediator may take on the role of an arbitrator without seeking further, *ex post* consent, the 'med-' process is not truly voluntary because the parties are not free to walk away, such as by choosing a different mediator, a different arbitrator, or by going to court.[19] In effect, instead of agreeing to a process in which mediation turns into arbitration, the parties have agreed to arbitration pure and simple – the only difference being that the arbitrator has been authorised to begin by facilitating settlement. From this standpoint, it might be argued that *ex ante* consent should never be sufficient for med-arb because it calls into serious question whether the process even deserves to be called 'med-arb' rather than arbitration *tout court*. Only *ex post* consent would appear to safeguard mediation's commitment to voluntariness and party self-determination.

These issues are largely left unaddressed by existing med-arb legislation. Of the 43 jurisdictions that permit same neutral med-arb with party consent, 36 do not distinguish between *ex ante* and *ex post* consent. Seven specifically contemplate that *ex ante* consent is sufficient for the mediator to switch roles (Australia, Bermuda, Brunei Darussalam, BVI, Hong Kong, Singapore, and Trinidad and Tobago). Notably, all are common law jurisdictions. Five of the seven have the following substantially identical provision:

> Where an arbitration agreement provides for the appointment of a mediator and further provides that the person so appointed shall act as an arbitrator in the event of the mediation proceedings failing to produce a settlement

---

[19] Nonetheless, in their survey of mediators from the International Academy of Mediators, Thomas Stipanowich and Zachary Ulrich reported that nearly half of the respondents had experience with med-arb 'where the parties agreed ahead of time to conduct mediation, and if mediation failed the mediator would switch to the rule of arbitrator': Thomas J Stipanowich and Zachary P Ulrich, 'Commercial Arbitration and Settlement: Empirical Insights into the Roles Arbitrators Play' (2014) 6 Yearbook on Arbitration and Mediation 1, 28.

acceptable to the parties ... no objection shall be taken to the appointment of such person as an arbitrator, or to his conduct of the arbitral proceedings, solely on the ground that he had acted previously as a mediator in connection with some or all of the matters referred to arbitration ....[20]

This provision is notable for several reasons. First, it expresses a very permissive attitude towards med-arb by making it clear that no further party consent is required for the mediator to act as the arbitrator. Second, the provision makes clear that in such circumstances the parties have also waived any objection to '[the arbitrator's] conduct of the arbitral proceedings', something that is not provided for in the Model Mediation Law and that is rarely seen in permissive med-arb provisions more generally. It remains unclear whether this language is limited to procedural objections raised during the arbitration phase or whether it also extends to any objections against enforcement of the resulting award. Assuming the latter, the waiver addresses a key objection to same neutral med-arb from the standpoint of arbitration values.

2.3.2.2 Prohibited

In a minority of 16 of the 59 states that have chosen to regulate same neutral med-arb, the mediator is outright prohibited from serving as an arbitrator in the same dispute. These jurisdictions are represented by the red bar in Figure 2.1(a). An example of such a jurisdiction is Brazil, whose mediation act provides that '[t]he mediator may neither act as an arbitrator nor as a witness in legal or arbitration proceedings concerning a dispute in which he/she has acted as a mediator'.[21]

It is difficult to say whether prohibiting same neutral med-arb evinces a hostility to combining mediation and arbitration. On the contrary, such an approach could be re-framed as broadly supportive of *different neutral* med-arb.[22] For example, many scholars who

---

[20] International Arbitration Act 1994 (Singapore), s 16(3). See also Arbitration Act 1986 (Bermuda), s 3(2); International Conciliation and Arbitration Act 1993 (Bermuda), s 14(1); Arbitration Act 2001 (Singapore), s 62(3); Arbitration Order 2009 (Brunei Darussalam), s 62; Arbitration Ordinance 2011 (Cap 609) (Hong Kong), s 32(3); Arbitration Act 2013 (British Virgin Islands), s 30. The origin of this provision can be traced to a 1982 amendment to the Hong Kong Arbitration Ordinance. See Arbitration Ordinance 1961 (Cap 341) (Hong Kong), as amended, ss 2A(2), 2A(2)(a).

[21] Law No 13140, 2005 (Brazil), s 7.

[22] Alberta Law Reform Institute, 'Uniform International Commercial Arbitration, Final Report 114' (6 March 2019) <www.alri.ualberta.ca/2019/03/uniform-international-commercial-arbitration-final-report-114/> accessed 14 August 2020, 60.

endorse med-arb have argued that the same neutral should not serve in both roles.[23]

The region best represented in this cohort is the Americas (6 jurisdictions), followed by Asia (5 jurisdictions), Europe (4 jurisdictions), Africa (1 jurisdiction) and Oceania (zero jurisdictions). A sub-regional breakdown shows that Southern America (Brazil, Colombia, Ecuador, Paraguay) and Western Asia (Azerbaijan, Bahrain, Jordan) have the highest concentration of such jurisdictions. There are 13 civil law and 3 common law jurisdictions falling within this category.[24]

It bears noting that although the law on the books in these jurisdictions prohibits same neutral med-arb without exception, as a practical matter courts may turn a blind eye in cases where the parties have expressly consented to it. For example, even though the text of Canada's UICMA prohibits the mediator from serving as an arbitrator in the same dispute without providing an exception for party consent, the Report of the Working Group on the UICMA notes that 'parties may expressly agree to it'.[25] Likewise, although the Austrian mediation law states that a member of 'a decision-making body in a conflict between the parties, may not act as a mediator in the same conflict',[26] some scholars have noted that 'an exemption from the prohibition of acting as a decision-making body is permitted' to allow for same neutral med-arb.[27]

2.3.2.3 No Provision

Of the 195 database jurisdictions, 136 have no provision regarding same neutral med-arb.[28] Among these, 55 jurisdictions have a mediation law that

---

[23] See eg Eric W Fiechter, 'Mediation – Casting Issues: Can or Should the Same Person Be Mediator, or Conciliator and Arbitrator?' (2008) 15 Croatian Arbitration Year Book 255, 261; Emilia Onyema, 'The Use of Med-arb in International Commercial Dispute Resolution' (2001) 12 American Review of International Arbitration 411.

[24] As a percentage, civil law jurisdictions are more likely than common law jurisdictions to outright prohibit same neutral med-arb (10.2 per cent versus 6.4 per cent of jurisdictions, respectively).

[25] Report of the Working Group on the Uniform Act on International Commercial Mediation (2005), para 25. On file with the author.

[26] Law on Mediation in Civil Law Matters 2003 (Austria), s 16(1).

[27] See Markus Roth and David Gherdane, 'Mediation in Austria: The European Pioneer in Mediation Law and Practice' in Klaus J Hopt and Felix Steffek (eds), *Mediation: Principles and Regulation in Comparative Perspective* (Oxford University Press 2013) 287.

[28] Nigeria is currently included within this figure because the Arbitration and Conciliation Act 1988 does not specifically address same neutral med-arb. See Arbitration and Conciliation Act 1988 (Nigeria), ss 37–42. As at the time of writing, however, a bill to amend the Arbitration and Conciliation Act was passed by the Senate and is now pending before the House of Representatives. The bill follows the Model Mediation Law's

was enacted *after* the first iteration of the Model Mediation Law in 2002, which permitted same neutral med-arb with the consent of the parties. It is difficult to know whether the fact that those jurisdictions did not follow the Model Mediation Law's approach implies hostility, support or indifference towards med-arb. Perhaps some countries did not consider the Model Mediation Law at all, although this seems unlikely given how often it is consulted during the drafting of mediation legislation around the world. Other countries may have had reasons to privilege alternative precedents over the Model Mediation Law. For example, the EU Directive is silent on same neutral med-arb, which likely explains why 70.0 per cent of European jurisdictions with a mediation law (both EU and non-EU) nonetheless fail to address the issue. By comparison, 56.0 per cent of Asian jurisdictions and only 26.7 per cent of African jurisdictions that have a mediation law failed to address same neutral med-arb.

2.3.3 Approaches to Arb-med

Of the 195 jurisdictions in the database, 31 (or 15.9 per cent) address situations where the proceeding starts off as an arbitration and the arbitrator switches hats to become the mediator. They are represented in yellow, green and red in Figure 2.2(a). Jurisdictions falling into the yellow column allow the arbitrator to attempt mediation with the consent of the parties, those in the green column encourage or require the arbitrator to do so regardless of party consent, and those in the red column prohibit same neutral arb-med outright. There are only two jurisdictions falling within the last category – a point of contrast to the med-arb context, where many more jurisdictions prohibit the same neutral from serving in both roles. The remaining jurisdictions, shown in grey, have no legislation specifically directed at same neutral arb-med.

From among the jurisdictions shown in yellow, green and red in Figure 2.2(a), the best represented region is Asia. As Figure 2.2(b) demonstrates, 34.0 per cent of Asian states have regulated same neutral arb-med, as compared with 16.7 per cent of jurisdictions in the Americas, 8.9 per cent in Europe, 8.3 per cent in Oceania and 5.8 per cent in Africa. A subregional breakdown shows that Eastern, Southeastern and Southern Asia are most likely to regulate same neutral arb-med (50.0 per cent,

provision on mediators serving as arbitrators; thus, assuming the bill passes in the House and is assented to by the President, Nigeria is poised to become a permissive same neutral med-arb jurisdiction. See Arbitration and Conciliation Act Cap A18 LFN 2004 (Repeal and Re-enactment) Bill 2018 (SB 427) (Nigeria), ss 75, 77.

2 SNAPSHOT OF NATIONAL LEGISLATION ON SAME NEUTRAL 43

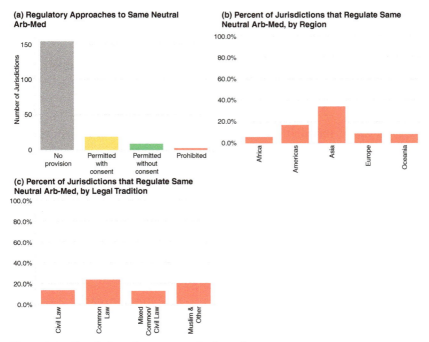

Figure 2.2   Regulation of same neutral arb-med

45.5 per cent and 44.4 per cent of jurisdictions, respectively), while Southern Europe and the Caribbean tend to regulate it the least (6.3 per cent and 7.7 per cent, respectively). Eastern Africa, Middle Africa, Southern Africa, and Northern and Eastern Europe do not appear to regulate same neutral arb-med at all.

The contrast to same neutral med-arb regulation is particularly striking. A comparison of Figure 2.1(b) and Figure 2.2(b) shows that in every region except Asia, same neutral med-arb is regulated *more* often than same neutral arb-med. In Africa this difference is most pronounced, at 42.3 per cent versus 5.8 per cent of jurisdictions, while in the Americas it narrows to 30.6 per cent versus 22.2 per cent. Asia is the only region where same neutral med-arb is regulated less frequently (26.0 per cent of states) than same neutral arb-med (36.0 per cent).

A similar pattern can be observed with respect to legal tradition. Figure 2.1(c) showed that a greater proportion of civil law than common law jurisdictions regulate same neutral med-arb (33.1 per cent versus 27.7 per cent). But Figure 2.2(c) reveals that when it comes to same neutral arb-med, the opposite is true: it is regulated by 23.4 per cent of common law jurisdictions but only 13.4 per cent (almost half) of civil law jurisdictions.

Sections 2.3.3.1–2.3.3.5 will describe the approaches to same neutral med-arb illustrated in Figure 2.2(a).

2.3.3.1 Permitted with Party Consent

In 19 of the 31 jurisdictions that regulate same neutral arb-med, arbitrators are permitted to mediate so long as they receive permission from the parties. These jurisdictions are represented by the yellow bar in Figure 2.2(a).

By far the greatest number of these jurisdictions are located in Asia (13 jurisdictions), followed by Africa (3 jurisdictions), the Americas (2 jurisdictions), Oceania (1 jurisdiction) and Europe (zero jurisdictions). All 11 common law jurisdictions that regulate same neutral arb-med take this approach, while only 6 out of 17 civil law jurisdictions do so. The two mixed common/civil law jurisdictions that regulate same neutral arb-med (the Philippines and Sri Lanka) also take this approach.

The low rate of regulation in Europe is somewhat surprising given the literature suggesting a high degree of receptivity to arbitrators facilitating settlement within Continental Europe. This disconnect could be explained by the fact that the law does not necessarily mirror cultural expectations or that national legislation may not fully capture what is considered legally permissible in a particular jurisdiction.[29] An alternative explanation is that settlement facilitation by arbitrators is not understood in Continental Europe as a form of same neutral arb-med at all, but rather as a function inherent in the arbitrator's role that does not need to be spelt out in the law.

As in the case of med-arb, the vast majority (73.7 per cent) of states that permit same neutral arb-med do not specify *when* party consent is necessary or sufficient. A good example of such a provision is the Indian Arbitration and Conciliation Act 1996, which provides: 'It is not incompatible with an arbitration agreement for an arbitral tribunal to encourage settlement of the dispute and, with the agreement of the parties, the arbitral tribunal may use mediation, conciliation or other procedures at any time during the arbitral proceedings to encourage settlement.'[30] This provision does not clarify whether the parties may agree *ex ante* (such as in a pre-dispute clause) to entrust the arbitrator to use mediation as he or she sees

---

[29] This appears to be the case, for example, in Austria. See discussion in Section 2.3.2.2.
[30] Arbitration and Conciliation Act 1996 (India), s 30.

fit during the course of the arbitration, or whether *ex post* consent is always necessary before the arbitrator may switch hats and become the mediator.

2.3.3.2 Permitted without Party Consent

A further 9 jurisdictions, depicted by the green bar in Figure 2.2(a), do not require the consent of the parties in order for the arbitrator to switch hats and attempt to facilitate a settlement. As compared with the approach outlined in Section 2.3.3.1, this approach expresses an even more permissive position towards same neutral arb-med.

Some jurisdictions following this approach make it clear that the arbitrators have either the power or the duty to order parties to attempt some type of settlement activity.[31] For example, Colombia's arbitration law states: 'Upon expiration of the term for transfer of exceptions of merit proposals against the initial claim or the counterclaim, ... the arbitral tribunal *will* indicate day and time to hold the conciliation hearing, to which both parties and their attorneys must attend. At the conciliation hearing the arbitral tribunal will urge the parties to resolve their differences through conciliation ....'[32] In other jurisdictions, it remains unclear whether the arbitrator's power or duty merely extends to *suggesting* mediation or some other type of settlement facilitation, and thus whether the decision to try this using the same – rather than a different – neutral ultimately remains in the parties' hands. For example, Brazil's arbitration law provides that '[t]he sole arbitrator or the arbitral tribunal shall, at the commencement of the procedure, attempt to reconcile the parties ....'[33] Does this mean that the arbitrator may compel parties to attempt mediation (that is, a mandatory mediation window, of the sort contemplated in Colombia) or that the arbitrator is just required to broach the subject of settlement with the parties and invite their participation?

Even if it is the latter, the problem is that, practically speaking, it is often difficult for parties to refuse a gentle nudge from the arbitrator to mediate. For example, in her empirical study of hybrid processes, Dilyara

---

[31] It is sometimes ambiguous whether the law in these jurisdictions contemplates that the arbitrator will change roles from an adjudicator to a settlement facilitator (mediator or otherwise), or whether it contemplates that the arbitrator *qua* adjudicator will – with varying degrees of assertiveness – encourage the parties to settle. Where only the latter was contemplated, I considered the jurisdiction as not regulating same neutral arb-med at all (see Section 2.3.3.5). In all other cases, I erred on the side of including the jurisdiction in order to capture as much hybrid process regulation as possible.

[32] Estatuto de Arbitraje Nacional e Internacional 2012 [Statute on National and International Arbitration] (Colombia), s 24 (emphasis added).

[33] Law No 9.307, 1996 (Brazil), s 21(4).

Nigmatullina reported the following concern expressed by a US lawyer: 'I have been involved in cases where arbitrators said: let me mediate this case. And my client ... was feeling tremendous pressure because he did not want to offend the arbitrator ... I think that's absolutely terrible for an arbitrator to say: let me mediate this and putting pressure on the parties.'[34] And even if consent is freely given to begin mediation, during the mediation window one or both parties may feel coerced into settling if they fear that by failing to do so they will fall out of the mediator-turned-arbitrator's favour. Worse, the arbitrator may issue a final award based on information obtained *ex parte*, during a private caucus. Thus, although it may appear less problematic for a binding decision-maker to become a mere facilitator rather than the other way around, same neutral arb-med raises the same basic concerns that attend same neutral med-arb. The reason is that there is always at least a possibility that the mediation window during arbitration will fail to produce a settlement, and thus that the parties will find themselves back in arbitration. In other words, arb-med always happens in the shadow of arb-med-arb. These issues will be explored in Section 2.3.3.3.

A number of observations may be made about the nine jurisdictions that permit arbitrators to order or suggest mediation without first receiving party consent. First, American jurisdictions that regulate same neutral arb-med are most likely to take this approach (four out of six jurisdictions, or 66.7 per cent), followed by European (50.0 per cent) and Asian (17.6 per cent) jurisdictions. African and Oceanian jurisdictions do not appear to follow this approach at all. Second, all countries falling into this cohort are civil law jurisdictions. For example, the American jurisdictions are all former colonies of Spain or Portugal located in Central and Southern America (Brazil, Colombia, El Salvador and Uruguay), which also helps explain the surprising fact that American jurisdictions are the best represented in this category. These findings are consistent with the observation that 'under the inquisitorial legal traditions of Continental Europe, facilitation of settlement is generally regarded as a desirable part of ... an arbitrator's role'.[35] On the other hand, Figures 2.2(b) and 2.2(c) show that European jurisdictions and civil law jurisdictions generally are very unlikely to enshrine this expectation of the arbitrator's role into formal law – perhaps for some of the reasons suggested in Section 2.3.3.1. Finally, China is one of

---

[34] Dilyara Nigmatullina, *Combining Mediation and Arbitration in International Commercial Dispute Resolution* (Routledge 2018) 172.

[35] Nigmatullina (n 34) 65; Michael E Schneider, 'Combining Arbitration with Conciliation' (1998) 8 ICCA Congress Series 57, 76.

the two Asian jurisdictions that take this approach (Indonesia is the other), which is consistent with evidence that arbitrators in China are encouraged, if not expected, to facilitate settlement.[36]

2.3.3.3 When Mediation Fails to Produce a Settlement: Regulating Arb-med as Arb-med-arb

What happens when the same neutral mediates during arbitration and the mediation fails? Should the same neutral automatically resume the role of arbitrator, or are further procedural protections warranted? These questions underscore the extent to which med-arb concerns are just as salient in a situation where mediation proceeds within an arbitration as it is where mediation precedes arbitration. Because there is always the possibility that an arb-med process will not result in settlement, the process is always effectively 'arb-med-arb' – that is, arbitration with med-arb embedded within it.

Only 8 of the 31 jurisdictions that regulate same neutral arb-med have focused on whether or under what circumstances the same neutral may resume the role of arbitrator if mediation during arbitration is unsuccessful. Two jurisdictions (Canada and Indonesia) specifically provide that the arbitrator may resume his or her role without incident. For example, Canada's UAA, which governs domestic arbitration, provides that the arbitral tribunal may use mediation if the parties agree but that an arbitrator 'may not be challenged or removed because the arbitral tribunal participated in [such] a process'.[37] These jurisdictions effectively take the position that no further procedural protections are required in order to resume arbitration, such as by requiring *ex post* consent during the embedded med-arb phase.

The remaining 6 jurisdictions implement one or both of the following procedural protections: (1) allowing the parties to object to the mediator resuming the arbitral role, and/or (2) requiring the mediator-turned-arbitrator to disclose the substance of any material *ex parte* communications during caucuses. Five of the six further provide that when the relevant procedural protection has been satisfied (that is, further consent or disclosure), the parties will be taken to have waived

---

[36] See eg Kun Fan, 'An Empirical Study of Arbitrators Acting as Mediators in China' (2014) 15(3) Cardozo Journal of Conflict Resolution 777, 787; Sally A Harpole, 'The Combination of Conciliation with Arbitration in the People's Republic of China' (2007) 24(6) Journal of International Arbitration 623, 623–24; Shahla Ali, 'International Arbitration and Mediation in East Asia: Examining the Role of Domestic Legal Culture and Globalization on Shaping East Asian Arbitration' (PhD thesis, University of California at Berkeley 2007) 201–2.
[37] Uniform Arbitration Act 2016 (Canada) (n 14), s 42(2).

any objections to the 'conduct of the arbitral proceedings' based on the fact that the same neutral served as both the arbitrator and the mediator.

Australia implements the first approach. All six Australian states, the Northern Territory and the Australian Capital Territory have each included the following identical provision in their domestic arbitration law:

> (4) An arbitrator who has acted as mediator in mediation proceedings that are terminated may not conduct subsequent arbitration proceedings in relation to the dispute without the written consent of all the parties to the arbitration given on or after the termination of the mediation proceedings.
>
> (5) If the parties consent under subsection (4), no objection may be taken to the conduct of subsequent arbitration proceedings by the arbitrator solely on the ground that he or she has acted previously as a mediator in accordance with this section.[38]

This provision contemplates two points at which consent must be given: to begin the mediation window and to resume arbitration. This is equivalent to taking the position that *ex ante* consent is *not* sufficient for same neutral med-arb; that is, in addition to agreeing *ex ante* to enter the embedded med-arb process, further *ex post* consent must be obtained before the mediator may resume the role of an arbitrator. This approach, which follows the recommendations of the CEDR Commission on Settlement in International Arbitration,[39] appears to give parties the greatest flexibility to avoid the problems identified in Section 2.1.

Australia also implements the second approach, giving it the distinction of having the most elaborate protections in the world for same neutral arb-med-arb.[40] The second approach is also followed in

---

[38] See Model Commercial Arbitration Act 2010 (Cth) (Australia) (n 14), ss 27D(4), (5). The International Arbitration Act 1974 (as amended in 2010) (Cth) (Australia) does not contemplate arb-med.

[39] CEDR Commission on Settlement in International Arbitration, *Final Report* (2009) <www.imimediation.org/download/102/public-libraries/31875/cedr-arbitration_commission_doc_final-nov-2009.pdf> accessed 15 April 2021, app II, s 7.3.

[40] In addition to requiring further consent by the parties in order to resume his or her role as an arbitrator, the arbitrator 'must, before conducting subsequent arbitration proceedings in relation to the dispute, disclose to all other parties to the arbitration proceedings so much of the information as the arbitrator considers material to the arbitration proceedings'. See eg Commercial Arbitration Act 2017 (ACT) (Australia), s 2D(7).

Brunei Darussalam, BVI, Hong Kong, the Philippines and Singapore, each of which has the following substantially identical provision:

> (3) Where confidential information is obtained by an arbitrator or umpire from a party to the arbitral proceedings during conciliation proceedings and those proceedings terminate without the parties reaching agreement in settlement of their dispute, the arbitrator or umpire shall before resuming the arbitral proceedings disclose to all other parties to the arbitral proceedings as much of that information as he considers material to the arbitral proceedings.
> (4) No objection shall be taken to the conduct of arbitral proceedings by a person solely on the ground that that person had acted previously as a conciliator in accordance with this section.[41]

Because they also provide that the aforementioned disclosure is sufficient to waive any objections to the 'conduct of the arbitral proceedings', unlike Australia these jurisdictions effectively take the position that *ex ante* consent to embedded med-arb can be sufficient. That is, as long as (1) the parties agree prior to the commencement of the mediation phase that the same neutral may serve first as the mediator and then as the arbitrator if no agreement is reached, and (2) the arbitrator makes the necessary disclosures, no further (*ex post*) consent from the parties is required in order to resume arbitration when the mediation fails.

Of these six jurisdictions, five are common law and one is a mixed common law/civil law jurisdiction. None are civil law, mixed civil law/Muslim or mixed civil law/customary jurisdictions. This is doubly significant in light of the fact that civil law jurisdictions in the database outnumber common law jurisdictions by a factor of 2.7 to 1.

2.3.3.4 Prohibited

Only 3 out of the 31 jurisdictions that regulate same neutral arb-med prohibit it outright (Afghanistan, Austria and Liechtenstein).[42] In the

---

[41] International Arbitration Act 1994 (Singapore) (n 20), ss 17(3), 17(4). See also Arbitration Act 2001 (Singapore) (n 20), ss 63(3), 63(4); Arbitration Order 2009 (Brunei Darussalam) (n 20), ss 63(3), 63(4); Arbitration Ordinance 2011 (Cap 609) (Hong Kong) (n 20), ss 33(4), 33(5); Arbitration Act 2013 (British Virgin Islands) (n 20), ss 31(4), 31(5). The Philippines has a similar provision that does not expressly contain the waiver language in clause (4): Alternative Dispute Resolution Act 2004 (Philippines), s 18; Implementing Rules and Regulations of the Alternative Dispute Resolution Act 2004 (Philippines), s 17.4.

[42] I note in passing that the Canadian province of Ontario also prohibits same neutral arb-med; however, it was not included in the database because it is a sub-national jurisdiction.

case of Afghanistan, the prohibition is clear: 'When requested by the parties, the Arbitral Tribunal shall not engage in Mediation with respect to disputes pending before it. However, the parties are free to appoint a third party as a mediator.'[43] Although the plain language of the Austrian mediation law states that '[a] person who himself is or has been party, party representative, counsellor or decision-making body in a conflict between the parties, may not act as a mediator in the same conflict',[44] as noted earlier it is possible that Austrian courts would condone – and perhaps even enforce – an agreement for same neutral arb-med. Liechtenstein has copied the Austrian provision into its mediation law.[45]

The relative paucity of jurisdictions that prohibit same neutral arb-med is in contrast to the med-arb context. Same neutral arb-med legislation tends to be overwhelmingly permissive; the main differences in approach cluster around whether or not party consent must be obtained before the arbitrator slips into the role of a mediator. By contrast, same neutral med-arb legislation is much less so. In 16 out of 59 states it is prohibited outright; of the remaining 43 states that permit it with party consent, 35 follow the Model Mediation Law approach of creating a default presumption prohibiting it unless the parties agree otherwise.

2.3.3.5 No Provision or Unclear

Of the 195 database jurisdictions, 154 have no legislative provision regarding same neutral arb-med. Of those, 67 are claimed by UNCITRAL as Model Arbitration Law jurisdictions. If, as discussed in Section 2.2.2, Article 19 or 28 of the Model Arbitration Law permits same neutral arb-med with the consent of the parties, it would follow that up to 67 additional jurisdictions might be added to the yellow bar in Figure 2.2(a) (assuming that their arbitration law contains the equivalent of Article 19 or 28).

In the remaining 10 jurisdictions, the settlement in the course of arbitration is contemplated but the law does not make clear whether the arbitrator him or herself may assume the role of the mediator. For example, the Taiwan Arbitration Act provides that '[d]uring the arbitral proceedings, the parties can resolve their dispute by means of conciliation or mediation', but does not clarify whether the same neutral may serve as the mediator and the arbitrator.[46] Likewise, the Czech Arbitration Law provides that '[i]n the course of the arbitral proceedings,

---

[43] Commercial Arbitration Law 2007 (Afghanistan).
[44] Law on Mediation in Civil Law Matters (Austria) (n 26), s 16(1).
[45] See Civil Law Mediation Act 2005 (Liechtenstein), s 12(1).
[46] See Arbitration Act 1998 (Taiwan), art 44.1.

2 SNAPSHOT OF NATIONAL LEGISLATION ON SAME NEUTRAL 51

the arbitrators shall encourage the parties to settle their dispute amicably'.[47] It is possible that this provision intends something short of the arbitrators themselves acting as mediators. Because these jurisdictions do not specifically permit or prohibit same neutral arb-med, they have been included in the grey bar in Figure 2.2(a).

2.4 Regulatory Patterns

2.4.1 Region and Legal Tradition

A number of broad observations may be drawn by comparing the regulation of same neutral hybrid processes by region and legal tradition. Figure 2.3(a) shows that Africa has the largest concentration of jurisdictions that regulate at least one type of same neutral hybrid process (46.2 per cent), followed by Asia (46.0 per cent), the Americas (36.1 per cent), Europe

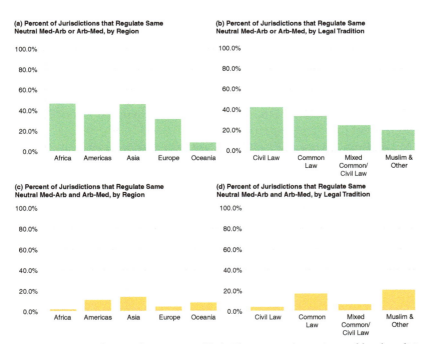

Figure 2.3 Regulation of same neutral hybrid processes by region and legal tradition

---

[47] Act No 216/1994 on Arbitral Proceedings and Enforcement of Arbitral Awards (Czech Republic), s 24(1).

(31.1 per cent) and Oceania (8.3 per cent). Figure 2.3(b) shows that a greater proportion of civil law jurisdictions (42.5 per cent) than common law jurisdictions (34.0 per cent) fall into this camp. Being an African or an Asian state therefore appears to be a very strong predictor of finding legislation governing same neutral med-arb or arb-med.

A different picture emerges, however, when we consider jurisdictions that have regulated *both* same neutral arb-med and med-arb. Figure 2.3(c) shows that Asia has the greatest concentration of countries that take a coordinated approach (14.0 per cent), while Africa has the least (1.9 per cent). Comparing Figure 2.3(b) and Figure 2.3(d) shows that although a greater proportion of civil law than common law jurisdictions regulate at least one type of same neutral hybrid process (42.5 per cent versus 34.0 per cent), a far greater percentage of common law jurisdictions regulate both (17.0 per cent versus 3.9 per cent).[48]

It is difficult to explain some of these findings if one assumes a close relationship between law and practice. For example, Europe has the highest concentration of developed economies and has passed mediation and arbitration legislation at the highest rates globally. Yet Figures 2.1(b), 2.2(b), 2.3(a) and 2.3(c) show that it is close to the bottom in terms of regulating same neutral hybrid processes. By contrast, because Africa is not known to be a hotbed for the use of such processes, it is somewhat surprising that the Western and Middle Africa sub-regions are the most likely of any sub-region in the world to regulate them (86.7 per cent and 77.8 per cent of states, respectively).[49]

My findings are also difficult to square with anecdotal and survey data specifically about arb-med – for example, that same neutral arb-med is well accepted in Continental Europe and Latin America, where judges are said regularly to facilitate settlement during the course of litigation.[50]

---

[48] Civil law jurisdictions also regulate same neutral med-arb more than common law jurisdictions, but the reverse is true for same neutral arb-med. See Section 2.3.3.

[49] Same neutral hybrid processes are regulated at substantially lower rates in other regions in Africa – from 0.0 per cent in Southern Africa up to 17.6 per cent in Eastern Africa.

[50] For example, in their study of 63 ICC cases resulting in consent awards between 2002 and 2005, Gabrielle Kaufman-Kohler and Victor Bonnin found that the arbitrators had facilitated settlement in 13 of those cases. Notably, the arbitrators in all 13 cases hailed from such jurisdictions. See Gabrielle Kaufmann-Kohler and Victor Bonnin, *Arbitrators as Conciliators: A Statistical Study of the Relation between an Arbitrator's Role and Legal Background* (International Council for Commercial Arbitration) <www.arbitration-icca.org/media/0/12319144605970/00950003.pdf> accessed 14 January 2018, 4. See also Bernd Ehle, 'The Arbitrator as Settlement Facilitator' in Olivier Caprasse (ed), *Walking a Thin Line – What an Arbitrator Can Do, Must Do or Must Not Do: Recent Developments and Trends* (Bruylant 2010) 80.

Figure 2.2(b) shows that only 8.9 per cent of European jurisdictions regulate same neutral arb-med, which is the lowest rate of regulation of any region other than Africa. Switzerland and Germany – often cited as hospitable jurisdictions for same neutral arb-med[51] – are not among those jurisdictions, nor is any civil law country in Eastern Europe or in the Nordic and Baltic states. Although Figure 2.2(b) also shows that a slightly higher percentage of jurisdictions in the Americas have regulated same neutral arb-med (16.7 per cent), it is still far from 50 per cent.[52] Worldwide, only 13.4 per cent of civil law jurisdictions regulate same neutral arb-med, which is about half the rate at which common law jurisdictions do so (23.4 per cent). Assuming that the law mirrors practice, this is also somewhat puzzling if it is true that common law practitioners are less favourable towards mixing arbitration and mediation using the same neutral.

On the other hand, as discussed in Section 2.3.3.2, civil law jurisdictions in Europe and Latin America are most likely to take the more liberal approach to same neutral arb-med, which allows the arbitrator to attempt mediation without first obtaining the consent of the parties. My findings are also consistent with the observation that East Asian arbitrators and parties, particularly those with links to China, are accustomed to and indeed actively encourage same neutral arb-med.[53] Of all the sub-regions of the world, Eastern and Southeastern Asia have the greatest proportion of states that regulate same neutral arb-med (50.0 per cent and 45.5 per cent, respectively).

2.4.2 Did East Asian Culture Influence the Spread of Same Neutral Hybrid Process Legislation in Other Regions?

Some commentators have theorised that (1) there has been a growth in the acceptance of same neutral hybrid processes over time and that (2) this growth can be explained largely by reference to culture – in particular, the influence of an East Asian (particularly Chinese) culture. For example, Nigmatullina argues that legislation in Canada, Australia,

---

[51] See Christian Bühring-Uhle, Lars Kirchhoff and Gabriele Scherer, *Arbitration and Mediation in International Business* (2nd edn, Kluwer Law International 2006) 110, fn 347; Kaufmann-Kohler and Bonnin (n 50); Thomas J Stipanowich and Véronique Fraser, 'The International Task Force on Mixed Mode Dispute Resolution: Exploring the Interplay between Mediation, Evaluation and Arbitration in Commercial Cases' (2017) 40(3) Fordham International Law Journal, 839, 854–55.

[52] Within the Americas, 19.0 per cent of civil law jurisdictions permit same neutral arb-med (with or without party consent) as compared with 15.4 per cent of common law jurisdictions.

[53] See n 36.

Hong Kong and Singapore allowing arbitrators to act as mediators in the same dispute reflects 'changes in the traditional Western approach [that] are, arguably, happening under the influence of East Asian cultures'.[54] Houzhi Tang argues that 'there is an expanding culture that favors combining arbitration with conciliation (mediation) in the world' and that '[t]his culture has been in existence in the East for a long time and is now expanding to the West'.[55] Other commentators are apt to shore up these claims by noting that the first wave of legislation permitting same neutral hybrid processes appeared along the pacific rim, in jurisdictions such as Hong Kong, California and British Columbia.[56]

Although culture unquestionably exerts an influence on law and legal practice, the extent to which East Asian culture in particular helps explain the rise of legislation in this area is far from clear. In 1989, Hong Kong became the first Eastern Asian jurisdiction to adopt a provision allowing arbitrators to act as conciliators in the same dispute. Yet there are even earlier examples of permissive same neutral arb-med legislation from countries outside Eastern Asia, such as Iraq (1969), Kuwait (1980), Australia (1984),[57] Canada (1986),[58] Bermuda (1986), the Netherlands (1986), California (1988) and Uruguay (1988).[59] The extended timeline in Figure 2.4 shows that Eastern and Southeastern Asian countries as a group were relative latecomers to such legislation.

---

[54] Nigmatullina (n 34) 76.

[55] Houzhi Tang, 'Is There an Expanding Culture that Favors Combining Arbitration with Conciliation or Other ADR Procedures?' (1998) 8 ICCA Congress Series 101, 101.

[56] M Scott Donahey, 'Seeking Harmony: Is the Asian Concept of the Conciliator/Arbitrator Applicable in the West?' (1995) 50 Dispute Resolution Journal 74, 77; Nabil N Antaki, 'Muslims' and Arabs' Practice of ADR' [2009] 2 NYSBA New York Dispute Resolution Lawyer 113, 113.

[57] See Conciliation and Arbitration Amendment Act 1984 (Cth) (Australia). The Act was adopted in all six states and in two territories. See Commercial Arbitration Act 1984 (NSW); Commercial Arbitration Act 1984 (Vic); Commercial Arbitration Act 1985 (NT); Commercial Arbitration Act 1985 (WA); Commercial Arbitration Act 1986 (ACT); Commercial Arbitration and Industrial Referral Agreements Act 1986 (SA); Commercial Arbitration Act 1986 (Tas); Commercial Arbitration Act 1990 (Qld).

[58] With the exception of Ontario and Nunavut, all Canadian provinces and territories – not just British Columbia – had passed international commercial arbitration acts in 1986 that permitted same neutral arb-med. See Uniform International Commercial Arbitration Act 1986 (Canada), s 6; International Commercial Arbitration Act 1986 (British Columbia), s 30.

[59] The earliest provision I have come across is from Australia's Conciliation and Arbitration Act 1904 (Cth), which governed industrial relations until it was repealed in 1988. In the original Act, s 23(2) provided that the Court of Conciliation and Arbitration 'shall make all such suggestions and do all such things as appear to it to be right and proper for reconciling the parties and for inducing the settlement of the dispute by amicable agreement'.

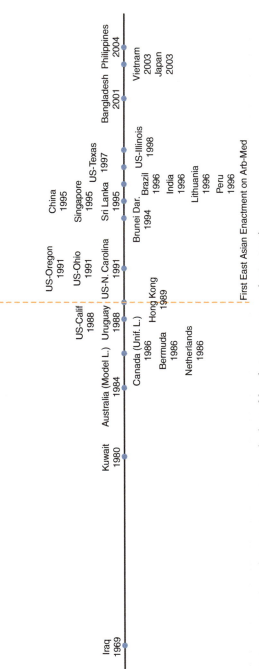

Figure 2.4 Timeline of permissive same neutral arb-med legislative enactments (1969–2004)

By contrast, given that the majority of jurisdictions in Figure 2.4 are common law jurisdictions, legal tradition rather than regional culture may be a better explanation for the origin of legislation favouring same neutral arb-med.

A similar story can be told about med-arb. Although the earliest examples of legislation permitting same neutral med-arb are from Hong Kong (1982), Australia (1984), Brunei Darussalam (1994) and Singapore (1995), the extent to which they influenced later enactments in other jurisdictions is questionable. With the exception of India (1996) and Hungary (2002), those later enactments all post-date UNCITRAL's publication of the first version of the Model Mediation Law in 2002. Recall that the Model Mediation Law permits same neutral med-arb with the agreement of the parties. National laws passed after 2002 that follow this approach are more likely to have been influenced by the Model Mediation Law (whose purpose, after all, is to promote international best practices in commercial mediation) than by the approach of any one country or region.

Here it might be argued that the Model Mediation Law itself could have been influenced by East Asian dispute resolution practices. But the *travaux préparatoires* do not explain the statute's permissive approach to same neutral med-arb as a response to the prevalence of the practice in any particular region of the world, let alone Eastern Asia.[60] Quite the opposite: they explain it in terms of modifying the UCR's absolute prohibition on the mediator acting as the arbitrator with a provision that allows parties to agree otherwise.[61] The intent behind the Model Mediation Law's approach was therefore to privilege party autonomy over immutable rules. There is no evidence in the *travaux* that the intention was to encourage a practice – whether associated with Eastern Asia or not – of mediators shifting seamlessly into the role of an arbitrator.

A further point is that if legislation is any guide, it is difficult to conclude that there is in fact 'an expanding culture that favors combining arbitration with conciliation (mediation) in the world'. Canada, for example, has shown signs of backpedalling from an earlier position favouring same neutral arb-med to one that is more lukewarm. In 2014, the Uniform Law Conference of Canada (ULCC) decided against retaining a provision in the 1986 Uniform International Commercial

---

[60] See eg United Nations General Assembly A/CN.9/460 (6 April 1999) paras 14–15.
[61] See eg United Nations General Assembly A/CN.9/468 (10 April 2000) paras 34–35; United Nations General Assembly A/CN.9/485 (20 December 2000) para 149; United Nations Commission on International Trade Law, Guide to Enactment and Use of the UNCITRAL Model Law on International Commercial Conciliation (2002) 78.

Arbitration Act that allowed the arbitrator to act as a mediator with the parties' consent. In 2019, the Alberta Law Reform Institute took the same decision in connection with proposed revisions to the Alberta International Commercial Arbitration Act 2000. The Institute's summary of its deliberations is illuminating:

> Apparently, using alternate dispute resolution techniques during an arbitration is very popular in Asian markets. One Project Advisory Committee member predicted that Alberta would not attract Asian parties if this provision were removed. Further, British Columbia is likely our biggest competitor with respect to attracting international commercial arbitration business and the BC Act retains this provision. Other Committee members indicated that, regardless of the impact that removing the provision has on attracting arbitration business, they agreed with the uniform approach.
> The ULCC Working Group was concerned about authorizing arbitrators to act in multiple roles, even with parties' consent . . .
> The ultimate consensus from the ULCC was not to carry this provision forward and to eliminate it from the Uniform Act 2014. Although mediation is to be encouraged, it is not the arbitral tribunal which should act in that capacity. An arbitrator must decide based only on a record of admissible evidence. When an arbitrator also serves as a mediator, it risks the arbitrator being exposed to inadmissible evidence from 'without prejudice' communications.
> ALRI concurs with this decision as well.[62]

These observations suggest that East Asian culture – or, more precisely, the desire to attract East Asian end-users – may have some influence on hybrid process legislation. But they also underscore how policy or ethical considerations, such as about arbitrators acting in multiple roles or the need for uniformity in the law, are equally important in shaping legislative choices.

Moreover, it is difficult to generalise about an East Asian approach to same neutral hybrid processes, and much less about whether that approach is uniformly favourable. During discussions around 2002 over amendments to the Hong Kong Arbitration Ordinance, for instance, the Hong Kong Mediation Council actually recommended removing existing sections in the Ordinance that permitted mediators and arbitrators to assume dual roles in the same dispute. The rationale was that 'these sections were alien to the way in which mediation was generally conducted in Hong Kong'.[63] Although the

---

[62] Alberta Law Reform Institute (n 22) 59–60.
[63] Hong Kong Institute of Arbitrators, Draft Report of the Committee of the Hong Kong Arbitration Law (June 2002) <www.hkiac.org/sites/default/files/ck_filebrowser/PDF/services/95.pdf> accessed 28 March 2021, 154.

sections were ultimately retained, the example illustrates that even in jurisdictions within the influence or control of China, there may be sharply dissenting views on the matter. Because legislative outcomes are based on majority vote, they do not necessarily reflect the full extent of those dissenting views, which may be substantial.

2.4.3 Innovation and Borrowing among Common Law Jurisdictions

Even though common law jurisdictions do not regulate same neutral hybrid processes at the highest rates overall, when they do so they appear both more attuned to the pitfalls of such processes and more inclined to innovate around them. For example, legislation around hybrid processes tends to refrain from addressing anything other than the narrow yes/no question of whether the same neutral may assume both roles. Only nine jurisdictions in the database (or 4.6 per cent) go the extra mile of regulating the circumstances under which the neutral may assume both roles – for example, by addressing what type of consent (*ex ante* or *ex post*) is sufficient or necessary in order for arbitration to follow mediation with the same neutral, or by providing for the neutral to disclose material information revealed in a private caucus before moving from the mediator to the arbitrator role. Significantly, eight of the nine are common law jurisdictions (Australia, Bermuda, BVI, Brunei Darussalam, Canada, Hong Kong, Singapore, and Trinidad and Tobago). The lone civil law jurisdiction is Indonesia.[64]

Common law jurisdictions are also more likely to borrow innovations from one another, sometimes lock, stock and barrel. For example, Bermuda, BVI, Brunei Darussalam and Singapore have all imported substantially the same intricate provisions permitting same neutral med-arb and arb-med (including those regarding required mediator disclosures) that derive from the 1982 and 1989 versions of the Hong Kong Arbitration Ordinance. Likewise, Sri Lanka, India, Bangladesh and several jurisdictions in the United States (California, Ohio, Oregon, North Carolina, Texas and Illinois) borrowed a provision from the 1986 version of the British Columbia International Commercial Arbitration Act which, among other things, permitted arbitrators to act as mediators and allowed any mediated settlement agreement to be recorded as an arbitral award on agreed terms.[65] By contrast, this type of borrowing is less evident among civil law jurisdictions.

---

[64] See Section 2.3.3.3.
[65] International Commercial Arbitration Act 1986 (British Columbia) (n 58), s 30.

2.4.4 Development Status

If region, legal tradition and culture do not provide compelling explanations for my findings or for the chronology of legislative enactments in Figure 2.4, what does? One way to begin answering this question is to revisit the assumption that jurisdictions legislate in this area in response to actual practices on the ground. Perhaps a bigger motivation is to be perceived as hospitable to law reform – for example, for purposes of encouraging foreign direct investment, moving up in the World Bank's Ease of Doing Business rankings, or complying with the terms of a loan from a development bank.

I hypothesised this to be most likely true in the med-arb context, since many developing countries have enacted mediation statutes at least in part for the aforementioned reasons. Alleviating court backlog is moreover a common development goal, and arbitration statutes may be perceived as less useful in this regard because arbitration (particularly international commercial arbitration) does not help reduce court caseloads in the same way and to the same extent as mediation.

To test this hypothesis, I used income level as a proxy for development status. I then categorised jurisdictions in the database based on whether they were high income, upper middle income, lower middle income or low income according to the World Bank's list of economies (as of June 2019).[66]

As shown in Figure 2.5(a), there is an almost perfectly inverse relationship between a country's income level and the propensity to regulate same neutral hybrid processes. Among low-income states, 55.2 per cent regulate some type of same neutral hybrid process (med-arb or arb-med), compared with 45.7 per cent of lower-middle-income, 26.3 per cent of upper-middle-income and 37.1 per cent of high-income jurisdictions. More so than region or legal tradition, therefore, being a low-income state is hands-down the best predictor of whether a jurisdiction will regulate same neutral med-arb or arb-med. Figure 2.5(b) reveals a strikingly similar pattern with respect to jurisdictions that regulate same neutral med-arb.

These results are consistent with the idea that low- and lower-middle-income countries may have passed mediation laws less in order to regulate pre-existing practices and more in order to promote (or appear to promote) the development of those practices from scratch. This explanation is corroborated by the fact that these countries have tended to copy wholesale from the Model Mediation Law, which permits same neutral

---

[66] See <https://datahelpdesk.worldbank.org/knowledgebase/articles/906519-world-bank-country-and-lending-groups> accessed 28 March 2021.

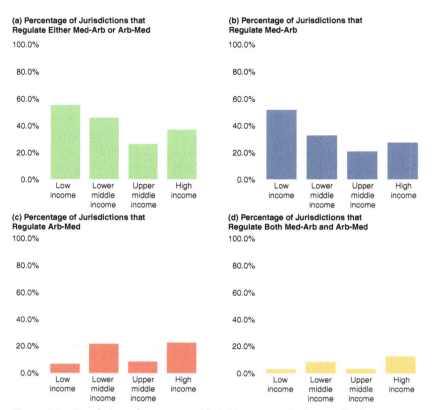

Figure 2.5 Regulation of same neutral hybrid processes by income level

med-arb with the consent of the parties. For example, among low-income countries with a mediation law, 62.5 per cent are Model Mediation Law jurisdictions. As one moves up the development ladder to lower-middle, upper-middle and high-income countries, these figures generally decline (33.3 per cent, 17.1 per cent and 22.5 per cent, respectively). In other words, the more developed a country is, the less it is likely to rely on off-the-rack model laws and the more it is likely to tailor legislation to actual regulatory needs. If so, and given that same neutral hybrid processes are relatively uncommon to begin with, it is also not surprising that upper-middle and high-income countries regulate them at the lowest rates.

By contrast, Figures 2.5(c) and 2.5(d) show that high-income jurisdictions are more likely to regulate same neutral arb-med, and to regulate *both* same neutral med-arb and arb-med. These findings, too, are consistent with my hypothesis. Most provisions regulating arb-med are contained in arbitration laws, which for reasons explained already have not featured as prominently as mediation law reform in development efforts. Moreover, the majority of arbitration law precedents – the most popular of which is the Model Arbitration Law – do not address same neutral arb-med. Thus, a state that has opted to regulate same neutral arb-med must have taken a deliberate step to depart from existing models in order to fill a regulatory need.

This may also explain why, in Figure 2.5(d), high-income jurisdictions are most likely to regulate *both* same neutral hybrid processes. If the law in those jurisdictions is more closely rooted in practice and, as I have argued, the same basic problems attend both processes, it is not surprising that those jurisdictions would have greater reason to legislate around both.

2.4.5 Other Observations

2.4.5.1 Emphasis on Same Neutral Med-arb More than Arb-med

As was true of the precedents, same neutral med-arb is regulated more often than same neutral arb-med: 59 states (or 30.3 per cent of the database) regulate the former and 31 states (or 15.9 per cent) regulate the latter.

This emphasis on same neutral med-arb is even further pronounced when one considers that same neutral med-arb is overwhelmingly regulated through mediation laws (or mediation sections of combined ADR laws), and *mutatis mutandis* for arb-med. There are 115 states with mediation laws and 192 states – almost double – with arbitration laws.[67] The upshot is that when a state chooses to regulate mediation, it addresses same neutral med-arb 51.3 per cent of the time; however, when a state chooses to regulate arbitration, it addresses same neutral arb-med only 16.1 per cent of the time.

2.4.5.2 Lack of Robust Hybrid Process Regulation

Overall, only 75 jurisdictions in the database (or 38.5 per cent) have chosen to regulate same neutral arb-med or med-arb. As Figures 2.1(b) and 2.1(c), 2.2(b) and 2.2(c) and 2.3 show, these processes are regulated in less than 50 per cent of states within any given region or legal tradition. Only in the following sub-regions have the majority of states (that is, more than 50 per cent) regulated at least one type of same neutral hybrid process: Western Africa (86.7 per cent), Middle Africa (77.8 per cent),

---

[67] If a state has a combined ADR law that addresses both arbitration and conciliation or mediation, it was counted as having both an arbitration law and a mediation law.

Northern America (66.7 per cent), Southeastern Asia (63.6 per cent) and Southern Asia (55.6 per cent). Looking just at same neutral med-arb, in only the first four of the foregoing sub-regions is it regulated by a majority of states. In no sub-region – not even Eastern or Southeastern Asia – has a majority of states regulated same neutral arb-med.[68]

2.4.5.3 Lack of Co-ordination and Consistency in the Regulation of Hybrid Processes

National laws also tend to reflect the approach of the precedents to regulate med-arb and arb-med in silos. Only 7.7 per cent of jurisdictions in the database regulate both same neutral arb-med and same neutral med-arb. As Figure 2.3(d) shows, a greater proportion of common law jurisdictions (17.0 per cent) than civil law jurisdictions (3.9 per cent) fall into this category.

Even where a country regulates both, it tends to do so in separate legal instruments. Same neutral arb-med tends overwhelmingly to be regulated in arbitration rather than mediation laws (90.3 per cent versus 6.5 per cent of the time) while same neutral med-arb tends to be regulated in mediation rather than arbitration laws (82.8 per cent versus 12.1 per cent of the time).[69] The upshot is that instead of regulating same neutral hybrid processes holistically, states do so largely from the perspective of the originating (that is, 'med-' or 'arb-') process. This can sometimes cause a lack of co-ordination and consistency, since arbitration and mediation law reformers often operate in different professional circles.

A good example here is Brazil. Brazil's Arbitration Law provides that '[t]he sole arbitrator or the arbitral tribunal shall, at the commencement of the procedure, attempt to reconcile the parties . . . .'.[70] At the same time, its Mediation Law provides that '[t]he mediator may neither act as an arbitrator nor as a witness in legal or arbitration proceedings concerning a dispute in which he/she has acted as a mediator'.[71] It is difficult to

---

[68] In the Eastern Asia and Australia & New Zealand sub-regions, exactly 50 per cent of states regulate at least one type of same neutral hybrid process. Note, however, that my database contains only two of the six jurisdictions in the Australia & New Zealand sub-region.

[69] As used in this sentence, 'mediation law' and 'arbitration law' include the mediation or arbitration part or chapter, as the case may be, of an omnibus ADR or Arbitration and Conciliation Act.

In two countries (Cape Verde and Vietnam), same neutral med-arb is regulated in both the mediation law and the arbitration law. In the Philippines, same neutral med-arb and same neutral arb-med are regulated in a generic section of an ADR Act. See Alternative Dispute Resolution Act 2004 (The Philippines) (n 41), s 18.

[70] Law No 9.307, 1996 (Brazil) (n 33), s 21(4).

[71] Law No 13140, 2015 (Brazil) (n 21), s 7.

comprehend why a state would take such diametrically opposite positions on the same basic combination of arbitration and mediation, based solely on which process preceded the other. It is moreover unclear whether Brazil's Mediation Law applies to mediation in the course of arbitration.[72] If it does, it creates intolerably conflicting demands on the neutral: on the one hand, the arbitrator has the authority if not the *duty* to 'attempt to reconcile the parties'; on the other hand, under the Mediation Law he or she would be absolutely prohibited from resuming the role of an arbitrator. This could potentially also jeopardise the efficacy of agreements to arbitrate, by giving one party the ability to sabotage an arbitration by refusing to settle during a mediation window.

Another example is the innovative provision in the arbitration laws of Australia, Brunei Darussalam, BVI, Hong Kong, the Philippines and Singapore requiring the arbitrator who receives material *ex parte* information during a mediation window to disclose it to the other side before resuming his or her role as the arbitrator. In all but one case, the provision is limited to disputes governed by a pre-existing arbitration clause, where the appointed arbitrator receives *ex parte* information during a mediation phase that takes place either prior to or after the commencement of arbitral proceedings.[73] It therefore does not apply to a situation where the parties initially only contemplate mediation and later authorise the mediator to arbitrate the dispute once a settlement is not forthcoming. The trouble is that there is no principled reason why the procedural safeguard of disclosure should be required in one context but not the other. A final award rendered pursuant to either process is equally exposed to challenge based on the arbitrator's receipt of *ex parte* communications.

2.5 Conclusion

This chapter has summarised some key findings regarding the regulation of same neutral hybrid processes from an examination of national arbitration and mediation laws of 195 jurisdictions. The key findings are as follows:

---

[72] Unlike other national mediation laws, Brazil's Mediation Law does not exclude mediation in the course of arbitration from its scope of application. If anything, the Mediation Law suggests broad applicability to all forms of mediation, the sole enumerated exception being '[m]ediation in labor relations'. See ibid, s 42.

[73] Only in the Philippines, whose ADR Act has a separate section devoted to hybrid processes, is it clear that the duty of disclosure applies in both contexts. See Alternative Dispute Resolution Act 2004 (The Philippines) (n 41), s 18; Implementing Rules and Regulations of the Alternative Dispute Resolution Act 2004 (The Philippines) (n 41), s 7.8(c).

- Overall, national law-making around same neutral hybrid processes does not appear to be a priority. Only 75 of the 195 jurisdictions in the database (or 38.5 per cent) have a law that regulates at least one type of process.
- As shown in Figure 2.3(a), the regions with the highest proportion of states falling into this category are Africa and Asia (46.2 per cent and 46.0 per cent, respectively), followed by the Americas (36.1 per cent), Europe (31.1 per cent) and Oceania (8.3 per cent). The sub-regions that regulate same neutral hybrid processes at the highest rates are Western Africa (86.7 per cent), Middle Africa (77.8 per cent), Northern America (66.7 per cent) and Southeastern Asia (63.6 per cent). Those that do so at the lowest rates are Northern Europe (10.0 per cent), the Caribbean (15.4 per cent) and Northern Africa (16.7 per cent). In terms of legal tradition, Figure 2.3(b) shows that a greater proportion of civil law jurisdictions (42.5 per cent) fall into this group than their common law counterparts (34.0 per cent).
- But the best predictor of whether a state will regulate at least one type of same neutral hybrid process is not region or legal tradition but rather development status (for which I used income level as a proxy). As shown in Figure 2.5(a), low-income states are most likely to regulate such processes (55.2 per cent), followed by lower-middle- (45.7 per cent), high- (37.1 per cent) and upper-middle-income (26.3 per cent) states. Taken together with the data by region and legal tradition, these figures suggest that legislation on same neutral hybrid processes is most common among the following categories of states, in order: low-income states, states located in Africa or Asia, lower-middle-income states, and civil law jurisdictions. It is least common among states in Oceania (8.3 per cent), Muslim and customary law jurisdictions (20.0 per cent) and mixed common/civil law jurisdictions (25.0 per cent).
- A slightly more nuanced picture emerges when one considers the regulation of med-arb and arb-med in isolation. As shown in Figure 2.1(b), states in Africa are most likely to regulate same neutral med-arb (42.3 per cent), followed by those in the Americas (30.6 per cent), Europe (26.7 per cent), Asia (26.0 per cent) and Oceania (8.3 per cent). But Figure 2.2(b) shows that almost the reverse is true for same neutral arb-med. Here, Asian states take the lead (34.0 per cent), followed by states in the Americas (16.7 per cent), Europe (8.9 per cent), Oceania (8.3 per cent) and Africa (5.8 per cent). A similar inversion can be observed with respect to legal tradition. Figures 2.1(c) and 2.2(c) show that, although a greater proportion of civil than common law

2 SNAPSHOT OF NATIONAL LEGISLATION ON SAME NEUTRAL 65

jurisdictions regulate same neutral med-arb (33.1 per cent versus 27.7 per cent), when it comes to same neutral arb-med, common law jurisdictions are almost twice as likely to regulate it than their civil law counterparts (23.4 per cent versus 13.4 per cent).
- Even though the same basic problems attend med-arb and arb-med before the same neutral, almost double the number of states in the database regulate the former than they do the latter (30.3 per cent versus 15.9 per cent). There is also a lack of co-ordination in the regulation of both processes, in the sense that (a) countries rarely regulate both and (b) even if they do, they do not always do so in a co-ordinated fashion.
- Although it is often said that combining mediation and arbitration using the same neutral is widely accepted in Continental European, Latin American and Eastern Asian cultures, this is only somewhat borne out by legislation.[74] Assuming that law-making mirrors culture, my findings lend qualified support only to the idea that Eastern and Southeastern Asian cultures are receptive to same neutral arb-med. Even so, as explained in Section 2.4.2 and Figure 2.4, it is difficult to conclude that those cultures were harbingers for permissive same neutral arb-med or med-arb legislation in other parts of the world.
- A smaller percentage of common than civil law jurisdictions regulate hybrid processes (34.0 per cent versus 42.5 per cent). But, as explained in Section 2.4.3, common law jurisdictions are much more likely to use law to craft creative solutions to the problems that attend such processes – for example, in the form of disclosure or *ex post* consent requirements before arbitration may follow mediation with the same neutral.

---

[74] See Sections 2.3.3.1 and 2.3.3.2.

PART II

Multi-tier Dispute Resolution in Asia

A

General Trends

3

Combinations of Mediation and Arbitration

The Case of China

WEIXIA GU

3.1 Introduction

Med-arb refers to the multi-tier dispute resolution of conducting mediation[1] in the course of arbitration. In Western jurisdictions, med-arb is controversial as, without proper safeguards, the hybrid process is particularly vulnerable to due process problems. The controversy has made med-arb less popular in the West. The due process concerns in the West, however, are not preventing med-arb from gaining popularity in Asia, where mediation has a strong cultural root. Japan, Hong Kong and Singapore, among others in East and Southeast Asia, have made certain provisions requiring med-arb to have proper procedure standards.[2] China, where med-arb is prevalent in the commercial dispute resolution system, is, however, lacking in this area.

In China, med-arb is popular for domestic as well as cross-border arbitrations. A typical med-arb procedure arises where the parties have entered into an arbitration and within the arbitration procedure have decided to mediate. Where mediation fails, arbitration resumes and an award is rendered. Although this process is more accurately known as 'arb-med-arb', this chapter focuses on the issues surrounding the resumption of arbitration after the mediation stage.

Despite its slowing economic growth in recent years, China does not seem to be seeing a decrease in arbitration caseloads. In 2016, 208,545

---

[1] Chinese law and rules of Chinese arbitration institutions translate the Chinese term of mediation (*tiaojie* 调解) as 'conciliation'. They are used interchangeably.
[2] Michael Pryles and Veronica L Taylor, 'The Cultures of Dispute Resolution in Asia' in Michael Pryles (ed), *Dispute Resolution in Asia* (3rd edn, Kluwer Law International 2006) 15–17.

cases were processed by the 251 arbitration institutions in China.[3] Compared to that in 2015, the caseload increased by 52 per cent.[4] China's leading arbitration institution, the China International Economic and Trade Arbitration Commission (CIETAC), handled 2,179 cases or 1 per cent of China's total arbitration caseload in 2016.[5] Statistics show that approximately 58 per cent of CIETAC's caseload was resolved by med-arb in 2016.[6]

The main difference between the med-arb used in domestic contexts and that used in cross-border disputes is the latter's additional international dimension. Med-arb is in many ways a medium that adds an international dimension, that is, arbitration, to the local product, namely, mediation.[7] Through cross-border med-arb, foreign parties are exposed not only to Chinese-styled mediation but also to the practices of Chinese arbitrators and arbitration institutions.

When attempting to understand the mediation stage within med-arb, we should consider how mediation is practised domestically in China as an independent dispute resolution method. This is because how mediation is conducted outside med-arb (for example, in judicial mediation and mediation by the People's Mediation Committees) contributes to how arbitration institutions think about the proper standard of mediation when designing and conducting their mediation stage of med-arb.

The literature shows that the Chinese approach to mediation is fairly different from the conventional, international understanding of it. Mediation as practised in Western jurisdictions is regarded as being co-operative, voluntary and party-centred. Mediators are expected to be mainly facilitators and to respect the autonomy and choice of the parties. Even in evaluative mediation in the West, mediators are required not to be adjudicatory.[8] However, Chinese mediation is more 'adjudicatory,

---

[3] China International Economic and Trade Arbitration Commission, *Zhongguo guoji shangshi zhongcai niandu baogao (2016)* [Annual Report on International Commercial Arbitration in China (2016)] <www.cietac.org/Uploads/201710/59df3824b2849.pdf> accessed 17 August 2020, 8.

[4] ibid.

[5] 'Statistics' (*China International Economic and Trade Arbitration Commission*) <http://cietac.org/index.php?m=Page&a=index&id=40&l=en> accessed 17 August 2020. This caseload figure excludes cases handled by the CIETAC Hong Kong Arbitration Center.

[6] Annual Report on International Commercial Arbitration in China (2016) (n 3) 13.

[7] Weixia Gu, 'When Local Meets International: Mediation Combined with Arbitration in China and Its Prospective Reform in a Comparative Context' (2016) 10(2) Journal of Comparative Law 84.

[8] Jacqueline M Nolan-Haley, *Alternative Dispute Resolution in a Nutshell* (4th edn, West Academic 2013) 60–63.

aggressive, and interventionist'.⁹ Some practitioners have commented that parties are forced into entering mediation during arbitration and some lawyers are even 'gaming' mediation to intentionally delay the proceedings and to seek more information from the other party.¹⁰ In the courts, parties enter into judicial mediation often due to pressure from the judge.¹¹ The judge is in turn under pressure of performance targets to settle cases through mediation.¹²

In the context of med-arb, this mediation culture translates into a more active med-arb management by the arbitrators. Fan conducted a survey of thirty-six active arbitrators from CIETAC, the Beijing Arbitration Commission (BAC) and the Wuhan Arbitration Commission (WAC) between 2011 and 2012 showing a glimpse of arbitrator attitudes towards med-arb and how such attitudes have affected the use of med-arb. According to Fan's study, 50 per cent of the respondents have recommended the parties to mediate in more than 90 per cent of the cases in which they acted as an arbitrator;¹³ more than 10 per cent of the respondents have recommended mediation in more than 70–90 per cent of the cases they arbitrated.¹⁴ As to parties, where both parties are Chinese, they are more likely to consent to med-arb than where foreign parties are involved.¹⁵ The survey also shows the reasons that the respondents chose to adopt a conciliatory role. Most respondents believed that 'the agreed outcome is easier to be voluntarily enforced than a decided outcome in an arbitral award'.¹⁶ The second and third cited reasons are that med-arb can reduce costs and improve efficiency and that mediation 'respects the free will and voluntariness of the parties'.¹⁷

How did the difference demarcating the Chinese and the Western approaches to mediation emerge? Compared to arbitration, mediation

---

⁹ Hualing Fu and Richard Cullen, 'From Mediatory to Adjudicatory Justice: The Limits of Civil Justice Reform in China' in Margaret YK Woo and Mary E Gallagher (eds), *Chinese Justice: Civil Dispute Resolution in Contemporary China* (Cambridge University Press 2011) 33.
¹⁰ Thomas J Stipanowich and others, 'East Meets West: An International Dialogue on Mediation and Med-arb in the United States and China' (2009) 9(2) Pepperdine Dispute Resolution Law Journal 395–96.
¹¹ Fu and Cullen (n 9) 33.
¹² ibid.
¹³ Kun Fan, 'An Empirical Study of Arbitrators Acting as Mediators in China' (2014) 15(3) Cardozo Journal of Conflict Resolution 777, 791.
¹⁴ ibid.
¹⁵ ibid 792.
¹⁶ ibid 790.
¹⁷ ibid.

is more culture-laden and less judicialised. Mediation's dependency on culture is a result of the aim to induce voluntary settlement by the parties, and appealing to the cultural background of the parties is a way of inducing that settlement. Arbitration, by contrast, is governed by international rules and norms created by the deliberations between potential users of various jurisdictions. It is designed to be an international dispute resolution method. In China, mediation is a product of its Confucian legal culture and the State governance to promote social harmony. Confucianism favours less contentious means of resolving disputes with an emphasis on mediation. While the ends are the same, the State governance to promote mediation is more instrumentalist. Mediation is used to promote better governability of the civil society and to reduce conflicts that might potentially reduce the legitimacy of the Party-State. It was not until the enactment of the Civil Procedure Law (1991) that cases were not required to be mediated first before adjudication by the People's Court when the former had failed.[18] Mediation is thus designed to meet the Confucian and governance objectives of dispute resolution in China. As a result, foreign users of med-arb may find Chinese mediation alien.

3.2 Procedural Defects

While the Chinese government has encouraged Chinese arbitration institutions to 'go abroad' (*zou chuqu* 走出去) and compete with regional institutions, the chronic problem with med-arb procedural defects has still not been resolved. This is in spite of the frequent and recent revisions to rules of various Chinese arbitration institutions. Despite recent updates to the regulations on arbitration, few have fundamentally addressed procedural irregularities long identified by scholars and practitioners, leaving the usual defects of actual and apparent bias and protection of confidentiality largely unmentioned.

3.2.1 Conflicting Roles of Arbitrator and Mediator

The main criticism of med-arb is the conflict of interest between the arbitral and mediatory roles assumed by the neutral. The concern is whether the neutral can remain impartial, given the different approaches

---

[18] Minshi Susong Fa (民事訴訟法) [Civil Procedure Law] (promulgated by the National People's Congress Standing Committee, 9 April 1991, effective 9 April 1991); Xianchu Zhang, 'Rethinking the Mediation Campaign' (2015) 10(2) Journal of Comparative Law 45.

and attitudes required for the two dispute resolution methods. It is the norm in China for the arbitrator to 'switch hats' and become the mediator when mediation occurs within the arbitration proceedings. In such case, arbitration is stayed and is resumed only when mediation fails.

A source of the conflict of roles is how an arbitrator, as opposed to a mediator, should conduct him/herself in the course of the proceedings. In the proceedings, the arbitrator takes on the role that decides on an appropriate award based on the merits of the submissions from both parties. It is a legal process in which the arbitrator must interpret relevant laws and apply them to facts, just as a judge would do in a court.[19] The mediator, by contrast, does not inquire into the appropriateness of a settlement reached by the parties. Instead, the mediator is more interested that the parties reach a settlement agreement developed on their own.

Because of the very different aims of the two forms of dispute resolution, the approach required of the neutral must not be the same in all stages of med-arb. A competent arbitrator should be disinterested and display a 'judicial temperament'.[20] She or he must observe the requirements of impartiality and general legal competence from which s/he draws respect from the party.[21] A good mediator, by contrast, should be sensitive to inter-party relationships so as to discover the needs of the parties that might hide below the mediatory exchanges (the so-called bottom lines). In facilitating settlement and communication between the parties, the mediator may take a more involved, personal approach. Practised separately as single-tier dispute resolution methods, even for the same subject matter, the dispute resolution process generally has no due process concerns. Theoretically, an arbitration proceeding can suffer no irregularities or biases, actual or apparent, when the same person switches hats between an arbitrator and a mediator if she or he can maintain the standards required of her/him in arbitration and mediation respectively. Due process concerns arise not from multi-tier resolutions per se but from the very human difficulty of partitioning information obtained in the two stages to ensure impartiality.

In China, the parties can request third-party mediation from an independent mediator.[22] But the mediatory role of the arbitrators is

---

[19] Paul E Mason, 'The Arbitrator as Mediator, and Mediator as Arbitrator' (2011) 28(6) Journal of International Arbitration 541.
[20] ibid 543.
[21] ibid.
[22] Sally A Harpole, 'The Combination of Conciliation with Arbitration in the People's Republic of China' (2007) 24(6) Journal of International Arbitration 623, 628.

generally assumed as a matter of practice. The med-arb rules of leading Chinese arbitration institutions with an international scope and with experience in cross-border arbitration, such as CIETAC, BAC, the Shanghai International Arbitration Center (SHIAC) and the Shenzhen Court of International Arbitration (SCIA), also reflect such assumption. The 2015 CIETAC Rules, for instance, state that '[w]ith the consents of both parties, the arbitral tribunal may conciliate the case in a manner it considers appropriate'.[23]

The rule empowers the tribunal to conduct mediation, but is silent on whether third parties can also mediate. It has been reported that CIETAC assembled an independent panel of mediators on the request of the party in one case.[24] The 2015 BAC Rules are more explicit with alternative arrangements. They provide for independent mediation at BAC's Mediation Center in accordance with the BAC Mediation Center Mediation Rules.[25] But such mediation is separate from the arbitral proceedings and thus is not a form of med-arb. As with self-settlement, parties who have reached a settlement agreement through the Mediation Center can request the arbitration tribunal to render an award based on that agreement,[26] allowing the agreement to be enforced in foreign jurisdictions under the New York Convention. With the approval of the BAC Chairperson and additional costs borne by the parties, the BAC Rules also allow international arbitrations to replace the arbitrator after mediation fails.[27] The explicit arrangement for a separate mediation mechanism and for allowing arbitrator replacement is rare among arbitration rules in China. Similar to other rules, though, the language of the CIETAC rules still does not expressly allow the possibility of mediation by independent mediators. The 2015 CIETAC Rules attempt to provide non-CIETAC mediation, but they only vaguely provide that 'CIETAC may, with the consents of both parties, assist the parties to conciliate the dispute *in a manner and procedure it considers appropriate.*'[28] It is unclear

---

[23] China International Economic and Trade Arbitration Commission, 'China International Economic and Trade Arbitration Commission Arbitration Rules' (2015) <http://cietac.org/index.php?m=Page&a=index&id=106&l=en> accessed 17 August 2020, art 47(2).

[24] Harpole (n 22) 627.

[25] Beijing Arbitration Commission, 'Beijing Arbitration Commission Arbitration Rules' (2015) <http://bjac.org.cn/english/page/ckzl/sz2015.html> accessed 17 August 2020, art 43.

[26] ibid, art 43(2).

[27] ibid, art 67(2).

[28] China International Economic and Trade Arbitration Commission Arbitration Rules (n 23), art 47(8) (emphasis added).

how the parties may be 'assisted' under this rule or what arrangements have been made under the rule.

Besides language in arbitration rules that tends to lead parties towards institutional med-arb, the parties may also choose their arbitrator to mediate because they are already familiar with the arbitrator, and the arbitrator is familiar with the facts and background of the dispute.[29] The parties can be sure that they can trust the arbitrator. Such an arbitrator will also allow quicker arbitration and award rendering if and when mediation fails.[30] However, whether trust and the saving of time and costs do draw parties into med-arb is dependent on the legal culture. Empirical evidence shows that mutual consent for med-arb is far more likely to be given when both parties are Chinese.[31] Presumably Chinese parties are more familiar with the med-arb process embedded in their dispute resolution culture, while foreign parties are less trusting of the process. Foreign parties might also expect an award rather than a settlement agreement by the end.[32]

3.2.2 Confidentiality

A more practical procedural concern has to do with confidentiality of information. The issue of due process arises when the neutral, as the mediator, reverts to becoming an arbitrator. In this process, the information obtained by the neutral during the mediation stage might, consciously or otherwise, rely on information provided by the parties during mediation.[33] Such information would not normally be communicated to the arbitrator in arbitration when practised alone. Mediators who practise evaluative mediation might also reveal to the parties the merits of their respective cases, which would not be known to the parties in arbitration until the award is rendered.[34]

Distinct from arbitration, mediation allows *ex parte* communication, or caucusing. Information given by a party to the neutral during caucuses is not known to the other party. The other party has no opportunity to

---

[29] Gu (n 7) 89.
[30] ibid.
[31] Fan (n 13) 792.
[32] ibid.
[33] Gu (n 7) 90.
[34] James T Peter, 'Med-arb in International Arbitration' (1997) 8(1) American Review of International Arbitration 83.

defend against such confidential information.³⁵ It is for the mediator to determine the truthfulness of the information and the extent to which that information should influence his or her decision in the arbitration stage to come should mediation fail. Parties might also use caucuses to privately influence the neutral in their favour in the subsequent arbitration. Because mediation may involve discussions into personal and emotional issues between the respective parties and the mediator, the neutral may become more sympathetic towards a particular party.³⁶ Admittedly, whether the parties will create bias through these interactions is dependent on the conduct of the individual neutral, but the fact that it cannot be certain that the neutral will not be biased indicates a gap in the regulation of med-arb. Indeed, partiality might only be known or become apparent to parties when mediation fails, at which point it is too late to remedy the proceedings.³⁷

The *Keeneye* case shows the potential dangers of caucusing in creating bias, actual or apparent. The dispute was related to a share transfer agreement. The tribunal, at the Xi'an Arbitration Commission (XAC) in China, was composed of a presiding arbitrator and two arbitrators nominated respectively by each side. After the first hearing, the tribunal suggested mediation to the parties and both sides expressed their consent. The tribunal also, on its own initiative, proposed that the respondents pay the applicants RMB 250 million as settlement. The tribunal then appointed XAC's Secretary-General and the arbitrator nominated by the applicants as mediators and to inform the parties of this proposal. The mediators contacted a person affiliated with the respondents. The person described himself to be 'a person related to (or affiliated with)'³⁸ (*guanxiren* 关系人) the respondents. According to the XAC Rules, '[w]ith the approval of the parties, any third party may be invited to assist the mediation, or they may act as the mediator'.³⁹ The mediators asked him to a private meeting at a restaurant in the Xi'an Shangri-la hotel. At the meeting, the Secretary-General asked the respondents' affiliate to 'work on' (*zuo gongzuo* 做工作) the respondents to get them to accept the settlement proposal. The respondents nonetheless rejected the settlement proposal. The arbitration tribunal reconvened after the failed mediation

---

³⁵ Gabrielle Kaufmann-Kohler, 'When Arbitrators Facilitate Settlement: Towards a Transnational Standard' (2009) 25(2) Arbitration International 198.
³⁶ Peter (n 34) 93.
³⁷ Gu (n 7) 89–90.
³⁸ *Gao Haiyan v Keeneye Holdings Ltd* [2011] 3 HKC 157 [22].
³⁹ ibid [21].

3 COMBINATIONS OF MEDIATION AND ARBITRATION: CHINA 77

and decided to award the respondents RMB 50 million. The respondents challenged the award before the Xi'an Intermediate People's Court. The Xi'an court upheld the award.

The enforcement of the award was then challenged in the Hong Kong Court of First Instance. The Hong Kong court refused enforcement on the grounds, among others, that the meeting over some 'wining and dining'[40] would 'cause a fair-minded observer to apprehend a real possibility of bias on the part of the Arbitration Tribunal'.[41] Although evidence showing actual bias was insufficient, the interactions during the Shangri-la meeting and the contrast between the proposed settlement and the award at the end were sufficient to constitute apparent bias.[42] This apprehension of bias was enough to render the enforcement of such award a contravention of Hong Kong's public policy, that is, 'the most basic notions of justice and morality of the Hong Kong system'.[43] The learned judge opined that '[t]he risk of a mediator turned arbitrator appearing to be biased will always be great'.[44] This decision was reversed when the party seeking enforcement appealed. The appellate court decided to allow enforcement on the basis that the enforcement court should have given greater weight to the decision handed down by the Xi'an court in the supervisory jurisdiction, which found no apparent bias and that the med-arb was properly conducted.[45]

It cannot be assumed that the same standard of apparent bias and deference applied by the Hong Kong Court of Appeal will be replicated by foreign courts. The appellate judgment questions whether the balancing exercise between promoting arbitration and ensuring that due process is observed is done right.[46] Indeed, it is the function of enforcement courts to review the arbitration and its procedure in light of the public policy in the jurisdiction of enforcement. If deference to the supervisory court is too readily relied upon, then the public policy ground to refuse award enforcement can only be applied in too narrow circumstances.

---

[40] ibid [67].
[41] ibid [3].
[42] Weixia Gu and Xianchu Zhang, 'The Keeneye Case: Rethinking the Content of Public Policy in Cross-Border Arbitration between Hong Kong and Mainland China' (2012) 42(3) Hong Kong Law Journal 1006.
[43] *Hebei Import & Export Corp v Polytek Engineering Co Ltd* [1998] 1 HKLRD 287 [47].
[44] *Keeneye* (n 38) [72].
[45] *Gao Haiyan v Keeneye Holdings Ltd* [2012] 1 HKLRD 627 [68].
[46] Gu and Zhang (n 42) 1023.

Unlike those in other jurisdictions, due process safeguards in med-arb rules are limited in China. A typical set of arbitration rules in China does not contain provisions specifically on the use of information arisen out of mediation. At most, the rules will provide only some safeguards that prohibit the parties from relying on any statement expressed during the mediation stage by the other party or the tribunal to support their case.[47] Generally, no provision will prevent the tribunal from relying on any information provided to them during the mediation stage to decide on an award. Even if such rules exist, adhering to them might be difficult in practice, since it amounts to keeping secrets from oneself.

Nonetheless, since the initial refusal to enforce the award in *Keeneye*, Chinese arbitration institutions have taken some steps to mitigate potential procedural irregularities. CIETAC revised its rules in 2012 to expressly state that, with the parties' consent, CIETAC may assist the parties to mediate the dispute 'in a manner and procedure it considers appropriate'[48] if they do not wish mediation to be conducted by the arbitral tribunal.[49] The previous CIETAC Rules (2005) had no suggestion that med-arb can be conducted by any other person or body than the tribunal. The change in the subsequent CIETAC Rules (2012) allows the parties to know that mediation by the arbitral tribunal is not the only option available.

In addition, no statutory safeguards targeting caucusing are available in Chinese law. This sets the Chinese statutory regime aside from other jurisdictions. Hong Kong, for example, has the Arbitration Ordinance that is based upon the UNCITRAL Model Law on International Commercial Arbitration 2006. The Ordinance allows for arbitrators to assume the role of mediators so long as the parties consent and have not withdrawn their consent in writing.[50] The Ordinance expressly provides for a disclosure safeguard: If and when mediation fails and the neutral has obtained confidential information from a party, they 'must, before resuming the arbitral proceedings, disclose to all other parties as much of that information as the arbitrator considers is material to the arbitral proceedings'.[51] Singapore's International Arbitration Act has a similar safeguard provision.[52] This safeguard allows both parties to know what

---

[47] See eg Beijing Arbitration Commission Arbitration Rules (n 25), art 42(5).
[48] China International Economic and Trade Arbitration Commission Arbitration Rules (n 23), art 47(8).
[49] ibid.
[50] Arbitration Ordinance (Cap 609) (Hong Kong), s 33(1).
[51] ibid, s 33(4).
[52] International Arbitration Act (Cap 143A) (Singapore), s 17(3).

information was given to the arbitrator and prompts the parties to defend against such information during the arbitral proceedings.

3.3 Regulation of Med-arb

Arbitration in China is regulated by several sources of law. These are statutes, judicial interpretations and guiding cases issued by the Supreme People's Court (SPC) and occasional regulations and circulars from the State Council. How med-arb is practised is also governed by the rules of individual arbitration institutions. However, the governance of med-arb is not well institutionalised and a bulk of its regulation relies on individual rules of arbitration institutions. This is one of the reasons why the procedural defects discussed earlier are still a pervasive problem when practising med-arb in China and why parties – especially foreign parties – are still suspicious of med-arb in China.

Statutes play only a small but nonetheless foundational role in regulating med-arb. The China Arbitration Law (2017) has had no major amendments[53] since its promulgation in 1994, and regulation of arbitration has been mainly achieved through the SPC's interpretations of the Arbitration Law throughout the years. Within the Arbitration Law, only Article 51 addresses med-arb and it does little to define how med-arb ought to be practised. But Article 51(1) does *require* Chinese arbitration institutions to provide for the procedure of med-arb: 'The arbitration tribunal may first conduct mediation before rendering an award. If the parties volunteer to be mediated, then the arbitration tribunal *shall* conduct mediation. When mediation fails, the tribunal shall duly render an award.'[54] The Article empowers all arbitration institutions in China to conduct med-arb, and both domestic and crossborder arbitration institutions include a med-arb clause in their arbitration rules that largely resembles the statutory language. Although the

---

[53] The first amendment to the Arbitration Law in 2009 changed two article numbers referencing the Civil Procedure Law (2007): Minshi Susong Fa (民事訴訟法) [Civil Procedure Law] (promulgated by the National People's Congress Standing Committee, 28 October 2007, effective 1 April 2008). The second amendment in 2017 concerned a minor change to the qualification of arbitrators: Minshi Susong Fa (民事訴訟法) [Civil Procedure Law] (promulgated by the National People's Congress Standing Committee, 27 June 2017, effective 1 July 2017).
[54] Zhongcai Fa (仲裁法) [Arbitration Law] (promulgated by the National People's Congress Standing Committee, 31 August 1994, effective 1 September 1995), art 51(1). The provision is translated by the author.

Article requires the tribunal to have regard for the intention of the parties to mediate to the extent that the tribunal is required to conduct mediation when the parties so request, it does not forbid the tribunal from conducting mediation even when a party decides against mediation. The issue of party consent is dealt with by arbitration rules. For instance, CIETAC's rules for commercial (2015) and investment (2017) arbitration expressly state that med-arb can proceed only with the consent of both parties, and that mediation must end when either party so requests.[55] BAC, SCIA and SHIAC have rules that stipulate the same.[56] In practice, according to Fan's survey, 77.8 per cent of the arbitrator respondents take the initiative to propose med-arb without being prompted by the party.[57] Suggesting med-arb is just a 'matter of good practice'.[58] However, the survey also found that these initiatives mainly take place during or after the main hearing.[59] Thus, parties are likely to have the opportunity to argue their case without entering the mediation stage.

3.3.1 Market-Based Regulation

As an institutional arbitration dominant jurisdiction,[60] China has de facto delegated the responsibility of arbitration regulation to the market through its 250-plus arbitration institutions. A danger in this regulatory approach is the inconsistency of the standards practised by arbitrators and the safeguards available to the parties among different Chinese arbitration institutions. Foreign investors are unlikely to arbitrate in local arbitration institutions that do not have much experience with cross-border disputes,

---

[55] China International Economic and Trade Arbitration Commission Arbitration Rules (n 23), art 47; China International Economic and Trade Arbitration Commission, 'China International Economic and Trade Arbitration Commission International Investment Arbitration Rules (For Trial Implementation)' (2017) <http://cietac.org/index.php?m=Page&a=index&id=390&l=en> accessed 17 August 2020, art 43.

[56] Beijing Arbitration Commission Arbitration Rules (n 25), art 67; Shenzhen Court of International Arbitration, '*Shenzhen guoji zhongcai yuan zhongcai guize*' [Shenzhen Court of International Arbitration Rules] (2016) <http://sccietac.org/index.php/Home/index/rule/id/798.html> accessed 17 August 2020, art 45; Shanghai International Economic and Trade Arbitration Commission, 'Shanghai International Economic and Trade Arbitration Commission Arbitration Rules' (2015) <http://shiac.org/upload/day_141230/SHIAC_ARBITRATION_RULES_2015_141222.pdf> accessed 17 August 2020, art 41.

[57] Fan (n 13) 791.

[58] ibid.

[59] ibid 795–96.

[60] China does not allow ad hoc arbitration. See Weixia Gu, *Arbitration in China: Regulation of Arbitration Agreements and Practical Issues* (Sweet & Maxwell 2012) 19–24.

and it is the institutions that focus on cross-border disputes that are paving the way in modernising and standardising Chinese med-ab regulation from a bottom-up approach.

Of all leading Chinese arbitration institutions, SCIA is the most innovative in dealing with med-arb. When SCIA split from CIETAC in 2012, its updated rules allowed parties to international commercial disputes and investment disputes relating to Hong Kong, Macau and Taiwan to submit their disputes to SCIA using UNCITRAL Rules in lieu of SCIA Rules.[61] Although this change was in line with CIETAC's 2015 Rules, which allow hybrid arbitration clauses specifying CIETAC arbitration using non-CIETAC arbitration rules, such as the UNCITRAL Rules,[62] it is the first time that Chinese arbitration rules have explicitly referred to the application of UNCITRAL rules. The revisions in the 2016 and 2019 SCIA Rules introduced the 'SCIA Guidelines for the Administration of Arbitration under the UNCITRAL Arbitration Rules' (SCIA UNCITRAL Guidelines), which further regulate how SCIA is to apply UNCITRAL Rules. This means that foreign parties might opt for UNCITRAL Rules with which they might be more familiar, rather than using the SCIA Rules.

With the UNCITRAL Rules, an arbitrator can be challenged 'if circumstances exist that give rise to justifiable doubts as to the arbitrator's impartiality or independence'.[63] If, within fifteen days from the date of the notice of challenge, the challenged arbitrator refuses to withdraw or the challenge is not agreed upon by all parties, then the challenging party may elect to pursue the challenge.[64] The SCIA UNCITRAL Guidelines specify that, in that case, the SCIA President will decide on the challenge.[65] However, besides this provision, there is no mention in the rules as to whether an arbitrator can also assume the role of a mediator. But, by virtue of Article 51(1) of the Arbitration Law, Chinese arbitration institutions are required to perform med-arb when both parties are willing and have consented to it. It is unclear whether using the UNCITRAL Rules would be consistent with Chinese statutory requirements. Although the UNCITRAL Arbitration Rules are silent as to med-arb, it might be useful to consider the position

---

[61] Shenzhen Court of International Arbitration Rules (n 56), art 3(4).
[62] China International Economic and Trade Arbitration Commission Arbitration Rules (n 23), art 4(3).
[63] UNCITRAL Arbitration Rules 2013, art 12(1).
[64] ibid, art 13(4).
[65] SCIA Guidelines for the Administration of Arbitration under the UNCITRAL Arbitration Rules (2019), art 7(3).

of the UNCITRAL Conciliation Rules on med-arb, which require the parties to mediation under the Conciliation Rules to 'undertake not to initiate, during the conciliation proceedings, any arbitral or judicial proceedings in respect of a dispute that is the subject of the conciliation proceedings, except that a party may initiate arbitral or judicial proceedings where, in his opinion, such proceedings are necessary for preserving his rights'.[66] Instead of including more detailed safeguards into their arbitration rules, SCIA and CIETAC seem to be moving away from med-arb, despite multi-tier resolution already being deeply embedded in Chinese arbitration culture.

Both SCIA and CIETAC have recently created mediation centres or set up schemes to allow for mediation by mediators other than the arbitral tribunal. SCIA has promoted what it calls the 'Diversified Harmonious Dispute Resolution' (DHDR). The term echoes an SPC opinion[67] issued in 2016 on the need to modernise and promote alternative dispute resolution systems as part of China's Fourth Five-Year Court Reform. In 2008, SCIA created its mediation centre to encourage mediation before and outside existing arbitration proceedings.[68] SCIA has since also advertised a combination of Hong Kong mediation and Shenzhen arbitration, as well as alternative arrangements under the Guangdong–Hong Kong–Macau Mediation Alliance.[69] CIETAC established its own mediation centre in May 2018.

3.3.2 Institutional Encouragement of Med-arb

The Chinese government has always encouraged med-arb. Requiring arbitration institutions to provide a mediation procedure in the Arbitration Law shows that the support for some form of arbitration-mediation hybrid procedure dates back to 1994.

For domestic arbitration, the SPC has made arbitral awards more difficult to be set aside by lower courts since 2018. The 'pre-reporting system',

---

[66] UNCITRAL Conciliation Rules 1980, art 16.
[67] Supreme People's Court, '*Zuigao renmin fayuan guanyu renmin fayuan jinyibu shenhua duoyuanhua jiufen jiejue jizhi gaige de yijian*' (最高人民法院关于人民法院进一步深化多元化纠纷解决机制改革的意见) [Supreme People's Court Opinion on the People's Courts Further Deepening the Reform of the Diversified Dispute Resolution Mechanism] [2016] Fa Fa 14.
[68] '*Huanan guozhong tiaojie zhongxin jieshao*' [Introduction to the SCIA Mediation Centre] (10 July 2014) <www.cnarb.com/Item/1245.aspx> accessed 17 August 2020.
[69] Xiaochun Liu, 'The Latest Innovation for Mediation in China – From the Perspective of SCIA' (*pkulaw.com*) <http://pkulaw.cn/fulltext_form.aspx?Gid=1510155206&Db=eqikan> accessed 17 August 2020.

formerly applied only to 'foreign-related cases', is now applied to arbitration without foreign elements conducted within mainland China.⁷⁰ According to the new provisions, when a first instance court has provisionally decided to declare an arbitration agreement invalid, to refuse the enforcement of an award or to vacate an award, it must first report such decision to its superior High People's Court (HPC). Only when the HPC agrees with the lower court's finding can the lower court render a decision to frustrate the arbitration outcome. Special rules apply when the decision to declare the arbitration agreement invalid, to not enforce or to vacate the award is made on the ground of public policy. In these circumstances, the HPC must in turn report the case to the SPC. Only when both the SPC and the HPC agree with the lower court's finding can the lower court render its decision to set aside the arbitral award.⁷¹

This new policy prevents lower courts from being over-zealous or subject to local protectionism and corruption. It also allows the SPC and the HPC to harmonise standards for setting aside awards nationally. Regarding med-arb, however, the pre-reporting system will make it more difficult for courts to set aside awards due to procedural irregularities that might emerge in Chinese med-arb procedures.

3.3.3 Factors Affecting Med-arb's Popularity in China

The market-based approach to regulating med-arb and the Chinese government's policy towards med-arb have painted the multi-tier resolution system in a positive light. But what of other factors?

3.3.3.1 Confucian Culture

Attributing the success of med-arb and mediation to the Confucian tradition for harmony is a trope in Chinese arbitration scholarship. Social actors are discouraged from actively asserting their rights and interests should others default their obligations.⁷² Legal actors are individuals only in the context of social relations. In dispute resolution,

---

[70] Supreme People's Court, *'Zuigao renmin fayuan guanyu zhongcai sifa shencha anjian baohe wenti de youguan guiding'* (最高人民法院关于仲裁司法审查案件报核问题的有关规定) [Relevant Provisions of the Supreme People's Court on Issues Concerning Applications for Verification of Arbitration Cases under Judicial Review] [2017] Fa Shi 21, art 2(2).

[71] ibid, art 3(2).

[72] Albert HY Chen, 'Confucian Legal Culture and Its Modern Fate' in Raymond Wacks (ed), *The New Legal Order in Hong Kong* (Hong Kong University Press 1999) 515.

therefore, this translates into a preference for more amicable, less adversarial processes. Thus, under Confucian legal thought, mediation is encouraged over litigation and arbitration to prevent societal contention and collapse of these social relations.

Before assessing the validity of this argument with regard to med-arb's popularity, cultural analysis of legal practices and norms warrants a caveat. This mode of analysis might fall victim to reductionism. It might be more accurate and useful to attribute the differences in practice between jurisdictions beyond references to cultural and traditional stereotypes. These stereotypes become less valid when parties appoint personnel from multiple legal cultures (such as appointing a foreign counsel or foreign arbitrators) and when arbitration institutions attempt to internationalise by adopting more widely accepted dispute resolution norms.[73] China may allow med-arb with the same personnel, but that does not mean that Eastern jurisdictions in general have less respect for due process. Japan, for instance, has taken greater steps than China to avoid due process issues while preserving med-arb as a popular means of dispute resolution. Contemporary reforms to Chinese arbitration and the design of arbitration and judicial institutions, as discussed earlier, are inspired by foreign countries, from both the East and the West.

This caveat does not mean that all cultural analyses are futile. Despite the fact that the behaviour of Chinese parties and the practices of Chinese arbitration institutions involved in cross-border arbitration can be seen as products of multiple legal traditions, the practices of arbitration and med-arb promoted by the Chinese government are distinctively Chinese. Cultural analyses are perhaps more accurately legal-political analyses that are influenced by traditional culture. After all, the way in which culture manifests itself in legal norms is shaped largely by the legal and political institutions that support arbitration.

3.3.3.2 Institutional Design

In China, the 'design from the top' (*dingceng sheji* 顶层设计) – to use a policy buzzword favoured by the Chinese government in promoting judicial reform – may be inspired by foreign trends, but legal reformers are very clear that such trends are specifically selected to reflect the needs of China and the Belt and Road Initiative (BRI). Indeed, one of the five

---

[73] Tai-Heng Cheng, 'Reflections on Culture in Med-arb' in Arthur W Rovine (ed), *Contemporary Issues in International Arbitration and Mediation: The Fordham Papers (2009)* (Brill 2010) 425.

basic principles expressed in the SPC's Diversified Dispute Resolution Opinion is that the 'diversified dispute resolution system with Chinese characteristics' must be perfected by 'basing it on the circumstances of the nation, reasonable adoption [of foreign experiences]'.[74]

The China International Commercial Court (CICC), for example, is inspired by other commercial courts around the world, such as Singapore's International Commercial Court.[75] Singapore's arrangement to set its commercial court within the highest court in Singapore is likely to have inspired the CICC's position within the SPC. But it is very unlikely that China will wholesale adopt international arbitral norms even when it would reconcile the differences in legal systems between Belt and Road jurisdictions. There are lines that China cannot cross. This is apparent from SPC Justice Gao Xiaoli's interview on the CICC. She noted that other commercial courts have foreign judges and have judgments in English despite it not being an official language of the country.[76] These are areas where China would find it hard to change, even when the Chinese legislature may remove such barriers by amending China's Judges' Law,[77] Arbitration Law and Civil Procedure Law.

Contemporary cross-border arbitration norms are primarily shaped by the need to attract foreign parties and investors to use Chinese arbitration services. Where there is no such demand, as in domestic arbitration, developments and reform lag behind. Some measures first implemented in 'foreign-related' arbitration were eventually applied to domestic arbitration, but reforms to domestic arbitration were conducted to make arbitration regulations more consistent within China[78] and to reflect the SPC's pro-arbitration judicial position.

The design of arbitration law, norms and institutions has affected how arbitrators approach arbitration and med-arb. In Fan's survey, mentioned

---

[74] Supreme People's Court (n 68).
[75] 'Dazao guoji shangshi fating sifa baozhang "yidaiyilu" jianshe' [Creating the International Commercial Court, Legal Protection for the Belt and Road Construction] (*China International Commercial Court*, 19 March 2018) <http://cicc.court.gov.cn/html/1/218/149/156/571.html> accessed 17 August 2020.
[76] ibid.
[77] Faguan Fa (法官法) [Judges' Law] (promulgated by the National People's Congress Standing Committee, 23 April 2019, effective 1 October 2019) <www.lawinfochina.com/display.aspx?id=30222&lib=law> accessed 2 April 2021.
[78] Relevant Provisions of the Supreme People's Court on Issues Concerning Applications for Verification of Arbitration Cases under Judicial Review (n 70). The preamble of the Provisions cites 'unifying adjudication benchmarks, protect the lawful interests of the parties in accordance with law and to ensure the development of arbitration' as its objects.

in Sections 3.1 and 3.3, the arbitrator respondents who believe med-arb to be appropriate (88.1 per cent of all respondents) have mostly given ease of enforcement of settlement compared to award, advantages in costs and efficiency, respect for party free will and voluntariness as the primary reasons for conducting med-arb.[79] These reasons are mostly technical and related to the efficiency of dispute resolution rather than to cultural factors. Only a few of such respondents (six out of thirty-two) stated that traditional Chinese culture has influenced them to conduct med-arb,[80] among whom one respondent also said that 'mediation reflects the local culture in China and therefore is more easily accepted by the Chinese'.[81] Though not representative, this respondent's response reflects how culture can manifest itself through the advantage of dispute resolution efficiency without being an influence to med-arb practices in China per se.

3.3.4 Overcoming Implementation Difficulties

Since the promulgation of the Arbitration Law in 1994, there has been no substantive amendment or regulations issued regarding the due process issues of med-arb. Med-arb has lingered in the rules of arbitration institutions without changes. But, on the whole, Chinese courts and the government remain supportive of multi-tier dispute resolution.

In late June 2018, the State Council issued the 'Opinion on Constructing "Belt and Road Initiative" Dispute Resolution Mechanism and Institutions' (the 'Mechanism and Institutions Opinion').[82] The Mechanism and Institutions Opinion stresses the need to build dispute resolution mechanisms and institutions that account for the inconsistencies of law and legal culture among the BRI jurisdictions. The solution suggested is a 'diversified' dispute resolution system to satisfy the range of disputes that the BRI will produce. 'Diversification' here is taken to mean the use of mediation, arbitration and litigation to resolve disputes, but these procedures may not necessarily be conducted by the same institution as in Chinese med-arb practice.

---

[79] Fan (n 13) 805.
[80] ibid.
[81] ibid.
[82] '*Guanyu jianli "yidaiyilu" zhengduan jiejue jizhi he jigou de yijian*' [Opinion on Constructing 'Belt and Road Initiative' Dispute Resolution Mechanism and Institutions] [2018] Zhong Ban Fa 19 <www.gov.cn/zhengce/2018-06/27/content_5301657.htm> accessed 17 August 2020.

The SPC established the CICC days after the Opinion was published. The CICC is governed by the 'Provisions of the Supreme People's Court on Several Issues Regarding the Establishment of the International Commercial Court' (the 'CICC Provisions'). The CICC consists of two courts: the First CICC in Shenzhen (Guangdong Province) and the Second CICC in Xi'an (Shaanxi Province). Shenzhen was chosen for handling BRI maritime-based disputes, due to its traditional role as a test bed for new legal and economic policies, and Xi'an was chosen for handling BRI land-based disputes, due to its historical position as the starting point of the historical Silk Road. The two new courts are permanent bodies within the SPC[83] and their judges are selected from senior judges who are familiar with international laws and norms and can use both English and Chinese in working proficiency.[84]

The CICC has jurisdiction over:

(1) international commercial cases with the subject matter worth more than RMB 300 million, where the parties have agreed in writing to choose the international commercial court for adjudication in accordance with Article 34 of the Civil Procedure Law (2017);
(2) first instance international commercial cases under the jurisdiction of the HPC that the HPC deems it should be adjudicated by the SPC, and the SPC has permitted so;
(3) first instance international commercial cases with national significance;
(4) applications for arbitration preservation measures under Article 14 of the CICC Provisions and applications to enforce or revoke an award from an international commercial arbitration; and
(5) any other international commercial cases the SPC deems the CICC should have jurisdiction over.[85]

'International commercial cases' are cases where:

(1) at least one party has a non-Chinese nationality, has no nationality, is a foreign enterprise or organisation;
(2) at least one party habitually reside outside of the People's Republic of China;

---

[83] Supreme People's Court, '*Zuigao renmin fayuan guanyu sheli guoji shangshi fating ruogan wenti de guiding*' (最高人民法院关于设立国际商事法庭若干问题的规定) [Provisions of the Supreme People's Court on Several Issues Regarding the Establishment of the International Commercial Court] [2018] Fa Shi 11, art 1.
[84] ibid, art 4.
[85] ibid, art 2.

(3) the subject matter is outside of the People's Republic of China; or
(4) the legal fact of creation, amendment or extinguishment of the commercial relationship occurred outside the People's Republic of China.[86]

For med-arb, the most important provisions are featured in Article 11 of the CICC Provisions:

> **Article 11** The Supreme People's Court shall establish an International Commercial Expert Committee (the 'ICE Committee'). This Committee shall include international commercial courts, and international mediation and arbitration institutions that meet the criteria to build with the International Commercial Court a dispute resolution platform that organically connects mediation, arbitration and litigation, so as to create a 'one-stop' international commercial dispute resolution mechanism.
>
> The International Commercial Court supports parties to resolve international commercial disputes by choosing what they believe to be an appropriate method within the dispute resolution platform that organically connects mediation, arbitration and litigation.

Article 11 allows international commercial disputes to be mediated and arbitrated in a single platform. The single platform does not imply that mediation and arbitration are to be conducted by the same personnel or institution, as in med-arb. Rather, Article 11 seems to suggest that mediations are to be conducted by mediation institutions and that arbitration is to be conducted by separate arbitration institutions. The platform merely provides a nexus between the dispute resolution methods. Details on how this 'one-stop' platform operates remain to be fine-tuned, and the SPC is expected to produce further regulations on this matter. However, the creation of this platform signals a move away from conducting arbitration and mediation under one roof and by the same neutral, a practice that has concerned foreign parties due to the potential for procedural irregularities.

3.4 How to Promote Med-arb under Belt and Road

Before asking how China can promote med-arb within the BRI context, we should ask what the most valuable and the least desirable features of cross-border arbitration are to users of arbitration. Then we should ask what China can do to make med-arb resolve those shortcomings and amplify advantages as perceived by potential parties.

---

[86] ibid, art 3.

In a recent survey conducted by Queen Mary University of London with respect to mainly European private practitioners, in-house counsels and arbitrators, the least valuable characteristic of cross-border arbitration was the cost involved.[87] Only 3 per cent of 922 respondents regarded it as one of the 'three most valuable characteristics of international arbitration' and 67 per cent regarded it as one of the 'three worst characteristics of international arbitration'.[88] 'Confidentiality and privacy' (36 per cent) and 'neutrality' (25 per cent) stood in the middle, while 'enforceability of awards' (64 per cent) and 'avoiding specific legal systems/national courts' (60 per cent) were considered the most valuable characteristics.[89]

The survey also asked respondents what factors they considered when choosing a seat. The 'general reputation and recognition of the seat' was considered the most important factor, followed by 'neutrality and impartiality of the local legal system', 'national arbitration law' and 'track record of enforcing agreements to arbitrate and arbitral awards'.[90] Despite being considered the worst part of cross-border arbitration, cost was regarded by only about 5 per cent of the respondents to be one of the top four factors in choosing a seat.[91]

Compared to the leading regional institutional rivalries on arbitration, namely, the Hong Kong International Arbitration Center (HKIAC) and SIAC, Chinese institutions such as CIETAC, BAC and SCIA are not as attractive as HKIAC and SIAC to foreign parties. As seen from the survey results, Chinese arbitration institutions should improve the neutrality and impartiality of med-arb as well as the enforceability of med-arb awards. Although the outcome of the *Keeneye* case could be an isolated one, its fact pattern has not been tested in courts other than those in Hong Kong. Other BRI jurisdictions may not give as much weight to deference to Chinese supervisory courts as courts in Hong Kong have done.

One suggestion is perhaps this: to improve the popularity and credibility of med-arb, Chinese courts should adopt stricter standards in

---

[87] Queen Mary University of London and White & Case LLP, *2018 International Arbitration Survey: The Evolution of International Arbitration* <www.arbitration.qmul.ac.uk/media/arbitration/docs/2018-International-Arbitration-Survey-The-Evolution-of-International-Arbitration-(2).PDF> accessed 2 February 2020, 7.
[88] ibid 7–8.
[89] ibid 7.
[90] ibid 11.
[91] ibid.

exercising their supervisory powers over med-arb awards that manifest due process issues. While it is advantageous for the development of commercial arbitration for Chinese courts to be supportive of the deficient med-arb practice and to make it difficult for med-arb awards to be set aside through the pre-reporting system, it does not promote confidence in foreign parties that Chinese courts are competent in reviewing the partiality of arbitrators when they also serve as a mediator, especially when 'neutrality and impartiality of the local legal system' is the second-most-considered factor in selecting the arbitration seat, according to the Queen Mary survey.

3.5 Conclusion

It is still too early to make conclusions as to whether med-arb in China will be impeded by due process issues under the BRI. But based on how Chinese arbitration institutions have operated thus far, the majority of its clients are not deterred by the potential issue of due process. To Chinese clients, the familiarity and the efficiency that Chinese med-arb brings allow them to 'go abroad' without bearing the costs of conducting commerce under unfamiliar laws.

For investment arbitrations, Chinese and foreign investors are still reluctant to use formal investor–state arbitration to assert their interests. Informal channels of dispute resolution through diplomacy and negotiation might yield better results for investors. It was suggested earlier that China could reconcile local practices with international standards in two ways under the BRI. Being an economic bloc proposed by China, the BRI has the potential to promote dispute resolution with Chinese characteristics. If China exports its med-arb norms of outcome-orientation and emphasises mediation, it might not need to modify its local med-arb practices much at all. In the end, promoting med-arb comes down to how crucial it is to address the due process defects of Chinese med-arb in the eyes of Chinese legislators and regulators, arbitration institutions and potential parties, both Chinese and foreign. If the development of med-arb in China over the past decade is any indication, it does not seem that due process issues are so pressing such that party familiarity and dispute resolution efficiency are to be subverted for higher standards of impartiality.

As hinted in Section 3.4, the Chinese courts and Chinese arbitration institutions should shift their mentality towards a more pro-arbitration stance and focus not only on the number of arbitral awards that are enforced overseas and in China but also on the quality of the processes through which arbitral awards are rendered. The establishment of the CICC could be an indication of such a shift in thinking, given that the judges sitting in the CICC have more international experience and greater awareness of due process issues. However, it remains to be seen whether the CICC and other related BRI-based legal initiatives are extending the practice of med-arb or signalling its demise.

Last but not least, in August 2019, China signed the United Nations Convention on International Settlement Agreements Resulting from Mediation (also known as the Singapore Mediation Convention) to show its commitment to promoting international commercial mediation within China, and to advocating the adoption of the same in transnational disputes arising out of the ambitious BRI development led by China. Despite the foregoing, China has never promulgated specific domestic laws to govern commercial mediations. The primary mediation-related legislations in China – the People's Mediation Law (promulgated in 2010)[92] and the Labour Dispute Mediation and Arbitration Law (promulgated in 2008)[93] – both appear to be geared towards resolving domestic civil disputes and facilitating social stability maintenance.

---

[92] Renmin tiaojie Fa (人民调解法) [People's Mediation Law] (promulgated by the National People's Congress Standing Committee, 28 August 2010, effective 1 January 2011) <www.lawinfochina.com/display.aspx?id=8266&lib=law> accessed 2 April 2021.

[93] Laodong zhengyi tiaojie zhongcai Fa (劳动争议调解仲裁法) [Labour Dispute Mediation and Arbitration Law] (promulgated by the National People's Congress Standing Committee, 29 December 2007, effective 1 May 2008) <www.lawinfochina.com/display.aspx?id=6584&lib=law> accessed 2 April 2021.

4

The Resolution of International Commercial and Financial Disputes

Hybrid Dispute Resolution in Hong Kong

JULIEN CHAISSE AND CARRIE SHU SHANG[*]

4.1 Introduction

Over the last decades, alternative dispute resolution (ADR) programmes have undergone rapid development. Unfortunately, many of these developments raise their own concerns. For example, arbitration has been criticised for favouring repeat appointments of the same persons as arbitrators, while mediation has faced constraints in cross-border enforcement. To overcome these shortcomings, parties have been increasingly attempting hybrid dispute resolution processes. Multi-tier dispute resolution clauses require parties to engage in one or more steps prior to commencing arbitration. A single step may involve mediation or negotiation between representatives of both parties. Sometimes parties may be required to take other steps prior to commencing arbitration. Dispute resolution clauses requiring parties to go through a sequence of different ADR modes to settle their dispute qualify as multi-tier dispute resolution clauses.[1]

Parties may favour this framework for several reasons. First, clients appreciate having the customised framework for the resolution of their disputes which a multi-tier dispute resolution clause ensures. Second,

---

[*] The research for this chapter has been funded by the General Research Fund Project No 11606820 ('Anatomy of Hong Kong's International Trade Law: Logic and Consequences of Unilateralism, Bilateralism, and Multilateralism') of the Hong Kong SAR Research Grants Council. The views expressed herein are the authors' own.

[1] George M Vlavianos and Vasilis FL Pappas, 'Multi-tier Dispute Resolution Clauses as Jurisdictional Conditions Precedent to Arbitration' in J William Rowley, Doak Biship and Gordon Kaiser (eds), *The Guide to Energy Arbitrations* (2nd edn, Law Business Research 2017).

multi-dispute resolution clauses help plan for potential disputes at the outset of the parties' relationship. Third, such clauses offer the opportunity to resolve a conflict prior to resorting to costly and time-consuming arbitration. Fourth, such clauses show both parties' commitment to attempting a resolution of their disputes in a peaceful non-adversarial manner before engaging in arbitration. The clauses can promote amicable dispute resolution and help foster long-term relationships. Consequently, many multi-tier dispute resolution clauses are seen in construction and other long-term contracts in which the parties wish to maintain a harmonious relationship over the duration of a project or joint venture.[2] However, one reason why parties may be indifferent to including such clauses in their contracts is because they can always opt for mediation or negotiation irrespective of a pre-existing arbitration agreement. Nevertheless, it may still be wise to negotiate a multi-tier dispute resolution clause because it is hard for parties to agree on anything once a dispute has arisen and their reactions when their relationship breaks down cannot be predicted.[3]

This chapter provides a general framework for understanding multi-tier dispute resolution in Hong Kong. The fostering of multi-tier dispute resolution is important towards maintaining Hong Kong's status as an international dispute resolution centre, especially as there is increasing competition from strong regional dispute resolution centres such as Singapore and emerging dispute resolution hubs like Shanghai, Shenzhen and Dubai. This chapter demonstrates that Hong Kong policy-makers need to expend significant effort incentivising the use of multi-tier dispute resolution by providing parties with cheaper and more flexible options.

This chapter first provides a comprehensive and critical account of the use of med-arb to resolve financial disputes in Hong Kong. Second, it explores the use of med-arb to resolve financial disputes in Hong Kong – from the Lehman Brothers Scheme to the establishment of the Financial Dispute Resolution Centre (FDRC). Third, it covers recent development in Hong Kong, including the potential impacts of Online Dispute Resolution and the Singapore Convention.

---

[2] Pui-Lam Ng and Audrius Banaitis, 'Construction Mediation and Its Hybridization: The Case of the Hong Kong Construction Industry' (2017) 9 Organization, Technology and Management in Construction 1528.
[3] See Piergiuseppe Pusceddu, 'PRIME Finance Arbitration – A Lighthouse Safe Harbour in the Mare Magnum of Financial Dispute Resolution' (2014) 3(1) Indian Journal of Arbitration Law 45.

4.2 Using Med-arb to Resolve Financial Disputes in Hong Kong: Searching for a Uniform Dispute Management Tool

Hong Kong is a centre of financial products and service innovation. As one of the world's major financial hubs, Hong Kong has bank-friendly laws and courts while its financial institutions employ many service professionals. On the other side of the equation, financial consumers have little bargaining power and may lack remedies when resorting to the courts. Over time, ADR (including arbitration and mediation) has been encouraged because it is not only faster and less contentious than traditional means of dispute resolution but also better at preserving long-term relationships. Nonetheless, using ADR for financial dispute resolution is only at its nascent stage. By making mediation mandatory in a majority of consumer disputes, Hong Kong's financial regulators have given ADR new momentum, leading to projections of its increased application in the coming years.

With increased financial and commercial awareness, consumers are also shifting towards more effective dispute resolution mechanisms. The present section first illustrates the historical development of ADR in Hong Kong through Civil Justice Reform (CJR) in 2009, the issue of Practice Direction 31 in 2010 and the enactment of the Mediation Ordinance (Cap 620) in 2012. Since the ADR industry in Hong Kong is largely self-regulated, this section will secondly shed light on the practical significance of the accreditation of mediators as a means of professionalising and standardising ADR practices among practitioners. Third, it provides a commercial perspective on the hybrid dispute resolution framework typically employed in Hong Kong and highlights the associated risks of such framework to the impartiality of the neutral. These risks have raised concerns over the efficacy of the existing framework. The judgment of the Hong Kong Court of Appeal in the *Gao Haiyan* case discussed in Section 4.2.2 aptly demonstrates the distrust among the business community of the arb-med and med-arb process.

4.2.1 Mediation in Hong Kong

Hong Kong incorporated the approach to mediation in the UNCITRAL Model Law on International Commercial Conciliation 2002 (the Model Law). According to Article 1 of the Model Law, 'mediation is a process where parties request a third person or persons ... to assist them in their attempt to reach an amicable settlement of their dispute arising out of or relating to a contractual or legal relationship'.[4] Due to the pressing needs of the legal community beginning in 2006, the Hong Kong government re-examined ADR development.[5] CJR of High Court procedures in 2009 included the promotion of mediation 'with a view to ensuring and improving access to justice at a reasonable cost and speed'. On 22 June 2012 the Mediation Ordinance was enacted, thereby signalling the government's desire to encourage parties to adopt mediation as a favoured ADR avenue. Unlike other jurisdictions, Hong Kong's regulation of mediation practices has been less formal and is mostly confined to the industry itself. In contrast to the UK's Rules of the Supreme Court (RSC) which were entirely replaced by a new set of rules (the Civil Procedure Rules (CPR)) following the Woolf Reforms, Hong Kong's Rules of the High Court (RHC) were only partly revised as a result of CJR and were not impacted by the enactment of the Mediation Ordinance after CJR. Under the current scheme, courts in Hong Kong encourage parties to consider out-of-court settlement mechanisms to resolve their disputes before taking legal action: 'Court action should be your last resort.'[6]

Hong Kong courts, including the Court of First Instance and the District Court, are also keen on promoting the use of mediation even after parties commence court proceedings. The judiciary in fact keeps a record of court cases that have been resolved through mediated settlements agreements. The 2017 judiciary statistics show that settlement of court-directed mediation cases was around 60 per cent, with a majority of court cases being resolved within six months of commencement.[7] The judiciary has also promoted mediation by encouraging parties to mediate proceedings already initiated in court or even before proceedings started. Practice Direction 31 (PD 31) came into effect in 2010 and applies to all civil proceedings in the Court of First Instance and the District Court. Under PD 31 the parties and their legal representatives have a duty to assist the court in resolving a case. PD 31 expressly warns parties that the court may depart from the common law practice that a losing party pays the winning side's litigation costs and may

---

[4] Shahla F Ali and John Koon Wang Kwok, 'After Lehman: International Response to Financial Disputes – A Focus on Hong Kong' (2009) 152 Richmond Journal of Global Law & Business 102.
[5] Danny McFadden, *Mediation in Greater China: The New Frontier for Commercial Mediation* (CCH Hong Kong 2013) 220.
[6] ibid 222.
[7] For overall statistics of mediation directed by the Hong Kong Judiciary, see 'Mediation Figures and Statistics' (*Hong Kong Judiciary*) <http://mediation.judiciary/hk/en/figures_and_statistics.html> accessed 7 September 2020.

instead penalise the winning party if it unreasonably fails to engage in mediation.[8]

Among mediation service providers, the Hong Kong Mediation Accreditation Association Limited (HKMAAL) was established as an umbrella body for standardising accreditation of the mediation profession in Hong Kong. It is essentially a member-established professional regulatory body that standardises professional qualifications for mediators in Hong Kong through a uniform accreditation process.[9] Although accredited and unaccredited mediators can practise in Hong Kong, accredited mediators have a reputational upper hand in gaining parties' recognition, in part because HKMAAL certifies that they have undergone a specified mediation training regime and attained a defined level of competence as a mediator. HKMAAL, in conjunction with mediation service providers in Hong Kong, further engages in promotional activities to heighten public awareness of accredited mediators. Consequently, even experienced mediators without HKMAAL accreditation will have a comparatively more difficult time breaking into the Hong Kong market, and those who wish to expand their ADR practice will usually seek HKMAAL accreditation.

4.2.2 Perceptions of Hybrid Dispute Resolution in Resolving Financial Dispute in Hong Kong

Overall, common law jurisdictions are widely recognised as being friendly to hybrid arbitration clauses.[10] For example, in the USA, hybrid clauses are generally treated as valid, except in some situations where there is an imbalance of bargaining power such as in respect of employment agreements and standard form consumer contracts.[11] Previously in Hong Kong, the use of mixed dispute resolution processes was more common in the construction industry, where a four-step dispute resolution process of engineer's decision (including expert determination), mediation, adjudication and arbitration has long been

---

[8] McFadden (n 5) 225.
[9] ibid 231.
[10] Carrie Menkel-Meadow, 'Regulation of Dispute Resolution in the United States of America: From the Formal to the Informal to the "Semi-Formal"' in Felix Steffek and others (eds) *Regulating Dispute Resolution: ADR and Access to Justice at the Crossroads* (Hart 2013) 424.
[11] Thomas J Stipanowich and Veronique Fraser, 'The International Task Force on Mixed Mode Dispute Resolution: Exploring the Interplay between Mediation, Evaluation and Arbitration in Commercial Cases' (2017) 40(3) Fordham International Law Journal 839.

generally accepted.¹² An independent expert certifier is often used to provide early review opinions (before mediators or arbitrators become involved) for the quicker resolution of a claim. During this type of dispute resolution process, mediation is seen as a necessary precondition to the implementation of arbitration or other procedures. However, outside the construction industry, med-arb and arb-med have not enjoyed the same level of recognition. This is despite med-arb receiving accolades because of its flexibility, cost-effectiveness, better incentives for parties to settle and arguably better arbitrated results.¹³ In an attempt to promote med-arb, the new Arbitration Ordinance (Cap 609) (AO) enacted in June 2011 expressly recognised that arbitrators could act as mediators in the same dispute.¹⁴ Section 33 of the AO established a framework for the arbitral tribunal's assumption of the role of mediator to facilitate settlement in pending arbitration proceedings. The section allows an arbitrator to act as a mediator after arbitration proceedings have commenced provided that all parties give their written consent.¹⁵ The section forbids challenges made against the arbitrator solely on the ground that he or she previously served as a mediator for the dispute submitted to arbitration.¹⁶ If the mediation fails, the arbitrator-mediator must disclose to all parties any confidential information obtained during the mediation that he or she considers 'material to the arbitral proceedings'.¹⁷ This disclosure requirement has led to criticism from practitioners who argue that the provision may discourage candid discussion during mediation proceedings.¹⁸

After the enactment of the AO, the High Court in *Gao Haiyan v Keeneye Holdings Ltd*¹⁹ effectively endorsed the use of med-arb in a case involving enforcement of a Mainland China arbitral award in Hong Kong. The award in the case had been rendered in a med-arb that had taken place pursuant to the rules of the Xi'an Arbitration Commission. In the course of the parties' arbitration, a mediation session

---

[12] Keyao Li and Sai On Cheung, 'The Potential of Bias in Multi-tier Construction Dispute Resolution Processes' in Paul W Chan and Christopher J Neilson (eds), *Proceedings of the 32nd Annual ARCOM Conference* (ARCOM 2016) 197.
[13] Ng and Banaitis (n 2).
[14] See Kun Fan, 'Mediation and Civil Justice Reform in Hong Kong' (2011) 27 International Litigation Quarterly 2; Kun Fan, 'The New Arbitration Ordinance in Hong Kong' (2012) 29 Journal of International Arbitration 719.
[15] ibid.
[16] ibid.
[17] ibid.
[18] ibid.
[19] [2011] 3 HKC 157.

took place over dinner at the Xi'an Shangri-la hotel in which a member of the arbitral tribunal and the Secretary General of the Xi'an Arbitration Commission, acting as mediators, met with a 'friend' of the respondent Keeneye. Neither of the actual parties to the arbitration were present at the mediation. The mediators proposed that Keeneye should settle its dispute with the claimant Gao by paying compensation of RMB 250 million to Gao. The mediators suggested that the friend should convey the mediators' suggestion to Keeneye and work on getting Keeneye to accept the settlement proposal. But Keeneye rejected the same. The arbitration continued without any complaint from Keeneye and the tribunal found in Gao's favour. Keeneye applied to the Xi'an Intermediate People's Court to set aside the arbitral award on the grounds that the Secretary General of the Xi'an Commission had manipulated the outcome of the arbitration. The Xi'an Court held that the mediation complied with the relevant arbitration rules. Keeneye's application to set aside the award at the seat of the arbitration thus failed. Gao then sought to enforce the arbitral award in Hong Kong. Keeneye opposed enforcement, arguing that it would be contrary to public policy to enforce the award as it was tainted by apparent bias. Although Reyes J confirmed that in principle there was nothing wrong with arb-med (provision for which had expressly been made in the AO), he concluded that the events at the Xi'an Shangri-la dinner gave rise to a reasonable apprehension of bias and that, as a matter of public policy, the award should not be enforced in Hong Kong. The Court of Appeal overturned the decision. By the leading judgment delivered by Tang VP, the Court of Appeal was of the view that the first instance judge should have deferred to the view of the Xi'an Intermediate People's Court, as the court of the arbitral seat, that there was nothing anomalous about the mediation which had taken place at the Shangri-la Hotel. As the supervisory court, the Xi'an court was in a better position than the Hong Kong court to assess whether or not the mediation had violated standards of due process in Mainland China.[20] The Court of Appeal's decision therefore suggests that, while many parties from Mainland China are familiar with arb-med and such process is popularly used in Mainland China, in Hong Kong there is a deep distrust of med-arb where the same person acts as mediator and arbitrator.

The core problem with arb-med lies in the risk of an appearance of bias on the part of a mediator when he or she resumes the role of arbitrator if a mediation fails. The Court of Appeal's enforcement of the award in the

---

[20] [2012] 1 HKLRD 627.

Gao Haiyan case might indicate that a Mainland Chinese-style mediation session occurring *ex parte* over dinner would not be contrary to Hong Kong public policy. Nonetheless, the case should be viewed with caution in light of the fact that Keeneye had not itself complained about the mediation during the resumed arbitration but had instead waited until setting aside proceedings before the Xi'an Court before it complained about apparent bias. Thus, Keeneye's continued participation in the arbitration proceedings could be regarded as a waiver of any entitlement subsequently to complain about the way in which the mediation was conducted.[21] Unsurprisingly then, even after *Gao Haiyan*, most legal practitioners and mediators in Hong Kong take a cautious approach to arb-med or med-arb in which a neutral acts as mediator and arbitrator in the same dispute, based on concerns as to the risks of breaching due process and losing impartiality. The worry is that the neutral's mind may be contaminated by confidential information obtained during the course of mediation. Nonetheless, pressure from competition among alternative Asian arbitral seats such as Singapore and the desire to provide dispute resolution services in support of Mainland China's Belt and Road Initiative (BRI) may in time make Hong Kong practitioners and parties more receptive to med-arb.[22]

4.3 State-Directed Financial Med-arb: From the Lehman Brothers Scheme to the Establishment of the Financial Dispute Resolution Centre (FDRC)

Dispute resolution literature suggests that ADR could work well in highly regulated industries such as the financial industry.[23] In particular, a

---

[21] 'Opposing the Enforcement of PRC Arbitral Award on Public Policy Ground? Not as Easy as You Think!' (*ONC Lawyers*) <www.onc.hk/en_US/opposing-the-enforcement-of-prc-arbitral-award-on-public-policy-ground-not-as-easy-as-you-think/> accessed 7 September 2020; cf the UNCITRAL Model Law on International Commercial Arbitration 2006, art 4:

> A party who knows that any provision of this Law from which the parties may derogate or any requirement under the arbitration agreement has not been complied with and yet proceeds with the arbitration without stating his objection to such non-compliance without undue delay or, if a time-limit is provided therefor, within such period of time, shall be deemed to have waived his right to object.

[22] ibid.

[23] 'Self-financed schemes are more likely to appear when a particular market is highly regulated, for example financial services': Pablo Cortes, *Online Dispute Resolution for Consumers in the European Union* (Routledge 2010), 70, 145. The UK has the Financial Ombudsman, the Office of the Telecommunication Ombudsman and the Energy Ombudsman: Rhoda James and Phillip Morris, 'The New Financial Ombudsman

structured mediation scheme could be useful in disputes between consumers and financial service providers for two reasons. First, an information asymmetry exists between consumers and financial institutions where the institutions understand their products more and have greater experience with dispute resolution processes. Second, the complex nature of financial services and products produced by various financial and insurance institutions requires the expertise of certain types of professionals as dispute resolvers. The present section traces the evolution of Hong Kong's FDRC by analysing the peculiar intersection of finance and dispute resolution, mainly due to the inefficacy of financial services regulators in setting up efficient consumer dispute resolution mechanisms against financial entities. The section then analyses the procedures and shortcomings of the regulatory framework governing hybrid resolution under the FDRC Scheme.

4.3.1 An Overview of the FDRC System Design

Hong Kong did not develop a uniform approach to resolving financial consumer disputes via mediation until recently. Hong Kong's dispute resolution system design closely follows the British model. However, although the UK has long enjoyed the successes of the Financial Ombudsman Service (FOS), an independent government body for resolving British consumers' disputes with their financial service providers, Hong Kong has never learnt from that experience.[24] Hong Kong's financial consumer dispute resolution design is largely based on the traditional consumer complaint route. This is despite the financial market's high numbers and high level of private participation at the retail level, all of which give rise to the 'quasi-gambling nature' and potential for conflict of the current design.[25] Usually, a Hong Kong customer in a dispute with

---

Service in the United Kingdom: Has the Second Generation Got It Right?' in Charles EF Rickett and Thomas GW Telfer (eds), *International Perspectives on Consumers' Access to Justice* (Cambridge University Press 2003) 169–71.

[24] See Shahla F Ali and Antonio Da Roza, 'Alternative Dispute Resolution Design in Financial Markets – Some More Equal Than Others: Hong Kong's Proposed Financial Dispute Resolution Center in the Context of the Experience in the United Kingdom, United States, Australia, and Singapore' (2012) 21(3) Pacific Rim Law & Policy Journal 486.

[25] Elizabeth Kantor and Philip Parrott, '"Gaps" Can End in Tears' (*Herbert Smith Freehills*) <http://hsfnotes.com/arbitration/wp-content/uploads/sites/4/2016/08/GapsCanEndInTears.pdf> accessed 7 September 2020.

a financial institution involving monetary loss has two options. The customer can file a complaint with the relevant financial institution or report the case to a regulator such as the Hong Kong Monetary Authority (HKMA) or the Securities and Futures Commission (SFC). But, while regulators can examine an institution's conduct and practices, they cannot adjudicate any financial remedy for the customer.[26] Hence, a customer may eventually have to take his or her monetary claim through the court system. The traditional system reveals its weakness when a large number of similar disputes must be handled simultaneously. One of the system's recent breakdowns was the 2008 financial crisis. After Lehman Brothers filed for chapter 11 bankruptcy in the USA, HKMA found that more than 48,000 Hong Kong investors had invested in structured products otherwise known as 'minibonds'[27] associated with Lehman Brothers'. These investments derived part of their value from the performance of an underlying asset. The total invested in minibonds amounted to HKD 20 billion. Lehman's bankruptcy caused these investments either to lose the majority of their value or to become entirely worthless. Aggrieved customers flooded the HKMA, seeking justice. To facilitate the settlement of disputes between investors and distributing banks, the HKMA engaged the Hong Kong International Arbitration Centre (HKIAC) to make mediation and arbitration services available under the Lehman Brothers-Related Products Dispute Mediation and Arbitration Scheme (the HKIAC Lehman Brothers Scheme).[28]

The HKIAC Lehman Brothers Scheme was open to investors who submitted complaints to the HKMA and whose complaints had been referred to the SFC. The SFC decided whether to take further action or whether a finding against a relevant individual or executive officer of a bank had been made.[29] The HKMA informed eligible investors in writing and paid the share of the fee for those services on behalf of (1) investors whose complaints

---

[26] See 'Complaints about Banks' (*Hong Kong Monetary Authority*, 28 August 2020) <www.hkma.gov.hk/eng/key-functions/banking-stability/complaints-about-banks.shtml> accessed 7 September 2020.

[27] The 'minibonds' were a form of credit linked note. See eg Bambos Tsiattalou, 'Understanding FCA's Ban on Speculative Mini-Bonds' *Financial Times* (London, 5 December 2019) <ftadviser.com/investments/2019/12/05/understanding-fca-s-ban-on-speculative-mini-bonds/> accessed 7 September 2020.

[28] See generally Gary Soo, Yun Zhao and Dennis Cai, 'Better Ways of Resolving Disputes in Hong Kong – Some Insights from the Lehman-Brothers-Related Investment Product Dispute Mediation and Arbitration Scheme' (2010) 9(1) Journal of International Business & Law 137.

[29] ibid.

had already been referred to the SFC and (2) investors whose complaints had resulted in a finding against an individual or executive officer by either the HKMA or the SFC.[30] For those ineligible for the HKMA-funded Scheme, HKIAC offered a similar service but it required investors and financial institutions to pay a fee and banks to consent to mediation.[31] According to statistics that the HKIAC provided to the HKMA, since the introduction of the HKIAC Lehman Brothers Scheme in November 2008, the HKIAC has received 351 referral cases, 291 of which have been completed. The completed cases consist of 91 successful mediations, 9 failed mediations, 147 withdrawn cases that had been settled between the banks and the investors before mediations began, and 44 cases for which the banks did not agree to mediation.[32]

Although the HKIAC Lehman Brothers Scheme was temporary, its successful operation led Hong Kong regulators to consider deficiencies in the then existing system. The Financial Secretary requested that the HKMA and the SFC prepare reports regarding issues arising from the crisis.[33] Both authorities realised that one issue raised by the crisis was the lack of a simple, efficient and effective means to resolve financial disputes.[34] Following their investigations and taking account of recommendations made by other departments, the authorities jointly proposed the establishment of the FDRC in February 2010. The FDRC's objective is to provide customers with an independent and affordable option for resolving monetary disputes with financial institutions amicably and in timely fashion, primarily through 'mediation first and arbitration next'.[35] The FDRC claims to be a 'one-stop shop' for resolving qualifying disputes between regulated financial entities and certain customers. FDRC membership is mandatory for all financial institutions authorised by the HKMA or licensed and registered by the SFC, obligating them to join mediation for qualified disputes.[36] Individuals and the increasing number of Hong Kong small businesses struggling with whether to bring claims against financial institutions and securities companies welcomed the

---

[30] ibid. See also Ali and Kwok (n 4).
[31] See Soo, Zhao and Cai (n 28).
[32] 'LCQ20: Mediation Service' (*info.gov.hk*) <www.info.gov.hk/gia/general/201102/23/P201102220246.htm> accessed 7 September 2020.
[33] Kantor and Parrott (n 25).
[34] ibid.
[35] 'Dispute Resolution Process' (*Financial Dispute Resolution Centre*) <www.fdrc.org.hk/en/html/resolvingdisputes/resolvingdisputes_fdrsprocess.php> accessed 7 September 2020.
[36] 'Financial Dispute Resolution Scheme (FDRS)' (*Financial Dispute Resolution Centre*) <www.fdrc.org.hk/en/html/aboutus/aboutus_fdrs.php> accessed 7 September 2020.

4 HYBRID DISPUTE RESOLUTION IN HONG KONG   103

change. The FDRC increased the options available to parties seeking relief in bank–investor disputes, providing a boost for ADR in Hong Kong and those wishing to avail themselves of its flexibility and options.[37]

4.3.2 The Current FDRC 'Mediation First, Arbitration Next' Process

The current FDRC process is mandatory for financial institutions that are members of the Financial Dispute Resolution Scheme (FDRS), a scheme that is co-administered by the HKMA and the SFC.[38] In Hong Kong more than 2,000 financial institutions are members of the FDRS, so it broadly covers all major financial service providers.[39] If a consumer wishes to file a complaint against a participating financial institution, involving a monetary claim arising out of a contract between the consumer and the institution or an act or omission of the institution in connection with any financial service provided to the consumer as an agent, such claim is considered a 'Standard Eligible Dispute' under the FDRS if the claimable amount is under HKD 1 million.[40] In initiating a request for dispute resolution, a consumer needs to lodge a complaint with the FDRC.[41] After a consumer files an application regarding a Standard Eligible Dispute, an FDRC case officer will verify if the application is within the scope of the FDRC Terms of Reference.[42] If the FDRC determines that the case is acceptable, both the claimant and the relevant financial institution will pay the required application fees for the mediation, which includes a one-time application fee (HKD 200) and a fixed-amount fee payable to an appointed mediator for a four-hour mediation session.[43] The mediator's fee depends on the claimable amount. After payment is received, a mediator will be appointed either by agreement of both parties or at the discretion of the

---

[37] 'Scope' (*Financial Dispute Resolution Centre*) <www.fdrc.org.hk/en/html/resolvingdisputes/resolvingdisputes_jurisdiction.php> accessed 7 September 2020.
[38] 'Financial Dispute Resolution Scheme (FDRS)' (n 36).
[39] ibid.
[40] See also Extended Eligible Disputes after the 2018 amendments: ibid.
[41] A dispute submitted as an 'Eligible Dispute' will have to go through the 'mediation first, arbitration next' process. Disputes submitted under the 'Extended' category can choose among 'mediation only', 'arbitration only' or 'mediation first, arbitration next'. See 'Terms of Reference' (*Financial Dispute Resolution Centre*) <www.fdrc.org.hk/en/html/aboutus/aboutus_tor.php> accessed 7 September 2020; FDRC Mediation and Arbitration Rules 2018, rr 2.1, 2.4, 3.2, 3.4.
[42] ibid.
[43] 'Fees' (*Financial Dispute Resolution Centre*) <www.fdrc.org.hk/en/html/resolvingdisputes/resolvingdisputes_scheduleoffees.pdf> accessed 7 September 2020.

FDRC.⁴⁴ If the mediation is successful, a mediated settlement agreement will be entered into by both parties.⁴⁵

Under the 'mediation first, arbitration next' process, if the mediation efforts prove futile and after the issue of a mediation certificate terminating the proceeding, the claimant can file a request for arbitration. Thereupon, the FDRC will appoint an arbitrator (who is usually different from the initially designated mediator) within sixty days of receiving the mediation certificate. The FDRC will usually conduct the arbitration on a 'documents-only' basis to save costs and time. Under exceptional scenarios, the arbitrator can call for an in-person hearing. An arbitration award will be entered into pursuant to relevant rules and the arbitration laws of Hong Kong. The award is final and binding on parties. Under Rule 3.12 of the FDRS Mediation and Arbitration Rules, parties can appeal against an FDRC arbitration award only on a point of law.⁴⁶ The maximum award that can be issued by an FDRC neutral is HKD 500,000. This is said to cover 'over 80% of the monetary disputes handled by the HKMA and about 80% of stock investors'.⁴⁷

At present, FDRC accepts only approximately thirty disputes annually, with slight variations among years.⁴⁸ Reasons behind such low acceptance rates are largely unrevealed. At its establishment, the Hong Kong Financial Services and the Treasury Bureau ambitiously estimated that the FDRC would process about 2,000 cases a year during the set-up stage, which is far more than the actual case intake numbers.⁴⁹ Putting FDRC case numbers in the context of the population of Hong Kong creates meaningful points of comparison. For example, in 2013, out of the thirty-one applications made to the FDRC, twenty-nine were accepted and one was rejected because it did not meet the Terms of Reference criteria for acceptance.⁵⁰ One application was under review.⁵¹ At the end of 2013, considering the population of

---

⁴⁴ ibid.
⁴⁵ ibid.
⁴⁶ FDRS Mediation and Arbitration Rules 2018, r 3.12.
⁴⁷ Financial Dispute Resolution Centre, 'Proposals to Enhance the Financial Dispute Resolution Scheme: Consultation Paper' <www.fdrc.org.hk/en/doc/Consultation_Document_ToR_EN.pdf> accessed 7 September 2020.
⁴⁸ 'FDRC Annual Report' (*Financial Dispute Resolution Centre*) <www.fdrc.org.hk/en/html/publications/annualreport.php> accessed 7 September 2020.
⁴⁹ 'Item for Financial Committee' (*Legislative Council*) <www.legco.gov.hk/yr10-11/english/fc/fc/papers/f11-23e.pdf> accessed 7 September 2020, para 16.
⁵⁰ Financial Dispute Resolution Centre, 'FDRC Annual Report 2013' <www.fdrc.org.hk/en/annualreport/2013/files/download/FDRC_annual_report.pdf> accessed 7 September 2020.
⁵¹ ibid.

Hong Kong was approximately 720 million, 0.043 out of every 10,000 Hong Kong people applied for mediation services from the FDRC during the whole year, a figure quite disproportionate to Hong Kong's vibrant financial scene.[52] This implies either that Hong Kong financial consumers were largely satisfied with the services they received or that they just do not intend to go through the FDRC process when faced with conflict with financial service providers.

Mediation is confidential in Hong Kong according to the MO[53] and no exception has been made to this principle under the FDRC Rules of Mediation.[54] Consequently, the FDRC does not publish its decisions except in selective scenarios, making any insight into the quality and style of services provided by the FDRC difficult. A general walk-through of an introduction to FDRC services suggests that complaints made to the FDRC are divided into 'applications' and 'public enquiries'. Pursuant to relevant definition in the FDRC rules, applications comprise complaints lodged by consumers at the FDRC to start a dispute resolution process, while public enquiries include anything from informational enquiries to informal complaints.[55] For example, in 2017, the FDRC received 775 public enquiries (with a majority of them involving complaints concerning financial products or services) while only 24 applications were filed.[56] In 2018, among 955 public enquiries, only 15 complaints were finally lodged and only 10 were accepted for the initiation of a formal FDRC mediation process.[57] A very small number of cases have proceeded to arbitration. The relevant case data are summarised in Table 4.1.

In Hong Kong, FDRC neutrals are private and professional mediators and arbitrators. Hybridisation of dispute resolution style appears to have been originally considered by the architects of the FDRC to increase flexibility in the dispute resolution process. This is evidenced by the use of the

---

[52] '2011 Population Census' (*Census and Statistics Department, the Government of the Hong Kong Special Administrative Region*, 25 February 2020) <www.censtatd.gov.hk /hkstat/sub/so170.jsp> accessed 7 September 2020.
[53] Mediation Ordinance (Cap 620) (Hong Kong), s 8.
[54] FDRC Mediation and Arbitration Rules 2018, rr 2.3, 2.5.
[55] Financial Dispute Resolution Centre, 'Consumer Fact Sheets 2018' <www.fdrc.org.hk/en/ html/publications/publications_factsheetleaflet.php> accessed 7 September 2020.
[56] Financial Dispute Resolution Centre, 'FDRC Annual Report 2017' <www.fdrc.org.hk /en/annualreport/2017/files/download/FDRC_annual_report.pdf> accessed 7 September 2020, 32.
[57] Financial Dispute Resolution Centre, 'FDRC Annual Report 2018' <www.fdrc.org.hk /en/annualreport/2018/files/download/FDRC_annual_report.pdf> accessed 7 September 2020, 28.

Table 4.1 *FDRC cases (2012–18)*

	2018	2017	2016	2015	2014	2013	2012
Public Enquiries	955	775	1111	1318	2004	2192	1054
Applications	15	24	39	21	35	31	16
Mediated and Settled	5	9	8	14	29	18	7
Proceed to Arbitration	3	1	3	3	1	1	1

*Compiled by authors.
Source: FDRC Annual Reports 2012–18.

'mediation first, arbitration next' slogan. Nonetheless, the med-arb version adopted by the FDRC is rigid and structured. Under the current FDRC Mediation and Arbitration Rules, an FDRC mediator will be appointed first. The mediator then commences and conducts the mediation process upon application of the consumer.[58] Only if for some reason the mediation is unsuccessful and later terminated will an arbitration proceeding be commenced at the financial consumer's request.[59] As financial ADR is usually fact-sensitive and may involve familiarity with complex and obscure provisions of banking and securities laws, a more flexible procedure for financial ADR should generally be encouraged. However, when the FDRC was established, the conduct of med-arb (as discussed in Section 4.3.2) or hybrid ADR procedures was not well known or much practised in Hong Kong.[60] Therefore, the FDRC Rules have artificially isolated mediation from arbitration proceedings. The current more formal and rigid 'mediation first, arbitration next' procedure, although creative, still makes it impossible for the same third-party neutral (1) to conduct the entire proceeding by switching hats if deemed necessary or (2) to engage in a wide range of ADR strategies as appropriate. This is in contrast to the operation of financial ombudsmen in many countries. In addition, under the FDRS, two separate neutrals need to be appointed if parties go through both mediation and arbitration. As flexibility is among the top reasons that ADR is used in resolving financial consumer disputes, the failure fully to exploit the full potential of med-arb sessions by the FDRC is disappointing.

---

[58] 'Terms of Reference' (n 41), r 19.1.1.
[59] ibid, r 19.11.
[60] Weixia Gu, 'The Delicate Art of Med-arb and Its Future Institutionalization in China' (2014) 31 UCLA Pacific Basin Law Journal 97.

4.4 Recent Developments: Potential Impact of Online Dispute Resolution and the Singapore Convention

This section will highlight the following: (1) the trend towards a digitised dispute resolution infrastructure, (2) the development of an online dispute resolution (ODR) scheme to enable ADR to take place despite safe-distancing restrictions imposed by the Hong Kong Government on account of COVID-19 and (3) the scope for harmonisation of hybrid dispute resolution in light of the coming into effect of the Singapore Convention on 12 September 2020.

4.4.1 Digitisation of Hong Kong's Dispute Resolution Infrastructure

Like many jurisdictions in the region, Hong Kong has spent enormous resources on digitising its dispute resolution infrastructure. In 2019 it was announced that a HKD 150 million platform – the Electronic Business Related Arbitration and Mediation (eBRAM) – would be launched to facilitate online arbitration and mediation.[61] The ambitious technology-enabled platform was envisaged to become an electronic intermediary for 'deal-making and dispute resolution including through negotiation, arbitration and mediation'.[62] The Hong Kong Government was positioning eBRAM to be the dispute resolution forum for China's BRI projects.[63] The platform has enabled online case filings through its e-portal, as well as a combination of e-negotiation, e-mediation and e-arbitration proceedings to be conducted entirely online.

4.4.2 COVID-19 Online Dispute Resolution Scheme

During the recent COVID-19 crisis, the Hong Kong Government announced an ODR scheme aimed at providing parties with a means of resolving their disputes without a need to meet face-to-face. In a press release, the Secretary of Justice Teresa Cheng SC explained that the ODR scheme was meant to cover COVID-19-related disputes in which the

---

[61] Alvin Lum, 'How Hong Kong Plans to Take Arbitration Online with New eBRAM Project' *South China Morning Post* (Hong Kong, 8 April 2019) <www.scmp.com/news/hong-kong/law-and-crime/article/3005025/how-hong-kong-plans-take-arbitration-online-new-ebram> accessed 7 September 2020.
[62] Nick Chan, 'eBRAM Centre: The Law Tech Deal-Making & Dispute Resolution Platform to Facilitate Cross-Border Trade' <www.lscm.hk/sites/summit2018/eng/wp-content/uploads/2018/10/Nick-Chan_eBRAM-Centre-3Oct2018_.pdf> accessed 7 September 2020, 2.
[63] ibid.

amount claimed is HKD 500,000 or less. This was to ensure that the programme benefited 'micro-, small and medium-sized-enterprises' (MSMEs) that may be adversely affected by the pandemic.[64] By targeting MSMEs, the scheme is in line with the Collaborative Framework on ODR of the Asia-Pacific Economic Cooperation (APEC).[65] Under the ODR scheme, at least one of the parties (either the claimant or the respondent) must be a Hong Kong resident or business if a dispute is to qualify for the programme. The preliminary design of the ODR scheme suggests that there will be a multi-tier dispute resolution mechanism following a gradually escalating process of 'negotiation-mediation-arbitration' steps.[66] The proposed COVID-19 ODR scheme has been integrated with eBRAM and will be operated through eBRAM. At the time of writing, no case statistics have been released regarding the success of the COVID-19 Online Dispute Resolution Scheme.[67]

4.4.3 *Singapore Convention on Mediation*

Another event that could impact on the dispute resolution ecosystem in Hong Kong will be the coming into effect of the Singapore Convention on Mediation, also known as the United Nations Convention on International Settlement Agreements Resulting from Mediation, on 12 September 2020. The People's Republic of China was among the initial forty-six signatories of the Singapore Convention. It is likely that the Chinese Central People's Government will ratify the Singapore Convention in due course and the Hong Kong Government will then take steps to implement the Singapore Convention as part of its domestic law, in light of the clear benefits that the instrument would bring to the enforcement of mediated settlement agreements across borders.[68] Accession by China to the Singapore Convention

---

[64] Teresa Cheng, 'Stand in Solidarity Against COVID-19' (*Department of Justice, the Government of the Hong Kong Special Administrative Region*, 11 April 2020) <www.doj.gov.hk/eng/public/blog/20200411_blog1.html> accessed 7 September 2020.

[65] 'APEC's Collaborative Framework for Online Dispute Resolution of Cross-Border Business-to-Business Disputes – Endorsed' (*Asia-Pacific Economic Cooperation*) <http://mddb.apec.org/Documents/2019/EC/EC2/19_ec2_022.pdf> accessed 7 September 2020.

[66] Teresa Cheng, 'COVID-19 Online Dispute Resolution (ODR) Scheme' (*Department of Justice, the Government of the Hong Kong Special Administrative Region*, 13 April 2020) <www.doj.gov.hk/eng/public/blog/20200413_blog1.html> accessed 7 September 2020.

[67] ibid; 'COVID-19 Online Dispute Resolution (ODR) Scheme' (eBRAM) <www.ebram.org/covid_19_odr.html> accessed 9 April 2021.

[68] Eunice Chua, 'Enforcement of Mediated Settlement Agreements in Asia – A Path towards Convergence' (2019) 15(1) Asian International Arbitration Journal 1.

would accordingly answer doubts as to whether Hong Kong mediated settlement agreements can be enforced elsewhere and thereby bolster Hong Kong's reputation as an international dispute resolution hub. The attraction of multi-tier dispute resolution, insofar as it combines mediation and arbitration, would likewise be boosted.

4.5 Conclusion

The legal community in Hong Kong used to take a more schematic approach towards ADR by viewing mediation and arbitration as separate and distinct processes. Although this view is not wrong, it needs to be updated to reflect increased demands from businesses to hybridise dispute resolution for efficiency and cost-effectiveness reasons. The competition from strong regional dispute resolution centres such as Singapore and emerging dispute resolution hubs like Shanghai, Shenzhen and Dubai will continue to challenge Hong Kong's status as one of the Asia-Pacific's leading dispute resolution venues. In neighbouring Singapore, for example, the Singapore International Arbitration Centre (SIAC), the Singapore International Commercial Court (SICC) and the Singapore International Mediation Centre (SIMC) have co-ordinated cross-institutional links and hybridised procedures. In Mainland China, in addition to arbitration centres constantly refining their rules, the recently established China International Commercial Court (CICC) has started to hybridise its dispute resolution processes. All these developments will exert pressure on Hong Kong's dispute resolution infrastructure to remain competitive. Overall, Hong Kong policy-makers probably will need to engage in significant efforts to incentivise the use of multi-tier dispute resolution to maintain Hong Kong's appeal as an international dispute resolution centre and provide parties with cheaper and more flexible options. However, significant challenges remain.

5
Multi-tier Dispute Resolution
Present Situation and Future Developments in Taiwan

KUAN-LING SHEN

5.1 Introduction

In contrast to countries in the West, traditional Taiwanese society did not seek to resolve disputes through litigation, and most Taiwanese people viewed lawsuits as perilous undertakings. Since the ancient times, ideas such as 'litigation finally is terrible' (Zhouyi), 'there must not be any litigation' (Confucius Analects), 'peace is best', or 'law should not enter the family' have been prevalent. On this account, instead of litigation, the society searched for other methods of dispute resolution. The Taiwanese society has long had a legal mentality of emphasising mediation over litigation. The mediation system used to be a major mechanism of conflict resolution in traditional agricultural society. However, since the lifting of martial law in 1987 and the progressive establishment of the 'legal state', which subjects the exercise of governmental power to the constraints of the law, coupled with judicial reform and the strengthened independence of the judiciary, the number of lawsuits in Taiwan has continued to increase year by year (see Table 5.1).[1] Thus, the Judicial Yuan has put much effort into promoting alternative dispute resolution (ADR) over the last few years, with strengthening court-annexed mediation and other out-of-court ADR being its landmark reforms.[2]

The average annual number of mediation cases in district courts was 106,994 from 2011 to 2017, with a steady rise of caseload every year (see Table 5.1). In comparison, the Chinese Arbitration Association (CAA)

---

[1] See eg the Annual Reports published by the Judicial Yuan at <www.judicial.gov.tw/tw/np-1260-1.html> accessed 23 September 2020.

[2] 'ADR *xunxi gonggao*' [ADR Bulletin] (*Judicial Yuan*) <www.judicial.gov.tw/tw/lp-1493-1.html> accessed 23 September 2020.

Table 5.1 *Number of cases resolved through mediation: Chinese Arbitration Association (CAA) versus district courts*

Year	CAA: Arbitration (cases)	CAA: Mediation (cases)	District Court: Mediation in the first instance (cases)
2011	109		82,190
2012	137		95,085
2013	144		101,472
2014	119		109,037
2015	103	3	111,562
2016	105	4	120,657
2017	142	2	128,953
Average	123	3	106,994

(Taipei) handled an average of 123 arbitrations annually from 2011 to 2017, and only 9 mediations in total from 2015 to 2017 (see Table 5.2).[3] The relatively low rate of usage of arbitration in Taiwan is due to several reasons. First, parties are more familiar with court-annexed mediation than arbitration as court-annexed mediation was introduced much earlier, in 1935, following amendments to the then Code of Civil Procedure. Arbitration has only been promoted since 1998 when the system was amended based on the UNCITRAL Model Law on International Commercial Arbitration 1985. Second, parties are generally inclined to trust the court-annexed mediators more than arbitrators. Third, court-annexed mediation requires no contractual consent in advance.

Court-annexed mediation assumes a vital role in Taiwan's ADR landscape.[4] Legislative attempts were made to boost the success rate of court-annexed mediations and address the practical difficulty to force a separate arbitration proceeding upon parties. The 1999 amendments to the Code of Civil Procedure incorporated the element of adjudication (an

---

[3] Statistics on arbitration cases during 2011–17 are provided by the CAA. The CAA website states that in the past 15 years, there was an average of 170 arbitration cases every year: 'About Us' (*Chinese Arbitration Association, Taipei*) <http://en.arbitration.org.tw/about.aspx> accessed 23 September 2020.

[4] Kuan-Ling Shen, 'Mediation in Taiwan: Present Situation and Future Development' in Carlos Esplugues and Louis Marquis (eds), *New Developments in Civil and Commercial Mediation* (Springer 2015).

Table 5.2 Number of different types of cases handled by the CAA

Year	Total	Construction	Securities	Maritime	Trade	Service	Private participation in infrastructure projects	Others (IP law, trust, labour or agency, family law, lease, broking)	Government entities as one of the parties	International
2000	182	141	10	3	20	3		5	129	27
2001	237	196	10	2	19	3		7	171	13
2002	211	173	5	2	22	2		7	140	16
2003	197	141	5	1	25	11		14	124	14
2004	189	143	2	3	19	12		10	121	9
2005	161	111	5	6	11	17		11	81	9
2006	132	94	3	0	16	11		8	71	10
2007	176	112	0	5	20	30		9	100	12
2008	209	155	4	2	16	16		16	140	10
2009	213	122	1	2	28	21		39	145	12
2010	185	129	2	2	20	8		24	102	12
2011	109	70	0	2	16	4		17	66	7
2012	137	74	10	4	14	12		23	61	8
2013	144	82	11	0	20	14		17	66	11
2014	119	73	1	1	21	11	6	6	74	11
2015	103	41	1	1	23	9	7	21	49	20
2016	105	52	2	4	16	11	10	10	35	9
2017	142	50	31	0	13	13	16	19	41	31

attribute derived from arbitration) into mediation,[5] thereby instituting a multi-tier model that blends together consensuality and adjudication, to the end of precluding ensuing litigations. This is a kind of med-arb model (or so-called quasi arbitration). If the parties cannot reach a settlement agreement during mediation proceedings, they may agree that the mediation proceedings will be converted into arbitration, in which the mediators assume the role of arbitrators and make a mediation proposal. Parties cannot object to and must abide by the proposal, similar to the nature of an arbitral award.

The subsequent analysis focuses on court-annexed mediation and compares it to hybrid processes of arbitration and other out-of-court mediations.

5.2 The Legalisation of Multi-tier Dispute Resolution in Taiwan

ADR refers broadly to dispute resolutions other than litigation.[6] Modes of ADR include negotiation, settlement, mediation and arbitration. It is not limited to out-of-court dispute resolutions. In-court non-contentious mechanisms of disposition, such as in-court settlement and court-annexed mediation, are also included.[7]

While diverse definitions of ADR exist, at the core of ADR is consensuality between parties. In stark contrast to court verdicts, which do not consider parties' consent, ADR hinges upon the consensus between parties, albeit with slight alterations in the matters that the parties may or shall consent to. For instance, in arbitration, parties enter the proceedings voluntarily, but the arbitral award comes from a neutral third party's

---

[5] Lian-Gong Chiou, *The Theory of Procedural Choice* (Sanmin 2000) 201.
[6] See Jacqueline M Nolan-Haley, *Alternative Dispute Resolution in a Nutshell* (4th edn, West Publishing 2013). Each nation has its own institution. For instance, in America, in-court ADR also encompasses 'mini-trial' and 'summary jury trial', which do not have a binding effect. In contrast, the term ADR is less broad in Japan as it is defined as 'procedures for resolution of a civil dispute between parties who seek, with the involvement of a fair third party, a resolution without using litigation': Act on Promotion of Use of Alternative Dispute Resolution (Act No 151 of 2004), art 1. See Yamamoto Kazuhiko and Yamada Aya, *Law of ADR & Arbitration* [in Japanese] (2nd edn, Yuhikaku 2015).
[7] In addition to the classification of in-court and out-of-court systems, ADR can also be categorised into three forms: (1) consensual procedures, (2) adjudicative procedures, and an in-between form, namely, (3) suggestive procedures. See Kuan-Ling Shen, 'Current Situation and Developments of Out-of-Court Dispute Resolution in Taiwan: Focus on Court-Annexed Mediation' in Jiunn-rong Yeh (ed), *East Asian Courts under Transformation: Changing Judicial Functions in Leading Cases* (National Taiwan University Press 2014) 118–19.

judgment. On the other hand, in mediation, the outcome or conclusion of a dispute is agreed upon by parties consensually. Mediators' advice does not bind the parties unless with their explicit or implicit consent.

ADR in Western countries flourished due to the failings of litigation. Lengthy proceedings and disproportionate expenses not only hinder the protection of parties' rights but also suffocate the judiciary with an enormous caseload. Ever since the promotion of ADR in the 1976 Pound Conference in America, mediation, of all forms of ADR, has gained the most attention.[8] Mediation has also developed into various forms. In addition to the facilitative mediation, there are also other forms such as evaluative mediation and transformative mediation.[9] In particular, evaluative mediation is most favoured in Taiwan.

Out-of-court dispute resolution has diversified lately. Apart from mediation and arbitration, there are hybrid models and multi-tier models which allow transition between different systems. In particular, transitions between consensual proceedings and adjudicative proceedings are made possible by proceedings such as mediation-arbitration (med-arb), arbitration-mediation (arb-med), negotiation-arbitration (neg-arb) and mediation-arbitration-mediation (med-arb-med).[10] Arb-med refers to the procedure where arbitration is converted into mediation. However, if the parties cannot reach a settlement agreement, the proceedings are converted back into arbitration. This is so-called arb-med-arb. Med-arb is a procedure in which parties that cannot reach an agreement in mediation can enter into arbitration, and in which the mediator assumes the role of arbitrator and makes the arbitral award. Neg-arb is where

---

[8] In the United States, the majority of empirical analyses of ADRs focus on mediation; see Frank EA Sander, 'Developing the MRI (Mediation Receptivity Index)' (2007) 22(3) Ohio State Journal on Dispute Resolution 599; Matthias Prause, 'A Methodology for the Determination of the MRI (Mediation Receptivity Index)' (2007) 22 Ohio State Journal on Dispute Resolution 610. In Germany, the enactment of the Mediation Act in 2012 also launched hermeneutic theorisation of mediation among scholars: Matthias Wendland, *Mediation Und Zivilprozess: Dogmatische Grundlagen einer Allegemeinen Konfliktbehandlungslehre* (Mohr Siebeck 2018).

[9] See Section 5.3 for detailed discussion. For analyses on different forms in American law, see Carrie Menkel-Meadow, *Mediation: Practice, Policy, and Ethics* (Aspen 2018) 113–17. For introduction to German law and Australian law, see Thomas Trenczek, 'Stand Und Zukunft Der Mediation – Konfliktvermittlung In Australien Und Deutschland' (2008) <https://waage-hannover.de/wp-content/uploads/2015/06/SchiedVZ_Trenczek_Stand_und_Zukunft_Mediation-Mskr2008.pdf> accessed 11 September 2020.

[10] Martin C Weisman, 'Med-arb: The Best of Both Worlds' (2013) 19 Dispute Resolution Magazine 40; Brian A Pappas, 'Med-arb and the Legalization of Alternative Dispute Resolution' (2015) 20 Harvard Negotiation Law Review 157.

parties first negotiate for a settlement, but follow this with arbitration if no settlement is reached.

ADR has also evolved from purely out-of-court proceedings to proceedings connected with court proceedings.[11] As such, court proceedings, which used to be rigid and uniform, have been refashioned to become a diversified and hybrid mechanism.[12] As a result, parties are endowed with a variety of options for resolving disputes. ADR should therefore be reinterpreted. The mechanisms conventionally categorised as ADR are not merely 'alternative' approaches but 'appropriate' approaches to resolve a conflict.[13] In Taiwan, the doctrine of procedural choice dictates that parties should have the freedom to agree to any ADR system. Such an agreement is considered a form of 'procedure contract'. Various dispute resolution procedures have also emerged in Taiwan. More analysis follows.

5.2.1   Court-Annexed Mediation

In Western countries, the following questions occasionally arise: Should judges be mediators? Is the role of judges changing, and should it be changing? The conventional role of the judiciary is to judge (not mediate), to apply the law (not interests), to evaluate (not facilitate), to order (not accommodate) and to decide (not settle).[14] However, these questions have never existed in Taiwan. Besides out-of-court mediation,[15] court-annexed mediation has existed in the Code of Civil Procedure since 1935. But there was no systematic theoretical framework underlying mediation. Contrary to mediation in traditional society, contemporary dispute resolution constitutes an element of procedural law.

---

[11] The Alternative Dispute Resolution Act of 1998 in the United States requires that all federal courts shall have at least one alternative dispute resolution programme in place.

[12] Carrie Menkel-Meadow, 'Regulation of Dispute Resolution in the United States of America: From the Formal to the Informal to the "Semi-Formal"' in Felix Steffek and others (eds), *Regulating Dispute Resolution: ADR and Access to Justice at the Crossroads* (Hart 2013) 424.

[13] Carrie Menkel-Meadow, 'Alternative and Appropriate Dispute Resolution in Context Formal, Informal, and Semiformal Legal Processes' in Peter T Coleman, Morton Deutsch and Eric C Marcus (eds), *The Handbook of Conflict Resolution: Theory and Practice* (Wiley 2014) 1–28.

[14] See David Spencer and Michael Brogan, *Mediation Law and Practice* (Cambridge University Press 2007) 391.

[15] For example, the Township and County-Administered City Mediation Act. For mediation in traditional society and during the Japanese rule, see Taisheng Wang, *See You in Court: Transformation of Taiwanese Conception of Justice during the Japanese Rule* (National Taiwan University Press 2017) 11–19.

Therefore, it must have its own legal basis, be procedurally justifiable and meet the threshold requirement of procedural guarantee.

Reforms to court-annexed mediation were conducted in 1999 based on the doctrine of rule of law and the requirement of procedural guarantee. Significant changes were made to court-annexed mediation, including expansion in the scope of *mandatory mediation* matters, improving the quality of mediators, establishing a med-arb (quasi-arbitration) system and referring actions pending in the court of first instance with the consent of both parties to mediation. Since 2007, such referral is extended to cases in the second instance as well.[16]

Subsequently, the law on family proceedings (Family Proceedings Act, officially known as the Family Act) was promulgated in 2012. This act is grounded on the theoretical backdrop of 'theory of adjudicative proceedings by type of dispute', 'theory of procedural choices' and 'theory of procedural transition'. As such, mediation for family cases is regulated by special procedural provisions. Likewise, 'court ruling by agreement'[17] and 'appropriate ruling'[18] are also in place. On this foundation, the

---

[16] See Section 5.2.1.1. For more detailed theorisation, see Chiou (n 5) 195.

[17] Family Proceedings Act, art 33:

> With regard to matters that are not subject to the parties' disposition, where the parties are very close to agreeing on their settlement or where the parties do not dispute the existence or inexistence of the transaction or occurrence that has given rise to the case, the parties may, by agreement, petition for a court ruling. Prior to making a ruling in accordance with the preceding paragraph, the court shall take into consideration the opinions of the mediators and the reports submitted by the family matter investigation officer. The court shall also investigate facts and necessary evidence on its own initiative, and it shall grant the parties or known interested parties an opportunity to speak on the results of the investigation. The Parties' motion for an oral argument proceeding shall be granted.

[18] ibid, art 36:

> Where a mediation on matters subject to the parties' disposition is not brought to a successful conclusion and there exists one of the following circumstances, the court shall make an appropriate ruling for the case, taking into consideration the opinions of the mediators, balancing the rights and interests of the parties, as well as considering the primary intentions of the parties and any other relevant circumstances: 1. where the parties, by agreement, motion for a court ruling; 2. where the parties, by agreement, motion for a joint ruling combining matters not subject to the parties' disposition but are related to, in connection with, or ancillary to the original claims; 3. where the parties are very close to agreeing on their settlement and differ only on matters related to, in connection with, or ancillary to the original claims, and where the court considers it necessary

Family Proceedings Act and the Labour Incident Act, implemented in January 2020, also reconstruct mediation proceedings for family cases and labour cases in an attempt to cater to the special needs and attributes of family cases and labour cases, with provisions requiring the parties to attempt mediation before the adjudication.[19]

The Commercial Disputes Act, which was finalised in late 2019, comes into effect in July 2021. This Act also requires mediation to be conducted by the Commercial Court before commercial cases are litigated, in a similar way to civil mediation, as discussed later in the chapter.[20]

5.2.1.1 Civil Mediation

Mediation for civil cases can be divided into two broad categories: compulsory mediation cases and voluntary mediation cases. Article 403 of the Code of Civil Procedure spells out eleven types of compulsory mediation cases. Before an action is initiated for these cases, it shall be subject to court-annexed mediation. For cases that do not mandate a pre-trial mediation, a party may apply for voluntary mediation before initiating the relevant action. Regardless of the category of the case, according to Articles 380 and 416 of the Code of Civil Procedure, a successful mediation has the same effect as a final and binding judgment. In-court mediation proceedings are generally conducted by a summary court judge. However, since Taiwan's judges are trained to deal with litigations and may not be unaccustomed to mediation proceedings, they may appoint one to three mediators to facilitate the mediation depending on the type of the dispute.

Apart from the settlement reached by the parties themselves, there are two newly introduced pathways leading to successful mediations. These pathways correspond to multi-tier dispute resolution.

5.2.1.1.1 Proposal of Mediation Terms by the Mediator with the Consent of Both Parties The first alternative is the med-arb system. According to Article 415-1 of the Code of Civil Procedure, with the consent of both parties, mediators may propose terms of settlement. The terms shall be forwarded to the judge for review and approval. The mediation shall be deemed successful if the terms are approved by the judge (Article 415-3 of the Code of Civil Procedure). In principle, the

---

to consolidate the handling of the matters concerned and has sought the consent from both parties.

[19] See Sections 5.2.1.2 and 5.2.1.3.
[20] Commercial Disputes Act, arts 20–32.

judge will respect and approve the mediation terms proposed by the mediators, and will only disapprove them in exceptional circumstances, for example, when the terms are contrary to public policy or cannot be enforced. The settlement has the same effect as a settlement in litigation (Article 416 of the Code of Civil Procedure). This is in essence mediation combined with informal arbitration. Some scholars refer to this as 'quasi-arbitration'[21] because the parties agree that the mediator act as an arbitrator to make decisions. As mediation is successful once the mediation terms are approved by the judge, if the parties agree to adopt this way to resolve their dispute, they cannot object to the terms proposed by the mediator.

5.2.1.1.2 Appropriate Resolution without the Objection of the Parties

The second alternative is via *court-proposed mediation resolution* without the objection of the parties. According to Articles 417 and 418 of the Code of Civil Procedure, '[i]f the parties are unable to, but are close to reaching an agreement (for example, in terms of money), the judge shall take all circumstances into consideration, consult with the mediators, balance the interests of the parties, and thereafter, subject to the main intent expressed by the parties, propose a resolution on its own initiative'. 'The proposed resolution shall be served upon the parties and the interested persons who have intervened. If no one raises an objection to it within ten days following the service, the mediation shall be deemed successful in accordance with that proposed resolution.'

It is noteworthy that such proposed resolution need not be in strict compliance with the substantive law. Instead, it can be tailor-made for the interests of the parties. As such, the nature of such proposed resolution is a non-contentious ruling. Moreover, upon any objection raised to the proposed resolutions, the litigation proceedings will be resumed (Article 418). In this sense, such a mechanism falls under the term of multi-tier dispute resolution as it synthesises mediation and the subsequent litigation.

5.2.1.2 Family Mediation

Family cases are governed by the special rules set out in the 2012 Family Proceedings Act. This Act lays particular emphasis on the expeditious and integrated handling of family disputes. This Act also heightens the significance and function of family mediation proceedings for the purpose of enabling the autonomously consensual resolution of disputes and restoring family harmony.

---

[21] Chiou (n 5) 88, 192–93.

Mediation proceedings for family matters shall be conducted by a family court judge, who may request voluntary assistance from other agencies or organisations. Judges may also appoint mediators to deal with disputes. For example, divorce mediations involving the custody of children are usually assigned to mediators who are social workers or have a therapist background. The family dispute mediation system can be seen as a multi-tier dispute resolution proceeding: first mediation, then a simplified adjudication or adjudicative procedure. Besides a settlement agreement, family mediation can be concluded through two means according to the nature of the case.

5.2.1.2.1 **Mediation to Ruling by Agreement** This method applies to matters that parties have no rights to reach an agreement upon, such as the determination of the validity of a marriage, the existence of an adoptive relation, or the acknowledgement of a child by the natural father. If parties are very close to agreeing on their settlement or where parties do not dispute the (non-)existence of the transaction or the (non-) occurrence that has given rise to the dispute, parties may, by agreement, petition for a court ruling without entering the litigation procedure (Article 33(1) of the Family Proceedings Act). The court will consider the parties' opinions but is not bound by them. The court will also investigate the facts and evidence and hear the parties' case. The court's ruling under this procedure has the same effect as a binding judgment (Article 35(1) of the Family Proceedings Act). However, this judgment is of a nature similar to a summary judgment, without necessarily being subject to public trial or oral debate, making it different from a judgment resulting from litigation.

5.2.1.2.2 **Appropriate Ruling with the Consent of Both Parties** A different set of procedures applies to matters that parties are capable of agreeing upon, such as matters concerning divorce, distribution of matrimonial property, and payments for living expenses or maintenance. If parties cannot reach an agreement, the case will proceed to litigation. However, if parties have agreed to move for a court ruling without litigation to get an expeditious and yet conclusive resolution, the court shall make an appropriate ruling after considering the opinion of the mediators (if any, although this is usually the case), the rights and interests of the parties, the primary intentions of the parties and any other relevant circumstances (Article 36 of the Family Proceedings Act).

To conclude, multi-tier dispute resolution methods that merge mediation and court decision are available for different types of family disputes. Such procedures transition from mediation to summary ruling and enable a speedy conclusion of conflicts that obviates the need for litigation. Notably, there is one difference between the two procedures described here. Since the former (that is, mediation to ruling by agreement) concerns one's identification and therefore involves public interest, the ruling shall be made in complete compliance with substantive laws rather than principles of equity. The same requirement is not applicable to the latter procedure of appropriate ruling with the consent of both parties.

5.2.1.3 Labour Mediation

Labour mediation in the new Labour Incident Act 2020 is distinguishable from mediation proceedings for regular civil cases. The Labour Incident Act has certain unique features distinct from similar mechanisms overseas. For instance, Japan's Act of Labour Trials merely prescribes pre-trial mediation and litigations, while Taiwan's Act goes further to lay down mechanisms for litigations and provisional remedies, and spell out the procedural and evidentiary linkages between mediation and litigation. As another example, Germany's Code on Labour Courts and Litigations provides only for judge-conducted negotiations, while Taiwan's labour mediation is conducted by a Labour Mediation Committee consisting of one judge and two professional mediators. In cases where the parties cannot reach an agreement, the mediation committee shall propose a resolution on its own initiative.

Unless otherwise provided by Article 16 of the Labour Incident Act, all labour cases shall be subject to labour mediation by the court before an action is initiated. For cases that do not mandate pre-trial mediation, a party may also apply for mediation before initiating an action (Article 16 of the Labour Incident Act). Furthermore, labour mediations are conducted by a Labour Mediation Committee. Such a committee comprises one judge from the labour court and two labour mediators who are equipped with expertise or experience in labour relations or employment affairs (Article 21 of the Labour Incident Act). This formation is designed to include both the legal perspective and specialised knowledge in the relevant fields. It is hoped that the installation of such procedures will pave the way for the autonomously consensual resolution of disputes between employers and employees.

Labour mediators are designated by the court based on their knowledge and experience. As these mediators are experts in labour relations or employment affairs (Article 20 of the Labour Incident Act), they contribute to the proceedings by providing observations, experience and knowledge of the practical issues in the relevant fields. Moreover, parties' opinions regarding whom to select shall also be respected. In cases where a party has objected to any of the appointed mediators, or where parties have agreed to appoint other appropriate persons, the judge may reappoint such agreed persons. This allows parties to put more faith in the mediation proceedings, thereby increasing the likelihood of reaching an agreement. In terms of deliberating mediation terms or proposing resolutions, mediators and the judge are on an equal footing, as the final outcome is decided by a majority vote (Article 27 of the Labour Incident Act).

The procedure of labour mediation is set out in Article 24 of the Labour Incident Act. A labour mediation shall be completed within three mediation sessions. The parties shall promptly present the facts and evidence before the end of the second session, unless due to reasons not imputable to the parties. The Labour Mediation Committee shall hear the parties' arguments, co-ordinate pertinent issues and evidence, elucidate possible outcomes at appropriate timings and facilitate settlement. The Committee may also, on motion or its own initiative, investigate facts and necessary evidence. The parties and known interested parties shall have an opportunity to speak on the results of the investigation.

Multi-tier dispute resolution as laid down in the Labour Incident Act is summarised as follows.

5.2.1.3.1 Proposal of Mediation Terms by the Labour Mediation Committee with the Consent of Both Parties

Similar to mediation for regular civil cases, if both parties intend to mediate but are unable to finalise the details of their agreement, then, with the consent of both parties, the Labour Mediation Committee may propose the terms of mediation. Since the judge is already a member of the mediation committee, there is no need for the judge to approve such terms. The mediation takes effect upon signature of the members of Labour Mediation Committee (that is, one judge and two mediators), which guarantees a speedy conclusion of the proceedings. This system, much like Article 415-1 of the Code of Civil Procedure, combines two phases: first mediation, then arbitration. The parties have procedural control over such a transition.

5.2.1.3.2 Appropriate Resolution without the Objection of the Parties

Article 28 of the Labour Incident Act addresses the situation where parties can neither reach an agreement nor agree to petition for proposed mediation terms. In order to allocate judicial resources sensibly and expedite the conclusion of labour disputes, Article 28(1) of the Labour Incident Act provides that 'the mediation committee shall take all circumstances into consideration, balance the interests of the parties, and thereafter, subject to the main intent expressed by the parties, propose a resolution on its own initiative'. The reasons for the resolution shall be summarily recorded. Since the resolution proposed according to this Article is not based on the consensus of parties, it naturally follows that the parties are endowed with an opportunity to raise objections to it. It is this opportunity that distinguishes the procedure of Article 28 from the aforementioned med-arb procedure (as prescribed in Article 27). Article 29 further provides that 'a party to the mediation or an interested person who has intervened may object to the proposed resolution provided in the preceding paragraph within a ten-day peremptory period following the service or notification thereof'. The mediation shall be deemed unsuccessful upon an objection raised to it within the statutory time limit. In cases where no objection is raised within the time limit, the mediation shall be deemed successful in accordance with that proposed resolution.

In the Labour Incident Act, mediation precedes litigation, but no clear line is drawn between these two processes. In the case of unsuccessful mediation, the proceedings transition to litigation promptly and the litigation procedure shall be resumed by the judge who has joined the Labour Mediation Committee (Article 29 of the Labour Incident Act). In this sense, mediation also operates as a process where the issues in dispute are sorted out. Since the judge is a member of the committee, by the time litigation is resumed, the relevant issues and evidence have already been sorted out during the mediation sessions. Therefore, the judge, with a full grasp of the case, can resolve the conflicts more promptly and more adequately. Furthermore, pursuant to Article 34 of the Act, in deciding a labour case, the court may take into account the factual or evidentiary investigation performed by the Labour Mediation Committee. Therefore, labour disputes are not resolved through two dissociated and disconnected proceedings. Quite the contrary: labour disputes are disposed of holistically, promptly and adequately through a synthesised process of 'first mediation, then litigation'. From this perspective, labour mediation also falls under the term 'multi-tier dispute resolution'.

To obviate prejudiced pre-judgment formed during mediation sessions, and to ensure that the parties can communicate genuinely, confidentiality of mediation proceedings is given statutory acknowledgement. However, exceptions are also permitted under circumstances where the protection of rights is a priority.

Specifically, the procedures of labour mediation shall be conducted privately (Article 25 of the Labour Incident Act). The judge, the court clerk and the mediators shall keep confidential all information learned by them in the course of handling mediation cases. If subpoenaed as a witness in future lawsuits, they may refuse to testify on such matters.

Likewise, no guidance provided by the mediators or the judge, and no representations or concessions made by the parties that are disadvantageous to themselves during the mediation proceedings may be admitted as the basis for making decisions in an action initiated as a result of an unsuccessful mediation (Article 30(1) of the Labour Incident Act). This provision also precludes admitting the relevant facts and evidence as a basis for judgment. The representations or concessions may not be admitted even on the grounds of being '[facts] known to the court' (as prescribed in Article 278 of Code of Civil Procedure). The transcripts of mediation may not serve as evidence either. Nevertheless, these provisions do not mean that no evidence introduced in mediation can be employed in the ensuing litigation. It is the communication during mediation that is entitled to privilege. Therefore, evidence introduced in mediation to substantiate one's claims or defences may still be introduced or presented during litigation.[22]

With respect to exceptions to the principle of confidentiality, since labour mediation also serves the function of organising the disputed issues, if parties have reached a binding agreement to narrow down the issues, their agreement shall be respected.[23] This way, their rights of procedural and evidentiary disposition are respected, reflecting the

---

[22] In balance of judicial fairness and confidentiality during mediation, a party who learns about a witness during mediation is not precluded by the privilege from subpoenaing that witness. See 'Uniform Mediation Act' (*National Conference of Commissioners on Uniform State Laws*) <www.uniformlaws.org/shared/docs/mediation/uma_final_03.pdf> accessed 20 August 2018.

[23] This stipulation is similar to art 7(1) of the Directive 2008/52/EC of the European Parliament and of the Council of 21 May 2008 on Certain Aspects of Mediation in Civil and Commercial Matters [2008] OJ L136/3 (European Union). See also G Gerhard Wagner, 'Sicherung der Vertraulichkeit von Mediationsverfahren durch Vertrag' [2001] Neue Juristische Wochenschrift 1399.

doctrine of 'procedural autonomy' in the statutory law. The Act authorises parties to establish a written agreement on the subject matters of the proceedings, the facts, evidence or other matters that are subject to the parties' own disposition (for instance, parties may agree not to introduce as evidence statements made by a third party during mediation sessions; they may agree to exclude a witness or to designate a specific person as the only witness; they may also establish any evidentiary contract that allocates the burden of proof or selects arbitral expert testimony). Parties shall be bound by the agreement so reached, unless they agree to amend the said agreement, or there are reasons not caused by the parties, or there are other circumstances that render such an agreement manifestly unfair (Article 30(2) of the Labour Incident Act).[24]

Besides, in deciding a labour case, the court may consider any factual or evidentiary investigation performed by or appropriate case-resolution proposals made by government-appointed mediators, a government-appointed mediation committee or a labour mediation committee of the court (Article 34 of the Labour Incident Act). The court may also take into account the injunctions or proposals made by such bodies.[25] However, if any self-disadvantageous representation or concession is involved, the court may choose not to admit such statements as the basis for making decisions unless parties have agreed otherwise. Therefore, only statements that are not self-disadvantageous and non-verbal objective behaviours can be considered as exceptions. To decide whether a specific piece of information is admissible, prudent interpretation on a case-by-case basis is needed.

Any communication or interaction for the purpose of mediation shall be in principle privileged. Likewise, to ensure that the parties may negotiate liberally, the mediation transcript shall be a succinct one rather than verbatim. Furthermore, if the court decides to weigh the aforementioned information in its deliberation, the parties shall be accorded an opportunity to present their arguments before the decision is made so as to prevent surprising judgments. Moreover, the facts,

---

[24] Similarly, art 7(1) of the Mediation Directive (n 23) provides for two exceptions.
[25] In the past, the Supreme Court in Taiwan held: 'As [party A] has applied to Taipei Municipal Government Procurement Complaint Reviewing Committee to mediate this contractual dispute, the mediation guidance provided by said committee may not be admitted as a basis for judgment': Supreme Court Civil Judgment Tai-shang-tzu 1183 (2012).

evidence, disposition or appropriate resolutions do not dictate the court's discretion. They are just factors that the court may consider.[26]

Labour mediation is multi-tiered. On the one hand, the Labour Incident Act strengthens the mediation committee's discretion. In cases where parties cannot reach an agreement, the committee shall propose appropriate resolutions on its own initiative. However, such resolutions take effect only when no objection is raised. In this sense, with consensuality being one of its significant features, this mechanism also falls under ADR. On the other hand, in light of the fact that this is still an in-court procedure, transition to subsequent litigation is facilitated. This promotes efficiency. In other words, the resolution of a labour dispute consists of, at most, four tiers: (1) a settlement agreement reached by the parties' consensus, (2) the committee's proposal of mediation terms with the agreement of the parties, (3) appropriate resolution proposed on the committee's own initiative and to which the parties do not object, and (4) the judgment made by the labour court. These four tiers are situated in different phases of conflict resolution. To put these four tiers on a spectrum, the parties have the most autonomy in tier (1), and the least in tier (4); the third independent body intervenes the most in tier (4), and the least in tier (1). It is noteworthy that the four tiers are not dissociated. Instead, they are interconnected and manifest the attribute of 'multi-tieredness' (see Figure 5.1). In conclusion, one can defensibly assert that mediation for labour disputes, when compared with regular civil mediations, has a stronger cohesion as well as a smoother transition with litigation procedure. After a year of operation, judicial statistics show that the proportion of successful labour mediations has increased significantly, up to 52.64 per cent.[27]

5.2.2 Mediation Out of Courts

Out-of-court administrative mediation takes many forms, some of which pertain to multi-tier dispute resolution. Some major examples are as follows.

5.2.2.1 The Government Procurement Act

Aware of the advantages of arbitration, namely, efficiency and professionalism, Taiwanese central administrative agencies have been vehemently

---

[26] Besides the aforementioned exceptions, should 'risks to public interests or order' also be included as an exception and therefore override the privilege of confidentiality? Further research is warranted.

[27] See the judicial statistics on labour incidents for 2020 at <www.judicial.gov.tw/tw/lp-1976-1.html> accessed 1 April 2021.

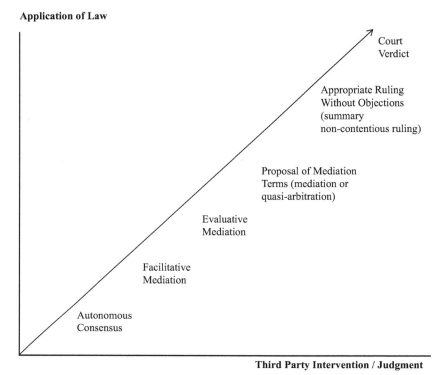

Figure 5.1 In-court resolution of labour disputes

advocating arbitration since 2006, in the hopes of offloading judiciary burden, enhancing administrative efficiency, boosting national competitiveness and according citizens procedural guarantee. Congressional attempts have also been made to expand the use of arbitration: mandatory arbitration is called for; many systems of 'first mediation, then arbitration' were stated and implemented.

Contractual disputes related to government procurement aptly exemplify this point.[28] When a government agency and a company are unable to reach an agreement over a contractual dispute, they may apply to the Complaint Review Board for Government Procurement (CRBGP) for mediation. The government agency concerned may not reject such an application submitted by a company. For disputes involving the

---

[28] Kuan-Ling Shen and In-Chin Chen, 'Arbitration, Procedural Choice, and Rights of Litigation: Issues about Mandatory Arbitration of Government Procurement Act Article 85-1 Paragraph 1' [2008] Taiwan Law Review 218–19.

performance of a public construction contract, it is stipulated in Article 85-1(1) of the Government Procurement Act that '[i]n the event that the entity and the supplier failed to reach an agreement over the dispute in relation to the performance of the contract in question, they may (1) apply to CRBGP for mediation, or (2) refer to an arbitration institution for arbitration'.

If parties apply for mediation, the provisions of mediation under the Code of Civil Procedures shall apply mutatis mutandis (Article 85-1(3) of Government Procurement Act). In other words, unless the parties have reached an agreement, mediators may exercise their discretion to propose a recommended solution in the name of the CRBGP. If the company does not agree with the proposal, it shall first be submitted to a higher authority for approval, along with the CRBGP and the company's reasoning (Article 85-3 of the Government Procurement Act). If parties are unable to reach an agreement but are close to reaching an agreement, the CRBGP may propose its own mediation proposal, taking into account all the circumstances, including the opinion of the mediation committee, and also seeking to balance the interests of the two sides while respecting the parties' wishes. Both parties, as well as other interested parties, shall have ten days from the day of proposal to raise objections. If objections are raised within the ten-day period, mediation is deemed to have failed. If, however, no objections are raised within the ten-day period, mediation is deemed to be successful (Article 85-4 of the Government Procurement Act). Professional mediation by the administrative authority is the most effective system for disputes related to public construction contracts, with the success rate reaching as high as 70 per cent.[29]

In the event that a mediation of construction works and technical services is unsuccessful because the entity does not agree with the CRBGP's proposed settlement terms, the entity may not object to the arbitration filed by the supplier. With regard to the multi-tier dispute resolution in the Government Procurement Act, it is stipulated in Article 85-1(2):

> In the event that the application for mediation is made by the supplier, the government agency may not object to such application. CRBGP shall offer

---

[29] For instance, in 2019, there were a total of 444 concluded mediation cases. Among those, 350 were resolved on substantive grounds (the other 94 were resolved on procedural grounds). Moreover, 274 cases were resolved by mediation where both parties agreed with the proposed suggestion by the CRBGP: *'Shenxuhui xiangguan tongji ziliao'* [Relevant Statistical Information of the Complaints Commission] (*Public Construction Commission, Executive Yuan*) <www.pcc.gov.tw/cp.aspx?n=F34923ABE419ADE0> accessed 20 September 2020.

suggestions or proposals for mediations of construction works and technical services. In the event that the mediation of construction works and technical services is unsuccessful due to the government agency not agreeing with the proposal or resolution for mediation proposed by CRBGP, the government agency may not object to the arbitration filed by the supplier.

In other words, the procedure follows the pattern of 'first mediation, then arbitration'. Nevertheless, this practice differs from the abovementioned pattern of 'first court-annexed mediation, then (quasi-)arbitration' in the sense that the former involves two independent proceedings, whereas in the latter, the mediators also act as arbitrators and propose mediation terms. As per the official notice of the Public Construction Commission, the mediation committee should try to make mediation proposals and resolve disputes. In order to prevent the mediation committee from 'expecting' subsequent arbitration procedures, as well as to prevent damage to the rights and interests of the authorities, it is specifically stated that the mediation committee should not be a follow-up arbitrator.[30]

Admittedly, such unilateral statutory arbitration is an apt response to government agencies' growing reluctance to go for arbitration.[31] However, there are doubts about this system in the literature. Some scholars are concerned about the fact that only suppliers have the procedural choice to opt for arbitration or mediation, while government agencies can only defer to suppliers' choices.[32] Moreover, arbitration awards are binding on parties and have the same force as a court judgment. It therefore invokes the concern that such non-consensual arbitration has restricted or infringed upon the parties' procedural rights. Besides, Article 53 of the Arbitration Act provides that '[a] dispute which according to other laws must be submitted to arbitration, may be governed mutatis mutandis by this Law unless otherwise specified by those other laws'. However, is it appropriate

---

[30] See the Official Notice No 09700479460 of Public Construction Commission on 12 December 2008.

[31] On 4 December 2002, the Transport Department even published an opinion on 'deleting of arbitration clauses in construction contracts and returning to the procurement law', causing a stir in the construction industry. See Yueduan Chen, '*Gongcheng caigou lvyue zhengyi yu xin zhongcai jizhi zhi tantao*' [A Discussion on Construction Procurement Contract Performance Disputes within the New Arbitration Framework] (2018) 13(2) *Gaoda faxue luncong* 7–8.

[32] Ai'e Chen and Congzhou Wu, '*Yi qiangzhi zhongcai tujing jiejue gonggong gongcheng caigou qiyue lvyue zhengyi zhi yanjiu*' [Research on Resolving Public Construction Procurement Contract Performance Disputes through Mandatory Arbitration] (2010) <www.ndc.gov.tw/News_Content.aspx?n=E4F9C91CF6EA4EC4&sms=4506D295372B4 0FB&s=D96F97CBFFF7BF8F> accessed 23 September 2020.

to apply procedural provisions governing voluntary arbitration to statutorily mandated arbitration? Further studies are warranted.[33]

5.2.2.2 The Financial Consumer Protection Act

Taiwan has witnessed a flood of financial consumer disputes in the wake of the 2008 financial crisis. In this context, the Financial Consumer Protection Act was promulgated to protect financial consumers' rights and to dispose of financial consumption disputes fairly, reasonably and effectively.

According to Article 13(2) of the Financial Consumer Protection Act, financial consumers shall approach a dispute by first filing a complaint with the respective financial services enterprise. If the financial consumer does not accept the disposition proposed by the enterprise, or the enterprise fails to handle the matter within the statutory time limit, the financial consumer may apply to the ombudsman to institute an ombudsman case. The ombudsman body shall first seek to institute mediation proceedings (Article 23(2) of the Financial Consumer Protection Act). If both parties reach an agreement or accept the terms proposed by the ombudsman board, the mediation is successful. Approximately 50 per cent of disputes are disposed of at this stage.[34]

In the case of unsuccessful mediation, after the ombudsman body entertains an application, the chairperson of the ombudsman committee shall appoint at least three ombudsman committee members as pre-examiners to carry out an inspection and prepare an inspection opinion (Article 25(1) of the Financial Consumer Protection Act). Once the parties accept the ombudsman's decision, the ombudsman case is resolved (Article 29(1) of the Financial Consumer Protection Act). In this case, the ombudsman body shall send the ombudsman statement and the associated case files for approval by the district court. Once approved, the ombudsman statement shall have the same force as a final and irrevocable civil judgment, and parties to the dispute shall not initiate legal proceedings again in connection with the ombudsman case (Article 30 of the Financial Consumer Protection Act). It is worth mentioning that financial consumer disputes often involve massive numbers of consumers, and it often requires professional knowledge about the financial industry. These attributes (that is, being highly

---

[33] Shen and Chen (n 28) 219–20.
[34] In 2019, the Financial Ombudsman Institution had a dispute resolution rate of 62 per cent for all financial consumer dispute-related complaints and ombudsman cases handled. It has also maintained a dispute resolution rate averaging or exceeding 50 per cent since 2012. See Financial Ombudsman Institution, '2019 Annual Report' (2020) <www.foi.org.tw/Article.aspx?Lang=2&Arti=1358&Role=1> accessed 20 September 2020, 25.

professional and involving a large class of people) necessitate not only the establishment of a specialised institution to handle such disputes but also the installation of a 'first mediation, then (quasi-)arbitration' system.

5.2.3 Arbitration and Mediation at the Chinese Arbitration Association (CAA)

5.2.3.1 Mediation to Arbitration

The 1961 Commercial Arbitration Law marked the genesis of arbitration in Taiwan. Following two slight revisions in 1982 and 1986, this act went through a major amendment in 1998 inspired by foreign legislation. Retitled the Arbitration Law, this law was anticipated to internationalise, liberalise and align Taiwan's arbitration with international movements. There are four arbitral institutions in Taiwan, among which the Chinese Arbitration Association (CAA) is perhaps the largest. With its dispute mediation centre, the CAA handles not only arbitration cases but also mediation cases. Parties may petition to the mediation centre to initiate mediation procedures. There are also several multi-tier dispute resolution mechanisms in place, which are explicated below. The CAA handled an average of 170 cases annually between 2000 and 2013, but, among them, only 12 cases per year on average were international cases.[35] Construction cases account for the majority of the cases. Moreover, the number of the cases in which an administrative agency is one of the parties has begun to decline since 2010. In contrast, international commercial cases gradually increased from 2013 to 2017 (see Table 5.2).

Facilitative mediation is in principle adopted. According to Article 25 of the CAA Mediation Rules, if parties cannot reach a settlement but request the mediator to give settlement recommendations, the mediator may give written recommendations with explanations to parties. If parties do not request the mediator to give settlement recommendations, the mediator may still give recommendations unless parties object to it. In court-annexed mediation for civil cases or labour cases, mediators can decide the approaches and the procedure may take the form of evaluative mediation. In contrast, in mediation conducted by arbitral institutions, parties have higher autonomy with regard to mediating approaches; parties may also refuse to adopt evaluative mediation.

---

[35] See CAA case statistics in 'Home' (*Chinese Arbitration Association, Taipei*) <http://en.arbitration.org.tw> accessed 11 September 2020.

According to Article 26 of the CAA Mediation Rules, 'in matters involving proprietary rights, the mediator may set specific settlement terms or prices that are selected from a number of acceptable terms or range of prices agreed on in writing by the disputing parties'. Similar to civil mediation and labour mediation, under such circumstances, the mediator performs 'quasi-arbitration', that is, makes judgments and specifies mediation terms. According to Article 27(1) of the CAA Mediation Rules, '[i]f a mediation settlement cannot be reached by mediation, the dispute may be submitted for arbitration, if the disputing parties consent to do so in writing'. Article 27(4) of the CAA Mediation Rules provides: 'Unless the disputing parties have approved in writing, the mediator shall not assume the role of an arbitrator.' In such a case, mediation and arbitration are two separate and independent proceedings. Unless the disputing parties have approved in writing, the mediator shall not assume the role of an arbitrator. If approved, the mediator acts as the arbitrator as the proceedings transition from mediation to arbitration (med-arb). What makes this mechanism unique is the respect accorded to the parties' self-determination, in that the parties have the final say in whether or not the mediator can also be the arbitrator.

Furthermore, for arbitration cases to which simplified procedures shall apply (pursuant to Article 36 of the Arbitration Act), Rule 2 of the CAA Rules on Pre-Arbitration Mediation for Simplified Procedure specifies that arbitration may be preceded by mediation. But such pre-arbitration mediation is not mandatory. It shall be implemented with both parties' agreement. Where mediation is not reached, the procedure shall proceed to arbitration as specified by Rule 8(1) of the same CAA Rules. In such a case, it is only with both parties' consent that the mediator can assume the role of an arbitrator in the subsequent arbitration phase.

5.2.3.2 Arbitration to Mediation

Before an arbitral award is made, an arbitrator may mediate a dispute if the disputing parties and the arbitrator believe that the dispute is suitable for reconciliation.[36] This transition from arbitration to mediation resembles civil procedure law's relevant regulations on 'court's referral to mediation upon the parties' agreement'.

---

[36] Art 28(4) of CAA Mediation Rules: 'An arbitrator may, before the arbitration award is made, apply these Rules to settle a dispute if the disputing parties and the arbitrator believe that the dispute is suitable for reconciliation.'

There are special regulations for arbitrating financial disputes. According to Articles 34 and 35 of the CAA Rules on Arbitration for Financial Disputes, the CAA may consider the nature of the dispute and advise the parties to mediate. During the process of arbitration, the CAA may, upon petition from both parties, refer the case to the mediation centre of the CAA.

As per Article 35(1) of the CAAI Arbitration Rules 2017,[37] if the parties settle their dispute with or without mediation before the tribunal makes the final award, the tribunal may record the settlement in the form of a consent award upon parties' request. This award shall have the same status and effect as any other award (Article 34 of the CAAI Arbitration Rules 2017). This stipulation combines arbitration with settlement or mediation. If parties have reached a settlement, then the arbitration award shall be made in accordance with the said settlement so as to respect the parties' autonomy. Seen in this light, such an arbitration award as made pursuant to the parties' settlement is not adjudicative.

5.2.3.3 Adjudication/Arbitration to Mediation for Construction Disputes

For construction disputes, where parties agree to submit their dispute to adjudication, the Dispute Adjudication Board and the CAA may convert the dispute adjudication process into a mediation process with both parties' consent that the members of the Board are mediators appointed by the parties. The dispute adjudication process terminates upon conversion into the mediation process (Article 16 of the CAA Rules of the Construction Dispute Adjudication Board, or the 'CAA Construction DAB Rules'). Where the mediators are all qualified arbitrators, the mediation agreement shall have the same force and effect as that of an arbitral settlement agreement, and therefore the same force and effect as that of an arbitration award. Where not all of the mediators are qualified arbitrators, upon the parties' request, the CAA may provide the premise for a notary to notarise such a mediation record pursuant to Article 13(1) of the Notary Act. In the absence of an agreement with regard to the effect of an adjudication, the parties may object to the adjudication within a twenty-eight-day period after being served the adjudication award. Also, according to Article 17(3) of the

---

[37] The CAAI Arbitration Rules 2017 have been adopted by the Chinese Arbitration Association, International (CAAI) to take effect from 1 July 2017. The Rules apply to arbitrations seated outside Taiwan Area, while the CAA Arbitration Rules 2001 continue to apply to arbitrations seated in Taiwan Area.

CAA Construction DAB Rules, with both parties' consent, the fact-finding results and grounds, documents and evidence employed in the adjudication award may be used in the ensuing mediation, arbitration or litigation as evidence.

Furthermore, after the parties petition for a review, the committee and the CAA may, upon petition from one party and consent from the other party, designate the committee's members as mediators and fill out consenting forms of designation. The reviewing procedure would then transit into mediation, and the reviewing procedure would be suspended (Article 15-1 of the CAA Rules of the Construction Dispute Review Board, or the 'CAA Construction DRB Rules'). According to Article 16 of the CAA Construction DRB Rules, where both parties disagree with the reviewing results, they may take further actions to resolve the dispute as agreed in their contract or as specified by law. In this case, both parties may require that the reviewing results be employed in the ensuing mediation, arbitration or litigation.

5.3   Global Perspectives

5.3.1   *Mediation Plus Litigation*

Mediation takes various forms, ranging from facilitative mediation, evaluative mediation to transformative mediation. **Facilitative mediation** was mainstream in the United States in the 1960s and 1970s. In this 'classic form' of mediation, mediators offer assistance by means of asking questions, clarifying viewpoints, pursuing interests, and discovering and contemplating options for resolution. Mediators may also narrow down options and encourage autonomously consensual decisions, without giving suggestions, personal opinions, perspectives or predictions about possible court judgments. Parties and mediators may discuss together or separately. Mediators are mainly responsible for ensuring sufficient communication, upon which the parties' consensus is built. In this form of mediation, it is the parties' (as opposed to the lawyers') dispositions and actions that lead to the final outcome. As such, mediators are not necessarily legal experts. However, in more recent forms of mediation, that is, evaluative mediation, mediators assume a more active role. They may analyse weak spots and risks for parties, and even predict possible court judgments, thereby fostering mutual consensus. Mediators may also propose official or non-official suggestions. Moreover, mediators not only consider parties' needs and interests but also evaluate each party's case based on legal concepts of fairness, taking into account the legal rights of the parties. In this sense, mediators are usually legal experts who perform shuttle diplomacy: that is, they convene with parties separately and help each party (and/or their lawyer) evaluate their case and possible expenses. **Evaluative mediation** is usually seen in pre-trial negotiation conducted by judges.[38] Moreover, there also exists transformative mediation, which lays emphasis on helping parties to fully realise the opposing party's needs. Thus, conflicts are no longer in passive and destructive impasse but in a positive and active flow of resolution. The parties' relationships are also repaired.[39]

In the United States, even though, traditionally, trials and mediations are separate,[40] Article 16 of the US Federal Rules of Civil Procedure (FRCP) does not prohibit the trial judge from participating in pre-trial or settlement conferences.[41] Recent court practice gradually acknowledges that trial judges may conduct mediation on pre-trial conferences.[42] Such a practice has incurred both criticism and support. Those against this practice believe that it compromises the neutrality of trial proceedings as there is a conflict of roles. Those in favour of such a practice believe that since judges are inherently authoritative and independent, they make excellent mediators. With judges' legal analyses, which are generally highly credible, parties can understand their cases better and may be more inclined to resolve their disputes; Lawyers also expect judges to provide legal analyses as neutral third parties; moreover, with judges participating in mediation (pre-trial conferences), parties are more willing to accept mediation suggestions as they might feel that they are 'having their day in court'. With regard to criticisms about possible risks or dangers that might arise when judges act as mediators (for example, forced mediation or pre-

---

[38] For more analysis on these two forms of mediation, see Leonard L Riskin, 'Understanding Mediators' Orientations, Strategies, and Techniques: A Grid for the Perplexed' (1996) 1 Harvard Negotiation Law Review 7.

[39] Robert A Baruch Bush and Joseph P Folger, *Promise of Mediation: The Transformative Approach to Conflict* (Jossey-Bass 2004) 41.

[40] Legal historian Taisheng Wang argues that to separate trial and mediation is a modern Western approach of resolving conflicts, which differs greatly from the practice of Taiwan during Qing dynasty under traditional Chinese law. See Wang (n 15) 11.

[41] There are views from both sides on this issue. For a more detailed report, see Ellen E Deason, 'Beyond "Managerial Judges": Appropriate Roles in Settlement' (2017) 78(1) Ohio State Law Journal 105–20.

[42] Wayne D Brazil, 'Judicial Mediation of Cases Assigned to the Judge for Trial' (2011) 17 Dispute Resolution Magazine 24.

judgment), these problems are not insoluble.[43] With an adequate code of conduct or ethical regulations, judges could be restrained from pressuring a party into reaching mediation or giving up their case.[44] With adequate restriction on admissibility of evidence, information gleaned during mediation sessions could also be barred from trial proceedings.[45]

Since every form of mediation has its own strengths and weaknesses, Taiwanese law does not specify or limit a certain form of mediation for court-annexed mediation. Depending on the case, the proceeding may take the form of facilitative mediation, evaluative mediation, transformative mediation or even a mixture of such forms. It is stipulated in the Code of Civil Procedure that the mediation shall be conducted peacefully and sincerely, and that appropriate mediation/guidance shall be provided to parties. An appropriate proposal could be recommended with a view to a fair and amicable resolution acceptable to the parties (Article 414 of the Code of Civil Procedure). It is also spelled out in the Labour Incident Act that a Labour Mediation Committee shall promptly hear parties' cases, sort out relevant issues and evidence, and inform parties of likely outcomes at an appropriate timing (Article 24(3) of Labour Incident Act). Therefore, there is no superior or universally applicable form of mediation. Elasticity should be given in choosing a certain form of mediation for an individual case. Factors such as the intensity of conflicts, the tension of interests and the necessity to apply the laws all influence such a choice.

Moreover, in cases where parties are unable to reach an agreement, the mediation committee in a labour mediation shall propose a resolution on its own initiative. Such a proposal assumes the nature of a non-contentious judgment. For cases where parties have a more aggressive argument or a higher sense of self-determination, facilitative mediation may suffice. However, in Taiwan, if parties do not hire lawyers or if parties are unequal in terms of resources or capacity (for example, in a labour case, an employer

---

[43] Dan Aaron Polster, 'The Trial Judge as Mediator: A Rejoinder to Judge Cratsley' (*Mediate. com*, March 2007) <www.mediate.com/articles/polsterD1.cfm/#4> accessed 20 August 2018.

[44] 'A judge may encourage and seek to facilitate settlement but should not act in a manner that coerces any party into surrendering the right to have the controversy resolved by the courts.' See 'Guide to Judiciary Policy' (*United States Courts*) <www.uscourts.gov/sites/default/files/vol02a-ch02_0.pdf> accessed 20 August 2018, ch 2.

[45] For example, in the United States, arts 4–6 of the Uniform Mediation Act privilege communication in mediation with confidentiality. Art 408 of the Federal Rules of Evidence stipulates: 'Evidence of the following is not admissible ... (1) furnishing, promising, or offering – or accepting, promising to accept, or offering to accept – a valuable consideration in compromising or attempting to compromise the claim; and (2) conduct or a statement made during compromise negotiations about the claim.'

is likely to have more resources and capacity than an employee), then there is a need to adopt evaluative mediation as well in order to protect the weaker party through the intervention of a neutral mediator's analysis. Also, in cases of impasse, parties may refer to the resolution proposed by the mediation committee and make a decision. It is noteworthy, though, that the parties have the final say on whether to accept the proposal or not, and that the parties bear the consequences once they choose to accept (or not accept) it. As such, there is no contravention to the fundamental philosophy of mediation.[46]

The relation between mediation and litigation has long been a matter of scholarly contention: the theory of distinction versus the theory of convergence, and continualism versus non-continualism, etc. Although comparative legal research[47] has been somewhat sceptical about the combination of mediation and arbitration, in Taiwan, court-annexed mediation has been statutorily acknowledged as being both 'consensual' and 'adjudicative', as discussed in Section 5.2.

This contention pertains to such issues as (1) whether the conductor (the mediator or the judge) remains the same after transition, (2) whether the information gleaned in mediation remains confidential, and (3) whether the information gleaned in mediation can be admitted as basis for judgment. Non-continualism asserts that mediation and litigation should be severed: the two procedures shall be conducted by different bodies; the information gleaned in mediation cannot be admitted as basis for judgment. As a result, the parties can engage in mediation with full genuineness. Conversely, continualism finds it preferable to let the same judge conduct mediation and litigation, for the reason that the judge would have a more comprehensive understanding of the case.[48] It can be observed from the developments in America and Germany that the relation between mediation and litigation has evolved significantly.[49] In the past, out-of-court mediation and litigation have been clearly separated. However, with the recent transformation of judges' role and functions, court-annexed mediation has emerged. Court-annexed mediation has also branched into

---

[46] For more explication on the principles of voluntariness, neutrality, self-responsibility, transparency and confidentiality in mediation, see Shen (n 4) 118.

[47] There are opposing views on this matter; see Deason (n 41).

[48] See Hsuan-Ju Chiu, 'New Constructions of Family Dispute Proceedings' [2002] Taiwan Law Journal 18–19; Kazimura Taiti and Tokuta Kazuyuki (eds), *Family Dispute Procedures* (2nd edn, Yuhikaku Publishing 2007) 46–47; Katiuti Shusuke, 'Relationship between Family Mediation and Family Litigation' [2010] Jurist 58.

[49] See Wendland (n 8).

two types: one where the same judge conducts both mediation and litigation, and the other where they are handled by different people.[50]

A country's culture, the citizens' legal awareness, the money and time needed for litigation, the citizens' confidence in judges, and other factors all influence the system that a jurisdiction would adopt. In jurisdictions (or particular cases) where the parties show more desire to protect their rights and strive for autonomous consensus, facilitative mediation may be sufficient to meet the parties' needs. But in Taiwan, when a party does not appoint a lawyer, or in labour cases where the employer is often better off with more bargaining power, then there is a need for the mediator to assess the situation under an evaluative mediation approach in order to protect the weaker party, as well as allowing the party to consider the 'appropriate resolution' proposed by the mediation committee if they find it difficult to propose their own solution. However, as the decision of whether to adopt these methods rests solely with the party, this does not pose a conflict with the basic principles of mediation.[51]

There is no definitive answer as to which doctrine (continualism or non-continualism) is better. What matters most is to extract the strengths from both doctrines and fashion a system that best suits each jurisdiction. On the one hand, Taiwan's law foregrounds the continuity between labour mediation and litigation in order to construct a multi-tier procedure with maximised efficiency. On the other hand, Taiwan's law specifies the confidentiality principle of mediation as well as its exceptions, lest unjustified leakage should compromise the function of mediation.

5.3.2 Mediation or Conciliation Plus Arbitration

When compared with court-annexed mediation, the combination of arbitration and mediation follows a different path of development. Since the formation of arbitration law in 1998 was primarily under the impact of the UNCITRAL Model Law on International Commercial Arbitration 1985, the design of Taiwanese arbitration tends to resemble relevant international arbitration regulations. On the one hand, facilitative mediation is in principle adopted. Unless requested by the parties, mediators do not offer mediation suggestions. Likewise, without consent from both parties, mediators do not propose resolutions. On the other

---

[50] See Brazil (n 42); Deason (n 41); Polster (n 40).
[51] On the basic principles of voluntariness, neutrality, self-determination, transparency and confidentiality in mediation, see Shen (n 7) 118.

hand, where the proceeding has entered into arbitration, a mediator cannot act as an arbitrator in the same proceeding unless otherwise agreed upon by the parties, which is very similar to Article 10(3) of the 2014 International Chamber of Commerce (ICC) Mediation Rules.

Different from court-annexed mediation, the selection of arbitration is founded upon parties' agreement (arbitration agreement or arbitration clause in contract). On that account, the transition from arbitration to mediation should hinge upon parties' procedural rights of choice, and vice versa. Likewise, whether the arbitrator and the mediator can be the same body is a decision that lies with the parties.

Regarding the enforceability of multi-tier dispute resolution clauses, that is, 'pre-arbitral procedural requirements', the Taiwanese Supreme Court practice has been inconsistent: there are two judicial opinions. The first opinion, while acknowledging the validity of such clauses, does not perceive pre-arbitration processes as a prerequisite to arbitration. For instance, Supreme Court Civil Judgment Tai-shang-tzu 992 (2004) held:

> Arbitration is a vital system deriving from the parties' autonomy in private law and from the parties' procedural choice to resolve private disputes. Thus, since the parties may reach an agreement to arbitrate their dispute, there are all the more reasons for them to reach an agreement to mandate a pre-arbitration process, thereby granting the other party sufficient time to weigh 'accepting compensation' against 'submitting to arbitration'. Not only is such an arbitral clause valid, it also serves to reduce procedural costs since it screens out conflicts that can be resolved through simpler processes such as out-of-trial settlement or third-party mediation. However, if a party finds it impossible to mediate, settle, or resort to other simpler procedures, or if parties agree to choose arbitration as the only resolution, then *they may submit to arbitration short of a pre-arbitration process. This does not violate the spirit of the arbitral agreement, nor does it contravene the nature of pre-arbitration processes.*
>
> (emphasis added)

Likewise, the Supreme Court held in Civil Ruling Tai-shang-tzu 1634 (2012):

> Lastly, a pre-arbitration process does not halt the effect of arbitral agreements, nor does it install extra procedural barriers to hinder arbitration. If a party (or both parties) finds it impossible to reach any consensus during pre-arbitration processes, they may submit to arbitration for an arbitral reward. *The opposing party may not apply set aside the arbitral reward on the grounds of lack of undertaking pre-arbitration processes.*
>
> (emphasis added)

5 MULTI-TIER DISPUTE RESOLUTION

The second opinion views pre-arbitration processes as a prerequisite to arbitration. Supreme Court Civil Judgment Tai-shang-tzu 671 (2003) is an example. Specifically, the court held:

> [I]f the parties agree in an arbitral agreement to undertake pre-arbitration processes before submitting to arbitration, the spirit of such an agreement is to accord the adversary party with sufficient time to weigh 'accepting compensation' against 'submitting to arbitration' and with the right to determine which disputes should be subject to arbitration. As such, a pre-arbitration agreement is a valid arbitral clause as it is founded on the parties' autonomy; it also serves to narrow down disputes and to screen out disputes unsuitable for arbitration. *If a party does not undertake the pre-arbitration process in compliance with the agreement, then the disputes could not be narrowed down. As such, the disputes are not the subject of the arbitral agreement as the parties did not intend to submit the dispute directly to arbitration. As a conclusion, they may not submit the dispute directly to arbitration.*
>
> (emphasis added)

If, under such circumstances, a party still litigates directly, then the other party may file a demurrer according to the Arbitration Act. This was affirmed in the Supreme Court Civil Ruling Tai-kang-tzu 1080 (2014). Specifically, the High Court (in the second instance) held:

> This court considered the following information: Article 22.1 of the parties' contract, which lays down 'regular connections and communications'; Article 22.2(1) and Article 22.3, which stipulate 'both parties may reach an agreement that any dispute pertaining to the prescription or performance of this contract shall be submitted to negotiation committee in compliance with this contract' and that '(1) if the dispute is not resolved after 30 days following the submission to negotiation, both parties agree to arbitrate; . . . (3) if arbitration is selected, the arbitration reward shall be final and binding, unless one party apply to court to set aside said reward. From the aforementioned information, this court infers that both parties agree that they shall first communicate, and then negotiate. Only when negotiation fails to resolve the dispute would they resort to arbitration. It is evident that both parties shall be bound by their arbitration agreement out of adherence to contracts. The interlocutory appellant in the present case litigated directly, the opposing party filed a demurrer on the grounds of Article 4(1) of Arbitration Act. New Taipei District Court rightfully ruled to suspend the litigation and ordered the interlocutory appellant to submit to arbitration within a certain time frame. There is no error in the application of the law.

As a result, the interlocutory appeal was denied by a ruling as the Supreme Court affirmed the High Court's judgment.

5.4 Conclusion

In summary, regarding multi-tier dispute resolution, Taiwan has had many legal provisions concerning court-annexed mediation in civil disputes, family disputes and labour disputes. Based on the legal principle of procedural choices, parties are free to choose the way of dispute resolution and restrict the actionability of the claim. If the parties expressly stipulate in the contract that they should 'first mediate, then arbitrate' or arrange other multi-tier dispute resolution procedures, those clauses should be legally binding and enforceable. The multi-tier dispute resolution clauses could bar a litigation or arbitration. If conciliation or mediation is an element of a dispute resolution mechanism containing an arbitration agreement, the parties shall attempt to mediate or conciliate before applying to arbitration in the same way as being the case in litigation. However, the effect of those clauses is not observed *ex officio*. A party has to raise the objection of non-compliance with the procedure. If an objection has not been raised at the early stage of arbitration, the arbitral award should not be set aside. If a party has raised the objection of breach of a pre-arbitral ADR clause in arbitration, the arbitral tribunal has to determine the enforceability of the ADR clause before deciding whether to commence the arbitration. When the ADR clause is confirmed by the arbitral tribunal, it should order the parties to attempt mediation or conciliation according to the ADR clause and stay the arbitral proceeding. However, if the arbitral tribunal found that there was no valid ADR clause and then made an arbitral award, this ruling on the ADR clause and thus the validity of the arbitral procedure are not reviewable by the court in proceedings concerning annulment or enforcement of the award. Otherwise, the purposes of ADR to reduce time and costs of procedure would not be achieved. Because the fulfilment of the ADR clause does not affect the arbitral agreement and the jurisdiction of the tribunal, non-compliance with the ADR clause should not be a reason to set aside the arbitral award.

Since a mediator's job is distinct from that of a judge or arbitrator, and since the operation of mediation relies heavily on the mediator's discretion, it then matters more to familiarise mediators with their duties in different roles, and to equip them with relevant knowledge and skills. That is, even though they are judges or arbitrators, they still need to have a solid grasp of various methods and forms of mediation. Only in this way can they switch between different proceedings based on the needs and interests of the parties in individual cases. ADR methods other than trials have diversified, and the once-rigid dichotomy between contentious trials and non-contentious proceedings should be modified. Court procedure should synthesise with other consensual means of dispute resolution, and, with multi-tiered transition, present parties with various options to resolve their individual conflict. These diverse and distinctive procedures should be given equal emphasis in order to guarantee a smooth operation. Under this trend, the traditional legal curriculum in Taiwan, which mainly trained students as judges who apply the laws and attorneys who argue and defend cases in courts, should be viewed as somewhat obsolete and in need of revamping. Modern legal education should highlight various dispute resolution proceedings and foster students' comprehensive professional skills, not only to litigate but also to mediate and to settle.

Even though Taiwan is not a member of the United Nations and did not participate in the Hague Convention on the Recognition and Enforcement of Foreign Judgments in Civil or Commercial Matters or in the New York Convention on the Recognition and Enforcement of Foreign Arbitral Awards, it has, through its national legislation, followed the Hague Convention and the New York Convention to recognise the judgments of foreign courts and arbitral awards in order to strengthen international trade. Obviously, Taiwan is still unable to sign the Singapore Convention on Mediation due to its special political status. Nevertheless, it can be expected that Taiwan will adopt a similar approach by transposing the Singapore Convention into national law, with specific provisions for the enforcement of international settlement agreements resulting from mediation, and setting out specific grounds for refusing to grant relief.

6

Perspectives and Challenges of Multi-tier Dispute Resolution in Japan

YUKO NISHITANI

6.1 Introduction

For parties involved in cross-border business transactions, it is important that an efficient and reliable dispute resolution system is available. Today, contracting parties refer not only to litigation but also to arbitration and, recently, to mediation as forms of alternative dispute resolution (ADR).[1] While litigation remains the primary tool in many cross-border cases,[2] arbitration has the advantages of being flexible, neutral, confidential, professional and expeditious. The readiness of enforcing arbitral awards across borders pursuant to the 1958 New York Convention, which has gained 168 contracting states,[3] adds to the attractiveness of arbitration compared with litigation.[4] On the other hand, mediation seeks a peaceful

---

[1] Arbitration, conciliation and mediation are arguably the oldest and most universally used amicable dispute resolution methods. Historically, they facilitated settlement of disputes in the absence of a state judiciary: Kazuhiko Yamamoto and Aya Yamada, *ADR Chûsaihô* [Law of ADR & Arbitration] (2nd edn, Nihon Hyôronsha 2015) 30.

[2] For the continuing relevance of litigation, see Carlos Esplugues, 'General Report: New Developments in Civil and Commercial Mediation – Global Comparative Perspectives' in Carlos Esplugues and Louis Marquis (eds), *New Developments in Civil and Commercial Mediation* (Springer 2015) 2.

[3] United Nations Convention on the Recognition and Enforcement of Foreign Arbitral Awards, New York (adopted on 10 June 1958, entered into force on 7 June 1959); for the status table, see 'Home' (*United Nations Commission on International Trade Law*) <https://uncitral.un.org> accessed 17 May 2021.

[4] Notably, quite a few jurisdictions, such as Indonesia and Thailand, do not recognise or enforce foreign judgments in the absence of treaties. Judgments recognition is also considerably restricted in Cambodia, Myanmar, the Philippines and Vietnam. See the national reports in Adeline Chong (ed), *Recognition and Enforcement of Foreign Judgments in Asia* (Asian Business Law Institute 2017); Anselmo Reyes (ed), *Recognition and Enforcement of Judgments in Civil and Commercial Matters* (Hart 2019). For the relationship between Mainland China and Japan, see eg Yuko Nishitani, 'Coordination of Legal

6 PERSPECTIVES AND CHALLENGES OF MDR IN JAPAN 143

settlement of disputes by involving third persons as mediators who can ensure neutrality and fairness and may help find a compromise solution. Mediation is flexible and cost- and time-efficient. It is tailored to the interests of the parties, susceptible to being voluntarily abided by, and supportive of preserving commercial relationships. Geared towards amicable solutions, mediation can duly complement litigation and arbitration, which are grounded on adversarial proceedings.[5]

Against this background, it is becoming a global phenomenon to employ a combined form of dispute resolution. A multi-tier dispute resolution (MDR) may constitute 'med-arb', 'arb-med' or 'arb-med-arb', all of which incorporate a stage of mediation seeking an amicable solution before or after commencing arbitral proceedings.[6] A typical MDR clause would primarily set out negotiation in good faith in case of disputes, provide for mediation when negotiation fails, and, finally, authorise to institute arbitration or litigation.

In Asia, the most advanced and sophisticated hubs for cross-border dispute resolution have so far been Hong Kong[7] and Singapore.[8] Seeking regional economic integration through the Belt and Road Initiative (BRI), Mainland China is also aspiring to become an important actor in international dispute resolution.[9] Other jurisdictions, including the Republic of Korea and Japan, are seeking to catch up with these regional centres. Against this background, this chapter expounds and analyses

---

Systems by the Recognition of Foreign Judgments – Rethinking Reciprocity in Sino-Japanese Relationships' (2019) 14(2) Frontiers of Law in China 193ff.

[5] Esplugues (n 2) 4ff; Aya Yamada, '*Minkan-gata ADR no Riyo to Sosho Tetsuzuki no Kankei*' [Use of Private Mediation and Its Relationship to Litigation] in Yoshinaka Toyoda and others (eds), *Wakai wa Mirai wo Tsukuru: Kusano Yoshiro Sensei Koki Kinen* [Settlements Make Future: Liber Amicorum Yoshiro Kusano for His 70th Birthday] (Shinzansha 2018) 35; Kazuhiko Yamamoto, '*ADR no Igi, Enkaku, Tenbo*' [Significance, History and Perspectives of ADR] in Japan Association of the Law of Arbitration and Alternative Dispute Resolution and Meiji University Law School (eds), *ADR no Jissai to Tenbo* [Practice and Perspectives of ADR] (Journal of Japanese Arbitration and ADR) (Shoji Homu 2014) 4ff.

[6] For recent developments with statistics, see Weixia Gu, 'Multi-tier Approaches and Global Dispute Resolution' (2020) 63 Japanese Yearbook of International Law 147–66.

[7] See Chapter 3 in this volume.

[8] See Chapter 8 in this volume. For the Singapore International Commercial Court (SICC), see Man Yip, 'The Singapore International Commercial Court: The Future of Litigation?' in Xandra Kramer and John Sorabji (eds), *International Business Courts: A European and Global Perspective* (Eleven International 2019) 129ff.

[9] See Weixia Gu, 'China's Belt and Road Development and a New International Commercial Arbitration Initiative in Asia' (2018) 51(5) Vanderbilt Journal of Transnational Law 1305, 1318ff.

some cardinal issues surrounding MDR in Japan. It focuses particularly on the enforcement of agreements to mediate in case of non-compliance by either party, the acceptability of arbitrators acting as mediators at the pre-stage of arbitration, and the enforceability of settlement agreements. It is hoped that this chapter sheds light on civil law perspectives on MDR that are different from common law jurisdictions.

6.2 ADR in Japan

In Japan, arbitration has seldom been employed in either international or domestic cases, despite the increasing use of arbitration worldwide and a long tradition of mediation and conciliation in Japan.[10] These dispute resolution mechanisms were ultimately institutionalised by the enactment of the 2003 Arbitration Act and the 2004 ADR Act.[11] The scarce use of arbitration presumably is owing to the fact that parties have preferred to have their disputes determined in judicial proceedings, which are reliable, efficient and transparent, and conducted by learned judges. Moreover, parties used to avoid designating Japan as situs of arbitration in international commercial cases, apparently due to lack of experience, unfamiliar arbitration climate, and the limited accessibility of information on the Japanese legal and judicial system.[12]

A couple of years ago, the Japanese government, Japan's arbitration and mediation institutions – such as JCAA,[13] JIMC[14] and JAA[15] – and

---

[10] Since the twelfth century, the feudalistic regimes of Kamakura and Tokugawa used conciliation so that local communities could settle their disputes themselves without disturbing the authority: Yasunobu Sato, *Commercial Dispute Processing and Japan* (Kluwer Law International 2001) 280. After the 1868 Meiji Restoration, in-court conciliation was introduced in 1922 for disputes over land and building leases, and rapidly extended to other areas. Today, judicial conciliation is generally used in civil and commercial matters, including labour and family matters. Outside the courts, mediation is conducted by private organisations as well as the central or local governments, particularly in financial and consumer, traffic accident and product liability cases: Yamamoto and Yamada (n 1) 111.

[11] Arbitration Act (Law No 138 of 1 August 2003); Act on Promotion of Use of Alternative Dispute Resolution (Law No 151 of 2004).

[12] See Yarik Kryvoi and Dai Yokomizo, 'Improving Arbitration Climate in Japan – Report and Recommendations' (*SSRN*) <https://papers.ssrn.com/sol3/papers.cfm?abstract_id=2865717> accessed 14 November 2020.

[13] Japan Commercial Arbitration Association (JCAA). See 'Home' (*Japan Commercial Arbitration Association*) <www.jcaa.or.jp/en/> accessed 14 November 2020.

[14] Japan International Mediation Center (JIMC). See 'Home' (*Japan International Mediation Center*) <www.jimc-kyoto.jp/> accessed 14 November 2020.

[15] Japan Association of Arbitrators (JAA). See 'Home' (*Japan Association of Arbitrators*) <https://arbitrators.jp/> accessed 14 November 2020.

6 PERSPECTIVES AND CHALLENGES OF MDR IN JAPAN   145

other stakeholders launched a campaign to overcome the current stalemate and promote Japan as a venue for international arbitration and mediation. The strategies include (1) establishing the necessary legal framework, facilities and centres to accommodate arbitral proceedings and mediation;[16] (2) providing educational programmes and training for (future) attorneys, arbitrators and mediators; (3) marketing the advantages of conducting arbitration and mediation in Japan; and (4) revising the JCAA Commercial Arbitration Rules to ensure confidentiality, transparency and efficiency.[17]

Further to this, in 2020 the Japanese legislature amended the Act on Foreign Lawyers[18] to extend the competence of foreign attorneys so as to represent Japanese clients in commercial arbitrations with foreign elements or those taking place abroad, and to enact detailed rules for foreign attorneys involved in international commercial mediation. Major legislative reforms are envisaged at present for the 2003 Arbitration Act[19] and other relevant statutes. Judging from a preliminary report published in July 2020 and the Interim Draft Proposal of 5 March 2021,[20] the Japanese legislative committee will presumably contemplate (1) rules on provisional measures taken by arbitral tribunals in Japan or abroad and the enforcement (*exequatur*) of such provisional measures along the lines of the 2006 amendments to the UNCITRAL Model Law on Arbitration,[21]

---

[16] The Japan International Dispute Resolution Centre (JIDRC) was opened in February 2018 as a venue for international commercial arbitration and mediation. See 'Home' (*Japan International Dispute Resolution Centre*) <https://idrc.jp/en> accessed 14 November 2020.

[17] 'Commercial Arbitration Rules (2019)' (*Japan Commercial Arbitration Association*) <www.jcaa.or.jp/en/arbitration/rules.html> accessed 14 November 2020; for further details, see eg Masato Dogauchi, '*Nihon Shoji Chusai Kyokai (JCAA) no atarashii ugoki – 3tsu no Shin Chusai Kisoku no Seko to*' [New Movements of the Japan Commercial Arbitration Association – Putting into Force of Three New Arbitration Rules] [2020] New Business Law 1141, 4ff; Kokusai Chusai Seido Kenkyukai [Working Group on International Arbitration], '*Wagakuni ni okeru Kokusai Chusai no Hatten ni mukete – Nihon Chusai no Kasseika wo Jitsugen suru 7tsu no Teigen*' [Towards Developments of International Arbitration in Japan – 7 Proposals for Enhancing Arbitration in Japan] [2018] New Business Law 1125, 4ff.

[18] Act on Special Measures concerning the Handling of Legal Services by Foreign Lawyers (Law No 66 of 23 May 1986; amended by Law No 33 of 29 May 2020).

[19] Arbitration Act (Law No 138 of 1 August 2003).

[20] See *Shoji Homu Kenkyukai* [Japan Institute of Business Law], '*Chusai Hosei no Minaoshi wo Chushin to shita Kenkyukai Hokokusho*' [Report of the Working Group on Amendments of the Arbitration Act etc] (*Japan Institute of Business Law* 2020) <www.shojihomu.or.jp/> accessed 14 November 2020; 'Chusaiho to no Kaisei ni Kansuru Chukan Shian' [Interim Draft Report on Reform of the Arbitration Act etc] <www.moj.go.jp/> accessed 17 May 2021.

[21] UNCITRAL Model Law on International Commercial Arbitration (adopted on 21 June 1985; amended on 7 July 2006).

and (2) rules with necessary safeguards for the enforcement of international settlement agreements resulting from mediation in light of the 2018 Singapore Convention on Mediation[22] and the 2018 UNCITRAL Model Law on Mediation (the '2018 Model Law').[23]

It remains to be seen how things will improve and whether these strategies and legislative measures will suffice to change the climate in Japan more favourably towards international arbitration and mediation. In any case, along this policy shift, academic voices have gradually become responsive to cross-border arbitration and mediation, and started to discuss various issues, including MDR methods.

6.3 Enforcement of Agreements to Mediate

6.3.1 Development of Case Law

6.3.1.1 Facts of the Case

An MDR method generally consists of 'med-arb' or 'arb-med', meaning that mediation is attempted before or after instituting arbitration. In the latter case, the method of 'arb-med-arb' may be employed to further confirm the settlement agreement reached in mediation in the form of an arbitral award. Instead of arbitration, parties may also agree to refer to litigation when mediation fails. To ensure the effectiveness of MDR agreements, it is of primary importance whether and to what extent such agreements can be enforced in case of non-compliance by either party. Light on this question was first shed through the Tokyo High Court judgment of 22 June 2011.[24]

This case concerned damages claims in the amount of USD 113 million brought by *X* to the Tokyo District Court. *X* was initially established in Japan as a joint venture of defendant Japanese companies *Y1* and *Y2*. *X* developed, designed, manufactured and sold electronic products using dynamic random access memory (DRAM). The sales in the US market were assigned to *X*'s US subsidiary *A*. *X* contended that *Y1* and *Y2*, as *X*'s former parent companies, had a dominant position over *X* and were therefore liable for a settlement payment made by *X* and *A* to several US companies for *A*'s violation of US antitrust law. To allocate the damage and costs resulting from the settlement payment and plea bargaining

---

[22] United Nations Convention on International Settlement Agreements Resulting from Mediation (adopted on 20 December 2018; open for signature since 7 August 2019).
[23] UNCITRAL Model Law on International Commercial Mediation and International Settlement Agreements Resulting from Mediation (adopted on 20 December 2018).
[24] Tokyo High Court, 22 June 2011, 2116 Hanrei Jiho 64.

made with the US Federal Trade Commission, X signed with Y1 and Y2 a 'Judgment Sharing Agreement Civil DRAM Cases' (JSA). The preliminary question raised by Y1 and Y2 was whether an MDR clause included in the JSA was binding upon the parties to refer to first good faith negotiations, then to mediation, prior to seizing the Japanese courts. The pertinent Article 9 of the JSA provided:

> This Agreement is governed in all respects by and shall be construed in accordance with laws of Japan. To the extent that any Party disagrees about how to allocate a Shared Resolution Amount (an 'Allocation Dispute') under this Agreement, *the Parties shall conduct good faith negotiations concerning any such dispute.* If such negotiations do not fully resolve the dispute within sixty (60) days of the commencement of such good faith negotiations, *any Party may then submit the matter to a neutral Japanese mediator.* The mediator shall be chosen by agreement of the Parties. If the Parties cannot agree on the selection of a mediator within thirty (30) days of the initiation of the mediation process, *any Party may submit a written request to the Japanese Commercial Arbitration Association ('JCAA') requesting the appointment of a mediator,* who shall be a native speaker of Japanese and shall be experienced in Japanese business matters. The selection of a mediator by the JCAA shall be binding on the Parties. Following the selection of a mediator, the Parties shall conduct a non-binding mediation pursuant to principles of Japanese business practice. *If mediation does not fully resolve the dispute, the Parties agree that any legal action to resolve any remaining issues shall be commenced in the courts of Japan.*[25]

The issue was whether the suit brought by the plaintiff, without abiding by the mediation clause precedent to litigation, could be upheld. Article 9 of the JSA provided that (1) the parties shall conduct good faith negotiations in case of disputes; (2) when the negotiations fail, any party may submit the matter to a mediator selected by both parties; (3) when the parties cannot agree on a mediator, any party may request the JCAA to appoint a mediator; and (4) when mediation fails, litigation shall be commenced. The judges at the first and second instance gave different answers.

In its judgment of 8 December 2010,[26] the Tokyo District Court judges considered that this clause provided for MDR with sufficiently detailed procedure, such as timelines to move to the next step and precise conditions for selecting a mediator. The judges opined that both parties were obliged to take the prescribed steps prior to instituting a lawsuit.

---

[25] Cited from the decision of the first instance (see n 26), emphasis added.
[26] Tokyo District Court, 8 December 2010, 2116 Hanrei Jiho, 68, Westlaw Japan No 2010WLJPCA12088010.

Accordingly, the judges dismissed the case on the ground that the seizure of the Japanese courts, without following the order of procedure agreed upon by the parties, was unlawful due to the bar to proceedings.

6.3.1.2 Tokyo High Court Judgment

Upon appeal, the Tokyo High Court reversed this judgment. As a premise, the judges stated that in Japan the validity and enforceability of procedural agreements precluding litigation had been granted only for 'agreements to arbitrate' and 'agreements not to sue', whereas the treatment of MDR clauses, like Article 9 of the JSA in the underlying case, had not yet been contemplated in academic writings or court decisions.

According to the Tokyo High Court judges, first, the absence of agreements to arbitrate or agreements not to sue constitutes a 'procedural requirement' for commencing court proceedings on the merits. Although valid procedural agreements restrict the parties' right of access to the courts pursuant to Article 32 of the Constitution,[27] agreements to arbitrate have binding effects, since arbitration serves to resolve the parties' disputes instead. Similarly, agreements not to sue is valid because the parties voluntarily give up their right of action and transform their substantive claims into 'natural obligations'. On the other hand, the JSA gives priority to bona fides negotiations and mediation before turning to court proceedings. Unlike arbitration, however, negotiations in good faith or mediation do not ensure resolving the parties' disputes in a final and conclusive way, especially when the parties are in dispute and their mutual trust is impaired. Nor do negotiations or mediation serve to interrupt the period of prescription (or statute of limitation). Thus, the judges reasoned that the JSA does not have the procedural effects of precluding litigation but solely constitutes an efforts clause or gentleman's agreement.

Second, the Tokyo High Court judges pointed out that, pursuant to Article 26(1) item (ii) of the ADR Act, court proceedings may be stayed up to four months upon application by both parties, who agree to refer to a certified dispute resolution process under the ADR Act.[28] According to

---

[27] Constitution of Japan (promulgated on 3 November 1946; entered into force on 3 May 1947).

[28] Act on Promotion of Use of Alternative Dispute Resolution (n 11), art 26(1) provides:

> Where a lawsuit is pending between the parties to a civil dispute which may be settled, the court in charge of the case may, upon the joint request of the parties to the dispute, make a decision that the legal proceedings shall be stayed for a period of not more than four months, in any of the following

the judges, this means, *a contrario*, that a suit brought to the courts without an agreed certified dispute resolution process previously having been conducted cannot be dismissed for lack of procedural requirement. Furthermore, under Article 26(1) item (ii) of the ADR Act, the stay of court proceedings is subject to the parties' joint application, and the judge still retains discretion to reject it. Thus, the Tokyo High Court held that the Japanese legal system is not yet ready to provide binding effects for a clause to mediate before private institutions, parallel to certified dispute resolution under the ADR Act. Thus, a suit brought to the courts without prior attempt of mediation is lawful and satisfies procedural requirements.

Third, the Tokyo High Court judges opined that the plaintiff company attempted conciliation before the Tokyo Summary Court and, after that failed, brought its claims to the Tokyo District Court, with a view to properly interrupting the period of prescription. Dismissing the plaintiff's case would amount to refusing its obtaining damages claims and obliging it to pay litigation fees (USD 173 million) twice if negotiations and mediation should fail. Thus, the judges contended to respect the plaintiff's right of action, instead of creating a new category of procedural requirements that would exclude the litigation at hand on the ground that agreed negotiations and mediation have not yet taken place.

For these reasons, the Tokyo High Court did not acquiesce to the defendants' preliminary objection and allowed the parties to move on to the proceedings on the merits.

6.3.2 Analysis

6.3.2.1 General Remarks

This 2011 Tokyo High Court judgment attracted attention among Japanese academics as the first case concerning the enforcement of a mediation clause as a condition precedent to litigation. Although a number of foreign jurisdictions – including the United States,[29] the

cases: (i) A certified dispute resolution procedure is being carried out for the dispute between the parties to the dispute; (ii) In addition to the case prescribed in the preceding item, the parties to the dispute have reached an agreement to achieve a resolution of the dispute through certified dispute resolution.

[29] See eg *Mortimer v First Mount Vernon Industrial Loan Association* No Civ AMD 03–1051, 2003 US Dist LEXIS 24698 (D Md, 19 May 2003); *Secala v Moore* 982 F Supp 609 (ND Illinois 1997).

United Kingdom,[30] Singapore,[31] Australia,[32] Germany,[33] France[34] and Switzerland[35] – are responsive to the binding effects of a mediation clause as a condition precedent to litigation or arbitration, Japanese case law has taken a different path. Considering the international trends favouring MDR, as represented by the 2018 Model Law,[36] the reasonings of the Tokyo High Court judges ought to be critically revisited. The following analysis focuses on the enforceability and procedural effects of agreements to mediate, whereas it has not yet been discussed in Japan whether and to what extent a bona fides negotiation clause could have binding procedural effects on the courts or arbitral tribunals.[37]

6.3.2.2 Enforcement of Agreements to Mediate

The Tokyo High Court judges opined that a clause requiring mediation precedent to litigation should be understood as an efforts clause or gentleman's agreement. This is because such a clause can be equated neither with arbitration agreements, which provide a final and conclusive dispute resolution with the effects of interrupting the period of prescription, nor with agreements not to sue, which turn substantive rights into natural obligations.

---

[30] See eg *Cable & Wireless plc v IBM United Kingdom Ltd* [2002] EWHC 2059 (Comm), [2002] 2 All ER (Comm) 1041.
[31] Mediation Act 2017 (Singapore), s 8.
[32] See eg *Hooper Bailie Associated Ltd v Natcon Group Pty Ltd* (1992) 28 NSWLR 194; *Aiton Australia Pty Ltd v Transfield Pty Ltd* (1999) 153 FLR 236; for further details, see Chapter 14 in this volume.
[33] *Bundesgerichtshof* (BGH), 4 July 1977, NJW 1977, 2263; BGH, 23 November 1983, NJW 1984, 669; cf BGH, 18 November 1998, NJW 1999, 647.
[34] *Cour de cassation*, 14 February 2003, no 00-19.423, 00-19.424.
[35] *Bundesgericht* (BG), 6 June 2007 (4A_18/2007); BG, 16 May 2011 (4A_46/2011).
[36] Regarding resort to arbitral or judicial proceedings, the 2018 Model Law, art 14 states:

> Where the parties have agreed to mediate and have expressly undertaken not to initiate during a specified period of time or until a specified event has occurred arbitral or judicial proceedings with respect to an existing or future dispute, such an undertaking shall be given effect by the arbitral tribunal or the court until the terms of the undertaking have been complied with, except to the extent necessary for a party, in its opinion, to preserve its rights. Initiation of such proceedings is not of itself to be regarded as a waiver of the agreement to mediate or as a termination of the mediation proceedings.

[37] The obligations to negotiate in good faith have been discussed only as a matter of substantive contract law or tort law: Tatsuya Nakamura, *Chusaiho no Ronten* [Issues on Arbitration Law] (Seibundo 2017) 205ff.

It should, however, be reminded that agreements to mediate are not meant to preclude dispute resolution by subsequent litigation or arbitration but solely to ensure that mediation is undertaken before turning to litigation or arbitration. In this respect, agreements to mediate substantially differ from agreements not to sue, which are justified as a contract creating an obligation to refrain from bringing a suit to the courts for the legal relationship concerned and eliminating the parties' procedural interests to institute court proceedings.[38] Considering that agreements to mediate do not deprive the party of the right of access to the courts pursuant to Article 32 of the Constitution, one could focus on party autonomy and assume contractual binding force of the agreements to mediate as a matter of substantive law. The primary decision of the parties at the conclusion of their contract to use MDR and give priority to less drastic, more peaceful methods deserves respect at a later stage of disputes leading to litigation or arbitration.[39] It would also allow proper allocation of tasks between different dispute resolution institutions. When, for example, the resolution of certain disputes requires expertise in that field, it would be reasonable for the parties to use ADR to obtain the necessary information and have the relevant issues clarified, prior to referring to litigation.[40]

6.3.2.3 Procedural Effects

Notably, the Tokyo High Court judges denied any procedural effects to agreements to mediate on the ground that they could not be equated with agreements to arbitrate or agreements not to sue. Yet, this reasoning would be tenable only when the enforcement of any procedural agreements should result in dismissal of claims, and not in stay of court proceedings. As is provided for in Article 26(1) item (ii) of the ADR Act and accepted in the majority of foreign legal systems[41] and arbitration practice,[42] the enforcement of agreements to mediate solely yields staying proceedings to wait for the outcome of mediation, instead of bringing about dismissal of claims

---

[38] Tsunahiro Kikui and Toshio Muramatsu (eds), *Konmentaru Minji Soshoho* [Commentary of the Code of Civil Procedure], vol 3 (2nd edn, Nihon Hyoronsha 2019) 12ff; Hajime Kaneko and others (eds), *Jokai Minji Soshoho* [Commentary of the Code of Civil Procedure] (2nd edn, Kobundo 2011) 735ff.
[39] Shunichiro Nakano, '*Minkan Chotei de Funso ga Kaiketsu sarenai toki ni Saiban Tetsuzuki wo Kaishisuru Mune no Goi no Koryoku*' [Effects of an Agreement to Institute Litigation When Disputes Cannot Be Resolved in Mediation by Private Institutions] [2012] 636 Hanrei Hyoron 171.
[40] Yamada (n 5) 38ff.
[41] See nn 29–35; for a comparative study, see Nakano (n 39) 169ff.
[42] Nakamura refers to the practice of ICC arbitration: Nakamura (n 37) 177ff.

henceforth. Furthermore, it would arguably be contradictory, as Nakano asserts, to authorise parties to agree to arbitrate or not to sue with strong preclusive effects of litigation, while rejecting any procedural effects for agreements to mediate precedent to litigation or arbitration. Thus, agreements to mediate in the sense of 'agreements not to sue temporarily' ought to be distinguished from other types of procedural agreements and provided with the effects of staying court proceedings.[43]

In this respect, Article 26(1) item (ii) of the ADR Act deserves special attention as the only relevant statutory provision in Japan. As the Tokyo High Court judges indicated, this provision has a narrow scope by calling for both parties' consent and leaving stay of court proceedings to the judge's discretion. The requirement of joint application derives from the Japanese legislature's concern over ordering the plaintiff who knocks on the court's door to first refer to certified ADR, which could run counter to the responsibility of the judiciary and infringe de facto upon the party's right of access to the courts.[44] Thus, an explicit consent by both parties was held necessary to ensure the parties' right to be heard.[45] It was also opined that the intent of resolving disputes by ADR alone would not suffice, as it cannot be equated with the intent of giving priority to ADR over a lawsuit, as the parties may well want to conduct both proceedings in a parallel way.[46] This would be particularly the case with the period of prescription, which instituting ADR itself cannot interrupt.[47]

---

[43] Nakano (n 39) 171; Yoko Hamada, '*Minkan no Chotei ni yotteha Funso ga Kaiketsu sarenai toki ni Saibansho ni okeru Hoteki Shudan wo Kaishi suru Mune no Goi ga aru Baai ni oite, Togai Minkan no Chotei no Tetsuzuki wo hezuni Teiki sareta Sosho ga, Sosho Yoken ni kakeru mono deha nai to sareta Jirei*' [A Lawsuit Brought to the Courts Without Prior Reference to Mediation Was Held to Fulfil Procedural Requirements, although the Parties Had Agreed to Commence Litigation Only When a Private Mediation Failed to Resolve Their Disputes] (2012) Shiho Hanrei Remarks 45, 101; Takeshi Ueda, '*Chotei Zenchi no Goi ha Shokyokuteki Soshoyoken ni naruka*' [Does an Agreement to Mediate Precedent to Litigation Constitute a Negative Procedural Requirement?] (2012) 690 Hogaku Seminar 144; Kazuhiko Yamamoto, '*ADR Goi no Koryoku – Soken Seigen Goi nit suite no Jakkan no Kento*' [Effects of ADR Agreements – Some Considerations on Agreements Limiting Right of Access to the Courts] in *ADR Hosei no Gendaiteki Kadai* [Legal Framework of ADR and Its Modern Challenges] (Yuhikaku 2018) 211. Nakamura, on the other hand, advocates dismissing claims in enforcing a mandatory agreement to mediate precedent to litigation: Nakamura (n 37) 184ff.
[44] Yamamoto and Yamada (n 1) 280.
[45] Toru Kobayashi, *Saibangai Funso Kaiketsu Sokushinho* [Act on Promotion of ADR] (Shoji Homu 2005) 135; Kotatsu Uchibori, *ADR Ho Gaisetsu to Q&A* [Commentary of the ADR Act and Q&A] (Bessatsu NBL No 101) (Shoji Homu 2005) 71.
[46] Yamamoto and Yamada (n 1) 281; Yamamoto (n 43) 212.
[47] Yamamoto (n 43) 214.

6 PERSPECTIVES AND CHALLENGES OF MDR IN JAPAN

This reasoning of the Japanese legislature to require parties' joint application may be suitable to agreements to mediate entered into by parties whereby there is a gap in bargaining power and information, such as a consumer and a company, and the consumer instituted a lawsuit without previously referring to ADR. As Nakano indicates, however, this premise would not apply to cross-border commercial disputes between large enterprises. As in the underlying case, when a defence is raised that ADR be ordered according to the parties' mandatory agreement to mediate precedent to litigation, the requirement of the parties' joint application could hardly be fulfilled.[48] Whether or not the legislature decided in a proper way back in 2003, today applying Article 26(1) item (ii) of the ADR Act *mutatis mutandis* to expand MDR would not satisfy the practical needs of international business transactions.

Against this backdrop, with a view to honouring an MDR clause and enhancing ADR, the courts ought to be provided with discretionary power *de lege lata* to order stay of court proceedings, once a mandatory mediation clause is invoked by the defendant. The legal basis for this could be either Article 275(1) of the Domestic Relations Case Procedure Act (DRCPA)[49] *mutatis mutandis*, which authorises the judge to exercise discretionary power to stay contentious court proceedings and give priority to in-court conciliation, or the usual practice of civil procedure to postpone fixing the date of court hearings.[50]

6.3.2.4 The Case at Hand

The remaining question is whether the JSA in the underlying case fulfilled the conditions to oblige the parties to conduct mediation precedent to litigation. This requires a careful investigation and assessment, given that a mandatory, binding mediation clause would be provided with the procedural effects of staying court proceedings in the author's

---

[48] Nakano (n 39) 171.
[49] Domestic Relations Case Procedure Act (DRCPA) (Law No 52 of 25 May 2011). Art 275(1) of the DRCPA provides the family court judge with discretionary power to stay contentious court proceedings, with a view to giving priority to in-court conciliation and waiting for its outcome. Other comparable rules are provided in art 5 of the Civil Conciliation Act (Law No 222 of 9 June 1951), art 25(1) of the Act on Securing etc of Equal Opportunity and Treatment between Men and Women in Employment (Law No 113 of 1 July 1972) and art 25-17 of the Construction Business Act (Law No 100 of 24 May 1949).
[50] Nakano (n 39) 171; Hamada (n 43) 101; Ueda (n 43) 144; Yamada (n 5) 39; Yamamoto (n 43) 216ff; on the principles, see also Nakamura (n 37) 188.

view. The defendant's behaviour is also considered in general, in order not to favour the party acting in bad faith. When the defendant is primarily responsible for the omission of mediation precedent to litigation – for example, by ignoring the plaintiff's request to respond to mediation or refusing to pay the fee – the court proceedings can go forward upon the plaintiff's request.[51]

In the underlying case, the Tokyo High Court judges pointed out that the plaintiff had attempted in-court conciliation at the Tokyo Summary Court for six months. While it is not clear why the plaintiff did not refer to the JCAA for the purpose of mediation pursuant to Article 9 of the JSA, the defendants did not suggest employing JCAA mediation either. After October 2010, mediation was conducted between the parties at the JCAA without success. Consequently, authors generally approve of the Tokyo High Court judgment not to acquiesce to the defendants' plea to preclude court proceedings pursuant to the JSA.[52]

6.3.2.5 Results

As has been discussed so far, in light of practical needs and parties' expectations when engaging in international commercial transactions nowadays, an MDR clause ought to be honoured and enforced when mediation is a condition precedent to litigation, unlike with the current Japanese case law. The judge ought to have discretionary power to stay court proceedings where it appears necessary and the mediation clause is sufficiently precise, mandatory and binding upon the parties. At the same time, to set a reasonable limit to the exercise of discretion, the judge should carefully assess the circumstances of the case and hear the opinions of the parties (art 274(1) of the DRCPA *mutatis mutandis*).

The reasonings expounded here apply to MDR methods grounded not only on litigation but also on arbitration. In the case of arbitration, it is the task of the arbitrators to determine whether to stay arbitral proceedings when the respondent invokes a mandatory mediation clause precedent to arbitration.

---

[51] Yamamoto puts forth that art 9 of the JSA did not presuppose a mandatory use of ADR or restrict the parties' right of action. Nor did it precisely define the procedure and the time frame of ADR, without mentioning whether to apply the JCAA Commercial Mediation Rules: Yamamoto (n 43) 219ff.

[52] Nakano (n 39) 171; Hamada (n 43) 101; Ueda (n 43) 144; Yamada (n 5) 40; Yamamoto (n 43) 225ff; cf Nakamura (n 37) 187 (advocating that the Tokyo High Court judges should have dismissed the claims in the underlying case).

6.4 Bridging between Mediation and Arbitration

In considering the functioning of MDR methods, the way of bridging between different steps arguably deserves a separate analysis. In the following, after an appropriate task division between mediators and arbitrators is examined, binding effects of settlement agreements resulting from mediation are discussed.

6.4.1 Tasks of Mediators and Arbitrators

In MDR, 'med-arb', 'arb-med' or 'arb-med-arb' is used to mutually complement and take advantage of the respective dispute resolution methods. This raises the question of whether the same person can conduct both mediation and arbitration, how the tasks ought to be divided between mediators and arbitrators, and to what extent the information provided in mediation can later be used in arbitration.

6.4.1.1 'Med-arb'

The usual form of combining mediation and arbitration is 'med-arb' in Japan. The parties ought to agree that the persons responsible for the procedure primarily act as mediators and seek to settle the parties, and that, once it fails, the same persons conduct an arbitration procedure and render an arbitral award. It can be profitable that the same persons, already familiar with the case, continue conducting arbitration and render the award. The mediators can also better assess the likely outcome of future arbitration during mediation beforehand, which allows the parties to understand the legal situation. Another advantage of 'med-arb' is that, although primarily grounded on a facilitative rather than an evaluative ADR in search of amicable solution, an arbitral award with binding effects can be rendered in case mediation fails.[53]

The drawback of 'med-arb' is, however, that the preliminary stage of mediation could become formal. Because parties are aware that, failing mediation, the same mediators will subsequently sit as arbitrators and render an award, parties may not co-operate, concede, admit their failure or absence of evidence, or provide necessary information. This may increase cases where mediation ends without success, possibly

---

[53] Luke Nottage, 'Arb-med and New International Commercial Mediation Rules in Japan' (*University of Sydney*, 21 July 2009) <https://japaneselaw.sydney.edu.au/2009/07/arb-med-and-new-international-commercial-mediation-rules-in-japan/> accessed 14 November 2020.

exacerbating the conflicts between the parties in the subsequent arbitration.[54]

The assessment of 'med-arb' differs throughout various legal systems as it depends on the physiognomy of mediation and the parties involved. Commercial parties will properly assess the pros and cons of 'med-arb' and make the most of it. For other parties to be able to freely discuss and negotiate in mediation, it would be advisable that different persons be appointed as mediators and arbitrators. In any case, the appointment of the same persons ought to be strictly conditioned on both parties' consent, as is provided in Article 13 of the 2018 Model Law and Article 27 of the 2020 JCAA Mediation Rules.[55] Furthermore, for the sake of due process, fairness and predictability, the information obtained in caucusing mediation (for example, possible amount of damages or other conditions for settlement) should not be revealed to the other party or used in arbitration unless both parties agree.[56] This is in line with Article 11 of the 2018 Model Law. This principle is of particular importance for Japan, given that caucusing is the usual form of private mediation, as well as in-court conciliation.[57]

The remaining question will be whether parties, after reaching a settlement agreement, can still institute arbitration to have it confirmed as an arbitral award, while theoretically there is no longer dispute between the parties. As Nottage and Garnett point out, some foreign legal systems see it as a hindrance to render an arbitral award based on the parties' settlement agreement.[58] As for Japan, however, it is readily accepted and common practice that settlement agreements reached in mediation be confirmed by the arbitral tribunal as an award, or by the judge as a judicial settlement pursuant to Article 275(1) of the Code of Civil Procedure (CCP).[59] These issues, crucial for some foreign jurisdictions,

---

[54] Yamamoto and Yamada (n 1) 421.
[55] 'Commercial Mediation Rules (2020)' (*Japan Commercial Arbitration Association*) <www.jcaa.or.jp/en/arbitration/rules.html> accessed 14 November 2020.
[56] Yamamoto and Yamada (n 1) 422ff; on the principles, see also Takeshi Kojima and Takashi Inomata, '*Chusai Tetsuzuki to Wakai & Chotei*' [Arbitration Procedure and Settlement & Mediation] in Kaoru Matsuura and Yoshimitsu Aoyama (eds), *Gendai Chusaiho no Ronten* [Issues of Modern Arbitration Law] (Yuhikaku 1998) 305.
[57] See Yamamoto and Yamada (n 1) 72ff, 169ff. See also Nottage (n 53).
[58] Luke Nottage and Richard Garnett, 'The Top 20 Things to Change in or around Australia's International Arbitration Act' in Luke Nottage and Richard Garnett (eds), *International Arbitration in Australia* (The Federation Press 2010) 149, 179. Garnett, therefore, suggests using the form 'arb-med', instead of 'med-arb'.
[59] Code of Civil Procedure (CCP) (Law No 109 of 26 June 1996).

will ultimately be overcome once it is established that settlement agreements become enforceable pursuant to domestic law or the 2018 Singapore Convention on Mediation.[60]

6.4.1.2 'Arb-med' and 'Arb-med-arb'

During the course of arbitration proceedings, after hearings and examinations, an amicable solution may appear appropriate for the parties involved. In the 'arb-med' procedure, the arbitrators assume the role of mediators to reach a settlement between the parties. In litigation, Japanese judges have discretionary power to switch to in-court conciliation *ex officio*,[61] which frequently occurs,[62] whereas arbitrators need to obtain both parties' consent to refer a dispute to mediation. Once authorised by the parties, the same arbitrators act as mediators. Arbitration proceedings are stayed during the course of mediation. Notably, any kinds of offers, admissions or other statements by the parties, or recommendations by the mediators made during the course of mediation, should not be used as evidence in the subsequently resumed arbitration proceedings, unless otherwise agreed by the parties (arts 58 and 59 of the 2019 JCAA Commercial Arbitration Rules).[63]

After mediation fails due to discordance of the parties or ends successfully by settlement, the arbitrators may resume arbitration proceedings and render an award. This procedure of 'arb-med-arb' to confirm settlement agreements has found a statutory ground in Article 38 of the Arbitration Act.[64] Once the parties settle during the course of arbitration proceedings, possibly by using a separate mediation, the arbitral tribunal

---

[60] See Section 6.4.2.
[61] Art 20(1) of the Civil Conciliation Act.
[62] Yamamoto and Yamada (n 1) 88.
[63] See n 17.
[64] Art 38 of the Arbitration Act states:

(1) If, during the course of the arbitration procedure, a settlement is arranged between the parties with regard to a civil dispute which has been referred to an arbitration procedure and both the parties have so petitioned, the Arbitral Tribunal may make a decision based on the agreed matters in the settlement.
(2) The decision set forth in the preceding paragraph shall have the effect of an Arbitral Award.
(3) In making the decision set forth in paragraph (1), an Arbitral Tribunal shall prepare a written decision in accordance with the provisions of paragraphs (1) and (3) of the following Article and indicate that such written decision is an Arbitral Award.
(4) If the consent of both parties has been obtained, an Arbitral Tribunal or one or more arbitrators who have been appointed by the Arbitral Tribunal may attempt to arrange a settlement for the civil dispute which has been referred to an arbitral procedure.

can be requested to lay down the settlement agreement in writing and render it as an arbitral award. This has the obvious advantage of obtaining *res judicata* effects for the settlement agreement, which becomes eligible to be recognised and enforced pursuant to the 1958 New York Convention throughout various countries.

6.4.1.3 Results

By combining the advantages of mediation and arbitration in a flexible way, and possibly litigation, the parties can select the most appropriate dispute resolution methods, with the help of arbitrators and mediators. Some legal hindrances that exist in other countries (for example, instituting arbitration after a settlement agreement has been entered into by the parties or using the same persons as mediators and arbitrators) do not seem to be present in Japanese law, arguably because of the long tradition of flexible combination between contentious court proceedings and in-court conciliation or private mediation.

6.4.2 Enforcement of Settlement Agreements

Once the parties reach a settlement agreement in mediation, the issue of how to make it legally binding and enforceable is crucial, lest the other party refuses to abide by the settled obligation. It is advantageous for the parties to use 'arb-med-arb' in this respect. In other cases of stand-alone mediation or certified ADR, there is not yet any statutory ground for rendering settlement agreements enforceable.

When enacting the 2004 ADR Act, it was debated whether to render a settlement agreement resulting from certified ADR enforceable, with a view to enhancing the use of ADR and ensuring efficient dispute resolution. The Japanese legislature eventually decided not to adopt such rules, considering that they were premature, subject to risk of abuse and not supported by practical needs. Under the current Japanese law, however, a title of compulsory execution extends to final and conclusive judgments, judicial settlements and records entered as a result of in-court civil conciliation or family conciliation, in addition to foreign judgments and foreign and domestic arbitral awards provided with an *exequatur* (art 22 of the Civil Execution Act).[65] Considering that

---

(5) The consent set forth in the preceding paragraph or the revocation thereof shall be made in writing, unless otherwise agreed by the parties.

[65] Civil Execution Act (Law No 4 of 30 March 1979).

ADR and judicial proceedings, as well as in-court conciliation and private ADR, are supposed to stand on an equal footing, the legislature should have allowed compulsory execution based on settlement agreements resulting from certified ADR.[66]

At present, the Japanese legislature is contemplating a legislative reform to make at least international settlement agreements enforceable, with a view to becoming an attractive venue for the resolution of cross-border commercial disputes.[67] Once international settlement agreements become enforceable in Japan, through amendment of the 2004 ADR Act or other relevant statutes, use of 'arb-med-arb' or judicial settlement may become obsolete, as a stand-alone mediation will suffice to confirm settlement agreements and make them legally binding. The 2018 Singapore Convention on Mediation, which ensures cross-border enforcement of settlement agreements resulting from mediation, has already attracted six contracting states and another forty-seven signatories.[68] It will be ideal if Japan also contemplates ratifying this successful international instrument in the near future.

Parallel to this, it will be considerable progress for the Japanese legal system to extend the scope of foreign judicial decisions or settlements to be recognised and enforced. Japan so far cannot enforce foreign judicial settlements on the ground that they do not qualify as 'judgments' for lack of authoritative judicial decision-making and *res judicata* effects (art 118 of the CCP).[69] New legislative reforms may gradually overcome this hindrance by extending the scope of the recognition and enforcement of foreign court decisions. This will ultimately lower the threshold for Japan to join the 2005 Hague Choice of Court Convention[70] and the 2019

---

[66] Yamamoto and Yamada (n 1) 285.
[67] See Section 6.2.
[68] For the status table, see 'Home' (n 3).
[69] Chuichi Suzuki, '*Gaikoku no Hishosaiban no Shonin, Torikesi, Henko*' [Recognition, Revocation and Alteration of Foreign Decisions in Non-contentious Matters] (1974) 26 (9) Hoso Jiho 1489; Hiroshige Takada, 'Article 200' in Masahiro Suzuki and Yoshimitsu Aoyama (eds), *Chushaku Minji Soshoho* [Commentary of the Code of Civil Procedure], vol 4 (Yuhikaku 1997) 357; Kazuhiko Yamamoto, 'Article 118' in Tsunahiro Kikui and Toshio Muramatsu (eds), *Konmentaru Minji Soshoho* [Commentary of the Code of Civil Procedure], vol 2 (2nd edn, Nihon Hyoronsha 2006) 513; Morio Takeshita, 'Article 200' in Hajime Kaneko and others (eds), *Jokai Minji Soshoho* [Commentary of the Code of Civil Procedure] (2nd edn, Kobundo 2011) 625. As a matter of domestic law, however, judicial settlements are enforceable like a final and conclusive judgment (art 267 of the CCP), even though they do not have *res judicata* effects.
[70] HCCH Convention of 30 June 2005 on Choice of Court Agreements.

Hague Judgments Convention,[71] which will enhance cross-border circulation of court decisions including judicial settlements.

6.5 Conclusion

Although Japan has a long tradition of conciliation and mediation, establishing and enhancing arbitration, in combination with mediation, is a recent development. It is a challenge for Japan to deal with cross-border dispute resolution and not just in relation to the language barrier and the civil law tradition. We have a lot to learn from our neighbouring countries in the Asia-Pacific region and would be grateful to continue working together.

As mentioned here, the Japanese government, Japan's arbitral institutions and other stakeholders have recently been making efforts to enhance the use of international arbitration in Japan. Legislative reforms will presumably lead to new rules stipulating provisional measures being ordered by arbitral tribunals, and to the enforceability of such measures as well as settlement agreements resulting from cross-border mediation. In order to accommodate international arbitration and mediation, further refinement of statutory rules, case law, practice and academic discussions will be necessary in Japan. Implementation of MDR methods will also need to be deliberated, particularly the enforcement of agreements to mediate precedent to litigation or arbitration, and methods of combining mediation and arbitration procedures. Further developments are anxiously awaited.

---

[71] HCCH Convention of 2 July 2019 on the Recognition and Enforcement of Foreign Judgments in Civil or Commercial Matters.

7

Might There Be a Future for Multi-tiered Dispute Resolution in Korea?

Challenges and Prospects

JOONGI KIM[*]

7.1 Introduction

Korea has one of the largest developed economies in the world, and cross-border trade and investment remain an integral part of its growth and prosperity. Effective resolution of the disputes that inevitably arise has become an important priority for Korean businesses. Given the efficiency that multi-tiered dispute resolution approaches offer, they serve as practical alternatives that should be considered. This chapter examines the use of multi-tiered approaches for resolution of disputes related to Korea, particularly within a cross-border context.

Unlike in other jurisdictions in Asia, multi-tiered clauses do not appear to be the preferred choice for dispute resolution for Korean parties. Med-arb, arb-med and med-arb-med, where combinations of mediation and arbitration are sequentially carried out, sometimes by the same person, are still uncommon in Korea. This is consistent with the fact that, relative to non-adjudicative approaches to resolving disputes such as negotiation and mediation, use of adjudicative approaches such as litigation and arbitration remains the preferred option. This state of affairs must take into account that arbitration itself has become an established, viable and robust option only within the past fifteen years. Furthermore, mediation remains a relatively under-developed alternative dispute resolution (ADR) method for both domestic and international disputes.

---

[*] The author would like to thank Solji Lim for her research assistance.

Currently, the under-utilisation of non-adjudicative approaches such as mediation stands as the most prominent barrier to the adoption of multi-tiered approaches. Whether the source of Korea's deviation from other East Asian countries in the use of non-adjudicative approaches is structural or cultural remains unclear. It can be most likely attributed to a host of reasons. Possible causes include socio-cultural biases, lack of experience and education, the weak structural environment and capacity, and the statutory framework. Measures are needed to enhance awareness, overcome ingrained biases, deal with concerns over justice and fairness, and balance the effectiveness of med-arb or other similar options. Experts stress the need to focus more on facilitative processes as opposed to the current system that stresses a more evaluation-based approach. Whether recent efforts for reforms will lay the foundations for multi-tiered approaches to prosper in the future remains to be seen.

This chapter explores the situation regarding use of multi-tiered dispute resolution first by providing an overview of dispute resolution in Korea. Next, it looks at the statutory and legal framework of arbitration and mediation, particularly from a cross-border perspective. It reviews the state of multi-tiered approaches in domestic and international commercial disputes. It then provides an analysis of multi-tiered approaches in international investment treaties.

7.2 Dispute Resolution in Korea

Within the span of fifty years, Korea has established itself as one of the leading economies and strongest democracies in the world. In the process, Korea now boasts exceptional rule of law, a highly competent and independent judiciary, and it consistently ranks among the top countries in terms of the enforcement of contracts.[1] The World Bank's Worldwide Governance Indicators, for instance, rank Korea third in Asia in terms of its rule of law, and its Ease of Doing Business rankings rate Korea second in the world in terms of enforcement of contracts. With its continuous economic growth, the need for effective dispute resolution remains an important priority.

Historically, much debate has focused on whether Koreans are culturally inclined towards adjudicative approaches to dispute resolution such

---

[1] Dohyun Kim and Chulwoo Lee, 'Dispute Resolution in South Korea' in Michael Palmer, Marian Roberts and Maria Moscati (eds), *Comparative Dispute Resolution* (Elgar 2020); for a more historic overview of the rise of civil litigation in Korea from 1906–2016, see Figure 7.1.

as litigation. A traditional view suggested that Koreans might be culturally averse to litigation but the modern view is that a compilation of factors have contributed to a substantial increase in civil litigation that has largely dispelled prior theories.[2] The changes have been spawned by political, social and non-cultural factors such as the increases in attorneys and judges, economic growth and democratisation. Kim and Lee, in particular, concluded that, instead of the transition to democratisation, '[e]conomic factors such as the GDP per capita have had stronger correlations with the litigation rate, while institutional factors such as the density of lawyers and judges have interacted with litigation frequency as both dependent and independent variables'.[3]

To assess the general state of affairs of Korea's general dispute resolution framework, it is worth analysing how litigious the county is relative to other similarly situated countries. Table 7.1 compares Korea with a host of civil law countries with advance economies. The countries were selected based on having both a population greater than 45 million and a GDP per capita more than USD 30,000. Civil law countries were chosen because they have a similar legal framework, particularly in terms of civil procedure. Although not as large

Table 7.1 *Civil litigation in leading civil law countries (2014–18) (cases per 100 persons)*

	2014	2015	2016	2017	2018
Spain	2.16	2.34	2.15	2.55	2.75
Italy	2.61	2.54	2.56	2.47	2.55
France	2.64	2.62	2.55	2.48	2.24
Korea	2.17	1.91	1.84	1.92	1.81
Germany	1.78	1.74	1.59	1.51	1.52
Taiwan	0.60	0.61	0.64	0.67	0.71
Japan	0.36	0.37	0.37	0.38	0.38

Source: Compiled by the author from Court of First Instance incoming civil and commercial litigious case lists.

---

[2] For an early traditional view that Koreans were averse to litigation, see Pyong-Choon Hahm, *The Korean Political Tradition and Law* (Royal Asiatic Society Korea Branch 1967); Pyong-Choon Hahm, *Korean Jurisprudence, Politics, and Culture*(Yonsei University Press 1986).
[3] Kim and Lee (n 1) 16.

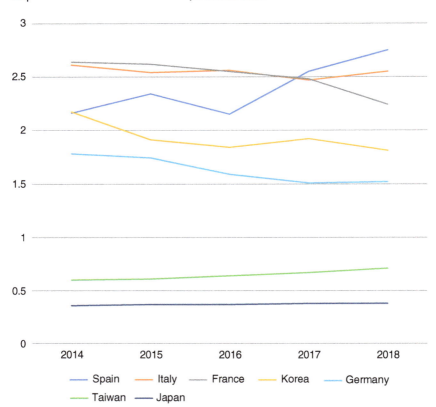

Figure 7.1 Civil litigation in leading civil law countries (2014–18) (cases per 100 persons)
Sources: EU Justice Scoreboard; Korean Supreme Court; Japan Supreme Court; KOSIS; OECD Stats; Taiwan Judicial Yuan Judicial Statistics Yearbook 2018.[4]

as Korea, Taiwan was included as being another example of civil law jurisdiction in Asia. These countries were all then compared based on factors such as population and economic size.

Table 7.1 and Figure 7.1 reveal several noteworthy trends. First, Korea consistently remains not one of the most litigious civil law countries and

---

[4] See <https://ec.europa.eu/info/policies/justice-and-fundamental-rights/upholding-rule-law/eu-justice-scoreboard_en>, <www.scourt.go.kr/supreme/supreme.jsp>, <www.courts.go.jp/english/index.html>, <https://kosis.kr/eng/>, <https://stats.oecd.org/> and <www.judicial.gov.tw/en/np-1806-2.html> all accessed 2 April 2021. Under the European Commission for the Efficiency of Justice (CEPEJ) methodology, litigious civil and commercial cases concern disputes between parties, for example, disputes about contracts, while non-litigious civil and commercial cases concern uncontested proceedings, for example, uncontested payment orders.

stands at about the average among those analysed. From a comparative standpoint, Korea has remained more litigious than Germany, Japan and Taiwan while being less so than Spain, Italy and France. Furthermore, as with the other advanced economies, litigiousness in Korea has remained relatively stable per capita with minor fluctuations on a yearly basis over the past five years. Finally, as with the other countries, other than Spain, a general decline in the amount of litigation can be seen.

Korea's and Taiwan's legal and civil litigation systems largely trace their roots from Japan through Germany. Even today, Korean scholars and courts often consult Japanese and German treatises, scholarship and court cases. Yet, despite this shared legal tradition, within Asia, Korea has been consistently far more litigious than both Japan and Taiwan, being 4.8 and 2.5 times greater, respectively, as of 2018. The gap with Taiwan has been declining as the number of cases in Taiwan has been increasing, although this could be because Taiwan has only recently reached a GDP per capita of USD 25,000.[5] Japan clearly stands as an outlier as the least litigious among the major civil law countries and also has had the smallest amount of fluctuation and change over the past five years.

When measured by the size of the economy, the general trends remain the same but overall a bit more pronounced (see Table 7.2 and Figure 7.2).

Table 7.2 *Civil litigation in leading civil law countries (2014–18) (cases per GDP USD million)*

	2014	2015	2016	2017	2018
Spain	64.5	66.9	57.7	64.4	67.8
Italy	72.1	68.9	64.2	59.0	59.5
France	65.7	64.0	59.3	55.3	48.0
Korea	63.4	52.1	48.0	48.3	44.1
Germany	37.8	36.5	31.4	28.4	28.0
Taiwan	26.2	26.8	27.6	26.7	27.5
Japan	9.3	9.1	9.4	9.3	9.2

Source: Compiled by the author from Court of First Instance incoming civil and commercial litigious case lists.

[5] Dohyun Kim, '*Sosong jeungganeun gyesok doel geosinga?: jesoyulkwa kyeongje yoin bunseok*' [Will the Increase of Litigation Continue? An Analysis of the Relationships between the Litigation Rate and Economic Factors] (2015) 48 *Beop gwa sahoe* [Korean Journal of Law and Society] 249–79.

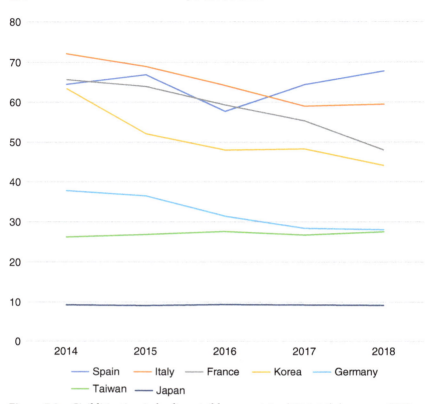

Figure 7.2 Civil litigation in leading civil law countries (2014–18) (cases per GDP USD million) Sources: EU Justice Scoreboard; Korean Supreme Court; Japan Supreme Court; KOSIS; OECD Stats; Taiwan Judicial Yuan Judicial Statistics Yearbook 2018.[6]

Other than Spain, a general decline in the amount of litigation can be seen. Litigiousness in Korea has also consistently declined when calculated from an economic growth perspective over the past five years. The decline in litigiousness is particularly pronounced in France and Korea, at 73 per cent and 70 per cent, respectively, within the same five-year period. This suggests that population plays a less determinative factor compared with the size and maturity of the economy.

These data confirm the results of Dohyun Kim's cross-country survey of sixteen countries based on 2012 data, which concluded that increase in economic size was the strongest contributor towards

[6] See the websites in n 4.

a linear, proportional increase in civil litigation.[7] He predicted that after the size of an economy reached a certain critical mass and a certain level of development was achieved, the level of civil litigation would no longer rise in a proportional fashion. Instead, his research suggested that a decline would occur in a reverse 'U' fashion starting from a peak of GDP per capita of USD 25,975.[8] More recent data confirm this general plateau or declining effect, particularly with the case of Taiwan, as mentioned already. Spain has been an outlier for at least the past couple of years.

Historically, although a comparative analysis has not been conducted, the effect on litigation must be considered within the context of the significant increase in the number of attorneys in Korea. From a structural standpoint, the increase in the supply of attorneys no doubt contributed to a dramatic increase in access to legal services, which may have contributed to the growth in civil litigation in the decades of the 1990s and the 2000s. The number of attorneys increased more than twelve-fold during the period 1990 to 2020 (see Table 7.3), from 2,741 to 31,974 for a population of approximately 50 million people. In 1990, there was 1 attorney for every 15,640 persons; in 2018, this ratio dropped to 1 attorney for every 1,614 persons. From a different perspective, the number of attorneys for 10,000 persons went from 0.83 in 1990 to 6.20 in 2018. This supply-side increase no doubt played a role in the increased demand for legal services. In addition, increased education provided to people, entities and businesses about their legal rights also made civil litigation far more accessible and affordable.

In contrast, one reason for the general decline in litigation in Korea in recent years might be the development of other forms of dispute resolution and the increasing diversification that is occurring. With its economic development, Korea could also be becoming more open to other forms of dispute resolution beyond the traditional options. Furthermore, the general sophistication of contract negotiators has increased, which no doubt has created more robust contracts and reduced the uncertainties that create disputes. Parties also no doubt have a better sense of the disadvantages of expensive litigation and are becoming more aware of the advantages of reasonable settlement by negotiation and other non-adjudicative approaches.

[7] ibid 272.
[8] ibid 272.

Table 7.3 *Number of attorneys in Korea (1990–2018)*

Year	1990	1995	2000	2005	2010	2015	2018
Attorneys	2,741	3,731	4,699	7,693	11,802	20,531	31,974
Population per one attorney	15,640	12,086	10,004	6,263	4,199	2,485	1,614
Number of attorneys per 10,000 persons	0.83	1.00	1.60	2.38	4.02	4.68	6.20

7.3 Arbitration and Mediation

Given Korea's initial proclivity to engage in formal adjudicative dispute resolution through the courts, with the growth in its economy, the potential need for Koreans to seek alternative means of dispute resolution such as arbitration and mediation would appear to be considerable. A diversification of the means of dispute resolution would give Korean parties far more options. It would be in line with Korean parties becoming among the most sophisticated users of dispute resolution in the world as its economy increasingly becomes one among the most advanced. Nevertheless, Korea has generally shown a preference for the more formal means of dispute resolution in the form of arbitration over mediation or negotiation, especially in relation to cross-border transactions. One might postulate that either a time lag exists or that other reasons account for this state of affairs.

7.3.1 Arbitration

Among the alternative means of dispute resolution, formal adjudication through arbitration has become the most preferred in cross-border dealings. Korean parties have become leading advocates for arbitration not only domestically but, more prominently, internationally.

Korean parties remain among the most active users of arbitration in all other major arbitral institutions such as the International Chamber of Commerce (ICC), the Singapore International Arbitration Centre (SIAC) and the Hong Kong International Arbitration Centre (HKIAC). At the ICC, for instance, Korean parties consistently have ranked among the top users of the institution, ranking twelfth in both 2018 and 2019. They were the second most active users in Asia, behind China, in 2018, and

Table 7.4 *KCAB arbitration cases (2010–19)*[9]

	2010	2011	2012	2013	2014	2015	2016	2017	2018	2019
Domestic arbitration	264	246	275	261	295	339	319	307	331	373
International arbitration	52	77	85	77	87	74	62	78	62	70
Total	316	323	360	338	382	413	381	385	393	443

the third most active users, behind India and China, in 2019.[10] At the SIAC, Korean parties ranked eleventh in 2018 and tenth in 2019. At the HKIAC, Korean parties ranked seventh in both 2018 and 2019. Anecdotal evidence suggests not only that there is a high incidence of Korean parties using these leading international institutions but also that the average quantum of the cases involving Korean parties is significantly large.

In terms of arbitral institutions, the Korean Commercial Arbitration Board (KCAB), established in 1966, is the country's oldest and largest dispute resolution institution devoted to handling arbitration and mediation. Under its guidance, arbitration and mediation have significantly expanded with consistent, yearly growth that in 2019 reached a record of 373 domestic cases and 70 international cases (see Table 7.4). The newly established KCAB International began its operation in April 2018 and since then oversees all international arbitration cases.

Several other domestic institutions offer arbitral services such as the Korean Christian Settlement and Arbitration Center, established in 2008, and the Korean Buddhist Conciliation and Arbitrator Center, established in 2015, but their arbitration caseloads are minimal and, if at all, they remain more focused on mediation.

7.3.2 *Mediation*[11]

Mediation in Korea can be broadly categorised into judicial mediation, administrative mediation and private mediation. Korea has been trying

---

[9] See <www.kcab.or.kr> accessed 2 April 2021.
[10] '2019 ICC Dispute Resolution Statistics' (*International Chamber of Commerce*) <https://iccwbo.org/publication/icc-dispute-resolution-statistics> accessed 2 April 2021.
[11] In Korea, as with other jurisdictions, much debate revolves around the definitional distinction between mediation and conciliation. Both terms are alternatively translated

to promote mediation primarily through top-down, government-led initiatives that have focused much of their attention on developing judicial mediation and administrative mediation. In terms of cross-border disputes involving international parties, however, judicial mediation and administrative mediation are less relevant and more emphasis needs to be placed on the development of private mediation. How to successfully achieve this goal remains one of the final puzzles in the development of ADR in Korea.

Judicial mediation involves mediation primarily conducted through the courts under the Judicial Conciliation of Civil Disputes Act (JCCDA).[12] In judicial mediation under the JCCDA, among the cases brought to the courts under standard civil litigation, cases can be referred to mediation by the courts or upon mutual agreement of the parties. In the original judicial mediation under JCCDA, judicial mediation can be conducted by a Conciliation Judge, the Standing Commission, the Conciliation Council or the relevant court.[13] Roughly, 8–9 per cent of all civil cases brought to the court are mediated under the JCCDA by these various mediators (conciliators). As testament to the lack of appetite for mediation among Korean parties, at present, the courts refer far more cases to judicial mediation as opposed to those initiated by the parties.

In contrast to this court-dominated and court-driven approach to mediation, court-annexed mediation is a process by which the court refers cases to external organisations. Under this scheme, parties can privately work out a resolution through external mediators who are not directly associated with the courts. While court-annexed mediation has made inroads as an alternative to full-fledged litigation, it still remains under-developed overall, particularly in cross-border disputes. Although statistics are not available, almost all of the cases reportedly involve disputes between domestic parties and few involve foreign parties.

Since 2010, the Seoul District Court has referred cases for mediation to more than seventeen external organisations such as the KCAB, the Seoul Bar

---

as *jojeong* [調停], *hwaui* [和議], *alseon* [斡旋] and sometimes *hwahae* [和解] in Korean and vice versa. This chapter will consider both mediation and conciliation together to constitute *jojeong* [調停], *hwaui* [和議] and *alseon* [斡旋] but will generally use the term mediation. For specific statutes or rules, it will follow the terminology chosen by the Korean Ministry of Government Legislation and the KCAB, respectively.

[12] Another type of judicial mediation concerns family-related disputes brought under the Family Litigation Act, but these will not be considered in this chapter.

[13] Judicial Conciliation of Civil Disputes Act, art 7.

Association (SBA), professional organisations and law schools.[14] Since then the Seoul District Court has referred a significant number of cases to the KCAB and the Seoul High Court has referred cases as well (see Table 7.5). In 2017, for instance, a record number of 1,220 cases were referred to the KCAB and, in 2019, 692 cases were referred. In May 2020, the Patent Court of Korea also designated the KCAB for court-annexed mediation. In terms of court-annexed mediation, the Mediation and Arbitration Center of the Seoul Bar Association has become the other leading venue designated by the Seoul District Court. It handled 1,633 cases in 2014, 1,830 cases in 2015, 2,067 cases in 2016, 2,324 cases in 2017, 2,304 cases in 2018 and 979 cases in 2019 (see Table 7.5).[15] While there was a significant decline in the number of cases in 2019, for the past four years the success rate has remained at around 12 per cent.[16] It appears, however, that there have been relatively few court-annexed mediation cases that have involved international parties.

Other institutions that have been designated for court-annexed mediation include the Korea Association of Beommusa Lawyer, Seoul Central District Beommusa Lawyer, the Korea Fair Trade Mediation Agency, the Korea Consumer Agency, the Content Dispute Resolution Committee,

Table 7.5 *KCAB and SBA court-annexed mediation cases (2010–19)*

	2010	2011	2012	2013	2014	2015	2016	2017	2018	2019
KCAB	281	705	593	809	959	767	827 (6*)	1,220	769	692
SBA					1,633	1,830	2,067	2,324	2,304	979
Total	281	705	593	809	2,592	2,597	2,900	3,544	3,073	1,671

* Cases referred from the Seoul High Court.
Sources: KCAB Annual Reports 2010–19; The Seoul Bar Association.[17]

---

[14] Jiyoung Park, *Minsa jojeong jedo ui ipbeopjeok gaeseon bangan* [Legislative Policy for the Improvement of Civil Conciliation] (2017) NARS Issue Report 310, Publication Registration No 31-9735020-000632-14 (National Assembly Research Service 2017) 13.

[15] Park (n 14) 14; Kim and Lee (n 1) 15, citing Seungtae Hwang and Inkook Kay, *Hangukhyeong daechejeok bunjaeng haegyeol (ADR) jedo ui baljeon banghyange gwanhan yeongu* [A Study for the Development of Korean-Style ADR Systems] (2016) Judicial Policy Research Institute Research Monograph 2016-04, Publication Registration No 32-9741568-000851-01 (Judicial Policy Research Institute 2016) 321.

[16] Based on data provided to the author by the Seoul Bar Association.

[17] See <www.kcab.or.kr> accessed 2 April 2021 and <www.seoulbar.or.kr> accessed 2 April 2021.

the Korea Exchange, the Korea Copyright Commission and others. These other institutions in total accounted for 1,552 cases in 2015 and 1,201 cases in 2016. They have been relatively successful.

The Korean Christian Settlement and Arbitration Center, for instance, which was established in 2008 and seeks to offer for free purely private mediation unconnected with the courts, has had a minimal amount of cases referred by the court with only twenty-two cases in 2015 and eleven cases in 2016.[18] This is despite the Center having a panel of highly respected mediators such as former judges and practitioners.

Administrative mediation concerns statutory mediation that occurs under the auspices of various administrative agencies, ministries or local governments in subject areas such as construction and real estate, consumer and finance, information and communication, press, traffic and transportation, intellectual property, environment, medical, education and labour. More than sixty mediation committees, commissions and institutions have been established for this purpose and operate through the regulations of the relevant statutes. Administrative mediation, however, is not geared towards cross-border disputes and focuses on domestic disputes.

In comparison with judicial mediation and administrative mediation, the more market-based private mediation remains under-utilised given the size and development of Korea's economy. The KCAB is at the forefront in addition to court-annexed mediation and also conducts private mediation based on its own Mediation Rules that were adopted in 2012 and the more informal *alseon*.[19] *Alseon*, which is not based on any rules and is less structured, has recently averaged more than 900 cases per year, and there have been far more cases than court-annexed mediation. Most notably, for the purposes of this chapter, international cases have accounted for approximately 11 per cent of the total *alseon* cases, although most of them involved smaller disputes worth less than USD 500,000. Furthermore, in recent years, the percentage of international cases has been steadily declining from a high of 26 per cent in 2010 to 7 per cent in 2019 (see Table 7.6). As for the KCAB's Mediation Rules, which are based on the UNCITRAL Conciliation Rules, they unfortunately have not been employed that often, with only a handful of cases per year. It also appears that none of the cases under the Mediation Rules involved any international parties.

---

[18] Kim and Lee (n 1) 15.
[19] The Mediation Rules provide for the Mediator to be appointed by KCAB if the parties cannot agree and for the mediator to present a mediation proposal at any time.

7 MIGHT THERE BE A FUTURE FOR MDR IN KOREA?

Table 7.6 KCAB 'private' mediation cases (2010-19)

	2010	2011	2012	2013	2014	2015	2016	2017	2018	2019
Domestic *Alseon* (Conciliation)	636	766	797	819	821	847	753	1,002	881	830
International *Alseon* (Conciliation)	165	149	141	97	95	92	137	99	80	59
KCAB Mediation Rules Cases				1	1	3	0	8	2	2
Total	801	915	938	917	917	942	890	1,109	963	891

Source: KCAB Annual Reports 2010-19.[20]

Overall, a multitude of reasons have been cited for the general weakness of non-adjudicative approaches to dispute settlement such as mediation, in particular private mediation. The reasons include lack of awareness, structural issues and cultural inclinations. In terms of the lack of awareness, according to one commentator, the reasons for the lack of mediation include 'a lack of knowledge regarding ADR and mediation among Korean citizens'.[21]

Structural constraints such as inexperience of attorneys, lack of incentives and passive reliance on the court-driven approach are also cited. One observer notes that 'many attorneys are not experienced in ADR or mediation'.[22] Another problem is that mediations are traditionally 'top-down' and led by judges through judicial mediation, and as a result 'are often not conducted until the latter half of the trial, instead of earlier in the case'.[23]

Although questioned by some leading experts, some believe that cultural factors may play a role in the lack of development of non-adjudicative approaches. Culturally, some commentators suggest that 'Korean culture, with a strong element of "face-saving" and pride, also may be characterised as having a "killer 'knock-out' instinct" that is triggered when a person feels clearly wronged.'[24] Similarly, the lack of

---

[20] See <www.kcab.or.kr> accessed 2 April 2021.
[21] Peter Robinson and others, 'The Emergence of Mediation in Korean Communities' (2015) 15 Pepperdine Dispute Resolution Law Journal 518.
[22] ibid.
[23] ibid.
[24] Andrew White and Saeyoun Kim, 'Early Resolution of Disputes in Korea: Negotiation, Mediation, and Multi-tiered Dispute Resolution' (2017) 15 Dispute Resolution Journal

parties voluntarily choosing court mediation could be because of '[t]he overall unripened ADR culture in Korea and the plaintiff's desire to not to be regarded as being "in a weak stance" at the starting line'.[25] 'Many Koreans also strongly favor receiving a court judgement [sic] from a judge, instead of resolving the problem with a mediator', who might be considered to lack the same stature and authority. Kim and Lee, for instance, surmise that 'Koreans have a weak disposition to submit themselves voluntarily to mediation'.[26] In contrast, Korea traditionally has a history where elders would resolve problems in their villages.[27]

7.4 International Treaties

In terms of multi-tiered dispute resolution, the most prominent area related to Korea, particularly in the cross-border context, can be found in international investment treaties.[28] Korea has entered into 102 international investment agreements (IIAs), mostly in the form of bilateral investment treaties and free trade agreements, with most of them providing for investor–state dispute settlement (ISDS). Among the IIAs, eighty-seven of them are bilateral investment treaties (BITs), one is a trilateral treaty and fourteen are free trade agreements (FTAs). Recently, Korea has been subject to a host of ISDS cases and Korean investors are increasingly bringing cases against other governments as well. Due to the confidential nature of some ISDS procedures, it is possible that some unreported cases might have occurred, but the use of mediation, conciliation or multi-tiered dispute resolution clauses remains unknown. While Korea was one of the original signatories of the Singapore Mediation Convention, it is still too early to evaluate the effects of this. Some hope that it can help serve as a catalyst for the adoption of a comprehensive mediation law.[29]

---

16. See also Robinson and others (n 21) 518 ('Koreans seem to have a strong "K.O." mentality, where they want to knock out the other party in a dispute instead of seeking a compromise').
[25] Jae-Seog Choi, 'Mediation Cases: Corporation-Related Disputes' (2019) 1 Asian Pacific Mediation Journal 99.
[26] Kim and Lee (n 1) 16.
[27] Nam Hyeon Kim and others, 'Community and Industrial Mediation in South Korea' (1993) 37 Journal of Conflict Resolution 361, 363–64.
[28] This analysis excludes disputes between countries under an IIA.
[29] Sun Ju Jeong, 'Singapore Convention on Mediation and Recognition and Enforcement of Settlement Agreement' (2020) 24 Civil Procedure 1, 8–9.

A closer analysis of Korea's IIAs shows that, with few exceptions, almost all of the IIAs first provide that when a dispute arises the parties should try to settle the dispute in an 'amicable way'.[30] The Korea–El Salvador BIT (2002) adds that efforts in an 'amicable way' should not be 'without prejudice to the negotiations which can be done through the diplomatic channels'.[31] Some IIAs alternatively provide that the parties should engage in consultation and negotiation to settle the dispute.

In terms of using a third party to help resolve the dispute, most IIAs do not mention non-adjudicative or multi-tiered approaches, or non-binding procedures. The Korea–Peru FTA (2011) is one of the few treaties that mentions that the parties may also pursue as an option the use of 'non-binding third party procedures', but it does not provide any further specification or qualification.[32] The recently ratified Korea–Central America FTA (2019) goes a step further and provides that 'consultation and negotiation' may include 'non-binding, third party procedures' and specifically suggests 'conciliation and mediation' as examples. No other IIAs explicitly mention non-binding third-party procedures.

For purposes of this chapter, the two prominent examples where mediation is explicitly mentioned as an option and basically provides for a multi-tiered dispute resolution structure are the Korea–Colombia FTA (2016) and the recently ratified Korea–Central America FTA. The Korea–Colombia FTA provides that the parties are free to '[refer] their dispute, by mutual agreement to *ad hoc* or institutional mediation or conciliation before or during an arbitral proceeding'.[33] The Korea–Central America FTA, as mentioned, includes 'conciliation and mediation' as examples of non-binding third-party procedures. In both cases, however, those are non-mandatory options that are merely suggestive in nature.

In recent years, Korea has been subject to a host of ISDS cases at the International Centre for Settlement of Investment Disputes (ICSID) and Korean investors are increasingly bringing ICSID cases as well. Two of the three cases brought against Korea at the ICSID have settled, the first one in 1990 and the second one in 2016.[34] None of the disputes involving

---

[30] Korea–Dominica BIT, art 8(1) provides for the phrase 'in a "friendly manner"'.
[31] Korea–El Salvador BIT, art 9(1).
[32] Korea–Peru FTA, art 9.16(2).
[33] Korea–Colombia FTA, art 8.17(2).
[34] The first case brought against Korea at ICSID, which happened to be a contract-based case, settled: *Colt Industries Operating Corporation v Republic of Korea* (ICSID Case No ARB/84/2). The second case was *Hanocal Holding BV and IPIC International BV v Republic of Korea* (ICSID Case No ARB/15/17).

Korea or Korean investors, however, have utilised the conciliation procedures under the ICSID Convention. While most IIAs provide for ISDS at the ICSID as an option, a number of the IIAs also provide for mutually agreed conciliation or arbitration based on the ICSID Convention even before both countries become members of ICSID.

Notably, one high-profile, potential ISDS case recently settled through mediation after a notice of intent for arbitration had been filed.[35] A Malaysian investor brought litigation against the Jeju Free International City Development Center (JDC) at the Seoul District Court and also filed a notice of intent to bring an arbitration against Korea. The parties successfully settled both cases pending in the Korean courts and awaiting the investment treaty arbitration through court-annexed mediation. The exact details of the settlement have not been revealed, but this recent success might bode well for the future use of mediation to settle investment treaty disputes. There are no other known cases of mediation or conciliation being attempted or used in this type of context.

7.5 Multi-tiered Dispute Resolution

While adjudicative forms of dispute resolution such as arbitration have become established in Korea with international arbitration becoming commonplace in international border transactions, as shown already, mediation remains relatively under-developed, particularly in terms of private mediation in the cross-border context. Given this lack of use of private mediation, the potential for non-adjudicative approaches to dispute resolution that includes the use of multi-tiered resolution does not appear promising in the short term. According to one commentator, multi-tiered clauses in Korea are 'mostly encountered in contracts involving stakeholders, including construction contracts and contracts involving state entities'.[36] Korea must continue to make progress towards making private mediation a more attractive option for parties engaged in cross-border deals. Towards this end, Korea did make the promising move of becoming one of the original signatories to the Singapore Mediation Convention, but much remains to be done, such as enacting a broad-based general mediation statute. As a general

---

[35] Cosmo Sanderson, 'South Korea Averts Treaty Claim over Island Resort' (*Global Arbitration Review*, 9 July 2020) <https://globalarbitrationreview.com/article/1228592/south-korea-averts-treaty-claim-over-island-resort> accessed 17 August 2020.

[36] John P Bang, 'South Korea' in Frederick A Acomb and others (eds), *Multi-tiered Dispute Resolution Clauses* (IBA Litigation Committee 2015) 186.

matter, definitional issues related to multi-tiered dispute resolution processes such as arb-med, med-arb or arb-med-arb that plague the field in other jurisdictions also exist in Korea given the lack of experience and examples.

7.5.1 International Multi-tiered Dispute Resolution

In Korea's version of the annual 'Queen Mary Survey' that was conducted in 2017,[37] the questionnaire asked what method of dispute resolution respondents preferred for international transactions. The survey results (see Table 7.7) provide the closest snapshot of the state of affairs in Korea pertaining to multi-tiered dispute resolution. Notably, respondents to the survey proclaimed an overwhelming preference for adjudicative approaches with the top choice being arbitration, with 70 per cent preferring it, and 11 per cent preferring litigation. Among the industries surveyed, only the financial and insurance sector showed a preference for international litigation over international arbitration.

Most notably, for this chapter, in terms of multi-tiered ADR options, only 8 per cent of the respondents said that they preferred 'international arbitration and ADR', whereas 5 per cent preferred 'international litigation and ADR'. According to the survey organisers, these two categories were designed to cover multi-tiered dispute resolution. Only 3 per cent preferred mediation by itself. By industry, in terms of international dispute resolution, the energy and resource sector as well as the manufacturing,

Table 7.7 *Korea's ADR survey*

Categories	Responses	Percentage
International arbitration	52	70
International litigation	8	11
International arbitration and ADR	6	8
International litigation and ADR	4	5
Other	2	3
Mediation	2	3

Source: KCAB and SIDRC Survey 2017 (on file with the author), p 8.

---

[37] On file with the author.

science and technology sectors were where one of the multi-tiered resolution methods was most preferred. In contrast, the results of the 2015 Queen Mary Survey showed that 56 per cent of the respondents preferred international arbitration alone, 34 per cent preferred international arbitration with ADR, and only 5 per cent preferred mediation alone.[38] Some commentators remain more optimistic and believe that '[a]lthough so far it has been rarely used in Korea, multi-tiered dispute resolution is slowly emerging in Korean companies' contracts'.[39]

Although not reflected in the survey, it is commonplace for Korean companies in the construction sector entering into overseas contracts to use the internationally established FIDIC contracts that provide for a Dispute Adjudication Board before arbitration.[40] In the cross-border context, this clearly represents the most active sector where multi-tiered dispute resolution is widely used.

7.5.2 Domestic Multi-tiered Dispute Resolution

Under the KCAB's current Domestic Arbitration Rules (2016), Article 38 provides that a party may at any time during the arbitration proceedings apply for mediation under the KCAB's Mediation Rules concerning the entire dispute or a portion thereof. If the parties agree to pursue mediation, then the arbitration will be suspended and the mediator must be someone different from the arbitrator. Hence, Article 38 does not allow the parties to choose the same person for both mediation and arbitration.[41]

Unlike the SIAC-SIMC Arb-Med-Arb Protocol, for instance, the KCAB does not provide at present for such a structured multi-tiered process. As noted by some commentators, as a general matter 'arb-med-arb has yet to see wide incorporation in contracts among Korean parties,

---

[38] Queen Mary University of London and White & Case LLP, '2015 International Arbitration Survey:
Improvements and Innovations in International Arbitration' <www.arbitration.qmul.ac.uk/media/arbitration/docs/2015_International_Arbitration_Survey.pdf> accessed 2 April 2021, 5.

[39] White and Kim (n 24) 24.

[40] Saeyoun Kim and Youngji Kim, 'Management of Overseas Construction Claims in Preparation for International Arbitration' (2013) 22 Korean Forum on International Trade and Business Law 103.

[41] KCAB's pre-2016 Domestic Arbitration Rules provided in art 18 that if the parties mutually agreed then the parties could refer a case to conciliation before the arbitration. Art 18 then provided that the KCAB Secretariat would appoint one to three conciliators. If the conciliation succeeded, then the conciliator would be deemed the arbitrator appointed by the parties and the settlement would be considered a consent award.

and it will take more time to raise awareness about the efficiency of such clauses'.[42] At the same time, nothing prevents the parties from agreeing to such a procedure while choosing the KCAB's mediation and arbitration rules for the mediation and arbitration processes, respectively, or designing their own arb-med-arb, med-arb or arb-med process. Notably, the KCAB's International Rules do not contain a similar provision concerning mediation or the prospects of multi-tiered dispute resolution.

Among domestic disputes, one example of multi-tiered dispute resolution can be found in the construction industry. The Construction Dispute Conciliation Committee was created under the auspices of the Minister of Land, Infrastructure and Transportation in 2014.[43] The Committee handled eight cases in 2016, and eight cases from July 2018 to June 2019.[44] The statute-based scheme provides first for negotiation, then mediation through the Committee or arbitration, then court litigation or arbitration.

7.5.3 General Matters

The enforceability of multi-tier dispute resolution clauses has not been robustly tested in Korea. The judicial treatment and the consequent enforcement issues remain uncertain. At present, no reported court cases could be found that have considered the enforceability of such clauses.[45]

The closest examples would be the judicial treatment of optional clauses that provide an option for mediation or arbitration.[46] A host of Supreme Court cases have delved into the enforceability of optional clauses. The Supreme Court has held that such clauses are not enforceable by themselves unless the parties subsequently agree upon one of the options.

In light of this, the key factors in a multi-tiered clause would be when does negotiation end, when does mediation end, and when is arbitration triggered? As White and Kim note, enforceability will depend upon whether the clause '(i) clearly requires mandatory negotiation or mediation as a condition precedent to arbitration or litigation, (ii) sets forth in detail the tier(s) of dispute resolution that must precede arbitration or

---

[42] John P Bang, Julia Jiyeon Yu and Umaer Khalil, 'The Current State of ADR in Korea' (2017) 72 Dispute Resolution Journal 27, 27, 32.
[43] Korean Framework Act on the Construction Industry.
[44] Minister of Land, Infrastructure and Transportation Report on Status and Activities of Committees, 31 December 2016, 33; Minister of Land, Infrastructure and Transportation Report on Status and Activities of Committees, 30 June 2019, 28.
[45] White and Kim (n 24) 25; Bang (n 36) 191.
[46] Joongi Kim, *International Arbitration in Korea* (Oxford University Press 2017) 64–88.

litigation, and (iii) sets forth the scope of disputes subject to the initial tier(s) of dispute resolution'.[47]

In terms of confidentiality, judicial mediation under JCCDA is subject to confidentiality and may not be invoked in subsequent litigation.[48] Given the lack of a general mediation statute, however, there are no comparable provisions for private mediation.

7.6 Conclusions

With the growth of its economy, Korea has become a leading user of various forms of resolution for its cross-border disputes. The use of adjudicative approaches such as litigation or arbitration, relative to non-adjudicative approaches such as negotiation and mediation to resolve disputes, remains the preference in Korea. The most preferred means has become international commercial arbitration, and, more recently, the use of investment arbitration has significantly increased. Other means of dispute resolution that combine mediation are gradually gaining currency and becoming more acceptable. Court-annexed arbitration that is referred to non-judicial institutions and other forms of institutional mediation has increased. Yet, private mediation and other options that are based on it, such as multi-tiered dispute resolution generally, remain under-utilised. The reasons for this appear to be manifold.

Some suggest that structural, environmental and capacity restraints have contributed to this state of affairs. Korea does not have an overarching law for private mediation. Instead, judicial mediation largely driven by the judiciary and administrative mediation that is primarily statute-based are the most frequently used forms of mediation. Legislative and regulatory reforms to promote the infrastructure for mediation should help, as was the case for arbitration in its early years.

Although questioned by many, others suggest that, from a socio-cultural perspective, Koreans prefer a more winner-takes-all attitude. A general lack of awareness due to lack of education, experience and expertise may be another issue. Given the sophistication of the Korean economy, it makes economic sense that Korean businesses should seek a more diverse range of dispute resolution options that utilise non-adjudicative approaches such as mediation and multi-tiered clauses. Some experts stress the need to focus more on 'facilitative process' as

---

[47] White and Kim (n 24) 25.
[48] Judicial Conciliation of Civil Disputes Act, art 23.

opposed to its 'currently highly evaluative system'.[49] The future for market-based solutions that utilise such means as multi-tiered clauses remains bright in the medium to long-term future of Korea's dispute resolution landscape. Whether the Singapore Mediation Convention can serve as a catalyst for change remains to be seen.

---

[49] White and Kim (n 24) 26.

8

Combinations of Mediation and Arbitration

The Singapore Perspective

MAN YIP

8.1 Introduction

In recent years, Singapore has been actively rethinking and reworking 'access to justice', with a strong focus on creating new options for dispute resolution and promoting the awareness of these options. The creation of the Singapore International Commercial Court in 2015 and the launch of the SIAC Investment Arbitration Rules in 2017 are testaments to Singapore's innovation through hybridisation of conventional dispute resolution mechanisms. Singapore's promotion of consensual resolution mechanisms saw the establishment of the Singapore International Mediation Centre (SIMC) and the Singapore International Mediation Institute (SIMI) in 2014, as well as its active support for the 2019 United Nations Convention on International Settlement Agreements Resulting from Mediation (the 'Singapore Convention on Mediation') which was signed in Singapore in August 2019.

Against this background, this chapter examines the judicial, regulatory and institutional support in Singapore for the twinning of mediation and arbitration as a form of multi-tier dispute resolution mechanism for commercial disputes. It is a hybrid approach that draws upon 'the strengths of both adversarial and consensual dispute resolution'.[1] In particular, this chapter critically analyses the SIMC-SIAC Arb-Med-Arb Protocol (the 'AMA Protocol'). Section 8.2 considers the enforcement of multi-tier dispute resolution clauses. Section 8.3 examines the statutory support for the arbitration-mediation dispute resolution approach and potential issues that require further attention. Section 8.4

---

[1] Vijaya Kumar Rajah, 'W(h)ither Adversarial Commercial Dispute Resolution?' (2017) 33 Arbitration International 17, 33.

critically analyses the AMA Protocol, which is Singapore's contribution towards improving the arb-med-arb mechanism.

8.2 Enforcement

The Queen Mary University of London and White & Case LLP 2018 International Arbitration Survey ('QMUL Survey 2018') findings reveal that 'there has been a significant increase in the combination of arbitration with ADR'.[2] Nearly half of the participants[3] to the 2018 survey preferred the hybrid approach, as compared to just 35 per cent in the 2015 survey findings.[4] This is unsurprising in view of the benefits of using mediation as a prerequisite to starting arbitration.[5] The mediation step allows for a 'cooling-off' period for parties, thereby avoiding the escalation of disputes for adversarial resolution as an immediate recourse.[6] It also has a filtering effect: only the 'truly' contentious issues in dispute proceed for resolution by arbitration.[7] Overall, thus, the mediation prerequisite increases the prospects of preserving the parties' commercial relationship. Indeed, the QMUL Survey 2018 findings support the general dispute-avoidance mentality of business parties. Within the in-house counsel sub-group, it is reported that there is 'a clear preference' for the twinning of international arbitration and alternative dispute resolution (ADR) (60 per cent) over international arbitration as a stand-alone mechanism.[8]

The enforceability of multi-tier dispute resolution clauses is thus a crucial consideration for business parties in deciding the precise dispute resolution mechanism. In the past, there was some uncertainty as to the enforceability of multi-tier dispute resolution clauses under Singapore law, by reason of the common perception that clauses requiring parties to

---

[2] Queen Mary University of London and White & Case LLP, *2018 International Arbitration Survey: The Evolution of International Arbitration* <www.arbitration.qmul.ac.uk/media/arbitration/docs/2018-International-Arbitration-Survey-The-Evolution-of-International-Arbitration-(2).PDF> accessed 2 February 2020, 5.
[3] Of the respondents to the survey, 25 per cent were from the Asia Pacific region: ibid 41.
[4] Queen Mary University of London and White & Case LLP (n 2) 5.
[5] Constance Castres Saint-Martin, 'Arb-med-arb Service in Singapore International Mediation Centre: A Hotfix to the Pitfalls of Multi-tiered Clauses' [2015] Asian Journal of Mediation 35, 37.
[6] Craig Tevendale, Hannah Ambrose and Vanessa Naish, 'Multi-tier Dispute Resolution Clauses and Arbitration' (2015) 1 Turkish Commercial Law Review 31, 33.
[7] ibid.
[8] Queen Mary University of London and White & Case LLP (n 2) 5.

negotiate in good faith were not enforceable.[9] For some time, the concerns of uncertainty and repugnancy towards the nature of adversarial dispute resolution – which were raised in respect of agreements to negotiate in good faith – had been extended to agreements to mediate as mediation was viewed as a form of assisted negotiation.[10] However, efforts to distinguish an agreement to mediate from an agreement to negotiate in good faith prevailed. In *Cable & Wireless plc v IBM United Kingdom Ltd*,[11] the English High Court held that an agreement to mediate was enforceable. More significantly, in *HSBC Institutional Trust Services (Singapore) Ltd v Toshin Development Singapore Pte Ltd*, the Singapore Court of Appeal refined the law by holding that a clause to negotiate in good faith, which is sufficiently certain, is valid and enforceable.[12] The Court stressed that the law should uphold commercial parties' *choice* of a particular form of dispute resolution[13] and rejected drawing a distinction between a 'negotiate in good faith' agreement and a mediation agreement.[14] It affirmed that such clauses 'promote consensus and conciliation in lieu of adversarial dispute resolution, values which the Singapore legal system should promote'.[15]

More recent developments clearly indicate that multi-tier dispute resolution clauses of different designs are generally enforceable under Singapore law.[16] Such a development is in line with the prioritisation of party autonomy in dispute resolution under Singapore law, as well as the active promotion of ADR in Singapore in recent years. The landmark decision was *International Research Corp plc v Lufthansa Systems Asia Pacific Pte Ltd*.[17] The case concerned a multi-tier mediation-arbitration

---

[9] *Walford v Miles* [1992] 2 AC 128, which was followed in Singapore: *United Artists Singapore Theatre Pte Ltd v Parkway Properties Pte Ltd* [2003] 1 SLR(R) 202; *Grossner Jens v Raffles Holdings Ltd* [2004] 1 SLR(R) 202; *Sundercan Ltd v Salzman Anthony David* [2010] SGHC 92.

[10] Joel Lee, 'Agreements to Negotiate in Good Faith' [2013] Singapore Journal of Legal Studies 212.

[11] [2002] EWHC 2059 (Comm), [2002] 2 All ER (Comm) 1041.

[12] [2012] 4 SLR 738 (the case concerned a multi-tier rent review mechanism contained in a lease agreement).

[13] ibid [45].

[14] ibid [43].

[15] ibid [45].

[16] See George M Vlavianos and Vasilis FL Pappas, 'Multi-tier Dispute Resolution Clauses as Jurisdictional Conditions Precedent to Arbitration' in J William Rowley, Doak Bishop and Gordon Kaiser (eds), *The Guide to Energy Arbitrations* (2nd edn, Law Business Research 2017).

[17] [2014] 1 SLR 130 ('*Lufthansa*').

dispute resolution mechanism. The pre-arbitral mediation mechanism involved a number of steps that progressively escalate the dispute for mediation by the more senior ranks of the respondent's management and the designated personnel of the counterparty. Disputes which could not be settled by mediation[18] were to be resolved by arbitration.

The *Lufthansa* decision clarified two crucial aspects of enforceability of multi-tier dispute resolution clauses. First, are such clauses generally enforceable from the perspective of certainty? On this question, the Court of Appeal agreed with the lower court's ruling that the preconditions for arbitration were certain and enforceable, noting the clear and mandatory language and the specificity as to the personnel involved in each pre-arbitral step.[19] The lack of specification as to the time frame or rules for each pre-arbitral step did not render the clause uncertain.[20] Clearly, the Court of Appeal took a commercially sensible, as opposed to technical, approach in assessing certainty of dispute resolution clauses.[21]

The second issue is this: are the pre-arbitral steps conditions precedent to the commencement of arbitration? If the pre-arbitral steps constitute conditions precedent, the arbitral tribunal constituted without fully complying with these steps and any resultant ruling would be subject to a jurisdictional challenge. In *Lufthansa*, the Court of Appeal was of the view that the pre-arbitral steps, in the form that they were drafted, were conditions precedent to the submission of disputes for arbitration.[22] The arbitration clause clearly specified that only 'disputes which cannot be settled by mediation pursuant to Clause 37.2, shall be finally settled by arbitration ...'.[23] The Court further affirmed that, in the absence of waiver, specific procedures prescribed as conditions precedent to arbitration or litigation must be fully complied with.[24] Disagreeing with the lower court, it held that the pre-arbitral steps had not been satisfied by the mere convening of '*some* meetings between *some* people in their respective organisations discussing *some* variety of matters'.[25] The decision

---

[18] The pre-arbitral steps were described as 'mediation' by the parties in their agreement.
[19] *Lufthansa* (n 17) [54].
[20] The specification of deadlines and time limits would, however, increase the chances of enforcement: see Lawrence Teh, 'Singapore' in Frederick A Acomb and others (eds), *Multi-tiered Dispute Resolution Clauses* (IBA Litigation Committee 2015) 172.
[21] Seng Onn Loong and Deborah Koh, 'Enforceability of Dispute Resolution Clauses in Singapore' [2016] Asian Journal of Mediation 51, 59.
[22] *Lufthansa* (n 17) [54].
[23] ibid [7], [54].
[24] ibid [62].
[25] ibid.

would thus assure the commercial parties that Singapore courts would hold parties to their agreement.

Lufthansa was followed in the subsequent case of *PT Selecta Bestama v Sin Huat Huat Marine Transportation Pte Ltd*,[26] which contains the following dispute resolution clause:

> Save for the matters set out in [the following] paragraph [concerning disputes over the quality of materials or workmanship], all disputes arising in connection with this contract including but not limited to the validity, the interpretation or the execution of this contract shall be settled amicably by negotiation. In case no settlement can be reached the parties hereto agree to submit all such disputes to the Governing Jurisdiction of the Courts Batam in Batam [*sic*].

In *PT Selecta*, the defendant argued that the Singapore proceedings ought to be stayed as the parties' contract contained an exclusive jurisdiction clause in favour of Batam courts and the plaintiff failed to prove that the breach may be justified by exceptional circumstances amounting to 'strong cause'.[27] It was held that the obligation to negotiate is a condition precedent to the commencement of litigation in a Batam court.[28] As parties had yet to attempt negotiation in the case, the obligation to pursue litigation in a Batam court was not engaged and the 'strong cause' test was thus irrelevant at that stage.[29]

Further, Singapore courts view a multi-tier dispute resolution clause as a unitary dispute resolution mechanism, as opposed to comprising severable and distinct dispute resolution mechanisms. For clauses which incorporate arbitration as one of the dispute resolution steps, the judicial characterisation bears practical significance for a party's ability to invoke section 6 of the Arbitration Act[30] or section 6 of the International Arbitration Act[31] (as the case may be)[32] to ask for a stay of court

---

[26] [2015] SGHCR 16 ('*PT Selecta*') [53].

[27] As to the 'strong cause' test, see *Vinmar Overseas (Singapore) Pte Ltd v PTT International Trading Pte Ltd* [2018] 2 SLR 1271.

[28] *PT Selecta* (n 26) [51]–[52].

[29] ibid [55]. The defendant did not argue whether the plaintiff's commencement of court proceedings in Singapore amounted to a breach of the obligation to negotiate, thereby entitling the defendant to enforce the exclusive jurisdiction agreement (see ibid [56]).

[30] Arbitration Act 2001 (Cap 10).

[31] International Arbitration Act 2002 (Cap 143A).

[32] The Arbitration Act governs arbitrations where the place of arbitration is in Singapore and where Part II of the International Arbitration Act does not apply (see Arbitration Act, s 3). The International Arbitration Act governs international arbitrations and non-international arbitrations where parties have agreed in writing that Part II of the International Arbitration Act or the UNCITRAL Model Law on International

proceedings commenced by the other party in breach of the clause. On a unitary dispute resolution mechanism characterisation, the entire multi-tier dispute resolution clause will be treated as an arbitration agreement for the purposes of section 6 of the Arbitration Act[33] and section 6 of the International Arbitration Act.[34] As such, the innocent party may ask for a stay of court proceedings that were commenced without first attempting the pre-arbitral steps such that the arbitration agreement is not engaged. This is an eminently sensible approach as the relevant legislative provisions aid in the enforcement, albeit in an indirect way, of the multi-tier dispute resolution clause. Putting enforcement considerations aside, the unitary dispute resolution mechanism view is also consistent with the reality of combined processes. As will be discussed in Sections 8.3 and 8.4, the combination of two processes inevitably means that the features of the separate processes are adapted and sometimes lost. In other words, the combined process is a different mechanism, and not the sum of the separate processes.

Relevantly, the Mediation Act 2017 further bolsters the enforcement of an agreement to mediate disputes by providing that the courts have a power to stay court proceedings commenced in breach of a mediation agreement.[35] This statutory power applies in respect of a dispute falling within the scope of a 'mediation agreement' which is defined by the legislation as simply 'an agreement by 2 or more persons to refer the whole or part of a dispute which has arisen, or which may arise, between them for mediation'.[36] Accordingly, this power may be invoked in a case where mediation is the pre-arbitral step in a multi-tier dispute resolution clause and one party has commenced court proceedings in breach of the agreed dispute resolution procedures.[37]

8.3 Regulatory and Institutional Support

The pro-enforcement attitude of the courts goes hand-in-hand with the strong regulatory and institutional support of multi-tier dispute resolution,

---

Commercial Arbitration 1985 shall apply to their arbitration (see International Arbitration Act, s 5).
[33] *Ling Kong Henry v Tanglin Club* [2018] SGHC 153.
[34] *Heartonics Corporation v EPI Life Pte Ltd* [2017] SGHCR 17 [80].
[35] Mediation Act 2017, s 8.
[36] ibid, s 4.
[37] Mediation Act 2017 applies only to 'a mediation that is wholly or partly conducted in Singapore' or where the agreement stipulates that the Mediation Act 2017 or Singapore law applies to the mediation (see s 6).

to which we now turn. We commence our analysis by tracing the rise of ADR[38] in Singapore, for this forms the foundation for the support of multi-tier dispute resolution mechanisms.

8.3.1 The Rise of ADR

The Singapore judicial system embraces the vision of 'a multi-door courthouse'[39] through the incorporation of various forms of ADR since 1994. Numerous seminal developments on mediation in Singapore legal practice are worth highlighting:[40]

- Court-based mediation was first implemented in the Subordinate Courts (which have now been renamed the State Courts) in 1994.
- In 1997, the Singapore Mediation Centre, which focused on private commercial mediation, was established.
- In 1998, the Community Mediation Centres were set up by the Ministry of Law to provide mediation for disputes arising between relatives, friends and neighbours.
- In 2011, the option of neutral evaluation – a process of assessing parties' legal rights by a neutral third party – was made available for all civil cases.[41]
- In 2013, mediation and counselling had been made mandatory for divorce cases involving parents with children under fourteen years of age.
- In 2014, the SIMC and the SIMI were established. The SIMC was set up to provide world-class mediation services for transnational commercial disputes, particularly those arising from business operations in Asia. The SIMI, on the other hand, is a professional standards body which offers a mediator credentialling scheme.
- From 2015, parties involved in matters falling under the Protection from Harassment Act and the Community Disputes Resolution Act 2015 may be referred for mediation, with or without their consent.

---

[38] In this chapter, 'ADR' shall refer to any means of non-litigation dispute resolution process, including mediation, neutral evaluation, conciliation and arbitration.
[39] Frank EA Sander, 'Varieties of Dispute Resolution' (1976) 70 FRD 111; Leo A Levin and Russell R Wheeler, *The Pound Conference: Perspectives on Justice in the Future* (West Publishing 1979).
[40] See also George Lim and Eunice Chua, 'Development of Mediation in Singapore' in Danny McFadden and George Lim (eds), *Mediation in Singapore: A Practical Guide* (2nd edn, Sweet & Maxwell 2017), ch 1; Andrew Phang, 'Mediation and the Courts – The Singapore Experience' [2017] Asian Journal of Mediation 14.
[41] Dorcas Quek Anderson and Chi Ling Seah, 'Finding the Appropriate Mode of Dispute Resolution: Introducing Neutral Evaluation in Subordinate Courts' (2011) Law Gazette 21.

8 COMBINATIONS OF MEDIATION AND ARBITRATION

- The Mediation Act 2017, a legislative framework for commercial mediation, came into force on 1 November 2017.[42] It contains four salient provisions: power of court to stay court proceedings pending the completion of mediation;[43] enforceability of mediated settlement agreements;[44] confidentiality and admissibility of mediation communications;[45] and applicability of exceptions under the Legal Profession Act (applicable to arbitration) to mediation.[46]

From this summary of seminal developments, it is clear that Singapore law promotes the use of mediation for resolving both commercial and non-commercial disputes.[47] In respect of commercial disputes, which forms the focus of this chapter, it would be unrealistic to expect that all disputes will be resolved amicably through ADR. Moreover, the enforceability of mediated settlement agreements, although enhanced to some degree by the Mediation Act 2017,[48] is still much more limited as compared with the degree of enforceability of arbitral awards under the New York Convention.[49] Save for mediated settlements that are reached in a mediation following the commencement of arbitration (and can be recorded in a consent award), mediated settlements are generally enforced as an agreement. The enforcement of such agreements overseas can be costly and time-consuming. Whilst the Singapore Convention on Mediation[50] mitigates some of these difficulties, it should not be missed that the Convention only applies to international commercial disputes. It also excludes settlement agreements that have been approved by a court or have been concluded in court proceedings, and are enforceable as a judgment in the state of the issuing court, as well as mediation agreements that have been recorded

---

[42] See Dorcas Quek Anderson, 'Comment: A Coming of Age for Mediation in Singapore?: Mediation Act 2016' (2017) 29 Singapore Academy of Law Journal 275.
[43] Mediation Act 2017, s 8.
[44] ibid, s 12 (recording of mediated settlement agreement as order of court).
[45] ibid, s 9 (restrictions on disclosure) and s 10 (admissibility of mediation communication in evidence).
[46] ibid, s 17.
[47] See, generally, Siyuan Chen and Eunice Chua, 'Singapore Civil Procedure' in Piet Taleman (ed), *International Encyclopedia of Laws* (3rd edn, Kluwer Law and Business International 2018).
[48] On conditions for the conversion of a mediated settlement into a court order under s 12 of the Mediation Act 2017, see Anderson (n 42) 287-88.
[49] In full, the 1958 United Nations Convention on the Recognition and Enforcement of Foreign Arbitral Awards. More than 150 countries are signed up to the New York Convention.
[50] At the time of writing, there are fifty-two signatories to the Convention.

and are enforceable as an arbitral award.[51] Moreover, there are uncertainties as to enforcement under the Convention.[52] With Qatar ratifying the Convention on 25 February 2020, following Singapore and Fiji, the Convention has come into force on 12 September 2020. It remains to be seen how popular this instrument will be going forward and whether the uncertainties can be satisfactorily resolved in the near future. Accordingly, it may still be prudent and sensible to combine mediation with arbitration in the dispute resolution clause, as opposed to relying on mediation alone, for some time to come. Relying on adversarial forms of dispute resolution alone (such as arbitration and litigation), on the other hand, ensures that an outcome would be reached in every case, but it does not facilitate the preservation of the parties' commercial relationship.[53]

In former Attorney-General VK Rajah, SC's words, thus, 'the future belongs to hybrid dispute resolution mechanisms which marry both adversarial and consensual forums'.[54] Accordingly, Singapore's promotion of ADR for the resolution of commercial disputes is carried out in conjunction with the promotion of multi-tier dispute resolution mechanisms. In Section 8.3.2, we turn to consider regulatory support for the hybrid dispute resolution mechanism that combines mediation and arbitration under Singapore law.

8.3.2 Regulatory Support

Both the Arbitration Act and the International Arbitration Act envisage that disputes may be resolved through the twinning of mediation and arbitration and provide support for the implementation of the procedures. Express legislative provision for mediation[55] appears 'unusual'

---

[51] Singapore Convention on Mediation, art 1(3).
[52] See Norton Rose Fulbright, 'The Singapore Mediation Convention: An Update on Developments in Enforcing Mediated Settlement Agreements' <www.nortonrosefulbright.com/en/knowledge/publications/b5906716/the-singapore-mediation-convention> accessed 14 August 2020.
[53] Bobette Wolski, 'ARB-MED-ARB (and MSAs): A Whole Which Is Less Than, Not Greater Than, the Sum of Its Parts' (2013) 6(2) Contemporary Asia Arbitration Journal 249, 258.
[54] Rajah (n 1) 32.
[55] The International Arbitration Act uses the terminology of 'conciliator' and 'conciliation', which are defined under s 16(5) to include reference to a mediator and mediation proceedings, respectively. The Arbitration Act uses the language of 'mediator' and 'mediation proceedings', which are defined under s 16(4) to include reference to a 'conciliator' and 'conciliation proceedings', respectively.

8 COMBINATIONS OF MEDIATION AND ARBITRATION

because mediation and like processes are considered 'purely voluntary' in other jurisdictions and are generally left up to the parties' own agreement or arrangements.[56] However, these legislative provisions are helpful in practice as they operate as 'gap-fillers' and/or clarification on the effect of such a hybrid mechanism. We now examine these provisions in detail.

First, both legislations provide for a mechanism to appoint a mediator in the event that the appointing party designated by the agreement 'refuses to make the appointment or does not make it within the time specified in the agreement or, if no time is so specified, within a reasonable time of being requested by any party to the agreement to make the appointment'.[57] Under the International Arbitration Act, the President of the Court of Arbitration of the Singapore International Arbitration Centre (SIAC) is given the power to appoint the mediator, on the application of any party to the said agreement. Similarly, under the Arbitration Act, the Chairman of the Singapore Mediation Centre may make the appointment in such circumstances.

Second, both the Arbitration Act and the International Arbitration Act, in identical language, prescribe default timelines for the conduct of the mediation.[58] These provisions ensure that the mediation agreement can be implemented in practice and help to overcome any issue of uncertainty with provisions that fail to provide for specific timelines.

Third, section 37 of the Arbitration Act and section 18 of the International Arbitration Act (referring to Article 30 of the UNCITRAL Model Law on International Commercial Arbitration 1985) provide that if the parties settle their dispute during the arbitral proceedings, the settlement agreement shall be recorded as a consent award by the arbitral tribunal, if so requested by the parties and not objected to by the arbitral tribunal.[59] For parties who choose SIAC arbitration, Article 32.10 of the SIAC Rules 2016 also makes clear that the arbitral tribunal 'may make a consent award recording the settlement' of the parties, if the parties so request.

Fourth, both legislations expressly allow for the appointment of the same person to act as both the mediator and the arbitrator.[60] Parties may agree to the same person acting as both mediator and arbitrator where

---

[56] Robert Merkin and Johanna Hjalmarsson, *Singapore Arbitration Legislation Annotated* (2nd edn, Informa Law 2016) 81.
[57] Arbitration Act, s 62(1); International Arbitration Act, s 16(1).
[58] Arbitration Act, s 62(4); International Arbitration Act, s 16(4).
[59] The provisions, on a literal reading, would not apply to a med-arb procedure as any settlement reached in the mediation phase is not reached in the course of an arbitration.
[60] Arbitration Act, s 62(4); International Arbitration Act, s 16(3).

mediation fails to help parties reach a settlement (the 'Same Person Model') on considerations of savings of time and costs because the mediator would not need to spend further time familiarising himself/ herself with the facts and issues when acting as arbitrator.[61] It is said that this model is particularly advantageous if parties are not confident that the pre-arbitral mediation will be successful.[62] However, the Same Person Model suffers from a number of shortcomings. As an arbitrator is better paid than a mediator, the third party who is to assume both roles sequentially is placed under a conflict of personal interest (of receiving more remuneration) and duty.[63] He/she might come under attack for not working as hard to bring both parties to a consensual settlement of their dispute out of the self-interest of wanting to receive more remuneration for his/her subsequent role as the arbitrator. Further, the conduct of the mediator (who later turned arbitrator) in the pre-arbitral mediation proceedings might give rise to allegations of procedural irregularities or other grounds (for example, apparent bias) to challenge the arbitral award or its enforcement.[64] Such complications/challenges do not arise in a model where different persons take on the roles of mediator and arbitrator.

Even if the mediator's conduct in the mediation proceedings is beyond reproach, there is a real risk that a mediator who has to then take on the function of an arbitrator may adjudicate the dispute under bias, having already formed his/her views as to the merits of the case based on the communications exchanged during the mediation proceedings or the parties' reasonableness in conduct.[65] Most crucially, parties may have divulged confidential information or made concessions in the course of the mediation proceedings on a 'without prejudice' basis – for example, during private meetings (caucus sessions)[66] – in hope of reaching an amicable settlement which did not ultimately materialise.[67] The information disclosed or the concessions made may operate to the disadvantage of the relevant party in the arbitral proceedings or increase the risk of bias

---

[61] Castres Saint-Martin (n 5) 39.
[62] ibid.
[63] ibid.
[64] See *Gao Haiyan v Keeneye Holdings Ltd* [2011] 3 HKC 157. The Hong Kong Court of First Instance found the conduct of the mediation proceedings by the mediator turned arbitrator to be irregular and concluded that the arbitral tribunal operated under apparent bias. The arbitral award was accordingly refused enforcement on the ground of public policy. This holding was reversed on appeal: [2012] 1 HKLRD 627.
[65] Castres Saint-Martin (n 5) 40.
[66] See Arbitration Act (n 30), s 63(2)(a); International Arbitration Act (n 31), s 17(2)(a).
[67] Merkin and Hjalmarsson (n 56) 82.

from the mediator-arbitrator. It cannot be assumed that the mediator-arbitrator can put aside the information that has been received in the mediation process when he/she is to take on the function of an arbitrator. In fact, cognitive psychology instructs that the contrary tends to happen.[68] Conversely, for fear of compromising their positions in the event of arbitration, parties may be unwilling to confide in the mediator who is to take on the function of the arbitrator subsequently, thereby diminishing the effectiveness of the mediation process.[69]

Such risks are more pronounced under Singapore law. Although the mediation communications are generally regarded as confidential,[70] both the Arbitration Act and the International Arbitration Act oblige the arbitrator, on the resumption of the arbitral proceedings, to divulge as much of the confidential information he or she received during the mediation proceedings to all parties to the arbitral proceedings as he or she considers material to the arbitration. In nearly identical language, section 63(3) of the Arbitration Act and section 17(3) of the International Arbitration Act provide:

> (3) Where confidential information is obtained by an arbitrator or umpire from a party to the arbitral proceedings during [mediation/conciliation] proceedings and those proceedings terminate without the parties reaching agreement in settlement of their dispute, the arbitrator or umpire shall before resuming the arbitral proceedings disclose to all other parties to the arbitral proceedings as much of that information as he considers material to the arbitral proceedings.

Clearly, the Singapore legislative model opts for transparency as a means of safeguarding against the risk of bias on the part of the arbitrator. It resurrects the norms of arbitrations: most notably, to ensure that information provided by one party will be communicated to the other party,[71] and that all parties to an arbitration have a right to be heard. Section 63(3) therefore ensures that all parties have a chance to respond to communications made in the mediation process that may potentially influence the arbitrator's decision-making process in the arbitration. Yet, this may diminish the utility of the mediation step for

---

[68] Ellen E Deason, 'Combinations of Mediation and Arbitration with the Same Neutral: A Framework for Judicial Review' (2013) 5 Yearbook on Arbitration and Mediation 219, 220.
[69] Castres Saint-Martin (n 5) 40.
[70] Arbitration Act (n 30), s 63(2)(b); International Arbitration Act (n 31), s 17(2)(b).
[71] Arbitration Act (n 30), s 63(3) essentially overrides the effect of private sessions that took place during mediation. See IBA Rules of Ethics for International Arbitrators, r 5.3.

defensive parties. It may also be that parties in mediation, being aware of the full disclosure to follow in the arbitral process, feel compelled to settle. As such, parties, in opting for a multi-tiered clause that combines mediation and arbitration, need to balance the risks against the benefits of adopting the Same Person Model. Parties should also carefully consider their selection of a professional to act as both the mediator and the arbitrator. The two roles require very different skill sets and not everyone is able to discharge both functions with competence.[72] More broadly, the foregoing analysis reveals that the combination of both mediation and arbitration does not always lead to the best of both worlds with no downsides. Hence, tactically, given the inherent limitations of the pre-arbitral mediation phase, some parties may use the mediation process to improve their chances of success in arbitration, by using the process to 'shape the views of the person who will become the ultimate fact finder'[73] or flush out the counterparty's position.

Of course, parties may choose to agree on the appointment of different persons to take on the functions of mediator and arbitrator. Such a model would be more costly and time-consuming but may better preserve, though not in entirety, the key advantageous features of both processes. In Section 8.4, we turn to look at the AMA Protocol, which generally appoints different persons for the two processes. Through a close scrutiny of this initiative, we explore in greater depth the difficulties that may arise with multi-tier dispute resolution mechanisms.

8.4 The AMA Protocol

On 5 November 2014, the SIAC and the SIMC jointly launched the AMA Protocol,[74] a three-stage mechanism that seeks to overcome or avoid the problems that commonly arise in the combined process of mediation and arbitration, including the ones discussed in Section 8.3.2. To summarise, at the first stage, the parties' dispute is submitted for arbitration before the SIAC. An arbitral tribunal is constituted. At the second stage, the arbitral tribunal orders a stay of the arbitration and the case is referred to mediation at the SIMC (within a prescribed eight-week mediation

---

[72] Deason (n 68) 224, 228–29.
[73] ibid 224.
[74] Singapore International Mediation Centre, 'SIAC-SIMC Arb-Med-Arb Protocol' <http://simc.com.sg/v2/wp-content/uploads/2019/03/SIAC-SIMC-AMA-Protocol.pdf> accessed 2 February 2020.

window)[75] pursuant to the SIMC Mediation Rules. At the final stage, as a general description, arbitration is resumed and the arbitral tribunal makes an award. But what precisely happens at this final stage depends on the outcome of the mediation at the second stage. If the mediation successfully led to a settlement, then the parties may ask the arbitral tribunal to record their settlement in a consent award at the final stage. If the mediation was unsuccessful, the parties settle the dispute through arbitration at the final stage.

8.4.1   Core Features of the AMA Protocol

The parties may agree to the application of the AMA Protocol at any time: in their contract, after the dispute has arisen or after arbitration has commenced. There are a number of key advantages of the AMA Protocol. First, the AMA Protocol lays down more specific procedures than the pre-existing med-arb or arb-med-arb processes which generally leave parties to determine for themselves the applicable timelines and procedures.[76]

Second, the arb-med-arb three-stage process ensures that the settlement agreement at the conclusion of a successful mediation can be recorded as a consent award and is enforceable under the New York Convention. The alternative multi-tier mechanism that begins with mediation and continues with arbitration poses two problems for the enforceability of the settlement agreement as a consent award.[77] Where the dispute has been settled by mediation, technically, there is no dispute between the parties to be submitted to arbitration.[78] In other words, the tribunal lacks jurisdiction to act. The lack of a dispute raises a separate question as to whether an award made on the basis of a mediated settlement agreement concluded before the commencement

---

[75] This period may be extended by the Registrar of the SIAC in consultation with the SIMC: see ibid, para 6.

[76] Alastair Henderson and Emmanuel Chua, 'Singapore International Mediation Centre Is Launched, Offering Parties an "Arb-med-arb" Process in Partnership with SIAC' (*Herbert Smith Freehills*, 11 December 2014) <https://hsfnotes.com/arbitration/tag/ama-protocol/> accessed 25 October 2018.

[77] See generally Yarik Kryvoi, 'Enforcement of Settlement Agreements Reached in Arbitration and Mediation' (*Kluwer Arbitration Blog*, 25 November 2015) <http://arbitrationblog.kluwerarbitration.com/2015/11/25/enforcement-of-settlement-agreements-reached-in-arbitration-and-mediation/> accessed 25 October 2018.

[78] Arbitration agreements typically stipulate that there must be a dispute between the parties in order that an arbitration may be commenced pursuant to the arbitration agreement.

of arbitration is enforceable under the New York Convention.[79] Article I(1) of the New York Convention provides that it applies to the recognition and enforcement of arbitral awards 'arising out of differences between persons, whether physical or legal'. If the dispute has been settled by mediation, there is no 'difference' of any kind between the parties. Where the arbitration is initiated before the commencement of mediation and stayed to enable the mediation to proceed as under the AMA Protocol, the aforesaid problems or uncertainties do not arise.[80]

Third, as the arbitral tribunal and mediator under the AMA Protocol are separately and independently appointed by the SIAC and the SIMC,[81] they are usually different persons, unless the parties agreed otherwise. As discussed in Section 8.3.2, this ensures greater impartiality on the part of the arbitral tribunal when the arbitration is resumed after an unsuccessful mediation as well as great effectiveness of the mediation process. It is also less likely that the arbitral award may be challenged in a setting-aside application or refused enforcement. Indeed, the mediation will be conducted in accordance with the SIMC rules on mediation,[82] thereby ensuring that the proceedings will abide by certain standards and be overseen by the SIMC. Of course, costs are likely to be higher for using different persons in the dispute resolution process.

8.4.2 Problems and Uncertainties

Notwithstanding the improved dispute resolution process under the AMA Protocol, uncertainties and problems remain. First, commentators have highlighted the silence of the AMA Protocol on the issue of jurisdictional objections.[83] This gives rise to uncertainty as to whether the

---

[79] See Christopher Boog, 'The New SIAC/SIMC AMA-Protocol: A Seamless Multi-tiered Dispute Resolution Process Tailored to the User's Needs' (*Singapore International Mediation Centre*, 14 April 2015) <http://simc.com.sg/the-new-siacsimc-ama-protocol-a-seamless-multi-tiered-dispute-resolution-process-tailored-to-the-users-needs/> accessed 25 October 2018.

[80] There is a question to be investigated, as a matter of principle, which is whether the technical differences between the two forms of multi-tier dispute resolution mechanisms should lead to differences in enforceability. See Wolski (n 53) 269. But we may prescind from this question now.

[81] 'SIAC-SIMC Arb-Med-Arb Protocol' (n 74), cls 4–5.

[82] See Singapore International Mediation Centre, 'Mediation Rules' <http://simc.com.sg/mediation-rules/> accessed 25 October 2018.

[83] Paul Tan and Kevin Tan, 'Kinks in the SIAC-SIMC Arb-Med-Arb Protocol' (*Law Gazette*, January 2018) <https://lawgazette.com.sg/feature/kinks-in-the-siac-simc-arb-med-arb-protocol/> accessed 14 August 2020.

8 COMBINATIONS OF MEDIATION AND ARBITRATION

objections should be raised pre-mediation or post-mediation. It has been pointed out that the AMA Protocol seems to assume that the arbitral tribunal has jurisdiction and requires a mandatory stay of arbitration after the filing of the Notice of Arbitration with the SIAC.[84] This reading is supported by clause 5 of the AMA Protocol:

> The Tribunal shall, after the exchange of the Notice of Arbitration and Response to the Notice of Arbitration, stay the arbitration and inform the Registrar of SIAC that the case can be submitted for mediation at SIMC. The Registrar of SIAC will send the case file with all documents lodged by the parties to SIMC for mediation at SIMC. Upon SIMC's receipt of the case file, SIMC will inform the Registrar of SIAC of the commencement of mediation at SIMC (the 'Mediation Commencement Date') pursuant to the SIMC Mediation Rules. All subsequent steps in the arbitration shall be stayed pending the outcome of mediation at SIMC.

Commentators thus suggest that the AMA Protocol, on balance, envisages that any jurisdictional objections will be raised post-mediation. This is, however, far from satisfactory. Parties may be less committed to reaching an amicable settlement during the mediation proceedings[85] if they are concurrently concerned with the jurisdiction of the tribunal and the possibility that their settlement agreement, even if reached, may not be recorded in a consent award.[86] In an article published on the SIMC website, but addressing a different issue, it is suggested that although the AMA Protocol 'does not expressly stipulate the extent to which parties are free to deviate from the standard process', '[i]t can ... be expected that party autonomy will be given precedence'.[87] The general force of the suggestion lends support to the argument that parties are given some flexibility to deviate from the standard process. However, the article is not a legally binding authority. It also does not discuss the issue of the extent to which party autonomy – and therefore deviation from the AMA Protocol – will be 'given precedence'.

Second, the AMA Protocol does not expressly provide for application for interim relief, for example, an order to preserve evidence or a freezing order. Relevantly, it is unclear whether parties may apply for such relief post-stay of arbitration, pending the conclusion of mediation. Where urgent relief is required, one 'less than ideal' solution is to terminate the

---
[84] ibid.
[85] Parties may refuse to participate in the mediation and even attempt to derail any mediation proceedings on the basis of jurisdictional objections.
[86] Tan and Tan (n 83).
[87] Boog (n 79).

mediation proceedings pursuant to clause 7 of the AMA Protocol to allow for the resumption of the arbitration.[88] An alternative solution,[89] which is less drastic but rather uncertain, is to apply to the court for interim relief pursuant to section 12A(6) of the International Arbitration Act. By way of background, section 12A of the International Arbitration Act extends to the Singapore High Court 'the powers that are conferred on an arbitral tribunal' to make the interim measures set out in sections 12(1)(c) to 12(1)(i) in connection with arbitral proceedings,[90] whether the arbitration is held in Singapore or abroad.[91] Exercise of the aforesaid powers is subject to sections 12A(3)–(6):

> (3) The High Court or a Judge thereof may refuse to make an order under subsection (2) if, in the opinion of the High Court or Judge, the fact that the place of arbitration is outside Singapore or likely to be outside Singapore when it is designated or determined makes it appropriate to make such order.
> (4) **If the case is one of urgency**, the High Court or Judge thereof may, on the application of a party or proposed party to the arbitral proceedings, make such orders under subsection (2) as the High Court or Judge thinks necessary for the purpose of preserving evidence or assets.
> (5) **If the case is not one of urgency**, the High Court or Judge thereof shall make an order under subsection (2) only on the application of a party to the arbitral proceedings (upon notice to the other parties and to the arbitral tribunal) made with the permission of the arbitral tribunal or the agreement in writing of the other parties.
> (6) **In every case**, the High Court or a Judge thereof shall make an order under subsection (2) only if or to the extent that the **arbitral tribunal**, and any arbitral or other institution or person vested by the parties with power in that regard, **has no power or is unable for the time being to act effectively**. (emphasis added)

If the application for interim measures from the Singapore High Court is 'not one of urgency' as falling under section 12A(5), the High Court may make such orders sought only where notice has been given to the other parties and the arbitral tribunal and where the arbitral tribunal's permission and the other parties' agreement in writing have been obtained. Importantly, whether the case is one of urgency or not, section

---

[88] Boog (n 79); Tan and Tan (n 83).
[89] Tan and Tan (n 83).
[90] *Maldives Airports Co Ltd v GMR Malé International Airport Pte Ltd* [2013] 2 SLR 449 [33].
[91] International Arbitration Act (n 31), s 12A(1)(b).

12A(6) imposes a threshold jurisdictional requirement on the order of interim measures by the Singapore High Court. For the purpose of our discussion, thus, the question is: can it be said in a stage 2 situation of the AMA Protocol that the arbitral tribunal 'has no power or is unable for the time being to act effectively' simply by reason of the stay of arbitration to allow a 'mediation window'? Commentators have observed that the provision for the appointment of an emergency arbitrator under the SIAC Rules[92] is likely to 'cut out pre-arbitration applications in most cases'.[93] By parity of reasoning, can it be said that the availability of clause 7 in the AMA Protocol to enable the premature termination of the mediation proceedings so that arbitration may resume would similarly cut out the necessity of section 12A applications? The clause 7 solution is more drastic and is therefore an inexact parallel to the appointment of an emergency arbitrator under the SIAC Rules. The idea is, however, very similar – it is possible for the arbitral tribunal to act in the circumstances. The more important point is that the lack of clarity on application for interim relief under the AMA Protocol is unsatisfactory. However, it has been pointed out that this aspect of uncertainty is unlikely to be a great cause for concern in practice because 'most mediations under the Protocol are completed within 1–2 days' and parties are thus unlikely to make applications for interim relief within 'that narrow window'.[94]

Third, arb-med-arb mechanisms – one of which being the AMA Protocol – have been criticised for not preserving the core features of both mediation and arbitration.[95] In particular, the features of party autonomy and the concomitant procedural flexibility inherent in arbitration do not appear to be explicitly taken into consideration in the AMA Protocol. One particular issue is the timing of the mediation process. If it takes place straight after the constitution of the arbitral tribunal, it is said that the parties enter mediation with their own, and often wildly different, perceptions of the justice of the case. They are less likely to reach settlement than if they have carefully thought through the merits of the case, for example, after they have completed written briefs.[96] This is the case for the AMA Protocol. However, it may be that the

---

[92] See Singapore International Arbitration Centre, 'SIAC Rules 2016' <https://siac.org.sg/our-rules/rules/siac-rules-2016> accessed 16 August 2020, sch 1, para 3.
[93] Merkin and Hjalmarsson (n 56) 71.
[94] Aziah Hussin, Claudia Kück and Nadja Alexander, 'SIAC-SIMC's Arb-Med-Arb Protocol' (2018) 11 New York Dispute Resolution Lawyer 85.
[95] Wolski (n 53) 267.
[96] ibid 266.

concerns are somewhat exaggerated. In commercial disputes, parties are likely to have sought the preliminary opinion of their lawyers before even commencing arbitration. In fact, many large multinational companies have able in-house counsel who would have advised the board of directors even before the engagement of external legal counsel. If the merits of the case were overwhelmingly in favour of one side, most parties would resolve the matter privately rather than initiate formal legal processes. It should also not be missed that commercial parties do often try to negotiate a private resolution between themselves at an early stage of a potential dispute, before lawyers are involved. As such, they are not completely unaware of the other side's basic position. The concerns may be exaggerated but they can be real, at least in some instances.

The follow-on question is can the parties deviate from the AMA Protocol (which provides for very specific steps and timelines) and design a process that better suits their own needs? It has been suggested that party autonomy is given precedence under the AMA Protocol and that parties 'may agree to insert a mediation phase after the first or even the second round of full written briefs, or even after the arbitration hearing, instead of after the response to the notice of arbitration'.[97] If the AMA Protocol indeed champions party autonomy, the way forward is for explicit provision of possible deviations from the standard process. This is not just for certainty. That a dispute resolution mechanism is described as a 'protocol' means that it lays down a set of formal rules to govern the process. To allow parties to deviate from the set of rules as they wish, so long as there is agreement between them, would transform the AMA Protocol into a mere model dispute resolution template. Further, the AMA Protocol is a collaborative initiative between the SIAC and the SIMC. It represents a standardised and co-ordinated dispute resolution process that both institutions are able to administer efficiently. Deviations will have an impact on the efficiency of the process, as both institutions would need to readjust the co-ordination and the processes they are in charge of. Significant deviations may mean that the process is no longer an application of the AMA Protocol but the application of a multi-tier dispute resolution process in which both the SIAC and the SIMC are involved. In any event, parties who are considering a deviation from the standard process should bear in mind that a later mediation phase in the arbitral process would mean that significant legal costs have been run up in the pre-mediation arbitral stage.

---

[97] Boog (n 79).

Since the SIMC's launch in November 2014, approximately one-fifth of more than fifty mediations that it has administered used the AMA Protocol.[98] Going forward, it will be interesting to carry out a study on the utilisation rate of the AMA Protocol, addressing questions concerning the popularity of including the AMA Protocol as a dispute resolution mechanism in parties' contracts as compared with post-dispute utilisation; the types of disputes for which the AMA Protocol is most frequently used; and the settlement rate for mediations conducted under the AMA Protocol. One interesting query, in particular, is the impact which the Singapore Convention on Mediation will have on the utilisation rate of the AMA Protocol. The Singapore Convention on Mediation is a UN treaty that is aimed at making it easier to enforce mediated settlement agreements across jurisdictions. The Singapore Convention on Mediation does not prescribe a specific mode of enforcement but sets out conditions for enforcement by a state. If a key advantage of the AMA Protocol (or generally the arb-med-arb process) is that it facilitates enforcement of the mediated settlement agreement through the mechanism of converting it into an arbitral award, the question is whether the popularity of the AMA Protocol may decline over time when there is a more direct means of enforcement. Of course, parties may choose the application of the AMA Protocol for its other advantages discussed in this chapter.

8.5 Conclusion

This chapter has discussed Singapore's support of multi-tier dispute resolution mechanisms for commercial disputes through three means: judicial enforcement of multi-tier dispute resolution clauses, regulatory support of such mechanisms; and institutional innovation to improve the combination of mediation and arbitration for the resolution of commercial disputes (the AMA Protocol). This chapter has also highlighted the inherent weaknesses or limitations of the combined processes, whether adopting a Same Person Model or the AMA Protocol which generally appoints different persons to take on the functions of mediator and arbitrator. The point is this: the combined process does not fully bear out the salient features of the separate processes. Something is lost in the combination, in exchange for other gains. Our expectations of what the combined process can do and how it should develop should accordingly be different from our

---

[98] Hussin, Kück and Alexander (n 94).

expectations of the separate processes. Readjustment of expectations will bring to the fore important research and law reform questions, such as:

1. Why should med-arb differ from arb-med or arb-med-arb in terms of enforceability of the consent award?
2. What are the real advantages of combined processes and for which kinds of disputes is each combined process most suitable?
3. What are the ethical or procedural issues arising from such combined processes that may need to be addressed through regulation or codes of conduct?
4. How would the combined dispute resolution process change our understanding and practice of mediation and arbitration as separate processes?
5. Should there be accreditation schemes for mediator-arbitrators (in other words, individuals who are to take on dual functions in the combined dispute resolution process), to the extent that the law continues to sanction the Same Person Model?

B

Specific Cases

9

HKIAC's Experience of the Use of Multi-tier Dispute Resolution Clauses

SARAH GRIMMER

9.1 Introduction

This chapter explores growing global interest in multi-tier dispute resolution options (Section 9.2) and whether that interest is reflected in parties' dispute resolution choices by examining, inter alia, more than a thousand arbitration clauses brought before the HKIAC between 2014 and 2018 (Section 9.3). The chapter also addresses 'med-arb' where the same neutral acts as mediator and arbitrator (Section 9.4) and the ways in which the 2018 HKIAC Administered Arbitration Rules are relevant to multi-tier dispute resolution (Section 9.5). It then reviews three recent international and regional developments that are likely to increase the demand for multi-tier dispute resolution options in different contexts (Section 9.6): (1) the Belt and Road Initiative (BRI, or the 'Initiative') and related establishment of the China International Commercial Courts (CICC); (2) the United Nations Convention on International Settlement Agreements Resulting from Mediation (the 'Singapore Mediation Convention'); and (3) the investment dispute mechanism agreed between the Hong Kong SAR and Mainland Chinese governments.

9.2 Current Global Interest in Multi-tier Dispute Resolution Options

'Multi-tier dispute resolution' refers to parties' agreement to attempt to settle their disputes through a sequence of methods beginning with non-adversarial, non-binding options such as negotiation and/or mediation, failing which, the dispute is determined via an adversarial and binding method, such as arbitration or litigation. This chapter focuses on multi-tier clauses that end with arbitration.

Multi-tier dispute resolution options are appealing for several reasons. They can enhance efficiency by facilitating early settlement or the reduction in scope of a dispute. When a non-binding method of dispute resolution precedes a binding one, parties are incentivised to agree a solution that is more or less acceptable to them, rather than face the imposition of a legal determination in respect of which they can be forced to comply by law. Multi-tier dispute resolution approaches can also increase the chances of parties preserving their business relationships; their ability to resolve a dispute amicably bodes well for future business dealings.

But there are also disadvantages. Multi-tier dispute resolution options may oblige parties to undertake futile efforts at amicable settlement, wasting time and money. A party may prefer that a dispute is resolved by binding decision rather than negotiated settlement so that it cannot be held responsible for or deemed complicit in the outcome. Multi-tier clauses must be carefully drafted; if not, they are vulnerable to abuse by parties wishing to delay matters and increase costs through procedural battles. During amicable discussions, a party may reveal information in good faith, only to have it used to its detriment or to inform the other side's strategy in later adversarial proceedings.

As several important surveys in recent years have shown, corporations are expressing an increased preference for combining 'amicable' or alternative dispute resolution (ADR)[1] methods with arbitration in the hopes of resolving disputes more cheaply and quickly than they perceive is possible through arbitration alone.

This general trend was evident in the 2018 International Arbitration Survey: The Evolution of International Arbitration by the Queen Mary University of London and White & Case LLP (the '2018 International Arbitration Survey'), in which 49 per cent of respondents chose a multi-tier mechanism as their preferred method of resolving cross-border disputes (up from 34 per cent in 2015).[2] The preference was most

---

[1] 'Amicable dispute resolution' refers to non-adversarial forms of dispute resolution such as negotiation, mediation and conciliation. 'Alternative dispute resolution' is a term sometimes used to refer to all dispute resolution methods that are 'alternatives' to court litigation, including arbitration. For the sake of this chapter, 'ADR' refers to amicable dispute resolution and does not include arbitration.

[2] Queen Mary University of London and White & Case LLP, *2018 International Arbitration Survey: The Evolution of International Arbitration* <www.arbitration.qmul.ac.uk/media/arbitration/docs/2018-International-Arbitration-Survey-The-Evolution-of-International-Arbitration-(2).PDF> accessed 26 February 2020, 5–6. This survey involved 922 respondents comprising private practitioners, full-time arbitrators, in-house counsel, experts,

pronounced among in-house counsel, 60 per cent of whom preferred arbitration combined with ADR as compared to the 32 per cent who preferred arbitration on its own.

Another important survey conducted through the Global Pound Conference Series 2016–17 ranked the priorities identified by respondents for future improvements in commercial dispute resolution as the use of non-adjudicative dispute resolution processes like mediation or conciliation before adjudicative processes, including arbitration (51 per cent), and the use of non-adjudicative processes in combination with adjudicative processes (45 per cent).[3] Interest in such options was spread across all stakeholder groups revealing a 'clear consensus' that combining processes, or mixed-mode dispute resolution, is 'the way forward'.[4]

It is evident from these two surveys that there is serious global interest in multi-tier dispute resolution and that interested parties wish to see it used more to enhance efficiency. Despite the interest in and broad consensus that multi-tier dispute resolution is desirable, another study conducted among eighty-one respondents between February and June 2014 (the 'Nigmatullina Survey') found that it is far from common; only one-third of participants in that survey had experienced a combination of mediation and arbitration in the previous five years and, for almost half of those who had, it constituted less than 10 per cent of their overall international commercial dispute resolution practice.[5]

The surveys also shed light on what leads to the use of multi-tier mechanisms and, importantly, what may detract from their use. This

---

academics, judges, third-party funders, government officials, economists, entrepreneurs, law students and others.

[3] Herbert Smith Freehills and PricewaterhouseCoopers, *Global Pound Conference Series: Global Data Trends and Regional Differences* <www.imimediation.org/research/gpc/series-data-and-reports/#6-gpc-series-data-and-reports> accessed 1 March 2020 (the 'Global Pound Report'), 13–14. This report is the result of a survey completed by more than 4,000 people who attended 28 conferences in 24 countries in 2016 and 2017. Those delegates and hundreds more who contributed data online voted on a series of twenty questions on dispute resolution.

[4] ibid 14.

[5] Dilyara Nigmatullina, 'The Combined Use of Mediation and Arbitration in Commercial Dispute Resolution: Results from an International Study' (2016) 33(1) Journal of International Arbitration 37, paras 50–52. The survey participants included international practitioners and legal academics predominantly from Europe and Asia/Pacific who attended the 2014 ICC Mediation Week and the APRAG 2014 Conference, as well as people who responded to a questionnaire published on LinkedIn or by the Arbitration Institute of the Stockholm Chamber of Commerce.

partially explains why, despite their great appeal, multi-tier clauses are not more frequently used.

According to the 2018 International Arbitration Survey, most interviewees observed (somewhat circularly) that multi-tier dispute resolution was resorted to because of a multi-tiered escalation clause in the relevant contract.[6] Others noted (but did not record experience of their use) that some institutional rules contain provisions asking arbitrators to instruct the parties to attempt settlement of their dispute, and verify whether meaningful attempts to settle were made.[7] According to the Nigmatullina survey, the most common triggers for using mediation-arbitration were (1) counsel's suggestions (66.7 per cent); (2) contractual provisions (51.9 per cent); (3) the initiative of one party (40.7 per cent); and (4) reference to an arbitral institution's model multi-tier clause (25.9 per cent).[8] Few experienced the use of combined mediation and arbitration pursuant to legislation (11.1 per cent).[9] Only two participants had experienced the combination of mediation and arbitration pursuant to an arbitration institution's rules, of whom only one had done so at the suggestion of the institution.[10]

What detracts from the use of multi-tier dispute resolution processes? In the 2018 International Arbitration Survey, it was apparent that while in-house counsel reported a greater preference for multi-tier mechanisms, external counsel preferred arbitration as a stand-alone method.[11] The Global Pound Report respondents indicated that external advisers were considered to be the primary obstacle to change in commercial dispute resolution practice.[12] Respondents thought this failure to promote ADR often stemmed from lawyers' unfamiliarity with multi-tier methods. Practitioners possibly lacked sufficient training to perform the varied roles required by mixed-mode dispute resolution and arbitral institutions may not have created sufficient incentives for them to gain such experience.[13] This may be different in certain jurisdictions, particularly where there exist rules requiring litigants to attempt mediation before pursuing civil lawsuits or where settlement facilitation by

---

[6] Queen Mary University of London and White & Case LLP (n 2) 6.
[7] ibid 6.
[8] Nigmatullina (n 5), para 55.
[9] ibid, para 57.
[10] ibid, para 58.
[11] Queen Mary University of London and White & Case LLP (n 2) 5.
[12] Herbert Smith Freehills and PricewaterhouseCoopers (n 3) 15–17.
[13] ibid 15–17.

a judge or arbitral tribunal is accepted practice.[14] The Nigmatullina survey identified a professional cultural divide between counsel who see themselves primarily as advocates and their instructing parties who expect advisers to help them resolve their dispute by the best means possible, including by facilitating ADR processes such as mediation (in advance of, in parallel with or integrated into litigation or arbitration). It was also noted that arbitrators were unlikely to refer parties to ADR of their own initiative, perhaps because they see their mandate as being primarily to resolve disputes through arbitration.[15]

What can be done to increase the use of multi-tier dispute resolution processes? In order to improve the frequency with which multi-tiered options are used, 51 per cent of respondents in the Global Pound Conference Report opted for legislation or conventions,[16] while 47 per cent chose protocols which promoted non-adjudicative processes.[17] This demonstrated a near universal recognition that parties should at least be encouraged, if not compelled, to explore non-adjudicative options.[18]

Four broad conclusions about the current state of multi-tier dispute resolution can be drawn from these surveys. First, efficiency is a key priority for parties in choosing dispute resolution processes, and multi-tier dispute

---

[14] For example, Mainland China (discussed more later), Switzerland, Germany, Austria. See Queen Mary University of London and White & Case LLP (n 2) 7. However, it is interesting to compare the situation in the common law jurisdiction of Hong Kong. Pursuant to Hong Kong's Civil Justice Reform of 2009, parties are required to consider mediation once court proceedings have been commenced. See Practice Direction 31 (Hong Kong). If a party refuses to mediate, it must provide a reasonable explanation for that refusal, failing which the Court may order it to pay a greater proportion of the other side's costs of the litigation once the case has concluded. Notwithstanding this, some in Hong Kong believe that mediation is still often seen as a 'box-ticking' exercise by lawyers and parties alike. See May Tai, Julian Copeman and Anita Phillips, 'Mediating Commercial Disputes: A Call to Action in Hong Kong' [2017] Asian Dispute Review 72, 73. However, according to statistics published by the Hong Kong government on the reforms, there has been a gradual increase in the number of mediations in litigation proceedings and a change in the profession towards an acceptance of mediation. The review also shows that, out of the mediated cases, 38 per cent resulted in agreements. See Legislative Council Panel on Administration of Justice and Legal Services, 'Review of the Implementation of Civil Justice Reform' <www.legco.gov.hk/yr14-15/english/panels/ajls/papers/ajls20150518cb4-964-5-e.pdf> accessed 26 February 2020, 3, 41–49, para 10, annex A, B.

[15] Queen Mary University of London and White & Case LLP (n 2) 6–7.

[16] See later discussion on the Singapore Mediation Convention in Section 9.6.2.

[17] Herbert Smith Freehills and PricewaterhouseCoopers (n 3) 20.

[18] For further discussion on enhancing the use of multi-tier dispute resolution, see Dilyara Nigmatullina, 'Aligning Dispute Resolution Processes with Global Demands for Change: Enhancing the Use of Mediation and Arbitration in Combination' [2019] Belgian Review of Arbitration 7.

resolution is believed to enhance it. Second, the search for cost-saving is driven primarily by in-house counsel for whom a tiered sequence of what are perceived as increasingly expensive methods of dispute resolution motivates them to seek the earliest possible resolution. Third, there is a global interest in the combined use of adjudicative and non-adjudicative processes. Finally, parties wish for greater collaboration from external lawyers in the dispute resolution process, and multi-mode options are part of that.

While they post-date the cited surveys, the Prague Rules on the Efficient Conduct of Proceedings in International Arbitration released in December 2018 (the 'Prague Rules')[19] may have an impact on the frequency with which arbitrators assist parties to settle, especially if they achieve similar ubiquity as the IBA Rules on the Taking of Evidence in International Arbitration 2010. Article 9 of the Prague Rules is pertinent: it provides that the arbitral tribunal may assist the parties in reaching an amicable settlement of the dispute at any stage of the proceedings, unless one of the parties objects. In addition, upon the prior written consent of all parties, any arbitrator may act as a mediator to assist in the amicable settlement of the dispute. If a settlement is not achieved within an agreed period, the arbitrator who acted as a mediator may continue to act as arbitrator in the proceedings upon the written consent of all parties, failing which he or she shall resign.

9.3 HKIAC's Experience of Multi-tier Dispute Resolution

HKIAC is the flagship arbitral institution in Hong Kong providing dispute resolution services in arbitration, mediation, adjudication and domain name dispute resolution, among other things.[20] Since its establishment in 1985, HKIAC has provided services in over 10,500 matters. As the administering institution for numerous dispute resolution proceedings, HKIAC has a unique vantage point in that it is privy to

---

[19] 'Rules on the Efficient Conduct of Proceedings in International Arbitration (Prague Rules)' (*Prague Rules*, 2018) <https://praguerules.com/prague_rules/> accessed 1 March 2020.

[20] Since 1997, HKIAC has served the statutory function of the appointing authority prescribed under the Hong Kong Arbitration Ordinance (Cap 609) (the 'Ordinance'). HKIAC has the following functions under the Ordinance: (1) determine the number of arbitrators where the parties have not reached an agreement on the matter (s 23); (2) appoint an arbitrator where a party fails to make an appointment, or the agreed appointment procedures fail to result in appointment of an arbitrator (s 24); (3) appoint a mediator if a person designated by an arbitration agreement fails to make the appointments (s 32).

thousands of dispute resolution clauses. From this position, it is possible to gauge whether the apparent high level of interest in multi-tier dispute resolution proceedings is reflected through the conclusion of a high number of multi-tier dispute resolution clauses.

In 2018, HKIAC conducted an internal survey of 1,252 dispute resolution clauses in disputes submitted to HKIAC between 1 January 2014 and 31 August 2018 (the 'HKIAC Survey').[21] The survey revealed that most clauses (82 per cent) provided for arbitration only, while 17 per cent of clauses referred to different and sequenced modes of dispute resolution.

Of the 17 per cent of clauses that referred to different and sequenced modes of dispute resolution, 13 per cent provided for negotiation followed by arbitration, 2 per cent provided for mediation followed by arbitration, and 1 per cent provided for some form of adjudication followed by arbitration.[22] Each of these categories is elaborated upon in Sections 9.3.1–9.3.5. The remaining few clauses, representing 1 per cent of the overall survey, could not be categorised; they referred to different modes of dispute resolution, but the modes were not sequenced in a clear fashion, providing, for example, for 'mediation and/or adjudication' or 'mediation or otherwise'.

One important note is that all the cases surveyed contained agreements to arbitrate, and almost all the disputes involved had been submitted to arbitration and thus had *not* been resolved during pre-arbitral steps.[23] The important qualification to the survey is thus that HKIAC has limited visibility over those cases in which the parties agree a multi-tier dispute resolution clause and successfully settle their dispute through one of the pre-arbitral dispute resolution methods.

9.3.1 Negotiation-Arbitration Clauses

As mentioned in Section 9.3, 13 per cent of clauses surveyed expressly provided for negotiation prior to arbitration.[24] The agreements in

---

[21] This represents a subset of all cases brought under HKIAC's auspices over the relevant time period, that is, those in which the parties agreed to HKIAC's administrative and appointing authority services in arbitrations. It has been chosen because in these cases HKIAC is provided with a copy of the contract containing the dispute resolution clause, which is not always the case in other matters, for example, fund-holding matters.

[22] For the purposes of this paper, 'adjudication' refers to a process in which the parties have empowered a third party to decide the dispute on a non-binding basis, which is subject to subsequent review by an arbitral tribunal or other body.

[23] Four cases were submitted to HKIAC during the mediation phase.

[24] The terms used in such clauses included 'friendly negotiations', 'consultations', 'amicable consultation', 'friendly discussion' or 'friendly consultations'.

question covered a wide range of commercial activity including corporate agreements, international sales contracts, construction deals, licensing agreements, professional services contracts, banking and finance agreements; no trend in terms of industry sector or type of underlying transaction was clearly discernible.

Among the clauses that provided for negotiation followed by arbitration, 42 per cent included a time period over which negotiations were to occur, following which a party could refer the matter to arbitration. Not all time limits were clear, however: 20 per cent of the subset did not identify a precise starting point from which the time period for negotiations would run or were unclear in some other way. While the challenges posed by unclear time limits are not insurmountable, they can lead to increased costs, delay and procedural challenges.

In the clauses that did include clear time limits, the time periods generally ranged from twenty to sixty days. The shortest time period was three hours for negotiations before a party could file an arbitration; that was found in a shareholders' agreement (similarly, in another shareholders' agreement, the parties provided for a three-hour mediation prior to arbitration).

Only 7 per cent of the clauses in this subset expressly identified the persons authorised to undertake negotiations. Most commonly, those persons were identified as senior executives, which is unsurprising given the benefit of decision-making authority being vested in any person undertaking settlement talks.

9.3.2 Mediation-Arbitration Clauses

Only 2 per cent of cases involved some form of mediation followed by arbitration. Notably, most clauses that provided for mediation followed by arbitration *also provided for negotiation* at the outset of the dispute and were thus *three*-tier dispute resolution clauses. Most were found in construction-related contracts with a smaller but not insignificant number found in professional services contracts. Within this subset of cases, only 21 per cent were solely 'mediation-arbitration' clauses referring the dispute directly to mediation (without reference to negotiation) followed by arbitration (hereinafter referred to as 'med-arb' clauses).

9.3.3 Negotiation-Mediation-Arbitration Clauses

Of the clauses that provided for negotiation, mediation then arbitration, two observations can be made. First, the clauses were well drafted (and noticeably *better* drafted than the 'med-arb' clauses). Eighty-six per cent contained clear time limits for each step in the mechanism. Ninety per cent identified the positions of the persons who would be qualified to negotiate an agreement.

Second, some of these clauses also included important ways to avoid wasted time and costs. Several clauses provided that, failing settlement by negotiation, any party could request mediation but that, if any other party rejected the request for mediation, the dispute could be referred immediately to arbitration. This relieves parties of having to 'go through the motions' of a mediation when at least one of them knows that it is futile. Rather, by unilateral request, a party can move the dispute directly to arbitration. Similarly, in another clause, the parties agreed that the matter could be referred to mediation but that, during the mediation, any party could refer the matter to arbitration.

Also, in other cases under this subset – mainly construction cases – the parties provided for the appointment by each side of a designated representative with authority to settle disputes shortly after the conclusion of the contract. In these clauses, the parties expressed that the representative was not to be involved in the day-to-day administration of the contract. In this way, the parties ensured that the person authorised to run the negotiations would be somewhat removed from the dispute.

In another case, the parties specified the qualities they wanted in a mediator. The case concerned a large hotel management agreement. The parties stipulated that the mediator had to have 'experience in the hospitality industry and operation of hotels and must not have any conflict of interest'. In this way, the parties expressed their preference for a mediator with industry experience.

9.3.4 *Mediation-Arbitration Clauses*

As previously mentioned, a smaller percentage of clauses provided for med-arb without first requiring negotiations. These clauses were found in a variety of traditional commercial agreements such as contracts for professional services, trading contracts, construction works and a shareholders' agreement. In these clauses, there was a high frequency of referral to a set of existing mediation rules. But what was most striking was the lower quality of drafting; only one clause contained clear time limits.

9.3.5 Adjudication-Arbitration Clauses

As noted, just 1 per cent of cases in the HKIAC Survey involved a form of adjudication. Eighty-one per cent of matters in this subset referred to adjudication then arbitration; the rest referred to adjudication, then mediation, then arbitration. All cases were construction disputes. One of the key observations in these cases was to whom the parties entrusted the adjudicatory function. Clauses differed in that disputes between an employer and a contractor were entrusted to the architect, the engineer or an interim disputes referee who would act as an independent expert. In another construction matter, any disputes between the contractor and the subcontractor would be decided first by the contractor but, if the subcontractor was not satisfied with the decision, it could refer the matter to mediation, failing which arbitration.[25]

9.4 'Med-arb' Where the Same Neutral Acts as Mediator and Arbitrator

One of the most frequently discussed issues in respect of med-arb is whether the person who acts as the mediator may also act as the arbitrator if the mediation fails. Concerns about this practice include that an arbitrator's impartiality may be affected by confidential information to which he or she becomes privy during private caucusing in mediation and the other party has no way of presenting its case in respect of such information. Attitudes to using the same person as mediator and arbitrator vary across jurisdictions. In Mainland China, for example, the practice of med-arb is a familiar one that aligns broadly with Chinese judicial tradition.[26] The tribunal may conduct the mediation in a manner it

---

[25] A detailed examination of the use of multi-tiered dispute resolution clauses in construction contracts, including the role that adjudicators, interim disputes referees, experts or dispute resolution advisers play, is beyond the scope of this chapter.

[26] Danny McFadden, 'Mediation/Arbitration' in Denis Brock (ed), *Arbitration in Hong Kong* (Sweet & Maxwell 2011), paras 5.033–5.034; Ning Fei and Joe Liu, 'Mediation Meets Arbitration – The Experience of Med-Arb in Mainland China and Hong Kong' (2014) 1(5) Alternative Dispute Resolution Law, 98, where they report on the combined use of mediation and arbitration in China-related disputes:

> Deeply rooted in the Chinese legal culture and tradition, the use of med-arb has long been favoured by Chinese parties as a dispute resolution practice that is in conformity with the core values that dominate the political philosophy and social life in China, such as harmony and disdain for conflict. These philosophical and social norms result in the wide use of med-arb for China-related disputes. According to the PRC State Council's

considers appropriate which in practice may include meeting with the parties collectively or privately.²⁷ If the mediation is not successful, the tribunal will resume its arbitral role. PRC Arbitration Law also supports the process. It provides that an arbitral tribunal may conduct mediation before issuing an arbitral award and that if the mediation is not successful, the tribunal shall make an award promptly.²⁸

By contrast, in Hong Kong, it is rare for parties to agree that the same person may act as mediator and later as arbitrator if there is no settlement.²⁹ Notwithstanding this, Hong Kong is one of the few jurisdictions that regulates this situation. Section 32 of the Hong Kong Arbitration Ordinance provides that, where the parties agree, the mediator may act as the arbitrator if the mediation fails. Section 33 provides that when an arbitrator acts as mediator, he or she may communicate with the parties collectively or separately and must treat any information obtained as confidential. If the mediation fails, before resuming the arbitral proceedings, the arbitrator must disclose to all other parties as much of that confidential information as he or she considers is material to the arbitral proceedings. This provision disincentivises parties from being forthcoming during the mediation and explains why, apart from fundamental due process concerns, med-arb using the same neutral is not practised in Hong Kong.

Notwithstanding this, HKIAC has administered a case in which the sole arbitrator made several proposals to the parties during an arbitration, two of which included him taking on the role of mediator. His

> statistics, out of 104,257 arbitration cases accepted by 225 PRC arbitration commissions in 2013, 60,112 cases [or 57.8 per cent] were concluded by med-arb.
>
> See also Gabrielle Kaufmann-Kohler and Fan Kun, 'Integrating Mediation into Arbitration: Why It Works in China' (2008) 4 Journal of International Arbitration 479.

²⁷ Fei and Liu (n 26) 98.
²⁸ Arbitration Law (PRC), art 51 provides: 'The arbitration tribunal may reconcile a case before passing the award. Whereas the parties concerned accept the reconciliation effort of their own accord, the arbitration tribunal may conduct the reconciliation. Should the reconciliation fail, the arbitration tribunal shall pass the ruling in time.' See also ibid 98.
²⁹ McFadden (n 26), para 5.095. In this regard, see the differing approaches of the Hong Kong courts in respect of an application to refuse enforcement of a PRC award resulting from an arbitration-mediation-arbitration procedure on the grounds of public policy (the award allegedly being tainted by bias) in *Gao Haiyan v Keeneye Holdings Ltd* [2012] 1 HKLRD 627 (Hong Kong Court of Appeal), 2 December 2011 (where the award was enforced); [2011] 3 HKC 157 (Hong Kong Court of First Instance), 12 April 2011 (where the award was refused enforcement). See also McFadden (n 26), paras 5.043–5.079.

proposals also included an important safeguard in respect of the enforceability of any award if mediation failed. The dispute was between an American party and a Mainland Chinese party and involved intellectual property rights. Related litigation was ongoing in the United States. The parties had attempted settlement talks at an earlier stage in the case. Following the substantive hearing, the sole arbitrator believed that another attempt at mediation would benefit the parties as it would allow them to try to resolve all their disputes at once and not just those that came within his mandate. The sole arbitrator made three proposals to the parties: first, he advised them that, pursuant to section 33 of the Hong Kong Arbitration Ordinance, they could agree that he act as the mediator. He proposed, however, that any mediation occur *after* he had finalised the arbitral award and placed it in escrow with the HKIAC. The advantage was that if the mediation failed, the award could be rendered to the parties without being compromised by the mediation process. The disadvantage was that the parties would not be saved award-drafting costs as they would if the arbitration were immediately suspended. Second, the sole arbitrator proposed that the parties appoint a co-mediator to help him mediate the dispute. That way the sole arbitrator would bring a detailed knowledge of the case to the mediation and help inform the other mediator of the case details in a more efficient manner, whereas the co-mediator could meet with the parties directly and be the recipient of any confidential information, thus leaving the sole arbitrator 'untainted'. Third, the sole arbitrator proposed that the parties appoint an independent mediator. The parties did not respond to the sole arbitrator's proposals and in due course he rendered a final award. Even after the arbitration had terminated, the parties continued to dispute related matters before US courts.

9.5 The Relevance of HKIAC's 2018 Administered Arbitration Rules to Multi-tier Dispute Resolution

On 1 November 2018, HKIAC promulgated the 2018 HKIAC Administered Arbitration Rules (the '2018 Rules') following a year-long process of revision, public consultation and deliberation.[30] The 2018 Rules facilitate multi-

---

[30] Hong Kong International Arbitration Centre, *2018 Administered Arbitration Rules* <www.hkiac.org/arbitration/rules-practice-notes/hkiac-administered-2018> accessed 26 February 2020.

tier dispute resolution proceedings in two ways. First, the 2018 Rules introduce a new Article 13.8 which provides:

> Where the parties agree to pursue other means of settling their dispute after the arbitration commences, HKIAC, the arbitral tribunal or the emergency arbitrator may, at the request of any party, suspend the arbitration on such terms as it considers appropriate. The arbitration shall resume at the request of any party to HKIAC, the arbitral tribunal or the emergency arbitrator.

This provision makes express the conditions under which parties can navigate from arbitration to a non-adversarial form of dispute resolution, be it negotiations, mediation, conciliation or otherwise after the arbitration has commenced. The condition is that there is an agreement between the parties to pursue another means of settling their dispute. The parties can opt for the other method at any time including (1) during the mandate of an emergency arbitrator; (2) before an arbitral tribunal is constituted, in which case the parties would seek suspension from HKIAC; or (3) after the constitution of the arbitral tribunal, in which case the request for suspension would be made to the arbitral tribunal. Critically, it also makes express that, at any time, a party may unilaterally trigger the resumption of the arbitration if it becomes apparent that the other method will not be successful.

Second, the 2018 Rules provide that parties may request the appointment of an emergency arbitrator prior to the commencement of the arbitration.[31] This has significance for multi-tier dispute resolution. It allows parties to seek emergency relief before having satisfied pre-arbitral dispute resolution steps. If, for example, a party is bound by a clause that provides for mandatory mediation for thirty days after which it may commence an arbitration, but it requires emergency relief before the thirty-day mediation is complete, it can apply for such relief while participating in the mediation. Under the 2018 Rules, the arbitration must be commenced within seven days of filing an application for the appointment of an emergency arbitrator, unless the emergency arbitrator extends this time limit. The satisfaction of a mandatory

---

[31] ibid, sch 4 para 1 provides: 'A party requiring Emergency Relief may submit an application ... for the appointment of an emergency arbitrator to HKIAC (a) before, (b) concurrent with, or (c) following the filing of a Notice of Arbitration, but prior to the constitution of the arbitral tribunal.' Sch 4 para 21 provides: 'The Emergency Arbitrator Procedure shall be terminated if a Notice of Arbitration has not been submitted by the applicant to HKIAC within seven days of HKIAC's receipt of the Application, unless the emergency arbitrator extends this time limit.'

mediation may be a circumstance in which an emergency arbitrator would extend the time limit within which a party is obligated to commence the arbitration. This provides an important avenue for parties to seek and obtain emergency interim relief without breaching mandatory pre-arbitral steps.[32]

9.6 International and Regional Developments that Increase the Importance of Multi-tier Dispute Resolution

While there is evidence of growing interest in multi-tier dispute resolution options by corporations, the clauses reviewed by HKIAC show that, in most cases, parties continue to agree upon arbitration as a singular option. That may change, however, as a result of several international and regional developments, discussed next.

---

[32] Different courts and arbitral tribunals have taken different approaches to the breach of pre-arbitral steps. It is outside of the scope of this chapter to discuss them; suffice it to say that they include that (1) pre-arbitral steps expressed in mandatory and certain terms are enforceable and may be considered as a condition precedent to arbitration (an agreement expressed in mandatory terms to have 'friendly discussions to resolve [a] claim ... [is] a condition precedent to the right to refer the claim to arbitration' (*Emirates Trading Agency LLC v Prime Mineral Exports Private Ltd* [2014] EWHC 2104 (Comm), [2015] 1 WLR 1145 [25], [64]); '[w]here the parties have clearly contracted for a specific set of dispute resolution procedures as preconditions for arbitration, those preconditions must be fulfilled' (*International Research Corp plc v Lufthansa Systems Asia Pacific Pte Ltd* [2014] 1 SLR 130 (Singapore) [61]–[63]); albeit not in the context of pre-arbitral steps: '... there is no good reason why an express agreement between contracting parties that they must negotiate in good faith should not be upheld' (*HSBC Institutional Trust Services (Singapore) Ltd v Toshin Development Singapore Private Ltd* [2012] 4 SLR 378 (Singapore) [40]); cf cases where agreements to negotiate (outside of the context of pre-arbitral-steps) have been found to be unenforceable for lack of certainty (*Hyundai Engineering & Construction Co Ltd v Vigour Ltd* [2005] 3 HKLRD 723 (Hong Kong), on appeal; [2004] 3 HKLRD 1 (Hong Kong); *Courtney & Fairbairn Ltd v Tolaini Brothers* [1975] 1 WLR 297 (UK); *Walford v Miles* [1992] 2 AC 128 (UK); *Cable & Wireless plc v IBM United Kingdom Ltd* [2002] EWHC 2059 (Comm), [2002] 2 All ER (Comm) 1041 (UK); *Wah (aka Alan Tang) v Grant Thornton International Ltd* [2012] EWHC 3198 (Ch), [2013] 1 All ER (Comm) 1226 (UK))); and (2) the effect of a breach of a pre-arbitral step constitutes an issue arising out of, or in connection with, the agreement containing the arbitration clause and thus, according to the principle of *kompetenz-kompetenz*, should be decided by the arbitral tribunal. It should thus not be seen as affecting the *jurisdiction* of the arbitral tribunal in the sense that a breach cannot destroy the arbitration agreement. An arbitral tribunal should consider a request for arbitration inadmissible if the parties agreed in a binding and unequivocal manner to first engage in other steps to resolve their dispute: see Alexander Jolles, 'Consequences of Multi-tier Arbitration Clauses: Issues of Enforcement' (2006) 72(4) Arbitration 329, 336, for an examination of Swiss, English, German and US case law, as well as some ICC arbitral awards. That compliance with a pre-condition is a question of admissibility which the tribunal is best placed to determine and does not raise any question of jurisdiction was recently confirmed by the Hong Kong High Court in *C v D* [2021] HKCFI 1474.

9.6.1 The Belt and Road Initiative and the China International Commercial Courts

9.6.1.1 Introduction

The first development is the BRI – a strategy launched by the Chinese government in 2013 as an official policy to stimulate economic development along an overland 'Silk Road Economic Belt' and a seaborne '21st Century Maritime Silk Road'.[33] It is overseen by China's National Development and Reform Commission, Ministry of Foreign Affairs and Ministry of Commerce under sanction from the State Council, the nation's chief administrative body. The Initiative encourages Chinese outbound investment, often through loan financing, in large-scale infrastructure projects that target resources and energy development, industrial capacity co-operation and financial co-operation in the relevant jurisdictions. It covers a wide range of commercial activity with a focus on infrastructure development and integrating trade corridors across Asia, the Middle East, Africa and Europe.

According to China's Ministry of Commerce, in 2017, China's direct investment in countries along the Belt and Road reached USD 20.17 billion.[34] Most BRI projects are being led by China's state-owned enterprises and policy banks. In addition, China has secured support

---

[33] In the Chinese language, the term *Yi Dai Yi Lu* (一带一路) (which literally means 'One Belt One Road') is used for the BRI. The Chinese government has launched an official Belt and Road Portal website at 'Belt and Road Portal' <https://eng.yidaiyilu.gov.cn> accessed 26 February 2020; 'Vision and Actions on Jointly Building Silk Road Economic Belt and 21st-Century Maritime Silk Road' (*Belt and Road Initiative – Hong Kong*) <www.beltandroad.gov.hk/visionandactions.html> accessed 26 February 2020. See also Julien Chaisse and Jędrzej Górski (eds), *The Belt and Road Initiative: Law, Economics, and Politics* (Brill 2018). For a list of 743 Belt and Road projects, see Nicolas de Loisy, *Transportation and the Belt and Road Initiative: A Paradigm Shift* (SCMO Research 2019).

[34] Ministry of Commerce of People's Republic of China, 'Report on Development of China's Outward Investment and Economic Cooperation' <http://images.mofcom.gov.cn/fec/201901/20190128155348158.pdf> accessed 26 February 2020. See also Aisha Nadar, 'Construction Arbitration in the Context of China's Belt and Road Projects' in Stavros Brekoulakis and David Brynmor Thomas (eds), *The Guide to Construction Arbitration* (Global Arbitration Review 2018), who reports (at 250) that 'from January 2015 to August 2017, Chinese companies have signed more than 15,300 new construction contracts in BRI countries with an aggregate project value of more than USD 300 billion'. See also Weidong Zhu, 'Some Considerations on the Civil, Commercial and Investment Dispute Settlement Mechanisms between China and the Other Belt and Road Countries' in Julien Chaisse and Jędrzej Górski (eds), *The Belt and Road Initiative: Law, Economics, and Politics* (Brill 2018) 608, where it is reported that (as of 2016) China's investment in Belt and Road countries had surpassed USD 50 billion and that total trade between China and other Belt and Road countries in 2014–16 exceeded USD 3 trillion.

from many international organisations and financial co-operation through the Silk Road Fund and the Asian Infrastructure Investment Bank, among others.[35] BRI investment projects are estimated to add over USD 1 trillion of outward funding for foreign infrastructure over the ten-year period from 2017.[36]

9.6.1.2   Dispute Resolution under the Belt and Road Initiative

In the context of the BRI, there is an obvious need for effective dispute resolution for Sino-foreign disputes. Hong Kong's traditional role as the venue for Sino-foreign dispute resolution is important as is HKIAC's long history of administering arbitrations between Chinese and non-Chinese parties. Each year, Mainland Chinese parties are amongst the most frequent users of HKIAC arbitration.[37] Arbitral awards emanating from Hong Kong and HKIAC have an excellent rate of enforcement in Mainland China.[38] Reflecting the growing number of cases involving Mainland Chinese parties at HKIAC, and possibly their growing bargaining power, HKIAC saw an increase in the number of cases between 2016 and 2018 in which the Chinese language was used and PRC law was selected as the governing law.[39]

From 2014 to 2019, HKIAC administered more than 650 cases involving a party from one of the original 65 Belt and Road jurisdictions (the 'BRI countries'). From 2014 to 2019, more than 100 of those cases involved at least 1 party from Mainland China and at least 1 party from a BRI country. The disputes were of a commercial, maritime, construction or corporate nature and the aggregate amount in dispute was USD 1.3 billion, and an increasing number clearly involve Belt and Road projects.[40]

---

[35] Nadar (n 34) 256.

[36] OECD, 'The Belt and Road Initiative in the Global Trade, Investment and Finance Landscape' in OECD, 'OECD Business and Finance Outlook 2018' (OECD Publishing 2018) <https://doi.org/10.1787/bus_fin_out-2018-6-en> accessed 23 September 2020.

[37] '2019 Statistics' (*Hong Kong International Arbitration Centre*) <www.hkiac.org/about-us/statistics> accessed 26 February 2020.

[38] See eg Teresa Cheng and Joe Liu, 'Enforcement of Foreign Awards in Mainland China: Current Practices and Future Trends' (2014) 31(5) Journal of International Arbitration 651; Meg Utterback, Ronghui Li and Holly Blackwell, 'Enforcing Foreign Arbitral Awards in China – A Review of the Past Twenty Years' (*King & Wood Mallesons*, 15 March 2016) <www.kwm.com/en/knowledge/insights/enforcing-foreign-arbitral-awards-in-china-20160915> accessed 26 February 2020.

[39] Hong Kong International Arbitration Centre (n 37).

[40] For an overview of HKIAC's experience administering disputes arising from Belt and Road projects, see Joe Liu and Othmane Benlafkih, 'Resolving Disputes from Belt and Road

9 HKIAC'S EXPERIENCE OF THE USE OF MDR CLAUSES 221

Amongst the Mainland Chinese parties on HKIAC's docket, in a given year between 10 per cent and 15 per cent are state-owned entities. Organs of the Chinese State enjoy Crown immunity in Hong Kong;[41] however, as confirmed by the Hong Kong courts in a 2017 judgment, a Chinese state-owned enterprise that enjoys powers of independent management and the capacity to assume civil liabilities independently is not covered by Crown immunity in Hong Kong.[42] As a result, the Hong Kong courts have enforced arbitral awards against Chinese state-owned enterprises. This is commercially relevant as many Chinese state-owned assets are located in Hong Kong. This further underscores Hong Kong's relevance to effective dispute resolution for parties from Belt and Road jurisdictions that are contracting with Chinese state-owned enterprises under the BRI.[43]

It has long been understood that China's legal culture places a greater emphasis on mediation than many other jurisdictions. Unsurprisingly, when addressing dispute resolution options for Belt and Road disputes – the common denominator of which is the presence of a Mainland Chinese party – there is much focus on integrating mediation into any process, including an ultimately adversarial one. Mixed modes of dispute settlement have been trumpeted by many as the preferred approach for BRI disputes.[44] For example, in May 2016, at the Conference of the

Projects' in *CDR Essential Intelligence: Belt & Road Initiative* (Global Legal Group Ltd 2020). See also Sarah Grimmer and Christina Charemi, 'Dispute Resolution along the Belt and Road' (*Global Arbitration Review*, 22 May 2017) <https://globalarbitrationreview.com/chapter/1141929/dispute-resolution-along-the-belt-and-read> accessed 25 August 2020.

[41] *The Hua Tian Long (No 2)* [2010] 3 HKLRD 611 (Hong Kong).

[42] *TNB Fuel Services Sdn Bhd v China National Coal Group Corp* [2017] 3 HKC 588 (Hong Kong).

[43] On the relevance of Hong Kong as a seat of arbitration in Sino-foreign disputes, see also Sarah Grimmer, 'Distinction and Connection: Hong Kong and Mainland China, a View from the HKIAC' (*Global Arbitration Review*, 24 May 2019) <https://globalarbitrationreview.com/insight/the-asia-pacific-arbitration-review-2020/1193369/distinction-and-connection-hong-kong-and-mainland-china-a-view-from-the-hkiac> accessed 25 August 2020.

[44] Guiguo Wang, *Dispute Resolution Mechanism for the Belt and Road Initiative* (Zhejiang University Press 2017) (otherwise known as the 'Bluebook'). In the Bluebook, the BRI Academy – an academic group comprising Chinese and international legal scholars and arbitration practitioners – published a proposal for a comprehensive dispute resolution mechanism which begins from the premise that current methods of dispute resolution are insufficient for the BRI and calls for a tailor-made mechanism. It envisions a multi-tier approach in which disputes are first referred mandatorily to non-adversarial methods of dispute resolution prior to arbitration. Art 6 of the Academy's proposed 'Belt and Road Arbitration Rules' provides that parties may not commence arbitral proceedings until they have exhausted the mediation or conciliation methods available to them as outlined in the Rules. The proposed Rules further provide that no admissions or concessions made in the

Presidents of the Supreme Courts of China and the Central and Eastern European Countries, the Supreme People's Court of China emphasised 'the application of mediation to settle disputes'.[45] The Supreme Courts of Central and Eastern European Countries agreed to 'actively consider applying mediation and other ADR mechanisms in their respective countries'.[46] It is considered that the need to resolve disputes between parties who are connected not only by their immediate contractual relationship but also by common participation in the transnational BRI project is of paramount importance. Many commentators therefore note the appeal of a resolution mechanism designed from the outset to preserve relationships.[47] Moreover, as the BRI involves states as well as state- and privately owned enterprises, it is believed that there is a need for an overall framework that is equally suited to resolving disputes between private entities as it is for those involving sovereign and state-owned entities, including investor–state disputes. Two factors are discernible from the approaches put forward by commentators in respect of BRI dispute resolution: (1) that of a 'one-stop-shop' dispute resolution forum; and (2) that of mediation or conciliation as a mandatory precondition for arbitration or litigation.

9.6.1.3 The China International Commercial Courts

In January 2018, the General Office of the Central Committee of the Communist Party of China and the General Office of the State Council issued an 'Opinion on Establishing the "One Belt, One Road" International Commercial Dispute Resolution Mechanism and Institutions'. This mandated the Chinese Supreme People's Court to establish two China International Commercial Courts in Shenzhen (Guangdong) and Xi'an (Shaanxi) (referred to collectively as the 'CICC').[48]

---

course of mediation may be adduced in evidence during subsequent arbitral proceedings, and that the mediator is prohibited from acting as arbitrator in those proceedings.

[45] Zhu (n 34) 614.
[46] ibid 614.
[47] Wang (n 44) 42.
[48] *'Guanyu jianli 'yidaiyilu' zhengduan jiejue jizhi he jigou de yijian'* [Opinion on Constructing 'Belt and Road Initiative' Dispute Resolution Mechanism and Institutions] [2018] Zhong Ban Fa 19 <www.gov.cn/zhengce/2018-06/27/content_5301657.htm> accessed 17 August 2020, as summarised in 'Notice of the General Office of the CPC Central Committee and the General Office of the State Council on Issuing the "Opinions Concerning Establishing BRI's International Commercial Dispute Resolution Mechanisms and Bodies"' (*People's Republic of China Central Government*, 27 June 2018) <www.gov.cn/zhengce/2018-06/27/content_5301657.htm> accessed 25 August 2020.

9 HKIAC'S EXPERIENCE OF THE USE OF MDR CLAUSES   223

The CICC was thus established to determine international commercial disputes between private entities. Its jurisdiction is voluntary. Article 8(1) of the CICC Procedural Rules (the 'CICC Rules') requires parties to explicitly consent to its jurisdiction.[49] The dispute in question must have some connection to China while it is expected that at least one party will be non-Chinese. To assist it in matters of foreign law, the CICC maintains a Panel of Experts made up of leading Chinese and international practitioners of international trade law and arbitration.[50] In this way, the CICC presents itself as a *forum conveniens* to which non-Chinese parties from across the BRI may submit disputes regardless of whether their underlying contract is governed by PRC law.

A stated aim of the CICC is to promote 'the linkage of mediation, arbitration and litigation' by means of a procedural framework that interacts responsively with the parties' intentions at each stage of the resolution process. Central to this is the notion of the 'one-stop-shop' institution. Under Article 17(3) of the CICC Rules, where parties agree to mediate a case under the CICC's jurisdiction, they may request a mediator to be appointed from the CICC Panel of Experts or they may jointly agree to have the matter referred to one of seven institutions designated by the CICC as 'one-stop-shop' institutions.[51]

Where a mediation is conducted by a mediator drawn from the Panel of Experts or from one of the designated institutions, and the parties reach a settlement, the CICC may, at the request of the parties, conduct a review and issue an official mediated settlement

---

[49] China International Commercial Court, *Procedural Rules for the China International Commercial Court of the Supreme People's Court (For Trial Implementation)* <http://cicc.court.gov.cn/html/1/219/208/210/1183.html> accessed 26 February 2020.

[50] 'Expert Directory' (*China International Commercial Court*) <http://cicc.court.gov.cn/html/1/219/235/237/index.html> accessed 26 February 2020.

[51] The seven institutions as of 30 January 2019 are all Mainland Chinese arbitral commissions: China International Economic and Trade Arbitration Commission; Shanghai International Economic and Trade Arbitration Commission (Shanghai International Arbitration Center); Shenzhen International Court of Arbitration; Beijing Arbitration Commission (Beijing International Arbitration Center); China Maritime Arbitration Commission; China Council for the Promotion of International Trade and China Chamber for International Commerce Mediation Center; and Shanghai Commercial Mediation Center. See Supreme People's Court, 'Notice on the Determination of the First International Commercial Arbitration and Mediation Agencies Incorporated into the "One-Stop" International Commercial Disputes Diversification Mechanism' <http://cicc.court.gov.cn/html/1/218/149/192/1124.html> accessed 25 August 2020.

agreement.⁵² It may further, if the parties so request, enter the settlement agreement as an official judgment of the court.⁵³ Where mediation is unsuccessful, the CICC Rules provide that the records of the mediation and any compromises made therein may not be used prejudicially against a party (without its consent) during the litigation proceedings.⁵⁴ For arbitration cases administered by any of the 'one-stop-shop' institutions, parties may apply to the CICC for interim measures including pre-action interim relief. Such applications will be referred to the CICC by the 'one-stop-shop' institutions, rather than by the parties.

The aim of the process is to offer a unified dispute resolution forum that supports mediation, arbitration and litigation. The process does not require a contractual mechanism agreed by the parties in the form of a multi-tier clause; rather, it seeks to achieve a similar process by offering a set of rules and procedures (under the general supervision of the CICC) into which the parties may opt after their dispute has arisen.⁵⁵ In this way, the process is vulnerable in that it relies in part on the disputing parties reaching consensus on procedural matters after a dispute has arisen. Experience in international arbitration shows that it can be very difficult for disputing parties to reach agreement on procedural matters post-dispute.

Given that the CICC Rules are largely based on Chinese civil law rules of procedure, it remains to be seen how they will operate in practice and whether foreign parties will opt for the CICC to resolve their international commercial disputes with Chinese parties.⁵⁶ The benefit for foreign parties would be the ability to obtain a Chinese judgment or award at the end of the process, making enforcement arguably easier on the Mainland than of a foreign arbitral award under the 1958 New York Convention or the special arrangements

---

⁵² CICC Rules, art 24.
⁵³ ibid.
⁵⁴ ibid, art 26.
⁵⁵ For information on the work of the CICC, see 'Zuigao fayuan guoji shangshi fating yi shouli yipi guoji shangshi jiufen anjian' [The China International Commercial Court of the Supreme People's Court Have Accepted to Hear a Batch of Cases on International Commercial Disputes] (*China International Commercial Court*, 29 December 2018) <http://cicc.court.gov.cn/html/1/218/149/192/1150.html<int_b> accessed 26 February 2020.
⁵⁶ Helen Tang and others, 'Supreme People's Court Issues Rules of Procedure for the China International Commercial Courts' (*Herbert Smith Freehills*, 7 December 2018) <https://hsfnotes.com/arbitration/2018/12/07/supreme-peoples-court-issues-rules-of-procedure-for-the-china-international-commercial-courts/> accessed 26 February 2020.

for enforcement of arbitral awards that apply as between Mainland China and Hong Kong and Macau.[57] The CICC began accepting cases in December 2018.[58]

9.6.2 Convention on International Settlement Agreements Resulting from Mediation

Another significant development in respect of mediation was the adoption on 20 December 2018 of the Singapore Mediation Convention.[59] To date it has been signed by fifty-three states and ratified by six.[60] It entered into force on 12 September 2020.

The Convention obliges ratifying states to enforce international settlement agreements resulting from mediation.[61] The objective of the Convention is that a mediated settlement will be as equally enforceable by virtue of the Convention as an arbitral award is by virtue of the 1958 New York Convention.[62]

The definition of what may be enforced under the Convention, that is, an international settlement agreement resulting from mediation, is broad. 'Mediation' is defined as the 'process ... whereby parties attempt to reach an amicable settlement of their dispute with the assistance of

---

[57] 'Arrangement Concerning Mutual Enforcement of Arbitral Awards between the Mainland and the Hong Kong Special Administrative Region' <www.doj.gov.hk/eng/topical/pdf/mainlandmutual2e.pdf> accessed 1 March 2020; 'Arrangement between the Mainland and the Macau Special Administrative Region on Reciprocal Recognition and Enforcement of Arbitration Awards' (*Região Administrativa Especial De Macau Gabinete Do Chefe Do Executivo*) <https://bo.io.gov.mo/bo/ii/2007/50/aviso22_cn.asp> accessed 1 March 2020; 'Publicação do Acordo sobre a Confirmação e Execução Recíprocas de Decisões Arbitrais entre o Interior da China e a Região Administrativa Especial de Macau' (*Região Administrativa Especial De Macau Gabinete Do Chefe Do Executivo*) <https://bo.io.gov.mo/bo/ii/2007/50/aviso22.asp> accessed 1 March 2020.

[58] For information on the work of the CICC, see n 54.

[59] 2019 United Nations Convention on International Settlement Agreements Resulting from Mediation.

[60] See 'Status: United Nations Convention on International Settlement Agreements Resulting from Mediation' (*United Nations Commission on International Trade Law*) <https://treaties.un.org/pages/ViewDetails.aspx?src=TREATY&mtdsg_no=XXII-4&chapter=22&clang=_en> accessed 23 September 2020.

[61] Singapore Mediation Convention (n 59), art 1. Art 2(3) of the Convention defines 'mediation' as 'a process ... whereby parties attempt to reach an amicable solution of their dispute with the assistance of a third person ... lacking the authority to impose a solution upon the parties to the dispute'.

[62] Timothy Schnabel, 'The Singapore Convention on Mediation: A Framework for the Cross-Border Recognition and Enforcement of Mediated Settlements' (2019) 19 Pepperdine Dispute Resolution Law Journal 1, 19.

a third person or persons ... lacking the authority to impose a solution upon the parties to the dispute'.[63] 'Settlement agreement' is referred to as 'an agreement resulting from mediation and concluded in writing by parties to resolve a commercial dispute'.[64] Settlement agreements must be signed and in writing, but beyond that the Convention sets no requirements as to formality or procedure. The dispute being settled must be commercial in nature and international. 'Commercial' is not defined, allowing for capacious future interpretation by courts. Some investor–state disputes that are also rightly considered commercial disputes may also be covered. 'International' is broadly defined: a settlement agreement is 'international' if at the time of the agreement the parties to it have their place of business in different states or if the subject matter of the dispute is located elsewhere than the parties.[65] The Convention will therefore most likely cover almost all non-adjudicative third-party-assisted dispute resolution processes in international commercial disputes.

The Convention contains in Article 5 grounds upon which a court may refuse to grant relief at the request of the disputing party against whom it is invoked. They relate first to the parties: that a party to the agreement was under some incapacity; second, to the agreement: it is null and void, inoperable, incapable of being performed, not binding, not final, subsequently modified, or it is the case that the obligations in the agreement have been performed or are not clear, or granting relief would be contrary to its terms; third, to the procedure: that a mediator failed to disclose circumstances that raise justifiable doubts as to his/her independence and impartiality and that failure has a material impact or undue influence on a party without which the party would not have entered into the agreement, or there was a serious breach by the mediator of standards that apply to him/her without which breach the parties would not have concluded the agreement. Article 5 also includes two additional grounds upon which the court may, on its own motion, refuse to grant relief: granting relief would be contrary to public policy; the subject matter of the dispute is not capable of settlement by mediation under the law of that contracting party.

The Article 5 grounds will no doubt provide good exercise to the courts of contracting states in the future. What may be considered a serious

---

[63] Singapore Mediation Convention (n 59), art 2(3).
[64] Singapore Mediation Convention (n 59), art 1(1).
[65] ibid.

breach of mediator standards under Article 5(1)(e) in one jurisdiction may be considered innocuous in another, for example.[66] As there is no concept of a 'seat' under the Convention, there is no one supervisory jurisdiction over the mediation process. The critical jurisdiction in terms of due process, public policy and whether a dispute may be mediated (cf 'arbitrability') will be that of the enforcing court. It will behove parties to understand the law in the enforcement jurisdiction early in the process so that they can safeguard their mediation accordingly. However, as we know from arbitration, it is not always possible or on the parties' minds to identify from the outset the jurisdictions in which enforcement may eventually be sought.

Notwithstanding that the definition of what the Convention covers is broad, it also contains limitations in its scope. It does not apply to consumer disputes or disputes under family, employment or inheritance law. It excludes mediated settlements that are enforceable as judgments or awards.[67] Article 8 allows states to make two types of declarations affecting their obligations under the Convention: first, a state may declare that it shall not apply the Convention to settlement agreements to which it is a party or to which any governmental agencies or any person acting on behalf of a governmental agency is a party.[68] This allows states to define the group of state actors that may enter into mediated settlement agreements that are then enforceable under the Convention.[69] Importantly, and particularly relevant to the BRI, this exemption was not intended to allow states to exempt state-owned enterprises from the

---

[66] For a discussion of the different legal frameworks for commercial mediation in China, Hong Kong, India and Singapore, see Eunice Cha, 'Enforcement of International Mediated Settlement Agreements in Asia: A Path towards Convergence' (2019) 15(1) Asian International Arbitration Journal 11.

[67] For discussion of the effect of these exclusions and their interplay with the 2005 Hague Convention on Choice of Court Agreements, the 2019 Hague Convention on the Recognition and Enforcement of Foreign Judgments in Civil or Commercial Matters and the 1958 New York Convention, see Schnabel (n 62) 25–28. See also Nadja Alexander and Shouyu Chong (eds), *The Singapore Convention on Mediation: A Commentary* (Global Trends in Dispute Resolution, vol 8) (Kluwer Law International 2019) 31–37 ('Article 1. Scope of Application').

[68] Singapore Mediation Convention (n 59), art 8(1)(a). To date, the Republic of Belarus, the Islamic Republic of Iran and the Kingdom of Saudi Arabia have made declarations under this Article: see United Nations Commission on International Trade Law (n 60).

[69] According to Schnabel (n 62) 56: 'Such a declaration would only have a limited reciprocal effect: if a Party exempts a particular set of its own state actors from being subject to the Convention in its courts, other Parties would have no obligation to permit those actors to seek relief under the Convention in their own courts.'

Convention's application.[70] Second, Article 8 allows states to declare that they 'apply this Convention only to the extent that the parties to the settlement agreement have agreed to the application of the Convention'.[71] Generally, the Convention applies by default unless the parties to a settlement agreement expressly opt out of it (per Article 5(1)(d) which allows refusal of enforcement where granting relief would be contrary to the agreement's terms). An Article 8(1)(b) declaration reverses the default application of the Convention, allowing states to apply the Convention on an 'opt-in' basis such that the Convention will apply only where the parties to the agreement have expressly provided for its application. If many states make an Article 8(1)(b) declaration, the scope of the Convention will be significantly reduced and dependent on parties expressly indicating their intention that it apply. That in turn will depend on parties being aware of the need to opt in in the first place.

Time will tell how broad the application of the Convention will be in terms of both the number of states that ratify it and the limiting effect of any declarations. The significant number of countries that have already signed it is encouraging in that respect. Time will also tell how significant an impact the Convention will have on the dispute resolution market. Given that most mediated settlement agreements (and indeed most settlement agreements generally) are complied with – this being inherent in their nature of being an agreed set of terms – it is difficult to measure the actual 'gap' that the Convention was written to fill. One imagines the number of international mediated settlement agreements that are not complied with to be relatively few, and, while enforcement challenges exist, recourse is available as legal title under contract law. Whatever the size of the gap, there is no doubt that the Convention will ease enforcement if widely adopted. As a result, it is likely that, for the enforcement advantage, informed disputants will use mediation more or increasingly introduce third parties into their settlement negotiations where otherwise they would not have, to bring any settlement agreement under the Convention. Another result is that dispute resolution institutions will need to be adept at providing evidence that a settlement agreement resulted from mediation to satisfy Article 4(1)(b)(ii) and (iii) of the Convention. Institutions may thus publish documents that mediators

---

[70] ibid 56–57.
[71] Singapore Mediation Convention (n 59), art 8(1)(b). To date, the Islamic Republic of Iran has made a declaration of this sort: see United Nations Commission on International Trade Law (n 60).

can sign to indicate that the mediation was carried out and attestations by the institution that administered the mediation.[72]

Given the importance of mediation in the Chinese dispute resolution landscape and the growing number of Sino-foreign transactions and disputes under the BRI, China's signing of the Convention is noteworthy.[73] Given the volume of commercial activity between Mainland China on the one hand and Hong Kong and Macau on the other, it will also be important for special arrangements to be entered into between the territories for the enforcement of mediated settlement agreements to mirror the Convention (similar to the arrangements entered into for the enforcement of arbitral awards that mirror the 1958 New York Convention).[74]

9.6.3 The Mediation Mechanism under the Closer Economic Partnership Arrangement between Mainland China and the Hong Kong SAR

The third development, a *regional* one, may also increase focus on mediation as a means of settling cross-border disputes. On 28 June 2017, the Hong Kong SAR and Mainland China updated their Closer Economic Partnership Arrangement (CEPA) with an Investment Agreement (the 'Agreement') to promote and facilitate investments by Mainland Chinese and Hong Kong SAR investors within their reciprocal territories. It provides for, among other things, substantive obligations of both sides to protect qualified investors and covered investments, including fair and equitable treatment, full protection and security, national treatment, most-favoured treatment and lawful expropriation.

---

[72] See eg Swiss Chambers of Commerce Association for Arbitration and Mediation, *Swiss Rules of Mediation* <www.swissarbitration.org/files/838/Swiss%20Rules%202019/Web%20versions%202019/Mediation%20Web%202019/mediation_2019_webversion_englisch.pdf> accessed 1 March 2020, art 16(5). Upon request the Secretariat 'shall provide the parties and the mediator with a mediation certificate confirming that the mediation took place and stating whether it led to a settlement'.

[73] One commentator identifies several areas in which China's current legal system will need to be adapted to ensure effective implementation of the Convention in China: see Wei Sun, 'Singapore Mediation Convention – Harmonization of China's Legal System with the Convention: Suggestions for the Implementation of the Convention in China' (*Kluwer Mediation Blog*, 2 March 2019) <http://mediationblog.kluwerarbitration.com/2019/03/02/singapore-mediation-convention-harmonization-of-chinas-legal-system-with-the-convention-suggestions-for-the-implementation-of-the-convention-in-china/> accessed 26 February 2020.

[74] See n 56.

Articles 19 and 20 of the Agreement include multiple mechanisms for settling disputes between an investor and the host government, one of which is mediation at the place of investment whereby an investor may submit an investment dispute arising from the Agreement to a mediation institution that has previously been designated by the host government and agreed to by the other government.[75] The Government of the Hong Kong SAR designated HKIAC's Mediation Council (HKIAC-HKMC) as one of the two mediation institutions authorised to administer disputes between a Mainland Chinese investor and the relevant authorities or institutions of Hong Kong under the Agreement.[76] HKIAC-HKMC will, among other things, facilitate the appointment of mediators from a list of designated mediators[77] and assist mediators in conducting mediations pursuant to rules produced by the Department of Justice of Hong Kong.[78]

To date, no mediations have been commenced under the Agreement, but it serves as an important instrument which includes mediation as an option for investor–state dispute resolution.

9.7 Conclusion

Parties are increasingly interested in using mixed-mode forms of dispute settlement for cross-border disputes. But this high level of interest is not

---

[75] The others are resolution through (1) amicable consultation between the disputing parties; (2) the complaint-handling mechanisms established by the respective authorities; (3) the function of notification and co-ordination of investment disputes established by the Committee on Investment of this Agreement; (4) administrative review; or (5) recourse to judicial proceedings.

[76] See 'Mainland and Hong Kong Closer Economic Partnership Arrangement (CEPA)' (*Trade and Industry Department of the Government of the Hong Kong Special Administrative Region*) <www.tid.gov.hk/english/cepa/investment/mediation.html> accessed 26 February 2020.

[77] 'List of Mediators of Hong Kong Mediation Council' <www.tid.gov.hk/english/cepa/investment/files/mediators_hkiac.pdf> accessed 26 February 2020. To be eligible, with some exceptions, mediators must (1) be accredited mediators; (2) who have mediated at least two cross-border commercial or investment disputes; (3) have at least three years' experience in an executive position at an institution involved in cross-border commerce and investment (or have equivalent credentials through academic qualifications or legal training); (4) be bilingual in Chinese and English; and (5) have completed relevant training.

[78] 'Investment Agreement under the Framework of the Mainland and Hong Kong Closer Economic Partnership Arrangement Mediation Rules for Investment Disputes' <www.tid.gov.hk/english/cepa/investment/files/HKMediationRule.pdf> accessed 26 February 2020.

yet matched by reality. Indeed, most clauses agreed in disputes under HKIAC's auspices provide for arbitration alone. Some believe that more effort on the part of external advisers, institutions, the broader dispute resolution community and governments is required for mixed-mode dispute resolution to gain greater traction. However, several very recent but significant developments – all coming out of Asia – indicate that change is already upon us. This is particularly so in the context of China's BRI with the creation of the CICC as a forum offering mixed modes of dispute settlement for international disputes. With respect to mediation, the conclusion of the Singapore Mediation Convention aims to render international mediated settlement agreements as enforceable as foreign awards and thus elevate international mediation to the pedestal that international arbitration has long enjoyed as the most preferred means of international dispute settlement. The dispute resolution mechanism adopted by the CEPA Agreement between Hong Kong and the Mainland also assigns mediation a central role in the resolution of cross-border investor–government disputes between the two jurisdictions. We will be able to measure the success of these recent and significant developments with time. In a future survey of dispute resolution clauses under HKIAC's auspices, multi-tier clauses may make a stronger showing.

10

The Use of Conciliation and Litigation by the Hong Kong Equal Opportunities Commission (EOC)

ANSELMO REYES AND WILSON LUI

10.1 Introduction

This chapter is an outlier among the other chapters in this book. The reason is that this chapter is not concerned with the resolution of commercial disputes. It focuses instead on affronts to the dignity of the person. More specifically, it looks into the use of hybrid dispute resolution to deal with complaints of discrimination, harassment and vilification on grounds of sex, race, disability or family status. The complaints may arise as a result of occurrences in the workplace or other venues, or by reason of systemic defects within community institutions. They often involve a person, group or company abusing their power and authority over another. In many jurisdictions, responsibility for handling such complaints is delegated to a bespoke government agency. In Hong Kong, the responsibility has been conferred by statute on the Equal Opportunities Commission (EOC). As with analogous bodies in other countries, the EOC is tasked with resolving complaints of discrimination through conciliation (mediation) followed (if the latter process proves unsuccessful, and if the complaint upon investigation warrants further action) by litigation. The question explored in this chapter is how an organisation such as the EOC can discharge its functions of conciliator (mediator), investigator and litigator. The difficulty is that the conflicts inherent in multi-tier dispute resolution when a person acts as mediator and decision-maker in the same dispute also confront the EOC and similar agencies in other parts of the world. The EOC and its sister organisations have to strike some balance between, on the one hand, maintaining neutrality and respecting the confidentiality of information imparted during a conciliation or mediation by an alleged wrongdoer and, on the other hand, ensuring that justice is done and those who engage in discrimination are held answerable for their wrongful conduct. The balance is not an easy one, and (as has been the position with the EOC since its inception) the public will often be critical, accusing the agency of taking too long to investigate, spending too much time to conciliate, and being too timid in deciding what cases it chooses to bring to court.

The catalyst for this chapter was an independent review of the EOC's complaint-handling process which the lead author was requested by the EOC in late October 2017 to undertake on a pro bono basis.[1] The review was conducted with the assistance of the junior author over the first half of 2018 and a final report (the External Report) with twenty-five recommendations was submitted on 30 November 2018.[2]

The EOC is an independent body established by the Hong Kong Government to promote equal opportunity and eliminate discrimination on grounds of sex, disability, family status and race.[3] The EOC

---

[1] However, the authors requested that, subject to (1) maintaining the confidentiality of those interviewed in the course of preparing the External Report and (2) the EOC giving final clearance after submission of the External Report, the authors be permitted to discuss the External Report and its conclusions in academic publications. By email dated 11 January 2019, the EOC gave the requisite clearance to the authors.

[2] In parallel with the authors' review, the EOC carried out its own internal process review. The EOC's process review resulted in a report dated 13 September 2019 (the 'EOC Report'): Equal Opportunities Commission, 'Report on Review of the Equal Opportunities Commission Governance, Management Structure and Complaint Handling Process' (*Equal Opportunities Commission*, 13 December 2019) <www.eoc.org.hk/EOC/Upload/UserFiles/File/Process_Review/EOCs_Review_Report_E.pdf> accessed 1 September 2020.

The External Report (consisting of the report proper and three annexes) appears as Appendix 7 to the EOC Report. The EOC discusses the authors' twenty-five recommendations in section 7 of the EOC Report. The EOC accepted only some of the authors' recommendations: see the EOC Report (n 2) 42–45. For an update (as at 10 June 2020) on the implementation by the EOC of the authors' recommendations (the 'EOC Update'), see 'LCQ5 Annex' (*info.gov.hk*, 10 June 2020) <https://gia.info.gov.hk/general/202006/10/P2020061000538_343171_1_1591784369710.pdf> accessed 1 September 2020.

The External Report observed that operational reviews or audits of the EOC's processes have been a staple over the twenty-odd years of the EOC's existence. It is thus unlikely that the External Report or, for that matter, the EOC Report will be the final word on the EOC's complaint-handling processes.

[3] For further background on the EOC, see Carole J Petersen, Janice Fong and Gabrielle Rush, *Enforcing Equal Opportunities: Investigation and Conciliation of Discrimination Complaints in Hong Kong* (Centre for Comparative and Public Law, The University of Hong Kong, 2003) and Katherine Lynch, 'Private Conciliation of Discrimination Disputes: Confidentiality, Informalism and Power' (paper presented at a conference on *Enforcing*

was established on 20 May 1996 following enactment of the Sex Discrimination Ordinance (Cap 480) (SDO) in 1995. Other anti-discrimination statutes (the Disability Discrimination Ordinance (Cap 487) (DDO), the Family Status Discrimination Ordinance (Cap 527) (FSDO) and the Race Discrimination Ordinance (Cap 602) (RDO)) have since also come into effect. The EOC oversees the implementation of the four statutes. The SDO forbids discrimination based on sex, marital status or pregnancy. The DDO forbids discrimination based on disability. The FSDO forbids discrimination based on family status. The RDO forbids discrimination on grounds of race. Harassment (including sexual harassment), discriminatory advertisements, instructions or pressure to discriminate, vilification (disparagement by reason of gender, race, status or disability) are all illegal under the four ordinances. All four statutes explicitly forbid the Hong Kong Government from engaging in the proscribed discriminatory acts.

The EOC fulfils its objective of eliminating discrimination and promoting equal opportunity by exercising the following principal functions:

(1) investigating complaints lodged under the four anti-discrimination statutes;
(2) encouraging conciliation between a complainant and the person against whom the complaint has been lodged (the respondent);
(3) providing legal assistance to victims of discrimination;
(4) promoting anti-discrimination and equal opportunity values and policies by implementing educational and publicity programmes and offering supporting resources;
(5) reviewing legislation and issuing guidelines; and
(6) conducting research on issues relevant to discrimination and equal opportunity.

There is little statutory guidance as to how the EOC is supposed to operate or how it is to interpret its scope of work. However, the EOC has an Internal Operating Procedures Manual (the 'IOP Manual') which contains details on how complaints are to be assessed, investigated, conciliated and legally assisted.

Equal Opportunities in Hong Kong: An Evaluation of Conciliation and Other Enforcement Powers of the EOC, June 2003). The External Report's recommendations build on Lynch's insights, especially those at Lynch (n 3) 15–16.

10.2 The Conduct of the EOC's Business

10.2.1 Structure

The EOC is overseen by a Board whose members are appointed by Hong Kong's Chief Executive. The Board has a chairperson and not fewer than four or more than sixteen other members. Members must not be public officers. The Board has authority to perform the functions and exercise the powers of the EOC. The Board has four committees. They are: (1) the Administration and Finance Committee (AFC), (2) the Community, Participation and Publicity Committee (CPPC), (3) the Legal and Complaints Committee (LCC) and (4) the Policy, Research and Training Committee (PRTC). Board members are usually assigned to at least one committee. The focus in this chapter will be on the LCC. The LCC provides advice to the chairperson and officers of the EOC, monitors and evaluates the EOC's conciliation work, oversees formal investigations, determines applications for legal assistance and decides on the issue of enforcement notices. The LCC additionally makes recommendations on matters arising out of formal investigations and on proposals for amending the anti-discrimination statutes.

The chairperson is in charge of the EOC's management. The chairperson is appointed on a three-year contract. The contract may be renewed, but this has rarely happened. The EOC has five divisions and two units. The divisions are the Complaint Services Division (CSD), the Legal Services Division (LSD), the Corporate Planning and Services Division (CPSD), the Corporate Communications Division (CCD) and the Policy, Research and Training Division (PRTD). The units are the Ethnic Minorities Unit and the Anti-Sexual Harassment Unit, which were set up in 2014 and 2021 respectively. A director, head or chief is in charge of each of the five divisions. Previously, there was a Chief Operating Officer (COO) who reported to the chairperson and acted as her or his deputy. It was envisaged that the COO would focus on internal management, enabling the chairperson to concentrate on the bigger picture, such as forging links with external organisations in Hong Kong and elsewhere, and mapping out a strategy for the EOC's future development. In May 2020, the COO was replaced by two executive directors, leading the enforcement divisions (CSD and LSD) and the operational divisions (other divisions and units) respectively.

The CSD is headed by a director (DCS). There are two sub-divisions (known as 'A' and 'B') within the CSD, each under the supervision of a Chief Equal Opportunities Officer (CEOO). The CEOOs are identified as CA or CB depending on which sub-division they head. Below them are (as at the time of the External Report) six Senior Equal Opportunities Officers (SEOOs), nine Equal Opportunities Officers (EOOs) and four Assistant Enquiry Services Officers (AESOs). The CSD is responsible for dealing with enquiries and complaints. It is usually the first port of call for a member of the public wishing to use the EOC's services. It is responsible for the conciliation and investigation of complaints. Having determined that a complaint falls within the EOC's statutory mandate, CSD officers endeavour to resolve the same through conciliation, by assisting the disputing parties to reach a legally binding settlement agreement. The CSD further undertakes self-initiated investigations (SIIs) (that is, investigations initiated by the EOC of its own motion in response to enquiries or complaints of a general nature from the public) of potential discriminatory practices within Hong Kong society. The LSD is headed by a director (identified as the Chief Legal Counsel). The director is assisted by (as at the time of the External Report) five Legal Counsel and two Assistant Legal Counsel. Following the failure of conciliation and upon a complainant applying for legal assistance, the LSD assesses whether the complaint merits the grant of legal assistance. The LSD can also provide general or specific advice on legal matters relating to Hong Kong's anti-discrimination statutes.

10.2.2 Conciliation

Where a complaint falls within the EOC's statutory jurisdiction, the EOC must investigate the complaint and it must attempt to conciliate it. The conciliation requirement is mandatory (see, for example, SDO, sections 64(1)(d) and 84(3)(b)).[4] As at the time of the External Report, the EOC

---

[4] The anti-discrimination statutes refer to 'conciliation' by the EOC. The IOP Manual distinguishes between conciliation and mediation thus:

> 5.3.1 Conciliation and mediation are terms that are often used interchangeably. Mediation is about disputing parties appointing a skilled third party – a mediator – to assist them to find a mutually acceptable solution to their differences. Conciliation is usually a mandatory court-annexed process that is found in legislation, and is more interventionist than private mediation, in that a conciliation officer has certain statutory obligations to promote.
>
> 5.3.2 Although both are 'voluntary' processes, in the sense that the parties must both desire to reach a settlement by finding a mutually acceptable solution to their dispute, conciliation pursuant to legislation generally requires the conciliation officer to use his/her best endeavours to bring the parties in a dispute to settlement whilst at the same time furthering the objectives of the legislation.

adopts a two-tier conciliation process: (1) early conciliation (which occurs before any investigation) and (2) post-investigation conciliation (also referred to as 'further conciliation'). Upon receiving a complaint, the CSD attempts early conciliation. Before any detailed investigation is undertaken, the complainant and the respondent (that is, the alleged wrongdoer) will be invited to conciliate their differences with the assistance of a CSD officer. If early conciliation succeeds, the case is closed. If early conciliation fails, the complaint undergoes detailed investigation with a view to a further attempt at conciliation, unless the complaint is withdrawn. Investigation is similarly a statutory duty of the EOC (see, for example, SDO, section 84(3)(a)). Investigation involves obtaining information on the complaint from the complainant and the respondent. The complainant is asked to furnish supporting evidence, including documentary and witness evidence. The EOC may issue notices to compel third parties to provide information for the purposes of investigation and conciliation, and a failure to comply with such notices without reasonable excuse will constitute a criminal offence. This power is found in section 5 (also referred to as 'Rule 5') of the four sets of Investigation and Conciliation Rules that serve as subsidiary legislation to the respective anti-discrimination statutes.[5] The EOC assesses a complaint in the course of conducting its investigation. It may as a result of assessment discontinue pursuing the complaint on the ground that it is frivolous, vexatious, misconceived or lacking in substance. It is for the CSD officer handling the complaint to consider whether investigation should be discontinued. Upon completion of the EOC's investigation, the parties attempt further conciliation. The success rate of further conciliation has been low, at around 5 per cent to 10 per cent. A likely reason for this is an unwillingness to conciliate due to the hardening of the parties' stances in the course of investigation.

10.2.3 Litigation

It is only after there has been no settlement of a complaint that an aggrieved person may apply to the EOC for assistance to bring court

---

In actuality, there is little to distinguish 'conciliation' as conducted by the EOC from what is conventionally understood as 'mediation'. The terms are therefore used interchangeably in this chapter.

[5] Namely, the Sex Discrimination (Investigation and Conciliation) Rules (Cap 480B), the Disability Discrimination (Investigation and Conciliation) Rules (Cap 487B), the Family Status Discrimination (Investigation and Conciliation) Rules (Cap 527A) and the Race Discrimination (Investigation and Conciliation) Rules (Cap 602B).

proceedings against the respondent. Applications for legal assistance must be made in writing. The EOC is bound by law to consider each application for assistance (see, for example, SDO, section 85(1)). But it is not obliged to grant assistance in every case. The Board has delegated to the LCC the authority to decide which cases should receive assistance and the type of assistance to be granted. For this purpose, the LSD prepares for the LCC a brief on a complaint. On the basis of the brief, the LCC determines whether legal assistance should be granted, and whether in full or only on a limited basis. The EOC has wide discretion as to which case it will assist. As it is a public organisation with only limited funds, it cannot assist every complaint. It must instead select cases which it believes will advance its objectives. Legal assistance is not limited to prosecuting a case in court. The EOC can decide to grant limited legal assistance, at least initially, for the purpose of advising a complainant on the strengths and weaknesses of a case and assessing whether a case is worth pursuing in court. When deciding which cases to pursue, attention must be accorded to cases (1) which raise a question of principle, (2) which a complainant cannot pursue on her or his own due to complexity or (3) which it would be unreasonable to turn down, having regard to the complainant's position vis-à-vis the respondent or third party (see, for example, SDO, section 85(2)). The IOP Manual (at paragraph 6.3.3) provides for the following factors to be considered when exercising the discretion to grant or refuse legal assistance:

(1) the strength of the evidence in the case;
(2) any question of principle involved;
(3) the complexity of the issues;
(4) the prevalence of the particular act/conduct;
(5) the attitude of the respondent during (or in respect of) conciliation;
(6) the conduct of the parties during conciliation;
(7) the educational value of assisting the case;
(8) the individual redress of the particular case;
(9) the positive/negative results that a court case could achieve;
(10) whether the case falls within an area which requires special attention or raises an issue which needs to be decided by a court;
(11) whether the matter was initially referred to the EOC for investigation and conciliation and a genuine attempt at conciliation was made;
(12) what implications the case has for the EOC's resources;
(13) whether EOC assistance is warranted in all the circumstances.

Despite the confidential nature of the conciliation stage, it appears from items (5) and (6) above that the sincerity, attitude and conduct of the respondent during conciliation play a role in the determination of legal assistance. If the EOC decides to grant assistance, the complainant will be advised of the nature of such aid and the terms and conditions of the same. There will a written agreement between the EOC and the complainant setting out the terms of the assistance. If the EOC decides not to grant assistance, the complainant is informed of the reasons. Persons refused assistance may apply for legal aid from the Legal Aid Department. They may also take the case to court themselves.

When deciding whether to grant legal assistance for the purpose of taking a case to court, the LCC has an unenviable responsibility. The LCC has to guard against granting legal assistance to trivial, frivolous or vexatious complaints with little or no realistic prospect. But the line between a frivolous or vexatious complaint and one which, albeit hard to prove, has merit will at times involve a judgement call on the LCC's part. The reality is that it is hard to prove a discrimination offence. For instance, many complaints involve alleged sexual harassment contrary to the SDO. Documentary evidence in such cases will often be scant. It will frequently come down to choosing between the oral testimony of the complainant and that of the respondent. Both parties will be subjected to intense cross-examination, if they elect to give evidence. For most victims, that alone would be a traumatic and daunting experience. To complicate matters, because of the gravity of such an accusation, which can have repercussions for a respondent's reputation, the court will require that the complaint be proved on a more stringent basis than the simple balance of probabilities.[6] The court will typically have to be satisfied that the complaint has been made out to something like the criminal law standard of beyond reasonable doubt. In those circumstances, it will be hard to distinguish, when determining whether to grant legal assistance, between a hopeless case which has little or no foundation as a matter of fact and law and a meritorious case for which, apart from the complainant's oral testimony, there is little evidence and which may result in failure at court.

---

[6] This is despite the District Court Ordinance (Cap 336) providing that the court in the exercise of its jurisdiction under each of the anti-discrimination statutes 'shall not be bound by the rules of evidence and may inform itself on any matter in such manner as it sees fit, with due regard to the rights of the parties to proceedings therein to a fair hearing, the need to determine the substantial merits of the case and the need to achieve a prompt hearing of the matters at issue between the parties'. See District Court Ordinance (Cap 336), ss 73B(5), 73C(5), 73D(5), 73E(5) on the proof of offences.

In coming to a decision on legal assistance, the LCC does not act as a court. It exercises an administrative discretion, not a judicial function. As seen from the IOP Manual, it needs to take into account a broad range of factors, not just the legal and evidentiary merits of a case. Such factors seemingly can include the respondent's attitude and bona fides during the conciliation stage, although this would be contrary to the conventional understanding of conciliation, whereby everything that happens in such process is supposed to remain confidential.[7] A more subtle factor that the LCC must at least bear in mind is that of moral hazard. That is because a large number of respondents at the receiving end of discrimination complaints are private individuals or MSMEs (micro-, small- and medium-sized enterprises).[8] Multinationals and government institutions can fend for themselves as respondents. But individuals or MSMEs will not necessarily have the means to engage lawyers to assist them during the conciliation process or, when legal proceedings are brought, to conduct a defence. This could lead to possible oppression where legal assistance is (say) mistakenly granted to fight an unmeritorious case with little or no realistic prospect of success in court. The complainant would have little incentive to settle because her or his costs would be covered by the EOC. Indeed, the complainant may be vindictive and relish putting the respondent in a difficult position financially through the instigation of litigation. The usual costs order in anti-discrimination court cases will be for each party to bear its own costs, unless the court is satisfied that the proceedings were brought maliciously or frivolously, or that there are special circumstances.[9] It is unlikely that the court will regard the fact that a respondent is an individual or an MSME as a special circumstance justifying a costs order against the EOC where a complainant has lost a case. Thus, a respondent may be in the position of having successfully defended against a case, only to find its finances seriously depleted by the experience.

---

[7] There are provisions in the anti-discrimination statutes protecting confidentiality: see, for example, SDO, s 84(6); Sex Discrimination (Investigation and Conciliation) Rules (Cap 480B), rr 6, 8. It is submitted that, as a cardinal principle and contrary to what the IOP Manual implies, all information imparted to a CSD officer by a respondent in the lead up to and during a conciliation should be sacrosanct. A CSD officer should not convey anything about what was said or done in connection with a conciliation (apart from the fact of its failure) to anyone.

[8] See Annex 3 of the External Report, at the EOC Report (n 2) 112. For earlier statistics, see Petersen, Fong and Rush (n 3), paras 14–15.

[9] See District Court Ordinance (Cap 336), ss 73B(3), 73C(3), 73D(3), 73E(3) on costs.

10.2.4 Complaints about the EOC's Complaint Handling

Between 2008 and 2017, the EOC received 424 applications for legal assistance. Over that period, the EOC processed 416 applications and legal assistance was granted in 193 cases (46.3 per cent). In 2018, the LCC granted legal assistance in thirty-two out of sixty-two cases (51.6 per cent). In 2019, the LCC granted legal assistance in twenty-three out of forty-one cases (56.1 per cent). The foregoing statistics indicate that the likelihood of a complainant receiving legal assistance to pursue a case in court is roughly 50 per cent. It would be meaningless to say, in a vacuum, whether 50 per cent is a good or bad ratio for the grant of legal assistance. A higher figure 'does not necessarily mean that society would be better off if [the EOC] were litigious'.[10] If a case is unmeritorious, it would be an abuse of process and a waste of taxpayers' money to bring it to court. It would also be unfair and oppressive to a respondent for the EOC to litigate a complaint that is frivolous or vexatious or has no real prospect of success. Nonetheless, from its establishment, the EOC has been regularly criticised for being insufficiently proactive in assisting complainants and taking their cases to court. It has repeatedly been suggested that the EOC is too focused on resolving cases through conciliation, rather than prosecuting cases in court.[11]

The External Report (at paragraph 5) characterised the problem as being at heart one of perception, pointing out:

> [T]here is a mismatch of perception between the public and the EOC. ... [T]his mismatch of perception needs to be addressed. It is far from ideal where the public, which funds an organisation through taxes, expects one type of service to be provided, but receives something else. The public seeks pro-active guidance from the EOC at an early stage on the strengths and merits of a complaint and how best the same might be resolved through conciliation, litigation or otherwise. The EOC, on the other hand, sees itself as a quasi-adjudicative body. It believes that, as such, it should maintain a scrupulous impartiality while investigating a complaint, attempting to conciliate the same, and (following unsuccessful conciliation) determining whether the complaint merits legal assistance to litigate the same in court. It is only if and when a decision is taken to grant legal assistance for the litigation of a complaint that the EOC truly

---

[10] Puja Kapai, 'The Hong Kong Equal Opportunities Commission: Calling for a New Avatar' (2009) 39 Hong Kong Law Journal 339, 344. Statistics are from the EOC website: <www.eoc.org.hk/eoc/graphicsfolder/inforcenter/papers/statisticlist.aspx>.
[11] ibid 342–44.

advises an aggrieved person on how best to conduct her or his complaint. But that stage will usually only come months down the road from the time when a complaint was first raised. In the meantime, the complainant is likely to feel alienated or discouraged by the whole process. Expecting to receive advice early on, the complainant instead finds oneself constantly called upon to answer probing questions, provide evidence, and justify the merits of one's complaint.

The External Report sought to bridge the gap in perception by making recommendations that would signal to the public that the EOC is a service-oriented entity, as opposed to 'an organisation that stands aloof'. In this light, the External Report (at paragraph 37) stressed that the EOC should

> not merely [be] provid[ing] conciliation services and facilities in the manner of (say) the Hong Kong Mediation Centre. Nor does it merely sit as a quasi-judicial body that determines whether discrimination complaints have legal merit. On the contrary, within the constraints set by the discrimination statutes, it exists to assist, as much as it can and to the best of its ability, members of the public having legitimate complaints about discriminatory conduct to resolve their complaints in a fair and equitable manner through conciliation and (where appropriate if conciliation fails) litigation.

A key change advocated by the External Report (at paragraph 38) was consequently that the EOC should,

> following failure of [early] conciliation, . . . grant legal assistance by way of initial legal advice . . ., especially where (as in many of the EOC's cases) there will be a power imbalance between a complainant and a respondent. It would be 'unreasonable' (applying the test in [SDO, s 85(2)(b), by way of example]) to expect a complainant in a position of power imbalance vis-à-vis a respondent to deal with a complaint unaided. . . . [I]t is likewise consonant with [SDO, ss 85(2) and (3), for instance] for the EOC to conduct detailed investigation into a complaint by way of 'any other form of assistance which the Commission may consider appropriate' ([SDO, s 85(3)(d)]), in particular where there is a disparity between the means of the complainant and the respondent.

Under the current system, a protracted and detailed investigation follows on from a failed 'early conciliation'. Thereafter, a further conciliation is attempted. But the result of this procedure has been that the complainant frequently feels victimised for a second time, as during the investigation stage she or he would have to recount (and so relive) the circumstances underlying a complaint. Further, the parties, in responding to each other's written accusations, often resort to emotional or vindictive language, thereby poisoning any prospect of settlement in the further conciliation. The External Report was concerned that, apparently in the interests of maintaining strict neutrality, the EOC does not provide an aggrieved person with legal advice on the merits of a complaint until months down the road after the further conciliation has failed and, even then, only if the LCC has decided to grant legal assistance to the aggrieved person. In such a situation, one can imagine the sense of frustration and helplessness of a member of the public who comes to the EOC for redress of a wrong to the dignity of her or his person. Such member instead finds that she or he must go through early conciliation, detailed investigation, further conciliation and a positive assessment by the LCC insofar as the grant of legal assistance is concerned before receiving any legal advice on the merits and weaknesses of her or his grievance.

On a given complaint, the EOC is bound by statute to undertake conciliation and investigation. If conciliation fails and investigation suggests that a case is meritorious, then legal assistance may be granted after an abortive further conciliation. The question is how the EOC can maintain neutrality and confidentiality when discharging its respective functions of conciliator, investigator and litigator. Insofar as conciliation is concerned, there would at the least be a conflict on a personal level. The CSD officer investigating a complaint is also the officer endeavouring to settle the complaint through further conciliation. It would be difficult for the officer to maintain fairness and impartiality as a conciliator while at the same time evaluating (judging) the truth or falsehood of each party's version of events. There would also be conflict on an organisational level. If conciliation proves abortive, the EOC must determine whether to grant legal assistance to the complainant and prosecute the respondent in court. How does the EOC ensure that confidential information conveyed by (say) the respondent during the conciliation stage does not affect its decision whether to grant legal assistance to a complainant? What about information obtained from the respondent or the latter's associates in the course of the CSD officer's investigation leading up to the failed further conciliation? Can such information, obtained at a time when the EOC was still attempting to reconcile the complainant and the respondent, be utilised in whatever way the EOC deems fit for the purpose of building up a court case on behalf of the complainant against the respondent? The External Report sought to tackle the foregoing issues within certain practical constraints. Of those constraints, the two most relevant to the present discussion were as follows:

(1) The anti-discrimination statutes (that is, the sources of the EOC's jurisdiction) were taken as a given. The External Report did not suggest how the ordinances might be improved, leaving that for others in the future.

(2) The EOC's existing organisational structure was taken as a given. The External Report did not (in contrast to previous reviews) propose a re-organisation of the EOC. It did not, for instance, venture into the ongoing debate on whether there should be a part-time non-executive chairperson and a full-time executive CEO at the apex of the EOC.

The External Report's key recommendations for resolving the conflicts are discussed in Section 10.4. Before then, it will be helpful to see how other countries have dealt (or not) with analogous conflicts in the operation of their equivalents to the EOC.

10.3 Comparative Perspectives

This section seeks to answer the questions posed about the EOC's conflicts at the end of Section 10.2 by looking into how similar bodies in four other jurisdictions have (if at all) resolved the conflict between conciliation and litigation. To this end, the handling of discrimination-related disputes by commissions in Australia, New Zealand, the UK and the USA will be contrasted with the Hong Kong system.

10.3.1 Australia

Australia has what might be thought to be a similar model to that of the EOC.[12] In fact, Hong Kong looked to the Australian model when designing its anti-discrimination legal regime.

The Australian Human Rights Commission (AHRC) is a statutory body established under the Australian Human Rights Commission Act

---

[12] The discussion here is limited to the federal discrimination legislation and the human rights watchdog at the federal level. Individuals can additionally lodge complaints at the state and territory level with the designated body in that state or territory. In some situations, complainants have to elect between engaging the federal or the state-level machinery. Otherwise, their complaint may be dismissed: Australian Human Rights Commission, 'Federal Discrimination Law' (*Australian Human Rights Commission*, 2016) 300–2, <https://humanrights.gov.au/sites/default/files/document/publication/AHRC_Federal%20Discrimination%20Law_2016.pdf> accessed 1 September 2020.

1986 (AHRCA). The AHRC is a collegiate body comprising a President and seven Commissioners, each responsible for an aspect of the AHRC's work.[13] The President, who is appointed by the Governor-General (as are the seven Commissioners), serves as the AHRC's chief executive officer. The AHRC is an independent agency. Staff handling complaints are not advocates representing a complainant or respondent. The AHRC does not have the power to decide whether unlawful discrimination has occurred. Instead, its role is to obtain both sides of the story and, where appropriate, help the parties to resolve their dispute.

A written complaint may be lodged with the AHRC, alleging that one or more acts or omissions have occurred involving unlawful discrimination. The requisite threshold is that a complaint should be 'reasonably arguable'. The AHRC 'must take reasonable steps to provide appropriate assistance to [a] person' where assistance is needed to formulate a complaint or reduce it to writing (AHRCA, section 46P). The complaint is referred to the President (AHRCA, section 46PD) who considers whether to enquire into the matter and attempt conciliation (AHRCA, sections 11(1)(aa) and 46PF(1)(c)). The President can at any time decide to investigate a complaint further, following a consideration of the matters in section 46PH of the AHRCA. Reasons should be given for the refusal or termination of an investigation. Such reasons might be that the complaint lacks merits or has been dealt with by another agency. An initial step of the AHRC's inquiry involves notifying the respondent of a complaint. The AHRC may ask the respondent to provide specific information or reply to the complaint. If the AHRC believes that a third party is capable of providing material information or producing relevant documents, it may serve a notice on that person requiring provision or production of the same (AHRCA, sections 21 and 46PI). Failure to comply without reasonable excuse is a criminal offence (AHRCA, sections 23 and 46PM). A 'reasonable excuse' is statutorily defined to include the ground that compliance 'might tend to incriminate the individual or to expose the individual to a penalty' (AHRCA, section 46PM(3)).

Many complaints go to conciliation. The AHRC acts as a neutral during the conciliation. The AHRC's role is to assist the parties to

---

[13] Namely, a Human Rights Commissioner, the Race Discrimination Commissioner, the Sex Discrimination Commissioner, the Age Discrimination Commissioner, the Disability Discrimination Commissioner, the National Children's Commissioner and the Aboriginal and Torres Strait Islander Social Justice Commissioner.

consider options for resolving a complaint and to provide information about possible terms of settlement. The AHRC will discuss with a complainant the options for resolving a grievance, including any available remedies. The AHRC will also inform the respondent about the benefits of conciliation. Conciliation will typically involve the conciliator attempting to resolve the parties' differences through a combination of exchanges by email, mail or telephone and caucuses or joint face-to-face meetings. The process is not conducted in public (AHRCA, section 46PK(2)). Parties are not supposed to focus on proving or disproving a complaint. The conciliator does not decide who is right or wrong or how the complaint should (as opposed to might) be resolved. The conciliator does not act as an advocate for either party. Instead, the conciliator allows the parties to state their viewpoints, ventilate the issues and settle the matter on their own terms. The conciliator can provide information about relevant laws and how similar cases have been resolved in the past. The conciliator decides when, where and how the conciliation is to be conducted (AHRCA, sections 46PJ and 46PK(1)). Failure to attend a conciliation upon service of the President's written notice is a criminal offence of strict liability (AHRCA, sections 46PJ(5) and 46PJ(6)). A party's reasonable expenses in attending the conference will be reimbursed (AHRCA, section 46PJ(7)). The AHRC may allow lawyers and others to participate in a conciliation. But legal professionals are not supposed to behave as if they were appearing for a client in court. They are instead supposed to 'help their client understand the benefits of conciliation' and 'assist their client to proactively consider a range of options to resolve the complaints, prioritise these options and explore areas for compromise'.[14] They should 'respect the difference between conciliation and an adversarial court process and refrain from actions such as cross-examination or seeking determination of legal issues'.[15] Confidentiality is important to enable both sides to engage in an open and frank exchange. It is maintained in the sense that information about what is said or done in the course of a conciliation cannot be used in any determination by the AHRC and later court actions concerning the complaint (AHRCA, sections 46PKA and 46PS(2)). The only exception is that a rejected offer of settlement may be considered when determining

---

[14] See 'Information for Advocates and Lawyers Participating in Conciliation' (*Australian Human Rights Commission*) <www.humanrights.gov.au/sites/default/files/conciliation_-_information_for_advocates_lawyers_-_april_2017.pdf> accessed 1 September 2020.
[15] ibid.

the incidence and quantum of costs in subsequent legal proceedings (AHRCA, section 46PSA).

Complaints can be resolved (among other means) by an apology, reinstatement in a job, compensation for pecuniary loss or injury to feelings, or the introduction of anti-discrimination policies in a company. If a complaint cannot be resolved, the conciliator may assist in further negotiations for a short period of time. A final round of information might be requested from the complainant, before the President decides whether to discontinue or terminate the case. If a complaint is terminated, the complainant may take it to the Federal Court.[16] An application to the court must be made within sixty days of the date of termination of the complaint (AHRCA, section 46PO).[17] In most circumstances, leave from the court is required (AHRCA, section 46PO(3A)). It should be noted that the AHRCA is an 'exclusive regime'. The court will not accept a case unless a complaint has first been made to the AHRC, the complaint has been terminated and a termination notice has been served.[18] The President of the AHRC can report a matter to the Federal Attorney-General if of the opinion that there has been an act of discrimination or a breach of human rights. The President's report should include recommendations on preventing the repetition or continuation of the impugned conduct and on remedial action to compensate for or reduce loss or damage (AHRCA, sections 29(2) and 35(2)).

The AHRC does not take a complaint to court. Nor can it help complainants to present their case in court, although it may help them to prepare the forms required for an application (AHRCA, section 46PT). A complainant will need to consult a lawyer or legal service provider if she or he wishes to litigate in the courts. Both the complainant and the respondent may apply to the Attorney-General for legal or financial assistance (AHRCA, section 46PU). The statutory test is twofold: (1) will refusing a person's application involve 'hardship to that person' and (2) is it 'reasonable' to grant the application 'in all the circumstances'

---

[16] But it must only be against the respondent in the complaint: see eg *Grigor-Scott v Jones* (2008) 168 FCR 450, and the complaint must be the same: AHRCA, s 46PO(3); *Desouza v Secom Australia Pty Ltd* [2013] FCCA 659.

[17] It has been said that there are 'strong public policy reasons' for the court to entertain bona fide claims relating to the infringement of human rights legislation: *Lawton v Lawson* [2002] FMCA 68. For the legal principles, see eg *Philips v Australian Girls' Choir Pty Ltd* [2001] FMCA 109. See also Australian Human Rights Commission (n 12) 317–32.

[18] Australian Human Rights Commission (n 12) 302–3.

(AHRCA, section 46PU(2))?[19] The President may provide the court with a written report on a complaint, excluding anything said or done during conciliation (AHRCA, section 46PS). When making a determination, a court is not bound by technicalities or legal forms (AHRCA, section 46PR), although procedural rules and legal principles should be taken into account.[20] If the court finds that there has been unlawful discrimination, it can impose such remedy as it thinks fit, including making any order set out in AHRCA, section 46PO(4). Examples are an order for employment or for compensation to be paid.

The AHRC has other powers. It can hold public inquiries (AHRCA, section 14). It can intervene in proceedings involving human rights issues when it considers it appropriate (AHRCA, section 11(1)(o)).[21] The Commissioners may also appear as *amicus curiae* in certain proceedings with leave of the adjudicating body. Such proceedings include those which may have a significant bearing on human rights or the administration of relevant laws and those for which it would be in the public interest that the Commissioners appear (AHRCA, section 46PV).[22]

In answer to the questions posed at the end of Section 10.2, the Australian model suggests that it may not be possible to reconcile the

---

[19] The limited data available from 2000 to 2010 indicate that the Attorney-General received twenty-seven applications for financial assistance. Of these, nine were granted, nine were refused pursuant to s 46PU(2) of the AHRCA, and nine did not proceed: Dominique Allen, 'Strategic Enforcement of Anti-discrimination Law: A New Role for Australia's Equality Commissions' (2010) 36(3) Monash University Law Review 103, 106.

[20] See eg *Zoological Board of Victoria v Australian Liquor, Hospitality and Miscellaneous Workers Union* (1993) 49 IR 41, 48 (Moore VP); *Maiocchi v Royal Australian and New Zealand College of Psychiatrists* [2014] FCA 301 [8].

[21] HRC has issued guidelines on when the Commission should intervene: 'Intervention in Court Proceedings: The Australian Human Rights Commission Guidelines' (*Australian Human Rights Commission*, 18 September 2009) <https://humanrights.gov.au/our-work/legal/intervention-court-proceedings-australian-human-rights-commission-guidelines> accessed 1 September 2020. The instances in which HRC intervened, together with HRC's submissions, are publicly available: 'Submission to Court as Intervener and Amicus Curiae' (*Australian Human Rights Commission*) <https://humanrights.gov.au/our-work/legal/submissions/submission-court-intervener-and-amicus-curiae> accessed 1 September 2020.

[22] HRC has issued guidelines on when the Commissioners should intervene: 'Commission Guidelines for the Exercise of the Amicus Curiae Function under the Australian Human Rights Commission Act (*Australian Human Rights Commission*, 18 September 2009) <https://humanrights.gov.au/our-work/legal/amicus-guidelines> accessed 1 September 2020. The instances in which the Commissioners intervened, together with the respective Commissioner's submissions, are publicly available: 'Submission to Court as Intervener and Amicus Curiae' (n 21).

EOC's roles. On a given complaint, the AHRC essentially acts purely as conciliator. If conciliation fails, the AHRC maintains its neutrality and does not switch hats to become the prosecutor of the complaint. It does not decide whether to grant legal assistance to a complainant. It may assist the court in various proceedings or conduct inquiries itself. But such proceedings or inquiries are unrelated to complaints in which the AHRC has acted as conciliator. Although superficially similar to the EOC system in Hong Kong, the Australian model keeps the AHRC's conciliation and litigation functions separate and distinct.[23]

10.3.2 New Zealand

The Human Rights Commission (HRC) is the independent Crown entity responsible for administering the Human Rights Act 1993 (HRA) on discrimination-related matters. The HRA protects persons from unlawful discrimination on various prohibited grounds (HRA section 21). It also makes certain behaviour unlawful, including sexual harassment, racial harassment, causing racial disharmony, and victimisation (HRA, sections 61–69). Under the HRA, the HRC is tasked with resolving complaints of unlawful discrimination (HRA, section 76(1)). It is required 'to facilitate the resolution of disputes ... by the parties concerned, in the most efficient, informal, and cost-effective manner possible'. There is no limit to the dispute resolution services that the HRC can provide (HRA, sections 77 and 78).

A complainant can phone or email the HRC for a discussion in the first instance. The initial conversation may help to clarify the issues and consider ways to resolve them. The conversation can lead to a formal complaint being lodged with the HRC. However, other means of recourse are available. HRC staff can discuss options to work out the optimal way forward. For example, a possibility might be to arrange for an aggrieved

---

[23] The two 'exceptions' are the South Australian Equal Opportunities Commission and the Western Australian Equal Opportunities Commission. Under the Equal Opportunity Act 1984 (SA), s 95C, the Commissioner may, at the request of the complainant or respondent, provide representation for that party in proceedings before the tribunal. Before 2009, the Commissioner had to assist a complainant (not a respondent) to present her or his complaint to the tribunal, if requested. This mandatory requirement was repealed following a review which considered the conflict between the Commissioner's impartiality in handling a complaint and the Commissioner's partisanship in representing the complainant. Under the Equal Opportunity Act 1984 (WA), s 93A(1), the Commissioner may arrange for legal representation or financial assistance for a complainant to appear in the Supreme Court or the State Administrative Tribunal. See Allen (n 19).

person to discuss the issue directly with the person or organisation concerned. A complaint can be lodged with the HRC by phone, fax, email or post. However, a complaint need not be in writing.

The HRC does not provide legal representation to a party. Nor does it form an opinion about whether there has been a breach of the HRA. It does not investigate matters or make findings as to whether conduct is discriminatory. The HRC's aim is instead to help in resolving disputes over actual or potential breaches of the HRA. This means that, to engage the HRC's services, a complainant does not need to show that there has been an actual breach of the law. In general, a complaint of discrimination must at least show a prohibited ground (such as sex or race) as influencing or being connected to the impugned conduct. The HRC will consider a range of factors when determining whether to offer a dispute resolution process (HRA, section 80), including whether there is another agency or process better suited to respond and whether there has been delay for more than twelve months. If the HRC decides to take no further steps, it must give reasons for its decision to the parties and inform them of their right to bring an action before the Human Rights Review Tribunal (HRA, section 80(4)).

The HRC has a dispute resolution process to resolve complaints of discrimination and harassment. The process allows parties (whether an individual, an MSME, a multinational company or a government agency) to receive necessary information (HRA, section 81) and to discuss a complaint in a fair, open and constructive manner. The service can take various forms, depending on what is best for the complaint. For example, (1) information can be provided to enable the parties to resolve the matter independently (self-help), (2) the parties may be directed to educational and other resources, and (3) mediation may be attempted, whether in writing, over the telephone or face-to-face. The HRC's mediators treat all persons impartially. The mediators assigned to complaints by the HRC will ensure that the parties understand the process and relevant legislation. They will suggest possible solutions. But they will not impose their views. The HRC does not determine whether actions or policies are discriminatory; it merely assists the parties to arrive at practical ways to address a complaint. The mediation process is entirely confidential. Statements during the mediation cannot be disclosed to anyone outside of that process unless agreed by all parties. Nor can any statements be used for any other purpose, whether by the mediator, the HRC or the parties (HRA, sections 85 and 86).

Complaints that cannot be resolved through the HRC's dispute resolution process can be heard by the Human Rights Review Tribunal (HRRT), an independent forum administered by the Ministry of Justice. While what happens during the HRC's dispute resolution process is confidential, proceedings before the HRRT are not. Proceedings are open to the public, although anonymity orders are possible (HRA, section 107).[24] A complaint is heard by the HRRT's chairperson and two members, after which a determination is made. The HRRT has the power to grant damages and other remedies (see, for example, HRA, section 92I(3)) and may refer the question of remedies to the High Court if the loss suffered exceeds the monetary limits of the District Court (HRA, sections 92R–92U).

The Office of Human Rights Proceedings (OHRP) may provide free legal representation for a complainant before the HRRT. Although the OHRP functions in similar ways to the LSD of Hong Kong's EOC, it is a separate part of the HRC. The OHRP is headed by the Director of Human Rights Proceedings who is required (see especially HRA, section 20(3)) to act independently of anyone, including the rest of the HRC and ministers of the Crown. The OHRP is staffed with two senior solicitors, a legal adviser and a legal executive or executive assistant.[25] The OHRP has limited resources and cannot provide representation to all who apply. The OHRP represents only plaintiffs, not defendants. The OHRP will reject an application for assistance if no attempt has been made to resolve the complaint through the HRC's dispute resolution process. Once the OHRP receives an application for assistance, it will request a copy of the HRC's complaint file, subject to the applicant's consent. An OHRP lawyer will review the file and discuss the complaint further with the applicant. The OHRP then decides whether to provide legal representation (HRA, section 92). Its decision with reasons (if representation is refused) will be set out in a letter to the applicant (HRA, section 92A(1)(b)). The OHRP aims to decide within sixty working days of receiving a complaint file from the HRC.[26] If legal assistance is refused, a complainant can take a case to the HRRT at his or her own expense. The decision to provide legal representation does not entitle a complainant to representation for an appeal or other proceedings. In

---

[24] See eg *Erceg v Erceg* [2016] NZSC 135, [2017] 1 NZLR 310; *Waxman v Pal (Application for Non-Publication Orders)* [2017] NZHRRT 4; *Director of Proceedings v Brooks (Application for Final Non-Publication Orders)* [2019] NZHRRT 33.
[25] 'About the Office of Human Rights Proceedings' (*Office of Human Rights Proceedings*) <www.hrc.co.nz/ohrp/about/> accessed 1 September 2020.
[26] 'Frequently Asked Questions' (*Office of Human Rights Proceedings*) <www.hrc.co.nz/ohrp/faqs/> accessed 1 September 2020.

each instance, the Director makes a fresh decision on legal representation. The Director may withdraw legal representation at any stage. The Director or the HRRT may send a case back to the HRC for mediation (HRA, sections 91(2) and 92D, respectively). In some cases, when the Director remits a matter for mediation, an OHRP lawyer may represent the complainant at the mediation.[27]

Some situations of discrimination and breaches of human rights cannot adequately be resolved through the HRC's dispute resolution service. The HRC has a wide range of powers to address these issues in ways that will have a greater long-term impact. For example, the HRC can conduct inquiries and bring civil proceedings (HRA, sections 5(2)(h) and 92E). An inquiry can raise community understanding of pertinent issues and result in recommendations to government and other agencies to address systemic discrimination.[28] The HRC can appear in civil proceedings (HRA, section 92H). The HRC also can intervene informally, for example, by facilitating a meeting between opposing groups, by providing education or training programmes, or by developing guidelines to assist organisations in understanding their responsibilities under the HRA.

New Zealand has accordingly answered the question posed at the end of Section 10.2 by having separate and distinct units within its HRC. There is the HRC proper, which conducts mediations in human rights or discrimination-related disputes, and, as an independent part of the HRC, there is the OHRP. Although the HRC's complaint file may be provided to the OHRP, that will simply identify the nature of the complaint. Nothing of what has happened or been communicated in an HRC mediation will be disclosed to the OHRP and it will be up to the OHRP's officers to conduct whatever investigations they deem appropriate to enable them to decide whether to grant assistance.

10.3.3 The UK

In the UK,[29] under the Equality Act 2006 (EA), as from 1 October 2007, the former Commission for Racial Equality, Equal Opportunities Commission, and Disability Rights Commission were amalgamated into the Equality and Human Rights Commission (EHRC). The EHRC is an independent

---

[27] ibid.
[28] For example, the Inquiry into the use and promotion of New Zealand Sign Language in 2013, and the Inquiry into Accessibly Public Land Transport in 2005.
[29] The discussion here is limited to England and Wales. Northern Ireland has its Equality and Human Rights Commission under the Northern Ireland Act 1998, s 68. Scotland has

statutory body sponsored by the Government Equalities Office. It is separate from and independent of the government, albeit accountable for its use of public funds. Section 3 of the EA states that the EHRC's general duty is to encourage and support the development of a society in which there is respect for equality, diversity and human rights. The EHRC's duties are set out in sections 8 and 9 of the EA. The EHRC also monitors and advises the government on the effectiveness of the UK's equality and human rights enactments (EA, section 11). It provides relevant information, advice, education and training (EA, section 13) to the public, publishes codes of practice (EA, section 14), and conducts inquiries (EA, section 16). The EHRC may investigate on its own initiative whether a person has committed an unlawful discriminatory act (EA, section 20). The person may be served with an unlawful act notice, specifying the unlawful act by reference to provisions of the Equality Act 2010. The notice can require the person served to propose an action plan for avoiding a repetition or continuation of the unlawful act or otherwise remedying the situation (EA, section 21(4)). If an individual disagrees with the unlawful act notice, he or she can appeal to the appropriate court or tribunal[30] within six weeks of the notice. The court or tribunal can then affirm, annul or vary the notice and make an order for costs and expenses. Alternatively, the EHRC and the person notified may enter into an agreement whereby the latter undertakes not to commit the unlawful act in return for the EHRC not proceeding against her or him (EA, section 23). The agreement is not treated as an admission by the relevant person. The EHRC may investigate whether a person has complied with an unlawful act notice or an undertaking (EA, section 20).

The EHRC may assist a person with a complaint that she or he has been the victim of an unlawful act (EA, section 28). The assistance may take the form of legal advice, legal representation or provision of facilities for the settlement of the dispute. The EHRC can itself commence (or intervene in) legal proceedings, if the subject matter is relevant to the performance of its functions (EA, section 30). Previously, by section 27 of the EA, the EHRC could arrange for conciliation services in respect of certain non-employment related disputes. But this power was repealed by section 64(1)(b) of the Enterprise and Regulatory Reform Act 2013. This

---

its Human Rights Commission under the Scottish Commission for Human Rights Act 2006.

[30] Typically, the county court or the Employment Tribunal: EA, s 21(7).

was apparently done to clarify the EHRC's remit.[31] The conciliation service had been available to parties to facilitate the settlement of disputes by agreement without recourse to legal proceedings. All information communicated to the conciliator was treated as confidential, not to be disclosed to others without the consent of the party making the communication. Administrative arrangements were made to prevent confidential information arising in a conciliation from being disclosed to the EHRC Commissioner or a member staff.

In summary, the EHRC is no longer responsible for carrying out the conciliation or mediation of discrimination-related disputes or deciding whether to initiate actions on behalf of a complainant.[32] An aggrieved person can now only (1) complain directly to the person or organisation involved, (2) engage on their own in mediation with such person or organisation, or (3) bring a claim in a court or tribunal. With respect to the last, the aggrieved person may seek assistance from the EHRC. Hence, the conflicts faced by the EOC in Hong Kong do not arise within the EHRC.

10.3.4 The USA

The US Equal Employment Opportunity Commission (EEOC) is responsible for enforcing federal anti-discrimination laws. It has authority to investigate charges of discrimination against employers covered by the legislation, that is, employers having at least fifteen employees (twenty employees for age discrimination cases). When a charge is filed, the EOOC will notify the respondent within ten days. There will be an electronic portal for the respondent to log in and access the details of the charge, together with information about the investigation. Mediation is the first stage of resolution that the EEOC will recommend. Almost all disputes are eligible.[33] The process is a voluntary one in which parties can discuss the charge. In practice, the parties elect to mediate at this early stage; otherwise, the charge proceeds to investigation. However, a 2020 ADR Pilot Scheme (also known as the 'ACT' Mediation Pilot Program) allows for

---

[31] See Explanatory Notes to s 64 of the Enterprise and Regulatory Reform Act 2013 <www.legislation.gov.uk/ukpga/2013/24/notes/division/5/4/3/1> accessed 1 September 2020.

[32] 'Discrimination: Your Rights' (*gov.uk*) <www.gov.uk/discrimination-your-rights/what-you-can-do> accessed 1 September 2020.

[33] The few exceptions include class and systemic charges, charges filed under the Genetic Information Non-Discrimination Act, or those filed solely under the Equal Pay Act. The EEOC also has the authority to withhold charges from mediation in cases where it serves the public interest to investigate the same. Under the 2020 ADR Pilot scheme, the only exceptions are disputes which the EEOC determines as devoid of merit.

mediation at any time during the process.³⁴ The Pilot Scheme permits the use of technology for virtual mediations, with reduced costs and improved accessibility during the COVID-19 outbreak.³⁵ The EEOC has given a wide range of reasons as to why mediation is preferred, including efficiency, neutrality and informality.³⁶ The goal is to ventilate an issue and reach a satisfactory settlement agreeable to all parties. The process does not involve fact-finding on the mediator's part. A settlement agreement does not constitute an admission of wrongdoing. The process is facilitated by the EEOC's use of Universal Agreements to Mediate (UAMs). It involves the EEOC and a respondent agreeing to mediate all relevant charges filed against the latter prior to investigation or litigation. Given the voluntary nature of mediation, the parties can opt out of mediation on a given charge even though a UAM has been signed. UAMs are confidential unless otherwise agreed.³⁷ Settlement can take various forms, such as the payment of compensatory or punitive damages. Limits on damages are applicable, depending on the respondent's size. If mediation is successful, there is no investigation. Mediation sessions are not recorded or transcribed. Notes taken during mediation are destroyed. If mediation is unsuccessful, information obtained during mediation cannot be used in an EEOC investigation.

During investigation, the EEOC will ask both parties to supply relevant documents. For a respondent, this may be a statement of position, information on personnel policies, or personnel files. The EEOC may request an on-site visit to view or photocopy materials and conduct interviews among management and employees. The EEOC investigator will evaluate the evidence to assess whether there is 'reasonable cause' to believe that unlawful discrimination has taken place. If the EEOC concludes that the evidence does not establish a violation, the complainant will receive a 'Dismissal and Notice of Rights' which is copied to the respondent. The former may then file

---

[34] 'Questions and Answers – 2020 ADR Pilot' (*US Equal Employment Opportunity Commission*) <www.eeoc.gov/questions-and-answers-2020-adr-pilot> accessed 1 September 2020.

[35] 'United States: EEOC Expands Voluntary Resolution Efforts with Temporary Mediation and Conciliation Pilot Programs' (*Mondaq.com*, 5 August 2020) <www.mondaq.com/unitedstates/employee-rights-labour-relations/972302/eeoc-expands-voluntary-resolution-efforts-with-temporary-mediation-and-conciliation-pilot-programs> accessed 1 September 2020.

[36] '10 Reasons to Mediate' (*US Equal Employment Opportunity Commission*) <www.eeoc.gov/10-reasons-mediate> accessed 1 September 2020.

[37] 'Questions and Answers Universal Agreements to Mediate (UAMS)' (*US Equal Employment Opportunity Commission*) <www.eeoc.gov/questions-and-answers-universal-agreements-mediate-uams> accessed 1 September 2020.

a lawsuit in a federal or state court within ninety days of receipt of the notification. If the EEOC decides that there is reasonable cause to believe that discrimination has occurred, the parties will receive a 'Letter of Determination' to that effect. The letter will invite the parties to settle the charge through an informal and confidential conciliation conducted under the EEOC's auspices.[38] This latter conciliation is voluntary. The parties work together with an investigator to develop a remedy for the discrimination. The investigator may take a more active role than the mediator in the initial mediation. The conciliation is effectively a process of negotiation whereby offers and counter-offers are made. Note in this connection that the EEOC is statutorily required to attempt to resolve findings of discrimination through 'informal methods of conference, conciliation, and persuasion'.[39] The EEOC therefore encourages parties to take advantage of the conciliation to resolve the charge informally, before the EEOC considers litigation. If conciliation fails, the EEOC may commence a lawsuit in the federal court. But litigation is a last resort. If the EEOC decides against litigation, the complainant will receive a 'Notice of Right to Sue' and may start an action in the federal court within ninety days. The EEOC does not assist the complainant in such action. The EEOC can also participate in ongoing litigation as *amicus curiae*. Further, the EEOC leads and co-ordinates the equal employment opportunity efforts of the federal government. It can conduct administrative hearings and issue appellate decisions on complaints of discrimination by federal employees and applicants for federal employment.

Among the jurisdictions surveyed, the EEOC model most closely resembles the situation of the EOC in Hong Kong. It conducts two levels of mediation or conciliation. There is an initial mediation before investigation begins. Confidential information disclosed during such process is not disclosed to anyone else. Thereafter, an investigation takes place and, if there is evidence of discrimination, an investigator conducts a proactive conciliation if the respondent is agreeable to such process. In light of the information obtained during the investigation, the investigator turned conciliator proposes possible remedies to the respondent who is taken to have engaged in wrongdoing. There is no pretence here of treating the respondent as an innocent party. If this robust conciliation fails or is rejected, litigation may ensue. The key step to forestalling conflicts of the sort identified in Section 10.2 is to ensure that the early

---

[38] 'What You Can Expect after a Charge Is Filed' (*US Equal Employment Opportunity Commission*) <www.eeoc.gov/employers/what-you-can-expect-after-charge-filed> accessed 1 September 2020.

[39] 42 USC § 2000e-5.

mediation process is kept confidential from those who conduct any later investigation, conciliation and litigation. There is also a difference from the way that the EOC conducts litigation. In Hong Kong, the EOC's role is analogous to that of a third-party funder in a commercial arbitration. If the EOC decides to provide legal assistance to a complainant, it will not be in the driving seat of the resulting District Court litigation; it takes its instructions from the complainant. In contrast, if the EEOC takes up a case against a respondent, it does so in its own right. The action is that of the EEOC, which has free rein to decide how to conduct its case.

10.4 Reconciling the EOC's Conflicting Roles

The EOC Report laudably resolves in paragraph 1 to adopt what the EOC calls a 'victim-centric approach as an integral part of its culture'. But the difficulty with this approach is how the 'victim' is to be identified in the first place. Thus, the Prelude to the EOC Report fairly observes:

> In the context of a discrimination case, a victim-centric approach is one which, while focused on operating within principles of fairness and impartiality to both parties in a complaint activated under the Anti-Discrimination Ordinances, nevertheless recognises and pays special attention to the needs of victims at all stages of the complaint handling process. An important, but related observation is that the victim could be the complainant, the respondent, or some other third party. Accordingly, for a complaint that alleges an act which is not unlawful and/or is otherwise frivolous, vexatious, misconceived and/or lacking in substance the EOC will seek to dismiss it, and to direct resources to the pursuit of appropriate cases for the victims as complainants.

If the respondent can be the victim of a false accusation by a complainant, how and when does the EOC decide on whom to focus its victim-centric approach? It appears that the only practical way to ascertain the true victim would be to conduct a detailed investigation. Thus, the EOC Report's 'victim-centric approach' in effect merely restates the problem inherent in the EOC's conflicting roles as conciliator, investigator and prosecutor. The real question remains how can the EOC carry out all its roles, acting as 'honest broker' in a conciliation, as an investigator assessing who the victim actually is, and as litigator prosecuting a case against a wrongdoer on behalf of an identified victim.

Of the twenty-five recommendations made by the External Report, seven were put forward as a way of reducing actual or potential conflicts of interest in the way that the EOC operates:

Recommendation (1)

The EOC should require all complainants to attempt what is now called 'early conciliation', such process should normally be completed within two to three months of the making of the complaint. Where this 'early conciliation' fails, the EOC should straightaway proceed to considering whether and (if so) in what form it should grant legal assistance to a complainant. To facilitate this change in operating procedure, it is suggested that what is now known as 'early conciliation' should simply be renamed as 'conciliation'.

Recommendation (3)

Following the failure of conciliation (formerly early conciliation), save in cases that plainly are outside of the EOC's remit or are frivolous, vexatious, misconceived or lacking in substance, limited legal assistance should normally be granted to a complainant to enable the EOC to perform one or more of these functions:

(a) providing initial advice to an aggrieved person on the strengths and weaknesses of a complaint,
(b) developing a plan in conjunction with an aggrieved person for bringing a complaint to court (including the degree of investigation required, the evidence to be gathered through such investigation, and the timetable to be followed), and
(c) in light of the results of the detailed investigation to be carried out, assessing in conjunction with the aggrieved person the legal merits, the strength of the evidence, and the likely outcome of any court proceedings.

Recommendation (6)

The EOC will need to ensure that [systems] are in place to prevent a CSD officer who has acted as conciliator on a complaint from later having anything to do with the detailed investigation and legal assessment of that same complaint. . . .

Recommendation (7)

In most cases, the EOC should target making a decision on whether or not to grant full legal assistance for the purposes of bringing a case to court within 6 months from the failure of conciliation.

Recommendation (11)

it should be a normal expectation that the LCC decides whether to grant full assistance within 9 to 12 months of a complaint being made or of a specific enquiry being classified as a complaint.

Recommendation (12)

The LCC should continue its practice of giving reasons for any refusal of full legal assistance. It will not normally be enough merely to issue a terse statement that a complaint lacks legal or evidentiary merit and no principle of importance is involved. Reasons can be succinct, but they should convey the gist of the considerations that the LCC has taken into account.

Recommendation (21)

A CSD officer who has conducted an abortive conciliation should refrain from communicating anything about the conciliation (apart from the fact that it failed) to anyone else.

Recommendations (1) and (3) were mentioned earlier.[40] The underlying rationale of Recommendation (1) was that the EOC's 'early conciliation process has been universally acknowledged as bringing about the speedy resolution of a significant number of complaints'. In contrast, for the reasons discussed already,[41] where, after an abortive 'early conciliation', the EOC conducts an investigation with a view to a further conciliation, that further conciliation exercise has largely been unsuccessful at resolving a dispute. The thinking was accordingly that there should be a serious attempt at conciliation early on and, if that was unsuccessful, the EOC should switch from its conciliation mode to its litigation mode. There could be a further conciliation, if the complainant and respondent so wished, at a later stage. But the EOC's role would then be to facilitate the parties having such further conciliation before an independent mediator (that is, someone unconnected with the EOC or (if from the EOC) a CSD officer with no previous involvement or knowledge of the relevant complaint). It seemed to the authors that once the EOC had gone into investigation mode following an abortive 'early conciliation', it would be inappropriate for the EOC (especially the EOC officer involved in the investigation) to act as mediator in respect of the same complaint. There would be a real risk of actual or apparent bias in such situation. Recommendation (3) picks up from Recommendation (1) and the failure of 'early conciliation'. It was meant to address the complaint that the EOC was not providing enough legal assistance to complainants. The idea was that, save when a complaint is plainly devoid of substance, following an abortive early conciliation, all complainants should be granted initial legal assistance by the EOC for the purpose of assessing the strengths and weaknesses of their case and mapping a way forward. Recommendation (3) was intended to deal

---

[40] See Sections 10.2.2 and 10.2.4.
[41] See Section 10.2.4.

with the mismatch of perceptions identified by the External Report. It was hoped that, as a result, complainants would feel a sense of 'ownership' over the progress of their complaint, in the sense of understanding the legal merits and evidential difficulties of the same and having a say in how their complaint was to be investigated and its forensic weaknesses addressed.

The EOC has apparently not accepted Recommendations (1) and (3). The EOC Report explained the EOC's reasons as follows (footnotes omitted):

> 7.5 The Independent Report proposes that following receipt of a complaint, the EOC should be focused on conciliating the case during the initial two to three months, and thereafter on granting some form of legal assistance for most of the complaints except those excluded by s 84(4) of the SDO and its equivalent in the other Ordinances. This would include cases where no unlawful act appears to have been committed, the complainant does not wish to proceed further, the 12-month time bar has lapsed or the complaint is frivolous, vexatious, misconceived and/or lacking in substance.
>
> In this connection, the Review Panel Members refer to the Anti-Discrimination Ordinances where it is stipulated that after complaint is lodged with the EOC, the EOC shall 'conduct an investigation into the act subject of the complaint ... and endeavour, by conciliation, to effect a settlement'. In the course of the Review, Panel Members observed that current statistics indicate that, following the proper classification of enquiries to complaints, around 50% of complaints received are in the category of not concerning unlawful acts, of being frivolous, vexatious, misconceived and/or lacking in substance. In certain cases, therefore the identified victim is the respondent (albeit there may not be discrimination of the proper victim). For example, in an actual case, a professional alleged that an institution was discriminating the professional in relation to certain matters, when in fact, the professional had committed multiple breaches of confidentiality under the guise of seeking to find the truth, which went way beyond common decency or acceptable behaviour. There were also other legal redress options available to the professional which were being pursued. The application was rejected on the basis that it was misconceived, as with a number of other complaints.
>
> If this particular proposal as mentioned above was broadly adopted, there is a risk, and we are referring to a risk only, in the minds of a fair-minded individual, and maybe even within the CSD that conciliation should be attempted in all cases. The Review Panel Members therefore recommend the CSD to continue to apply the

current investigation procedures under the Anti-Discrimination Ordinances and IOP.

7.6 In addition, and more importantly, from the legal perspective, Review Panel Members note that during this suggested initial conciliation period of two to three months suggested under the recommendations, 'evidence of anything said or done by any person in the course of conciliation under this section (including anything said or done at any conference held for the purposes of such conciliation) is not admissible in evidence in any proceedings under this Ordinance except with the consent of that person' (privilege). If Professor REYES's recommendations were adopted, then after two to three months and a very initial investigation, where conciliation fails, there would be a real risk that the LSD would inherit a case with no evidence from the respondent as everything said and done would have been for conciliation. There would therefore be significant duplication of efforts required and funding requirements to investigate to obtain the evidence again. This would again create a double burden for the victim having to start from the beginning, would prolong the time of processing and the respondent could well come up with a different version of facts. There was consensus between Review Panel Members and EOC key staff that that this proposal would likely be difficult to work in practice.

The authors respectfully disagree. The authors do not see how what is stated in paragraph 7.5 of the EOC Report has any bearing on the rationale underlying Recommendations (1) and (3), which are the most significant proposals made by the External Report. It is unclear, for instance, how the giving of limited assistance following a failed early conciliation can logically give rise to a risk (of whatever magnitude) that 'conciliation should be attempted in all cases'. It is likewise difficult to follow the reasoning in paragraph 7.6 of the EOC Report. It is suggested there that, after early conciliation, the LSD would 'inherit a case with no evidence from the respondent as everything said and done would have been for conciliation' with the result that 'there would ... be significant duplication of efforts required and funding requirements to investigate to obtain the evidence'. It is true that any 'investigation' prior to early conciliation would be minimal. The External Report (at paragraph 23) put it thus:

> [Recommendation 1] means that there would no longer be the protracted and cumbersome detailed investigation and conciliation process that is presently undertaken by the CSD. Instead, at this early stage in the handling a complaint, a CSD officer would only conduct such preliminary investigation as may be necessary to glean the essential facts of

a complaint in order to conduct a neutral 'early conciliation' between the complainant and respondent. To avoid confusion, there no longer being a subsequent 'conciliation' stage if 'early conciliation' fails, it is suggested that what is now known as 'early conciliation' might be more simply renamed as 'conciliation'.

Detailed investigation would commence straightaway, if what the EOC now calls 'early conciliation' were to fail. In those circumstances, it is hard to see what 'duplication of efforts' there would be or how the complainant would be twice vexed by investigators. The 'investigation' carried out prior to 'early conciliation' would be no more than to ascertain relevant facts and matters, that is, to find out what any mediator would have to know to carry out a mediation.

Nonetheless, the authors have stated above that the EOC has 'apparently' rejected Recommendation (3). That is because the picture is not wholly clear. Notwithstanding what is said in paragraphs 7.5 and 7.6 of the EOC Report, the EOC Report (at paragraph 13) states:

> The victims of discrimination should be given the opportunity, following an unsuccessful conciliation, to meet a legal professional from the LSD team. This would be after LSD's review of the facts and evidence up to the stage of conciliation which are not subject to privilege. The purpose of the meeting is for the LSD to provide the victim with an analysis of what the gaps in the case are and in relation to which the LSD would need further information and/or would need to investigate for the purpose of providing an impartial legal analysis to the LCC to assist the LCC to determine whether to grant legal assistance, and the extent of such, (limited or full assistance) depending on the legal and policy considerations of the LCC. The Review Panel Members believe that this aspect is important to the victim-centric approach and EOC should seek to reorganise its resources and/or seek Government funding to achieve this objective. The Chairperson is recommended to make this a priority item at the A&FC [Administration and Finance Committee] for effective resourcing.

The foregoing suggests that, after a failed further conciliation, the victim (presumably, this refers to the complainant) is to be given legal assistance of some sort. While it is not apparent from the EOC Report on what basis the complainant is to be identified as the victim following an unsuccessful conciliation, this will likely be as a result of the detailed investigation conducted between the early and further conciliation. That investigation will possibly filter out complainants whose accusations are obviously trivial, frivolous or vexatious, leaving only genuine complainants to be dealt with as proposed in paragraph 13. This is similar to Recommendation (3) of the External Report, except that the relevant legal assistance is given at a later stage under the EOC Report's scheme. Recommendation (3) would be more generous and provide some legal assistance to all bona fide complainants following early conciliation.

The authors query whether, consistently with its role as 'honest broker' in a conciliation, the EOC can conduct a detailed investigation of the merits of a case while conciliation proceedings remain in progress. More pertinently, what paragraph 7.6 of the EOC Report does not address is the problem of reconciling the EOC's role (in particular, that of its CSD officers) as investigator (digging into the facts and ascertaining what actually did or did not happen) and conciliator (avoiding making value and other judgements of the parties' respective cases). Nor does paragraph 7.6 address confidentiality. The EOC Report suggests that information obtained by a CSD conciliator in the course of preparing for further or perhaps even early conciliation can be passed on to the LSD for use in putting together a case against a respondent. But, if so, that would contradict the EOC's apparent acceptance of Recommendation (21). The EOC Report (at paragraph 8.4) instead makes its own recommendations to address the concerns just indicated:

(ix) As to the investigation processes undertaken by CSD, it is wrong in principle for the CSD to investigate a case only for the purpose of conciliation. The Anti-Discrimination Ordinances state where a complaint is lodged the EOC shall conduct an investigation into the act, and endeavour by conciliation to effect a settlement. The Review Panel Members cannot equate this to a leap of logic that the investigation should be for the purpose of conciliation. This is because there is a need to have a holistic view of a case prior to attempts at conciliation. This is part of the art of case management. . . .

(x) On the issue of preservation of the victims' privilege which attaches to conciliation only, CSD should explain up-front that the victim should seriously consider agreeing to release anything said and done by the victim where conciliation fails, otherwise the case would not be on firm grounds for legal assistance.

(xi) On the other hand, the CSD should limit investigations over respondents and potential respondents which attract privilege for conciliation. The CSD has powers of investigation under applicable rules and regulations under the Anti-Discrimination Ordinances. These allow for it to obtain information and evidence generally from a respondent, potential respondents and/or third parties. The CSD should be ready to use its powers as regulator for effectiveness in discharging its regulatory objectives.

The authors do not believe that the EOC's recommendations meet their concerns. The issue is perception. The fact that the EOC has powers to compel the respondent and third parties to provide evidence is neither here nor there. If the conciliation is to be conducted as a truly voluntary exercise, the respondent must not feel compelled or pressured to provide incriminating information or evidence in relation to her or his case while conciliation is ongoing. No one denies that the EOC has the power and the duty to investigate complaints. The question is how any detailed investigation is to be conducted in a way that does not undermine the EOC's role as conciliator. The External Report proposed that detailed investigation commence immediately after a failed early conciliation. At that point, the EOC would cease to be conciliator and act as investigator. A complainant can, of course, agree to have her or his confidential information made available for use in litigation. But, to safeguard the respondent's confidentiality, the External Report proposed that the CSD officer involved in conciliation should not also be the EOC officer conducting the investigation and should not disclose information communicated by the respondent during the conciliation to the EOC officer conducting the investigation.

The EOC distinguishes between what happens in a conciliation session (whether early or further conciliation) and the information obtained by the conciliator in the lead-up to such conciliation session (including any information obtained from a respondent). The EOC accepts that what happens within the confines of a conciliation session is to be treated as sacrosanct, but considers that what happens in the lead-up (including information obtained from the respondent or the respondent's associates in the course of investigation through resort to Rule 5) is regarded as fair game for use in subsequent court proceedings. It is submitted that such distinction is untenable in practice. A conciliator should always be neutral as a matter of principle and should not be (or be seen to be) compiling a dossier for potential use against a respondent in court litigation. Information obtained by a conciliator, whether before or during a conciliation session, should be treated as confidential. From the survey in Section 10.3, such strict approach has been consistently and uncompromisingly adhered to in Australia, New Zealand, the UK and the USA. The USA's EEOC may conduct conciliation following investigation of a complaint, but that is conducted on the footing that the respondent has engaged in wrongdoing and the conciliation is directed towards finding a suitable way of remedying the complainant's grievances. Recommendations (6) and (21) were put forward by the External Report as a means of maintaining the confidentiality of the early conciliation process. Where a CSD officer conducts an unsuccessful early conciliation, it will be necessary to ensure that the same officer is not involved in any ensuing investigation of the relevant complaint. Further, a system would need to be in place so that confidential information communicated by a respondent in early conciliation (including the lead-up to such conciliation) is not recorded in any file to which the investigating team might have access. The EOC says that it has accepted Recommendation (21). But the reality (as discussed) seems to be otherwise. According to the EOC Report and Update, the EOC is still studying Recommendation (6). The EOC Update adds: 'In 2019/20, the conciliation success rate for complaint cases was about 70%. The EOC is of the view that the current practice has not had any adverse impacts on investigation and conciliation.' It is unclear how the comment in the EOC Update has any bearing on Recommendation (6). The issue of confidentiality in a conciliation is a matter of principle, not statistics.

Recommendations (7), (11) and (12) were intended to reinforce the necessity of the EOC deciding whether to give full (as opposed to merely limited) assistance within a reasonable time from the lodging of a complaint or the elevation of an inquiry into a complaint *and* the failure of early conciliation. The authors submit that, in most cases, a complainant should know where she or he stands in terms of full legal assistance and the pursuit of a complaint in court within nine to twelve months of a complaint being submitted. In the interests of transparency, Recommendation (12) stressed the need to provide a complainant with more than merely perfunctory or 'pro forma' reasons for a refusal of legal assistance. According to the EOC Report and Update, Recommendations (7) and (11) are being considered by the EOC. The EOC Update adds: 'At present, the EOC will inform the applicant of legal assistance within 3 months upon receipt of his/her application whether legal assistance will be granted or not.'

Recommendation (12) has not been accepted. According to the EOC Report, the reason for this is as follows:

> 7.7 The Independent Report also proposes that legal advice sought by EOC on any case could be disclosed to the Complainant on request. The LCC had previously discussed this and viewed that the danger of revealing internal legal advice to the EOC to the complainant, which is based on a neutral and impartial assessment of the facts, would in fact amount to a waiver of privilege, and open up all files to the respondent institution which is being sued. This may have unintended consequences, and the matter is best left for consideration on a case-by-case basis.

The authors do not see how the foregoing reason has any bearing on Recommendation (12). From time to time, the LCC seeks advice from counsel on the merits of a case. On occasion, where legal assistance has been refused following advice from counsel, a complainant has asked to see counsel's opinion and (in a few cases) the instructions given to counsel. Ultimately, the question of whether a complainant should be allowed to see counsel's legal advice is a different one from whether the complainant should be given the gist of the LCC's reasons for rejecting an application for legal assistance. Paragraphs 59 to 62 of the External Report commented comprehensively on whether counsel's advice should be shown to a complainant, but it made no recommendation in respect of the same. Recommendation (12) simply dealt with the provision of reasons to a complainant. The authors remain of the view that, as a matter of principle, a complainant is entitled to know at least the gist of the LCC's reasons for refusing assistance. Nor do the authors believe that a fear that a disappointed applicant will ask to see counsel's advice (if such was sought) justifies the LCC in giving no reasons or only vague reasons for rejecting assistance. In all jurisdictions surveyed in Section 10.3, reasons are required to be given where legal assistance is refused or where an agency decides not to pursue a complaint before a court or tribunal.

In summary, it will be seen that the EOC has rejected Recommendations (1), (3) and (12) and is still considering Recommendations (6), (7) and (11) more than a year after the External Report was submitted. These six recommendations were among the crucial reforms proposed by the External Report, especially as means of dealing with the conflicts of interest and the related confidentiality problems inherent in the exercise of the EOC's multiple functions. In light of the reasons that have been put forward as grounds for rejecting Recommendations (1), (3) and (12), the authors are not sanguine that even the recommendations still under consideration will be accepted. If it is to perform its roles of conciliator, investigator and litigator effectively, the EOC has to confront the conflicts inherent in them. At a minimum this would mean:

(1) putting in place a system that fully respects the integrity and confidentiality of the entire conciliation process (not just what happens during a conciliation session); and
(2) ensuring that information gathered during the conciliation process is not disclosed to those involved in the detailed investigation and assessment of a complaint for the purpose of granting legal assistance.

But that is only the bare minimum. The authors suggest that, where an aggrieved person approaches the EOC with a complaint which is not obviously trivial, frivolous or vexatious, such person is entitled, in keeping with the EOC's role of redressing discrimination, to some assessment of the merits and weaknesses of her or his complaint at an early stage. A complainant should not have to wait until an abortive early conciliation, a detailed investigation and an abortive further conciliation have all transpired before receiving even some legal guidance. That would be too long. The mismatch in perceptions highlighted in Section 10.2 means that the EOC is currently perceived by the public as being overly aloof from and judgemental of complainants. Such perception will ultimately deter complainants from raising their grievances and hinder the EOC from fulfilling its statutory mission of 'working towards the elimination of ... discrimination and harassment and promoting equality of opportunity'.[42] Recommendations (1) and (3) were intended to demonstrate that it is possible to bridge the gap in perception.

10.5 Conclusion

There are divergent views on how precisely the EOC should handle discrimination complaints. The bottom line must, however, be that the EOC is ultimately answerable to the public and should meet the public's expectations. It should be service-oriented. It is not in the position of a judge who of necessity maintains a distance from a case, and its parties, in order to determine (and be seen to determine) the case impartially in accordance with the law. Within the constraints of the anti-discrimination statutes, the EOC exists to assist the public to conciliate or otherwise resolve their legitimate complaints of discriminatory conduct and affronts to their personal dignity. The discharge of such functions calls for the EOC not just to weigh evidence and apply the law but also to display empathy, sensitivity and understanding (the hallmarks of a good mediator). The conflicting demands of the EOC's roles of conciliator, investigator and litigator are not readily reconciled. No jurisdiction (whether Australia, New Zealand, the UK or the USA) has found a complete answer. But it is of little help to say that the task of reconciling the conflicts is difficult or impossible. However imperfect,

---

[42] See the preamble to the SDO.

a system needs to be worked out that will enable the EOC to cater to the public's needs and perceptions effectively and fulfil its objective of eradicating discrimination in Hong Kong. As EOC celebrated its 25th anniversary in May 2021, this is only becoming a more pressing issue.

PART III

Multi-tier Dispute Resolution in the Wider World

11
Multi-tier Commercial Dispute Resolution Processes in the United States

THOMAS J STIPANOWICH*

11.1 Introduction

The rich and complex landscape of commercial dispute resolution in the United States has dramatically changed in the course of four decades of development in public and private conflict management that have been characterised as The Quiet Revolution.[1] This wave of change was primarily motivated by frustrations with the costs, delays, uncertainty and inflexibility of litigation[2] and the commensurate need for process alternatives that could effectively serve various priorities of disputing parties, including efficiency, economy, finality, privacy and confidentiality, intervention by experts, and enhanced control by one or both parties over process and outcome.[3]

---

* My thanks to Anselmo Reyes, Weixia Gu and participants in the Hong Kong University Symposium 'Multi-tier Approaches to the Resolution of International Disputes: A Global and Comparative Study' (September 2018), the Straus Institute and the Hagler Institute of Advanced Study and the Colleges of Law and Architecture at Texas A&M University, where I was a Visiting Fellow at the time this work commenced. I also thank Carson Bennett, Pepperdine Caruso School of Law Class of 2019; Derek McKee, Texas A&M School of Law Class of 2019, and Zachary Remijas, Pepperdine Caruso School of Law Class of 2021, for their research assistance.

[1] See Linda R Singer, 'The Quiet Revolution in Dispute Settlement' (1989) 7 Mediation Quarterly 105; Thomas J Stipanowich, 'Living the Dream of ADR: Reflections on Four Decades of the Quiet Revolution in Dispute Resolution' (2017) 18 Cardozo Journal of Conflict Resolution 513 <http://ssrn.com/abstract=2920848> accessed 1 September 2020. See also Randall Kiser, *How Leading Lawyers Think: Expert Insights into Judgment and Advocacy* (Springer 2011). Kiser states that '[b]eginning in the mid-1980s, with the widespread adoption of alternative dispute resolution programs in federal and state courts, mediation became an integral component of [the] system of "liti-gotiation"': ibid 203 (interior quotation marks added).

[2] See David B Lipsky and Ronald L Seeber, 'In Search of Control: The Corporate Embrace of ADR' (1998) 1 University of Pennsylvania Journal of Labor and Employment Law 133, 139–42.

[3] See Craig A McEwen, 'Managing Corporate Disputing: Overcoming Barriers to the Effective Use of Mediation for Reducing the Cost and Time of Litigation' (1998) 14

Much attention has been given to the evolution of discrete process formats involving forms of third-party intervention – mediation,[4] arbitration[5] and non-binding evaluation.[6] Very often, however, commercial disputes are resolved through the *interplay of processes*: the mixing and matching of forms of adjudication with approaches intended to promote negotiated settlement.[7]

Thus, commercial contracts often include tiered or stepped dispute resolution schemes that comprise multiple, varied mechanisms for resolving conflict – the focus of this chapter. For business parties, a variety of motivations prompted the quest for 'alternative dispute resolution' (ADR).[8] These included saving time, saving money, greater party control, greater satisfaction with process and outcome, more durable resolutions, protecting privacy and confidentiality, preserving relationships and employing third-party expertise in

---

Ohio State Journal of Dispute Resolution 1, 7–8; John Lande, 'Failing Faith in Litigation? A Survey of Business Lawyers' and Executives' Opinions' (1998) 3 Harvard Negotiation Law Review 1, 35–36.

[4] In the United States, commercial mediators engage in a wide variety of approaches for the resolution of disputes; choices of approach may reflect mediators' individual preferences, the influence of lawyers, or other circumstances and may vary by region. See Thomas J Stipanowich, 'Insights on Mediator Practices and Perceptions' [2016] Dispute Resolution Magazine 4 <http://ssrn.com/abstract=2759982> accessed 1 September 2020. See also Thomas J Stipanowich and Véronique Fraser, 'The International Task Force on Mixed Mode Dispute Resolution: Exploring the Interplay between Mediation, Evaluation and Arbitration in Commercial Cases' (2017) 40(3) Fordham International Law Review 839, 876–77 (discussing evaluative and non-evaluative approaches in mediation) <http://ssrn.com/abstract=2920785> accessed 1 September 2020.

[5] Thomas J Stipanowich, 'Reflections on the State and Future of Commercial Arbitration: Challenges, Opportunities, Proposals' (2014) 25 American Review of International Arbitration 297 <http://ssrn.com/abstract=2519084> accessed 1 September 2020.

[6] Non-binding evaluation principally refers to '[n]on-adjudicative (nonbinding) evaluative processes [which] involve an advisory assessment by a third party neutral of the likely outcome of a dispute being adjudicated, the merits of the case, and/or the value of an asset or claim': Stipanowich and Fraser (n 4) 872. Non-binding evaluation may involve any of the following processes: advisory appraisal, advisory expert determination, advisory/non-binding arbitration, conciliation, dispute boards, early neutral evaluation and facilitative mediation, among others: Stipanowich and Fraser (n 4) 872–76.

[7] See Renate Dendorfer and Jeremy Lack, 'The Interaction between Arbitration and Mediation: Vision vs. Reality' (2007) 1 Dispute Resolution International 1.

[8] Thomas J Stipanowich and J Ryan Lamare, 'Living with ADR: Evolving Perceptions and Use of Mediation, Arbitration and Conflict Management in Fortune 1,000 Corporations' (2014) 19 Harvard Negotiation Law Review 1, 36–40 (summarising and analysing the results of the 2011 survey of Fortune 1,000 corporate counsel and comparing the results to a similar 1997 survey) <http://ssrn.com/abstract=2221471> accessed 1 September 2020.

dispute resolution.⁹ To varying degrees, all of these goals were cited as reasons why parties used ADR.¹⁰

Perceptions that mediation may be especially useful in promoting various business priorities in ADR[11] appear to be linked to growth in the use of mediation by major companies. In a 1997 survey of Fortune 1,000 corporate counsel, 87 per cent of respondents stated that their companies had recently used mediation; by 2011, that number had climbed to 98 per cent,[12] with 83 per cent having used mediation in commercial or contractual disputes.[13] At that time more than 85 per cent indicated that their companies were likely or very likely to use mediation in the future.[14]

These trends are reflected in the experience of the International Institute for Conflict Prevention and Resolution (CPR). Founded in the early days of The Quiet Revolution, CPR coalesced corporate counsel and other attorneys to exploring avenues for more effective management of business conflict.[15] Although CPR developed and promoted a variety of initiatives and dispute resolution tools, including the CPR Pledge, mediation gradually became a primary emphasis. Contractual mediation clauses are a central element of CPR's master guide Drafting Dispute Resolution Clauses,[16] and the promotion of business mediation has long been CPR's chief international 'export'.[17]

If mediation was the principal focus of development in The Quiet Revolution, binding arbitration claimed pride of place as a widely favoured adjudicative alternative to litigation of business disputes founded on private contract.[18] Through much of the twentieth century in the USA, arbitration was broadly perceived as an efficient,

---

[9] ibid.
[10] ibid.
[11] ibid 37, table D.
[12] ibid 41, chart F.
[13] ibid 45, chart G.
[14] ibid 49, table L.
[15] See Dennis Campbell, 'International Dispute Resolution' (2010) 31A Comparative Law Yearbook of International Business 59.
[16] See Kathleen M Scanlon, *Drafting Dispute Resolution Clauses: Better Solutions for Business* (International Institute for Conflict Prevention & Resolution 2006).
[17] See eg Nancy Nelson and Thomas J Stipanowich, *Commercial Mediation in Europe: Better Solutions for Business* (International Institute for Conflict Prevention & Resolution 2004).
[18] In 2001, the Report of CPR's Commission on the Future of Arbitration observed: 'If adjudication by a third party is required, a well-conducted arbitration proceeding usually is preferable to litigation.' See Thomas J Stipanowich and Peter Kaskell (eds), *Commercial Arbitration at Its Best: Successful Strategies for Business Users* (ABA 2001) 5–6.

expeditious and relatively inexpensive process of private adjudication run by and for businesses.[19] In recent decades, however, American commercial arbitration has gradually taken on more of the trappings of litigation, including expanded pre-hearing discovery, more motion practice and greater emphasis on legal standards in decision-making.[20] Arbitration rules, and sometimes arbitration timetables and related budgets, ballooned to accommodate enhanced due process.[21]

More businesses preferred mediation as the path to achieving key business goals like efficiency, economy, privacy, satisfactory results, and preservation of business relationships, and mediation's perceived advantage may have been sharpened as arbitration tended to become more like litigation.[22] In the 1997 Fortune 1,000 survey, 'mediation-arbitration' (which normally would be understood as a dispute resolution process in which both processes had been employed)[23] had been recently used by 40 per cent of respondents' companies in 1997; by 2011 this figure had risen to 51 per cent.[24] Resort to both mediation and arbitration in the course of resolving a particular conflict is probably even more likely in current US practice and is a probable contributor to recent trends towards higher rates of settlement during arbitration.[25]

Given these developments, it is not surprising that parties began to use these and other dispute resolution processes in tandem through the mechanism of tiered or stepped dispute resolution provisions. These approaches require parties initially to attempt to settle a dispute through informal means such as direct negotiation or mediation, and to litigate or arbitrate only if the informal mechanisms are unsuccessful in resolving disputes.[26]

---

[19] See Jill I Gross, 'Justice Scalia's Hat Trick and the Supreme Court's Flawed Understanding of Twenty-First Century Arbitration' (2015) 81 Brook Law Review 111, 117–19.

[20] See Thomas J Stipanowich, 'Arbitration: The "New Litigation"' [2010] University of Illinois Law Review 1.

[21] ibid.

[22] Stipanowich and Lamare (n 8) 37, table D.

[23] ibid 40–41.

[24] ibid 41, chart F.

[25] Thomas J Stipanowich and Zachary P Ulrich, 'Commercial Arbitration and Settlement: Empirical Insights into the Roles Arbitrators Play' (2014) 6 Yearbook on Arbitration and Mediation 1, 16–17 <http://ssrn.com/abstract=2461839> accessed 1 September 2020.

[26] Some tiered provisions also include a preliminary step during which the parties negotiate without a mediator. See Section 11.1.

11.2 Why Tiered Dispute Resolution Processes Are Widely Used in Commercial Contracts

11.2.1 The Case for Stepped Approaches

Contractual relationships are particularly suitable settings for tailored dispute resolution processes,[27] and prototypes of tiered dispute resolution have been employed in labor, construction and mercantile settings.[28] Early in The Quiet Revolution, provisions for tiered (stepped) dispute resolution with mediation as a preliminary stage began to appear in standard form construction contracts.[29] Today, tiered dispute resolution processes comprising multiple separate approaches to resolving relational conflict in sequence (such as negotiation, mediation and arbitration) are frequently found in various kinds of commercial contracts.[30]

11.2.1.1 Constructive 'Funnelling' of Conflict

Some years ago, a group of experienced commercial advocates and arbitrators convened by CPR began a book of guidelines on binding arbitration of business disputes by advising parties that '[m]ost disputes are best resolved privately and by agreement' and that principals should be engaged in efforts to informally negotiate disputes, first directly and then, if necessary, with the help of a mediator or evaluator.[31] Only after these steps should the parties resort to arbitration. Even then, however, 'the door to settlement should

---

[27] Stipanowich and Lamare (n 8) 10. CPR is today known as the International Institute for Conflict Prevention & Resolution.

[28] See eg *Fluor Enterprises Inc v Solutia Inc* 147 F Supp 2d 648, 649–50 (SD Tex 2001) (involving agreement 'mandat[ing], first, a detailed process by which a dispute will proceed upward through the management hierarchy of each company in an effort to resolve the matter in a process less adversarial than litigation', failing which resolution, the agreement next provides for formal mediation): Nelson and Stipanowich (n 17).

[29] Thomas J Stipanowich, 'The Multi-door Contract and Other Possibilities' (1997) 13 Ohio State Journal on Dispute Resolution 303, 330. See eg *MCC Development Corp v Perla* 81 AD 3d 474, 916 NYS 2d 102 (NY App Div 2011) (construction contract providing that the architect's decision is a condition precedent to mediation, and completion of mediation is a condition precedent to arbitration); *Bombardier Corp v National Railroad Passenger Corp* 298 F Supp 2d 1 (DDC 2002) (incorporating contract claims procedures including dispute resolution board).

[30] See eg *Halter Marine Inc v OK Shipping Ltd* No Civ A 98-3184, 1998 US Dist LEXIS 18771 (ED La, 25 November 1998) (provisions requiring parties to confer in good faith and to refer technical issues to an expert as agreed in the contract prior to arbitration); *Estrada v CleanNet USA Inc* No C 14-01785 JSW, 2015 WL 833701 (ND Cal, 24 February 2015) (dealing with franchise agreements involving three-tiered dispute resolution provision including requirements of direct negotiation, mediation and arbitration).

[31] Stipanowich and Kaskell (n 18) 5–6.

remain open; arbitrators should encourage the parties to discuss settlement and, if appropriate, to employ a mediator'.[32]

These recommendations envision a multi-step 'funnelling' mechanism for dispute resolution that accommodates the varied priorities of businesses. When it comes to dealing with conflict with another commercial party, business interests might include a degree of control over the resolution,[33] an efficient and economical path to resolution,[34] privacy and confidentiality,[35] and/or a result that is perceived as fair or advantageous,[36] all of which are often effectively realised through direct negotiations.[37] If, however, direct negotiations fail, dispute resolution proceeds by stages to methods involving increasingly robust intervention by third parties and a commensurate reduction in party control, informality, economy and efficiency. If, for example, the parties proceed to engage a mediator, the principals may remain fully engaged in the process, retaining control over the final outcome and expectations of privacy and confidentiality, although mediators may affect the dynamics of negotiation in several ways, including influencing the final outcome.[38] Should mediation also end in impasse and the parties move on to arbitration, procedures are more rigorously formal, adversarial, lawyer-driven and extended in duration and may or may not be confidential; control over the outcome is ceded to the adjudicator(s) – preferably experts – whose decision is likely to be final.[39] And whatever one may say about the ability of arbitrators to fashion remedies appropriate to the circumstances, the practical reality is that commercial arbitrators tend to adhere to the safe ground of recognised judicial remedies rather than exercise creativity at the risk of extended judicial review and possible vacatur.[40] Therefore, while binding arbitration

---

[32] ibid.
[33] Lipsky and Seeber (n 2) 139.
[34] ibid 142.
[35] See Susan Oberman, 'Confidentiality in Mediation: An Application of the Right to Privacy' (2012) 27 Ohio State Journal on Dispute Resolution 539.
[36] See Rebecca Hollander-Blumoff, 'Just Negotiation' (2010) 88 Washington University Law Review 381, 400–1.
[37] Some variations begin with 'stepped negotiations' comprising multiple stages of negotiation involving successive pairings of negotiators at different levels in company management.
[38] Depending on the circumstances, moreover, there may be some ceding of control to legal advocates at the mediation stage.
[39] See Lisa B Bingham, 'Mandatory Arbitration: Control over Dispute-System Design and Mandatory Commercial Arbitration' [2004] Law & Contemporary Problems 221, 224–25.
[40] See Thomas J Stipanowich and Zachary P Ulrich, 'Arbitration in Evolution: Current Practices and Perspectives of Experienced Commercial Arbitrators' (2014) 25 American

may be perceived as preferable to litigation for business parties, the latter are usually best served by arriving at a negotiated settlement.

11.2.1.2 Benefits of Early Negotiation

By avoiding the rancor and 'spiraling adversarialism' that is sometimes a by-product of adjudication, negotiating an early settlement may produce more satisfactory results while enabling parties to maintain or restore relationships. A negotiated settlement may permit parties to promote their business interests through integrative terms and 'in-kind' trade-offs that could not be obtained through litigation or arbitration.[41] Early settlement gives parties the opportunity to air their differences and explore solutions in private, avoiding the publicity and visibility that may accompany public litigation (and, in some cases, arbitration). Finally, research has shown that negotiated or mediated settlements are more likely to be more sustainable and complied with voluntarily than decisions by third-party arbitrators or judges.[42]

Although there are no reliable data on the general effectiveness of multi-step dispute resolution clauses in commercial contracts, many are firmly convinced of their benefits. For example, an appropriately structured arrangement for stepped negotiations may facilitate early direct engagement by and discussions between party representatives who can view issues in dispute with some degree of detachment.

11.2.1.3 Benefits of Early Mediation

If unaided efforts to negotiate are unsuccessful, a mediator at the bargaining table may provide important value as a referee, an agent of reality and a creative adviser.[43] Mediators are often especially attuned to the opportunities in relational disputes to employ interest-based co-operative approaches, 'expanding the pie' through trade-offs and non-monetary integrative terms, and perhaps even

---

Review of International Arbitration 395; Thomas J Stipanowich, 'Arbitration and Choice: Taking Charge of the "New Litigation"' (2009) 7 DePaul Business and Commercial Law Journal 383, 426, fn 212.

[41] See Nelson and Stipanowich (n 17).

[42] See eg Craig A McEwen and Richard J Maiman, 'Small Claims Mediation in Maine: An Empirical Assessment' (1981) 33 Maine Law Review 237, 260.

[43] See Jacqueline M Nolan-Haley, 'Lawyers, Non-lawyers and Mediation: Rethinking the Professional Monopoly from a Problem-Solving Perspective' (2002) 7 Harvard Negotiation Law Review 235, 281.

repairing or improving a relationship.[44] In addition to helping resolve commercial disputes earlier and/or more effectively, they may assist parties in developing a customised process for resolving their disputes,[45] predict the potential consequences if the issues in dispute are adjudicated in court or in arbitration, and provide other value.[46]

In response to an informal survey, a Washington DC-area mediator who had conducted hundreds of commercial mediations indicated that, in his experience, pre-adjudication mediation was a highly efficient and effective way of settling disputes.[47] Where cases did not settle outright, mediation helped to 'sharpening the issues' for resolution.[48]

11.2.1.4 Taking the Onus off Parties

From the early days of The Quiet Revolution, it was suggested that contractual provisions for negotiation or mediation of disputes, like court directives to mediate, were necessary to obviate the need for a party to propose negotiation or mediation – actions that might be viewed as reflecting doubts about the strength of the party's own case.[49]

11.2.1.5 Tailored Frameworks for Dispute Resolution

Besides creating early opportunities for reflection and discussion that might act as a 'safety valve' for companies facing what could become a protracted legal fight,[50] pre-dispute procedures give parties the opportunity to co-operatively develop templates tailored to their own specific circumstances and priorities.

Models for multi-tier dispute resolution clauses in commercial contracts may be found in CPR's detailed Master Guide,[51] guidelines published by leading institutional providers of commercial dispute

---

[44] Dwight Golann, 'Is Legal Mediation a Process of Repair – Or Separation? An Empirical Study, and Its Implications' (2002) 7 Harvard Negotiation Law Review 301, 311–18.

[45] See Paul M Lurie and Jeremy Lack, 'Guided Choice Dispute Resolution Processes: Reducing the Time and Expense to Settlement' (2014) 8 Dispute Resolution International 167.

[46] See Nelson and Stipanowich (n 17).

[47] Email from Adrian L Bastianelli III, Partner, Peckar & Abramson PC, Washington DC, to author (2 March 2019).

[48] ibid.

[49] This remains a concern for some parties. Edna Sussman and Victoria A Kummer, 'Drafting the Arbitration Clause: A Primer on the Opportunities and the Pitfalls' (2012) 67(1) Dispute Resolution Journal 30.

[50] John DeGroote, 'The Multi-step Dispute Resolution Clause: A Few Reasons Clients Like Them' (*Mediate.com*, April 2010) <www.mediate.com/articles/DeGrooteJbl20100405.cfm> accessed 29 August 2020.

[51] See Scanlon (n 16).

resolution services,⁵² and other sources for practitioners.⁵³ Multi-step approaches involving negotiation are frequently employed in certain arenas of conflict, such as building design and construction, and may be embodied in widely used standard contract templates.⁵⁴

11.2.2 Concerns about Pre-dispute Tiered Provisions

However, opinion among lawyers and other dispute resolution professionals is far from unanimous regarding contractual stepped dispute resolution provisions. The author's informal survey of experienced commercial lawyers and dispute resolution professionals revealed sharply conflicting perspectives regarding the utility of such arrangements.

Critiques of contractual commitments to negotiate or mediate disputes in advance of arbitration or litigation often begin with the observation that, given the obvious benefits of negotiated settlement in business disputes and the pervasive use of mediation, parties and counsel will employ these processes anyway at the appropriate time, in the appropriate circumstances, without the need for pre-dispute contractual mandates.⁵⁵

Second, negotiation and mediation are most likely to be effective if parties participate willingly. If parties are at the settlement table only to comply with contractual requirements, some argue, such preliminaries may do nothing more than delay the start of adjudication.⁵⁶ Contractual arrangements for stepped negotiations may be too cumbersome and produce unintended consequences. For example, although stepped processes calling for negotiations moving up successive rungs of the corporate ladder are sometimes employed in construction claims resolution procedures, some long-time mediators complain that, in some cases,

---

⁵² See eg JAMS, *JAMS Clause Workbook: A Guide to Drafting Clauses for International and Cross-Border Commercial Contracts* (2018) 10–12; American Arbitration Association, *Drafting Dispute Resolution Clauses: A Practical Guide* <www.adr.org/sites/default/files/document_repository/Drafting%20Dispute%20Resolution%20Clauses%20A%20Practical%20Guide.pdf> accessed 29 August 2020.

⁵³ See eg 'General Contract Clauses: Alternative Dispute Resolution (Multi-tiered)' (*Thomson Reuters Practical Law Commercial Transactions*) <https://content.next.westlaw.com/9-555-5330> accessed 1 September 2020.

⁵⁴ See Thomas J Stipanowich, 'Managing Construction Conflict: Unfinished Revolution, Continuing Evolution' (2014) 34(4) Construction Law 13, 25–27.

⁵⁵ One experienced Los Angeles mediator argues: 'If mediation is a good and logical approach to resolving a dispute, won't smart people perceive that is in their interest to do it at the time?': Telephone interview with Jeff Kichaven, mediator (28 March 2019).

⁵⁶ Email from Buckner Hinkle to author (28 March 2019).

such procedures may prevent timely solutions and increase costs,[57] or even cause project managers to feel disempowered.[58]

Third, critics of contractual dispute resolution provisions sometimes contend that the decision to come to the bargaining table or to employ a mediator, and the timing of such decisions, hinge on specific circumstances that may not become apparent until disputes arise or thereafter. Although most commercial disputes are likely to be settled through negotiation at some point, some argue that negotiation and mediation may not be fruitful in advance of adjudication. The optimal moment for informal settlement, some argue, may occur at some point during the adjudicative process as they learn more about the case and their chances in adjudication.[59]

Yet another set of concerns respecting pre-dispute agreements to negotiate or mediate involves issues of enforcement. Parties who deliberately employ such provisions may be focused primarily on the utility of platforms for informal bargaining and not on what happens if one or both parties do not follow the prescribed steps. In the latter case, however, the provisions themselves may become the nub of controversy and fodder for judicial intervention, with potential delay or disruption of the dispute resolution process.[60]

Section 11.3 will explore the treatment of tiered process in US courts and arbitration. We will posit some guidelines for the use of tiered processes, taking account of the potential benefits and concerns discussed already.

11.3 Tiered Processes in the Courts and Arbitration

Parties may include contractual provisions for negotiation or mediation without much concern for their legal enforceability. After all, in many cases parties pursue negotiation and/or mediation, with or without contractual requirements, and reach a settlement without resort to adjudication or, alternatively, move to the final (adjudication) stage without bickering over procedures. Nevertheless, parties are advised to consider enforcement issues if pre-adjudication steps are sufficiently important that they may desire judicial assistance in compelling another party to participate. At the same time, they should be aware that provisions to negotiate or mediate disputes prior to adjudication are a double-edged sword; as

---

[57] Stipanowich (n 54) 15.
[58] Stipanowich (n 29) 338.
[59] ibid 365.
[60] See Section 11.2.

discussed later, a claimant's failure to comply with such provisions may be employed by defendants to delay or even derail adjudication.

11.3.1 Basic Enforceability Issues

Courts in the USA remain far from uniform in their handling of provisions obligating the parties to negotiate or mediate in an attempt to settle disputes arising under or related to commercial contracts. Some courts have concluded that an agreement to negotiate at a later date is an unenforceable agreement to agree.[61] Most often, however, it is understood that an agreement to negotiate or mediate contractual disputes is binding as a commitment to come to the table and engage in some way, but not necessarily to reach an agreement; nothing more is required or expected of its participants than their assent to discussion of the dispute at hand.[62]

When provisions in a contract for the negotiation or mediation of disputes arising under that instrument are enforced, the proper foundation is the common law of contracts in the absence of any applicable statute.[63] Although some courts have improperly enforced mediation provisions under the terms of the Federal Arbitration Act (FAA) or state arbitration statutes,[64] 'the law of arbitration is in nearly every respect an illogical foundation for the enforcement of mediation agreements'.[65]

---

[61] *Space Tech Development Corp v Boeing Co* 209 F App'x 236, 240 (4th Cir 2006) (finding 'obligation to negotiate and good faith and arrive at an acceptable LLC Agreement is an "agreement to agree" that is unenforceable under Virginia law'); *77 Construction Co v UXB International Inc* No 7:13-CV-340, 2015 WL 926036, 4 (WD Va, 4 March 2015) (refusing to enforce 'an agreement to attempt to settle their claims, or an agreement to negotiate at a later date').

[62] Peter N Thompson, 'Good Faith Mediation in the Federal Courts' (2011) 26 Ohio State Journal on Dispute Resolution 363.

[63] *Advanced Bodycare Solutions LLC v Thione International Inc* 524 F 3d 1235, 1241 (11th Cir 2008) (noting that contractual mediation provisions 'might be specifically enforceable in contract or other law'); *Gate Precast Co v Kenwood Towne Place LLC* No 1:09-CV-00113, 2009 WL 3614931, 5 (SD Ohio, 28 October 2009). In some states there may be legislation affecting the enforceability of an agreement for dispute resolution. See eg *Templeton Development Corp v Superior Court* 144 Cal App 4th 1073, 1079 (2006) (applying California Civil Procedure Code para 410.42, rendering void and unenforceable a provision in a construction contract 'which purports to require any dispute between the parties to be litigated, arbitrated, or otherwise determined outside this state', to deny enforcement to mediation provision).

[64] See eg *Fisher v GE Medical Systems* 276 F Supp 2d 891, 894–96 (MD Tenn 2003).

[65] *Advanced Bodycare* (n 63) 1240 (quoting Thomas J Stipanowich, 'The Arbitration Penumbra: Arbitration Law and the Rapidly Changing Landscape of Dispute Resolution' (2007) 8 Nevada Law Journal 427, 446). See also *Harrison v Nissan Motor Corp* 111 F 3d 343, 350–52 (3d Cir 1997) (FAA does not apply to Lemon Law informal dispute resolution

Contractual provisions for negotiation or mediation of disputes often call upon parties to engage in good faith.[66] There remains, of course, the question of what constitutes 'good faith' participation at the bargaining table – a question that often arises in mediation pursuant to a court order.[67] While there are no generally accepted standards for good faith in negotiation or mediation, parties' good faith obligations may be directly related to the specific activities associated with a process; in the case of mediation, these would include helping to select a mediator; co-ordinating a schedule and preparing mediation-related materials; and appearing at a mediation session and having a representative with some authority to settle.[68] In addition, some courts have sanctioned parties for failing to listen to and communicate with other parties or the mediator regarding the dispute, failing to engage in bargaining or responding to offers to settle, engaging in offense or abusive conduct, or employing mediation for unfair advantage.[69] Of course, parties drafting provisions for negotiation or mediation have the opportunity to identify expectations and establish a foundation for 'good faith' inquiries, in either their basic agreement or the incorporated procedures.

In the USA, efforts to police bad faith in mediation may run up against policies supporting confidentiality in mediation.[70] Nevertheless, courts addressing allegations of bad faith in mediation often admit evidence from mediation proceedings, including the testimony of mediators.[71]

---

procedures); *Trujillo v Gomez* No 14cv2483 BTM (BGS), 2015 US Dist LEXIS 51068 (SD Cal, 17 April 2015) (citing *Advanced Bodycare* (n 63) for the proposition that mediation agreements may not be enforced under the Federal Arbitration Act); *Heston v GB Capital LLC* No 16cv912-WQH-RBB, 2016 US Dist LEXIS 113355 (SD Cal, 23 August 2016), affirmed in No 16cv912-WQH-AGS, 2018 US Dist LEXIS 3210 (SD Cal, 5 January 2018) (compelling arbitration but not mediation, citing *Trujillo v Gomez* (n 65)).

[66] See eg *Swartz v Westminster Services Inc* No 8:10-cv-1722-T-30AEP, 2010 US Dist LEXIS 93107, 2–4 (MD Fla, 8 September 2010); *Kernahan v Home Warranty Administrator of Florida Inc* 199 A 3d 766 (2019); *N-Tron Corp v Rockwell Automation Inc* No 09–0733-WS-C, 2010 US Dist LEXIS 14130, 12–13 (SD Ala, 18 February 2010); *Fluor Enters v Solutia Inc* 147 F Supp 2d 648, 650 (SD Tex 2001).

[67] Thompson (n 62) (discussing concepts of good faith in federal court decisions regarding court-directed mediation). In the words of a Second Circuit decision, '[i]f the parties fail to reach ... a final agreement after making a good faith effort to do so, there is no further obligation': *Adjustrite Systems Inc v GAB Business Services Inc* 145 F 3d 543, 548 (2d Cir 1998).

[68] Thompson (n 62) 394–403.

[69] ibid 404–10.

[70] ibid 374, 404–10.

[71] ibid 410–17.

11.3.2 Judicial Remedies for Non-compliance with Preliminary Stages of Tiered Processes

Where courts have found contractual negotiation or mediation provisions to be valid and enforceable, the manner in which they address non-compliance under such agreements is likewise inconsistent across different jurisdictions. Although the conventional common law remedy for breach of contract is damages, there are usually significant problems with quantifying damages for breach of an agreement to negotiate or to mediate.[72] Courts have therefore tended to resolve issues of non-compliance via other means, including a stay of litigation, dismissal of claims, or summary judgment.

A number of courts have invoked the power to judicially stay proceedings pending the parties' completion of efforts to mediate their dispute.[73] In *Swartz v Westminster Services Inc*, the court stayed litigation in response to a motion to dismiss for failure to comply with a contractual mediation requirement in the parties' contract.[74] The court held that '[t]he law is clear that when confronted with an objection that a plaintiff has initiated litigation without satisfying arbitration or mediation requirements, courts routinely stay rather than dismiss the proceedings to allow for implementation of the agreed-upon dispute resolution mechanism'.[75] Ordering a stay of adjudication is a prudent manner of promoting participation in mediation in accordance with terms of the parties' agreement since the approach may avoid the potentially harsh consequences of dismissals and summary judgment and, furthermore, allows a court to retain jurisdiction in order to monitor the situation pending compliance.

In other cases, courts have granted motions to dismiss actions by parties who have failed to comply with contractual provisions for

---

[72] See *Ervin v Nashville Peace & Justice Center* 673 F Supp 2d 592, 612 (MD Tenn 2009) (breach of an agreement to mediate cannot be a basis for a claim for damages); cf Lye Kah Cheong, 'A Persisting Aberration: The Movement to Enforce Agreements to Mediate' (2008) 20 Singapore Academy of Law Journal 195, 208–11 (summarising developments in the UK and Commonwealth courts).

[73] See *Getchell v Suntrust Bank* No 6:15-cv-1702-Orl-TBS, 2016 US Dist LEXIS 23238, 8 (MD Fla, 25 February 2016) (staying proceedings 'so the parties can perform their contractual obligation to mediate'). The court's order ultimately resulted in the plaintiff's voluntary dismissal of the suit.

[74] *Swartz* (n 66); but see *Cumberland & York Distributors v Coors Brewing Co* 01-244-P-H, 2002 US Dist LEXIS 1962, 11–12 (D Me, 7 February 2002) (denying dismissal and ordering arbitration following the invalidation of a mediation provision for lack of a material term, rather than staying litigation and retaining jurisdiction over the matter).

[75] *Swartz* (n 66) 3.

mediation of disputes.⁷⁶ This is a common response where the contract makes mediation a condition precedent to adjudication.⁷⁷ In *Tattoo Art Inc v TAT International LLC*, the court granted a motion to dismiss the plaintiff's complaint without prejudice because the plaintiff failed to properly initiate mediation requirements before filing suit.⁷⁸ After finding the pre-litigation mediation provision to be unambiguous, the court concluded that 'until one of the parties either requests mediation and that request is denied or mediation commences and fails', the dispute was not ripe for litigation and therefore merited dismissal.⁷⁹ A court may decline to dismiss an action on such grounds where the consequences might be unduly harsh.⁸⁰

In a few cases, courts have resorted to the draconian remedy of dismissal of an action with prejudice or summary judgment against parties that have failed to comply with contractual obligations to mediate, thereby leaving the non-compliant party no option to refile their

---

⁷⁶ See *SOR Technology LLC v MWR Life LLC* No 3:18-CV-2358 JLS (NLS), 2019 US Dist LEXIS 146817, 13 (SD Cal, 28 August 2019) emphasizing that 'the dismissal is without prejudice so that Plaintiff may refile its claims once it has fulfilled its obligation to mediate prior to filing suit'); *Bank of America NA v SFR Investments Pool 1 LLC* No 2:15-cv-0693-GMN-VCF, 2016 US Dist LEXIS 11526, 6 (D Nev, 31 January 2016) ('because these claims were not submitted to mediation prior to the filing of this action, the Court lacks subject matter jurisdiction, and will dismiss these claims without prejudice'). See also *Willis Corroon Corp of Utah v United Capital Insurance Co* 97-2208 MHP, 1998 US Dist LEXIS 23226, 1, 19-24 (ND Cal, 5 January 1998) (granting a motion to dismiss for filing the action one day prematurely because the parties' agreement for pre-litigation mediation required a thirty-day 'standstill' after mediation).

⁷⁷ '[F]ailure to mediate a dispute pursuant to a contract that makes mediation a condition precedent to filing a lawsuit warrants dismissal': *Delameter v Anytime Fitness Inc* 722 F Supp 2d 1168, 1181-82 (ED Cal 2010) (quoting *Brosnan v Dry Cleaning Station Inc* C-08-02028 EDL, 2008 US Dist LEXIS 44678, 2 (ND Cal, 6 June 2008), citing *B&O Manufacturing Inc v Home Depot USA Inc* C 07-02864 JSW, 2007 US Dist LEXIS 83998, 8 (ND Cal, 1 November 2007)); *Centaur Corp v ON Semiconductor Components Industries LLC* 09 CV 2041 JM (BLM), 2010 US Dist LEXIS 8495 (SD Cal, 2 February 2010) (dismissing the lawsuit as 'premature' since the parties had not yet satisfied the condition precedent by engaging in mediation); *Stone & Webster Inc v Georgia Power Co* 968 F Supp 2d 1, 9-10 (DDC 2013) (granting a motion to dismiss the action without prejudice for failure to satisfy the condition precedent of mediation).

⁷⁸ *Tattoo Art Inc v TAT International LLC* 711 F Supp 2d 645, 651 (ED Va 2010). See also *3-J Hospitality LLC v Big Time Design Inc* 09-61077-CIV-MARRA/JOHNSON, 2009 US Dist LEXIS 100601, 3-4 (SD Fl, 27 October 2009) (holding that the plaintiff's failure to mediate, which was a condition precedent to litigation prior to filing suit, required dismissal of the case); *Mortimer v First Mount Vernon Industrial Loan Association* No Civ AMD 03-1051, 2003 US Dist LEXIS 24698, 3 (D Md, 19 May 2003) (same).

⁷⁹ *Tattoo Art* (n 78) 650.

⁸⁰ See eg *N-Tron Corp* (n 66).

complaint.[81] In *Primov v Serco*,[82] the Supreme Court of Virginia upheld the dismissal with prejudice of a breach of contract complaint by an employee for failing to comply with a contractual provision calling for the parties to mediate prior to bringing suit.[83] The trial court reasoned that the contract clearly established mediation as a condition precedent to filing suit – a condition which the employee failed to satisfy. The Virginia Court found no abuse of discretion in the lower court's dismissal, noting that the employee had filed his breach of contract claim on two separate occasions without ever requesting mediation; on the first occasion, moreover, he had withdrawn his claim right before trial when faced with a demand from the defendant to do so based in part on his failure to mediate.

Some court decisions have enforced provisions in contractual dispute resolution agreements denying awards of attorney fees to parties who failed to participate in mediation.[84] A court might also direct an award of attorney fees to a party forced to bear the consequences of an opponent's failure to comply with a dispute resolution provision.[85]

---

[81] See eg *DeValk Lincoln Mercury Inc v Ford Motor Co* 811 F 2d 326, 336–37 (7th Cir 1987) (upholding grant of a summary judgment against the plaintiff on the basis of its failure to comply with a 'mediation' provision that was a condition precedent to litigation). But see *Bombardier Corp* (n 29) 4–5 (finding that the dispute resolution procedure contained in the contract was not a condition precedent because it was not clearly defined as such), appeal denied in 333 F 3d 250 (DC Cir 2003).

[82] *Primov v Serco Inc* 296 Va 59, 817 SE 2d 811 (Va 2018).

[83] The parties' contract stated (at ibid 813):

> The parties shall attempt in good faith to resolve any dispute arising out of or relating to this Agreement promptly by confidential mediation. If the dispute has not been resolved by mediation within 60 days of a written request to mediate made by one of the parties, then either party may bring suit in the state or federal courts located in Fairfax County, Virginia.

[84] See *Lange v Schilling* 163 Cal App 4th 1412, 1418 (2008) (enforcement of term providing that, if any party commenced an action without first attempting to resolve the matter through mediation, or refused to mediate after a request was made, then that party would not be entitled to recover attorney fees, even if they would otherwise be available); *Frei v Davey* 124 Cal App 4th 1506, 1508 (2004) (enforcing agreement for attorney fees conditioned on participation in mediation by denying award of attorney fees); *Leamon v Krajkiewcz* 107 Cal App 4th 424 (2003) (same).

[85] See eg *Delameter* (n 77) 1180–81 (noting that the defendant was entitled to seek attorney fees for having to defend against a motion for summary judgment by the plaintiff who had failed to comply with the mediation provision).

11.3.3 Respective Roles of Arbitrators and Courts

When a party to a multi-step process fails or refuses to participate in contractually mandated negotiation, mediation or other dispute resolution process that is preliminary to arbitration, those circumstances may raise questions regarding the enforceability of the arbitration agreement.[86] A party seeking to enforce the arbitration agreement may also argue that issues surrounding compliance in preliminary 'steps' should be decided not by a court but by the arbitrator(s).[87] Such scenarios have spawned a growing body of federal and state court decisions under arbitration statutes.

In *Kemiron Atlantic Inc v Aguakem International Inc*,[88] the Eleventh Circuit Court of Appeals affirmed a district court order denying a motion to enforce an arbitration provision and stay a suit where neither party requested mediation, a preliminary step in the parties' dispute resolution agreement. Kemiron had sued Aguakem for breach of contract for the sale of chemicals; it also pleaded unjust enrichment and sought a declaratory judgment. Aguakem's motion to stay Kemiron's suit pending arbitration pursuant to the Federal Arbitration Act (FAA) was denied by the district court on the basis that there was no duty to arbitrate until the parties had first mediated their dispute; the Eleventh Circuit panel likewise concluded that the agreement to arbitrate was 'conditioned by the plain language' of the provision requiring mediation before arbitration.[89] *Kemiron*'s interpretation of the multi-step dispute resolution provision might appear rational on its face, but it is inconsistent with the strong FAA policy supporting broad enforceability of arbitration agreements and ignores repeated US Supreme Court directives respecting the relative spheres of courts and arbitrators with regard to arbitrability determinations.

---

[86] See eg *Halter Marine* (n 30) (enjoining the defendant from pursuing arbitration until the pre-arbitration settlement-oriented options, including conferring in good faith and submitting disputes to the American Bureau of Shipping for resolution, are exhausted). See also Stipanowich (n 65).

[87] See eg *In re R & R Personal Specialists of Tyler Inc* 146 SW 3d 699, 704–05 (Tex App 2004). But see *Tekmen & Co v S Builders Inc* 04C-03-007 RFS, 2005 Del Super LEXIS 181 (25 May 2005).

[88] *Kemiron Atlantic Inc v Aguakem International Inc* 290 F 3d 1287 (11th Cir 2002). See also *In re Pisces Foods LLC* 228 SW 3d 349, 351 (Tex App 2007) (where the multi-step agreement provided that '[i]f you have a work-related problem that involves a legally protected right that could not be settled through Steps 1, 2, or 3 of the Program, you may request arbitration,' the effect of failure to comply with the preliminary steps was a matter for judicial determination).

[89] *Kemiron* (n 88) 1291.

In *John Wiley & Sons Inc v Livingston*,[90] the Court made clear that arbitration law charges courts with the responsibility to determine whether there is a valid arbitration agreement and whether a particular issue is within the scope of that agreement,[91] in which case it falls to the arbitrator(s) to address all subsequent issues, procedural and substantive, leading to a final award on the merits, including questions about compliance with procedures for properly invoking and maintaining a claim.[92] Since the Court's pronouncement of respective spheres of authority in *John Wiley & Sons*, these principles have been repeatedly and forcefully restated,[93] with the Court repeatedly emphasising the limitations on the judicial role in enforcing arbitration agreements while underlining the far-reaching authority of arbitrators under broad-form arbitration clauses.[94] In *Howsam v Dean Witter Reynolds Inc*, the Court made it plain that judicial questions of arbitrability were of 'limited scope … applicable in the kind of narrow circumstance where contracting parties would likely have expected a court to have decided the gateway matter',[95] but not to '"procedural" questions which grow out of the dispute and bear on its final disposition[96] … [as well as] "allegations of waiver, delay, or a like defense to arbitrability"'.[97] The Court went on to explain that limiting the judicial role to such 'narrow circumstance[s] … avoids the risk of forcing parties to arbitrate a matter that they may well not have agreed to arbitrate'.[98]

Of course, when it comes to divining the respective responsibilities of courts and arbitrators on matters of arbitrability, the intent of the parties

---

[90] *John Wiley & Sons Inc v Livingston* 376 US 543 (1964).
[91] ibid 547.
[92] ibid 557–58.
[93] See *Green Tree Financial Corp v Bazzle* 539 US 444 (2003); *Howsam v Dean Witter Reynolds Inc* 537 US 79 (2002).
[94] See *Moses H Cone Memorial Hospital v Mercury Construction Corp* 460 US 1, 24–25 (1983) ('[A]ny doubts concerning the scope of arbitrable issues should be resolved in favor of arbitration …'). For a typical 'broad-form' clause, see *Collins & Aikman Products Co v Building Systems Inc* 58 F 3d 16, 20 (2d Cir 1995) ('The clause … submitting to arbitration "[a]ny claim or controversy arising out of or relating to th[e] agreement", is the paradigm of a broad clause' (quoting *David L Threlkeld & Co v Metallgesellschaft Ltd* 923 F 2d 245, 251 (2d Cir 1991)).
[95] *Howsam* (n 93) 83.
[96] ibid 84 (quoting *John Wiley* (n 90) 557).
[97] ibid (quoting *Moses H Cone* (n 94) 24–25).
[98] ibid 83–84.

controls.[99] In the event that the parties have clearly stated their intention that courts and not arbitrators will address issues surrounding negotiation, mediator or other preliminaries to arbitration in a multi-step agreement, that intention should be honored. Hence, some courts concluded that contractual provisions that specifically make mediation a 'condition precedent' to arbitration create justiciable arbitrability issues if a party refuses or fails to mediate.[100] Under dicta in *Howsam* supporting a narrow view of arbitrability, however, even 'conditions precedent' are normally expected to fall within the purview of arbitrators and not courts[101] – a conclusion that reinforces important federal policies supporting the enforcement of agreements to arbitrate (although it may be troublesome to scholars of contract).[102] A number of decisions have cited *Howsam* in support of determinations that contractual dispute resolution requirements that are or may be conditions precedent to arbitration should be addressed by arbitrators.[103]

Such judicial conclusions are likely to be reinforced by the fact that most arbitration rules provide arbitrators with virtually plenary authority regarding jurisdictional and enforcement issues.[104] *Contec Corp v Remote Solution Co*[105] follows the strong majority rule that when parties to an

---

[99] See ibid 85.
[100] See *Welborn Clinic v Medquist Inc* 301 F 3d 634, 638 (7th Cir 2002) (stating that '[i]f there is a condition precedent, it must be met before a court may compel arbitration'); *HIM Portland LLC v DeVito Builders Inc* 317 F 3d 41 (1st Cir 2003).
[101] See *Howsam* (n 93) 85.
[102] See generally Thomas J Stipanowich, 'Of "Procedural Arbitrability": The Effect of Noncompliance with Contract Claims Procedures' (1989) 40 South Carolina Law Review 847.
[103] See eg *Dialysis Access Center LLC v RMS Lifeline Inc* 638 F 3d 367, 383 (1st Cir 2011); *Lumbermens Mutual Casualty Co v Broadspire Management Services* 623 F 3d 476, 480–81 (7th Cir 2010); *JPD Inc v Chronimed Holdings Inc* 539 F 3d 388, 392–93 (6th Cir 2008). See also *Metzler Contracting Co LLC v Stephens* 774 F Supp 2d 1073, 1088 (D Haw 2011) (involving provision in the construction contract identifying the architect's initial decision as a condition precedent to arbitration).
[104] When the parties' agreement incorporates by reference institutional rules that grant the arbitral tribunal the power to rule on its own jurisdiction, questions about a condition precedent fall squarely within the purview of the arbitrator to determine. See *Footprint Power Salem Harbor Development LP v Iberdrola Energy Products Inc* 651963/2018, 2018 NY Slip Op 30794(U) 3 (NY Sup Ct, 1 May 2018). The Supreme Court strongly reinforced the contractual delegations of authority to arbitrators to resolve matters of arbitrability in *Henry Schein Inc v Archer and White Sales Inc* 139 S Ct 524, 526 (2019) (holding that when the parties have contractually delegated to an arbitrator authority to address a question of arbitrability, a court may not override this delegation even if it thinks that the argument in favor of arbitrability is 'wholly groundless').
[105] *Contec Corp v Remote Solution Co* 398 F 3d 205 (2d Cir 2005).

arbitration agreement 'explicitly incorporate rules that empower an arbitrator to decide issues of arbitrability, the incorporation serves as clear and unmistakable evidence of the parties' intent to delegate such issues to an arbitrator'.[106]

The concept that, under the FAA, arbitrators and not courts should decide whether a condition precedent to arbitration has been fulfilled was reaffirmed by the US Supreme Court in *BG Group plc v Republic of Argentina*.[107] The court in *Chorley Enterprises*[108] cited *BG Group* and *Howsam* in support of a determination that arbitrators rather than courts must decide questions associated with a mediation clause as a condition precedent to arbitration; decisions within the 4th Circuit have followed *Chorley*,[109] while some courts in other circuits are beginning to follow suit and refusing to follow previous circuit precedent that left the court to decide on preconditions.[110] This position is also supported by the

---

[106] ibid 208. In *Cafarelli v Colon-Collazo* CV055000279S, 2006 Conn Super LEXIS 1833 (20 June 2006), a Connecticut court held that the dispute about whether steps in a multi-step dispute resolution clause had been satisfied was an issue for an arbitrator due to the 'all-embracing' language in the contract: 7. '[L]anguage such as disputes . . . arising out of or related to . . . creates almost limitless jurisdiction': 8. Accordingly, the dispute about whether 'mediation as a condition precedent to arbitration' has been satisfied was to be determined by an arbitrator: 5–6 (emphasis omitted).

[107] *BG Group plc v Republic of Argentina* 572 US 25, 34–37 (2014).

[108] *Chorley Enters v Dickey's Barbecue Restaurants Inc* 807 F 3d 553 (4th Cir 2015); certificate denied, 136 S Ct 1656 (2016) (USA).

[109] *Ungava Techs v Innerspec Techs* 6:17-cv-6, 2017 US Dist LEXIS 83392, 9 (WD Va, 31 May 2017) ('But that provision [regarding a duty to negotiate] addresses the preconditions to arbitration, the satisfaction of which is a matter for the arbitrator.') (following circuit precedent in *Chorley* (n 108) and referencing *BG Group* (n 107)); *Arctic Glacier USA Inc v Principal Life Insurance Co* PX 16-3555, 2017 US Dist LEXIS 93822, 19 at fn 4 (D Md, 19 June 2017) (noting in a footnote that arguments about how the parties failed to negotiate and mediate before pursuing arbitration 'do[] not disturb the Court's jurisdiction because this issue of pre-conditions is properly resolved by the arbitrator'); *Anderson Group Co Inc v MC Hotels LLC* 0:17-cv-1564-TLW, 2017 WL 7513223, 3 at fn 3 (DSC, 16 October 2017) (noting in a footnote that, '[t]o the extent that the Subcontract requires the parties to mediate as a condition precedent to arbitration, the Fourth Circuit has very clearly stated that arbitrators – not courts – must decide whether a condition precedent to arbitrability has been fulfilled' (quotations omitted)).

[110] See eg *Dimattina Holdings LLC v Steri-Clean Inc* 195 F Supp 3d 1285, 1289 (SD Fla 2016) (relying on *Howsam* (n 93) and *BG Group* (n 107) to decline to follow the 11th Circuit's precedent in *Kemiron* (n 88)); *Brandao v Jan-Pro Franchising International Inc* 17-P-636, 2018 Mass App Unpub LEXIS 263, 2 at fn 5 (22 March 2018) (citing Chorley (n 109) for the proposition that 'whether such a condition precedent has been satisfied *may be* for the arbitrator to determine' (emphasis added)). See also *Dustex Corp v Board of Trustees of the Municipal Electric Utility of Cedar Falls* 13-CV-2087-LRR, 2014 US Dist LEXIS 82842, 32 (ND Iowa, 18 June 2014) (holding that 8th Circuit precedent maintains that 'whether a condition precedent has been satisfied is [a] procedural, rather than

Restatement (Third) of the US Law of International Commercial Arbitration.[111] Despite this trend under the FAA, however, some judicial decisions applying state arbitration laws may instead allocate responsibility for dealing with procedural preconditions to arbitration to courts.[112]

11.4 Developing Effective Tiered Dispute Resolution Provisions

Although tiered or stepped dispute resolution provisions are frequently employed in commercial contracts, such options are often embraced without much forethought regarding their operation and enforcement. Effective choice-making is rendered more difficult by uncertainties associated with judicial handling of agreements to negotiate or mediate as well as the inherent complexities of multi-step arrangements.[113]

Conscientious drafters will want to focus on the basic functionality of the multi-tier dispute resolution system – that is, to tailor a process that effectively serves the goals and intent of the parties. They should ask key questions, including, 'Who should be at the table, and for how long?' 'Might there be multiple levels of negotiation?' 'Should there be

---

substantive' issue that should be handled by the arbitration panel) (citing *El Dorado School of District No 15 v Continental Casualty Co* 247 F 3d 843, 847 (8th Cir 2001) and *John Wiley* (n 90) 557 ('Once it is determined... that the parties are obligated to submit the subject matter of a dispute to arbitration, "procedural" questions which grow out of the dispute... should be left to the arbitrator.')).

[111] Restatement (Third) US Law of International Commercial Arbitration Proposed Final Draft (2019), paras 2–19.

[112] See eg *Emerald Green Grp LLC v Norco Construction Inc* 155336/2014, 2014 WL 3107904 (NY Sup Ct, 1 July 2014) (directing a stay of arbitration pending obtaining of the architect's decision as a condition precedent to mediation, and completion of mediation as a condition precedent to arbitration) (citing *County of Rockland v Primiano Construction Co* 51 NY 2d 1, 8–9 (1980) (whether there is any preliminary requirement or any condition precedent to arbitration to be complied with are questions for judicial determination)); *In re Lakeland Fire District v East Area General Contractors Inc* 16 AD 3d 417, 418 (NY App Div 2005) (the contractor's failure to comply with the contractual conditions precedent in the form of the architect's decision and mediation requires the court to permanently stay the arbitration). See also *Hubbard Construction Co v Jacobs Civil Inc* 969 So 2d 1069, 1071–72 (Fla Dist Ct App 2007) (issues regarding the conditions precedent to arbitration are to be resolved by the court).

[113] See Jacqueline Nolan-Haley, 'Mediation: The "New Arbitration"' (2012) 17 Harvard Negotiation Law Review 61, 87 (noting that 'as mediation has become a less voluntary process mandated by the courts, parties have been more likely to challenge the enforceability of their mediated agreements') (citing James R Coben and Peter N Thompson, 'Disputing Irony: A Systematic Look at Litigation about Mediation' (2006) 11 Harvard Negotiation Law Review 43).

mediation or other third-party intervention at some point?' 'How does one move on from one step to another?' 'If we speak of "good faith" participation, what do we mean?'

However the tiered process is configured, it should offer users a clear and cohesive administrative platform for dispute resolution. The creative urge to develop customised multi-step dispute resolution processes must be tempered with care, since one-off provisions sometimes lead to collateral conflict. Terminology should be used consistently at all stages, and the beginning and end of each stage or step should be clearly defined.[114] The problem with lack of crystal clarity is exemplified by *Fluor Enterprises Inc v Solutia Inc*,[115] in which questions regarding the 'commencement' of mediation in a contractual provision for tiered dispute resolution resulted in competing motions for summary judgment and judicial parsing of the agreement and incorporated terms. Parties should also ensure that they clearly comply with their planned process, such as formally requesting mediation,[116] or take other necessary steps to implement the plan.[117]

Finally, one must remember that the opportunities for negotiation or mediation are not necessarily limited to a period of weeks or months before adjudication. Consideration might be given to whether, instead of (or in addition to) being a preliminary step to adjudication, mediation might be employed concurrently with arbitration.[118] Similarly, there

---

[114] A cautionary tale may be found in *ex parte Industrial Technologies* 707 So 2d 234 (Ala 1997), in which parties failed to clarify when and to what extent their agreed dispute resolution process was mediation, and what was arbitration.

[115] *Fluor Enterprises Inc v Solutia Inc* 147 F Supp 2d 648 (SD Tex 2001).

[116] See *Tattoo Art* (n 78) 647; *MB America Inc v Alaska Pac Leasing Co* 367 P 3d 1286, 1289–91 (Nev 2016).

[117] If a construction contract provides that the project architect's decision is a condition precedent to mediation or arbitration, the failure of parties to identify the architect in the contract has resulted in litigation, with varied outcomes. For example, in *Tillman Park LLC v Dabbs-Williams General Contractors LLC* 679 SE 2d 67, 71 (Ga Ct App 2009), the court concluded:

> [W]hether failure of the owner to name an architect . . . results in failure to meet a condition precedent thereby dispensing with the agreements arbitration requirement, or whether it results in an impossibility to satisfy the condition precedent thereby dispensing with the condition precedent requirement is a question that the agreement does not unambiguously answer and which statutory rules of construction do not resolve.

Therefore, it was up to the trial court as the trier of fact to determine the intent of the parties: ibid 71.

[118] See eg American Arbitration Association, *Commercial Arbitration Rules and Mediation Procedures* <www.adr.org/sites/default/files/CommercialRules_Web.pdf> accessed 29

might be value in employing a 'standing' mediator to offer real-time conflict management during the course of a construction project or other business relationship.[119] A contractual provision calling for the appointment of a mediator early in the dispute resolution process sets the stage for facilitation of the entire dispute resolution process.[120]

11.5 Single Neutral Med-arb and Arb-med in US Practice

No discussion of multi-tier dispute resolution is complete without some reference to circumstances in which a single neutral plays the roles of mediator and arbitrator in the course of resolving disputes.[121] Conventional opinion in the USA disfavours mixed roles for neutrals, reflecting dominant cultural perspectives and practices.[122] Many US practitioners and scholars argue that if a mediator is expected to assume an arbitral role if settlement is not achieved, parties may be strong-armed into reaching a resolution, or communicate less candidly with the neutral. If the matter proceeds to arbitration, moreover, some fear that any award may be tainted by communications made during *ex parte* discussions during mediation.[123] Keeping third-party facilitation of settlement separate from the adjudicative function also reinforces the pre-eminent role of legal advocates in the resolution of disputes.

On the other hand, it appears that, for one reason or another, many US neutrals have been given the opportunity to play mixed roles in the

---

August 2020, stating that '[s]ubject to the right of any party to opt out, in cases where a claim or counterclaim exceeds $75,000, the rules provide that the parties shall mediate their dispute upon the administration of the arbitration or at any time when the arbitration is pending'.

[119] Thomas J Stipanowich, 'Beyond Getting to Yes: Using Mediator Insights to Facilitate Long-Term Business Relationships' (2016) 34(7) Alternatives to the High Cost of Litigation 97.

[120] Paul Lurie, 'Using the Guided Choice Process to Reduce the Cost of Resolving Disputes' (2014) 9 Construction Law International 18.

[121] See generally Thomas J Stipanowich, 'Arbitration, Mediation and Mixed Modes: Seeking Workable Solutions and Common Ground on Med-arb, Arb-med and Settlement-Oriented Activities by Arbitrators' (2021) 26 Harvard Negotiation Law Review (forthcoming) <http://ssrn.com/abstract=3689389> accessed 1 September 2020.

[122] See Kristen M Blankley, 'Keeping a Secret from Yourself? Confidentiality When the Same Neutral Serves Both as Mediator and as Arbitrator in the Same Case' (2011) 63 Baylor Law Review 317; Brian A Pappas, 'Med-arb and the Legalization of Alternative Dispute Resolution' (2015) 20 Harvard Negotiation Law Review 157.

[123] Blankley (n 122) 332–37; Ellen E Deason, 'Combinations of Mediation and Arbitration with the Same Neutral: A Framework for Judicial Review' (2013) 5 Yearbook on Arbitration and Mediation 219, 228–29; Pappas (n 122) 177–78.

course of resolving disputes, at least occasionally, and a few dispute resolution professionals have developed a level of expertise with mixed roles.[124] It is perhaps natural that, as attorneys and neutrals have amassed experience with mediation and arbitration and become accustomed to employing these and other dispute resolution processes in combination, some have experimented with the possibilities afforded by having neutrals engaged in dual roles.[125] In such circumstances, experts suggest, parties should exercise special deliberation and caution. These realities are mirrored in the most authoritative statement regarding US perspectives on the subject of med-arb and the role of arbitrators in settlement, the Final Report of the CPR Commission on the Future of Arbitration.[126]

---

[124] This is illustrated by results from a survey of experienced arbitrators, all members of the US College of Commercial Arbitrators, conducted by the Straus Institute (at Stipanowich and Ulrich (n 40) 464–65):

> Those 59 Survey respondents who indicated they were at least 'sometimes' concerned with the informal settlement of cases before them were asked about their experiences changing roles or playing multiple roles (that is, as both an arbitrator and mediator) in a particular case. Of those 59 individuals, just under half (45.8%) indicated that they had 'sometimes' mediated a dispute in which they had been appointed an arbitrator . . .

An earlier survey of lawyers and arbitrators regarding international commercial arbitration indicated that some US respondents did become involved in settlement-related activities, although US respondents were much less likely to participate directly in settlement negotiations than their German counterparts. See Christian Bühring-Uhle, Lars Kirchloff and Gabriele Scherer, *Arbitration and Mediation in International Business* (2nd edn, Kluwer Law International 2006) 111–28.

[125] One US neutral with extensive experience in arrangements for med-arb, John Blankenship, acknowledges the special considerations associated with such processes, but says that voiced concerns over-emphasise the potential impact on arbitration and pay too little attention to how to effectively mediate. In his own experience, settlement usually occurs during the mediation phase: Email from John Blankenship to author (20 April 2020) 2.

[126] Stipanowich and Kaskell (n 18) (offering guidance for single neutral med-arb and arb-med-arb).

12

Multi-tiered Dispute Resolution Clauses

An English Perspective

EVA LEIN

12.1 Introduction

Multi-tiered dispute resolution clauses or 'escalation clauses'[1] in complex and high-value contracts have become increasingly popular in practice, also from an English perspective.[2] They appear in various types of contracts and across industries (construction in particular) and typically follow a two- or three-step approach, obliging the parties to first engage in non-binding processes such as negotiations and mediation. Only as a last resort, once the parties are unable to resolve their dispute at an antecedent stage, they engage in either arbitration or court proceedings.[3] The set sequence of more and less formal dispute resolution mechanisms, ideally combined with fixed time frames, helps de-escalate situations in which contractual relations did not go to plan, before the parties engage in lengthy and costly formal dispute resolution which might harm their business relationship. Both negotiations and mediation, either as an alternative of 'tier one' or coupled as 'tier one

---

[1] Also called '(multi-)step' or 'ADR first' clauses. See Klaus Peter Berger, 'Law and Practice of Escalation Clauses' (2006) 22 Arbitration International 1, 1; Gary Born, *International Commercial Arbitration* (2nd edn, Wolters Kluwer 2014) 278–79.

[2] See eg *Ohpen Operations UK Ltd v Invesco Fund Managers Ltd* [2019] EWHC 2246 (TCC), [2020] 1 All ER (Comm) 786; *Wah (aka Alan Tang) v Grant Thornton International Ltd* [2012] EWHC 3198 (Ch), [2013] 1 All ER (Comm) 1226.

[3] Michael Pryles, 'Multi-tiered Dispute Resolution Clauses' (2001) 18 Journal of International Arbitration 159. Arbitration is increasingly popular. For instance, according to the latest LCIA report (19 May 2020), their caseload in 2019 has grown by 25 per cent compared to the previous year. The Court recorded its highest ever case number (406 cases): see London Court of International Arbitration, '2019 Annual Casework Report' (19 May 2020) <www.lcia.org/media/download.aspx?MediaId=816> accessed 19 November 2020.

and two' of a multi-tiered clause,[4] allow for consensual solutions, reduce costs and avoid stigma.[5]

One of the reasons why escalation clauses which provide for 'ADR first' have become more popular is the increasing promotion in recent years of mediation as a viable alternative to court litigation and arbitration.[6] Mediation is all the more interesting for parties since the entry into force of the Singapore Convention[7] is giving settlements reached in mediation proceedings a binding and enforceable character. National civil procedure rules also increasingly require the courts to encourage out-of-court solutions between the parties.[8] A multi-tiered approach is therefore increasingly common.

Those clauses frequently directly involve corporate executives with authority to conduct negotiations and with an interest in amicably settling a dispute or representatives with specific knowledge, for example, technicians or engineers in construction contracts.[9]

The encouragement of consensual dispute resolution is now more important than ever in light of the COVID-19 crisis, which is unprecedented in recent history. The pandemic calls for 'breathing

---

[4] Julian DM Lew, Loukas A Mistelis and Stefan M Kröll, *Comparative International Commercial Arbitration* (Wolters Kluwer 2003) 8ff.

[5] Klaus Peter Berger, *Private Dispute Resolution in International Business* (Wolters Kluwer 2006) 2ff.

[6] Catharine Titi and Katia Fach Gómez, *Mediation in International Commercial and Investment Disputes* (Oxford University Press 2019).

[7] 2019 United Nations Convention on International Settlement Agreements Resulting from Mediation (the Singapore Convention). In the future, the Singapore Convention might challenge the role of the New York Convention which guarantees the enforceability of arbitral awards across a vast array of states.

[8] See, for England, *Halsey v Milton Keynes General NHS Trust* [2004] EWCA Civ 576; *McParland & Partners Ltd v Whitehead* [2020] EWHC 298 (Ch), [2020] Bus LR 699 [42]. A party's refusal to engage in mediation or other ADR mechanisms can have costs implications: see *Wales (t/a Selective Investment Services) v CBRE Managed Services Ltd* [2020] EWHC 1050 (Comm), [2020] Costs LR 603 [24]ff. See also Civil Procedure Rules (CPR), r 1.4:
(1) The court must further the overriding objective by actively managing cases.
(2) Active case management includes –
  (a) encouraging the parties to co-operate with each other in the conduct of the proceedings; . . .
  (e) encouraging the parties to use an alternative dispute resolution procedure if the court considers that appropriate and facilitating the use of such procedure; . . . .

[9] Oliver Krauss, 'The Enforceability of Escalation Clauses Providing for Negotiations in Good Faith under English Law' [2015–2016] (2) McGill Journal of Dispute Resolution 142, 145.

space'[10] in contractual relations, and non-contentious forms of dispute resolution are encouraged between parties to avoid a 'plethora of disputes' before the courts.[11] A multi-tiered clause does precisely that. It obliges the parties to attempt reasonable out-of-court solutions and to avoid reaching the last stage of their dispute resolution arrangement. Multi-tiered clauses can therefore play an important role in mitigating COVID-19-related contractual disputes provided they are well drafted. Several institutions such as the Centre for Effective Dispute Resolution (CEDR)[12] propose model clauses[13] to provide a detailed and certain framework for the parties.

---

[10] See William Blair, Eva Lein, Louise Gullifer and Judy Fu, 'Breathing Space, Concept Note 2 on the Effect of the 2020 Pandemic on Commercial Contracts, September 2020 Update' (*British Institute of International and Comparative Law*) <www.biicl.org/breathing-space> accessed 14 November 2020. It highlights steps to minimise the risk of a deluge of disputes in the current pandemic and to increase the prospect of constructive outcomes.

[11] See eg Cabinet Office, 'Guidance on Responsible Contractual Behaviour in the Performance and Enforcement of Contracts Impacted by the COVID-19 Emergency' (7 May 2020) <https://assets.publishing.service.gov.uk/government/uploads/system/uploads/attachment_data/file/883737/_Covid-19_and_Responsible_Contractual_Behaviour__web_final___7_May_.pdf> accessed 14 November 2020. This is updated as of 30 June 2020: Cabinet Office, 'Guidance on Responsible Contractual Behaviour in the Performance and Enforcement of Contracts Impacted by the COVID-19 Emergency (published 7 May 2020): Update, 30 June 2020' (30 June 2020) <https://assets.publishing.service.gov.uk/government/uploads/system/uploads/attachment_data/file/899175/__Update_-_Covid-19_and_Responsible_Contractual_Behaviour_-_30_June__final_for_web_.pdf> accessed 14 November 2020. Co-operation duties have also been introduced by national emergency legislation: see eg Einführungsgesetz zum Bürgerlichen Gesetzbuche [Introductory Act to the Civil Code] (1994, as amended in 2020) (Germany), art 240 paras 3(2), 3(4), which encourages the renegotiation of contractual terms in consumer credit contracts.

[12] 'Home' (*Center for Effective Dispute Resolution*) <www.cedr.com> accessed 14 November 2020.

[13] CEDR Model ADR Clauses for Commercial Contracts (2020 Edition) states:

> If any dispute arises in connection with this agreement, a director [or other senior representatives of the parties with authority to settle the dispute] will, within [14] [working] days of a written request from one party to the other, meet in a good faith effort to resolve the dispute.
>
> If the dispute is not wholly resolved at that meeting, the parties agree to enter into mediation in good faith to settle such a dispute and will do so in accordance with the CEDR Model Mediation Procedure. Unless otherwise agreed between the parties within 14 [working] days of notice of the dispute, the mediator will be nominated by CEDR. To initiate the mediation a party must give notice in writing ('ADR Notice') to the other party[ies] to the dispute, referring the dispute to mediation. A copy of the referral should be sent to CEDR.

Despite the advantages that multi-tier dispute resolution clauses present, various issues remain problematic.[14] From an English perspective, the enforceability of these agreements has been contested in the courts in instances in which one of the parties failed to observe the multi-tiered procedure, the clause lacked certainty, or the negotiation stage was subject to the principle of good faith.[15] The delimitation of the different escalation stages can give rise to controversy, where the process or model to be employed remains unclear and open for further argument. In practice, parties often take less care in drafting dispute resolution clauses than in setting out complex contractual arrangements, and therefore risk entering a dispute about the dispute resolution procedure. Another problem can arise when parties seek injunctive relief from a jurisdiction requiring arbitration proceedings to commence within a given time frame, which effectively hinders a party from observing the multi-tiered procedure. Lastly, the question arises as to the consequences of a breach of such agreements. Hence, there is a risk that multi-tiered clauses cause problems

> [If there is any point on the logistical arrangements of the mediation, other than the nomination of the mediator, upon which the parties cannot agree within 14 [working] days from the date of the ADR Notice, where appropriate, in conjunction with the mediator, CEDR will be requested to decide that point for the parties having consulted with them.]
>
> Unless otherwise agreed, the mediation will start not later than [28] [working] days after the date of the ADR Notice. ...
>
> No party may commence any court proceedings/arbitration in relation to any dispute arising out of this agreement until it has attempted to settle the dispute by mediation and either the mediation has terminated or the other party has failed to participate in the mediation, provided that the right to issue proceedings is not prejudiced by a delay.

The Model ADR Clauses are at <www.cedr.com/wp-content/uploads/2020/02/Model-ADR-Clauses-for-Commercial-Contracts-2020.docx> accessed 19 November 2020.

[14] See Didem Kayali, 'Enforceability of Multi-tiered Dispute Resolution Clauses' (2010) 27(6) Journal of International Arbitration 551; Lianne Sneddon and Amanda Lees, 'Frequently Asked Questions: Is My Tiered Dispute Resolution Clause Binding?' (*Ashurst*, 1 February 2013) <www.ashurst.com/en/news-and-insights/legal-updates/frequently-asked-questions-is-my-tiered-dispute-resolution-clause-binding/> accessed 14 November 2020; Gary Born and Marija Šćekić, 'Pre-arbitration Procedural Requirements: "A Dismal Swamp"' in David D Caron and others (eds), *Practising Virtue: Inside International Arbitration* (Oxford University Press 2015) 227.

[15] Simon Hart, 'England' in Frederick A Acomb and others (eds), *Multi-tiered Dispute Resolution Clauses* (IBA Litigation Committee, 1 October 2015) <www.ibanet.org/Document/Default.aspx?DocumentUid=9C6E21DE-043C-44C9-BE75-94CADECCF470> accessed 14 November 2020, 63, 65.

of interpretation and consequently delay dispute resolution in time-sensitive situations or in the event of an unsuccessful ADR stage. Parties could also use them tactically to their own advantage.

12.2 The Perspective of the English Courts: A Chronology

In the English courts, the enforceability of agreements to negotiate, of agreements to mediate or settle a dispute amicably and of combinations thereof has been challenged for reasons of uncertainty.[16] Such challenge is usually brought when the ADR stage(s) were ignored or considered unsuccessful by one of the parties.[17]

Although it has been voiced that English courts should not accentuate uncertainty and unenforceability,[18] but on the contrary focus on the parties' intentions, the requirements for the enforceability of multi-tiered clauses, in particular the question of the binding and enforceable nature of a pre-arbitration or pre-litigation procedure, have been subject to strict criteria. Such agreements need to set out the dispute resolution mechanism in a detailed and unambiguous manner to be enforceable under English law.[19] The case law shows that requirements as to drafting are rather challenging.

Where a clause provides for a merely optional ADR stage, for example, as indicated by the use of the term 'may' in the clause, it will be unenforceable due to lack of certainty.[20]

But even in cases in which the ADR stage is mandatory, problems can arise. These clauses can take slightly different forms and require the parties to attempt dispute resolution via 'friendly discussions', 'good faith negotiations', 'amicable settlement' or another specified manner, for example, via 'mediation'.[21]

---

[16] Sai Ramani Garimella and Nizamuddn Ahmad Siddiqui, 'The Enforceability of Multi-tiered Dispute Resolution Clauses: Contemporary Judicial Opinion' (2016) 24(1) IIUM Law Journal 166. See also Maryam Salehijam, 'Enforceability of ADR Agreements: An Analysis of Selected EU Member States' (2018) 21 International Trade Business Law Review 255, 255–76.

[17] See the cases cited in this section.

[18] *Cable & Wireless plc v IBM United Kingdom Ltd* [2002] EWHC 2059 (Comm), [2002] 2 All ER (Comm) 1041.

[19] See eg *Wah v Grant Thornton* (n 2).

[20] Paul D Friedland, *Arbitration Clauses for International Contracts* (2nd edn, JurisNet 2007) 123.

[21] See also Krauss (n 9) 145ff.

In English law, agreements to negotiate were regularly considered unenforceable.[22] In *Walford v Miles*,[23] the sellers of a company agreed to conduct exclusive negotiations with one potential purchaser, terminating any negotiations with any competitor. The agreement was considered too broad and hence invalid due to lack of certainty. The court refused to imply that either party could conclude negotiations for 'proper reasons' as this would amount to an obligation to act in good faith, which was, at the time, traditionally not a principle recognised under English law and considered a 'too open concept' to provide certainty as to the negotiation process.[24]

On the contrary, it was held in a later decision (*Cable & Wireless v IBM*)[25] that mediation clauses were enforceable, at least in cases in which the contractual clause in question refers to a specific, sufficiently detailed and clear procedure (here, a procedure provided for by a recognised mediation institution (CEDR)).[26] The parties to a global IT services agreement had fallen into dispute, but the court held that they were obliged to participate in the pre-litigation ADR process they had agreed upon in their contact. The court distinguished between an agreement to negotiate (unenforceable due to an uncertain outcome of the negotiations) and an agreement engaging in an ADR process which requires co-operation in the appointment of a mediator, submission of documents to the mediator and attendance at the mediation. In *Cable &*

---

[22] See *Courtney & Fairbairn Ltd v Tolaini Brothers (Hotels) Ltd* [1975] 1 WLR 297.
[23] *Walford v Miles* [1992] 2 AC 128.
[24] Hart (n 15) 65.
[25] *Cable & Wireless v IBM* (n 18).
[26] ibid. The relevant clauses state:

> [clause 41:] The Parties shall attempt in good faith to resolve any dispute or claim arising out of or relating to this Agreement or any Local Services Agreement promptly through negotiations between the respective senior executives of the Parties who have authority to settle the same pursuant to Clause 40.
> If the matter is not resolved through negotiation, the Parties shall attempt in good faith to resolve the dispute or claim through an Alternative Dispute Resolution (ADR) procedure as recommended to the Parties by the Centre for Dispute Resolution. However, an ADR procedure which is being followed shall not prevent any Party or Local Party from issuing proceedings.
> [clause 40:] ... Neither Party nor any Local Party may initiate any legal action until the [dispute escalation] process has been completed, unless such Party or Local Party has reasonable cause to do so to avoid damage to its business or to protect or preserve any right of action it may have.

Wireless v IBM, the parties were agreeing to a clear procedure intended to contemplate litigation only as a last resort.

In *Holloway v Chancery Mead Ltd*,[27] a dispute concerning the sale and development of a house, basic conditions for multi-tiered clauses were set out by the court. The claimants sought to refer pecuniary disputes relating to defects in the house to a specific multi-tiered arbitration scheme[28] and the question was whether it was a condition precedent for the dispute to be referred to conciliation. The court held that seller–buyer disputes of that kind did not fall under the conciliation scheme. The court nonetheless set out a number of criteria for escalation clauses which included the requirement for the dispute resolution process to be sufficiently certain without need for any further agreement; for the process of selection and remuneration of the person to resolve the dispute to be defined; and for the model of the process to be set out with sufficient certainty.[29]

A subsequent decision in *Wah (aka Alan Tang) v Grant Thornton International Ltd*[30] follows and clarifies this approach. The contract in

---

[27] *Holloway v Chancery Mead Ltd* [2007] EWHC 2495 (TCC), [2008] 1 All ER (Comm) 653.
[28] ibid. The relevant clause (clause 24) states:
    24.1 If any dispute shall arise between the Seller and the Buyer touching or concerning the construction or setting out of the dwelling house and/or the property either party shall at the written request of the other seek to resolve such dispute (and if to the extent that the subject matter of the dispute comes within the scope of the NHBC Dispute Resolution Service) through conciliation by the NHBC.
    24.2 If and to the extent that the dispute falls outside the scope of the NHBC Dispute Resolution Service, such dispute shall be and is hereby referred to arbitration in accordance with the NHBC Arbitration Scheme current at the date hereof.
    24.3 Disputes or parts of dispute which fall outside the ordinary scope of the NHBC Arbitration Scheme shall be referred to arbitration and the rules applicable to those disputes or parts of disputes shall be determined by the Arbitrator.
    24.4 If disputes or parts of disputes which fall outside the scope of the NHBC Arbitration Scheme are concurrent with disputes which fall within that scope, then all disputes shall be dealt with by the same arbitrator at the same time.
    24.5 A determination by an NHBC investigator shall not prevent a party from subsequently referring the same dispute or part thereof to arbitration.
    24.6 The making of a determination by an NHBC investigator shal l be a condition precedent to any right to refer the matter to arbitration in accordance herewith save that the condition can be waived by consent of the parties.
[29] *Holloway* (n 27) [81].
[30] *Wah v Grant Thornton* (n 2).

question contained a quite detailed clause that required conciliation prior to arbitration and referred to 'amicable conciliation of an informal nature'. The court found the relevant provisions to be too equivocal in respect of the process and of the parties' obligations to be considered enforceable. The language of the clause was mandatory and provided for disputes to first be referred to the chief executive in order to find a solution by way of conciliation. In case the dispute remained unsolved, the clause provided for a referral to a panel formed by members of the board. It was also stipulated in the clause that 'no party may commence any arbitration procedures in accordance with this Agreement' until either the panel had concluded that it could not resolve the dispute or a month had passed since it had received the request for conciliation.

In *Wah*, the court clarified that an enforceable clause needs to meet the following requirements: (1) a sufficiently certain and unequivocal commitment to commence a process; (2) distinct and objectively ascertainable steps that each party needs to follow to put the process in place; (3) a sufficiently clearly defined process so that it can be objectively assessed what is the minimum required of the parties in terms of participation in the dispute resolution process and when or how this process or 'stage' will be properly exhausted or terminable without breach.

In the case, it remained unclear to the court how the conciliation process before the chief executive and the panel would take place and how the parties were to take part in the process of participation. Also, the prohibition of commencing arbitration until the conciliation stage is unsuccessfully concluded was understood as defining a cut-off moment rather than a prohibition of arbitration in case the pre-arbitration stage could not be completed.

Furthermore, the court took a position as to negotiations in good faith. It considered the decision in *Petromec Inc v Petroleo Brasileiro SA Petrobras* in which the Court of Appeal recognised the difficulty of determining 'when a requirement to negotiate in good faith has been satisfied (the concept of bringing negotiations to an end in bad faith being "somewhat elusive")' but concluded that the court should not deny enforcement on that ground as 'the difficulty of a problem should not be an excuse for a court to withhold relevant assistance from the parties by declaring a blanket enforceability of the obligation'.[31] The court did not follow this reasoning in *Wah*, highlighting that *Walford v Miles* had

---

[31] ibid [54]. See also *Petromec Inc v Petroleo Brasileiro SA Petrobras* [2005] EWCA Civ 891, [2006] 1 Lloyd's Rep 121.

not been reversed by the Supreme Court and that the negotiations in *Petromec* were of a very limited scope.[32]

In *Sulamerica CIA Nacional De Seguros SA v Enesa Engenharia SA*,[33] the dispute resolution clause in question required mediation prior to arbitration but the procedure to appoint a mediator was not set out, although the mediation clause was fairly detailed.[34] Contrary to *Cable & Wireless v IBM* and *Holloway*, in which the court clarified that an agreement to enter into a prescribed mediation procedure can give rise to a binding obligation, 'provided that matters essential to the process do not remain to be agreed',[35] clause 11 in the present case contained 'no unequivocal undertaking to enter into a mediation, no clear provisions for the appointment of a mediator and no clearly defined mediation process'.[36] As there remained essential matters for the parties to define,

---

[32] ibid [54].
[33] *Sulamerica CIA Nacional De Seguros SA v Enesa Engenharia SA* [2012] EWCA Civ 638, [2013] 1 WLR 102.
[34] ibid [5], where the relevant clauses are reproduced:

11. Mediation

If any dispute or difference of whatsoever nature arises out of or in connection with this Policy including any question regarding its existence, validity or termination, hereafter termed as Dispute, the parties undertake that, prior to a reference to arbitration, they will seek to have the Dispute resolved amicably by mediation.

All rights of the parties in respect of the Dispute are and shall remain fully reserved and the entire mediation including all documents produced or to which reference is made, discussion and oral presentation shall be strictly confidential to the parties and shall be conducted on the same basis as without prejudice negotiations, privileged, inadmissible, not subject to disclosure in any other proceedings whatsoever and shall not constitute any waiver of privilege whether between the parties or between either of them and a third party.

The mediation may be terminated should any party so wish by written notice to the appointed mediator and to the other party to that effect. Notice to terminate may be served at any time after the first meeting or discussion has taken place in mediation.

If the Dispute has not been resolved to the satisfaction of either party within 90 days of service of the notice initiating mediation, or if either party fails or refuses to participate in the mediation, of if either party serves written notice terminating the mediation under this clause, then either party may refer to the Dispute to arbitration.

Unless the parties otherwise agree, the fees and expenses of the mediator and all other costs of the mediation shall be borne equally by the parties and each party shall bear their own respective costs incurred in the mediation regardless of the outcome of the mediation.

[35] *Cable & Wireless v IBM* (n 18); *Holloway v Chancery Mead* (n 27); *Sulamerica* (n 33) [33].
[36] *Sulamerica* (n 33) [33].

the clause could not create a binding obligation for the parties and therefore did not establish an 'effective precondition to arbitration'.[37]

In *Emirates Trading Agency LLC v Prime Mineral Exports Private Ltd*,[38] a case concerning the purchase of iron ore, the key question was whether an obligation to seek dispute resolution by friendly discussion and within a limited period of time as a condition precedent to arbitration in a two-level clause is enforceable.[39] The clauses stated: '[I]f no solution can be arrived at between the parties for a continuous period of four weeks ... then the non-defaulting party can invoke the arbitration clause.' Emirates Trading Agency argued that the arbitral tribunal lacked jurisdiction to hear the dispute as the dispute resolution clause contained a mandatory requirement to engage in time-limited negotiations before arbitration. The condition precedent had not been satisfied as there was no 'continuous period of 4 weeks of negotiations to resolve the claims'.

Based on the criteria in *Wah*, the clause was considered enforceable by the court. The court rejected the argument that negotiations had to run continuously for a period of four weeks, as the clause was referring to a time limit rather than to the duration of the discussions themselves. It was therefore part of the condition precedent that negotiations were held during the four weeks prior to arbitration, regardless of whether those negotiations were continuous or not.

Interestingly, the court referred to the principle of good faith during negotiations and stated that the obligation to seek to resolve disputes by friendly discussions must imply an obligation to do so in good faith. It concluded that an escalation clause in an existing and enforceable contract requiring the parties to first attempt dispute resolution by friendly discussions within a limited period of time is enforceable. The enforcement of such a clause was also considered to be in the

---

[37] ibid.
[38] *Emirates Trading Agency LLC v Prime Mineral Exports Private Ltd* [2014] EWHC 2104 (Comm), [2015] 1 WLR 1145.
[39] ibid [3], where the relevant clause is reproduced:
   11. Dispute Resolution and Arbitration
   11.1 In case of any dispute or claim arising out of or in connection with or under this LTC including on account of a breaches/defaults mentioned in 9.2, 9.3, Clauses 10.1(d) and/or 10.1(e) above, the Parties shall first seek to resolve the dispute or claim by friendly discussion. Any party may notify the other Party of its desire to enter into consultation to resolve a dispute or claim. If no solution can be arrived at in between the Parties for a continuous period of 4 (four) weeks then the non-defaulting party can invoke the arbitration clause and refer the disputes to arbitration. ...

public interest as commercial parties expect courts to enforce their freely assumed engagement to avoid potentially expensive and time-consuming arbitration.[40]

A very recent English case concerning a framework agreement for the provision of digital services (*Ohpen Operations v Invesco*)[41] provides further guidance on the enforceability of three-staged clauses which contain an agreement to negotiate and mediate as a precondition to litigation. In *Ohpen*, the parties included the following multi-tiered clause:

11.1 Internal Escalation

11.1.1 The Parties will first use their respective reasonable efforts to resolve any Dispute that may arise out of or relate to this Agreement or any breach thereof, in accordance with this Clause. If any such Dispute cannot be settled amicably through ordinary negotiations within a timeframe acceptable to Client and Ohpen, either Party may refer the Dispute to the Contract Managers who shall meet and use their reasonable efforts to resolve the Dispute.

11.1.2 During the Development and Implementation Phase, any disputes shall firstly be handled by the persons as described in Clause 22.1. If such escalation does not lead to resolution of the Dispute, then the Dispute shall be escalated to the executive committees of respectively Client and Ohpen. If escalation to the executive committee does not lead to resolution of the Dispute, then the Dispute shall be referred for resolution to mediation under the Model Mediation Procedure of the Centre of [Effective] Dispute Resolution (CEDR) for the time being in force. If the Parties are unable to resolve the Dispute by mediation, either Party may commence court proceedings.

11.1.3 If any such Dispute that arises after Commencement Date is not resolved by the Contract Managers within ten (10) Business Days after it is referred to them, either Party may escalate the Dispute through the hierarchy of the committees, as set out in the chapter on governance of Schedule 2 (Service Level Agreement), who will meet and use their respective reasonable efforts to resolve the Dispute.

---

[40] 'The obligation to seek to resolve disputes by friendly discussions must import an obligation to seek to do so in good faith. In traditional terms such an obligation goes without saying and is necessary to give business efficacy to the contract. In modern terms that is what the contract would be reasonably understood to mean.': *Emirates Trading* (n 38) [51]. See also Krauss (n 9) 154.

[41] *Ohpen Operations* (n 2).

11.1.4 Ohpen shall continue to provide the Services and to perform its obligations under this Agreement notwithstanding any Dispute or the implementation of the procedures set out in this Clause. Client's payment obligations that are listed in Schedule 3 (Pricing) shall not be halted during the resolution of any Dispute.

11.2 Jurisdiction

If a Dispute is not resolved in accordance with the Dispute procedure, then such Dispute can be submitted by either Party to the exclusive jurisdiction of the English courts.

Due to problems in the contractual relationship, the parties agreed that their primary obligations under the framework contract had been terminated, but they did not agree on which party had been in breach of contract. Ohpen started a damages claim in the courts and Invesco asked for a stay of the proceedings to be able to enforce the mediation clause which it considered to be a mandatory precondition to litigation. The argument put forward by Ohpen was that the termination of the framework agreement also affected the dispute resolution clause. However, based on the doctrine of separability, the court considered the dispute resolution clause separately and found the clause to be enforceable. The court based its reasoning on the following criteria:[42]

(1) The wording of the agreement must create an enforceable obligation mandating that parties shall engage in ADR processes;
(2) The obligation needs to be clearly drafted and state unambiguously that it is meant to be a condition precedent to arbitration or litigation;
(3) The dispute resolution procedure in the agreement does not have to be formal, but it must be sufficiently clear and certain, by reference to objective criteria, including methods to appoint a mediator or to determine any other necessary step in the process without the need for any further agreement between the parties;
(4) The court has a discretion to stay proceedings which were initiated in breach of an enforceable agreement;
(5) When exercising this discretion, the court will balance (i) the public policy interest in upholding any contractual agreement between parties with (ii) any overriding objective to assist parties in resolving their disputes efficiently and effectively.

It was underlined by the court that there is a 'clear and strong policy in favour of enforcing alternative dispute resolution provisions and in

---

[42] See ibid [32].

encouraging parties to attempt to resolve disputes prior to litigation',[43] provided that agreements are drafted meticulously based on detailed and mandatory terms. The court further stated: 'Where a contract contains valid machinery for resolving potential disputes between the parties, it will usually be necessary for the parties to follow that machinery, and the court will not permit an action to be brought in breach of such agreement.' As in earlier cases,[44] this is confirmed where a model procedure (such as provided for by CEDR) is employed.[45] It emerges from *Ohpen* and earlier case law that English courts will consider and pronounce a stay of proceedings where the ADR stage of an enforceable multi-stage clause is disregarded by a party.

12.3 Criteria for the Enforceability of Multi-tiered Clauses

From an English perspective, following the line of case law and the recent decision in *Ohpen*, the question of enforceability of multi-tiered clauses is developing, but within strict criteria.[46] Although multi-tiered clauses have been assessed on a case-by-case basis, some criteria have been repeatedly assessed by the courts and can be distilled from the English case law as follows:

12.3.1 Sufficient Certainty

The obligations of the parties need to be clearly set out and there must not be a need for any further agreement between the parties. A multi-tiered clause needs to provide sufficient objective criteria defining the negotiation and/or mediation stages[47] so that the parties and the court can understand without further clarifications how negotiations are to be conducted and how a mediator is appointed, remunerated and which mediation process is to be followed. It is recommended that the parties follow a defined ADR procedure, ideally a procedure suggested by

---

[43] ibid [58].
[44] *Sulamerica* (n 33) [36].
[45] *Ohpen Operations* (n 2) [53].
[46] While other jurisdictions such as Singapore have already had a pro-enforcement attitude, see Maryam Salehijam, 'Challenges of Mediation – The Need to Address the English Approach to Agreements to Mediate' (*Courts and Tribunals Judiciary*) <www.judiciary.uk/wp-content/uploads/2018/02/challenges-of-commercial-mediation-maryam-salehijam-cjc-adr.pdf> accessed 14 November 2020, 3.
[47] *Wah v Grant Thornton* (n 2) [57].

a recognised mediation institution such as CEDR or the new London Chamber of Arbitration and Mediation (LCAM), so that neither the description of the mediation process nor the mediation provider leaves any room for uncertainty.[48] Although the dispute resolution process stipulated in the multi-tiered clause does not need to be formal,[49] it is clearly not enough to simply refer to 'amicable dispute resolution by mediation' (or by negotiation, or both).[50] English case law demonstrates that clauses based on CEDR mediation proceedings have been considered enforceable on a regular basis,[51] whilst 'self-made' clauses carry the risk of uncertainty.

Nonetheless, courts (and arbitral tribunals) keep discretion to enforce an agreement to mediate and to stay proceedings. They will do so when it is the common intention of the parties to refrain from formal dispute resolution within a set period of time,[52] but this requires a clear and unequivocal expression of such intention in the dispute resolution clause. Courts and tribunals have discretion not to stay proceedings, notably if parties do not seem to intend making a reasonable or genuine attempt to resolve their dispute via negotiation or mediation or if they seem to intend to use the stay of proceedings as a delay tactic.[53]

12.3.2 Precise Definition of the Escalation Stages

An objectively determinable procedure also requires a clear determination of the negotiation and mediation stages including a time frame within

---

[48] See 'Home' (*Centre for Effective Dispute Resolution*) <www.cedr.com> accessed 14 November 2020; 'Home' (*London Chamber of Arbitration and Mediation*) <https://lcam.org.uk> accessed 14 November 2020.
[49] See *Ohpen Operations* (n 2) [32].
[50] See the arguments in *Wah v Grant Thornton* (n 2) [49]ff.
[51] *Ohpen Operations* (n 2); *Sulamerica* (n 33).
[52] cf CPR r 26.4:
> (1) A party may, when filing the completed directions questionnaire, make a written request for the proceedings to be stayed while the parties try to settle the case by alternative dispute resolution or other means.
> (2) If all parties request a stay the proceedings will be stayed for one month and the court will notify the parties accordingly.
> (2A) If the court otherwise considers that such a stay would be appropriate, the court will direct that the proceedings, either in whole or in part, be stayed for one month, or for such other period as it considers appropriate. . . .

[53] See an example from the High Court of Singapore: *Yashwant Bajaj v Toru Ueda* [2018] SGHC 229 (Singapore).

which the parties have to attempt ADR and refrain from arbitration or litigation. It needs to be clear when negotiations start (usually with a written request made by one of the parties) and within which time limit they need to be conducted (typically within a continuous period of either fourteen days or four weeks). This time limit is a crucial element when assessing the certainty of a multi-tiered clause. It further defines and delimits the parties' agreement not to engage in formal dispute resolution. It is therefore crucial to clarify when negotiations have failed and proceedings move to the next stage, ideally by notifying the other party in writing. Otherwise, there is a risk of a dispute around the question of whether or not the next escalation stage had been reached.[54]

The parties should therefore either use preformulated clauses of established institutions or ensure that they address the following points: description of the tiers and the respective procedure; method of negotiations; place and method of mediation; language; selection of negotiators and/or mediators; description of the parties' obligations (attendance, co-operation duties, minimum hours or sessions for negotiation or mediation); division of costs; consequences of a breach of the clause by disrespecting or shortening the escalation stages (stay, damages claim, etc).[55] In current contract practice, however, clauses rarely address all of these issues.

12.3.3 Good Faith during the Negotiation Stage

A recurrent problem during the negotiation stage of a multi-tiered clause is the role of good faith. There is no unanimous view of the role and content of good faith in English contract law.[56] It is being referred to as a standard of fair and open dealings[57] and an overall standard of behaviour which is not considered commercially unacceptable by reasonable and honest parties in the given contractual context.[58] Due to its vague character and potentially broad impact, the question arises of how good

---

[54] See the aforementioned case law; cf Krauss (n 9).
[55] See also in detail Salehijam (n 46) 6.
[56] As opposed to eg US law, see Restatement (Second) of the Law of Contracts, para 205: 'Every contract imposes upon each party a duty of good faith and fair dealing in its performance and its enforcement.'
[57] *Interfoto Picture Library Ltd v Stiletto Visual Programmes Ltd* [1989] QB 433, 439; *CPC Group Ltd v Qatari Diar Real Estate Investment Co* [2010] EWHC 1535 (Ch) [246].
[58] *Yam Seng Pte Ltd v International Trade Corporation Ltd* [2013] EWHC 111 (QB), [2013] 1 All ER (Comm) 1321 [145].

faith can be reconciled with multi-tiered clauses in which the different escalation stages are to be clearly defined, sufficiently certain and subject to a time limit to render them enforceable. The idea of subjecting negotiations to a principle as vague as good faith led the courts to challenge negotiation clauses in some of the abovementioned English decisions.[59]

However, two points should be made in this respect. First, there is a difference between cases in which good faith has been referred to as an express duty, agreed upon between the parties, and those in which it has been considered an implied term. It has been confirmed in case law that the parties who wish to impose a duty of good faith must do so expressly.[60]

Second, a difference should be made between negotiations before a contract is concluded and negotiations during the dispute resolution stage, following an existing contractual arrangement between the parties. During negotiations, before the conclusion of a contract, there is no general principle of good faith under English contract law, which adheres to the idea of 'freedom to contract and freedom from contract' and assesses negotiations from a much more economically focused and less moral perspective than continental legal systems. English law addresses contractual unfairness on a case-by-case basis, not based on a general duty of good faith.[61] However, where parties are in an existing contractual relationship, the idea of good faith has a different connotation. In that context, it has been accepted in *Yam Seng v ITC* that implying a duty of good faith into an existing contractual relationship based on the presumed intention of the parties is possible as it would not limit the parties' contractual freedom.[62]

The decision in *Emirates Trading* confirms this approach. The court found an obligation to resolve disputes by friendly discussions to imply an obligation to do so in good faith as this is 'necessary to give business efficacy to the [existing] contract'.[63] It therefore considered clauses which provide dispute resolution by friendly discussions in good faith and within a limited period of time to be enforceable.

---

[59] See Section 12.2.
[60] *Compass Group UK v Mid Essex Hospital Services NHS Trust* [2013] EWCA Civ 200, [2013] BLR 265 [105]. See also Krauss (n 9) 154.
[61] See *Walford v Miles* (n 23) 138; *Interfoto Picture Library Ltd* (n 57) 439.
[62] *Yam Seng Pte Ltd* (n 58) [131], [148], [153].
[63] *Emirates Trading* (n 38) [51].

It has also been suggested that the UK Cabinet Office's guidance on 'responsible contractual behaviour' following the COVID-19 crisis[64] may contribute to the development of the good faith principle in England.[65] Although the government guidance has no binding character, it is a stark reminder that the parties to contracts 'should act responsibly and fairly' in performing and enforcing contracts, which includes, in particular, scenarios in which they are 'commencing, and continuing, formal dispute resolution procedures, including proceedings in court';[66] and when 'requesting, and responding to, requests for mediation or other alternative or fast-track dispute resolution'.[67] In its updated guidance from 30 June 2020, the government stresses the need for an 'equitable adjustment or accommodation in contractual arrangements impacted by COVID-19 to be considered in preference to a formal dispute' and 'strongly encourages parties to seek to resolve any emerging contractual issues responsibly, through negotiation, an early neutral evaluation or mediation, before these escalate into formal intractable disputes'.[68]

12.3.4 Mandatory Procedure

The wording of the multi-tiered clause must create an enforceable obligation mandating that parties shall engage in ADR processes. The clause therefore needs to be clearly drafted and unambiguously state that the ADR stage(s) are meant to be a condition precedent to arbitration or litigation (as indicated by the use of the word 'shall'; or by stating that litigation or arbitration may start 'only if' the pre-arbitration or pre-litigation mechanism is employed by the aggrieved party; or by clarifying that the aggrieved party has the 'obligation' to use ADR before starting arbitration or litigation).[69] It is in particular necessary to clearly determine whether or not the negotiation stage (negotiations via technical experts, dispute boards, etc) is supposed to be mandatory.[70]

---

[64] 'Guidance on Responsible Contractual Behaviour' (n 11).
[65] See eg 'COVID-19 and Duties of Good Faith under English law' (*Dechert*, 25 June 2020) <www.dechert.com/knowledge/onpoint/2020/6/covid-19-and-duties-of-good-faith-under-english-law.html> accessed 14 November 2020.
[66] 'Guidance on Responsible Contractual Behaviour' (n 11).
[67] ibid, point 15.
[68] 'Guidance on Responsible Contractual Behaviour: Update, 30 June 2020' (n 11), points 12 and 13.
[69] See also ICC Case No 9984; Salehijam (n 46) 6.
[70] See eg ICC Cases Nos 4230 and 10256; Kayali (n 14) 567.

12.3.5 Severance of the Tiers

Dispute resolution clauses are separable from the main contract.[71] However, in multi-tiered clauses, another question arises, which is whether the unenforceability of one tier of an escalation clause automatically causes the other tiers to also be invalid.

In *Wah*, the court found that the clauses in a multi-tier process were interconnected and intertwined, with the result that an invalid mediation clause also rendered the negotiation clause unenforceable. The argument was put forward that it is not possible to

> extrapolate from a clause those parts of it which [the court] considers are sufficiently certain to be enforceable and treat that as being the enforceable content of the clause. That would be to re-write the contractual bargain struck. [T]he court must be satisfied that each part of the clause which was intended to be operative can be given certain legal content and effect.[72]

12.3.6 Law Applicable to Multi-tiered Agreements

Another question related to the interconnection of the tiers is which law applies to a multi-tiered dispute resolution clause. It has been raised in *Sulamerica* with respect to the arbitration tier of the clause.[73]

In *Sulamerica*, the parties had expressly agreed that their insurance policy was to be governed exclusively by the law of Brazil, which seemed to point strongly towards an implied choice of Brazilian law as the proper law of the dispute resolution clause. This clause included a mediation agreement and an arbitration clause (clauses 11 and 12). The court found that both clauses had to be read in conjunction with each other and in light of the choice of law clause in the contract. Where the parties subject their contract to a chosen law (here, Brazilian law), the mediation clause should also be governed by that law. But even when the mediation and arbitration tiers are intertwined and the

---

[71] *Fiona Trust & Holding Corp v Privalov* [2007] UKHL 40, [2007] 4 All ER 951. See also *Enka Insaat Ve Sanayi AS v OOO Insurance Company Chubb* [2020] UKSC 38, [2020] 1 WLR 4117. However, it has been noted by the Supreme Court that it does not follow from the separability principle 'that an arbitration agreement is generally to be regarded as a different and separate agreement from the rest of the contract or that a choice of governing law for the contract should not generally be interpreted as applying to an arbitration clause'.
[72] See *Wah v Grant Thornton* (n 2) [53].
[73] *Sulamerica* (n 33) [7]ff.

mediation clause is an effective precondition to arbitration, the arbitration clause remains separate. It is therefore possible that the two tiers are subject to different laws. The court considered the factors advocating in favour of an implied choice of Brazilian law as law applicable to the arbitration agreement, but found closer ties to the law of the seat of the arbitration. By choosing the seat, the parties would accept that the law of the seat (here, English law) applies to the proceedings and this tends to suggest that the parties intended the law of the seat to govern all aspects of the arbitration agreement, including matters relating to its formal validity and the jurisdiction of the tribunal. Furthermore, and more importantly, the application of Brazilian law would have led to the observance of formalities that ran counter to the parties' intention as expressed in their dispute resolution clause.

On this last point, determination of the applicable law to an arbitration agreement, the UK Supreme Court very recently took a landmark decision in *Enka v Chubb*.[74] The case concerned a damages claim due to a fire in a power plant. It was brought in Moscow, but the underlying contract contained an arbitration clause stipulating that 'the Dispute shall be finally settled under the Rules of Arbitration of the International Chamber of Commerce', and 'the place of arbitration shall be London, England' (clause 50.1). Enka tried to prevent the Russian claim via an anti-suit injunction issued by the London Commercial Court.

The central question arose as to which law governs the validity and scope of an arbitration agreement when the law applicable to the contract containing it differs from the law of the seat of the arbitration.

The Supreme Court set out the rules for two scenarios: first for the case in which the parties have not specified the law governing the arbitration agreement but have chosen the law applicable to the main contract. That choice would, 'in the absence of good reason to the contrary', also apply to the arbitration agreement,[75] to provide certainty and consistency and to avoid unnecessary complexities and artificialities.[76]

Second, in the absence of choice as to either the main contract or the arbitration agreement, 'the court must ... determine, objectively and irrespective of the parties' intention, with which system of law the

---

[74] *Enka v Chubb* (n 71).
[75] ibid [43].
[76] ibid [53]. It is likely that the second argument in *Sulamerica* would still qualify as 'a good reason to the contrary'.

arbitration agreement has its closest connection'.[77] As a general rule, the arbitration agreement is most closely connected with the law of the seat of the arbitration.[78] This solution would guarantee certainty and give effect to commercial purpose.[79]

In *Enka*, the parties had not determined the applicable law to the merits. The conclusion therefore was that the arbitration agreement is governed by English law as the law of the seat of the arbitration. This decision will be relevant for the future assessment of the arbitration tier of multi-tiered clauses.

12.4 Conclusions

In recent years, English courts have established strict criteria for the assessment of multi-tiered dispute resolution clauses. They need to be clearly drafted and not leave any room for interpretation as to their mandatory character, the procedure to follow and the set time frames for each escalation stage. Parties should also consider the law applicable to their dispute resolution agreement. There are numerous pitfalls in the drafting process and extra caution needs to be taken to ensure that the clause does not pose problems as to the commencement of arbitration or litigation. Such clauses are often so-called late-night clauses which bear the risk of a controversy about the dispute resolution procedure when they are badly drafted and consequently pathological.

In light of this, it should therefore, on the one hand, be considered whether a multi-tiered clause is in the parties' interests. On the other hand, a pre-arbitration or pre-litigation stage avoiding costly and lengthy proceedings can be of huge value to the parties. There is a trend towards ADR even in the context of normal court or arbitration proceedings. Courts must, where appropriate, encourage ADR before admitting certain types of cases. This debate is all the more relevant in the current COVID-19 crisis during which the UK government is strongly encouraging parties to commercial contracts to engage

---

[77] ibid [118].
[78] ibid [119].
[79] ibid [119]ff. See also Lawrence Collins and Jonathan Harris (eds), *Dicey, Morris & Collins on the Conflict of Laws* (15th edn, Sweet & Maxwell 2012), rule 64(1)(b) and para 16–016; David St John Sutton, Judith Gill and Matthew Gearing (eds), *Russell on Arbitration* (24th edn, Sweet & Maxwell 2015), para 2–121.

in negotiations and mediation and to avoid a deluge of cases brought before the courts.

Hence, the parties have to balance their interests in such a clause against the potential risks. The advantages of multi-tiered clauses seem, however, to outweigh the disadvantages if the strict drafting criteria set out by the English courts are observed by the parties.

13

Multi-tier and Mixed-Method Dispute Resolution in Canada

From Obscurity to Prominence in a Single Generation

JOSHUA KARTON AND MICHELLE DE HAAS

13.1 Introduction: The Evolving Canadian Environment

Not long ago – well after the careers of today's senior counsel and judges began – mediation was almost unheard of in Canada outside of family and labour/employment disputes. Beginning in the 1980s, commercial mediation's popularity began to rise, along with that of alternative dispute resolution (ADR) processes more generally.[1] Multi-tier dispute resolution agreements have correspondingly risen to prevalence.[2]

Courts throughout the judicial hierarchy have recognised the benefits of ADR, and have emphasised that fair and just outcomes can sometimes be best achieved through consensual dispute resolution processes. For example, in *Hryniak v Mauldin*, the Supreme Court of Canada observed that the process of litigation can impose 'unnecessary expense and delay' and thus 'can *prevent* the fair and just resolution of disputes'.[3]

---

[1] Pierre Bienvenu and Martin Valasek, 'Canada: Arbitration Guide: IBA Arbitration Committee' (*International Bar Association*, 2018) <www.ibanet.org/Document/Default.aspx?DocumentUid=5A3BA1C8-73A9-4EBD-A160-69D43D25A8FA> accessed 10 September 2020.

[2] Vasilis FL Pappas and George M Vlavianos, 'Multiple Tiers, Multiple Risks – Multi-tier Dispute Resolution Clauses' (2018) 12(1) Dispute Resolution International 5, 6; Bryan Duguid, 'Multi-tiered Dispute Resolution: Stepping Carefully' (*Mondaq*, 20 August 2008) <www.mondaq.com/canada/x/65050/Arbitration+Dispute+Resolution/MultiTiered+Dispute+Resolution+Stepping+Carefully> accessed 10 September 2020; Mary Comeau, 'In Defense of Tiered Dispute Resolution Clauses' (*ADR Perspectives*, 17 December 2019) <http://adric.ca/adr-perspectives/in-defence-of-tiered-dispute-resolution-clauses/> accessed 10 September 2020.

[3] *Hryniak v Mauldin* 2014 SCC 7 [24] (emphasis in original).

Legislatures have taken up the same banner, motivated partly by access to justice concerns and a belief in the value of consensual dispute resolution, but also by a desire to ease judicial caseloads. Today, all ten provinces and three territories of Canada, and the federal government, encourage litigating parties to settle, including by mediation. They have established judicial and institutional supports for pre-trial mediation, and four provinces impose mediation as a mandatory precondition to the setting of a trial date in court. Med-arb and other combined dispute resolution processes have been slower to catch on, although their popularity has risen recently, with institutional rules adapted specifically for med-arb and a novel professional designation introduced in 2019.

However, Canada's attitude towards ADR retains some ambivalence. Canada was not among the signatories to the Singapore Convention on Mediation, nor is there any momentum towards accession. In Canada's federal system, jurisdiction over dispute resolution rests with the provinces and territories, which enact most of the relevant legislation and which administer the courts; the federal government may be waiting to see what interest the provinces and territories have.[4] After all, Canada did not sign the 1965 ICSID Convention until 2006, nor ratify it until 2013, once all ten provinces had enacted implementing legislation. Legislatures and courts continue to toggle between a policy-informed desire to promote ADR and a resistance to change.

This chapter describes the recent evolution of multi-tier and mixed-method dispute resolution processes in Canada from obscurity to prominence. It begins by considering judicial treatment of multi-tier dispute resolution agreements – how the courts interpret and enforce parties' choice of multi-tier dispute resolution (Section 13.2). Next, it considers legislative interventions to support multi-tier dispute resolution, in particular the mandatory pre-trial mediation that prevails in some provinces (Section 13.3). Finally, it assesses the current state of play for med-arb and other mixed-method dispute resolution processes (Section 13.4).

---

[4] Douglas Harrison, 'Singapore Convention a Big Boost for International Mediation' (*The Lawyer's Daily*, 17 December 2019) <www.thelawyersdaily.ca/articles/17194> accessed 10 September 2020. Since dispute resolution is a matter of provincial jurisdiction in Canada, for the Singapore Convention to become effective, it would have to be ratified by the federal government and enacted into legislation by the provinces individually.

13.2 Multi-tier Dispute Resolution Agreements: Usage, Interpretation and Enforcement

Reliable statistics are hard to come by, but the number of reported cases involving multi-tier dispute resolution clauses has risen markedly since the 1990s, along with the greater visibility of commercial mediation in Canada. This section reviews the treatment of such clauses by the courts, dealing primarily with their interpretation and enforcement. It also considers a set of issues that arise when the rules of contractual interpretation that apply to multi-tier clauses interact with other doctrines espoused by Canadian courts.

For the most part, Canadian courts treat multi-tier dispute resolution clauses like they would any other contractual terms: they are enforceable unless one of the general exceptions to enforceability applies (such as unconscionability) and they are interpreted according to the general rules of contractual interpretation. The main interpretive issue that arises is whether the lower (usually consensual) tiers in a multi-tier dispute resolution process constitute mandatory preconditions (or 'conditions precedent') to the higher tiers, as well as what constitutes fulfilment of those preconditions. These issues are determined based on (1) the parties' intentions, so that a court or arbitral tribunal's role is primarily one of contractual interpretation, and (2) whether the preconditions are sufficiently 'certain' or 'definite' to be enforceable. Absent clear language and sufficient certainty, Canadian courts typically interpret lower tiers in a multi-tier clause *not* to be mandatory preconditions of the higher tiers.

Before discussing those requirements and some related issues, we observe that Canadian courts simply ignore the lower tiers of multi-tier clauses with surprising frequency. The most prominent example may be *Uber Technologies v Heller*, a recent Supreme Court of Canada decision dealing with arbitration, where the Court consistently referred to a multi-tier agreement with mediation and arbitration stages as an 'arbitration clause'. The mediation stage played no role in the judgment except when it came to estimating the total costs of dispute resolution under the agreement.[5]

There are numerous cases involving multi-tier clauses that culminate in arbitration where the pre-arbitration stages are simply not addressed by the courts.[6] For the most part, these can be explained by judicial

---

[5] *Uber Technologies v Heller* 2020 SCC 16.
[6] *NetSys Technology Group AB v Open Text Corp* [1999] CanLII 14937 (ONSC); *Cecrop Co v Kinetics Sciences Inc* 2001 BCSC 532; *Canada (Attorney General) v Marineserve MG Inc*

deference to arbitration and respect for arbitral competence-competence. In one particularly striking case, although the dispute resolution agreement described mediation as a 'condition precedent' to arbitration and the parties had not mediated, the court nevertheless stayed litigation and referred the parties to arbitration on the basis that that arbitration clause was not void, inoperative or incapable of being performed – without ever mentioning mediation except for once quoting the full dispute resolution clause.[7] Possibly, these cases are holdovers from an earlier era when mediation was less well established in Canada (or they were decided by judges trained in that era).

13.2.1 Interpretation of Multi-tier Dispute Resolution Clauses

The rules of contractual interpretation that apply in Canada's common law provinces mostly follow the modern rules of contractual interpretation across the common law world. However, there are two exceptions to this general characterisation.

The first has to do with the standard of review on appeal (including on appeal from a domestic arbitration award on a point of law). Traditionally, in Canada as in other common law jurisdictions, contractual interpretation was considered a pure question of law, so interpretations of contractual terms were reviewable *de novo*. In 2014, in *Sattva*, the Supreme Court overturned this long-standing characterisation, holding that contractual interpretation is a mixed question of law and fact and, therefore, attracts a deferential standard of review in recognition of the trial court's pre-eminent role in establishing the facts of a dispute.[8] Under *Sattva*, contractual interpretation by a trial court or arbitrator will be overturned only if it is 'unreasonable'.[9]

2002 NSSC 147; *Aradia Fitness Canada Inc v Dawn M Hinze Consulting* 2008 BCSC 839; *Goel v Dhaliwal* 2015 BCSC 2305; *Ts'Kw'Aylaxw First Nation v Graymont Western Canada Inc* 2018 BCSC 2101.

[7] *Ts'Kw'Aylaxw* (n 6) [33]–[37].

[8] *Sattva Capital Corp v Creston Moly Corp* [2014] 2 SCR 633 [50]. See also *Teal Cedar Products Ltd v British Columbia* 2017 SCC 32.

[9] ibid. In *Canada (Minister of Citizenship and Immigration) v Vavilov* 2019 SCC 65, the Supreme Court of Canada altered the standard of review on appeal from decisions of administrative tribunals and where a statutory right of appeal to the courts exists. It is not clear whether *Vavilov* applies to domestic commercial arbitration awards appealed on a point of law, and the sparse case law interpreting *Vavilov* thus far is inconsistent. See eg *Buffalo Point First Nation v Cottage Owners Association* 2020 MBQB 20; *Cove Contracting Ltd v Condominium Corp No 012 5598 (Ravine Park)* 2020 ABQB 106; *Ontario First Nations (2008) Limited Partnership v Ontario Lottery and Gaming Corporation* 2020

The second exception applies only to standard form and other contracts of adhesion, especially but not only consumer and employment contracts. Canadian common law courts employ their powers to interpret contracts as one means – in practice, the primary means – of controlling contractual unfairness. Canadian courts follow an explicit policy of interpreting onerous terms narrowly (including dispute resolution clauses that impose onerous costs or procedures on weaker parties), so as to reduce their scope of application.[10]

With respect to multi-tier clauses more specifically, Canadian courts focus on the particular language used to describe the various tiers of the process, according to those words' ordinary meanings – even in Québec, which follows civil law approaches to contractual interpretation. Consistent with Canadian courts' pro-access to justice and pro-arbitration policies (policies that are occasionally in tension with each other),[11] they tend to construe lower tiers as non-mandatory absent express language designating them as preconditions to arbitration or litigation. In practice, for a requirement of mediation or negotiation to be enforceable as a precondition to arbitration or litigation, the parties must demonstrate such an intention by using clear wording with a mandatory meaning. Words such as 'shall' or 'must' (as opposed to 'may' or 'can') are crucial to establishing a mandatory precondition.[12]

ONSC 1516; *Northland Utilities (NWT) Limited v Hay River (Town of)* 2021 NWTCA 1. In *Wastech Services Ltd v Greater Vancouver Sewerage and Drainage District* 2021 SCC 7, a majority of the Supreme Court expressly declined to decide whether *Vavilov* applies to arbitral awards: [46], although three concurring judges would have held that it does: [121]. If *Vavilov* indeed applies to appeals from domestic commercial arbitration awards, it would impose a 'correctness' standard to appeals on matters of law and of mixed fact and law. If the correctness standard applies, instead of the reasonableness standard in *Sattva*, courts deciding appeals from domestic arbitration awards would not defer to the tribunal's decision but would instead review it *de novo*.

[10] Such instances of judicial control often invoke the *contra proferentem* principle. Although *contra proferentem* is ostensibly a neutral rule for choosing among equally plausible meanings of an ambiguous term, the Supreme Court held in *Jesuit Fathers of Upper Canada v Guardian Insurance Co of Canada* [2006] 1 SCR 744 that contracts may be construed *contra proferentem* to correct for 'an imbalance in negotiating power': [28].

[11] As in *Uber*, where the Supreme Court invalidated a dispute resolution agreement whose costly processes were seen as inhibiting access to justice.

[12] *Canadian Ground Water Association v Canadian Geoexchange Coalition* 2010 QCCS 2597 (the court reads 'may' as giving the parties the option to mediate, but it is not mandatory if neither party requests it). See also *Suncor Energy Products Inc v Howe-Baker Engineers Ltd* 2010 ABQB 310; *Advanced Construction Techniques Ltd v OHL Construction Canada* 2013 ONSC 7505; *PQ Licensing SA v LPQ Central Canada Inc* 2018 ONCA 331.

For example, in *Cityscape v Vanbots*, the mediation and consultation processes stipulated in the dispute resolution agreement were held merely to provide expeditious options for resolving disputes. The applicant was not barred from initiating arbitration although neither consultations nor mediation had taken place.[13] The court observed that arbitration clauses are to be given a 'large, liberal and remedial' interpretation in order to realise the intention of the parties to arbitrate disputes.[14] Moreover, the court held, the broad submission to arbitration of all disputes concerning 'the interpretation, application or administration of the contract' demonstrated the parties' intention to have access to arbitration, unrestricted by the other methods of dispute resolution mentioned in the contract.[15]

Similarly, in *Canadian Ground Water*, section 10.2 of the agreement stipulated that the parties should first seek to resolve disputes by negotiation but that, if negotiations failed, 'either party may request that a mediator be appointed'.[16] Section 10.3 provided that if a mediator was appointed or the dispute was not resolved within twenty-one days after a request for mediation, either party could refer the dispute to arbitration.[17] The court read these provisions as providing an *option* to mediate. If a party exercised that option, twenty-one days later either party could proceed to arbitration. But where there had been no request for mediation, either party could resort to arbitration at any time.[18]

Cases where mediation or negotiation was held to be a mandatory precondition to arbitration or litigation all involve language clearly expressing such an intention. In *PQ Licensing*, the dispute resolution clause provided that, 'before resorting to arbitration, litigation or any other dispute resolution procedure ...[, the parties] will first attempt in good faith to settle the dispute or claim by non-binding mediation'.[19] The court found that arbitration did not become an 'appropriate' remedy until the precondition of mediation had been satisfied.[20] The same result can be seen in *Suncor*, where the parties' arbitration clause stated that 'if the parties are unable to resolve the dispute by mediation ... then the

---

[13] *Cityscape Richmond Corp v Vanbots Construction Corp* [2001] OJ No 638, 8 CLR (3d) 196 [21].
[14] ibid [19].
[15] ibid [21], [23], [32].
[16] *Canadian Ground Water* (n 12) [4].
[17] ibid.
[18] ibid [14].
[19] *PQ Licensing* (n 12) [9].
[20] ibid [47].

dispute shall be finally resolved by arbitration'.[21] The court held that arbitration could be invoked only after mediation had failed to resolve the dispute.[22] Where the wording is vague or ambiguous, the courts will view arbitration or litigation as unconstrained by any listed prerequisites.[23]

13.2.2 Enforceability of Consensual Tiers in a Multi-tier Clause

Most multi-tier dispute resolution clauses involve consensual dispute resolution procedures in the initial tiers. For these steps to constitute mandatory preconditions to arbitration or litigation, they must be separately enforceable. Canada maintains the traditional common law suspicion of 'agreements to agree'[24] that has been abandoned in other common law jurisdictions. Bare agreements to negotiate are not enforceable; if they do not incorporate some objective, ascertainable standard by which to judge whether 'negotiation' has occurred, they are void for lack of certainty.[25] That standard could be an objective substantive benchmark (such as a clause providing that the parties must negotiate as to a 'fair market price'),[26] an objective procedural benchmark (such as a deadline after which negotiations may be abandoned and arbitration or litigation commenced) or a third party guarantor of the process (such as designation of an independent institution to administer mediation). We consider agreements to negotiate and to mediate in turn.

An agreement to negotiate is unenforceable for lack of certainty unless there is an objectively ascertainable criterion by which to measure

---

[21] *Suncor* (n 12) [53].
[22] ibid. Similar language was also decisive in *Jakobsen v Wear Vision Capital Inc* 2005 BCCA 147 [3]; *Yukon Energy Corp v Chant Construction Co* 2007 YKSC 22 [25]–[27]; *Advanced Construction* (n 12) [179]; *3289444 Nova Scotia Ltd v RW Armstrong & Associates Inc* 2016 NSSC 330 [9], [40].
[23] See eg *Cityscape* (n 13) [19]–[21].
[24] As expressed in the famous trilogy of English Court of Appeal cases on definiteness: *May & Butcher Ltd v The King* [1934] 2 KB 17 (HL); *WN Hillas & Co Ltd v Arcos Ltd* (1932) 147 LT 503 (HL); and *Foley v Classique Coaches Ltd* [1934] 2 KB 1 (CA) (UK).
[25] *Empress Towers Ltd v Bank of Nova Scotia* 1990 CanLII 2207 (BCCA) 6–7; Didem Kayali, 'Enforceability of Multi-tiered Dispute Resolution Clauses' (2010) 27(6) Journal of International Arbitration 551, 574. See also *Sattva* (n 8) [49] (stating that the goal of contractual interpretation is to ascertain the objective intent of the parties).
[26] The classic case expressing this doctrine is *Empress Towers* (n 25), where the dispute resolution clause in a commercial lease provided that 'rental for any renewal period ... shall be the market rental prevailing at the commencement of that renewal term as mutually agreed between the Landlord and the Tenant'.

whether the parties have in fact negotiated and whether negotiations have ended. 'Good faith' or 'best efforts' do not suffice as such a criterion since they are subjective, which is to say that they depend on the subjective intentions of the parties. For an agreement to negotiate disputes to be enforceable on its own and as a precondition to arbitration or litigation, the parties must set out the process of negotiations to a degree of specificity not required in other jurisdictions.[27] As Kayali describes, 'what is enforced in [negotiation] procedures is not cooperation and consent but participation in a process from which cooperation and consent may come'.[28] For example, in *Alberici*, a contractual obligation to make 'all reasonable efforts' to negotiate was held unenforceable, since the clause set out neither a time frame for the negotiations nor any objective criterion by which to measure compliance.[29]

An agreement to mediate necessarily involves the participation of a neutral third party, which renders such an agreement more certain than an agreement to negotiate. However, Canadian courts have only consistently enforced agreements to mediate when they invoked established rules of procedure and/or an independent mediation provider.[30] For instance, in *PQ Licensing*, the mediation step of a multi-tier clause was held to be enforceable because it called for mediation under the auspices of the American Arbitration Association.[31]

13.2.3 Exceptions to the Enforceability of Multi-tier Clauses

Even if lower tiers of a multi-tier clause satisfy the requirements of enforceability, Canadian courts may nevertheless excuse the parties' failure to complete those tiers. First, a court may find that further attempts to satisfy a precondition to arbitration or litigation would be futile, or that a party insisting on a precondition is doing so only to delay

---

[27] Kayali (n 25) 569.
[28] ibid, citing *Hooper Bailie Associated Ltd v Natcon Group Pty Ltd* (1992) 28 NSWLR 194 (New South Wales) [206].
[29] *Alberici Western Constructors Ltd v Saskatchewan Power Corp* 2015 SKQB 74 [67]. Note that the presence of a time limit for negotiations, while relevant, is not necessarily decisive to make a negotiation tier enforceable. See *L-3 Communications SPAR Aerospace Ltd v CAE Inc* 2010 ONSC 7133 [2]; *3289444 Nova Scotia* (n 22) [6]–[9].
[30] Kayali (n 25) 554.
[31] *PQ Licensing* (n 12) [9]. See also *Jakobsen* (n 22), where a mediation tier was upheld as a mandatory precondition to arbitration when it called for a 'structured negotiation conference ... under the Commercial Mediation Rules of the British Columbia International Commercial Arbitration Centre'.

proceedings. Second, Canadian courts have recognised an estoppel-type doctrine to the effect that a party who has refused to engage in or failed to pursue a dispute resolution process that otherwise would have constituted a precondition to litigation may not invoke that process as a 'shield' to avoid litigation.

13.2.3.1 Futility and Bad Faith

Where pursuing a consensual dispute resolution process would be futile, Canadian courts have shown themselves willing to sweep aside such preconditions and permit the parties to proceed directly to arbitration or litigation.[32] For example, in *IWK*, after refusing to engage in the first two stages of the agreed ADR process (consultation and mediation), the respondent attempted to raise the parties' failure to complete those steps as a bar to arbitration.[33] The court refused to stay the arbitration that the claimant had commenced.[34] The claimant would effectively be deprived of its right to access arbitration by being compelled to engage in 'hopeless' preconditions, which presented no realistic chance of yielding a resolution.[35]

Similarly, in *Cityscape*, a construction contract provided that any disputes could be resolved by negotiation, mediation and then arbitration.[36] The parties agreed to commence mediation, but the respondent changed its position, asserting that it would only mediate certain issues, then vacated the worksite and commenced arbitration.[37] The court enforced the parties' agreement to arbitrate despite the mediation precondition not having being satisfied. It interpreted the agreement to mediate as providing an opportunity for expeditious resolution of the disputes arising between the parties; absent co-operation by the respondent, this option could not serve its expeditious purpose and so should not be enforced.[38] In general, where preconditions to arbitration or litigation are unlikely to yield a resolution to the dispute, particularly when this is due to one party's recalcitrance, Canadian courts will permit claimants to proceed directly to arbitration or litigation.

---

[32] *Advanced Construction* (n 12) [222]; *IWK Health Center Northfield Glass Group Ltd* 2016 NSSC 281 [6].
[33] *IWK* (n 32) [6].
[34] ibid [117]–[118].
[35] ibid [90].
[36] *Cityscape* (n 13) [4].
[37] ibid [17]–[18].
[38] ibid.

This case law is consistent with Canadian courts' broader tendency to avoid formalistic interpretations that would hinder the meaningful attempts at resolution intended by the contracting parties.[39] In *Telus v Wellman*, the Supreme Court observed that a primary purpose of the Ontario Arbitration Act is to 'encourage parties to resort to arbitration as a method of resolving their disputes in commercial and other matters, and to require them to hold to that course once they have agreed to do so'.[40] It follows that enforcing preconditions that would hinder the operation of the parties' chosen dispute resolution process would be contrary to the purpose of the Arbitration Act.

13.2.3.2 Preconditions as Shields to Litigation or Arbitration

Some courts have resolved factually similar situations on a different legal basis. Where one party refuses to participate in obligatory dispute resolution processes, it may be prevented from invoking the agreement to prevent arbitration or litigation. Some courts have even held that arbitration agreements (which would otherwise oust court jurisdiction) cannot be used as 'shields' to avoid litigation where the parties have demonstrated negligible concern for the arbitration process they chose.[41]

For example, in *Yukon Energy*, the parties agreed to mediation followed by arbitration.[42] The court refused to grant a stay of arbitration, even though it found that the preconditions to arbitration had not been met. The first stage of the dispute resolution agreement required the parties to mediate with a project consultant, and the respondent had the exclusive responsibility to appoint that consultant. The respondent later sought a stay of arbitration on the ground that the mediation had not occurred.[43] The court held that the respondent 'cannot rely on the non-fulfillment of any conditions precedent as a bar to the referral of disputes to arbitration, where those preliminary steps were prevented by [its] acts or omissions'.[44]

---

[39] See eg *Canadian Ground Water* (n 12) [12]; *L-3 Communications* (n 29) [24]; *IWK* (n 32) [98]–[100]; *Consolidated Contractors Group SAL (Offshore) v Ambatovy Minerals SA* 2017 ONCA 939 [38], [46]–[55].

[40] *Telus Communications Inc v Wellman* 2019 SCC 19 [82].

[41] See eg *Benner & Associates Ltd v Northern Lights Distribution Inc* [1995] OJ No 626 [20] (party's failure to pursue pre-litigation steps constituted 'undue delay').

[42] *Yukon Energy* (n 22) [3].

[43] ibid [8], [29].

[44] ibid [27].

13.2.4 Multi-tier Clauses and Limitation Periods

The commencement and expiry of limitation periods are often contested in cases with multi-tier dispute resolution agreements; if preliminary processes are dragged out, when arbitration or litigation is finally commenced the limitation period may have expired.[45] The question presented is whether the limitation period should commence when the dispute first arose or when the preconditions to arbitration or litigation were or should have been completed. Although the result depends on the statutory language applicable in the province, limitation periods to initiate litigation or arbitration generally do not commence until the preconditions have been met (or when it becomes futile to pursue consensual dispute resolution processes).[46]

For example, in *PQ Licensing*, mediation was held to be a precondition to arbitral jurisdiction, and the court upheld the arbitrator's conclusion that the limitation period to initiate arbitration commenced only after mediation had failed to produce a settlement.[47] Section 5(1)(a)(iv) of Ontario's Limitations Act allows postponement of the commencement of the limitation period until a claimant reasonably knows that legal action is appropriate. When there is a condition precedent to arbitration or litigation, reasonable knowledge that legal action is appropriate does not arise until the precondition is fulfilled or has become futile.[48]

13.2.5 Multi-tier Clauses and Deference to Arbitrators

When a court is called upon to interpret a multi-tier dispute resolution agreement that culminates in arbitration, the outcome turns not only on the way the court itself would interpret the contractual terms but also on the degree of deference it will accord to the tribunal. If the tribunal has not yet had a chance to rule on its jurisdiction, according to the competence-competence doctrine courts will normally stay litigation and refer the parties to arbitration so that the tribunal can decide whether any preconditions to arbitral jurisdiction have been met. If an arbitral award has already been issued, Canadian courts tend to defer to arbitrators'

---

[45] Pappas and Vlavianos (n 2) 7.
[46] *L-3 Communications* (n 29) [23].
[47] *PQ Licensing* (n 12) [9].
[48] ibid. See also *407 ETR Concession Co v Day* 2016 ONCA 709. In Alberta, however, the Limitations Act provides that a limitation period commences when a party knows or ought to know that it has a claim, which has been interpreted to mean the time *before* the first stages of a multi-tier dispute resolution processes have commenced.

decisions on the satisfaction of preconditions even though such decisions are arguably jurisdictional in character, in which case they should not be accorded deference.

13.2.5.1 Multi-tier Arbitration Clauses and Competence-Competence

If an arbitral tribunal has not yet determined whether it has jurisdiction over a dispute, courts will not normally intervene until after the tribunal has had an opportunity to rule on its jurisdiction, including whether any preconditions to arbitration have been met.[49] Accordingly, if a dispute arises as to the interpretation of a multi-tier arbitration clause, and the tribunal has not yet issued an award, courts will normally stay any related litigation.

This is evident in several cases, such as *Yukon Energy*, where the court dismissed an application for a stay of court proceedings in favour of arbitration, reasoning that 'whether the non-fulfillment of the preliminary steps in the dispute resolution process is a bar to arbitration ... is a matter to be determined by the arbitral tribunal and not this Court'.[50] Similarly, in *Nordion*, the parties had agreed to mediation followed by arbitration. Since none of the exceptions to competence-competence applied, the court stayed litigation to allow the tribunal to consider all issues related to its jurisdiction.[51]

Three exceptions to competence-competence have been recognised in Canada. The first two, introduced by the Supreme Court in *Dell v Union des consommateurs* and affirmed in *Seidel v Telus*, provide that a court may decide jurisdictional questions itself, without referring them first to arbitration, if the dispute raises pure questions of law or questions of mixed fact and law that require only superficial consideration of the evidence in the record. In 2020, the Supreme Court added a third exception in *Uber Technologies v Heller*: a court may refuse to stay litigation and determine the tribunal's jurisdiction itself if 'there is a real prospect that, if the stay is granted, the challenge may never be resolved by the arbitrator'.[52] *Uber* involved a multi-tier clause in UberEats's standard driver contract; the combined cost and inaccessibility of the mediation

---

[49] See eg *Seidel v Telus Communications Inc* 2011 SCC 15 [28]–[31], [114]; *Dell Computer Corp v Union des consommateurs* 2007 SCC 34 [43].
[50] *Yukon Energy* (n 22) [27].
[51] *Nordion Inc v Life Technologies Inc* 2015 ONSC 99 [71]. See also *Leeds Standard Condominium Corp No 41 v Fuller* 2019 ONSC 3900 [14].
[52] *Uber* (n 5) [44].

and arbitration stages led the court to find that, if it stayed litigation, the case would never actually be resolved by mediation or arbitration.[53]

13.2.5.2 Multi-tier Arbitration Clauses at the Setting-Aside or Enforcement Stage

After an arbitral tribunal issues an award, whether a partial award on jurisdiction alone or a final award that includes a determination on jurisdiction, that award is subject to setting-aside proceedings in the courts of the seat of arbitration and to enforcement proceedings elsewhere. Under the domestic and international arbitration legislation of the federal government and all ten provinces, lack of jurisdiction is a ground for setting aside and for non-enforcement of awards. Moreover, when a court reviews an arbitral award under Canada's arbitration legislation, it pays no deference to the tribunal and decides jurisdictional matters *de novo*.[54] Nevertheless, Canadian courts appear hesitant to reconsider arbitrators' determinations that preconditions to arbitration have been met, consistently characterising the satisfaction of preconditions as a procedural rather than a jurisdictional matter. Effectively – without saying so and perhaps without ever actually considering the matter – Canadian courts appear to consider the satisfaction of preconditions to be a procedural matter relating to admissibility, not a question of jurisdiction.[55]

For example, in *Consolidated Contractors*, the arbitrator held that he had jurisdiction on the ground that the (uncompleted) lower tiers of a dispute resolution agreement were not true preconditions to arbitration.[56] The claimant applied to the courts in Ontario, the seat of arbitration, to set aside the award.[57] The Ontario Court of Appeal held that procedural issues relating to arbitral proceedings were 'preeminently matters for the arbitrators to decide and the court must view the determination with deference'.[58] Accordingly, the court declined to reconsider the arbitrator's finding that the lower tiers of the dispute resolution

---

[53] ibid [47].
[54] *The United Mexican States v Cargill Inc* 2011 ONCA 622.
[55] For a rare example of a Canadian court taking seriously the distinction between jurisdiction and admissibility, see *The United Mexican States v Burr* 2020 ONSC 2376 [140]–[145] (upholding a NAFTA tribunal's determination that a dispute over whether investors submitted their consent to arbitration in the appropriate form and at the appropriate time were matters of admissibility rather than jurisdiction).
[56] *Consolidated Contractors* (n 39) [43].
[57] ibid [34].
[58] ibid [43].

process were not preconditions to arbitral jurisdiction, and upheld the award.[59] Courts across the provinces have consistently deferred to arbitrators' interpretations of arbitration agreements on this basis, whether tribunals have found that they have jurisdiction[60] or that they lack it.[61]

13.3 Judicial and Institutional Support for Mediation

As the profile of mediation has grown in Canada, judicial and regulatory support for mediation – on its own and as a precursor to arbitration or litigation – has grown as well. Today, all of the provinces maintain some publicly endorsed framework for sending the parties to pre-trial mediation, and four of the ten provinces, collectively accounting for two-thirds of Canada's population, now impose ADR processes, typically mediation, as a mandatory precondition to access to the courts. A Canadian Department of Justice study reviewing these programmes found that mediation processes reduced expenses and delays by as much as 30 per cent, depending on the circumstances.[62] Moreover, mediation improved participants' perceptions of fairness and satisfaction by up to 25 per cent.[63]

From its beginnings in the 1990s, mandatory ADR has expanded rapidly in line with the more general adoption of ADR in Canada.[64] The pioneer was Saskatchewan, which made amendments to its Queen's Bench Act in 1994 that imposed mediation as a precondition to litigation. Ontario's experience with mandatory mediation began in 1999,[65]

---

[59] ibid.
[60] See eg *Canadian Ground Water* (n 12); *PQ Licensing* (n 12).
[61] See eg *Jakobsen* (n 22).
[62] Austin Lawrence, Jennifer Nugent and Cara Scarfone, 'The Effectiveness of Using Mediation in Selected Civil Law Disputes: A Meta-analysis' (*Department of Justice*, 7 January 2015) <www.justice.gc.ca/eng/rp-pr/csj-sjc/jsp-sjp/rr07_3/index.html> accessed 10 September 2020, 27.
[63] ibid 27.
[64] Julie MacFarlane and Michaela Keet, 'Civil Justice Reform and Mandatory Civil Mediation in Saskatchewan: Lessons from a Maturing Program' (2005) 42(3) Alberta Law Reports 677, 678.
[65] ibid 678; Canadian Forum on Civil Justice, 'Ontario Mandatory Mediation Program (Rules 24.1 and 75.1)' (*Canadian Forum on Civil Justice*, 21 November 2013) <https://cfcj-fcjc.org/inventory-of-reforms/ontario-mandatory-mediation-program-rules-24-1-and-75-1> accessed 10 September 2020; 'Public Information Notice – Ontario Mandatory Mediation Program' (*Government of Ontario, Ministry of the Attorney General*, 9 September 2019) <www.attorneygeneral.jus.gov.on.ca/english/courts/manmed/notice.php> accessed 10 September 2020.

Alberta's in 2000,⁶⁶ and British Columbia's in 2001.⁶⁷ In some other provinces, most notably Québec and Nova Scotia, pre-trial mediation is not mandatory for all disputes, but courts are empowered to send the parties to mediation as they see fit.

The stated motivations for the provinces' mandatory mediation programmes have been twofold: to improve access to justice by avoiding the costs and delays associated with traditional court litigation, and to reduce the burden on public resources by reserving only serious or complex cases for the courts.⁶⁸ The provinces that have adopted mandatory mediation have seen high rates of resolution of disputes.⁶⁹ Where the parties attempt to bypass mandatory mediation, courts have consistently stayed litigation and referred the parties to mediation.⁷⁰

It is important to note that these programmes impose a precondition only to *litigation*. Mediation is not mandatory per se but is mandatory if the parties want access to the courts. If they choose arbitration, the mandatory mediation programmes do not apply. Since arbitration is popular for resolving commercial disputes among Canadian parties and between Canadian and foreign parties (and is incorporated in many standard form contracts), the impact of the mandatory mediation programmes is greatest in non-commercial civil litigation such as personal injury lawsuits.

---

[66] Provincial Court Act, ss 65–66; Mediation Rules of the Provincial Court – Civil Division, s 2(1); Alberta Rules of Court, s 4.16(1).

[67] Notice to Mediate (General) Regulation, ss 3, 5.

[68] MacFarlane and Keet (n 64) 679; Julia Quigley, Graham Sharp and Janelle Souter, '"Action" to Justice: Addressing Access to Justice in the Saskatchewan Court of Queen's Bench' (*University of Saskatchewan, College of Law*, February 2016) <https://law.usask.ca/documents/research/deans-forum/13_Superior CourtandCourtProcesses_PolicyDiscussionPaper_2016DeansForum.pdf> accessed 10 September 2020, 4.

[69] Province of Saskatchewan Ministry of Justice and Attorney General, 'Annual Report (2007–2008)' <http://publications.gov.sk.ca/documents/9/33067-JAG-07-08.pdf> accessed 10 September 2020, 26.

[70] Examples of such cases include: *Slater v Amendola* 1999 CarswellOnt 3049, [1999] OJ No 3787; *Kneider v Benson, Percival, Brown* 2000 CarswellOnt 990, 95 ACWS (3d) 1049; *Timmins Nickel Inc v Marshall Minerals Corp* 2001 CarswellOnt 1762, [2001] OTC 369; *Davidson v Richman* 2003 CarswellOnt 509, [2003] OJ No 519; *Rogacki v Belz* 2003 CarswellOnt 3717, [2003] OJ No 3809; *Rudd v Trossacs Investments Inc* 2006 CarswellOnt 1417, [2006] OJ No 922; *Latstiwka v Bray* 2006 ABQB 935; *Chase v Great Lakes Altus Motor Yacht Sales* 2010 ONSC 6365; *Calyniuk Restaurants Inc v DC Holdings Ltd* 2012 SKQB 160; *Cioffi v Modelevich et al* 2018 ONSC 7084.

13.3.1 Provinces with Mandatory Mediation

The four provinces that have implemented mandatory mediation have slightly different programmes. The Saskatchewan Queen's Bench Act provides that 'after the close of pleadings in a contested action or matter that is not a family law proceeding, the local registrar shall arrange for a mediation session, and the parties shall attend the mediation session before taking any further step in the action or matter'.[71] If one party fails to participate in a mandated mediation process, the other party may enter a certificate of non-compliance and the court may order the non-compliant party to pay the other party's costs associated with the mediation.[72]

Since the enactment of Saskatchewan's mandatory mediation programme, approximately 80 per cent of all non-family civil litigation actions in Saskatchewan have been mediated.[73] The Ministry of Justice reported that in 2007–08, 53 per cent of all non-family civil cases were resolved through the mandatory mediation programme, and that there had been a steady increase in the successful resolution rate year-on-year.[74] A 2005 study showed widespread support for mandatory mediation; participants generally saw it as achieving its objectives of providing faster and more suitable settlement of civil matters.[75] The same study concluded that Saskatchewan has experienced a significant culture shift towards greater interest and confidence in mediation.[76]

Ontario first introduced mandatory mediation in 1999, through amendments to its Rules of Civil Procedure.[77] The programme started as a pilot project in Toronto and Ottawa, Ontario's two largest cities. The programme's stated objectives were to reduce time and costs and to improve the quality of outcomes.[78] Agreements reached through mandatory mediation are legally binding; if a party fails to comply with the agreed terms, the other party may, at its option, seek a court order enforcing the mediated settlement or continue with litigation as if no agreement had been reached.[79] The final report on the pilot project,

---

[71] Queen's Bench Act, s 42(1.1).
[72] ibid, ss 42(3)–(5).
[73] MacFarlane and Keet (n 64) 682.
[74] Province of Saskatchewan, Ministry of Justice and Attorney General (n 69) 26.
[75] MacFarlane and Keet (n 64) 688.
[76] ibid 688.
[77] Rules of Civil Procedure, s 24.1.
[78] Megan Marrie, 'Alternative Dispute Resolution in Administration Litigation: A Call for Mandatory Mediation' (2010) 37(2) The Advocates' Quarterly 149, 154.
[79] Government of Ontario, Ministry of the Attorney General (n 65).

published in 2001, found that the programme had achieved its goals of saving litigants time and money and creating a more flexible and creative civil justice system.[80] Most lawyers and litigants who took part in the programme rated it positively.[81] On this basis, the programme was made permanent, and in 2002 it was expanded to include Essex county, which contains the city of Windsor.

In British Columbia, parties to non-family civil litigation may request mediation, which then becomes a mandatory precondition to a trial.[82] Parties must attend a mediation session but need not settle the dispute or even make good faith efforts to settle.[83] A party may apply for an exemption from mediation where it would be 'materially impracticable or unfair', but exemptions have only rarely been granted; there appear to be only two reported cases involving such applications between 2001 and 2015.[84] Parties to disputes before the BC Supreme Court (a court of first instance for higher-stakes disputes, where most commercial litigation takes place) may also, at any time before trial, request a settlement conference, during which the judge may themselves informally mediate or refer the parties to mediation.[85]

Alberta's mandatory ADR programme began in 1998 with a pilot programme in Calgary and Edmonton, the province's two large cities, and quickly spread.[86] As of 1 January 2019, parties are required to participate 'in good faith' in some form of dispute resolution process before a trial may be scheduled. That process is usually mediation, but it may also be arbitration or a settlement conference presided over by a judge, although not an informal bilateral negotiation.[87] These rules

---

[80] Robert G Hann and others, 'Evaluation of Ontario Mandatory Mediation Program (Rule 24.1)' (*Legislative Assembly of Ontario*, 12 March 2001) <www.ontla.on.ca/library/repository/mon/1000/10294958.pdf> accessed 10 September 2020, 67. See Alex Wellington, '"Exquisite Examples" of Creative Judicial Dispute Resolution: The Potential of Alternative Dispute Resolution for Intellectual Property Cases' (2011) 23 Intellectual Property Journal 289, 316–17.

[81] Marrie (n 78) 157.

[82] British Columbia Notice to Mediate (General) Regulation, ss 3, 5.

[83] ibid, ss 15, 23; *Matsqui First Nation v Canada (Attorney General)* 2015 BCSC 1409 [8]–[9].

[84] ibid [2]. The court notes that the 'materially impracticable' requirement is similar to the exemption requirements in Rule 4.16 of Alberta's Rules of Court, which include futility and unlikelihood of settlement as grounds for exemption: ibid [12]–[14].

[85] British Columbia Supreme Court Civil Rules, s 5-3(1)(o).

[86] 'Alberta Provincial Court Civil Claims Mediation' (*Canadian Forum on Civil Justice*, 24 October 2013) <https://cfcj-fcjc.org/inventory-of-reforms/alberta-provincial-court-civil-claims-mediation/> accessed 10 September 2020.

[87] Alberta Rules of Court, s 4.16(1).

were suspended in 2013 on the ostensible grounds that there were insufficient resources to administer them,[88] but mandatory ADR was restored as of 1 September 2019.[89]

13.3.2 Mandatory Mediation and Multi-tier Dispute Resolution Agreements

Given the robust system of mandatory mediation in four of Canada's six most populous provinces, the case law interpreting that legislation in the context of multi-tier dispute resolution agreements is surprisingly sparse. The few reported cases show that courts consistently refer the parties to mediation so long as the court's jurisdiction is not ousted by an arbitration agreement. Although parties may be exempted from mandatory mediation in all of the provinces that implement it, the exemptions have been interpreted narrowly.

In the cases where exemptions were granted, the courts invariably found that requiring mediation would not serve the objectives of the mandatory mediation programme: to save time and costs for parties and for the judicial system. For example, an exemption was granted in *Welldone Plumbing, Heating & Air Conditioning (1990) v Total Comfort Systems* on the basis that a previous mediation held before the plaintiff filed suit had been unsuccessful, so requiring further mediation would add time and costs without achieving the objectives of the Act.[90] In *Calyniuk Restaurants v DC Holdings*, the mandatory mediation was scheduled but the defendant objected that the plaintiff was represented by someone with no power to enter into a binding settlement.[91] The court held that, under the mandatory mediation statute, a corporate officer is assumed to be an agent with the authority to bind the

---

[88] Court of Queen's Bench of Alberta, 'Notice to the Profession: Mandatory Dispute Resolution Requirement Before Entry for Trial' (*Alberta Courts*, 12 February 2013) <https://albertacourts.ca/docs/default-source/qb/npp/notice-to-the-profession-public–mandatory-dispute-resolution-requirement-before-entry-for-trial–2013–01.pdf?sfvrsn=5664ac80_4> accessed 10 September 2020.

[89] Court of Queen's Bench of Alberta, 'Notice to the Profession & Public – Enforcement of Mandatory Alternative Dispute Resolution Rules 8.4(3)(A) and 8.5(1)(A)' (*Alberta Courts*, 2 July 2019) <https://albertacourts.ca/qb/resources/announcements/notice-to-the-profession-public–enforcement-of-mandatory-alternative-dispute-resolution-rules-8.4(3)(a)-and-8.5(1)(a)> accessed 10 September 2020.

[90] *Welldone Plumbing, Heating & Air Conditioning (1990) v Total Comfort Systems* 2002 SKQB 475 [12]–[13].

[91] *Calyniuk* (n 70) [6], [9].

company.⁹² On that basis, it found that the mediation requirement had been fulfilled, so the plaintiff could proceed with litigation.⁹³

A case of particular interest in the COVID-19 era, when online dispute resolution has become so much more common, is *Chase v Great Lakes Altus Motor Yacht Sales*. The applicant sought an exemption from the personal attendance requirement for mediation under Rule 24.1.11(1) of the Ontario Rules of Civil Procedure.⁹⁴ The court denied the application, reasoning that the personal attendance requirement is clearly outlined in the legislation, and that a mediation held in person is more likely to be successful than one held by telephone.⁹⁵ The objectives of the statute therefore supported strict enforcement of the physical presence requirement.⁹⁶ Several provinces have suspended physical presence requirements during the current COVID-19 pandemic; it is not clear whether they will be restored after the pandemic runs its course.

A final wrinkle is presented by cases containing multi-tier clauses that culminate in arbitration. If a court finds that the tribunal lacks jurisdiction, is mediation still required before a trial? None of the various provincial statutes providing for mandatory pre-trial mediation addresses this situation. In principle, therefore, the mandatory mediation provisions should apply equally where the parties intended to litigate from the outset and where one party first pursued arbitration but the arbitration agreement was invalid or the tribunal otherwise exceeded its jurisdiction. On the other hand, requiring mediation where the parties have already attempted to pursue a form of binding third-party adjudication seems futile or wasteful.

We could find no reported case from a province that maintains a mandatory mediation programme in which the court found that an arbitration agreement was invalid and then referred the parties to mediation. In these cases, the courts seem to neglect the mandatory mediation requirements altogether; the courts focus only on the issue of arbitral versus court jurisdiction. For example, in *Suncor*, the parties had agreed to engage in good faith negotiations, followed by mediation and finally arbitration.⁹⁷ Negotiations occurred, but mediation did not.⁹⁸ The court

---

⁹² ibid [23].
⁹³ ibid [30]. A similar result was obtained in *Skvaridlo v Cross Country Saskatchewan Assn Inc* 2015 SKQB 356 [4].
⁹⁴ *Chase* (n 70) [1], [5].
⁹⁵ ibid [18].
⁹⁶ ibid [28]–[30].
⁹⁷ *Suncor* (n 12) [53].
⁹⁸ ibid [47].

held that the limitation period to initiate arbitration had expired but that the claimant could proceed in court; the judgment never mentions Alberta's mandatory ADR programme.[99] We can only speculate as to the reasons for this phenomenon, but, since the legislation enacting the mandatory mediation programmes emphasises the speed and low cost of mediation, it seems likely that judges believe that if the parties have already litigated over the validity of an arbitration agreement, little is gained by requiring them to mediate before they may access the courts.

13.3.3 Provinces without Mandatory Mediation

Ontario, British Columbia, Alberta and Saskatchewan remain the only provinces with mandatory pre-trial mediation programmes. However, judicial and institutional support for mediation is strong across all ten provinces, beginning in the 1990s and becoming widespread in the 2000s.

Québec's experience is typical. In 2003, Québec adopted regulations to provide litigants with greater access to mediation prior to litigation. These efforts have evolved over the years. Québec's Code of Civil Procedure, as amended in 2016, directs parties to 'consider private prevention and resolution processes' such as negotiation, mediation or arbitration, prior to proceeding with litigation.[100] In the same year, Québec implemented the Platform to Assist in the Resolution of Litigation Electronically (PARLe), a pilot project that provides consumers and sellers with ADR options, including negotiations and mediation.[101] The PARLe project is voluntary, but it has seen considerable success, leading to settlements in approximately 70 per cent of cases in its first year.[102] However, there has been no serious discussion of mandating mediation outside of family law and consumer small claims disputes.[103]

Other provinces now provide comparable institutional support for mediation. For example, in Manitoba, voluntary mediation for civil matters has been offered since 1994 through the Manitoba Judicially Assisted Dispute Resolution (JADR) programme, which has reported

---

[99] ibid [55].
[100] Québec Code of Civil Procedure, art 1.
[101] Paul Fauteux, 'Online Dispute Settlement: Quebec on a Promising Path' (2019) 28(1) Canadian Arbitration and Mediation Journal 19.
[102] ibid 23.
[103] ibid 19.

an annual success rate of 85–95 per cent.[104] Similarly, in Nova Scotia, mediation at the trial level is voluntary but may be provided by judicial referral to a publicly administered mediation programme.[105] In Newfoundland, courts have had the power to refer the parties to mediation in non-family law cases since 2003.[106]

13.4 Med-arb and Other Mixed-Method Dispute Resolution Procedures

There is little history in Canada of med-arb or other forms of single-tier mixed-method dispute resolution.[107] As in other common law jurisdictions, many Canadians are made uneasy by the notion that an arbitrator may also act as a mediator in the same case.[108] The concerns most often raised are the same as elsewhere: that an arbitrator who acts as mediator may become biased by access to sensitive information that otherwise would not have been disclosed, and may therefore lose their neutrality; and conversely that mediation may lose much of its value in promoting amicable resolution when the parties know that their mediator could later impose a binding outcome.[109] Nevertheless, interest in med-arb among ADR practitioners has increased dramatically.[110] Although med-arb and arb-med-arb processes remain uncommon in practice, there is now growing legislative and institutional support for them.

---

[104] ADR Institute of Alberta Mediation Advocacy Task Force, 'White Paper 2016' (*ADR Institute of Alberta*, 15 March 2016) <https://adralberta.com/resources/Documents/White%20Paper%202016/WP%20May%2010,%202016.pdf> accessed 10 September 2020, 47.

[105] 'The Court of Appeal: Judicial Mediation Program' (*The Courts of Nova Scotia*) <https://courts.ns.ca/Appeal_Court/NSCA_mediation_program.htm> accessed 10 September 2020.

[106] Rules of the Newfoundland and Labrador Supreme Court, r 37A.

[107] Bobette Wolski, 'ARB-MED-ARB (and MSAs): A Whole Which Is Less Than, Not Greater Than, the Sum of Its Parts' (2013) 6(2) Contemporary Asia Arbitration Journal 249, 262–63.

[108] Brian A Pappas, 'Med-arb and the Legalization of Alternative Dispute Resolution' (2015) 20 Harvard Negotiation Law Review 157, 160. See also David Farmer and Steven Kley, 'Med-arbs – Practical Considerations for Getting the Best of Both' (*ADR Institute of Canada*, May 2018) <https://adric.ca/adr-perspectives/med-arbs-practical-considerations-for-getting-the-best-of-both> accessed 10 September 2020; Lauren Tomasich, Eric Morgan and Sarah Firestone, 'Two Hats, or Not Two Hats?' (*ADR Institute of Canada*, 17 December 2019) <http://adric.ca/adr-perspectives/two-hats-or-not-two-hats> accessed 10 September 2020.

[109] ibid 173; Wolski (n 107) 259–60.

[110] Pappas (n 108) 163.

That evolution is exemplified by the changes made to the Uniform Arbitration Act (UAA), promulgated by the Uniform Law Conference of Canada (ULCC). The UAA is intended to apply to domestic arbitrations; there is already substantial uniformity among the provinces' international commercial arbitration statutes, all of which enact the UNCITRAL Model Law on International Commercial Arbitration.[111] Article 42 of the UAA's current (2016) version provides:

(1) If the parties and the arbitral tribunal agree, the arbitral tribunal may use mediation, conciliation or another technique to assist the parties to settle a matter in dispute.
(2) An arbitrator may not be challenged or removed because the arbitral tribunal participated in a process under subsection (1).
(3) For certainty, subsection (2) applies if the arbitration process continues after or concurrently with a process under subsection (1).

The previous version of the UAA, adopted in 1990, gave legislatures two options, one that permitted med-arb with the parties' consent and one that prohibited arbitrators from serving as mediators in the same case. The official commentary to Article 42 of the UAA 2016 shows the drafters' ambivalence about med-arb and their ultimately lukewarm embrace of it:

> There was a divergence of opinion as to whether the new Act should prohibit, permit or encourage arbitrators to also act as mediators in the course of an arbitration ... While it is generally preferable for commercial arbitrators, at least, not to play a dual role, modern Canadian domestic practice is that, provided that suitable precautions are taken, 'mediation-arbitration' should not be prohibited.[112]

The provincial statutes largely permit, but do not actively encourage, the use of consensual dispute resolution methods during an arbitration process.[113] As long as both parties consent, most provincial statutes governing domestic arbitrations permit the same person to act as both mediator and arbitrator.[114] For example, section 35(1) of Alberta's

---

[111] However, only Ontario and British Columbia have updated their International Commercial Arbitration Acts to take account of the 2006 amendments to the UNCITRAL Model Law.
[112] Uniform Law Conference of Canada, 'Uniform Arbitration Act (2016)' (1 December 2016) <www.ulcc.ca/images/stories/2016_pdf_en/2016ulcc0017.pdf> accessed 10 September 2020.
[113] Provincial arbitration statutes address this; however, the Federal Commercial Arbitration Act remains silent on this issue. See the Federal Commercial Arbitration Act.
[114] Alberta Arbitration Act, s 35; International Commercial Arbitration Act, s 5; Saskatchewan Arbitration Act, s 36; International Commercial Arbitration Act, s 4;

Arbitration Act provides that 'members of an arbitral tribunal may, if the parties consent, use mediation, conciliation or similar techniques during the arbitration' and subsection (2) provides that '[a]fter the members of an arbitral tribunal use a technique referred to in subsection (1), they may resume their roles as arbitrators without disqualification'.[115] Identical or similar provisions have been enacted in Saskatchewan,[116] Manitoba,[117] New Brunswick,[118] Nova Scotia[119] and Québec.[120]

Other provinces have taken a more cautious approach. Section 35 of Ontario's Arbitration Act provides that 'members of an arbitral tribunal shall not conduct any part of the arbitration as a mediation or conciliation process or other similar process that might compromise or appear to compromise the arbitral tribunal's ability to decide the dispute impartially'.[121] However, this is a default provision; section 3 permits parties to contract out of section 35, either expressly or by implication.[122]

Perhaps surprisingly, given its extensive cultural and business links with Asia and desire to attract Asia-related disputes,[123] British Columbia's domestic arbitration legislation did not even address the possibility of med-arb until 1 September 2020, when a new domestic Arbitration Act came into force. These amendments bring into BC's Arbitration Act the same wording already found in its International Commercial Arbitration Act: 'It is not incompatible with an arbitration agreement for an arbitral tribunal to encourage settlement of the dispute and, with the agreement of the parties, the arbitral tribunal may use

---

Manitoba Arbitration Act, s 35; International Commercial Arbitration Act, s 5; New Brunswick Arbitration Act, s 35; International Commercial Arbitration Act, s 6; Nova Scotia Commercial Arbitration Act, s 38; International Commercial Arbitration Act, s 6; British Columbia International Commercial Arbitration Act, s 30. Some of these provisions are based on the 1990 version of the UAA.

[115] Alberta Arbitration Act (n 114), s 35.
[116] Saskatchewan Arbitration Act (n 114), s 36.
[117] Manitoba Arbitration Act (n 114), s 35.
[118] New Brunswick Arbitration Act (n 114), s 35.
[119] Nova Scotia Commercial Arbitration Act (n 114), s 38.
[120] Québec Code of Civil Procedure, art 620.
[121] Ontario Arbitration Act, s 35.
[122] ibid, s 3.
[123] Joshua Karton, 'Beyond the "Harmonious Confucian": International Commercial Arbitration and the Impact of Chinese Cultural Values' in Chang-fa Lo, Nigel NT Li and Tsai-yu Lin (eds), *Legal Thoughts between the East and the West in the Multilevel Legal Order* (Springer 2016) 519, 538.

mediation, conciliation, or other procedures at any time during the arbitral proceedings to encourage settlement.'[124]

Identical or similar provisions appear in the International Commercial Arbitration Acts of Alberta,[125] Saskatchewan,[126] Manitoba,[127] New Brunswick[128] and Nova Scotia.[129] However, legislative endorsement of med-arb for international disputes is not uniform. Ontario, whose domestic Arbitration Act provides that, by default, arbitrators may not also act as mediators, makes no mention of med-arb in its International Commercial Arbitration Act.[130]

Case law concerning med-arb agreements in Canada is almost exclusively confined to labour/employment or family law disputes, where med-arb-type processes are more established. We therefore cannot state with certainty how a Canadian court might respond to, for example, an application for enforcement of a foreign arbitration award where the arbitrator previously acted as a mediator during the proceedings, in either a med-arb or an arb-med-arb procedure. A handful of reported cases exist where the courts have interpreted med-arb agreements in domestic commercial disputes. In these cases, the courts treat med-arb agreements as arbitration clauses for such purposes as competence-competence,[131] confidentiality[132] and enforcement.[133] Based on these cases, and on Canada's generally deferential attitude towards arbitration, it is likely that awards generated through med-arb or arb-med-arb will be enforceable across Canada so long as it is clear that the parties consented to the procedure.

In sum, the statutory landscape is permissive of med-arb but does little or nothing to encourage it. Canadian common law reflects this neglect of med-arb, both in the sparseness of the case law and in its treatment of

---

[124] British Columbia International Commercial Arbitration Act (n 114), s 30(1); Arbitration Act, s 47(1).
[125] Alberta International Commercial Arbitration Act (n 114), s 5.
[126] Saskatchewan International Commercial Arbitration Act (n 114), s 4.
[127] Manitoba International Commercial Arbitration Act (n 114), s 5.
[128] New Brunswick International Commercial Arbitration Act (n 114), s 6.
[129] Nova Scotia International Commercial Arbitration Act (n 114), s 6.
[130] Ontario International Commercial Arbitration Act, sch 5.
[131] *Government of Saskatchewan v Capitol Steel Corp* 2017 SKQB 302 [36].
[132] *Mann v Elphick* 2015 BCSC 1853 [26], [30].
[133] *Conmac Enterprises Ltd v 0928818 BC Ltd* 2018 BCSC 360 [12], [47] (the med-arb practitioner's arbitration decision was upheld, and held to the same standards as any other arbitration agreement); cf *Cricket Canada v Syed* 2017 ONSC 3301 [37], [52] (the award dealt with issues outside the scope of the parties' submission to arbitration).

med-arb as a sub-category of arbitration, with which Canadian courts are more familiar.

By contrast, at the institutional level, there has been a much more enthusiastic embrace of med-arb. All of the Canadian institutions that administer arbitrations promote arbitration and mediation alike as desirable methods of dispute resolution. They all promulgate rules of arbitration and mediation and provide in their arbitration rules for the possibility of combining mediation and arbitration in a single procedure.

The leading Canadian institution for international commercial disputes, the Vancouver International Arbitration Centre (VanIAC), makes no mention of med-arb in its Domestic Commercial Arbitration Rules.[134] Interestingly, the rules that were in force until 1 September 2020 (when VanIAC was called the British Columbia International Commercial Arbitration Centre (BCICAC)) provided that '[t]he arbitration tribunal may encourage settlement of the dispute and, with the written agreement of the parties, may conduct mediation, conciliation, facilitation or other appropriate procedure(s)'.[135]

VanIAC's International Commercial Arbitration Rules, which were not amended when BCICAC was recreated as VanIAC, contain provisions analogous to the old BCICAC domestic rules but also go further,[136] stipulating:

> Where an arbitration agreement provides:
> (a) for the appointment of a conciliator or mediator; and
> (b) that the conciliator or mediator shall also act as arbitrator in the event of the conciliation or mediation failing to produce a settlement, a party shall not object to the appointment of a conciliator or mediator as arbitrator solely on the ground that the person acted as conciliator or mediator in connection with some or all of the matters referred to in the arbitration.[137]

---

[134] 'Domestic Commercial Arbitration Rules of Procedure' (*Vancouver International Arbitration Centre*) <https://vaniac.org/arbitration/rules-of-procedure/domestic-arbitration-rules/> accessed 9 October 2020.

[135] 'Domestic Commercial Arbitration Rules of Procedure' (*British Columbia International Commercial Arbitration Centre*) <https://vaniac.org/arbitration/rules-of-procedure/previous-domestic-commercial-arbitration-rules-of-procedure/> accessed 9 October 2020, r 37(1).

[136] 'International Commercial Arbitration Rules of Procedure' (*Vancouver International Arbitration Centre*) <https://vaniac.org/arbitration/rules-of-procedure/international-commercial-arbitration-rules-of-procedure/> accessed 9 October 2020, r 33.

[137] ibid, r 11(3).

The ADR Institute of Canada (ADRIC) has been the most energetic promoter of med-arb. Its Arbitration Rules have long encouraged settlement using language similar to that of VanIAC's International Commercial Arbitration Rules.[138] However, in December 2019, it promulgated procedural rules specifically for med-arb, the first of their kind in Canada.[139] These rules incorporate ADRIC's arbitration and mediation rules by reference but prevail over those rules where they conflict. They set out procedures tailored to the med-arb process, covering such matters as maintenance of the mediator-arbitrator's independence and neutrality, protection of confidential information disclosed during the mediation phase, and the transition from the mediation to the arbitration phase. The ADRIC Med-Arb Rules explicitly contemplate a two-stage process with mediation followed by arbitration, and would not work well with an arb-med or arb-med-arb process.

Accompanying the new Med-Arb Rules, ADRIC has introduced a professional designation, the 'Chartered Mediator-Arbitrator' (C. Med-Arb), also the first of its kind in Canada. The statement of purpose accompanying the new C. Med-Arb designation is telling. It observes:

> Med-Arb is a distinct, innovative standalone process that is not well known or understood by consumers of ADR services compared to mediation and arbitration. Med-Arb is not merely the merging of separate mediation and arbitration processes, but a unique process designed to meet the needs of particular disputants ... As part of ADRIC's roles of protecting the public and promoting best practices in ADR, the need for a designation to certify competence, experience and skills specifically in Med-Arb has been determined to be extremely important, especially as the use of Med-Arb is expanding in many areas of substantive disputes.[140]

This statement displays an awareness that med-arb is not popular in Canada, and that many practitioners are suspicious of it. It goes beyond simply reassuring sceptical practitioners and affirms the value of med-arb and the specificity of the skills needed to conduct it effectively and efficiently.

---

[138] 'ADRIC Arbitration Rules' (*ADR Institute of Canada*) <https://adric.ca/rules-codes/arbrules> accessed 10 September 2020, s 4.27.1.

[139] 'ADRIC Med-arb Rules' (*ADR Institute of Canada*) <https://adric.ca/rules-codes/adric-med-arb-rules> accessed 10 September 2020.

[140] 'Principles, Criteria, Protocol and Competencies Required for the Designation Chartered Mediator-Arbitrator (C. Med-Arb)' (*ADR Institute of Canada*) <https://adric.ca/wp-content/uploads/2020/05/ADRIC_CMed-ARB_Criteria-1.pdf> accessed 10 September 2020, 2.

The ADRIC Med-Arb Rules and the C. Med-Arb designation are too new to know whether they will be embraced by the broader legal profession in Canada. However, they do indicate significant enthusiasm for med-arb within the ADR community, which is likely to translate into at least somewhat wider acceptance in the future.

13.5 Conclusion

Historically, Canadian lawyers were hesitant to advise their clients to try mediation and other forms of ADR, and Canadian courts were hesitant to relinquish their dominant role in dispute resolution. Starting in the 1980s, and accelerating in the 1990s, judicial settlement conferences, mediation and ADR more generally have achieved broad acceptance from the bar, the judiciary and legislatures.[141] The benefits of ADR are now well recognised: reduction of time and cost of dispute resolution, restoration of amicable relations among disputing parties, and – perhaps most important from the point of view of legislatures – reduction of caseloads in the public courts.

Today, every province maintains a public system of referral to mediation before a lawsuit will be set down for trial. In four provinces, pre-trial mediation is mandatory, subject only to narrow exceptions. If anything, those exceptions reinforce the pro-ADR policy of the modern Canadian judiciary, as courts will generally release parties from their obligation to mediate (or find that the obligation has been fulfilled) only where doing so promotes quick and efficient dispute resolution.

As the profile and popularity of ADR mechanisms, especially mediation, have risen in Canada, multi-tier dispute resolution agreements have themselves become more prevalent. The courts' attitude towards multi-tier agreements is supportive but not particularly sophisticated. While the generally applicable rules of contractual interpretation apply equally to multi-tier dispute resolution agreements, clear trends are identifiable: Canadian courts tend to interpret lower tiers of dispute resolution agreements as optional, absent clear, express language designating them as mandatory preconditions to arbitral or judicial jurisdiction; they will not enforce consensual tiers of multi-tier agreements unless those tiers incorporate ascertainable or objective criteria to assess compliance, such as time limits or references to the mediation rules of an established institution; they defer to arbitral tribunals to decide whether

---

[141] MacFarlane and Keet (n 64) 679–80.

lower tiers constitute mandatory preconditions to arbitration and, if so, whether those preconditions have been satisfied; whether as a cause or consequence of that deference, Canadian courts treat the satisfaction of preconditions to arbitration as a matter of procedure or admissibility, not of jurisdiction; and finally, when they find that parties to an arbitration agreement (whether or not as part of a multi-tier clause) may proceed to litigation, they do not refer them to mediation, even in provinces that mandate pre-trial mediation.

The Canadian dispute resolution bar has only recently and unevenly begun to overcome its misgivings about mixing multiple methods of dispute resolution in a single proceeding. While med-arb, arb-med-arb and similar procedures remain uncommon, their popularity is growing. Such methods are expressly permitted by legislation in most of the provinces, and awards produced through a med-arb or arb-med-arb procedure are generally enforceable so long as the parties' consent to the procedure is established. ADR institutions and professional associations have embraced med-arb more enthusiastically, most notably ADRIC, the leading domestic provider of arbitration and mediation services. In 2019, ADRIC introduced tailored rules of procedure for med-arb, along with a new professional designation, the Chartered Mediator-Arbitrator. Mixed-method dispute resolution now appears poised for significant growth over the next decade.

14

Multi-tier Dispute Resolution in Australia

A Tale of 'Escalating' Acceptance

RICHARD GARNETT

14.1 Introduction

The Australian approach to multi-tier dispute resolution and 'arb-med' clauses has been one of progressive and incremental acceptance. In the case of multi-tier clauses that typically provide for negotiation, followed by mediation and then arbitration or litigation, the movement towards recognition has come through a series of judicial decisions dating from the 1990s. By contrast, the current version of arb-med or arb-med-arb was introduced into Australian law pursuant to uniform Australian State and Territory domestic arbitration legislation dating from 2010. There is presently no scope for parties to choose arb-med in an international arbitration seated in Australia.

A multi-tier dispute resolution clause typically involves a series of steps or tiers with fixed time frames for the transfer of the dispute from one step to another. The clause normally starts with an obligation to negotiate (often involving senior executives of both parties), followed by mediation and then concluded by arbitration or litigation. The aim of such clauses is to avoid the 'escalat[ion] of disputes to adversarial proceedings' by providing the opportunity to resolve them in a cheaper, quicker, less formal and less disruptive manner.[1] It is also considered that express provision of consensual methods of dispute resolution in an agreement encourages parties to use such methods rather than simply resorting to

---

[1] James H Carter, 'Part 1 – Issues Arising from Integrated Dispute Resolution Clauses' in Albert van den Berg (ed), *New Horizons in International Commercial Arbitration and Beyond* (Kluwer Law International 2005) 446; Klaus Peter Berger, 'Law and Practice of Escalation Clauses' (2006) 22 Arbitration International 1, 1; Vijaya Kumar Rajah, 'W(h)ither Adversarial Commercial Dispute Resolution?' (2017) 33 Arbitration International 17, 33.

litigation as a default response.² Furthermore, having adversarial methods at the end of the process also helps focus the mind of the parties during negotiation and mediation as they may be more inclined to settle the disputes to avoid the more coercive and expensive procedures. Such a concern may be less present where negotiation and mediation are only 'freestanding'.³

As several of the other chapters in this volume have noted, a major problem with multi-tier dispute processes is their enforceability; specifically, the enforcement of the early tiers of negotiation and mediation.

Prior to the 1990s in Australia, mediation and negotiation clauses were both generally unenforceable on the basis that it was considered 'futile to seek to enforce something which requires the co-operation and consent of a party when such co-operation and consent cannot be enforced'.⁴ In essence, the voluntary nature of such clauses made courts reluctant to issue orders directing parties to comply with them.

14.2 Mediation Agreements

The first real sign of liberalisation came in the 1992 decision of the Supreme Court of New South Wales in *Hooper Bailie Associated Ltd v Natcon Group Pty Ltd*.⁵ This case concerned a construction contract that contained an arbitration clause. A dispute arose, an arbitrator was appointed, and then the parties agreed to refer certain matters to mediation. During the process of mediation, a provisional liquidator of one of the parties (Natcon) sought to continue with the arbitration. The court granted Hooper Bailie's application to stay the arbitral proceedings based on the agreement to mediate. Such an agreement was held to be enforceable where it is sufficiently certain, which would be the case where the terms were clear as to what was expected of the parties and the mediator in terms of the process. In a much-quoted statement, the judge said that when a mediation agreement was being enforced what was enforced 'was not co-operation and consent but participation in a process from which co-operation and consent might come'.⁶ The judge in *Hooper Bailie* was, however, careful to say that a mediation agreement was distinct from

---

² Carter (n 1).
³ Rajah (n 1) 33.
⁴ *Hooper Bailie Associated Ltd v Natcon Group Pty Ltd* (1992) 28 NSWLR 194, 206.
⁵ ibid.
⁶ ibid; *WTE Co-Generation v RCR Energy Pty Ltd* [2013] VSC 314 [39].

both an 'agreement to agree' and an agreement to negotiate in good faith, neither of which was considered enforceable.

The requirement that a mediation agreement be sufficiently certain to be enforceable was further considered by the same court in *Elizabeth Bay Developments Pty Ltd v Boral Building Services Pty Ltd*.[7] *Elizabeth Bay* concerned a construction contract that contained a multi-tier dispute resolution clause that provided for mediation administered by the Australian Commercial Disputes Centre (ACDC), as a precursor to arbitration. After Boral ceased work on the project, Elizabeth Bay terminated the contract and commenced proceedings in the Supreme Court of New South Wales for damages for breach. Boral sought a stay based on the mediation clause, relying on the *Hooper Bailie* case.

The court noted that the ACDC had a set of guidelines for mediation of commercial disputes and a mediation agreement, but they were not consistent. Also, the mediation clause in this case did not incorporate the relevant guidelines and, in the court's view, was probably uncertain on this basis. Furthermore, even if the clause did incorporate the guidelines, it was still unenforceable for uncertainty. The ACDC guidelines required the parties to sign a mediation agreement but did not directly refer to the ACDC mediation agreement. Consequently, the obligation to enter into a mediation agreement that was consistent with the mediation guidelines was too vague to be enforceable.

In addition, the ACDC mediation agreement had another element of uncertainty as it contained a confirmation by the parties that they would 'attempt in good faith to negotiate toward achieving a settlement of the dispute'. The inclusion of such a duty to negotiate in good faith rendered the mediation agreement obscure and unclear.

The next major decision, *Aiton Australia Pty Ltd v Transfield Pty Ltd*,[8] concerned a contract containing a multi-tier dispute resolution clause that consisted of negotiation, followed by mediation and then expert determination or litigation. After Aiton commenced proceedings against Transfield for damages under Australian statute, Transfield sought a stay, relying on the dispute resolution clause. The court, approving the decisions discussed earlier, found that a mediation agreement could be enforced if it operated as a condition precedent to litigation or arbitration and was sufficiently certain.

---

[7] (1995) 36 NSWLR 709.
[8] [1999] NSWSC 996.

For a mediation agreement to be certain there are three requirements.[9] First, there cannot be stages in the process where agreement is required on some course of action before the process can proceed – otherwise the term is an 'agreement to agree'. Second, the administrative processes for selecting a mediator and determining the mediator's remuneration should be included in the clause; where the parties cannot agree, selection by a third party is required. Third, the clause needs to set out the process of mediation to be followed or incorporate the rules for mediation by reference. In *Aiton*, the judge found the mediation clause to be void for uncertainty because there were no provisions dealing with the remuneration to be paid to mediators.

More recently, mediation clauses in multi-tier agreements have been held unenforceable where (1) no process had been provided for the conduct of the mediation;[10] (2) not all parties to the dispute were parties to the mediation clause and not all claims were covered by the clause;[11] and (3) the mediation clause was optional in nature only because 'either party' had the right to elect mediation.[12] The conclusion that only 'mandatory' mediation clauses are enforceable is questionable since it is well accepted, by contrast, that an optional *arbitration* clause is enforceable. Such a clause crystallises into a binding arbitration agreement upon one party's asserting its right to arbitrate.[13] Why cannot a mediation clause be treated in the same manner?

14.3 Negotiation Agreements

The judge in *Aiton v Transfield*[14] also considered the first stage in the multi-tier clause, which provided for good faith negotiations between designated officers of the parties to resolve the dispute. The judge found this negotiation clause to be unenforceable because it was not separable from the mediation clause – they were intended to walk (and fall) together as a staged procedure.[15]

---

[9] ibid [69].
[10] *Skills Tiling v Trio Construct (Civil)* [2014] VMC 4.
[11] *Elizabeth Chong Pty Ltd v Brown* [2011] FMCA 565.
[12] *Termguard Pty Ltd v Statewide Pest Control Pty Ltd* [2016] WASC 359; *Roberts v Morphett Constructions Pty Ltd* [2018] NSWCATAP 33 (no obligation to mediate).
[13] *PMT Partners Pty Ltd (in liq) v Australian National Parks and Wildlife Service* (1995) 184 CLR 301.
[14] *Aiton* (n 8).
[15] ibid [71].

Significantly, however, the judge was not prepared to find the negotiation clause invalid on uncertainty grounds. Departing from the earlier expressed view in *Elizabeth Bay*, he drew a distinction between an 'agreement to agree' and a good faith negotiation clause with only the former clause being unenforceable.[16] Although such a statement was strictly obiter, it does suggest a departure from the previously negative position on negotiation clauses.

This optimism was confirmed in the very significant 2009 decision of the New South Wales Court of Appeal in *United Group Rail Services Ltd v Rail Corp of New South Wales*.[17] The multi-tier provision in issue in this case first involved a requirement that the parties' senior representatives 'meet and undertake genuine and good faith negotiations with a view to resolving the dispute or difference'. If the dispute could not be resolved by negotiation, then the parties were required to refer the dispute to the 'Australian Dispute Centre' for mediation. If mediation could not resolve the dispute within forty-two days, the dispute would be submitted to arbitration.

A dispute arose with both parties accepting that the 'steps' of dispute resolution were mandatory and that the mediation clause was unenforceable because the Australian Dispute Centre did not exist. United Group, however, argued before the court that the arbitration clause was invalid because the earlier stage negotiation clause was unenforceable, similar to the 'walk and fall together' principle applied in *Aiton*. The court held that a clause providing for negotiations in good faith is valid and enforceable. Such a clause can be interpreted as an obligation to behave in a particular manner in the conduct of an essentially self-interested commercial activity: the negotiation of resolution of a commercial dispute.[18] The conduct required by good faith is for parties to take an 'honest and genuine approach to settling a ... dispute'.[19] An example of bad faith in negotiations would be where a party pretended to negotiate, 'having decided not to settle what is recognised to be a good claim, in order to drive the other party into an expensive arbitration that it believes the other party cannot afford'.[20]

A good faith negotiation clause is, however, different from an 'agreement to agree', which is incomplete in lacking essential terms.[21]

---

[16] ibid [153].
[17] [2009] NSWCA 177; (2009) 74 NSWLR 618.
[18] ibid [71].
[19] ibid [73].
[20] ibid.
[21] ibid [56], [64].

Such an approach has been welcomed by commentators for its encouragement of parties to treat negotiations in a constructive and serious way rather than as an empty and futile gesture.[22] As noted, the advantages of resolving a dispute by negotiation are obvious and the *United Group* decision is a valuable endorsement of this method of dispute resolution. Another commentary has, however, been more critical of the case, suggesting that a duty to negotiate in good faith may lack reality in a self-interested business world[23] and, further, that seeking to compel compliance with an inherently voluntary activity may be unproductive and only delay resolution of the parties' dispute.[24]

The *United Group* case, while upholding the validity of a duty to negotiate in a multi-tier dispute resolution clause, does not address the question of whether such a duty is a 'jurisdictional precondition' to arbitration or litigation (the last stage of the process). What this expression means is that the failure by a party to comply with the duty to negotiate would result in the arbitral tribunal or court having no jurisdiction and any resulting award or judgment being void.

A subsequent English decision, *Emirates Trading Agency LLC v Prime Mineral Exports Private Ltd*,[25] adopted the reasoning of *United Group* on the status of good faith negotiation clauses, finding the clause whereby the parties 'shall first seek to resolve the dispute or claim by friendly discussion' to be enforceable. So, the influence of Australian law extends beyond Australia. Importantly, however, the English Commercial Court in *Emirates Trading* went further by declaring that the obligation to negotiate was a precondition to the arbitral tribunal's jurisdiction[26] (arbitration being the last stage in the process), although no breach of the obligation was found.

Courts in later Australian cases have confirmed the enforceability of agreements to negotiate in good faith, where part of a multi-tier dispute resolution process. Again, courts have not addressed the issue of whether

---

[22] Didem Kayali, 'Enforceability of Multi-tiered Dispute Resolution Clauses' (2010) 27(6) Journal of International Arbitration 551, 570; Leon Trakman and Kunal Sharma, 'The Binding Force of Agreements to Negotiate in Good Faith' (2014) 73 Cambridge Law Journal 598.

[23] Louis Flannery and Robert Merkin, '*Emirates Trading*, Good Faith and Pre-arbitral ADR Clauses: A Jurisdictional Precondition' (2015) 31 Arbitration International 63, 90.

[24] Simon Chapman, 'Multi-tiered Dispute Resolution Clauses: Enforcing Obligations to Negotiate in Good Faith' (2010) 27 Journal of International Arbitration 89, 94, 98.

[25] *Emirates Trading Agency LLC v Prime Mineral Exports Private Ltd* [2014] EWHC 2104 (Comm), [2015] 1 WLR 1145.

[26] ibid [64].

negotiation is a jurisdictional precondition to arbitration or litigation as the only relief sought by claimants has been a temporary stay of the arbitration or litigation to allow the negotiation to proceed.[27]

In *Downer EDI Mining Pty Ltd v Wambo Coal Pty Ltd*,[28] the court enforced a clause where the parties agreed, within five days after exchange of statements in relation to a dispute, to 'hold a meeting and attempt to resolve the dispute'. The negotiation clause was expressed to be a precursor to expert determination. Specifically, the court found the expression 'attempt to resolve the dispute' to be sufficiently certain, even though no reference was made to 'good faith'.[29] Interestingly, the court noted, while before the *United Group* case parties had complained about the *presence* of good faith in agreements, now they were objecting to its absence.

The court in *Downer* also rejected an argument that the negotiation clause was unenforceable because of futility. It was noted that even where a negotiation clause was prima facie valid and enforceable, the court still retained a discretion not to give effect to the clause where it would be unjust to the claimant. However, a heavy burden exists on a party seeking to avoid enforcement.[30] Hence, for the futility argument to succeed, the claimant would have to show that the parties had embarked upon negotiations but it was 'pointless to continue'. The court found in *Downer* that while the parties had engaged in some 'informal and unstructured negotiations' which had so far not been unsuccessful, those negotiations could still conceivably bear fruit in a more formalised setting.[31]

A similar outcome was reached in *Santos Ltd v Fluor Australia Pty Ltd*.[32] A futility defence was again rejected where on the evidence the parties had successfully settled disputes in the past and the claimant had shown no good reason why it had not initiated the negotiation process in respect of the current dispute.[33] The dispute concerned a discrete legal question – the construction of a contract – which would be clearly suitable for court determination. Yet the parties, 'for commercial reasons', had chosen alternative dispute resolution and this choice must

---

[27] See eg *Aiton* (n 8) [26]; *WTE* (n 6) [39].
[28] [2012] QSC 290.
[29] ibid [21].
[30] ibid [15], [28].
[31] ibid [29].
[32] [2016] QSC 129.
[33] ibid [27].

be respected. Furthermore, enforcing good faith negotiation clauses also furthers the public interest by avoiding unnecessary use of court time and reducing the costs of litigation.[34] The public and private interests supporting the enforcement of good faith negotiation clauses are clearly emphasised here.[35]

Note that in the case of negotiation and mediation agreements, the granting of a stay of court proceedings 'only suspends access to the court until the agreed process has been followed. If a party then undertakes the agreed process and no agreement is reached, the jurisdiction of the Court may still be invoked.'[36]

14.4 'Agreements to Agree': Growing Acceptance?

It was noted in the *Hooper Bailie, Aiton* and *United Group* cases that 'agreements to agree', that is, clauses which leave it up to the parties to agree a process for resolving a dispute, were considered unenforceable. Yet, in at least two other Australian cases 'agreements to agree' appear to have been enforced, which may suggest a possible re-evaluation of this issue.

Computershare Ltd v Perpetual Registrars Ltd (No 2)[37] involved a clause that provided that the parties 'must endeavour in good faith ... (a) to resolve the dispute or (b) to agree on (i) a process to resolve all or at least part of the dispute without arbitration or court proceedings (for example, mediation, conciliation, executive appraisal or ... expert determination); (ii) the selection and payment of any third party to be engaged by the parties; (iii) the involvement of any dispute resolution organisation'. Finally, after a ten-day period has expired, a party that has complied with the clause may terminate the dispute resolution process by giving notice to the other party.

The court did not directly address the question of whether it was enforcing an 'agreement to agree' but rather saw the entire clause as an agreement to negotiate in good faith. Yet, there was a key difference between the dispute resolution provisions here and those in *United Group*. In *United Group* the parties agreed to negotiate in good faith

---

[34] ibid [28].
[35] Compare *Contrast Constructions Pty Ltd v Allen* [2020] QCAT 194 [39] where a negotiation clause was not enforced where there was no prospect of the dispute resolution process 'achieving any useful outcome'.
[36] *Onslow Salt Pty Ltd v Buurabalayji Thalanyji Aboriginal Corp* [2018] FCAFC 118 [24].
[37] [2000] VSC 233.

alone whereas in *Computershare* the parties were given an option to negotiate either to resolve the dispute or to agree on an alternative process for dispute resolution. The court interpreted this option as merely *informing* the negotiation process, yet the provision did leave it to the parties to determine whether another method of dispute resolution should be employed.

In *Passlow v Butmac Pty Ltd*,[38] a similar clause provided that if a dispute was not resolved by negotiation then 'the parties must ... within ... 14 days ... seek to agree on a process for resolving the dispute through means other than litigation or arbitration'.

The court here directly confronted the 'agreement to agree' objection, finding that the above clause was enforceable because it provided 'a certain end to the process'. The provision was framed by a time limit, after which the right of the parties to refer the dispute to arbitration was triggered.[39] Hence, because the agreement was not open-ended and had a fixed endpoint, it was necessarily complete.[40] Since the agreement in *Computershare* was similarly constructed, this reasoning provides another basis for supporting the decision in that case.

The most recent statement on the enforceability of an 'agreement to agree' is found in *WTE Co-Generation v RCR Energy Pty Ltd*.[41] The court there had to consider a clause that provided that 'in the event the parties have not resolved the dispute then within ... 7 days a senior executive ... of the parties must meet to resolve the dispute or to agree on methods of doing so ..... If the dispute has not been resolved within 28 days of service of the notice of dispute, that dispute may be referred to litigation.'

This provision is similar to that in *Computershare* and also contains an endpoint whereby the parties may refer the dispute to litigation upon expiry of a certain time period (which was regarded as decisive of validity in *Passlow*). Nevertheless, the court refused to enforce the clause for two reasons. First, the process was uncertain because once the operation of the provision was triggered, the parties were required to do one of two things: either meet to resolve the dispute or agree on methods of doing so. No process was prescribed as to which option was to be pursued. Second, the clause was incomplete as an 'agreement to agree'. No method was prescribed for resolving the dispute and the clause required the parties' further agreement as to which method should be employed before the

---

[38] [2012] NSWSC 225.
[39] ibid [16].
[40] ibid [20].
[41] [2013] VSC 314.

process could proceed. The *Aiton* and *United Group* cases were cited with approval for the principle that an 'agreement to agree' was unenforceable because it was incomplete. However, neither *Computershare* nor *Passlow* was referred to by the court on this issue.

There therefore remains a division of opinion among Australian courts as to the enforceability of 'agreements to agree'. Given the general trend in Australia in favour of enforcing dispute resolution stages within multi-tier clauses, it may be thought that the view in *Passlow* and *Computershare* may ultimately prevail. Certainly, there seems to be a fine distinction between an agreement to negotiate in good faith, which is generally expressed, and one which suggests to the parties, as part of the negotiation process, that they may wish to consider entering another agreement on dispute resolution. Arguably, this is merely a suggestion to the parties to inform the process of negotiation and if such a process is limited by time, after which the parties may resort to litigation or arbitration, it seems hard to see why party autonomy should not be upheld. Advisers should, however, perhaps avoid including such provisions until the matter is authoritatively determined in Australia.

14.5 Severance of the Tiers

A point that was touched on in the *Passlow* case,[42] but not resolved, was whether unenforceability of one tier of a multi-tier clause automatically results in the invalidity of subsequent tiers, such as an arbitration clause. In *Passlow*, the court did not have to consider this argument, since the earlier tier was found to be enforceable in any event.

However, in *Aiton*, discussed in Section 14.2, the court did find that the clauses in a multi-tier process are interconnected and intertwined, with the result that an invalid mediation clause also renders unenforceable the negotiation clause. In *United Group*, by contrast, the court found, as a matter of contractual interpretation, that the negotiation and mediation clauses are severable from the arbitration clause, such that the invalidity of the first or second tiers would not affect the third.[43]

So, Australian courts have largely considered the question of whether an arbitration clause is rendered invalid by failure of earlier tiers as a matter of contractual construction. The issue is, however, whether this approach is consistent with the well-recognised principle that an

---

[42] *Passlow* (n 38).
[43] *United* (n 17) [96].

arbitration clause is separable from the contract in which it is contained.[44] According to the separability doctrine, a finding of invalidity of the principal contract (or any term of such contract) has no effect on the status of the arbitration clause.

The key question is whether the interconnected argument is more analogous to an attack on the validity of the principal contract or a challenge to the validity of the arbitration clause itself. If separability means that the arbitration clause is separable from all other provisions in the contract, then arguably a successful challenge to the enforceability of an earlier tier in a multi-tier clause should not affect the status of the arbitration clause whose validity must be determined independently.[45]

14.6 Arb-med or Arb-med-arb

From 2010 onwards, the Australian States and Territories enacted new uniform legislation for domestic arbitration, for example, in New South Wales, the Commercial Arbitration Act 2010 (CAA). This legislation includes provisions authorising arb-med and arb-med-arb[46] as methods of dispute resolution which are closely based on rules adopted in Singapore and Hong Kong.[47]

Arb-med is the procedure whereby the arbitrator assumes the role of mediator to facilitate settlement of the dispute submitted to arbitration. The procedure is often said to offer the 'best of both worlds' for parties: if they can reach a consensual solution then a binding settlement agreement may be signed. If no such agreement is achieved, then resort can be had to arbitration to obtain a binding and enforceable award.[48] Arb-med has been generally supported by Australian lawyers based on the potentially significant savings in costs and time provided by using the same person as arbitrator and mediator on the same matter, who has continuous knowledge of the dispute.[49] Nevertheless, Australian arbitrators have

---

[44] See Commercial Arbitration Act 2010 (NSW), s 16.
[45] This is the view of Flannery and Merkin (n 23) 95 at fn 133.
[46] Arbitration followed by mediation and arbitration followed by mediation and then arbitration.
[47] See International Arbitration Act (Cap 143A) (Singapore), s 17 and the current Arbitration Ordinance (Cap 609) (Hong Kong), s 33.
[48] Doug Jones, *Commercial Arbitration in Australia* (2nd edn, Thomson Reuters 2013) 344.
[49] See eg Luke Nottage, 'Arb-Med in Australia: The Time Has Come' (2007) 5 ADR Reporter 8; Campbell Bridge, 'Med-arb and Other Hybrid Processes: One Man's Meat Is Another Man's Poison' (2014) 1(4) Australian Alternative Dispute Resolution Law Bulletin 76, 77–78.

little or no experience of acting as mediators in the same matter[50] (compared to the position in some Asian jurisdictions such as Japan)[51] and so there will be a period of adjustment. Some commentators have suggested that Australian parties will be reluctant to use the process,[52] although analogous systems exist in other Australian legislation.[53] Commentators, however, have considered that it is preferable that any combined process begin with arbitration rather than mediation. The problem with a process commencing with mediation is that if it succeeds, then there is no longer any dispute capable of being resolved by arbitration and producing an enforceable consent award.[54]

There are no arb-med provisions in the Australian legislation for *international* commercial arbitration,[55] an omission that has been criticised for its failure to take account of the diverse needs of international parties.[56] In theory, parties could incorporate an arb-med or arb-medarb process into an international arbitration agreement with an Australian seat, but, in the absence of statutory authorisation, any award following a failed mediation may be susceptible to challenge on natural justice or public policy (bias) grounds in the courts of both Australia and foreign countries.[57] This risk is particularly great where

---

[50] Clyde Croft, 'Alternative Dispute Resolution in Arbitration: Is Arb-med Really an Option?' <www.supremecourt.vic.gov.au/about-the-court/speeches/alternative-dispute-resolution-in-arbitration-is-arb-med-really-an-option> accessed 16 August 2020.

[51] Luke Nottage, 'Arb-med and New International Commercial Mediation Rules in Japan' (*University of Sydney*, 21 July 2009) <https://japaneselaw.sydney.edu.au/2009/07/arb-med-and-new-international-commercial-mediation-rules-in-japan/> accessed 16 August 2020.

[52] Jones (n 48) 350.

[53] See eg Land and Environment Act 1979 (NSW), s 34, cited in Jones (n 48) 354.

[54] Luke Nottage and Richard Garnett (eds), *International Arbitration in Australia* (Federation Press 2010) 179. This position may change with the wide adoption of the United Nations Convention on International Settlement Agreements Resulting from Mediation (the Singapore Convention on Mediation), which was opened for signature on 7 August 2019 and entered into force on 12 September 2020. The aim of the Convention is to increase the enforceability of settlement agreements that arise from mediation so as to create a counterpart to the New York Convention on the recognition and enforcement of foreign arbitral awards. Currently only six states, Belarus, Ecuador, Fiji, Qatar, Saudi Arabia and Singapore, have ratified the Convention, but each state may apply the Convention to a party to a settlement agreement whose place of business is not in a Contracting State, such as Australia.

[55] International Arbitration Act 1974 (Cth).

[56] Luke Nottage and Richard Garnett, 'Top 20 Things to Change in or around Australia's International Arbitration Act' (2010) 6 Asian International Arbitration Journal 1, 35; see n 47 for a comparison of Singapore and Hong Kong.

[57] Luke Nottage, 'International Commercial Arbitration in Australia: What's New and What's Not' (2013) 30 Journal of International Arbitration 465, 489.

the arb-med process in its mediation phase permits 'caucusing' (*ex parte* communications with individual parties).

The relevant provisions on arb-med are found in section 27D of the CAA, which some commentators have criticised for being too prescriptive and limiting parties' autonomy to design their own arb-med process.[58] The central provision is section 27D(1), which permits an arbitrator, with the parties' consent in writing, to act as a mediator. 'Mediator' is defined in section 27D(8) to include 'a conciliator or other non-arbitral intermediary between parties'. Section 27D(1) is uncontroversial with the writing requirement ensuring that the parties' will is clearly expressed; if there any concerns about the integrity of the process, consent will be refused.

Section 27D(2) provides that an arbitrator, when acting as a mediator, may communicate separately with the parties (caucusing is therefore allowed) and, unless otherwise agreed, treat any information obtained in the course of communications as confidential. Such a provision recognises a clear difference between arbitration and mediation: in arbitration the arbitrator must stand apart from the parties and impose a decision based on the legal rights and duties whereas in mediation it is accepted that a mediator may adopt more flexible strategies or 'creative possibilities'[59] in seeking to resolve the dispute.

Section 27D(3) provides that the mediation terminates by agreement of the parties, by the withdrawal of a party or by the decision of the mediator. This provision is in accord with customary mediation practice.

Section 27D(4) is an important provision and provides that where an arbitrator who has acted as mediator wishes to resume the arbitration, he or she must obtain the written consent of all parties on or after termination of the mediation. Section 27D(5) then provides that where consent is given under (4) no objection may be taken to the arbitrator's subsequent conduct of the arbitration solely on the ground that the arbitrator previously acted as a mediator. Section 27D(4) is a natural justice or due process provision. If a party is concerned about an arbitrator's impartiality after the mediation phase, perhaps because of information obtained, the party may refuse to allow the mediator to continue as arbitrator.

---

[58] Mark Goodrich, 'Arb-med: Ideal Solution or Dangerous Heresy?' (2016) Construction Law Journal 370, 378; cf Nottage and Garnett (n 56) 37 who advocate only one agreement in writing that commits the parties to retain the arbitrator even if the mediation fails but with no caucusing permitted to ensure due process.

[59] Alan Limbury, 'Don't be Scared, This Is the Future – Avoiding the Pitfalls of Arb-med-arb' (2014) 1(4) Australian Alternative Dispute Resolution Law Bulletin 84.

This provision has been supported[60] on the ground that it will encourage parties to speak 'frankly and freely in the mediation phase without fear of retribution in any subsequent arbitration'. Other commentators, however, fear that section 27D(4) will have the opposite effect in that it may encourage risk averseness on the part of parties. Since a party will not know what material has been imparted to the mediator by the other party, it may err on the side of caution and refuse consent to the mediator acting as arbitrator. So, the problem of natural justice is addressed in section 27D(4) but at the expense of the workability of med-arb.[61] Equally, giving a party an effective veto over whether a mediator can continue as an arbitrator could be used as a weapon to delay or frustrate the process[62] and 'empower ulterior motives'.[63]

Section 27D(4) was recently considered by the Supreme Court of New South Wales in *Ku-ring-gai Council v Ichor Constructions Pty Ltd*.[64] *Ichor* is the first and so far only Australian decision on section 27D and comments made by the court on the provision's scope and effect may have relevance not only for Australia but also for Singapore and Hong Kong where similar rules exist.[65]

Ichor concerned a construction contract that contained an arbitration clause. After the arbitration commenced, the parties agreed in writing to the arbitrator assuming the role of mediator under section 27D(1) of the CAA. The arbitrator then conducted the mediation and put a proposal to the parties for settlement, which was rejected. After the mediation terminated, the parties continued with submissions and purported to treat the former mediator now as arbitrator. Significantly, however, no written consent of the parties as required by section 27D(4) was obtained before recommencement of the arbitration. At the conclusion of submissions, the former mediator reserved his decision.

Ichor then brought proceedings, claiming that any award handed down would be invalid as the arbitrator had no mandate to continue the arbitration following termination of the mediation. The court agreed,

---

[60] ibid 84.
[61] Robert Angyal, 'Med-arb – Past, Present and Future' <www.bar.asn.au> accessed 16 August 2020, para 26.
[62] Goodrich (n 58) 380.
[63] George Pasas, 'The Arbitrator as Mediator: *Ku-ring-gai Council v Ichor Constructions Pty Ltd* [2018] NSWSC 610' (2019) 29 Australian Dispute Resolution Journal 266, 271. The single agreement model advocated by Nottage and Garnett (n 56) 37 was intended to overcome the difficulty of obtaining a second agreement after a failed mediation.
[64] [2018] NSWSC 610.
[65] See n 47 above.

finding that the requirement for express written consent in section 27D (4) could not be substituted by conduct of the parties in participating in the arbitration such as to create an implied or inferred consent. The requirement of certainty under the legislation demanded that section 27D(4) be strictly adhered to.[66]

The Council also argued that Ichor had waived the requirement of written consent under section 27D(4) by its conduct in continuing with the arbitration. The allegation of waiver was based on section 4 of the CAA, which implements Article 4 of the UNCITRAL Model Law on International Commercial Arbitration 2006 (the Model Law). Section 4 provides that 'a party who knows that any provision of this Act from which the parties may derogate or any requirement under the arbitration agreement has not been complied with and yet proceeds with the arbitration without stating the party's objection to such non-compliance without undue delay ... is taken to have waived the party's right to object'.

The argument was again rejected by the court, who said that for waiver under section 4 to apply, the party must have had actual knowledge of the legal requirement said to be waived. On the facts here there was no evidence that Ichor knew of the obligation to obtain consent in writing under section 27D(4). The court also observed that the above waiver argument assumed that section 27D(4) was 'a provision from which the parties may derogate', that is, it was not a mandatory rule. The court noted other provisions in the CAA that are clearly 'derogable' because language such as 'unless otherwise agreed by the parties' is used. No such wording is present in section 27D(4) which led the court to suggest (without deciding the issue) that Parliament may not have intended it to be a provision from which derogation by the parties was possible.

In 2019, the Council filed an application for leave to appeal to the New South Wales Court of Appeal from the first instance decision.[67] Ichor's response was that the application was incompetent because the court's power to determine whether the arbitrator's mandate had been terminated was derived from section 14(2) of the CAA, a decision on which was not subject to appeal to a higher court. The Council, however, argued that the court's power to make the orders arose from sections 9 and 17J of the CAA, which contained no such restriction. Sections 9, 14 and 17J are almost identical to Articles 9, 14 and 17J of the Model Law.

---

[66] cf Pasas (n 63).
[67] *Ku-ring-gai Council v Ichor Constructions Pty Ltd* [2019] NSWCA 2.

Section 14 provides:

> (1) If an arbitrator becomes in law or in fact unable to perform the arbitrator's functions or for other reasons fails to act without undue delay, the arbitrator's mandate terminates if the arbitrator withdraws from office or if the parties agree on the termination.
> (2) Otherwise, if a controversy remains concerning any of these grounds, any party may request the Court to decide on the termination of the mandate.
> (3) A decision of the Court under subsection (2) that is within the limits of the authority of the Court is final.

Section 9 provides:

> It is not incompatible with an arbitration agreement for a party to request, before or during arbitral proceedings, from a court an interim measure of protection and for a court to grant the measure.

Section 17J provides:

> (1) The Court has the same power of issuing an interim measure in relation to arbitration proceedings as it has in relation to proceedings in courts.
> (2) The Court is to exercise the power in accordance with its own procedures taking into account the specific features of a domestic commercial arbitration.

The Court of Appeal found in favour of Ichor. The orders made by the first instance court, including the determination that the arbitrator had acted as mediator and the parties had not given written consent to the arbitrator continuing the arbitration, were not 'interim measures of protection' within the terms of sections 9 and 17J. The Court of Appeal referred to the legislative history of Article 9 of the Model Law to show that the term 'interim measures of protection' referred to orders such as pre-award attachments, measures relating to the protection of trade secrets and proprietary information, measures relating to the subject matter of the dispute and those intended to secure evidence. The common element with all such measures was that they are 'designed to facilitate and protect the arbitration process'.[68] Further, when Article 17J was added to the Model Law in 2006, it was not intended to extend the type of relief that could be granted by the court.[69]

---

[68] ibid [63].
[69] ibid [64].

In the present case, questions relating to whether the arbitrator's mandate had been terminated, whether Ichor had consented to the continuation of the arbitration by the mediator or whether a mediation had taken place all concerned the central issue of whether the arbitration had been terminated.[70] They were not orders designed to protect the arbitration process.

Consequently, the proceeding did not involve 'interim measures' under section 17J but instead was a matter falling within section 14(2) of the CAA. The case concerned the question of whether the arbitrator had become in law unable to perform the arbitration under section 14(1), with the court's power to adjudicate enlivened under section 14(2).[71]

The next question for the Court of Appeal was whether the first instance court's decision was 'final', within the terms of section 14(3). The Court of Appeal found that it was, as 'final' means 'not subject to appeal'. This result was reached despite section 14(3) not including the words 'which decision shall be subject to no appeal' from the original Article 14(3) of the Model Law.[72] Parliament intended that there should only be a limited court review of matters under section 14 so as to avoid 'unnecessary delay or expense' within the terms of section 1C(1) of the CAA.[73]

Finally, the Court of Appeal said that even if the application for leave to appeal had been competent, in its discretion, it still would have refused leave. The court first felt that it would be undesirable to grant leave where the effect would be to 'delay the progress of the arbitral process to which the parties have agreed to resolve their dispute'.[74] Second, in terms of substance, the applicant's objections in relation to section 27D had little merit. In particular, the first instance court's conclusion that section 27D(4) requires the express written consent of the parties before the mediator may proceed with the arbitration was entirely logical in circumstances where such person may have received confidential information during the mediation and may have expressed views on the merits of the proceedings at that time.[75]

The overall effect of the Court of Appeal decision is to make it difficult for a party to appeal any decision by a court in relation to the arb-med-arb

---

[70] ibid [65].
[71] ibid [66].
[72] ibid [71].
[73] ibid [71], [74].
[74] ibid [79].
[75] ibid [81].

provisions in the CAA. Such an outcome is welcome in encouraging finality of dispute resolution and is also consistent with the general trend in international commercial arbitration to limit judicial review of arbitral awards and orders. The only query after the decision is the earlier expressed concern regarding section 27D(4), namely, how the requirement of express consent may be used by a party to obstruct the arbitral process after mediation.

Returning to the remaining arb-med-arb provisions in the CAA, section 27D(5) provides that the parties' consent in section 27D(4) acts as a form of waiver of any objection to the subsequent conduct of the arbitration on the basis that the arbitrator previously acted as a mediator. This provision is slightly ambiguous in that it may suggest that a party loses all its rights to challenge an arbitrator or an award on natural justice grounds once the party has given its consent.[76] That reading, however, would be too broad: if an arbitrator, for example, proceeded to conduct the reference in a biased manner or denied a party natural justice or procedural fairness, then the arbitrator and/or the award may be challenged under section 12 and section 34 of the CAA, respectively.[77] Section 18 of the CAA, which requires the arbitral tribunal to treat the parties with equality and provide each with a reasonable opportunity to present its case, is almost certainly a mandatory rule that cannot be waived by the parties.[78] What section 27D(5) precludes is a party raising a bias objection *simply* on the ground that the arbitrator had previously acted as mediator in the same matter.

Section 27D(6) provides that if the parties do not consent to the mediator continuing as arbitrator under section 27D(4) then the mandate of the arbitrator is terminated and a substitute arbitrator is required to be appointed. The appointment of a substitute arbitrator is unavoidable where the parties' consent is withheld, but it does raise the same problems of disruption, delay and wasted costs that occur in conventional arbitration where a substitute is appointed after an arbitrator withdraws or dies.[79]

Section 27D(7) is another key provision that provides that 'if confidential information is obtained from a party during mediation proceedings ... the arbitrator must, before conducting subsequent arbitration proceedings ... disclose to all other parties to the arbitration

---

[76] Goodrich (n 58) 380.
[77] As occurred in *Hui v Esposito Holdings Pty Ltd* [2017] FCA 648.
[78] *Noble China Inc v Lei* (1998) 42 OR (3d) 69.
[79] See Commercial Arbitration Act 2010 (n 44), s 15.

proceedings so much of the information as the arbitrator considers material to the arbitration proceedings'.

Section 27D(7) has both mandatory and discretionary elements, mandatory in the sense that the arbitrator *must* disclose certain information but discretionary in the sense that the provision leaves it up to the arbitrator to determine when such information is 'material'. Some commentaries have suggested that the definition of what is 'material' imposes an unreasonable burden on mediators and may expose them to court challenges as to what information should or should not have been disclosed.[80] Arguably, however, such a duty of disclosure is no more onerous than that which rests on an arbitrator to disclose possible conflicts of interest prior to accepting an appointment or to make determinations during the reference regarding questions of weight and admissibility of evidence. The view, therefore, that all information disclosed in the mediation should be disregarded in the arbitral process[81] seems excessive.

A more serious problem raised by this subsection is that it does not specify *when* the arbitrator must make disclosure, specifically, whether it should be before or after the parties have consented to the mediator acting as arbitrator. Commentaries suggest that the provision should be read as requiring disclosure before the parties give their consent so that any consent is necessarily fully informed. Otherwise, the problem mentioned here will occur again: that is, a risk-averse party will refuse to give consent to the mediator continuing as arbitrator.[82]

While this analysis ensures that parties are fully informed when giving their consent, it has been suggested that such an approach may stifle the effectiveness of the earlier mediation.[83] The concern is that parties may err on the side of minimal disclosure and candour in the mediation out of fear that such material may be used against them in any subsequent arbitration.[84] Equally, a mediator who is aware that he or she may be appointed in a subsequent arbitration may be 'less robust' in the mediation,[85] with commentators acknowledging that a mediator in arb-med must be more

---

[80] Goodrich (n 58) 379; Bobette Wolski, 'Re-assessment of QCAT's Hybrid Hearing and Arb-med-arb under Section 27D of the Commercial Arbitration Act' (2014) 3 Journal of Civil Litigation and Practice 156, 166.
[81] cf Goodrich (n 58).
[82] Wolski (n 80) 162.
[83] Angyal (n 61), para 34.
[84] Wolski (n 80) 166; Goodrich (n 58) 379.
[85] George Golvan, 'What Do Clients Really Want – Hybrid Procedures, the New Frontier of Alternative Dispute Resolution' (2014) 1(4) Australian Alternative Dispute Resolution Law Bulletin 80, 81.

'facilitative' than 'evaluative'.[86] Specifically, expressions of opinion on the merits of a party's case or summing up parties' positions, which may be appropriate in a 'freestanding' mediation, are undesirable in arb-med.

While it is acknowledged that the nature of mediation may be different and more constrained in an arb-med process, the 'shadow' of possible future arbitration nevertheless may act as a beneficial discipline on the parties. It can serve to remind them of the costs and disharmony that may accompany an adversarial procedure and so encourage settlement.[87] Ultimately, the process of mediation may itself benefit through increased prospects of settlement. Moreover, the linking of mediation and arbitration has the further advantage of allowing a mediation settlement to be recorded as a consent arbitral award which can be enforced under arbitration legislation.[88]

14.7 Conclusion

Australia appears as a generally progressive and welcoming jurisdiction in respect of multi-tier dispute resolution and arb-med procedures. There have, however, been only limited court decisions so far, particularly on arb-med. Also, all the developments have been in the sphere of domestic dispute resolution; it will be interesting to see how courts apply these principles to cross-border disputes. The approach of the courts and the legislatures, nevertheless, has been to recognise that the doctrine of party autonomy should be given wide scope in commercial dispute resolution with intervention justified only to protect parties from cases of contractual uncertainty or lack of procedural due process.

---

[86] Jones (n 48) 345, 355; Bridge (n 49) 78; Limbury (n 59) 85.
[87] Wolski (n 80) 167; Rajah (n 1) 33.
[88] Rajah (n 1) 32; the arbitration process must, however, have commenced, with the tribunal having jurisdiction over the dispute, for an enforceable award to be created. See Jones (n 48) 355.

15

Praised, but Not Practised

The EU's Paradoxes of Hybrid Dispute Resolution

JULIEN CHAISSE[*]

15.1 Introduction

Over the last few decades, alternative dispute resolution (ADR) programmes in the European Union (EU) have undergone rapid development.[1] Unfortunately, many of these developments in the use of ADR have raised their own concerns.[2] For example, arbitration has been criticised for favouring repeat appointments of the same persons as arbitrators, while mediation has faced constraints in cross-border enforcement. To compensate for the void left by these incomplete solutions, a hybridisation of dispute resolution processes has been called for.

Construction contracts have been a significant beneficiary of the multi-tier dispute resolution mechanism, essentially because construction disputes involve huge claims and the parties are therefore more inclined to resolve disputes via ADR than they are to shell out for the costs of adjudication proceedings.[3] To illustrate, these contracts contain preconditions to refer

---

[*] The author thanks Professor Christoph Hermann, Professor Eleftheria Neframi and Mr Xueliang Ji for comments on earlier drafts of this article. Thanks also to Mr Urmil Shah for his excellent research assistance. The views expressed herein are the author's own.

[1] Giuseppe De Palo and Mary B Trevor, *Arbitration and Mediation in the Southern Mediterranean Countries* (Kluwer 2007).

[2] Lilian Edwards and Caroline Wilson, 'Redress and Alternative Dispute Resolution in EU Cross-Border E-commerce Transactions' (2007) 21 International Review of Law, Computers & Technology 3; Elisabetta Silvestri, 'Alternative Dispute Resolution in the European Union: An Overview' [2012] Herald of Civil Procedure 166; Michael Bogdan, 'The New EU Regulation on Online Resolution for Consumer Disputes' (2015) 9 Masaryk University Journal of Law & Technology 155; Eva Storskrubb, 'Alternative Dispute Resolution in the EU: Regulatory Challenges' (2016) 24 European Review of Private Law 1.

[3] Elizabeth Kantor and Philip Parrott, '"Gaps" Can End in Tears' (*Herbert Smith Freehills*) <http://hsfnotes.com/arbitration/wp-content/uploads/sites/4/2016/08/GapsCanEndInTears/pdf> accessed 7 September 2020.

conflicts to dispute boards[4] and the success ratio of such boards stands at 97 per cent. The FIDIC Red, Yellow and Silver Books Model, often referred to during formation of construction contracts, advises a tiered dispute resolution mechanism: *Firstly*, the claim is submitted to the engineer for determination. *Secondly*, in case of lingering aggrievement, the case goes on to a dispute adjudication board for a decision. *Thirdly*, in case a party remains unhappy, the case proceeds to amicable settlement. *Lastly*, it goes to arbitration.[5] Even HM Treasury's draft 2012 Standardisation of PF2 Contracts provides for a tiered dispute resolution process. In this case, parties *firstly* refer their dispute to consultation between the authority concerned and the contractor. *Secondly*, on failure, reference is made to expert determination. *Lastly*, if a party remains dissatisfied, adjudication is preferred.[6]

Multi-tier dispute resolution clauses require parties to engage in one or more steps prior to commencing arbitration.[7] A single step may involve mediation or negotiation between representatives of both parties. Sometimes parties may be required to take several steps prior to commencing arbitration.[8] Dispute resolution clauses requiring parties to go through a sequence of different ADR modes to settle or determine their dispute qualify as multi-tier dispute resolution clauses.[9] Parties may favour this framework for several reasons. First, clients appreciate having

---

[4] They are a set of independent professionals who review the facts and make either recommendations or binding decisions.

[5] Leo Grutters and Brian Samuel Barr, *FIDIC Red, Yellow and Silver Books: A Practical Guide to the 2017 Editions* (Sweet & Maxwell 2018).

[6] HM Treasury, 'Standardisation of PF2 Contracts' <https://assets.publishing.service.gov.uk/government/uploads/system/uploads/attachment_data/file/207383/infrastructure_standardisation_of_contracts_051212.pdf> accessed 7 September 2020.

[7] Craig Tevendale, Hannah Ambrose and Vanessa Naish, 'Multi-tier Dispute Resolution Clauses and Arbitration' (2015) 1 Turkish Commercial Law Review 31.

[8] Vasilis FL Pappas and George M Vlaivanos, 'Multiple Tiers, Multiple Risks – Multi-tier Dispute Resolution Clauses' (2018) 12(1) Dispute Resolution International 5.

[9] Michael Pryles, 'Multi-tiered Dispute Resolution Clauses' (2001) 18 Journal of International Arbitration 159; Stefan Krennbauer, 'Enforceability of Multi-tiered Dispute Resolution Clauses in International Business Contracts' (2010) 1 Yearbook on International Arbitration 199; Tevendale, Ambrose and Naish (n 7); George M Vlaivanos and Vasilis FL Pappas, 'Multi-tier Dispute Resolution Clauses as Jurisdictional Conditions Precedent to Arbitration' in J William Rowley, Doak Biship and Gordon Kaiser (eds), *The Guide to Energy Arbitrations* (2nd edn, Law Business Research 2017); Ewelina Kajkowska, *Enforceability of Multi-tiered Dispute Resolution Clauses* (Hart 2017); Katarina Tomic, 'Multi-tiered Dispute Resolution Clauses: Benefits and Drawbacks' [2017] Journal of Legal and Social Studies in South East Europe 360. For an EU perspective, see David JA Cairns, 'Mediating International Commercial Disputes: Differences in US and European Approaches' (2005) 60 Dispute Resolution Journal 3.

a customised framework for the resolution of their disputes which a multi-tier dispute resolution clause ensures. Second, multi-dispute resolution clauses help the parties to plan for potential disputes at the outset of their relationship.[10] Third, such clauses offer the opportunity to resolve conflict prior to resorting to costly and time-consuming arbitration methods. Multi-tier dispute resolution clauses help in the speedy and efficient disposal of disputes without the parties having to resort to relatively expensive modes of adjudication. The only drawback would be that consensual settlement cannot take place without the presence of both parties, unlike arbitration or court proceedings.[11] Fourth, such clauses show both parties' commitment to attempting a resolution of their disputes in a peaceful and non-adversarial manner before engaging in arbitration. Such clauses can accordingly promote amicable dispute resolution and help foster long-term relationships. Not surprisingly then, many multi-tier dispute resolution clauses are seen in construction and other long-term contracts in which the parties would wish to maintain a harmonious relationship over the duration of a project or joint venture.[12]

---

[10] Businesses may segregate their disputes as per the customised dispute resolution clause. For instance, they may prefer not to spend funds on labour disputes by arbitrating them and would therefore try to resolve them first by mediation, thereby adhering to the specific needs of their relationship. For a detailed reference, see James H Carter, 'Issues Arising from Integrated Dispute Resolution Clauses' in Albert Jan van den Berg (ed), *New Horizons in International Commercial Arbitration and Beyond* (ICCA Congress Series No 12, 2005) 446; Klaus Peter Berger, 'Law and Practice of Escalation Clauses' (2006) 22 Arbitration International 1; Didem Kayali, 'Enforceability of Multi-tiered Dispute Resolution Clauses' (2010) 27(6) Journal of International Arbitration 551. See *International Research Corp plc v Lufthansa Systems Asia Pacific Pte Ltd* [2013] 1 SLR 973 (Singapore) [40]. The Singapore Court emphasised that such multi-tier clauses are 'in the public interest as they promote the consensual disposition of any potential disputes' and 'serve a useful commercial purpose in seeking to promote consensus and conciliation in lieu of adversarial dispute resolution', which are values that the legal system should promote.

[11] The advantage of mediation is that it is speedy and cost-efficient. Also, approximately 70 per cent of the disputes are generally resolved. That said, although the preconditions to litigation or arbitration may be speedy and cost-efficient, one might ask, why not just have a negotiation or mediation clause? The reason for a multi-tier dispute resolution clause is that a party cannot be compelled to attend a negotiation or mediation, or, rather, the negotiation or mediation process cannot proceed in the absence of one of the parties. Therefore, the next step (whether litigation or arbitration) can commence and proceed, regardless of whether a party participates in the initial stage of negotiation and mediation, provided only that the non-participating party has been sufficiently notified.

[12] Carlos Esplugues, 'Mediation in the EU after the Transposition of the Directive 2008/52/EC on Mediation in Civil and Commercial Matters' in Carlos Esplugues

However, one reason why parties may be indifferent to including such clauses in their contracts is because parties can always opt for mediation or negotiation irrespective of a pre-existing agreement. Further, how such clauses have been drafted is important and can cause later problems. This is because, depending on how they are worded, preconditions to litigation or arbitration may be held to be mandatory or optional. Nonetheless, on balance, it may still be wise to include a multi-tier dispute resolution clause because it is hard for parties to agree once a dispute has arisen and their reactions when their relationship breaks down cannot be predicted.[13] In practice, commercial contracts can consist of numerous permutations of hybrid resolution including expert advisory mediation,[14] facilitative mediation, wise counsel mediation,[15] evaluative mediation,[16] tradition-based mediation[17] and transformative mediation.[18] The Panel of Recognised International Market Experts in Finance (PRIME Finance), established as a not-for-profit institute to resolve complex

(ed), *Civil and Commercial Mediation in Europe (Volume II: Cross-Border Mediation)* (Intersentia 2014).

[13] William W Park, 'Arbitration in Banking and Finance' (1998) 17 Annual Review of Banking Law 213. See Piergiuseppe Pusceddu, 'PRIME Finance Arbitration-A Lighthouse Safe Harbour in the Mare Magnum of Financial Dispute Resolution' (2014) 3 (1) Indian Journal of Arbitration Law 45. In EU dispute resolution, preconditions to litigation or arbitration must be expressly mentioned in the dispute resolution clause for any resulting settlement agreement to be validly enforced. See *Emirates Trading Agency LLC v Prime Mineral Exports Private Ltd* [2014] EWHC 2104 (Comm), [2015] 1 WLR 1145 (UK); *Medissimo v Logica*, decision no 12-27.004, 20 April 2014 (France); *International Research Corp plc v Lufthansa Systems Asia Pacific Pte Ltd* [2014] 1 SLR 130 (Singapore) where the tribunal declined jurisdiction to arbitrate on the ground that the precondition to negotiate had not been clearly expressed, so it was not possible to ascertain whether such process had been followed. This lack of certainty stems from the fact that the Mediation Directive does not address whether an agreement to mediate as a condition precedent to arbitration is enforceable within the national courts of member states. See F Peter Phillips, 'The European Directive on Commercial Mediation: What It Provides and What It Doesn't' (*Business Conflict Management*) <www.businessconflictmanagement.com/pdf/BCMpress_EUDirective.pdf> accessed 7 September 2020.

[14] Nadja Alexander, 'The Mediation Metamodel: Understanding Practice' (2008) 26 Conflict Resolution Quarterly 97.

[15] Nadja Alexander, 'The Mediation Meta-model: The Realities of Mediation Practice' (2011) 12(6) ADR Bulletin: The Monthly Newsletter on Dispute Resolution 126.

[16] James J Alfini, 'Evaluative versus Facilitative Mediation: A Discussion' (1996) 24 Florida State University Law Review 919.

[17] Alexander (n 14).

[18] Robert A Baruch Bush, 'Handling Workplace Conflict: Why Transformative Mediation' (2001) 18 Hofstra Labor and Employment Law Journal 367.

financial disputes through institutional process, also offers mediation based on the 1980 UNCITRAL Conciliation Rules.[19]

The background to the formation of the Singapore Mediation Convention[20] was a proposal of UNCITRAL Working Group II[21] on having a mechanism for the recognition and enforcement across borders of mediated settlement agreements, along the lines of the New York Convention[22] for the recognition and enforcement of foreign arbitral awards, that could lead to an upsurge in the adoption of mediation. Attempts had been made to facilitate the recognition and enforcement across borders of mediated settlement agreements.[23] What was envisaged was a convention that would enable a uniform regime for the enforcement of settlement agreements in different countries. The Singapore Convention was thus adopted with a view to promoting the widespread international enforceability of mediated settlement agreements.[24] It is generally considered as an instrument to facilitate the use of mediation as an alternative method of resolving international trade disputes and a means of bringing consistency to the international framework of mediation, thereby contributing to the United Nations Sustainable Development Goals (SDGs).[25]

---

[19] Pusceddu (n 13). For a brief overview of PRIME, see 'PRIME Finance' (*Norton Rose Fulbright*) <www.nortonrosefulbright.com/en/knowledge/publications/11ad2a93/prime-finance> accessed 7 September 2020.

[20] 2019 United Nations Convention on International Settlement Agreements Resulting from Mediation.

[21] David C Sawyer, 'Revising the UNCITRAL Arbitration Rules: Seeking Procedural Due Process under the 2010 UNCITRAL Rules for Arbitration' (2011) 1 International Commercial Arbitration Brief 24.

[22] Ahdieh Alipour Herisi and Wendy Trachte-Huber, 'Aftermath of the Singapore Convention: A Comparative Analysis between the Singapore Convention and the New York Convention' (2019) 12 American Journal of Mediation 154.

[23] For a brief overview of the UNCITRAL Working Group work, see Christina Hioureas and Shrutih Tewarie 'A New Legal Framework for the Enforcement of Settlement Agreements Reached through International Mediation: UNCITRAL Concludes Negotiations on Convention and Draft Model Law' (*EJIL: Talk!*, 26 March 2018) <www.ejiltalk.org/a-new-legal-framework/for-the-enforcement-of-settlement-agreements-reached-through-international-mediation-uncitral-concludes-negotiations-on-convention-and-draft-model-law/> accessed 7 September 2020; for a general overview, see Martin Svatos, 'The UNCITRAL Draft Convention on the Enforcement of Mediated Settlement Agreements: The Dawn of Cross-Border Mediation?' <http://forarb.com/wp-content/uploads/2017/04/Georgetown-mediation.pdf> accessed 7 September 2020.

[24] Elisabetta Silvestri, 'The Singapore Convention on Mediated Settlement Agreements: A New String to the Bow of International Mediation' (2019) 2 Access to Justice in Eastern Europe 5.

[25] Michael McIlwrath, 'UNCITRAL to Consider Proposal for Convention on Enforcement of Mediated Settlements' (*Kluwer Arbitration Blog*, 7 July 2014) <http://arbitrationblog.kluwerarbitration.com/2014/07/07/uncitral-to-consider-proposal-for-convention-on-

The peculiarity of directives under EU law is that they oblige member states to frame domestic enactments,[26] but without dictating the means by which the directed outcome is to be attained. Such manner of delegated legislation provides the necessary flexibility to design laws in a manner which suits the social, economic, political, technological and legal circumstances of each member state.[27] The EU has always been committed to encouraging member states to resort to mediation as an alternative and efficient mode of dispute resolution; however, not until 2008 did the member states adhere to the proposal.

This chapter offers an assessment of the EU ongoing effort to establish a basic regulatory framework for mediation that member states will have to transpose into their domestic legal orders. More than twelve years since the implementation of the Mediation Directive,[28] the biggest limitation with the framework has been the enforcement of settlement agreements. Considering the novelty of hybrid dispute resolution, it is essential to understand its viability under the existing legal framework. Addressing the peculiarities of (and implementing an enforcement mechanism for) such agreements is a necessity considering the changing dimensions of global dispute resolution. This chapter considers the compatibility of the decade-old EU mediation framework with such novel mode of dispute resolution and attempts to align both with each other.

15.2 The Genesis of the EU's Minimum Regulatory Standards for Mediation Legislation

The EU effort to establish minimum regulatory standards for mediation legislation reached a first positive outcome in the form of the 2008 Directive on Certain Aspects of Mediation in Civil and Commercial

---

enforcement-of-mediated-settlements/> accessed 7 September 2020. The Singapore Convention addresses the lack of uniformity in the enforcement of mediated settlement agreements in the context of SDG 16, which aims to promote peaceful and inclusive societies for sustainable development, provide access to justice for all, and build effective, accountable and inclusive institutions at all levels.

[26] AJ de Roo and RW Jagtenberg, 'ADR in the European Union: Provisional Assessment of Comparative Research in Progress' in Loïc Cadiet and others (eds), *Médiation et Arbitrage: Alternative Dispute Resolution: Alternative à la Justice ou Justice Alternative? Perspectives Comparatives* (LexisNexis 2005).

[27] Nadja Alexander, *International and Comparative Mediation: Legal Perspectives* (Wolters Kluwer 2009) 75–76.

[28] See Section 15.2.

Matters (the Mediation Directive).²⁹ The Mediation Directive was passed with the clear objective of facilitating efficient dispute resolution and reducing the externalities of time and cost associated with traditional court-based litigation,³⁰ thereby securing the rights of parties in an amicable manner.³¹ There is very little discourse on the intersection between the Directive and hybrid modes of dispute resolution, which gives scope for one to experiment when working out the compatibility of such novel mode of resolution with existing legal norms.

15.2.1 The Objectives of the EU Mediation Directive

The EU passed the Mediation Directive to incentivise the use of mediation for resolving disputes in civil and commercial matters. To determine the exact meaning of the phrase 'civil and commercial matters', reference must be made to EU Regulation 44/2001/144.³² In 2017 the European Parliament passed a resolution (the EU Resolution) to implement the Directive within the EU.³³ However, the Resolution left the manner of implementing the Directive to the individual member states of the EU. For instance, individual states were given the discretion to determine how to enforce settlement agreements.³⁴

The Mediation Directive was instituted under the aegis of Article 81 of the Treaty on the Functioning of the European Union (TFEU) and applies to cross-border and domestic disputes.³⁵ It was intended to provide a framework within the EU for the use of mediation, which it defined as 'a structured process, however named or referred to, whereby two or

---

[29] Directive 2008/52/EC of the European Parliament and of the Council of 21 May 2008 on Certain Aspects of Mediation in Civil and Commercial Matters [2008] OJ L136/3.
[30] Giuseppe De Palo, Ashley Feasley and Flavia Orecchini, 'Quantifying the Cost of Not Using Mediation – A Data Analysis' <www.europarl.europa.eu/document/activities/cont/201105/20110518ATT19592/20110518ATT19592EN.pdf> accessed 7 September 2020.
[31] Ashley Feasley, 'Regulating Mediator Qualifications in the 2008 EU Mediation Directive: The Need for a Supranational Standard' [2011] Journal of Dispute Resolution 333.
[32] Esplugues (n 12).
[33] European Parliament Resolution of 12 September 2017 on the Implementation of Directive 2008/52/EC of the European Parliament and of the Council of 21 May 2008 on Certain Aspects of Mediation in Civil and Commercial Matters (the 'Mediation Directive') (2016/2066(INI)) [2018] OJ C337/2 (European Union).
[34] Esplugues (n 12).
[35] Opinion of the European Economic and Social Committee on the Proposal for a Directive of the European Parliament and of the Council on Certain Aspects of Mediation in Civil and Commercial Matters (COM(2004) 718 final – 2004/0251 (COD)) [2005] OJ C286/1, 5; Treaty on the Functioning of the European Union [2012] OJ C326/47.

more parties to a dispute attempt by themselves, on a voluntary basis, to reach an agreement on the settlement of their dispute with the assistance of a mediator'.[36] The Mediation Directive, which came into force on 13 June 2008,[37] aims 'to facilitate access to alternative dispute resolution and to promote the amicable settlement of disputes by encouraging the use of mediation and by ensuring a balanced relationship between mediation and judicial proceedings'.[38] It represents an intentional effort on a pan-European scale to achieve a degree of homogeny and predictability in the treatment of mediated resolutions of commercial disputes.

15.2.2 The Mediation Directive Impact on Multi-tier Dispute Resolution

The Directive applies universally to all member states except Denmark and, thus, the habitual residences of the parties to mediation should be different because it is applicable in instances of cross-border disputes.[39] Recital 8 of the Directive does not impose any impediment on member states in implementing the provisions in their internal mediation processes. For example, the Directive is applied uniformly for internal and external mediation disputes in Ireland.

While the Directive is strictly applicable to 'civil and commercial matters',[40] it disregards disputes involving third-party obligations including those under customs, revenue and administrative matters of government and public policy[41] disputes arising under employment and personal laws.[42] While Article 5 obligates member states to develop the existing state of mediation, Article 6 encourages the judiciary to refer matters for mediation. Article 9, on the other hand, calls for information about the process to be made available on public platforms to increase transparency.

Since the object of mediation is to settle disputes amicably without reference to courts, Article 1 provides that the process should not be regarded as an alternative to court litigation. Although enforceability of

---

[36] Directive 2008/52/EC (n 29), art 1(1).
[37] Steven Friel and Christian Toms, 'The European Mediation Directive – Legal and Political Support for Alternative Dispute Resolution in Europe' (2011) 2 Bloomberg Law Reports – Alternative Dispute Resolution 3.
[38] ibid.
[39] Denmark is not bound by the Directive, as acknowledged in Directive 2008/52/EC (n 29), recital 30.
[40] ibid, art 1(2).
[41] Friel and Toms (n 37).
[42] ibid.

the settlement agreement is provided by a number of member states through submission to public notary, homologation and forming it as part of a court judgment, Article 6 specifically states that settlement agreements shall be enforceable.[43]

Recital 13 makes clear that the process of mediation is largely unregulated as parties have the autonomy to organise the process in the manner they wish and the judiciary should ascertain opportunities for mediation as far as possible and practicable.[44]

In short, the Mediation Directive standardised several provisions. First, it put forward simple definitions of 'mediation' and 'mediator',[45] which did not raise any problems with the national laws or the different practices of member states. Second, the Directive harmonised minimum guarantees for the enforcement of settlement agreements reached through mediation, basic confidentiality principles that cover the mediator and his or her administrative staff, and the prevention of limitation or prescription period expiration when mediations take place.[46] All EU states have implemented these provisions with only a few minor differences. An important factor in making mediation a success story is its quality. The Directive has addressed this issue through:

- the encouragement of voluntary Codes of Conduct (and other quality control mechanisms);[47]
- the initial and further training of mediators[48] (which some member states have promoted through frameworks of accreditation and registration); and
- the provision of information about mediation, especially to the general public.[49]

---

[43] The Mediation Directive is implemented in the UK by way of part 78 of the Civil Procedure Rules, which states that the written agreement, if any is arrived at by the parties, can be annexed to any application to court for a mediation settlement enforcement order.
[44] Directive 2008/52/EC (n 29), recital 8.
[45] ibid, art 3.
[46] Gordon Blanke, 'The Mediation Directive: What Will It Mean for Us?' (2008) 74 Arbitration 441, 442.
[47] EU member states have adopted different quality control mechanisms as the Mediation Directive provides them a large degree of freedom to ensure the quality of mediation services. Consequently, some member states have adhered to the minimum requirement of simply having a Code of Conduct (namely, the European Code of Conduct for Mediators adopted by Portugal and Cyprus), whereas others have gone ahead to set up mediator accreditation procedures and mediator registries. For a detailed reference, see Feasley (n 31).
[48] Directive 2008/52/EC (n 29), art 4(2).
[49] Esplugues (n 12).

15.3 Are Member States Ready for Hybrid Dispute Resolution? The Challenge of Framework Directives

The EU Resolution of 12 September 2017 deals with the implementation of the Mediation Directive. The European Parliament, while passing the Resolution, was mindful of the fact that, despite the object of Article 1 being to achieve harmony between mediation and judicial process, the process is used on average in less than 1 per cent of litigation matters.[50]

15.3.1 EU Member States' Role in Effective Mediation

Despite the Mediation Directive and the EU Resolution, the use of mediation throughout the EU has remained minimal. While mediation has flourished in countries such as the UK and the Netherlands, basic problems exist in countries such as Estonia and the Czech Republic as a result of national legislation that inadequately differentiates between mediation and conciliation.[51] Nonetheless, the Mediation Directive has

---

[50] Among several factors, the definition of the term 'ADR' has led to considerable confusion within the Irish justice system where there is lack of clarity as to what dispute resolution mechanisms can be included or excluded. Further, the unpredictable enforcement practices among the varied national laws of EU member states constitute a serious hindrance for businesses trading between member states. See generally Brette L Steele, 'Enforcing International Commercial Mediation Agreements as Arbitral Awards' (2006–07) 54 ULCA Law Review 1385; Guiguo Wang, 'Mediation in the Globalised Business Environment' (2009) 17(2) Asia Pacific Law Review 47.

[51] Esplugues (n 12). In the case of the Czech Republic, before enactment of the Mediation Act 2012, there were procedural overlaps between mediation and conciliation processes. Court-referred conciliation was the formal mode of alternative dispute resolution other than arbitration. The amended Code of Civil Proceedings introduced a role for the mediator, but not for the purpose of conducting mediation.

In the case of Estonia, the Mediation Directive was implemented by way of the Conciliation Act 2010. It uses the terms 'mediation' and 'mediator', which are not defined in the Act. The terms 'mediation' and 'conciliation' are synonymously used in the 2010 Act and resorting to mediation is a voluntary process as enshrined under art 11. Enforcement of a mediated settlement agreement depends upon the role of the mediator. Thus, if the agreement is reached through an attorney acting as mediator, it is enforceable if authorised by a county court. If the mediator is neither a notary nor an attorney, the agreement can be enforced only if the relevant court has determined that the mediator's character ensures impartiality and independence, as provided under the act. Estonia's signing of the Singapore Mediation Convention would therefore be of significance as that would consolidate the process of enforcement of mediated settlement agreements and differentiate between the processes of mediation and conciliation.

For a detailed reference, see Giuseppe De Palo and others, '"Rebooting" the Mediation Directive: Assessing the Limited Impact of Its Implementation and

had some impact and currently all EU states have mediation-related regulations. Prior to 2008, Bulgaria and Scotland did not have laws concerning mediation.[52] In other countries, such as Germany and France, the Mediation Directive has helped bring mediation back into favour for academic and practical use.[53]

Because the Mediation Directive provides that its objectives should be addressed 'by any means Member States consider appropriate', leaving the details to national legislators, the EU currently contains a multitude of solutions involving legal provisions and self-regulatory practices.[54] Table 15.1 summarises how the Directive has been implemented in some member states.

15.3.2 Improving the Use of and Access to Hybrid Dispute Resolution by Reference to the Practices of Member States

Hybrid dispute resolution presents a distinct perspective of resolving conflicts in jurisdictions which often confuse adversarial and non-adversarial modes of dispute resolution. The blurred distinction requires clarification. As it is said that the raison d'être of ADR is the principle of freedom and flexibility, it is essential to look at the effectiveness of this novel mechanism of ADR in the EU. There are a number of ways to improve the use of and access to hybrid dispute resolution in the EU by reference to the practices adopted by the member states, including better enforcement of such multi-tier contracts,[55] ensuring

---

Proposing Measures to Increase the Number of Mediations in the EU' <www.europarl.europa.eu/RegData/etudes/etudes/join/2014/493042/IPOL-JURI_ET(2014)493042_EN.pdf> accessed 7 September 2020.

[52] Kevin Wright and others, 'Parental Experiences of Dealing with Disputes in Additional Support Needs in Scotland: Why Are Parents Not Engaging with Mediation?' (2012) 16 International Journal of Inclusive Education 1099.

[53] Esplugues (n 12).

[54] See Directive 2008/52/EC (n 29), recital 25.

[55] As far as Belgium is concerned, BS 22.III.2005 (21 February 2005) inserted art 1725 into the Belgian Judicial Code; it states that every contract can have a mediation clause, through which the parties oblige themselves to turn to mediation first, before resorting to other forms to solve their dispute. However, the law does not oblige the parties to come to a resolution as such an obligation would interfere with a party's right of access to a judge, in line with the voluntary principle. As far as the enforcement mechanism is concerned, there exists no prescribed sanction in the event of breach of the terms of the hybrid dispute resolution, and the absence of such mechanism acts a prime hindrance to the enforcements of a hybrid dispute resolution clause. For a detailed reference, see Benoit Allemeersch, 'Een geactualiseerde inleiding tot de bemiddelingswet' in Raf Van Ransbeeck (ed), *Bemiddeling* (Die Keure 2008) 30.

Table 15.1 *Enforcement of the Mediation Directive by countries*

Country name	Status of implementation of the Mediation Directive
Belgium	Articles 1724 to 1737 of the Belgian Judicial Code complies with the Directive.
France	Pursuant to the Time Limitations Act 2008, French mediation law complies with the Directive.
Germany	The German law on mediation is not fully compliant with the Directive due to lack of provisions on ensuring quality of mediation, enforceability of settlement agreements and refusal of mediator to adduce evidence.
Italy	Articles 185 and 420 of the Italian Code of Civil Procedure, Article 16.D Lgs 2003 n 5 and Legislative Decree no 28/2010 making mediation of certain disputes mandatory comply with the Directive.
Poland	The Polish Code of Civil Procedure 2005 complies with the Directive.
Romania	Romanian Law 192/2006 formulated on the basis of the draft version complies with the Directive.
Slovenia	The Slovenian Mediation in Civil and Commercial Matters Act 2008 complies with the Directive.
Spain	The Spanish Commercial Mediation Bill 2010 models on the lines of the Directive.
United Kingdom	The English law on mediation complies with the Directive.

Source: Elaborated by the author from publicly available law, regulations and sources.

different personnel for both settlement and adjudication proceedings,[56]

Similarly, under Bulgarian national law, there is no sanction for the non-performance of a contractual obligation, such as an obligation to negotiate. It is suggested that there should be a strong mechanism for enforcement to ensure that the parties adhere to their obligations to negotiate or mediate, in order to increase the utility of hybrid dispute resolution agreements.

[56] Under Czech law and practice, a person can act as mediator in settlement proceedings and as arbitrator in relation to the same dispute. However, such practice can lead to a conflict of interest on the part of the person acting as mediator and arbitrator. The practice may erode the foundation principle of arbitration whereby an arbitrator must act impartially despite any confidential information that he or she has received during the settlement proceedings. Segregating such information from one's mind is a highly subjective exercise. Accordingly, ensuring that different persons act as mediator and arbitrator in

written clauses,[57] use of unambiguous language,[58] and application of the rules of a specified institutional body.[59]

Most EU member states suffer from the lack of enforcement of hybrid dispute resolution agreements because of a lack of deterrence for the breach of such contracts. In contrast, for example, under Cypriot law and practice, a party who ignores non-adversarial dispute resolution as agreed under a dispute resolution clause and instead unilaterally commences litigation faces dismissal of its court action on grounds of premature litigation.[60] Such deterrence can go a long way in legitimising the practice of acceptance of hybrid dispute resolution.

Nonetheless, deterrence by means of legislation or court practice is not sufficient. Care still needs to be taken in the drafting of hybrid dispute resolution agreements. The relevant clauses should require the parties to attempt negotiation or mediation as a condition precedent to approaching courts or arbitral tribunals. Such mandatory clauses can be made enforceable only when assertive words such as 'must' or 'shall' are used.[61]

---

a dispute can help maintain the integrity of the arbitral process and thereby the parties' confidence in it.

[57] The *Cour de cassation* of France in *Clinique du Golfe v Le Gall*, 6 May 2003, Semaine Juridique, G, 11 February 2004, II 10021, no 01–01291 (France) ruled that trade practice and model contract clauses will not be sufficient to enable a court to infer the existence of a dispute resolution clause in a contract. Article 1341 of the Italian Civil Code provides that arbitration clauses are ineffective unless specifically approved in writing by the parties to the dispute. For a detailed Italian perspective, see Gino Gorla, 'Standard Conditions and Form Contracts in Italian Law' (1962) 11 American Journal of Comparative Law 1.

[58] The *Cour de cassation* of France in *Placoplâtre v SA Eiffage TP*, 6 February 2007, comments by J Béguin, Semaine Juridique, E&A, 30 August 2007, no 05–17573 (France) ruled that a reference to 'consultation', which on its face would be limited to deciding whether or not to resort to arbitration, could not be equated to 'conciliation', which aims at resolving the dispute altogether.

[59] It is a common practice in agreements to specify the applicability of institutional rules governing a particular mode of dispute settlement.

[60] International Bar Association Litigation Committee, 'Multi-tiered Dispute Resolution Clauses' <www.ibanet.org/Document/Default.aspx?DocumentUid=9C6E21DE-043C-44C9-BE75-94CADECCF470> accessed 7 September 2020.

[61] In ICC Case No 9984, Preliminary Award of 7 June 1999, the word 'shall' obliged both the parties to attempt amicable settlement before approaching the tribunal. Similarly, in ICC Case No 10256, Interim Award of 8 December 2000, the word 'may' implied a discretion to attempt amicable settlement by engaging an expert.

The dispute resolution clause can contain other requirements (for example, fixing the number of mediators and their fees; specifying which party is to bear which costs and in what proportion; or stipulating how many attempts have to be made or how long negotiation or mediation is to be undertaken before adjudication may be commenced). This kind of clarity is generally considered good drafting practice, resulting in better

Imposition of a time limit for the settlement proceedings is also a way forward for the convenience of parties. Imposing a time limit for negotiation or mediation when drafting a clause will ensure that a party does not string out non-adversarial dispute resolution processes to delay having to fulfil a contractual commitment. If peaceful resolution is not possible within the stipulated period, the settlement proceedings can smoothly move into an adjudication phase. Under the Estonian Code of Civil Procedure 2006, pre-trial proceedings have been mandated before parties have recourse to the courts,[62] which may order extrajudicial costs for the breach of any such preliminary stage[63] or impose an obligation on one party to reimburse the opponent's consequential damages as a result of that party having acted in bad faith by prematurely engaging the court.

A one-shot solution to the impeding issue of harmonised enforcement of hybrid and non-hybrid dispute resolution agreements would be EU member states acceding to the Singapore Convention. However, it remains to be seen whether the EU has the competence to become a signatory to the Convention as a regional economic integration organisation (REIO). The prerogative lies with the European Council. But the prognosis for the EU acceding to the Convention is far from optimistic. This is because the EU was the only country opposed to UNCITRAL Working Group II's draft of the Singapore Convention, stating that each country's domestic legislation was better suited to determine that country's enforcement regime.[64]

15.4 Hybrid Dispute Resolution Still in the Making

The framework for mediation in EU law is not only diverse but fragmented, having separate regulations for enforcement of judgments

---

enforcement of settlement agreements. See *Wah (aka Alan Tang) v Grant Thornton International Ltd* [2012] EWHC 3198 (Ch), [2013] 1 All ER (Comm) 1226 (UK) where it was held that, for positive and negative obligations to be enforceable, an agreement must objectively specify the preconditions in detail to enable the court to ascertain whether such conditions have been followed by the parties.

[62] Code of Civil Procedure 2006 (Estonia), s 3(3). See generally Dorcas Quek Anderson, 'Mandatory Mediation: An Oxymoron? Examining the Feasibility of Implementing a Court-Mandated Mediation Program' (2010) 11(2) Cardozo Journal of Conflict Resolution 479, 485–86.

[63] Code of Civil Procedure (Estonia) (n 62), s 144.

[64] Timothy Schnabel, 'The Singapore Convention on Mediation: A Framework for the Cross-Border Recognition and Enforcement of Mediated Settlements' (2019) 19 Pepperdine Dispute Resolution Law Journal 1, 60.

arising out of challenges to mediation. Since the Mediation Directive applies not only within the context of intra-EU mediations, ascertaining the interpretation of enabling parts of the Mediation Directive is essential to determine the exact scope of its application to hybrid dispute resolution. Passing a directive does not automatically result in increased instances of ADR in the EU. Concerted efforts have to be made by the legislature and the judiciary to promote this model, so as to enable the EU to compete with advanced jurisdictions increasingly employing complex modes of dispute resolution for resolving commercial and financial disputes. In this connection, the EU enacted a new regulation in 2012 on jurisdiction and the recognition and enforcement of judgments in civil and commercial matters,[65] which aims at improving mediation practice (see Section 15.4.1). Subsequently, the 2014 Rebooting Study (that is, 'Rebooting the Mediation Directive: Assessing the Limited Impact of Its Implementation and Proposing Measures to Increase the Number of Mediations in the EU') provided a detailed analysis of the impact of the Mediation Directive on various EU member states. It took into consideration an empirical study of 816 experts from all over Europe to ascertain the reasons behind the lack of effectiveness in implementation of the Directive (see Section 15.4.2). More recently, in the latest institutional effort to promote mediation in the EU, the European Parliament adopted a new resolution on building EU capacity in conflict prevention and mediation (see Section 15.4.3).

15.4.1 *Jurisdiction, Recognition and Enforcement of Judgments in Civil and Commercial Matters*

This section focuses on Regulation (EU) No 1215/2012 of the European Parliament and of the Council of 12 December 2012 on Jurisdiction and the Recognition and Enforcement of Judgments in Civil and Commercial Matters[66] (popularly known as Brussels I Recast)[67] and its relationship with the Mediation Directive.

The now repealed Council Regulation (EC) No 44/2001 of 22 December 2000 on Jurisdiction and the Recognition and Enforcement

---

[65] Guido Carducci, 'The New EU Regulation 1215/2012 of 12 December 2012 on Jurisdiction and International Arbitration: With Notes on Parallel Arbitration, Court Proceedings and the EU Commission's Proposal' (2013) 29 Arbitration International 467.
[66] [2012] OJ L351/1. See also ibid.
[67] Peter Hay, 'Notes on the European Union's Brussels-I "Recast" Regulation' (2013) 1 The European Legal Forum 1.

of Judgments in Civil and Commercial Matters (sometimes known as Brussels I)[68] was one of the EU legislator's most important private international law instruments. Besides unifying grounds of jurisdiction, it ensured the efficient recognition and enforcement of judgments rendered in EU member states. More generally, it facilitated judicial co-operation in civil and commercial matters. The Regulation applied to all EU member states (including Denmark). Article 1(2) of the Mediation Directive explicitly states that it applies 'in cross-border disputes, to civil and commercial matters'.[69] This implies that, for the Mediation Directive to be applied harmoniously across borders, the meaning of 'cross-border' and of 'civil and commercial matters' must be clearly established. To determine the exact meaning and scope of the notion of 'civil and commercial matters', reference initially had to be made to Council Regulation (EC) No 44/2001. Following repeal, that regulation has now been subsumed within Regulation (EU) No 1215/2012,[70] which likewise deals with jurisdiction and the recognition and enforcement of judgments in civil and commercial matters Reference also needs to be made to the case law of the European Court of Justice (CJEU).[71]

This relationship with Brussels I Recast has two consequences. Firstly, in countries where mediation is designed to be solely applicable to 'civil and commercial' disputes, a dispute can be compulsorily referred to mediation in cases with a cross-border dimension, whereas it would remain outside the scope of compulsory mediation in purely domestic cases.[72] For example, the referral of disputes to mediation is considered as belonging to public law. This may cause some problems even in cases of cross-border disputes when no specific adaptation has been envisaged by a national legislator. Secondly, matters outside the notion of 'civil and commercial matters' as developed by the CJEU in connection with Council Regulation (EC) No 44/2001 may be included in the notion of 'civil and commercial matters' by national law.[73] The expression 'civil and commercial matters' is not defined within the Mediation Directive itself. However, a perusal of the entire Mediation Directive gives an impression that it was not intended

---

[68] [2002] OJ L12/1.
[69] Directive 2008/52/EC (n 29), art 1(2).
[70] Hay (n 67).
[71] Esplugues (n 12).
[72] ibid.
[73] I Queirolo, L Carpaneto and S Dominelli, 'Italy' in Carlos Esplugues, José Luis Iglesias Buhigues and Guillermo Palao Moreno (eds), *Civil and Commercial Mediation in Europe (Volume I: National Mediation Rules and Procedures)* (Intersentia 2012) 259.

to apply internally within member states. Thus, for example, matters between two French companies or between two German companies would be unaffected by the Mediation Directive.[74]

It is also important to appreciate the relationship between the Mediation Directive and the Consumer ADR Directive.[75] Due to Article 114(3) of the TFEU, consumer protection concerns (such as health, safety and environmental protection) have primacy and enjoy a higher level of protection taking into account approximation of measures under Article 114(1). By contrast, since civil and commercial matters will not necessarily fall within the category of health, safety, environmental and consumer protection, legislation made pursuant to the Mediation Directive may not have primacy over legislation made under the Consumer ADR Directive. Accordingly, by virtue of Article 81 of the TFEU, it would not be possible for there to be a uniform enforcement mechanism of mediation among member states. The extent of enforcement would depend (among other matters) on how the Consumer ADR Directive has been implemented in a member state. In effect, the Consumer ADR Directive goes a step further than the Mediation Directive as a result of Article 114 of the TFEU.[76]

15.4.2 The 2014 Rebooting Study

In 2013 the EU Parliament commissioned a study examining the implementation of the Mediation Directive.[77] The successful study proposal chosen by the EU Parliament (called the 'Rebooting Study') was presented in Brussels and published in 2014. The Rebooting Study was divided into

---

[74] See Carlos Esplugues, 'Access to Justice or Access to States Courts' Justice in Europe? The Directive 2008/52/EC on Civil and Commercial Mediation' (2013) 38 Revista de Processo (RePro) 304.
  Although, in an academic sense, the Mediation Directive strictly applies only to cross-border disputes, it is expected to have an impact on disputes within a member state, disputes between EU parties and non-EU parties, and disputes involving foreign elements. This is because many member states are unlikely to distinguish cross-border disputes from other disputes. See Friel and Toms (n 37).
[75] Directive 2013/11/EU of the European Parliament and of the Council of 21 May 2013 on Alternative Dispute Resolution for Consumer Disputes and Amending Regulation (EC) No 2006/2004 and Directive 2009/22/EC [2013] OJ L165/53; Naomi Creutzfeldt, 'Implementation of the Consumer ADR Directive' (2016) 5(4) Journal of European Consumer and Market Law 169.
[76] 'Directive 2013/11/EU (Directive on Consumer ADR) – Issues Emerging from the Meetings of the ADR Expert Group' <http://ec.europa.eu/transparency/regexpert/index.cfm?do=groupDetail.groupDetailDoc&id=18896&no=3> accessed 7 September 2020.
[77] De Palo and others (n 51).

four parts dealing respectively with time and cost,[78] effectiveness of pro-mediation features,[79] and legislative[80] and non-legislative[81] measures to improve the existing scenario of mediation in the EU. The third part of the study was the most significant as respondents were asked to suggest specific legislative measures which would have the effect of increasing access to mediation. The responses revealed that most existing measures were ineffective and the regulatory features in member states were not the decisive factors in the lack of utilisation of mediation in the EU.

The Rebooting Study presented suggestions for resolving the perceived mischief.[82] Proposals included the following:

1. **Voluntariness vs mandatory** – There was general agreement that the lack of a compulsory mediation regime was the primary factor hindering

[78] In part I 'Time & Cost Savings Study', the questions dealt with the estimated number of mediations conducted annually in member states; the existence of a balanced relationship between mediation and judicial proceedings; the average monetary value of mediation claims; the average cost incurred by the parties in conducting mediations; and the average time to complete a mediation. The data indicated that, if all cases in the EU first went to mediation, there would be successful outcomes in 50 per cent of them; an average of 240 days would be saved; and in successful mediations there would be time savings of up to 354 days. The results suggested that there would be monetary savings of around EUR 30–40 billion at a 50 per cent success rate. However, the majority of member states reported fewer than 500 cases per year (with the exception of the UK, the Netherlands and Denmark, which collectively reported more than 10,000 cases annually, and Italy, which registered 200,000 cases yearly). The average duration of a mediation was 43 days compared to 566 days for litigation. Calculated as per the World Bank's Ease of Doing Business 2014 Report, the cost of a mediation (EUR 3,371) would be relatively lower than that of courts (EUR 9,179).

[79] In part II 'Effectiveness of Pro-mediation Features', the Rebooting Study deals with features such as extent of confidentiality, court referral mediations, mediator accreditation system, enforcement of settlement agreements, economic incentives for mediation, mandate for preliminary informational sessions, mandatory recourse to mediation, existence of online mediation, and duty of attorneys to inform clients about existence of mediation.

[80] In part III 'Single Most Effective Legislative Measure', the Rebooting Study deals with the single most effective legislative measure which can drastically increase the effectiveness and utilisation of mediations in the EU.

[81] In part IV 'Non-legislative Measures', the Rebooting Study's respondents were asked to rate whether the effectiveness of mediations can be increased by applying non-legislative measures and the majority response indicated the contrary. Some non-legislative measures deliberated were pertaining to mediation advocacy education, implementing pilot projects for greater access to civil and commercial mediations, universal mediator certification and accreditation, appointment of mediation champions or ambassadors and having 'settlement week' programmes to increase public knowledge of mediation, creation of an EU ADR agency to promote mediation, and incentives for professional mediators.

[82] De Palo and others (n 51), s 3.2.4.

the growth of mediation. There was disagreement on the types of disputes which should go to mediation. However, there was overall consensus that the judiciary should more frequently refer disputes to mediation.
2. **Lack of knowledge and promotion** – Most lay persons are unaware of the benefits of mediation as a tool of ADR. The issue can be solved by an aggressive and largely uniform publicity campaign to promote mediation, with funding from the EU as well as member states.
3. **Incentives and sanctions** – Deterrent sanctions can enhance the attractiveness of mediation. Incentives can be given to encourage parties using the mechanism to arrive at meaningful solutions, rather than simply using mediation in bad faith as a delaying tactic.
4. **Uniformity in enforcement** – Uniform enforcement of mediated settlement agreements among member states, especially within the international business sector, can mitigate forum shopping practices. On the contrary using domestic courts or international arbitrations increases the likelihood of treaty shopping (as parties will choose the best forum depending on the enforcement conditions). One of the proposals in this regard was regulation of mediation to handle cross-border referrals to help promote mediation and harmonise the framework of cross-border cases and settlement agreements.
5. **Education on mediation** – Several experts emphasised university-level programmes aimed towards more areas of study than just law, and the introduction of mediation education within secondary schools. It was also suggested that judicial systems should have mediation components during the training of judges.
6. **Regulation of mediation** – It was suggested to establish a regulatory body to ensure uniform mediation examination, accreditation and testing standards.
7. **Governmental support** – Experts suggested that measures such as complex cultural and governmental differences must be worked on and that the EU must take the lead in implementing the Mediation Directive.

The EU Rebooting Study concluded with two important measures to increase access to mediation and achieve the objectives of the Directive.[83] Firstly, opt-out mandatory mediation should be introduced on a pilot basis and, secondly, the use of a Balanced Relationship Target Number

---

[83] ibid.

(BRTN) should be initiated, whereby member states would be obligated to log a minimum number of mediations annually to achieve the desired balance between mediation and court litigation.

It is often contended that, despite the compelling observations of the 2014 Rebooting Study, the BRTN proposal could not be effected, and there are fewer evidences for meaningful assessment as member states were given liberty to implement the Directive until 2011; however, it is also argued by counterparties that the Directive has still been significantly implemented by certain member states, affirming the pro-mediation spirit.

15.4.3 The 2019 European Parliament Resolution

In 2019, the European Parliament adopted a new resolution on building EU capacity in conflict prevention and mediation, which is the latest institutional attempt to accelerate use of mediation within the EU.[84] The resolution shows the European Parliament's commitment to increasing the use of mediation for resolving civil and commercial disputes within the EU. In this respect, the European Parliament resolution recognises the positive steps that members have taken since the enactment of the Mediation Directive and recommends steps that members can take in the future to enhance the adoption of mediation. More precisely, the European Parliament resolution recommends five key initiatives: (1) increasing the accessibility of mediation through informative and participatory campaigns and co-operation between mediation professionals in implementing best practices; (ii) developing uniform quality standards to facilitate better mediation services; (3) creating national registers of mediation proceedings; (4) undertaking research to understand the obstacles to accessibility of foreign mediation agreements and develop promotion activities; and (5) extending mediation into other civil and administrative areas not already covered in the Directive.

The resolution is a modest contribution as it is non-binding and remains merely suggestive of a political desire to act in a given area.[85] In fact, the resolutions are instruments that enable European institutions to suggest guidelines for co-ordinating national legislations or administrative practices in a non-binding manner. The member states have no legal obligation to follow such resolutions.

---

[84] European Parliament Resolution of 12 March 2019 on Building EU Capacity on Conflict Prevention and Mediation (2018/2159(INI)) (European Union).

[85] M Kengyel, V Harsági and Z Nemessányi, 'Hungary' in Esplugues, Buhigues and Moreno (n 73) 232.

15.5 Conclusion

The roots of the Directive lie in the members states' concerns pertaining to litigation costs, pendency of cases and enforcement issues arising out of cross-border dispute resolution. Except in the case of two member states, use of mediation pursuant to the Directive has largely been voluntary, which has acted as a major impediment to its accessibility and promotion.

Incentivising the use of multi-tier dispute resolution in the EU raises challenges. The Mediation Directive has been promulgated to encourage greater acceptance of mediation, but field responses have varied. Some general suggestions are made here. Firstly, parties should be more actively encouraged to attempt mediation, with the state perhaps playing a stronger role. Secondly, improvement of the training and selection processes for qualified mediators needs to continue. Mediation requires special skill sets that are not commonly used in other dispute resolution proceedings. Hybrid processes set an even higher bar on the neutral because of the possibility of changing hats from mediator to arbitrator in the course of seeking to resolve a dispute. Thirdly, the uncertainty of cross-border enforcement of mediated settlement agreements has always deterred potential users from committing to the inclusion of a hybrid dispute resolution clause in their commercial agreements. Accession by the EU to the Singapore Convention would enable counsel to be more at ease when recommending mediations to their clients.

16

Multi-tier Dispute Resolution in Russia

ALEXANDER MOLOTNIKOV

16.1 Introduction

Multi-tier dispute resolution clauses[1] are provisions in contracts that provide for distinct stages, involving separate procedures, for dealing with and seeking to resolve disputes. Such clauses typically provide for certain steps to be taken and efforts to be made by the parties prior to commencing arbitration or litigation. These initial steps are aimed at reaching an amicable settlement of disputes in order to avoid arbitration or litigation. Multi-tier dispute resolution is used in Russian practice. But it must be recognised that Russian procedural legislation in support of alternative dispute resolution (ADR) is still in the making. The rules of law governing pre-trial settlement of disputes have undergone many changes recently. Nonetheless, the legislature has been undecided for some time on the precise categories of dispute in respect of which a mandatory claim procedure or protocol should be established. Lawmakers have therefore revised the law in a disorderly fashion and that has generated intense criticism from the professional community. Given the present confused situation, it is hoped that (and no one would be surprised if) a further set of amendments to procedural legislation will be made in the near future. The main aim of pre-trial dispute regulation in Russia is to reduce the number of cases submitted to the courts. However, the backlog of cases before the courts continues to be as it was before the implementation of the most recent legislative amendments and the pre-trial settlement of disputes still remains mostly formal insofar as procedure is concerned (whether entered into as a result of mandatory requirements under the law or settled out of court by the parties). In the minds of Russian lawyers, pre-trial dispute resolution procedures are merely

---

[1] For dispute resolution in Russia generally, see Dimitri Dedov and Alexander Molotnikov (eds), *Dispute Resolution in Russia: The Essentials* (Statut 2019).

a necessary prerequisite to filing a claim in court and not to be regarded as a serious means of resolving a legal problem or conflict.

On the whole, there are no specific provisions in Russian law regulating pre-trial dispute resolution procedures. While the 2002 Commercial Procedure Code[2] contains some detailed rules, the 2002 Civil Procedure Code[3] provides only general provisions according to which pre-trial dispute resolution procedures should be adhered to in accordance with the law or the terms of a contract. There are three main components to be found in pre-trial dispute resolution procedures in existing legislative regulation and business practice: (1) pre-trial complaint, (2) mediation and (3) negotiations. Unfortunately, there is no diversity of means for pre-trial dispute resolution in Russia in comparison to (say) France. On the other hand, even the use of existing modes causes many practical problems.

This chapter will start with an overview of the Russian judicial system. It will then review the institutions already mentioned and analyse modern judicial practice in their application. It will conclude with practical recommendations for the improvement of pre-trial dispute resolution in Russia.

16.2 Overview of the Russian Judicial System

Under Article 4 of the 1996 Law on the Judicial System,[4] there are federal courts and courts of the constituent entities of the Russian Federation. The federal courts include the Constitutional Court and the Supreme Court. The latter heads the system of courts of general jurisdiction and arbitration courts. Courts of general jurisdiction and *arbitrazh* courts[5] form two relatively autonomous sub-systems. The highest judicial body of these courts is the Supreme Court. The courts of the constituent entities of the Russian Federation include constitutional (statutory) courts and justices of the peace (*mirovoy sudya*) who are judges of general jurisdiction. The proceedings in courts of general jurisdiction and the

---

[2] Commercial Procedure Code of Russian Federation, 'Rossiyskaya gazeta', No 137, 27 July 2002.
[3] Civil Procedure Code of Russian Federation, 'Rossiyskaya gazeta', No 220, 20 November 2002.
[4] Law on the Judicial System (No 1-FKZ of 31 December 1996), 'Rossiyskaya gazeta', No 3, 6 January 1997.
[5] The expression *arbitrazh* should not be confused with 'arbitration' in the sense of a mode of alternative dispute resolution. The *arbitrazh* courts in Russia are in fact commercial courts.

commercial courts are similar. Thus, it suffices to focus here on proceedings in the commercial courts.

The *arbitrazh* court process consists of six stages: (1) proceedings in the commercial court of first instance, (2) proceedings before the court of appeal, (3) proceedings before the court of cassation, (4) proceedings in the order of supervision, (5) revision on newly discovered circumstances in relation to judicial acts that have entered into force and (6) execution of judicial acts. The process of commencing proceedings in commercial courts of first instance is provided in chapter 13 of the 2002 Commercial Procedure Code. It contains information about the content of the statement of claim and the submission of a claim. The statement of claim may be submitted in written or electronic form. Electronic form means filing necessary documents via the online service of the commercial courts (*Moi Arbitr* at my.arbitr.ru). Part 2 of Article 125 of the Commercial Procedure Code sets out the requirements for a statement of claim. Article 126 prescribes the documents to be submitted with that pleading. In accordance with Article 127, after submission of the statement of claim, the judge decides whether to accept the claim within five days of the date of submission. If the statement of claim meets all statutory requirements, the claim is accepted and the judge passes a ruling to mark the commencement of proceedings. But, if the requirements are not met, the judge may not accept the statement of claim. Depending on the requirements which a claimant has failed to meet, the judge may (1) decline the statement of claim, (2) leave the statement of claim 'without action' or (3) return the statement of claim. At the commencement of proceedings, the court designates a special date when preparations for trial will be discussed with the judge. This date is an important stage. Under part 1 of Article 133 of the Commercial Procedure Code, the tasks involved in preparing a case for trial are (1) determining (a) the nature of the disputed legal relationship and the legislation to be applied and (b) the circumstances that are important for a proper consideration of the case, (2) resolving the issues relating to the composition of persons involved in the case and other participants in the trial process, (3) rendering assistance to the persons participating in the case insofar as presenting the necessary evidence is concerned, and (4) attempting to reconcile the parties. Only after the judge is satisfied that a case is ready for trial will he or she pass a ruling appointing the case for trial.

Following a trial on the merits, the court of first instance delivers its judgment in the name of the Russian Federation. After that parties may file an appeal and apply for cassation. Cassation is divided into two steps.

The first cassation takes place in the commercial circuit courts, while the second cassation is before the Supreme Court Chamber for Commercial Disputes. The difference between appeal and cassation is that the appeal court re-examines the merits of the case while the commercial circuit court is empowered to remit a case for a new trial before the court of first instance or appeal. The Commercial Court of Appeal allows a new appeal on the basis of the evidence available at first instance and additional evidence adduced on appeal.

16.3 Multi-tier Dispute Resolution and the Courts

The 2002 Civil Procedure Code sets out all the relevant regulations governing civil proceedings before courts of general jurisdiction, including processes of multi-tier dispute resolution. Under paragraph 7 of Article 132, a party should attach, to the statement of claim, proof confirming the implementation of pre-trial protocols for resolving a dispute, where such protocols are compulsory under federal law or the terms of a contract. The Civil Procedure Code does not itself identify any situations when pre-trial protocols are mandatory. But special rules can be found in other laws. For example, under Article 797 of the 2002 Civil Code, if a case concerns the carriage of goods, the claimant consignor can appeal to the court only after the respondent carrier has completely or partially refused to satisfy the claim or the plaintiff does not receive a response to a demand within thirty days. If the claimant (1) fails to observe mandatory pre-trial protocols for settling a dispute or (2) does not submit documents evidencing compliance with such protocols, the court will return the statement of claim (paragraph 1 of part 1 of Article 135 of the Civil Procedure Code) or, if the statement of claim was accepted for production, will leave it without consideration (paragraph 2 of Article 222 of the Civil Procedure Code).

Multi-tier dispute resolution clauses are indirectly enforced by the commercial courts through similar rules as those just mentioned. Part 5 of Article 4 of the Commercial Procedure Code provides that disputes may be submitted to the arbitration court only after the parties have taken the requisite steps for pre-trial settlement within a period of thirty days from the date when a demand was sent. Unfortunately, in practice, a waiting period of thirty days without the possibility of going to court entails a significant risk that a counterparty acting in bad faith will violate the rights of a claimant acting in good faith. In particular, within thirty days, an unscrupulous party may take actions aimed at creating obstacles to further legal proceedings (including the disposal of assets and going into voluntary liquidation or bankruptcy). At the same time, the bona fide party will be deprived of the possibility of applying for preliminary interim measures, as such applications are tied to the mandatory pre-trial procedure for settling disputes. To counteract this possibility, it should be sufficient to establish a moratorium of a mere seven or ten days, since it should be obvious within that period whether a bona fide debtor intends to satisfy the claimant's demands or has reasonably arguable grounds for not doing so. If the pre-trial procedure for settling a dispute is not stipulated by law, the parties can voluntarily establish such a regime by incorporating the same as a term of their contract. By such term, they would prescribe a pre-trial dispute resolution (including a multi-tier process) that must be initiated before process is brought before the court. In such clause, the parties can themselves identify special conditions, such as (for instance) fixing the time to answer a demand and the methods for notifying a claim. A dispute can then be referred for resolution by the commercial court only after such voluntarily agreed procedures have been carried out. There are accordingly two types of disputes as matter of general jurisdiction as well as regards the jurisdiction of the commercial courts: (1) disputes which should be negotiated on a mandatory basis before they can be referred to state courts, despite the absence of any agreement on this by the parties, and (2) disputes which are mandatory to negotiate by agreement of the parties. It is important to note that the parties cannot exclude a claim procedure through an agreement (contract), but they have the right to change the time limit and the procedure for pre-trial settlement of a dispute. Thus, the thirty-day period can be reduced or increased by contract.

An important requirement concerning court pre-trial dispute resolution protocols is that they require that the parties submit evidence of compliance with them and the judicial authorities are obliged to consider the evidence so adduced. Compliance must be documented on the basis of Articles 125 and 126 of the Commercial Procedure Code. Save in limited cases, there is no official list identifying the documents that must be adduced by an applicant to the arbitration court in order to prove that a pre-trial protocol for settling a case has been observed. Therefore, in practice there will be many questions about whether the documents presented are sufficient and whether a party has acted reasonably and in good faith. Disputes over the answers to such questions may affect a party's right to judicial protection. Moreover, the absence of evidence of compliance or the insufficiency thereof will automatically lead to the impossibility of considering the case on the merits. Note that the law equates evidence of a claimant's compliance with pre-trial settlement protocols with the *sending* of a notice of the underlying claim to the respondent. The fact that the respondent did not actually receive notice of the claim would therefore not be a basis for treating the pre-trial protocol as having been disregarded.

16.4   General Requirements for Regulated and Non-regulated Clauses

The absence of standards for proofs of compliance with mandatory pre-trial procedure in the Commercial Procedure Code has caused difficulties in practice. As a general rule, the following steps should suffice to confirm compliance with pre-trial protocols:

(1) Sending notice of a claim (including potential related actions which might be brought) by mail (Russian Post) to the respondent's usual address at least thirty days before the envisaged filing date;
(2) Attaching a copy of the notice sent to the respondent to the claim filed before the court together with:
   (a) documents confirming dispatch of the notice,
   (b) a checklist,
   (c) receipt of payment and
   (d) documents (for example, a delivery receipt) confirming delivery of the notice of claim to the respondent.[6]

The general procedure for filing a claim must comply with the requirements of part 1 of Article 165 of the 1996 Civil Code (dealing with legally significant messages) taking into account the clarifications in clauses 63 to 67 of the Resolution of the Plenum of the Supreme Court No 25 dated 23 June 2015 (dealing with the application by the courts of certain provisions of section I of part I of the Civil Code).[7] A contract may

---

[6] 'Mandatory Claim Dispute Resolution Procedure (by Goltsblat BLP)' (*SPS 'Konsul'tantPlyus'* – *Consultant Plus Reference Legal System*). It does not follow from the Commercial Procedure Code that the delivery documents of the notice of claim must be attached without fail, but, in the absence of an established judicial practice on this matter, it is advisable to do so.
[7] Resolution of the Plenum of the Supreme Court of the Russian Federation, No 25, 23 June 2015, 'On the Application by the Courts of Certain Provisions of Section I of Part One of the Civil Code of the Russian Federation', 'Rossiyskaya gazeta', No 140, 30 June 2015.

provide that legally significant messages (including claim notices) must be sent by one party to the other at a specified address or by a particular method. In such cases, sending the message to another address or by a different method will not be considered appropriate even if the person who sent the message did not know and had no reason to know that the address indicated in the contract was not true. It is thus advisable to fix the terms of pre-trial settlement procedures with some precision in a contract. In particular, parties should pay attention to the following matters when agreeing a multi-tier arbitration clause. The parties should state what a notice of claim is supposed to contain. The parties should set out how a notice of a claim is to be sent and how a response to the notice is to be made and what the response should contain. They should identify any specific addresses to which documents should be sent and the legally relevant items that must accompany a claim or response. Finally, the parties should fix deadlines for all relevant acts.

16.5 Rules of Setting Out Multi-tier Resolution Clauses for Non-regulated Disputes

There are two ways of including a multi-tier dispute resolution clause in a contract. The first is simple and most commonly used. The parties simply state that any dispute arising out of their contract is to be resolved through negotiation. The second is to set out a detailed dispute resolution procedure. In most cases, the simple courts will treat the simple clause as non-mandatory. To be regarded by the courts as mandatory or enforceable, a clause must normally be of the second type. According to the current practice of the courts of general jurisdiction, such a clause should at least set out a claim procedure and the time allowed for responding to a notice of claim.

Several cases illustrate the futility of including the first type of clause in a contract. For example, the *arbitrazh* court of the Udmurtskaya Region in a ruling of 3 May 2017[8] referred to a general clause whereby the parties agreed to 'resolve their disputes or differences arising from the contract through negotiations'[9] but failed to provide any evidence of adherence to such clause by the parties. In a ruling of 26 January 2017,[10] the *arbitrazh* court of the Penzinskaya Region accepted the fact that accounts, acts,

---

[8] Ruling of *arbitrazh* court of Udmurtskaya region, 3 May 2017, Case No A71-1815/2017.
[9] ibid.
[10] Ruling of *arbitrazh* court of Penzinskaya region, 26 January 2017, Case No A49-15015/2016.

invoices, protocols and references were sent to the respondent as evidence of compliance with pre-trial settlement protocols even though the same provision as in the foregoing case was included in the contract.[11] In a ruling of the 10th *arbitrazh* Court of Appeal dated 27 March 2018,[12] the parties had agreed an even vaguer clause to the effect that they would resolve their disputes through negotiations *in a spirit of mutual respect and cooperation.*[13]

Such clauses are routinely held to be unenforceable with the sole aim of confirming the parties' mutual understanding but not giving rise to any possibility of judicial protection in case of non-compliance. As confirmed by court practice, in order to have an enforceable clause, parties need to agree the precise details of their bespoke pre-trial settlement protocol. Thus, according to a ruling of the Supreme Arbitration Court dated 13 November 2009,[14] the mandatory elements of an agreed pre-trial settlement procedure are the timing of claims and the detailed procedure for their consideration.[15] As the *arbitrazh* court of the Penzinskaya Region stated in a ruling dated 16 November 2016,[16] the pre-trial procedure for settling a dispute implies: (1) a special written conciliation procedure, (2) a procedure for settling a dispute by the disputants themselves, (3) details as to the sending of an appropriate settlement proposal and (4) details as to sending a response to the settlement proposal. A distinctive feature of the pre-trial settlement of a dispute is that one party should send the other party a written document. Without such action, the requirement of a pre-trial procedure would not be met.[17]

Courts sometimes ignore a mandatory pre-trial procedure for settling a dispute. In its ruling of 23 July 2015,[18] the Russian Supreme Court stated that, according to paragraph 8 of part 2 of Article 125, part 7 of Article 126 and paragraph 2 of part 1 of Article 148 of the Commercial Procedure Code, pre-trial arbitration is a method that allows the restoration of violated rights and legitimate interests voluntarily within a short space of time without the additional expense of having to pay state duty.

---

[11] ibid.
[12] Ruling of 10th *arbitrazh* Court of Appeal, 27 March 2018, Ruling No 10АП-2025/2018, Case No A41-87102/17.
[13] ibid.
[14] Ruling of Supreme Arbitration Court, 13 November 2009, Ruling No SAC-14616/09.
[15] ibid.
[16] Ruling of *arbitrazh* court of Penzinskaya region, 16 November 2016, Case No A49-9323/2016.
[17] ibid.
[18] Ruling of Russian Supreme Court, 23 July 2015, Case No A55-12366/2012.

Such procedure serves as an additional protection of rights.[19] At other times, overly complicated pre-trial dispute resolution clauses may abuse the rights of a counterparty. For example, a complex claim procedure can be a negotiating trap used by one party to delay a trial. There may be different ways in which damages and a debt are advanced in a claim and the other party may take a lengthy period of time to respond to such claims. As a result, the party owing money or liable for compensation can delay payment, at a cost of that party having to bear only relatively little interest.

16.6 Mediation Procedure

Mediation can be used as one stage of a multi-tier dispute resolution procedure. Mediation is primarily regulated by the Federal Law on Alternative Procedure for Dispute Resolution with Participation of a Mediator 2010 (the Mediation Law).[20] Under part 1 of Article 4 of such law, if the parties have agreed to use mediation and have chosen not to refer the dispute to a court within the agreed period for mediation, the court will recognise the binding nature of such obligation until the same is fulfilled. According to Articles 3 and 7 of the Mediation Law, mediation is voluntary, so the parties cannot be forced to resort to mediation, in contrast to where there has been a violation of the mandatory pre-trial settlement protocol for a dispute.[21]

There are two types of written mediation agreements under the Mediation Law: (1) an agreement to resort to mediation pursuant to Article 7, and (2) an agreement to implement mediation. The first is a general framework agreement. If such clause is included in a contract, it means that parties have agreed to use mediation to resolve their dispute. No details are stated in such a clause. The agreement to implement mediation is more detailed and can include the provisions as to (1) the subject matter of the dispute, (2) the mediator, (3) the mediation procedure, (4) the allocation of mediation-related costs and (5) the time

---

[19] ibid. In the case itself, the Supreme Court did not find an intention on the defendant's part voluntarily and promptly to resolve the dispute out of court. The party instead filed a petition to leave the statement of claim 'without action' a year and a half after the institution of the action. The aim of such petition was to delay the resolving of the dispute and encroach on the claimant's legitimate rights.

[20] Federal Law on Alternative Procedure for Dispute Resolution with Participation of a Mediator (Mediation Procedure) (Federal Law No 193-FZ dated 27 July 2010), 'Rossiyskaya gazeta', No 168, 30 July 2010.

[21] See Commercial Procedure Code (n 2), arts 148 pts 1–2.

frame for mediation. Further, there are two forms of mediation: pre-judicial mediation and judicial mediation. Pre-judicial mediation can be of two types: (1) mediation as prescribed by law for certain categories of disputes and which the parties are obliged to undertake prior to going to court and (2) mediation as agreed by the parties and imposing an obligation to attempt mediation before going to court. Judicial mediation is applied during a litigation process and takes place on the recommendation of the court after the parties have commenced proceedings there.

Judicial proceedings play a significant role in the reconciliation of the parties before the start of the trial. The Civil Procedure Code obliges a judge to invite parties to settle their dispute at the stage of preparing a case for trial. One of the goals of the stage of preparation for trial is reconciliation of the parties.[22] The judge takes steps to facilitate the parties entering into a settlement agreement. The parties may settle their dispute at any stage of the preparation for trial stage. Any settlement agreement reached by the parties is approved by the judge if the provisions of the settlement agreement do not contradict the law and do not violate the rights of other persons.[23] The judge's approval makes such agreement binding on the parties. According to part 1 of Article 169 of the Civil Procedure Code, the court may postpone the proceedings for a period not exceeding sixty days at the request of both parties if they decide to undertake mediation. Similar provisions are contained in the Commercial Procedure Code. So, as already stated, one of the tasks of preparing a case for a trial is reconciliation of the parties.[24] The judge's task is to clarify to the parties their right to submit the dispute to the *arbitrazh* court and the right to seek the assistance of the mediator. The judge must also ensure that the parties understand the consequences of embarking upon a mediation. Russian courts usually indicate to the parties that they have a right to refer a dispute to mediation. Nonetheless, despite the existence of the Mediation Law, mediation is not actually popular in Russia. According to a report of the Supreme Court of Russia, the low popularity is due to (1) a lack of qualified mediators so that the practice of mediation is not widespread, (2) a lack of awareness of mediation as a result of minimal (if any) publicity and educational work by government offices, (3) the high cost of professional mediation services and (4) the unwillingness of the parties' legal

---

[22] Civil Procedure Code (n 3), art 148 para 5.
[23] ibid, art 39 pt 2.
[24] Commercial Procedure Code (n 2), art 133 pt 1.

representatives to advise or consider mediation for fear that they would receive less in fees as a result of the settlement of a dispute.

16.7 Negotiation as Part of a Multi-tier Dispute Resolution Clause

As mentioned, clauses such as 'the parties will resolve all disputes through negotiations' are widespread in Russian contracts. Negotiations are in fact a real alternative to pursuing a court claim procedure and the presence of a term on negotiation in the contract opens up the possibility of choosing negotiation as an obligatory means for settling disputes. In comparison to a rigid dispute resolution protocol, negotiation has a self-evident advantage. It is much faster than pre-trial procedures of sending a claim and awaiting an answer. However, problems can arise (including the necessity of documenting negotiations). This means that counterparties often refuse to negotiate.

The proper recording of negotiations is important. This issue is connected with the confirmation of compliance by a party with pre-trial protocols for settling a dispute in court. Negotiations are conducted either orally in person or by different means of communication (correspondence, email, video, etc). Oral negotiations usually end up with the preparation of written documents (for instance, minutes of meetings). But when negotiations are held by different means of communications, the parties should take care about other types of evidence. In this case audio and video recordings and electronic documents can also confirm the fact of negotiation. There is no uniformity in Russian court practice concerning the issue of whether email letters are confirmation of compliance with a claim resolution protocol. For example, the *arbitrazh* court of the Central District in a Ruling dated 25 December 2015[25] acknowledged that an exchange of letters through electronic communication was evidence of negotiations having taken place between the parties.[26] In contrast, the *arbitrazh* court of the Far Eastern District in a ruling dated 22 January 2016[27] deemed the exchange of letters by emails as evidence of non-compliance with a dispute resolution protocol.[28]

---

[25] Ruling of *arbitrazh* court of Central district, 25 December 2015, Case No A35-11066/2014.
[26] ibid.
[27] Ruling of *arbitrazh* court of Far Eastern district, 22 January 2016, Case No A73-6268/2015.
[28] ibid.

Negotiations require the participation of all parties in a conflict. That is why the key evidence confirming the fact of negotiations is a document drawn up by the parties. Such document should include the date and subject matter of the negotiations and the persons taking part in the same. The outcome of the negotiations can be included in the document, but this is not compulsory. The law only links the right to bring a claim to the fact that negotiations took place and does not have regard to any negative result. That is the reason why Russian courts do not treat telephone calls as admissible evidence of negotiations. For example, the federal *arbitrazh* court of the Northwest District in a ruling dated 14 December 2006[29] stated that 'the courts have rejected the company's reference to telephone negotiations, since it was impossible to establish the content of the negotiations from the information presented by the telephone company in the case file'.[30] It is interesting that the *arbitrazh* court of the Volgo-Vyatka District returned a claim because no documents were attached to the statement of claim to establish the fact that the parties had conducted pre-trial telephone negotiations.[31] In another ruling, the Moscow city court stated that 'the clause under which the parties are to enter into negotiations is not equivalent to a setting out of a pre-trial claim procedure by the parties'.[32] Negotiations are not treated as part of pre-trial dispute resolution as a matter of Russian law. A pre-trial dispute clause should include clearly defined conditions, procedures and provisions for the filing and consideration of the claim.[33] The same conclusion was reached by the International Commercial Arbitration Court of the Chamber of Commerce and Industry of the Russian Federation (ICAC) in case No 108/2011. The ICAC there pointed out that, despite the procedure of pre-trial settlement having been agreed by the parties, their agreement was silent on precisely how the settlement negotiations were to be conducted. The ICAC was adamant that the procedure for pre-trial settlement of disputes in the parties' agreement could not be equated with the mandatory claim procedure in form or substance and in actuality the parties had not agreed to a mandatory

---

[29] Ruling of *arbitrazh* court of Northwest district, 14 December 2006, Case No A56-17842/2006.
[30] ibid.
[31] Ruling of *arbitrazh* court of Volgo-Vyatka district, 27 October 2016, Case No A43-15711/2016.
[32] Ruling of Moscow city court, 30 May 2017, Case No 33–14571/2017.
[33] ibid. The same position can be found in Ruling of Russian Supreme Court, 26 April 2017, Case No A56-7889/2016.

dispute resolution procedure.[34] On the other hand, there have also been instances of judicial practice whereby the court has mixed up pre-trial procedure for settling a dispute and the institution of negotiations. For example, the Moscow city court in a ruling dated 14 August 2017 reasoned:

> [T]he bank sends a corresponding request signed by an authorized representative of the lender. The borrower is obliged to return the amount of the debt and pay the principal interest within five calendar days from the date following the date of delivery of the claim to the borrower. Thus, the contract provides for a negotiation process, a pre-trial procedure for settling a dispute has been established.[35]

On that basis, it is submitted that the issue of whether negotiations in Russia are a separate part of pre-trial dispute resolution remains controversial. This situation is likely to stay the same until changes to the law are made. A further issue that will need to be discussed is the confidentiality of the information shared among the parties during negotiations. There is no judicial ruling where such questions of confidentiality have been considered by the courts. For now, to protect their interests, parties should include a confidentiality clause in their contracts. Otherwise, where the negotiations prove abortive, any concessions made by a party during such negotiations may be treated as evidence in a later trial.

16.8 Conclusion

Russian legislation on multi-tier dispute resolution clauses remains a work in progress. Despite this and due to the needs of businesses, considerable judicial practice concerning such clauses exists. Most of the issues that have arisen are still controversial. But relatively recent judicial rulings provide an opportunity to work out an effective general framework for pre-trial dispute resolution in Russia.[36]

---

[34] Ruling of ICAC, 30 September 2013, Case No 108/2011.
[35] Ruling of Moscow city court, 14 August 2017, Case No 33-30776/2017.
[36] For further discussion, see Dedov and Molotnikov (n 1).

17

Multi-tier Dispute Resolution under OHADA Law

JUSTIN MONSENEPWO

17.1 Introduction

Victor Hugo wrote: 'All human wisdom holds in these two words: conciliation and reconciliation; conciliation of ideas, reconciliation of men.'[1] One field in which we can obverse the reconciliation of parties and the conciliation of ideas is that of multi-tier dispute resolution[2] mechanisms. As arbitration has come under criticism in the last years, the use of multi-tier dispute resolution clauses has significantly increased in practice. To cope with this reality and to address the issues related to arbitration, the OHADA Council of Ministers has adopted new texts in respect of multi-tier dispute resolution. This chapter examines the legal regime applicable to multi-tier dispute resolution under OHADA law. To do this, it first briefly presents the purpose, the institutions and the main instruments of OHADA. It also examines the rules governing multi-tier dispute resolution before and after the OHADA Council of Ministers meeting on 23 and 24 November 2017.[3] In addition, it analyses the new regime governing multi-tier dispute resolution

---

[1] Victor Hugo, *Discours d'ouverture du Congrès littéraire international de 1878* (Calmann Lévy 1878) 7.

[2] This chapter uses the terms 'multi-tier dispute resolution' and 'med-arb' to designate any alternative dispute resolution mechanism that combines mediation and arbitration in sequence in a single case. See Sarah Benzidi, 'Med-arb: How to Mitigate the Risk of Setting Aside or Refusal of Recognition and Enforcement of a Med-arb Award' (2017) 10 American Journal of Mediation 1, 2.

[3] On 23 November 2017, the OHADA Council of Ministers revised the Arbitration Rules of Procedure of the CCJA. Moreover, it adopted a new Uniform Act on Arbitration and a new Uniform Act on Mediation. All these texts entered into force on 23 February 2018. They all encompass provisions in respect of multi-tier dispute resolution and constitute an overall reform of provisions on alternative dispute resolution mechanisms under OHADA law.

under the new Uniform Act on Arbitration, the revised Arbitration Rules of Procedure of the CCJA and the new Uniform Act on Mediation. Lastly, it identifies the challenges to enforceability of multi-tier dispute resolution in the OHADA region.

17.2 Presentation of the Organisation for the Harmonisation of Business Law in Africa (OHADA)

17.2.1 Purpose and Institutions of OHADA

The *Organisation pour l'Harmonisation en Afrique du Droit des Affaires* (the Organisation for the Harmonisation of Business Law in Africa) is an African supranational organisation which was created on 17 October 1993 by fourteen Central and Western African states[4] to increase their attractiveness to foreign investments. As indicated in the preamble and Article 1 of the OHADA Treaty,[5] OHADA aims at creating simple, modern and harmonised business regulations in Africa.[6] To achieve this goal, OHADA has five institutions: (1) the Conference of Heads of State and Government (*Conférence des Chefs d'Etat et de Gouvernement*),[7] (2) the Council of Ministers (*Conseil des Ministres*),[8] (3) the Common Court of Justice and Arbitration (*Cour Commune de Justice et d'Arbitrage*, CCJA),[9] (4) the

---

[4] Benin, Burkina Faso, Cameroon, Central African Republic, Chad, Comoros, Congo, Côte d'Ivoire, Equatorial Guinea, Gabon, Mali, Niger, Senegal and Togo. Guinea Bissau, Guinea Conakry and the Democratic Republic of Congo later became members of the organisation. All these countries are francophone, except for Cameroon (which is bilingual: English and French), Equatorial Guinea (which is also bilingual: Spanish and French) and Guinea-Bissau (Portuguese).

[5] Treaty on the Harmonisation of Business Law in Africa (the 'OHADA Treaty') (OHADA). The OHADA Treaty was signed in Port Louis on 17 October 1993 and revised in Quebec on 17 October 2008.

[6] Joseph Issa-Sayegh, 'Quelques Aspects Techniques de l'Intégration Juridique: l'Exemple des Actes Uniformes de l'OHADA' [1999] Uniform Law Review 5, 20; Claire Moore Dickerson, 'Harmonizing Business Law in Africa: OHADA Calls the Tune' (2005) 44 Columbia Journal of Transnational Law 17; Peter Winship, 'Law and Development in West and Central Africa (OHADA)' (2016) SMU Dedman School of Law Legal Studies Research Paper No 272, 3.

[7] The OHADA Treaty, art 27(1).

[8] ibid, arts 27(2)–30; Joseph Issa-Sayegh, Paul-Gérard Pougoué and Filiga Michel Sawadogo, *OHADA: Traité et Actes Uniformes commentés et annotés* (Juriscopte 2014) 51.

[9] The OHADA Treaty, arts 14–26, 31–32; *Règlement de Procédure de la Cour Commune de Justice et d'arbitrage* [Rules of Procedure of the Common Court of Justice and Arbitration], Journal Officiel (OHADA) no 4, 1 November 1997, 9; *Règlement No 01/2014/CM/OHADA Modifiant et Complétant le Règlement de Procédure de la Cour Commune de Justice et d'arbitrage du 18 Avril 1996* [Rule No 001/2014/CM/OHADA Amending and

Regional School for Magistrates (*Ecole Régionale Supérieure de la Magistrature*, ERSUMA)[10] and (5) the Permanent Secretariat (*Secretariat Permanent*).[11]

The Conference of Heads of State and Government was added by the revision of the OHADA Treaty that was adopted in Quebec on 17 October 2008 (art 27(1) of the OHADA Treaty). It is composed of heads of state and government of the member states and is chaired by the head of state or government whose country chairs the Council of Ministers.[12] It has jurisdiction over all matters in respect of the OHADA Treaty (art 27(1) of the OHADA Treaty).[13] The Council of Ministers is composed of the ministers of justice and finance of the member states (art 27(2) of the OHADA Treaty). Except for decisions regarding adoption of Uniform Acts, which require unanimity under Article 8 of the OHADA Treaty, the decisions of the Council of Ministers are taken by an absolute majority of the member states which are present and voting (art 30 of the OHADA Treaty). The Council of Ministers may determine the areas of business law to be harmonised (art 2 of the OHADA Treaty). Moreover, it appoints the Permanent Secretary (art 40(3) of the OHADA Treaty), the General Director of the ERSUMA (art 41(4) of the OHADA Treaty) and the members of the CCJA (art 31(1) of the OHADA Treaty). In addition, the Council of Ministers has a legislative function. As a legislative body, it approves the annual programme of harmonisation of business law and unanimously adopts Uniform Acts (arts 4 and 8 of the OHADA Treaty).[14]

Supplementing the Rules of Procedure of the Common Court of Justice and Arbitration of 18 April 1996] (OHADA). See Issa-Sayegh, Pougoué and Sawadogo (n 8) 77, 1465.

[10] The OHADA Treaty, art 41. See Issa-Sayegh, Pougoué and Sawadogo (n 8) 58–59.

[11] The OHADA Treaty, art 40. See Issa-Sayegh, Pougoué and Sawadogo (n 8) 57–58.

[12] The OHADA Treaty, art 27(2). The Presidency of the Council of Ministers shall be chaired by the states parties, each for a one-year term to rotate among the states parties in alphabetical order. Adhering states shall hold the presidency of the Council of Ministers for the first time in the order of their accession after all previous states parties have served. If a state party cannot serve as the Council of Ministers' chair during a year prescribed therefor, the Council appoints the state party that is, pursuant to the prior paragraphs, next in line for the chair. When the state party that was previously unable to serve as chair considers that it is able so to serve, it shall promptly so inform the Permanent Secretariat, requesting that the Council of Ministers takes appropriate action.

[13] See Inès Fèviliyé, 'La Révision du Traité de l'OHADA' (2009) Revue Congolaise de Droit et des Affaires 1, 40.

[14] Djibril Abarchi, 'La Supranationalité OHADA' (2000) 37 Revue burkinabé de droit 7; Joseph Issa-Sayegh, 'La portée abrogatoire des Actes Uniformes de l'OHADA sur le droit interne des Etats-Parties' (2001) 40 Revue Burkinabè de Droit 51, 57; Parfait Diedhou, 'L'article 10 du Traité de l'OHADA: quelle portée abrogatoire et supranationale?' (2007) 12(2) Revue de droit uniforme 265.

Headquartered in Yaoundé, Cameroun, the Permanent Secretary is the executive body of OHADA (art 40(1) of the OHADA Treaty). It is directed by a Permanent Secretary appointed by the Council of Ministers for a term of four years, renewable once (art 40(1) of the OHADA Treaty). Pursuant to Article 40(2) of the OHADA Treaty, the Permanent Secretary represents OHADA and assists the Council of Ministers. He or she is mainly responsible for assessing the areas where the unification of business law is necessary. Moreover, the Permanent Secretary plays a key role in the adoption process of Uniform Acts.[15] Attached to the Permanent Secretary of OHADA, the ERSUMA is a training and documentation centre on OHADA law (art 41(1) of the OHADA Treaty).

The CCJA is composed of nine judges.[16] However, considering the size of the tasks and the availability of finances, the Council of Ministers may decide to set a higher number of judges (art 31(2) of the OHADA Treaty).[17] The CCJA has four main functions. First, it reviews the drafts of the Uniform Acts. According to Articles 6 and 7 of the OHADA Treaty, the CCJA controls the consistency of the drafts of the Uniform Acts with the OHADA Treaty before the Council of Ministers adopts them. Second, the CCJA plays the role of an arbitration centre. As such, it supervises institutional arbitration pursuant to Articles 21 to 26 of the OHADA Treaty, the Uniform Act on Arbitration, and the Arbitration Rules and the Rules of Procedure of the Common Court of Justice and Arbitration. In that capacity, the CCJA appoints or confirms arbitrators, receives information in respect of the conduct of proceedings, and reviews draft awards. Further, it rules on disputes which may arise with respect to the recognition and execution of those awards. Third, the CCJA may be consulted by any member state, the Council of Ministers or any national court on the interpretation and uniform application of the OHADA Treaty, the regulations, the Uniform Acts and the decisions of OHADA (art 14(1) of the OHADA Treaty). Fourth, the CCJA is

---

[15] See Section 17.2.2.1.
[16] Rule No 001/2014/CM/OHADA Amending and Supplementing the Rules of Procedure of the Common Court of Justice and Arbitration of 18 April 1996 (n 9), art 1.
[17] Under art 31(3) of the OHADA Treaty, judges of the CCJA are elected for a non-renewable term of seven years. They are elected by the Council of Ministers from among the nationals of the member states and must be either: (1) magistrates having at least fifteen years of professional experience and satisfying their countries' criteria for service in senior judicial position, or (2) lawyers who are members of the Bar of a member state and have at least fifteen years of professional experience, or (3) law professors who have at least fifteen years of professional experience.

a court of final appeal (art 14(3) of the OHADA Treaty). As such, it rules on decisions in civil and commercial matters that are taken by appellate courts of the member states in all matters pertaining to the application of OHADA law. The judgments of the CCJA are directly enforceable in all member states as if they were judgments of a national court. In no case may a national decision contrary to a judgment of the CCJA be executed in a territory of a member state (art 20 of the OHADA Treaty).

17.2.2 Instruments of OHADA

To unify business law in Africa, OHADA adopts (1) Uniform Acts and (2) regulations.

17.2.2.1 Uniform Acts

Uniform Acts are the main instruments of OHADA.[18] They are unified legal provisions that regulate a specific area of OHADA law. They are directly applicable in the member states and override all national contrary provisions. As of October 2018, the Council of Ministers has adopted ten Uniform Acts:

1. the Uniform Act Relating to Commercial Companies and Economic Interest Groups,[19] which entered into force on 1 January 1998 and was revised on 5 May 2014;
2. the Uniform Act Relating to General Commercial Law,[20] which entered into force on 1 January 1998 and was revised on 15 May 2011;

---

[18] As to the adoption process of the Uniform Acts, it is worth noting that, pursuant to art 6 of the OHADA Treaty, the Permanent Secretary is in charge of preparing the Uniform Acts. It is also responsible for circulating the draft versions of the Uniform Acts to the governments of the member states, which then have ninety days (starting on the date of receipt of such draft) to submit their written comments (art 7(1) of the OHADA Treaty). Upon expiration of that period, the Permanent Secretary sends a report, a draft version of the Uniform Act, and the comments of the member states to the CCJA. The CCJA controls the consistency of the drafts of the Uniform Acts with the OHADA Treaty within sixty days starting on the date of receipt of a request for opinion (art 7(3) of the OHADA Treaty). Upon expiration of the new deadline, the Permanent Secretariat completes the final draft of the Uniform Act and ensures its publication in the Official Gazette of OHADA after its adoption by the Council of Ministers (arts 7(4) and 9 of the OHADA Treaty).
[19] The Uniform Act Relating to Commercial Companies and Economic Interest Groups, Journal Officiel (OHADA) no 2, 1.
[20] The Uniform Act Relating to General Commercial Law, Journal Officiel (OHADA) no 23, 1.

3. the Uniform Act Organising Securities,[21] which entered into force on 1 January 1998 and was revised on 15 May 2011;
4. the Uniform Act Organising Simplified Recovery Procedures and Enforcement Measures,[22] which entered into force on 31 August 1998;
5. the Uniform Act Organising Collective Proceedings for Clearing of Debts,[23] which entered into force on 1 January 1999;
6. the Uniform Act on Arbitration of 23 November 2017, which entered into force on 15 March 2018,[24] replacing the Uniform Act on Arbitration of 11 March 1999;
7. the Uniform Act on the Harmonisation of the Accounts of Enterprises,[25] which entered into force in two phases – (1) as to the personal account of the enterprises, on 1 January 2001; (2) as to the consolidated accounts and the combined, on 1 January 2002 – and was revised on 26 January 2017;
8. the Uniform Act on Contracts for the Carriage of Goods by Road of 22 March 2003,[26] which entered into force on 1 January 2004;
9. the Uniform Act on Cooperatives of 15 December 2010,[27] which entered into force on 15 May 2011; and
10. the Uniform Act on Mediation of 23 November 2017, which entered into force on 15 March 2018.[28]

17.2.2.2 Regulations

Regulations are adopted by the Council of Ministers to complete and to implement the OHADA Treaty (art 4 of the OHADA Treaty). They are of the same nature as the OHADA Treaty.[29] They are directly applicable in

---

[21] The Uniform Act Organising Securities, Journal Officiel (OHADA) no 22.
[22] The Uniform Act Organising Simplified Recovery Procedures and Enforcement Measures, Journal Officiel (OHADA) no 6, 1.
[23] The Uniform Act Organising Collective Proceedings for Clearing of Debts, Journal Officiel (OHADA) no 7, 1.
[24] The Uniform Act on Arbitration, Journal Officiel (OHADA) Numéro Spécial (15 December 2017) 15.
[25] The Uniform Act on the Harmonisation of the Accounts of Enterprises, Journal Officiel (OHADA) no 10, 1.
[26] The Uniform Act on Contracts for the Carriage of Goods by Road, Journal Officiel (OHADA) no 13, 3.
[27] The Uniform Act on Cooperatives, Journal Officiel (OHADA) no 23.
[28] The Uniform Act on Mediation, Journal Officiel (OHADA) Numéro Spécial (15 December 2017) 5.
[29] Joseph Issa-Sayegh and Jacqueline Lohoues-Oble, *Harmonisation du droit des affaires* (Collection Droit uniforme africain) (Bruxelles 2002) 112.

all member states. As of January 2018, the Council has adopted the following regulations:

1. the Rules of Procedure of the Common Court of Justice and Arbitration of 18 April 1996, as amended by Rule No 001/2014/CM/OHADA of 30 January 2014;[30]
2. the Arbitration Rules of the Common Court of Justice and Arbitration as amended on 23 November 2017;[31]
3. the Financial Regulations of the OHADA Institutions;[32] and
4. the OHADA Staff Regulations.[33]

17.3 Provisions Related to the Multi-tier Provisions under OHADA Law

17.3.1 The Use of Multi-tiered Dispute Resolution in the OHADA Region before 2017

Before the adoption of the Uniform Act on Mediation, there was no provision on multi-tier dispute resolution under OHADA law. Neither the Uniform Act on Arbitration (with respect to so-called ad hoc arbitration)[34] nor the Arbitration Rules of Procedure of the CCJA (in respect of institutional arbitration)[35] regulated situations where the parties have agreed to engage in negotiation, mediation or some other form or combination of alternative dispute resolution prior to commencing

---

[30] See n 9.
[31] The Arbitration Rules of the Common Court of Justice and Arbitration as amended on 23 November 2017, Journal Officiel (OHADA) Numéro Spécial (15 December 2017) 29.
[32] The Financial Regulations of the OHADA Institutions, Journal Officiel (OHADA) no 8, 14.
[33] The OHADA Staff Regulations, Journal Officiel (OHADA) no 5, 18.
[34] In ad hoc arbitration, the proceedings are administered by the disputing parties. Under OHADA law, the ad hoc arbitration is governed by the Uniform Act on Arbitration. For more details on ad hoc arbitration under OHADA law, see Antoine Delabrière and Alain Fenon, 'La constitution du tribunal arbitral et le statut de l'arbitre dans l'Acte uniforme OHADA' (2000) Revue Penant numéro spécial no 833, 155.
[35] In institutional arbitration, the proceedings are monitored by the CCJA, which plays the role of an arbitration centre. Under OHADA law, institutional arbitration is governed by arts 21 to 26 of the OHADA Treaty, and the Arbitration Rules of Procedure of the CCJA. See Affoussiatta Bamba, 'La procédure d'arbitrage devant la Cour Commune de Justice et d'Arbitrage' (2000) Revue Penant numéro spécial no 833, 147. For an analysis of the Arbitration Rules of Procedure of the CCJA, see René Bourdin, 'Le Règlement d'arbitrage de la Cour Commune de Justice et d'Arbitrage' (1999) 5 Revue Camerounaise de l'Arbitrage 10.

arbitration. This can be explained by the significance given to arbitration. Indeed, since the creation of OHADA in 1993, arbitration has been praised for its expedition and flexibility, to the extent that the preamble and Article 1 of the OHADA Treaty expressly mention 'the promotion of arbitration as an instrument to settle contractual disputes' as one of the goals of OHADA.[36] Moreover, the importance given to arbitration by the founders of OHADA is also evidenced by the fact that Articles 21 to 26 of the OHADA Treaty contain provisions on institutional arbitration, which is uncommon for treaties founding international organisations. Thanks to unification through OHADA of rules pertaining to arbitral proceedings as well as to recognition and enforcement of arbitral awards, it is no surprise that arbitration has been hailed as one of the most efficient forms of adversarial dispute settlement in the OHADA region. National courts enforce arbitration agreements.[37]

Nevertheless, despite the lack of a legislative framework on med-arb under OHADA law, the use of multi-tiered dispute resolution clauses is not uncommon in practice in the OHADA region. Indeed, there are already several arbitration centres in the OHADA region which permit and provide 'med-arb'[38] services. For instance, the *Cour d'Arbitrage de la Côte d'Ivoire* (CACI) is a dispute resolution centre located in Abidjan (Ivory Coast). Created within the Chamber of Commerce and Industry of Ivory Coast, it aims at providing economic operators with alternative means of settling their disputes, including arbitration, arbitral review, accelerated debt collection and mediation. Med-arb is indirectly governed by Article 15 of the Rules of Mediation of the CACI: 'If the parties have also agreed to resort to arbitration under the CACI Arbitration Rules, any interested party may proceed with the arbitration when the mediation has ended under Article 11.'[39] Article 11 of the Rules of

---

[36] Yves Guyon, 'Conclusion' (2004) 205 Les petites affiches 59, 59.

[37] *Société de Manufacture de Côte d'Ivoire dit MACABI v May Jean-Pierre* [2005] CCJA, 1st chamber, Ohadata J-05-357 (OHADA); *FKA v HAM* [2006] CCJA, 1st chamber, Decision no 9, Ohadata J-07-23 (OHADA); *Kabou Henriette (BTM) v Société Sahel Compagnie (SOSACO)* [2008] Court of Appeal of Ouagadougou, civil and commercial chamber, Judgment no 116 of 19 May 2006, Ohadata-J-09-25 (OHADA); *Commercial Bank of Cameroon (CBC) v Kenmogne* [2006] Tribunal de Grande Instance of Mifi, Judgment no 79/civ, Ohadata J-07-70 (OHADA).

[38] Unless otherwise indicated, this chapter uses the term 'med-arb' to designate any alternative dispute resolution mechanism that combines mediation and arbitration in sequence in a single case. See Benzidi (n 2) 2.

[39] The original version in French reads: '*Dans l'hypothèse où les parties ont également convenu de recourir à l'arbitrage dans le cadre du règlement d'arbitrage de la CACI, il appartient le cas échéant, à toute partie intéressée, de mettre en œuvre la procédure d'arbitrage, dès lors que*

Mediation of the CACI provides that the mediation ends with either the signature of the parties' settlement or the refusal of at least one of the parties to continue the mediation process. To encourage parties to use multi-tier dispute resolution clauses, Article 32.5 of the Arbitration Rules of Procedure of the CACI provides that arbitration fees are halved if the parties have engaged in negotiation or mediation prior to commencing arbitration under the auspices of the CACI.[40]

Similarly, in Senegal, the Arbitration, Mediation, and Conciliation Rules of the *Chambre de Commerce, d'Industrie et d'Agriculture de Dakar* (CCIAD) ('CCIAD Rules') encompass templates of multi-tiered dispute resolution clauses which allow parties to engage in negotiation, mediation or any form of combination of alternative dispute resolution prior to commencing arbitration. The CCIAD Rules highlight that the primary purpose of the centre is the search for amicable solutions by easing the enforcement of multi-tiered dispute resolution clauses.[41] Moreover, Article 39(1) of the CCIAD Rules allows the arbitral tribunal to stay the arbitral proceedings to give the parties an opportunity to reach an agreement through mediation. If the parties reach an agreement, the arbitral tribunal then records the agreement in an award on agreed terms ('*sentence d'accord parties*'). Article 39(1) does not specify whether the arbitrator may act as mediator. Similar provisions can be found in Article 34 of the Rules of Arbitration of the *Centre d'Arbitrage du Groupement Interpatronal du Cameroun* (GICAM)[42] and Article 20 of the Rules of Arbitration of the *Centre d'Arbitrage du Congo* (CAC).[43]

---

la médiation aura pris fin pour l'une des raisons évoquées à l'article 11 ci-dessus.' See 'The Mediation Rules of Procedure of the CACI' <www.courarbitrage.ci/download/47/reglements/838/Reglement%20Mediation%20CACI.pdf> accessed 11 October 2018.

[40] 'The Arbitration Rules of Procedure of the CACI' <www.courarbitrage.ci/download/2/reglements/840/Arbitrage.pdf> accessed 11 October 2018.

[41] 'Reglement d'Arbitrage, de Mediation et de Conciliation du Centre d'Arbitrage de la CCIAD' [The Arbitration, Mediation, and Conciliation Rules of the CCIAD] <https://docplayer.fr/66350819-Reglement-d-arbitrage-de-mediation-et-de-conciliation-du-centre-d-arbitrage-de-la-cciad.html> accessed 2 April 2021. The French version reads: '*Ce présent règlement privilégie totalement la recherche des solutions amiables en prévoyant une clause passerelle avec l'arbitrage en cas d'échec de la médiation.*'

[42] The GICAM is the most prominent arbitration centre and the most representative organisation of the private sector in Cameroon. See 'The Rules of Arbitration of the GICAM' <www.legicam.cm/media/upload/2019049/reglement-darbitrage-cmag-1.pdf> accessed 2 April 2021.

[43] Located in Brazzaville, the CAC is one of the most important arbitration centres in the Republic of Congo. See 'The Rules of Arbitration of the CAC' <http://cac-rdc.org/reglement-darbitrage/> accessed 12 October 2018.

17.3.2 Multi-tiered Dispute Resolution under OHADA Law after 2017

17.3.2.1 New Provisions in Respect of Alternative Dispute Resolution

Arbitration has long been regarded as one of the most efficient forms of adversarial dispute settlement in the OHADA region. However, arbitration has recently come under heavy criticisms for becoming slow and expensive.[44] Indeed, parties in the OHADA region have become increasingly disenchanted with lengthy and costly arbitration proceedings,[45] to the point that it is now regarded as the 'new litigation'.[46] To address these issues related to arbitration, the OHADA Council of Ministers adopted in November 2017 three key instruments that revolutionise OHADA's legal arsenal on alternative dispute resolution.[47] More particularly, it adopted a new Uniform Act on Arbitration and a Uniform Act governing mediation, which is defined as 'any process, regardless of its name, in which the parties request a third party to assist them in reaching an amicable settlement of a dispute, a conflicting relationship or a disagreement arising out of or relating to a legal, contractual, or other relationship involving natural or legal persons, including public entities or states'.[48] Moreover, it also revised the Arbitration Rules of Procedure

---

[44] Filiga Michel Sawadogo, 'Les 20 ans de l'Organisation pour l'harmonisation en Afrique du droit des affaires (OHADA): bilan et perspectives' in L Cadiet (ed), Droit et attractivité économique: le cas de l'OHSADA (IRJS 2013) 29; Gaston Kenfack Douajni, 'Bilan et perspectives de l'arbitrage OHADA 20 ans après la création de l'OHADA' (2014) 48 Rev Burkinabède droit 158.

[45] See generally Thomas J Stipanowich, 'Arbitration: The "New Litigation"' [2010] University of Illinois Law Review 1. See also Achille Ngwanza, 'L'essor de l'arbitrage international en Afrique subsaharienne: les apports de la CCJA' (2013) 3 Revue de l'ERSUMA 31, who uses the term *'liturgie de l'arbitrage'* (liturgy of arbitration).

[46] Brian A Pappas, 'Med-arb and the Legalization of Alternative Dispute Resolution' (2015) 20 Harvard Negotiation Law Review 157, 159.

[47] The 45th session of the Council of Ministers of OHADA took place in Conakry (Republic of Guinea) on 23 and 24 November 2017. See 'Final Communique of the 45th Session of the Council of Ministers of OHADA' (*OHADA.com*, 25 November 2017) <www.ohada.com/actualite/3856/communique-final-de-la-45e-session-du-conseil-des-ministres-de-l-ohada.html> accessed 18 October 2018.

[48] The original French version of that provision reads: '... *tout processus, quelle que soit son appellation, dans lequel les parties demandent à un tiers de les aider à parvenir à un règlement amiable d'un litige, d'un rapport conflictuel ou d'un désaccord (ci-après le « différend ») découlant d'un rapport juridique, contractuel ou autre ou lié à un tel rapport, impliquant des personnes physiques ou morales, y compris des entités publiques ou des Etats'*. For a similar definition of the concept of mediation, see Otto J Hetzel and Steven Gonzales (eds), *Alternative Dispute Resolution in State and Local Governments: Analysis and Case Studies* (ABA Book Publishing 2015) 8.

of the CCJA. This represents another option that may be used in addition or as an alternative to arbitration clauses. In contrast with arbitration, mediation offers a less expensive alternative, more flexible remedies, an informal setting which allows participants to express their concerns freely, and an agreed solution, rather than a solution which is imposed on the parties.[49] The adoption of the Uniform Act on Mediation occurred after several member states had also adopted domestic legislation on mediation. This is the case of Senegal, with its Decree no 2014-1653 of 24 December 2014 on Mediation and Conciliation.[50] Similarly, Ivory Coast also adopted an Act on Mediation on 20 June 2014. Interestingly, the new Uniform Act on Arbitration (art 8-1), the revised Arbitration Rules of Procedure of the CCJA (arts 20 and 21-1) and the new Uniform Act on Mediation (arts 4(3) and 15) contain provisions allowing the combination of mediation and arbitration, which is a novelty under OHADA law.

17.3.2.2 Variations of Combinations of Mediation and Arbitration

The provisions in the Uniform Act on Arbitration, the Arbitration Rules of Procedure of the CCJA, and the Uniform Act on Mediation offer different variations of combinations of mediation and arbitration.

17.3.2.2.1 The Med-arb Model Under Article 15 of the Uniform Act on Mediation, the parties may agree not to initiate, during a given period or until the occurrence of a specified event, any arbitral or judicial proceeding relating to a dispute which has arisen or may arise in connection with their legal relationship.[51] In this two-stage dispute resolution mechanism, arbitration is conducted only if the mediation does not result in

---

[49] Stephen B Goldberg, 'The Mediation of Grievances under a Collective Bargaining Contract: An Alternative to Arbitration' (1982) 77 Northwestern University Law Review 270, 290. However, the fact that parties are free to end the session without agreement can be regarded not only as an advantage but also as a disadvantage. Indeed, the mediator has no 'real' power; hence, the parties may approach mediation without seriousness and use it only to gain information or delay further proceedings. See Sherry Landry, 'Med-arb: Mediation with a Bite and an Effective ADR Model' (1996) 63 Defense Counsel Journal 263, 264.
[50] For an in-depth analysis of Decree no 2014-1653, see Jean-Louis Corréa, 'La médiation et la conciliation n droit sénégalais: libres propos sur un texte réglementaire' (2017) Bulletin de droit économique 1.
[51] Whether or not the same person can act as mediator and arbitrator is examined later in the chapter.

settlement of the dispute.[52] Article 15 of the Uniform Act on Mediation must be read in conjunction with Article 21-1 of the Arbitration Rules of Procedure of the CCJA (in respect of institutional arbitration) and Article 8-1 of the Uniform Act on Arbitration (in respect of ad hoc arbitration), which provide that in the presence of an agreement requiring the parties 'to follow a stage of dispute resolution prior to arbitration', the arbitral tribunal must examine whether such prior procedure was completed. It is important to note that the provisions in Article 15 of the Uniform Act on Mediation, Article 21-1 of the Arbitration Rules of Procedure of the CCJA and Article 8-1 of the Uniform Act on Arbitration Law do not contain limitations on the med-arb clause.[53] Further, unlike Article 15 of the Uniform Act on Mediation which is silent on that question, Article 21-1-1 of the Arbitration Rules of Procedure of the CCJA and Article 8-1 of the Uniform Act on Arbitration specify that the arbitral tribunal cannot examine that question *proprio motu*: at least one of the parties must raise the issue of non-compliance with the multi-tiered dispute resolution clause. Neither article determines in which form a party can raise such an objection. Nonetheless, it can be inferred from Article 21 of the Arbitration Rules of Procedure of the CCJA that such an objection can be raised in the answer to the arbitration request (reading arts 6(b), (c) and (d) in conjunction with art 5(e) of the Arbitration Rules of Procedure of the CCJA).

Article 21-1-2 of the Arbitration Rules of Procedure of the CCJA and Article 8-1(2) of the Uniform Act on Arbitration provide that if the prior stage has not been initiated, the arbitral tribunal must suspend the

---

[52] Allan Barsky, '"Med-arb": Behind the Closed Doors of a Hybrid Process' (2013) 51 Family Court Review 637, 637–38.

[53] Conversely, under French law, the *Cour de cassation* ruled that the clause must be written in the contract between the parties and cannot be inferred from model contracts. See *Clinique du Golfe v Le Gall, Cour de cassation*, 6 May 2003, Semaine Juridique, G, 11 February 2004, II 10021, no 01-01291 (France). It is worth noting that under French law, the *Clinique du Golfe* decision dealt with a dispute between a doctor and a private hospital; the med-arb clause was derived from model contracts prepared by the Unions and commonly used. However, it had not been incorporated into the contract even by reference. Compare this with the case *Cour de cassation*, 28 April 2011, comments by M Billiau, Semaine Juridique, G, 26 September 2011, doctr 1030, para 8, where a med-arb clause in an architect's contract requiring prior submission of the dispute to the architect's regional association structure for their opinion was found enforceable. The same clause had not been incorporated by way of reference in the agreement between the buyer and the seller of the property. In contrast, the arbitration agreement must be made in writing, or in any other form evidencing its existence, in particular, by reference to a document containing the agreement (art 3-1(4) of the Uniform Act on Arbitration).

proceedings for such time as it sees fit so as to enable the most diligent party to implement this step. In contrast, if the prior stage has been initiated, the arbitral tribunal must ascertain the failure of that prior stage and continue the arbitral proceeding. As per Article 12(1) of the Uniform Act on Mediation, the mediation has failed if there is a written statement of the mediator indicating, after consultation with the parties, that new mediation efforts are no longer justified, or when one of the parties no longer participates in the mediation meetings despite repeated reminders by the mediator (art 12(1)(b)). Similarly, the mediation process has failed if the parties notify the mediator in a written statement that the mediation process is terminated. It is also the case if one party notifies to the other party and the mediator in a written statement that the mediation process is terminated (arts 12(1)(c) and (d) of the Uniform Act on Mediation).[54] Lastly, Article 12(1)(e) of the Uniform Act on Mediation provides that the mediation process ends upon expiration of the mediation period initially agreed upon by the parties, unless the parties decide to extend this period in agreement with the mediator.[55]

17.3.2.2.2 The Arb-med Model Article 4(3) of the Uniform Act on Mediation allows arbitrators, acting in agreement with the parties, to stay the arbitral proceedings and to refer the parties to mediation to resolve their dispute.[56] In that case, the arbitral tribunal determines the duration of the mediation process. In case the mediation ordered by the arbitral tribunal ends without the parties reaching an agreement pursuant to Article 12(3) of the Uniform Act on Mediation,[57] the arbitral proceedings must resume. Nevertheless, if the mediation process results in a settlement, the parties (or the most diligent party with the express agreement of the other party) may request that the arbitral tribunal crystallise the settlement in an award on agreed terms ('*sentence d'accord parties*'). This provision pays strict adherence to the axiom that 'the best agreement is an agreement which the parties themselves reach'.[58] It is

---

[54] In both cases, the mediation process is terminated on the date that declaration has been made (arts 12(1)(c) and (d) of the Uniform Act of Mediation).
[55] Art 12(2) of the Uniform Act on Mediation provides that parties may prove the end of the mediation process by any means.
[56] Whether a mediator can act as an arbitrator for the same dispute without bias is examined later in the chapter.
[57] In this case, the mediation period mentioned in art 12(1)(e) of the Uniform Act on Mediation is that determined by the arbitral tribunal according to art 4(3) of the same Uniform Act.
[58] Landry (n 49) 264.

worth noting that the first sentence in Article 16(8) of the Uniform Act on Mediation excludes the recognition and enforcement of an award on agreed terms ('*sentence d'accord parties*') from the scope of application of the Uniform Act on Mediation.[59] Therefore, the recognition and enforcement of an award on agreed terms ('*sentence d'accord parties*') is governed by the Uniform Act on Arbitration (in the case of ad hoc arbitration)[60] and Article 25 of the Arbitration Rules of Procedure of the CCJA (in the case of institutional arbitration).[61] In comparison, Article 20 of the 1996 version of the Arbitration Rules of Procedure of the CCJA already addressed the situation where, during arbitral proceedings, the parties settle the dispute and the arbitral tribunal records the settlement in the form of an arbitral award on agreed terms: 'If the parties reach an agreement during the course of the arbitral proceedings, they may request that the arbitrator confirm that agreement in the form of an arbitral award by consent.'[62]

However, Article 4(3) of the Uniform Act on Mediation and Article 20 of the Arbitration Rules of Procedure of the CCJA do not have the imperative tone found, for instance, in Article 30 of the UNCITRAL Model Law on International Commercial Arbitration 2006. Indeed, it cannot be said with absolute certainty that Article 4(3) of the Uniform Act on Mediation and Article 20 of the Arbitration Rules of Procedure of the CCJA oblige the arbitral tribunal to comply with the parties' desire. Other arbitration rules use formulations which are similar to that found in Article 4(3) of the Uniform Act on Mediation and Article 20 of the Arbitration Rules of Procedure of the CCJA. For instance, the arbitration rules of the Court of Arbitration of the Ivory Coast (CACI) provide that the arbitral tribunal may grant an award on agreed terms. Similarly, the arbitration rules of the *Centre d'Arbitrage, de Médiation et de Conciliation de la Chambre de Commerce, d'Industrie et d'Agriculture de Dakar* (CCIAD) as well as the arbitration rules of the arbitration of the *Centre d'Arbitrage du Groupement Interpatronal du Cameroun* (GICAM) provide that the parties may request that the arbitral tribunal record the agreement in the form of an award on agreed terms; the arbitral tribunal is not obliged to comply with the parties' desire.

---

[59] Jean-Marie Tchakoua, 'Le statut de la sentence arbitrale d'accord parties: les limites d'un déguisement bien utile' (2002) 7 International Business Law Journal 775, 775–76; Issa-Sayegh, Pougoué and Sawadogo (n 8) 208.
[60] See the Uniform Act on Arbitration (OHADA), arts 30–34.
[61] See the Arbitration Rules of Procedure of the CCJA, arts 30–31.
[62] The UNCITRAL Model Law on International Commercial Arbitration 2006, art 30.

17.3.2.2.3 Conservatory and Interim Measures Article 15(1) of the Uniform Act on Mediation provides that where the parties have agreed to mediate and have expressly agreed not to initiate, during a given period or until the occurrence of a specified event, the arbitral tribunal must give effect to that agreement. Nonetheless, Article 15(2) of the same Uniform Act specifies that this provision does not apply to situations where a party considers initiating, for provisional and protective purposes, a procedure for the safeguarding of its rights. The same provision underlines that the initiation of such a procedure must not be considered per se as a waiver of the mediation agreement or as an end to the mediation procedure. In respect of arbitration, Article 13(4) of the Uniform Act on Arbitration also contains a similar provision.[63] However, this principle was already sanctioned by national courts before the adoption of the Uniform Act on Arbitration.[64]

17.3.3 Challenges of Med-arb in the OHADA Region

17.3.3.1 Combination of Mediation and Arbitration with the Same Neutral

Under the chapeau '*incompatibilités*' (incompatibilities), article 14(1) of the Uniform Act on Mediation provides that, unless otherwise agreed by the parties, the mediator may not assume the functions of arbitrator or expert in a dispute that has been or is the subject of the mediation procedure or in any other dispute arising out of the same legal relationship or related to this one. This provision in Article 14(1) of the Uniform Act on Mediation resembles that in Article 7(2) of the Mediation Rules of the Arbitration Institute of the Stockholm Chamber of Commerce and in Article 10(3) of the Mediation Rules of the International Chamber of Commerce (ICC). However, unlike the ICC Mediation Rules, the Uniform Act on Mediation does not require a *written* agreement of the parties.

The general principle laid down in Article 14(1) of the Uniform Act on Mediation is that the same neutral cannot act as both arbitrator and

---

[63] Kenfack Douajni, 'Les mesures provisoires et conservatoires dans l'arbitrage OHADA' (2000) 8 Revue Camerounaise de l'Arbitrage 3.
[64] *TSA v Promoto* [1997] Supreme Court of Ivory Coast, Decision no 317/197, (1999) 5 Revue Camerounaise de l'Arbitrage 16; *Alliation Property Inc v Sirpi Alustel Construction et Société Elf Serepca* [1998] TPI Douala, Ordonnance de référé no 40, (1999) 4 Revue Camerounaise de l'Arbitrage 13; *Société Wanson v Société d'Etudes et de réalisation pour l'industrie caféière et cacaoyère (SERIC)* [1997] Court of Appeal of Abidjan, civil and commercial chamber, Decision no 484, (1998) 1 Revue Camerounaise de l'Arbitrage 10.

mediator. In addition, Article 14(2) of the Uniform Act on Mediation provides that the mediator cannot act as counsel in a dispute that has been or is the subject of the mediation process, or in any other dispute arising out of or related to the same legal relationship.[65] The confirmation of this principle in the Uniform Act on Mediation aims at avoiding the bias which the same neutral acting as mediator and arbitrator might have.[66] Similarly, the Arbitration, Mediation, and Conciliation Rules of the CCIAD also encompass a similar provision: 'The parties and the mediator must agree that the latter shall not perform the functions of arbitrator, representative, or counsel of a party in arbitral or judicial proceedings related to the dispute.'[67]

Nevertheless, the phrase 'unless otherwise stipulated' in Article 14(1) of the Uniform Act on Mediation allows parties to agree that the same neutral can act as both arbitrator and mediator in the same dispute.[68] Therefore, if agreed by the parties, both the mediation and the arbitration proceedings may be conducted by the same person who will first attempt to mediate their dispute and then will arbitrate in case mediation fails. The Uniform Act on Mediation does not provide many details in this regard. Nevertheless, depending on the agreement of the parties, many variations are possible. This includes, for instance, the possibility for the parties to agree after the mediation stage whether the mediator will continue and render a decision as an arbitrator.

Allowing the parties to determine whether the same neutral can act as both mediator and arbitrator is in line with the principle that the parties should be in control of the alternative dispute resolution proceedings. Indeed, parties must be able to design their own processes in an attempt to best serve their process needs. Moreover, if the matter goes from mediation to arbitration, the arbitrator has the advantage of already being familiar with the case and can possibly render a more agreeable award. Even in a situation where the parties have not reached a conciliated agreement, med-arb can increase efficiency as no efforts

---

[65] It is important to note that parties are not allowed to derogate from the provision in art 14(2) of the Uniform Act on Mediation.

[66] Kristen M Blankley, 'Keeping a Secret from Yourself? Confidentiality When the Same Neutral Serves Both as Mediator and as Arbitrator in the Same Case' (2011) 63 Baylor Law Review 317, 320.

[67] The original version in French reads: 'Les parties et le conciliateur s'engagent à ce que ce dernier ne remplisse pas les fonctions d'arbitre, de représentant ou de conseil d'une partie dans une procédure arbitrale ou judiciaire liée au différend objet de la médiation.'

[68] This can also depend on the rules of the applicable institution. Under art 3 of the Uniform Act on Mediation, such rules prevail over the agreements of the parties.

will be invested in informing two separate neutrals (a mediator and an arbitrator). In addition, combining mediation and arbitration with the same neutral allows parties to capitalise on settlement opportunities as they arise, therefore providing time flexibility. However, it must be conceded that the provision in Article 14(1) of the Uniform Act on Mediation is not without drawbacks. One of the biggest difficulties is that the neutral might impermissibly decide the arbitral case based on confidential or privileged information learned during mediation.[69] Hence, parties and their advocates might fear that their statements made during mediation could be used against them in arbitration. Hence, they will carefully guard their statements, which will make the information needed for a reasonable settlement unavailable.[70]

17.3.3.2 Drafting of Multi-tiered Resolution Clauses under OHADA Law

Despite the new provisions on med-arb, challenges to multi-tiered resolution clauses may arise if they are ill-drafted, vague and uncertain in their wording. In that case, in their interpretation of the real intention of the parties, courts might declare such clauses non-binding for the parties. To increase the chances of enforcement in the OHADA region, it is important that the multi-tiered resolution clause be drafted[71] in a way which indicates the parties' intention to be bound by the commitment therein. In this regard, the provision of deadlines, the use of mandatory language[72] would help the court to identify the intent of the parties in being bound by the multi-tiered resolution clause. The multi-tiered resolution clause should precisely indicate the different stages that parties wish to undertake before litigation or arbitration. This will ensure that the courts will uphold the intention of the parties as expressed in the agreement and in accordance with Articles 4(3) and 15 of the Uniform Act on Mediation.

---

[69] Blankley (n 66) 321.
[70] There is an unanswered question, beyond the scope of this chapter, as to the appropriate standard of professional liability to which a neutral acting as both mediator and arbitrator should be held.
[71] It is important to note that the provision in art 15 of the Uniform Act on Mediation does not contain several limitations on the med-arb clause. See n 53.
[72] Under French law, see, for instance, *Placoplâtre v SA Eiffage TP*, 1st civil section of the *Cour de cassation*, 6 February 2007, comments by J Béguin, Semaine Juridique, E&A, 30 August 2007, no 05-17573 (France) [16]; *Knappe Composites v Art Métal*, 3rd civil section of the *Cour de cassation*, 29 January 2014, no 13-10833 (France).

17.4 Conclusion

Multi-tier dispute resolution offers the advantage of allowing parties to reach an amicable settlement in accordance with African traditional values, which favour social harmony. This is reflected in concepts such as *'ubuntu'*,[73] *'palabre'*,[74] *'ubushingantabe'* (in Burundi), *'ntumbu'*, *'kibaku'*[75] and *'agacaca'* (in Rwanda). It joins mediation's flexibility (by leaving some room for settlement) with arbitration's finality (by guaranteeing a final resolution of the conflict).[76] The new provisions of the Uniform Act on Arbitration, the Arbitration Rules of Procedure of the CCJA and the Uniform Act on Mediation will allow the enforcement of multi-tier dispute resolution clauses in the OHADA region.[77] Therefore, it is likely that there will be more consciousness of the benefits that this type of clause may provide to parties as they will slowly become more present in contractual relationships in the OHADA region. Nevertheless, in spite of the new provisions on med-arb, challenges to the enforcement of multi-tier dispute resolution clauses may arise if they are ill-drafted and vague, at least until there are decisions of the CCJA on this subject. Hence, the chances of enforcement of such clauses may increase if they are drafted in a way which clearly indicates the parties' intention to be bound by the commitment therein.

---

[73] The term *'ubuntu'* means the search for conciliation through dialogue, the search for truth and reparation. See Émile-Derlin Kemfouet, 'Droit des libertés publiques comparé: une nouvelle: avant sa disparition annoncée, la Cour Africaine des Droits de l'Homme et des peuples rend son premier arrêt (Affaire Michelot Yogogombaye c. République du Sénégal)' (2011) 45(1) Revue juridique Thémis 151, 156.

[74] This concept emanates from the colonial context where the 'palabra' was a sort of concertation in which the European commander and the black leader sat; it consisted of a long, complex and often incoherent and contradictory customary debate, due to the need for an interpreter whose knowledge of the European language was approximate.

[75] See Nsimba Yi Masamba Sita, *Le ntumbu ou le kibaku: vers une théorie formelle du contrôle social* (Thèse de doctorat en criminologie, Université Catholique de Louvain, Brussels 1989) 74.

[76] Edna Sussman, 'Developing an Effective Med-arb/Arb-med Process' [2009] 2(1) New York Dispute Resolution Lawyer 71, 71–74; Blankley (n 66) 325.

[77] There is so far no case law regarding the enforcement of multi-tiered resolution clauses since the entry into force of the Uniform Act on Mediation.

PART IV

Conclusion

18

Making Multi-tier Dispute Resolution Work

ANSELMO REYES

18.1 Introduction

The chapters of this book have been testimony to the resilience and the attraction of multi-tier dispute resolution in different parts of the world.[1]

[1] During his keynote speech at the first SIAC Virtual Congress on 2 September 2020, Chief Justice Sundaresh Menon of Singapore alluded to this trend against the backdrop of the present discontent with international arbitration. Referring to the 'eye-wateringly high cost' of international arbitration and its lack of speed and efficiency as experienced today, the Chief Justice continued (at para 48):

> [M]ost obviously, these shortcomings are deeply corrosive of business confidence in international arbitration, which in turn tarnishes arbitration's legitimacy. Chief Justice James Allsop of the Federal Court of Australia recently warned that if arbitration cannot live up to its promise as an efficient and cost-effective means of dispute resolution, then it 'simply will not find favour with commercial parties'. A harbinger of arbitration's loss of favour can be found in the 2018 QMUL [Queen Mary University of London] survey itself, in that users now appear increasingly willing to explore dispute resolution options beyond arbitration. 49% of respondents reported that their preferred approach to dispute resolution was not international arbitration alone, but rather a combination of international arbitration and ADR which, in this context, likely encompasses mediation. This preference was far more pronounced in the in-house counsel subgroup, 60% of whom favoured combining international arbitration and ADR, with only half of that voting for arbitration as a standalone option. That is a marked difference from the findings of the 2015 [QMUL] survey, in which only 34% preferred a combination of the two. The authors of the 2018 survey conclude that users are 'increasingly resorting to various forms of ADR in the hope that a swifter and more cost-efficient resolution can be found to disputes before having them resolved by arbitration'.

The keynote speech is available as Sundaresh Menon, 'Arbitrator's Blade: International Arbitration and the Rule of Law' (*Supreme Court of Singapore*, 2 September 2020) <www.supremecourt.gov.sg/docs/default-source/default-document-library/siac-virtual-congress-2020–arbitration%27s-blade–international-arbitration-and-the-rule-of-law-(020920-as-

This final chapter will focus on the most problematic of multi-tier dispute resolution modes, that is, the situation where the same person acts as mediator and arbitrator in a dispute. Contributor after contributor to this book has identified that form of hybrid dispute resolution as being difficult because of the potential for breaches of confidentiality and conflicts of interest. For the analysis in this chapter, purely as a matter of shorthand to avoid constant repetition when referring to this problematic mode of hybrid dispute resolution, the term 'med-arb' will be defined and used here to denote the form of hybrid procedure where the same person acts as mediator and arbitrator in a dispute *and* the dispute resolution process commences with mediation, moving on to arbitration if and only if mediation proves abortive.[2] The question to be explored is whether 'med-arb' in the narrow sense just defined may be made to work effectively in commercial disputes as a means of hybrid dispute resolution, despite its perceived shortcomings. Can the problems of med-arb be overcome or mitigated to a level that would make it widely acceptable? That issue will be tackled on three fronts: (1) how to ensure the enforceability of med-arb clauses; (2) whether med-arb can be conducted in a way that circumvents or at least minimises its associated risks; and (3) how to facilitate enforcement of the outcomes of med-arb. Overall, the discussion here will very much be in favour of med-arb in the sense just defined. The conclusions reached in respect of the narrow case of med-arb can then be generalised to apply to all forms of multi-tier dispute resolution. The hope is therefore that the measures advocated here will (if adopted) enhance the attractiveness of hybrid dispute resolution generally, thereby accelerating the trend (observed by many contributors to this book) towards greater use of multi-tier dispute resolution.

---

delivered).pdf> accessed 1 October 2020. For further statistics on user preferences in relation to multi-tier dispute resolution, see section 9 ('Hybrid Dispute Resolution Mechanisms') in Singapore International Dispute Resolution Academy (SIDRA), *International Dispute Resolution Survey: 2020 Final Report* <https://sidra.smu.edu.sg/sites/sidra.smu.edu.sg/files/survey/index.html> accessed 5 October 2020.

[2] For a conceptual discussion of terms 'multi-tier dispute resolution', 'arb-med-arb', 'arb-med' and 'med-arb', see Chapter 1 in this volume. This present chapter has benefitted from the exhaustive analysis of med-arb in Dilyara Nigmatullina, *Combining Mediation and Arbitration in International Commercial Dispute Resolution* (Routledge 2018), especially the discussion of procedural modifications to same neutral med-arb (ch 7).

18.2 Bothering about Med-arb

At the outset, one might ask 'Why bother about med-arb at all?' Med-arb enjoys wide popularity in Mainland China as a means of settling commercial and non-commercial disputes. But, although permitted in many jurisdictions, it is seemingly not much used anywhere else. It is also far from being the only way of conducting a hybrid dispute resolution. A dispute may equally be resolved by engaging different persons to act as mediator and arbitrator. That mode of proceeding would not give rise to problems of confidentiality or conflict of interest. Why then should a government enacting laws to regulate multi-tier dispute resolution or a lawyer drafting a multi-tier dispute resolution clause waste time contemplating use of the same neutral as mediator and arbitrator? Why opt for med-arb despite its risks? Why do things the hard way?

On a practical level, there is an obvious answer. Med-arb will almost certainly cost significantly less and take less time when compared to the situation where different persons act as mediator and arbitrator in the same dispute. Where two persons have to be instructed to provide dispute resolution services, the parties could be paying for the time taken by each person to become familiar with the facts, matters and nuances of a dispute. Inevitably, a mediation having failed, the person then appointed as arbitrator will need time to become acquainted with the background material previously mastered by the individual previously engaged as mediator. In contrast, in med-arb, the mediator can move seamlessly into 'arbitrator mode' once a mediation proves abortive. In the post COVID-19 era, when financial resources will be tight due to global recession, commercial parties will be anxious to have in place a cost- and time-efficient means of resolving their differences, to enable them to safeguard cash flow and get on with business. It is submitted that a med-arb clause would be the obvious way of addressing those concerns.[3]

---

[3] Justice Patricia Bergin has argued, however, from a study of ninety-eight cases referred by the Supreme Court of New South Wales to mediation between 1 January 2006 and 1 June 2007 (sixty-five cases from the Commercial List and thirty-three cases from the Technology and Construction List), that:

> the majority of commercial litigants prefer to have the capacity to make the more precise judgment about the strengths and weaknesses of their cases before they settle at mediation. This is supported by the raw figures that show that 60% of the cases referred to mediation at an advanced stage of the litigious process settled compared to less than 30% when referred earlier, either at the preliminary or intermediate stage.

On a psychological level, commercial parties do not necessarily just wish the rights and wrongs of their differences to be determined on strict legal merit. Paradoxically, in many commercial disputes, the operative law is obvious and not actually in disagreement. It is instead the parties' versions of the facts and surrounding circumstances that are divergent and hotly disputed. Parties are thus frequently more concerned that the judge or arbitrator hearing their case fully comprehends the 'justice' of their position: grievances that have been undermining a contractual relationship over time; recent events that have led to irretrievable breakdown; good faith efforts to stave off that breakdown in the face of the other's intransigence; and frustration, hurt and a sense of betrayal at how the other has behaved. The problem is that neither the court nor the tribunal is a suitable venue for venting concerns of that nature. Litigation and arbitration are subject to rules of pleading and evidence that strictly limit what can be adduced to that which is relevant as a matter of law. Contractual liability in commercial contracts is a question of delivering a result or using best endeavours to achieve that result. Whether a party has met its obligations to produce an agreed outcome is judged objectively. One has either fulfilled one's promise or not. A party's motivations and feelings of hurt or disappointment are immaterial to the determination of such outcome and so are rigorously excluded from the purview of the court or tribunal. The parties will not be permitted to digress into such matters. Likewise, subjective understandings formed in the course of negotiations or during a contract's performance will normally be regarded by a court or tribunal as legally irrelevant background which it would be a waste of time and money even to consider. Med-arb, to the extent to which its inherent difficulties can be overcome, offers a way of having one's cake and eating it. All the background matters which the parties may regard as important if their side of a dispute is to be understood, but which the court or tribunal will disregard, can be communicated to the mediator. The parties will at least have the chance during the mediation to ventilate their real concerns, however meaningless those may be from the viewpoint of a judge or

---

See PA Bergin, 'Mediation in Hong Kong: The Way Forward: Perspectives from Australia', paper delivered at the Hong Kong International Arbitration Centre (HKIAC) (30 November 2007) <www.supremecourt.justice.nsw.gov.au/Documents/Publications/Speeches/Pre-2015%20Speeches/Bergin/bergin301107.pdf> accessed 1 October 2020, para 66.

On that basis, while med-arb may mean a significantly lower cost if mediation is tried early and proves successful, arb-med may be preferable in that cases are more likely to settle where mediation is attempted after the close of pleadings or memorials in the arbitration.

arbitrator. If the mediation breaks down, the parties will additionally have some comfort that, consciously or subconsciously, the mediator turned arbitrator will not be oblivious to their underlying motivations and aspirations and the nuances underlying their predicaments.

Making med-arb work consequently involves balancing between formality and informality.[4] The more formal the structure and rules of a dispute resolution process, the more such process will simply be litigation or arbitration by another name. Imposing too much formality (whether through legislation, institutional rules or the terms of a dispute resolution clause) will detract from the practical and psychological benefits of med-arb. Adherence to rules brings with it economic and emotional costs. But imposing no structure at all will mean that the problems inherent in med-arb will not be addressed. If the mediation stage is successful, there is possibly nothing to worry about. However, what if the mediation fails and the mediator now acting as arbitrator issues an award? In the absence of some formal structure constraining the initial mediation, there is a real risk that the award may be set aside or refused enforcement on due process or public policy grounds.[5] The benefits of med-arb would be lost.

---

[4] For an overview of the tensions between informality and formality in the development of ADR (including mediation), see generally Michael Palmer, 'Formalisation of Alternative Dispute Resolution Processes: Some Socio-legal Thoughts' in Joachim Zekoll, Moritz Bälz and Iwo Amelung (eds), *Formalisation and Flexibilisation in Dispute Resolution* (Brill 2014) 17–44. The author is indebted to Professor Palmer for drawing his chapter to his attention. Professor Palmer concludes (at 42–43):

> We have noted that the growing use of 'ADR' may result in a greater degree of formalisation in hitherto informal justice processes, creating problems of inflexibility, rigidity and so on, from which ADR is meant to offer release. This is the contradiction of formalisation. External pressures such as professional rivalry, the state as the representative of the public interest, the location of much of ADR discourse in law schools and legal practice, and the determination on the part of even ADR 'experts' to continue to see the court as the most natural forum for the resolution of civil disputes, all encourage this development. Internal pressures of institutionalisation are also at work, as we have seen: for the revolutionary message of ADR to be put into practice, problems are encountered and compromises have to be made that may well come to undermine the 'origin myth' as Fitzpatrick calls it. As a result, there has, in many ways, been a co-option of the ADR movement by specialists trained in legal rules and procedures.

The requirement to observe due process in any ensuing arbitration means that the mediation stage of med-arb will be subject to the same pressures of 'formalisation' identified by Professor Palmer.

[5] For example, because the neutral took into account confidential information imparted by a party during the mediation which the other (losing) party did not have a reasonable

The situation described at the end of the last paragraph encompasses what happened in the Hong Kong case of *Gao Haiyan v Keeneye Holdings Ltd*,[6] whose facts have been set out and discussed in Chapters 1, 3 and 4.[7] The author was the first instance judge in the case. In his judgment, having identified the problems inherent in med-arb, the author stated:[8] '[L]abelling a process as mediation does not mean that anything goes. There are appropriate and inappropriate ways of conducting mediations. The would-be mediator must ensure at all times, especially when one might act as arbitrator later on, that nothing is said or done in the mediation which could convey an impression of bias.' Because of the overly informal way that the mediation had been conducted in *Gao Haiyan*, the author concluded that there was apparent bias. This meant that, as a matter of domestic (that is, Hong Kong) public policy,[9] enforcement of the relevant award should be refused. The Court of Appeal disagreed. It held that, by failing in the arbitration to complain about the mediation, the respondents had waived the right to object to the award on the ground of apparent bias.[10] The Court of Appeal was further of the view that the author should have accorded greater weight to the decision of the Xi'an Intermediate People's Court (the court of the seat of arbitration) which had refused to set aside the award because '[f]rom the evidence provided to this court ..., it is not sufficient to prove that [the mediator] had manipulated ... the arbitral award of this

---

opportunity to rebut in the arbitration or because the neutral conducted the mediation in a way that gave rise to a reasonable apprehension of bias as an arbitrator. In practice, lack of due process and the presence of apparent bias are often elided together in challenges to an award. Thus, the typical argument would be that there was a real risk of the mediator-arbitrator's mind being subconsciously influenced by information which was imparted to her or him by one party during the mediation stage but which was not disclosed to the losing party. As a result, the losing party would claim to be under a justifiable apprehension that its case was not fairly determined by the mediator-arbitrator in the award.

[6] At first instance, [2011] 3 HKC 157 (Reyes J); on appeal, [2012] 1 HKLRD 627 (Tang VP, Fok JA, Sakhrani J).
[7] Sections 1.4.1, 3.2.2 and 4.2.2.
[8] *Gao Haiyan v Keeneye Holdings Ltd* [2011] 3 HKC 157 [79].
[9] The award in the case was a Mainland award. Hong Kong being part of China, the 1958 United Nations Convention on the Recognition and Enforcement of Foreign Arbitral Awards (the 'New York Convention') was not applicable. However, under the Arbitration Ordinance (Cap 341) then in force, the grounds for refusing enforcement of a Mainland award were identical to the grounds for refusing enforcement in Articles V(1) and V(2) of the New York Convention.
[10] The first instance judgment had also considered the question of waiver, but held for various reasons (with which the Court of Appeal disagreed) that there had been no waiver.

case'.[11] The difficulty with the Court of Appeal's analysis is that, even if there had been waiver, it should not have affected the public policy ground for refusing enforcement. An enforcing court cannot be estopped from applying (much less be regarded as having waived the application of) its domestic public policy to refuse enforcement of an award. On the contrary, whatever may or may not have happened in an arbitration or before a supervisory court in a setting aside application, an enforcing court remains under a duty to apply its domestic public policy. In *Gao Haiyan*, the Hong Kong court was thus obliged to apply Hong Kong (not Xi'an or Mainland China) public policy in deciding whether to enforce the award. If the question of whether there was apparent bias is treated as a mere question of whether due process had been observed in the Xi'an arbitration, the Court of Appeal may have a point. The Xi'an court having decided that there had been no procedural impropriety, that would be the end of the story. A Hong Kong judge should (as the Court of Appeal stressed) defer to the supervisory court on the issue of due process, not just as a matter of comity but more pertinently on the basis of issue estoppel.[12] However, the Court of Appeal's decision would be inapposite, if (as the author believes can frequently be the case) issues of adherence to an overly informal procedure and apparent bias may be closely linked and raise issues of public policy as well as due process.[13]

Chapter 1 of this book hails *Gao Haiyan* as a case where an award which was the output of a hybrid dispute resolution process was enforced. But there is a dark side to *Gao Haiyan*. An inevitable complaint against a med-arb which has been too informally conducted will be that there was a lack of

---

[11] Quoted at *Gao Haiyan v Keeneye Holdings Ltd* [2012] 1 HKLRD 627 [39].

[12] On issue estoppel and res judicata, see Anselmo Reyes, 'Recourse against Awards, Applications to Resist Enforcement and Tactical Considerations: Some Lessons from Singapore and Hong Kong Law' (2020) 63 Japanese Yearbook of International Law 127–46. In terms of the New York Convention, a lack of due process would be an Article V(1) ground for refusing to enforce an award. Public policy, however, is an Article V(2) ground. The enforcing court can of its own motion raise public policy as a ground for refusing enforcement of an award. Accordingly, in contrast to Article V(1) grounds which are for a respondent to raise when resisting enforcement of an award, an enforcing court cannot be estopped from raising (or deemed to have waived) public policy as a basis for refusing to enforce an award.

[13] As a matter of practice, parties seeking to set aside an award or resist its enforcement will not confine themselves to alleging that there has been a lack of due process. They will usually submit in the alternative that, because there was an absence of due process, the enforcing court should not recognise the award as a matter of public policy. In respect of the latter, parties will typically argue that, if an award is tainted by apparent bias, it would be contrary to the fundamental norms of the enforcing state to enforce the award since justice must not only be done but also be seen to be done.

adherence to due process and consequent apparent bias on the mediator-arbitrator's part. A party may object for those reasons to the integrity of the entire arbitral stage of the med-arb. The mediator turned arbitrator may or may not accept the objection. If the objection is upheld, the benefit of med-arb will be lost. There will have to be a fresh arbitration before a different tribunal. Time and cost will certainly be wasted. If the objection is rejected, that will not be the end of the story. The dissatisfied party can make the same objection in an application for recourse against the award in the seat of arbitration or when resisting enforcing of the award in another country. The objection having been raised (albeit rejected) in the arbitration stage of the med-arb, there will be no question of the right to object having been waived. Assume now that the objecting party's application to set aside the award in the seat has failed. That party will not necessarily be estopped from raising its objection again before the enforcing court. If (in distinction to what the Court of Appeal held in *Gao Haiyan*) an enforcing court accepts that a question of domestic public policy is triggered, it will not be bound by the findings of the foreign supervisory court on apparent bias. The enforcing court will instead have to assess whether there was apparent bias from its own point of view and, if it finds that there was, whether enforcement of the award should be refused as a matter of domestic public policy. The upshot is that in most New York Convention jurisdictions, with the possible exception of Mainland China where med-arb is commonly used in commercial disputes, an informal med-arb process poses significant risks when mediation is unsuccessful and arbitration culminates in an award. Unless proper care has been taken by the neutral during the med-arb process, there could be serious impediments to enforcing the resulting award.

Med-arb crudely conducted will have a significant bearing then on the enforceability of any resulting award. If too much informality is anathema to med-arb, what are the minimum formalities that will need to be in place to maximise the utility of the med-arb process? The sum total of those minimum features would constitute the 'minimalist approach' mentioned in the discussion that follows. The challenge is to come up with a minimalist approach which will enable commercial parties who opt for med-arb to derive as much of the practical and psychological benefits of that process as possible.

18.3 Enforcing Med-arb Clauses

There is no problem about enforcing arbitration agreements. In many jurisdictions, the mere reference to 'arbitration' as a means for resolving disputes arising in connection with a commercial contract will, without more, be enough to constitute an enforceable arbitration agreement.[14] There is no need to specify a seat of arbitration, a governing law or procedural rules for the arbitration, or even how many arbitrators there should be and how individual arbitrators are to be appointed. The arbitration statute in many jurisdictions will fill in the requisite details, in default of an agreement between the parties as to how their arbitration is to be carried out.

But the same is not true of mediation or hybrid dispute resolution clauses involving mediation. There may be at least two reasons for the lack of legislation. The first is that mediation is supposed to be a voluntary process. Accordingly, countries may hesitate at enacting a statute which compels a party to abide by (say) a mediation or med-arb clause and to initiate mediation despite the party being unwilling to mediate for whatever reason. The second has, at least historically, been a preoccupation among common law (rather than civil law) jurisdictions. That is the view (frequently supported in common law courts by invoking the House of Lords' decision in *Walford v Miles*)[15] that an agreement to mediate is nothing more than 'an agreement to agree' and so unenforceable for lack of certainty. More recently, however, this second reason has become less of an obstacle. The courts in several common law jurisdictions have held that agreements to mediate with particular characteristics are sufficiently certain to be enforceable.[16]

---

[14] See eg *Hobbs Padgett & Co (Reinsurance) Ltd v JC Kirkland Ltd* [1969] 2 Lloyd's Rep 547, 549 (Salmon LJ).

[15] [1992] 1 AC 128, where Lord Ackner (at 138C) famously stated: 'The reason why an agreement to negotiate, like an agreement to agree, is unenforceable, is simply because it lacks the necessary certainty.'

[16] See eg in England, *Cable & Wireless plc v IBM United Kingdom Ltd* [2002] EWHC 2059 (Comm), [2002] 2 All ER (Comm) 1041 (holding that a mediation agreement was sufficiently certain where it provided for the parties to attempt to resolve their disputes in good faith through an ADR procedure recommended by the Centre for Effective Dispute Resolution (CEDR) in London); in Singapore, *HSBC Institutional Trust Services (Singapore) Ltd v Toshin Development Singapore Pte Ltd* [2012] 4 SLR 738 (holding that a mediation agreement was sufficiently certain where it required the parties to negotiate in good faith) and *International Research Corp plc v Lufthansa Systems Asia Pacific Pte Ltd* [2014] 1 SLR 130 (holding (albeit obiter) that a multi-tier dispute resolution clause was sufficiently certain as the agreed preconditions to arbitration had been set out 'in mandatory fashion and with specificity'); in New South Wales, *Aiton Australia Pty Ltd v Transfield Pty Ltd* [1999] NSWSC 996 (holding that a mediation agreement was enforceable insofar as it was mandatory, specifying the procedure to be followed in the mediation and setting out how a mediator was appointed). See further the analysis of the foregoing cases and others like them in Chapters 8 (Section 8.2), 12

To deal with the both reasons just canvassed, the law of a state could specify that agreements to mediate are enforceable insofar as they are 'mandatory' in nature. Agreements to mediate would be 'mandatory' in nature to the extent that they *require* the parties to attempt in good faith to resolve their disputes through mediation. The legal principle just identified is in actuality the position that has been reached in Singapore as a result of *HSBC Institutional Trust Services*.[17] The Court of Appeal in that case equated a requirement of 'good faith' with one to use 'best endeavours'. Contractual provisions to use 'best endeavours' being routinely enforced by the courts without difficulty, there was no reason to regard an obligation to use 'good faith endeavours' any differently. By similar logic, there should be nothing unworkable or impractical about the 'good faith' requirement

> (Section 12.2) and 14 (Section 14.2). Of the leading common law jurisdictions covered in this book, only Hong Kong now appears to adhere to the narrow construction of a mediation clause as an agreement to agree. See *Hyundai Engineering & Construction Co Ltd v Vigour Ltd* [2005] 3 HKLRD 723 (Rogers VP, Le Pichon and Yuen JJA). At first instance [2004] 3 HKLRD 1, the author had pointed out (at [83]) that there were difficulties with Lord Ackner's approach in *Walford v Miles*:
>
>> Why [as Lord Ackner stated] is the Court able to assess whether 'best endeavours' have been used to reach a final agreement, but not whether negotiations have been conducted 'in good faith' towards final agreement? I doubt that there is any conceptual difficulty (as opposed to the usual problems of proof or evidence which would exist in any case) with the objective assessment of either category of negotiations. At heart, the Court must pose the same question which it regularly asks, namely, whether applying an objective standard the parties have acted reasonably in all the circumstances in carrying out a mutually agreed activity [such as mediation].
>
> But the Court of Appeal (at [27]) was adamant:
>
>> When taken as a whole it is clear that what was being said [by Lord Ackner] was that a court is not in a position to determine the good faith or otherwise of negotiations because a party is entitled to negotiate in any way it feels fit. In the first place it is inevitably acting in its own best interests and in the second place the tactics of negotiation may vary from person to person. In some cases, part of a negotiating tactic maybe to call off the negotiations hoping that better terms would be offered.
>
> The Court of Final Appeal (*Vigour Ltd v Hyundai Engineering and Construction Co Ltd* (unreported, FAMV 4/2006, 22 May 2006)) (Bokhary, Chan and Ribeiro PJJ) refused leave to appeal against the Court of Appeal's decision. But it left open the possibility of revisiting the enforceability of mediation agreements in a later case: 'The points of law put forward on behalf of the applicant are not reached in the peculiar circumstances of this case. We refrain from saying anything that might prejudge any of those points, which may yet reach the Court in some other case in the future.' No such case has come before the Court of Final Appeal to date.

[17] *HSBC Institutional Trust Services* (n 16).

being proposed here. Whether a person has acted in good faith by, for instance, refusing outright to engage in mediation can be evaluated by reference to normal standards of fairness and honest dealing, as well as ordinary commercial morality and practice.[18] It is accepted that there may be limits to how far one can go in evaluating whether a party has acted in good faith. For example, suppose that a party walks out of a mediation after only a few hours. Because of the principle of confidentiality, a court would not be able to look into what actually happened in the mediation to assess whether the walk-out was from genuine motives or simply stage-managed to create an impression of complying with a contractual requirement to mediate. But such limitation would simply be a consequence of a lack of admissible evidence, a common situation in court cases. The limitation would have nothing to do with whether an agreement to mediate is or is not certain enough to be enforceable.

Some jurisdictions (for example, New South Wales) posit additional requirements that an agreement to mediate must meet to be enforceable. Thus, there may be a requirement that a mediation clause identify the procedural rules that would apply to any mediation or specify how many mediators there should be and how they are to be appointed. However, if one is taking a minimalist approach, it is suggested that a good faith requirement will suffice. Using good faith as a touchstone, a court could decide, in much the same way that it assesses whether a party has acted reasonably or used best endeavours, whether a particular procedure or mediator proposed by a party, but rejected by the other, would constitute a mediation within the terms of the parties' agreement. If push comes to shove, a court can (as in Hong Kong)[19] exercise a power, by way of enforcing a mediation agreement, to direct that the parties engage a particular mediator at a given rate. The court might possibly order that a mediation pursuant to a mediation agreement be conducted pursuant to a specified body of rules (such as CEDR or ICC rules). But it may be better to leave it to the mediator appointed by the parties or designated by the court to decide on an appropriate procedure.[20]

---

[18] cf ibid [47].
[19] See, for instance, *Resource Development Ltd v Swanbridge Ltd* (unreported, HCA 1873/2009, 31 May 2010) (Registrar KW Lung); *Hak Tung Alfred Tang v Bloomberg LP* (unreported, HCA 198/2010, 16 July 2010) (Registrar KW Lung); *Upplan Co Ltd v Li Ho Ming* [2010] 6 HKC 457 (Registrar KW Lung); *C Y Foundation Group Ltd v Leonara Yung* [2012] 2 HKC 448 (Registrar KW Lung).
[20] cf art 7(2) of the UNCITRAL Model Law on International Commercial Mediation and International Settlement Agreements Resulting from Mediation 2018 (the 2018 Model Law).

The proposal put forward here is that 'the law of a given state specify' certain matters in connection with mediation agreements. Such a result can be attained by legislation or through the decision of a court. Of the two methods, the former would be the most direct means of achieving the desired effect.[21] The latter method suffers from the drawback that the court will have to wait for a case squarely to raise the issue of enforceability of an agreement to mediate before it can definitively rule on the matter. When legislating for the enforceability of mediation agreements, a country might, for the avoidance of doubt, include a provision mandating the observance of good faith in connection with agreements to mediate. Such provision would be analogous to Article 2A of the UNCITRAL Model Law on International Commercial Arbitration 2006 (the 2006 Model Law). In that way, unless they expressly state (which is unlikely) that there is no need to observe good faith in carrying out an agreement to mediate, the parties to a mediation agreement will automatically be under an obligation to carry out the same in good faith. It was observed earlier that, in the past, common law jurisdictions treated mediation clauses as uncertain agreements to agree. This may have been because, in contrast to civil law jurisdictions, the common law does not as a matter of law imply a duty obligation of good faith into contracts.[22] Given that many civil law jurisdictions require parties to observe good faith in the performance of contractual obligations, the last suggestion may be otiose for civil law jurisdictions.

The foregoing recommendations would ensure that agreements to mediate (including med-arb clauses) are generally enforceable. But even where there is an applicable law along the lines discussed, commercial parties drafting a med-arb clause should pay close attention to how the relevant

---

[21] The 2018 Model Law does not contain a provision making agreements to mediate enforceable. Art 5(2) of the 2018 Model Law merely provides: 'If a party that invited another party to mediate does not receive an acceptance of the invitation within 30 days from the day on which the invitation was sent, or within such other period of time as specified in the invitation, the party may elect to treat this as a rejection of the invitation to mediate.' The consequences of the rejection are not specified.

[22] On good faith at common law, see generally *Yam Seng Pte Ltd v International Trade Corporation Ltd* [2013] EWHC 11 (QB), [2013] 1 All ER (Comm) 1321; *Greenclose Ltd v National Westminster Bank plc* [2014] EWHC 1156 (Ch), [2014] WLR(D) 173 [150] ('[T]here is no general doctrine of good faith in English contract law and such a term is unlikely to arise by way of necessary implication in a contract between two sophisticated commercial parties negotiating at arms' length.'); *Compass Group UK v Mid Essex Hospital Services NHS Trust* [2013] EWCA Civ 200, [2013] BLR 265 [105]. ('[T]here is no general doctrine of 'good faith' in English contract law, although a duty of good faith is implied by law as an incident of certain categories of contract. . . . If the parties wish to impose such a duty they must do so expressly.')

provision is worded. Three dangers might be highlighted here. First, there has been a trend in arbitrations for respondents to object to a tribunal's jurisdiction on the basis of non-compliance with the preconditions to arbitration in a multi-tier dispute resolution clause. For instance, a common problem is where a mediation obligation in a hybrid dispute resolution clause is open-ended, not imposing a defined time period for mediation. Such situation leaves it open for a respondent to complain that it has not closed the door on mediation. The respondent alleges that it remains willing and able to mediate and so the commencement of arbitration is premature. A second danger is where only some differences are to go to mediation, while others are to be resolved in another forum. This type of formulation may spark disagreements over whether a particular dispute is to be resolved through mediation or in some other way.[23] Third, one must be careful to ensure that a med-arb clause allows a party to commence arbitration proceedings in the event that the initial mediation is unsuccessful or, for some reason, the mediation part of the med-arb clause turns out to be ineffective. One would not want to fall into the situation where the mediation and arbitration portions of a med-arb clause are found to be ineffective or inoperative by a court.

Professor Hiro Aragaki has noted that some jurisdictions have simply banned med-arb (in the narrow sense defined in this chapter) outright.[24] Despite the difficulties of med-arb, that would seem to be a draconian and unnecessary approach. It goes beyond the minimalist approach sketched out here. The objective of Section 18.4 will be to show that there are ways of conducting med-arb so as to circumvent its problems or at any rate mitigate them to an acceptable level. If there are such ways, there should be no need to legislate a blanket prohibition of med-arb.

18.4 Addressing Med-arb's Difficulties

Hong Kong's Arbitration Ordinance (Cap 609) (AO) suggests a possible method of conducting med-arb in section 33 which provides:

> (1) If all parties consent in writing, and for so long as no party withdraws the party's consent in writing, an arbitrator may act as a mediator after the arbitral proceedings have commenced.

---

[23] See eg *Inghams Enterprises Pty Ltd v Hannigan* [2020] NSWCA 82 (holding by a majority that a claim for unliquidated (as opposed to liquidated) damages fell outside the scope of a multi-tier dispute resolution clause).
[24] See Chapter 2 in this volume.

(2) If an arbitrator acts as a mediator, the arbitral proceedings must be stayed to facilitate the conduct of the mediation proceedings.

(3) An arbitrator who is acting as a mediator –

    (a) may communicate with the parties collectively or separately; and

    (b) must treat the information obtained by the arbitrator from a party as confidential, unless otherwise agreed by that party or unless subsection (4) applies.

(4) If –

    (a) confidential information is obtained by an arbitrator from a party during the mediation proceedings conducted by the arbitrator as a mediator; and

    (b) those mediation proceedings terminate without reaching a settlement acceptable to the parties, the arbitrator must, before resuming the arbitral proceedings, disclose to all other parties as much of that information as the arbitrator considers is material to the arbitral proceedings.

(5) No objection may be made against the conduct of the arbitral proceedings by an arbitrator solely on the ground that the arbitrator had acted previously as a mediator in accordance with this section.

A few preliminary remarks might be made about section 33. First, section 33 strictly applies only where an arbitration has been commenced and thereafter the arbitrator takes on the role of mediator. Thus, it really covers only 'arb-med' or 'arb-med-arb', using those terms here to describe a sequence of arbitration and mediation followed in the course of a given hybrid dispute resolution process. Section 33 does not on its terms deal with med-arb as defined for the purposes of this chapter. Second, section 33 is exclusive. If section 33 is to be used to validate a process wherein the same person is acting as mediator and arbitrator, then once an arbitration has commenced, the only way that the arbitrator may also act as mediator in the same dispute is by fulfilling the conditions imposed by section 33. Third, section 33 does not prevent an award from being challenged on the ground (say) that, in the resumed arbitration, the arbitrator inadvertently failed to disclose material confidential information.

What happens if something like the procedure in section 33 is adapted to med-arb? Where the mediation is unsuccessful, section 33 will not on its strict terms preclude a party from objecting to an award on the basis that arbitrator met in caucus (that is, on a one-to-one basis) with the other side during the abortive mediation. The court may, by analogy with section 33(5), rule that, the objecting party having agreed to the mediator also acting as arbitrator, the mere fact of the arbitrator having met separately with the other party should not be a sufficient basis to set aside an award. But that will be a matter of argument before the court. More pertinently, since section 33 does not prevent an award from attack on the ground that material confidential information was not disclosed by the mediator turned arbitrator, an award can still be challenged for material non-disclosure by the arbitrator, even if the med-arb process is conducted along section 33 lines. The difficulty is that, in real life, it often happens that information initially thought to be irrelevant at the start of an arbitration subsequently assumes critical importance when the issues are better understood. An arbitrator may easily fail to disclose a confidential fact that she or he regarded as immaterial when an arbitration resumes after a failed mediation, only to find that very fact assuming increasing importance as the arbitration proceeds. What happens then? At the point when it dawns on the arbitrator that some confidential fact is material, it may be too late to disclose the same without throwing the whole arbitration into jeopardy with consequent adverse effects in time and cost. Another common scenario is that an arbitrator forgets a piece of confidential information that was disclosed during the abortive mediation, only to recall the piece of material information well into the resumed arbitration. Belated disclosure at that point may likewise have significant consequences on the arbitration. In short, it would seem that there are just too many risks associated with a section 33-style med-arb. If the mediation is successful, of course there will be no problem. But if the mediation fails, embarrassing situations may arise.

Mr Haig Oghihian has suggested a different approach as a way out.[25] His method may more accurately be described as a form of 'arb-med' in the sense that a mediation is followed by an arbitration. The arbitrator conducts the arbitration to the point of writing an award. The arbitrator places the award in a sealed envelope and deposits the latter with an independent third person. The arbitrator informs the parties that the award has been written and offers to resolve the dispute by mediation. If the mediation is successful, the envelope containing the award is destroyed. If the mediation is unsuccessful, the envelope is opened and the award therein is made available to the parties. Mr Oghihian is the first person to acknowledge that his approach would not be suitable for every arbitration.[26] An obvious drawback would be that the costs of the entire

---

[25] Haig Oghigian, 'The Mediation/Arbitration Hybrid Concept in Dispute Resolution (Med/arb)' <https://journal.arbitration.ru/analytics/the-mediation-arbitration-hybrid-concept-in-dispute-resolution-med-arb-/> accessed 1 October 2020.

[26] Personal communication to the author.

arbitration will have been incurred before any mediation. In a complex commercial matter, the costs of such an exercise may be significant. Most, if not all, of the practical benefit of med-arb will thus have been lost, even if the ensuing mediation is successful. Nor is it clear that the parties will reap the psychological benefit posited in Section 18.2. It would be unusual if, having fought tooth-and-nail during the arbitration stage, the parties should still be seeking the understanding and empathy of the arbitrator-mediator or the other party. In all probability, each side will have exhausted themselves doing battle in the arbitration and would prefer just to know the ultimate outcome without further ado. There is also a real question as to whether, having already decided the case, the arbitrator can still act as an 'honest broker' between the parties so as to facilitate a resolution of their dispute. One of the most powerful tools in a mediator's arsenal is reality testing. There would be something artificial in an arbitrator-mediator engaging in genuine reality testing with one or other party when the arbitrator-mediator already has irretrievably committed to an actual outcome. It is submitted that Mr Oghigian's method would be appropriate only for simple commercial matters where the arbitrator can readily pick up the material facts and write an award after brief submissions from the parties. In those circumstances, the initial arbitration stage may not involve much time and cost and the parties may still be prepared to settle.

The 2019 Interactive Arbitration Rules (the IAR)[27] of the Japan Commercial Arbitration Association (JCAA) offer scope for a variation on Mr Oghigian's method. The IAR stipulates:

> *Article 48. Arbitral Tribunal's Active Role in Clarifying Parties' Positions and Ascertaining Issues*
>
> 1. At a stage as early as possible in the arbitral proceedings, the arbitral tribunal shall draft a document containing a summary of each Party's positions on factual and legal grounds of the claim and the defense ('Positions') and the factual and legal issues that the arbitral tribunal tentatively ascertains arising from the Positions ('Issues'). The arbitral tribunal shall present such document to the Parties, and give the Parties an opportunity to comment on the Positions and the Issues within a time limit fixed by the arbitral tribunal.
> 2. Within the time limit fixed by the arbitral tribunal under Article 48.1, the Parties shall provide their comments in writing on the Positions

---

[27] Available at <www.jcaa.or.jp/en/common/pdf/arbitration/Interactive_Arbitration_Rules2019 _en.pdf> accessed 1 October 2020.

and the Issues specifying which parts of the Positions and the Issues they agree or disagree with.
3. The arbitral tribunal may revise the Positions and the Issues taking into account the comments provided by the Parties under Article 48.2.
4. The arbitral tribunal may use the revised Positions under Article 48.3 as the Parties' positions set forth in the arbitral award.
5. Notwithstanding Article 48.4, during the further course of the arbitral proceedings, if a Party finds further amendments to be required, the Party may request in writing that the Positions be amended. Unless the arbitral tribunal rejects the request because of delay, the arbitral tribunal may use such amended Positions as the Party's position set forth in the arbitral award.

Article 48 was modelled on an analogous procedure employed by the Japanese court which has had wide approval and been found to facilitate resolution of disputed issues.[28]

A possibility would be for the tribunal, during the IAR Article 48 process, to attempt to mediate and resolve in whole or part the parties' differing positions on the issues. It would be consistent with the tribunal's proactive role as mandated by Article 48 for it to engage in hardcore reality testing of the parties' stances. Skilfully and carefully executed, such reality testing would not constitute the tribunal descending into the arena. The exercise would be little different from the reality testing that judges routinely engage in when they roll up their eyes at a party's hopeless submissions and invite counsel to move on to their best point. The key difference between a 'mediation' during the IAR Article 48 process and a conventional mediation would be that, in the former, the

---

[28] The practice of a court informing the parties of its provisional views on a case for the purposes of encouraging settlement and obviating the need for a final judgment is not just a feature of modern Japanese civil procedure. It has traditionally been a hallmark of the civil law generally. Thus, the reconciliation of parties, as opposed to the declaration of an outright winner, has historically been a significant aspect of French judicial procedure. In a private communication, Professor Peter Stein drew the author's attention to 'the provisional character of some judgements of civil law courts'. In Professor Stein's view, the reason was that 'because of known difficulties in enforcing a judgment contained in a final decree, the judges sometimes preferred to persuade the parties voluntarily to agree to accept such a compromise rather than proceed to final judgement'. See Peter Stein, *Legal Institutions: The Development of Dispute Settlement* (Butterworths 1984). On the judge's duty of conciliation in modern French civil procedure, see, for instance, Pierre Catala and François Terré, *Procédure civile et voies d'exécution* (2nd edn, Presses universitaires de France 1976) 349, 365–66; Gérard Couchez, *Procédure civile* (12th edn, Armand Colin 2002) 238–39. The civil law practice of using provisional judgments to encourage settlement would accordingly seem to be a relatively early form of multi-tier dispute resolution.

tribunal should not meet separately with the parties and receive confidential communication from a party in caucus. Everything said or communicated in writing by one party to the tribunal would be said in the presence of or copied to the other party. Both sides would then have the opportunity to deal with whatever the other has said. Depending on the tribunal's skill or ability as mediators, it would be possible to a greater or lesser degree for the tribunal to entertain submissions which are not strictly relevant as a matter of legal principle but which may be important towards fully understanding a party's position on an issue. In other words, mediation during the IAR Article 48 process can incorporate informal elements and need not be confined to establishing purely formal positions on law and fact.

By the touchstone of the minimalist approach discussed, the IAR Article 48 mediation process may be regarded as unnecessarily formal. Like Mr Oghigian's solution to the difficulties inherent in med-arb, a drawback to the IAR Article 48 process is the need to start an arbitration. In terms of sequence, the IAR Article 48 process is an arb-med or possibly arb-med-arb process. It is not med-arb. It might be queried why it is necessary to start an arbitration. To achieve potentially greater saving in time and cost and to enhance informality and flexibility from the outset, the parties can start directly with mediation. The only limitation on such mediation would be the prohibition against meeting the parties in caucus. A party would be free to communicate whatever it would like about its stance during a case, but everything it says or writes must be done in the presence of (or simultaneously made known to) the other party. If the initial mediation fails, each side would know what has been communicated to the other and could tailor its submissions during the arbitration stage accordingly. The parties having agreed to the mediator acting as arbitrator, they would not be able subsequently to object to such process having been followed. It is accepted that some, perhaps many, mediations are successful because the mediator is able to meet privately with each side and discuss the parties' respective positions in confidence. But, if med-arb is not to be devilled by its inherent contradictions, something must give. It is submitted that dispensing with caucus meetings with the mediator would be an acceptable price to pay to maintain the integrity of the med-arb process. It would be consonant with the minimalist approach. It might be that such sacrifice is not conducive to all disputes. But in that case the parties can always opt to have different individuals acting as mediator and arbitrator.

It would be worthwhile, to place the foregoing discussion in context, to consider a further option, albeit one that is neither med-arb nor arb-med. Dr Nobumichi Teramura has argued[29] that commercial parties should be more willing to have their disputes settled by *ex aequo et bono* arbitration, that is, arbitration in which the tribunal renders an award in accordance with what it considers to be fair and just in all the circumstances. Although *ex aequo et bono* arbitration is possible under the rules of most arbitral institutions, parties never opt for it. Such mode of proceeding is thought to be too uncertain in outcome. Dr Teramura suggests, however, that *ex aequo et bono* proceedings are in actuality constrained in their outcomes and thus far from arbitrary and unpredictable. Because of their relative informality, such proceedings instead offer a prospect of 'cutting to the quick' and arriving at a robust rough-and-ready, but eminently practical, resolution of the parties' commercial disputes. The only point being made here is to ask rhetorically whether, instead of choosing med-arb, it would be better for parties simply to agree to *ex aequo et bono* arbitration. The process would be more informal than conventional arbitration. Parties would have free rein to make their real concerns known to the arbitrator, unconstrained by formal rules of procedure and evidence. The process may or may not be less expensive than med-arb, depending on whether the initial mediation of a med-arb is successful. The downside (and it is a major one) is that, unlike med-arb where parties may accept or reject rough-and-ready solutions thrown up by the mediation process, the parties in an *ex aequo et bono* arbitration are bound to accept what the arbitrator awards by way of a resolution of their dispute.

Empirical research may shed light on whether, a mediation having failed, parties would generally prefer to have their dispute decided (1) strictly in accordance with their respective legal rights or (2) in a rough-and-ready manner in accordance with what the mediator turned arbitrator believes to fair and just in all the circumstances. If the latter is the case, while the parties may find a pure *ex aequo et bono* arbitration to be too uncertain and hesitate to opt for such as a means of resolving their disputes, they may be prepared to contemplate med-arb where the ensuing arbitration is conducted on an *ex aequo et bono* basis. The mediator turned arbitrator would then be entitled, subject to the parties' submissions in the course of the arbitration, to take full account of the informal

---

[29] Nobumichi Teramura, *Ex Aequo et Bono as a Response to the 'Over-Judicialisation' of International Commercial Arbitration* (Wolters Kluwer 2020).

elements raised by the parties during the mediation stage. Note that, in any case, for the reasons already canvassed, in this type of med-arb, it will still be necessary to prohibit caucus meetings during the mediation stage.

Even if med-arb is conducted along the lines suggested here, much will continue to depend on the personality, skill and authority of the mediator-arbitrator. Whether acting as mediator or arbitrator, the person appointed by the parties must at all times maintain her or his neutrality. She or he must not seem to descend into the arena or side with one or other party.[30] This is easier said than done. Mediation is frequently characterised as a 'non-adversarial' or 'non-confrontational' process which enables parties to maintain established relationships. That may be correct as a general statement. But, in the author's experience, mediations can be (and often are) stressful. Parties will come to a mediation in seemingly implacable mood. They will read out prepared non-conciliatory opening statements that make clear that they expect the other side to make substantial concessions before they will budge an inch from firmly entrenched positions. Mediations may even need to reach a moment of crisis, where everything seems hopeless, before slowly the parties work out some sort of settlement. Gone are the days when mediators simply act as post-boxes, dutifully conveying the offers and counteroffers of each party and nothing more. A more evaluative (as opposed to purely facilitative) style of mediation is coming to be increasingly favoured.[31] At any rate, today's mediator will likely have to engage in tough, extensive reality testing throughout the mediation of a commercial dispute. The mediator-arbitrator will thus have to enjoy the respect of the parties such that, if she or he questions the wisdom of a position taken by one or other party, her or his opinion and authority will carry weight. In such environment, unless the mediator-

---

[30] For instance, art 7(3) of the 2018 Model Law requires that a mediator 'maintain fair treatment of the parties', while art 18 of the 2006 Model Law stipulates that an arbitrator should treat the parties with 'equality' and provide each party with 'a full opportunity' of presenting its case.

[31] In Hong Kong, for instance, a Special Committee on Evaluative Mediation has been established to look into the greater use of evaluative mediation 'so as to provide more choices in terms of mediation techniques to mediators and end-users of mediation in Hong Kong'. See Department of Justice, '2018 Policy Initiatives of the Department of Justice' (CB(4)20/18–19(01)), paper prepared for a discussion of the Legislative Council Panel on Administration of Justice and Legal Services on 29 October 2018 (*Legislative Council of the HKSAR*, October 2018) <www.legco.gov.hk/yr18-19/english/panels/ajls/papers/ajlscb4-20-1-e.pdf> accessed 1 October 2020, para 49.

arbitrator is careful, she or he can convey an impression of badgering a party, through over-robust reality testing and evaluative commentary, to accept propositions advanced by the other side. If the mediation collapses and an arbitration ensues, any perception of 'badgering' may lead to the eventual award being challenged for actual or apparent bias by the losing party, despite the mediation having otherwise been conducted as recommended in this section. An inept mediator-arbitrator will put the integrity of an award at risk, no matter how impeccable the procedure followed in the med-arb may have been in theory.

18.5 Enforcing Med-arb's Outputs

Section 18.2 highlighted the risk of an award not being recognised or enforced if the med-arb process was conducted in too loose and informal a manner. It is hoped that the proposals in Section 18.4 will adequately deal with the problem.

That leaves the enforcement of a mediated settlement agreement in international commercial disputes. An obvious solution to the question of enforcement of such settlement agreements, one that has been endorsed in other chapters of this book, is accession to the 2019 United Nations Convention on International Settlement Agreements Resulting from Mediation (the Singapore Convention). This came into effect on 12 September 2020. As at that date, there were six contracting states to the Singapore Convention (Singapore, Belarus, Ecuador, Fiji, Qatar and Saudi Arabia). In addition to those countries, forty-seven states have signed the instrument and presumably will accede to it in due course. This section will confine itself to three observations in relation to the Singapore Convention.

First, the problem of enforcing mediated settlement agreements internationally should be seen in perspective and not overblown. If parties voluntarily agree to settle their dispute and enter into an agreement to that effect, there will be a high likelihood of compliance with the agreement. A rule of thumb is that in 90 per cent of cases, arbitral awards are honoured.[32] The corresponding percentage for mediated settlement agreements should be higher. Difficulties in enforcing mediated

---

[32] See eg this 2008 report: Queen Mary University of London and PricewaterhouseCoopers (PwC), 'International Arbitration: Corporate Attitudes and Practices' (2008) <www.imimediation.org/research/gpc/series-data-and-reports/#6-gpc-series-data-and-reports> accessed 1 October 2020, 2, 8, 13.

settlement agreements internationally will probably arise only in well under 10 per cent of cases. The real issue is a matter of perception. The lawyer drafting a dispute resolution clause in a client's international commercial contract will be asked about enforcement by the client. In the past, the lawyer would have answered that arbitral awards are enforceable in the 164 countries that have acceded to the New York Convention and judgments may be enforced pursuant to treaties or conventions (such as the 2005 Hague Convention) to which a relevant state is party. Until recently, the lawyer would have had to acknowledge that there was no analogous convention for mediated settlement agreements. Such answer would have deterred the client, out of an abundance of caution, from opting for a mediation or med-arb clause, even if the risk of non-compliance with a mediated settlement agreement is low. At most, the client might opt instead for an arb-med-arb clause, so that any mediated settlement agreement reached in the event of a dispute might be enforced through the New York Convention by means of an arbitral award embodying the terms of the parties' settlement. The Singapore Convention dramatically changes the picture. Once a substantial number of countries have acceded, the Singapore Convention existence will assure clients that mediated settlement agreements are readily enforceable and thereby overcome any reluctance to incorporate a mediation or med-arb clause in their contracts. There will be no need to safeguard the enforceability of any mediated settlement agreement that parties might reach, by setting up an arbitral tribunal (and incurring the time and costs thereof) before engaging in mediation.

Second, a number of states may hesitate to join the Singapore Convention because it treats mediated settlement agreements in international commercial disputes preferentially to mediated settlement agreements in domestic commercial disputes.[33] In many countries, including Singapore, a mediated settlement agreement in a domestic commercial dispute can be enforced only by suing the defaulting party for breach of the relevant agreement.[34] In contrast, Article 4 of the

---

[33] The author understands that Professor Masato Dogauchi has made this point in relation to Japanese law at a 2019 conference in Japan.

[34] In common law jurisdictions (including Singapore), however, it may be relatively straightforward to apply for summary judgment against the party breaching a domestic mediated settlement agreement. In other words, at the same time as writ is served, the claimant would take out a summons for summary judgment on the ground that there is no arguable defence to the claim. The summary judgment procedure may even be just or nearly as swift and effective in enforcing a mediated settlement agreement as the procedure envisaged in art 4 of the Singapore Convention.

Singapore Convention envisages that each contracting state will have a simple procedure in place for enforcing international mediated settlement agreements. When deciding whether to accede to the Singapore Convention, countries may therefore have to consider whether there are valid grounds for treating international and domestic mediated settlement agreements differently or, perhaps, whether a system such as that in Article 4 of the Singapore Convention should be established for domestic mediated settlement agreements.

Third, countries may additionally be nervous about joining the Singapore Convention because they take the view that the instrument can be used to facilitate organised crime (such as money laundering). Such concern has recently been expressed by Justice Hamid Sultan bin Abu Backer of the Court of Appeal in Malaysia:[35]

> It must be emphasised that: (a) even in domestic disputes a settlement agreement to be enforced through a court system must pass the test that the agreement is valid and enforceable. It is often seen as a cardinal test to sustain the rule of law; (b) whether an agreement is valid and enforceable is a separate exercise of judicial power and is not subject to party autonomy concept. This strict procedure is maintained in arbitration, statutory adjudication and even in court mediated settlement. However, it is not patent under the Convention. The enforcement procedure appears to be administrative in nature and if there is no objection the enforcement will go through. It will create a fertile opportunity to enforce agreements which may be related to severe violation of rule of law; (c) unlike an arbitration award, a settlement agreement will not set out the facts and grounds of decision for the enforcement court to be appraised of any breach of rule of law inclusive of criminal element related to the settlement; (d) jurisprudentially, fast-tracked enforcement within a framework where the rule of law is perceived to be compromised may naturally lead to unavoidable anarchy; (e) international commercial settlements may be for a substantial amount in quantum. Settlement agreements in breach of rule of law and enforcement in lightning speed with the support of electronic communication may result in fund disappearing overnight and there could be an avalanche of victims. Proper mechanism to check rule of law will indeed be welcomed; and (f) compromise deeds are dangerous when allowed to be enforced in other jurisdictions. It can

---

[35] See Haji Hamid Sultan bin Abu Backer, 'Singapore Mediation Convention: Is the Rule of Law Intact?' (*CIArb Features*, 6 September 2019) <www.ciarb.org/resources/features/singapore-mediation-convention-is-the-rule-of-law-intact/> accessed 1 October 2020. The article concludes: 'The [Singapore] Convention is a welcomed move in the evolution of ADR and enforcement of its orders. However, there must be safeguards to ensure the Rule of Law is not compromised'. In a footnote, the judge cautions that his article should 'be seen and read as food for thought only.'

lead to fraud and without knowledge of parties 'fraudulent settlement deeds', can be registered and enforced. It may even lead to a scam.

For example, in a case of illegal logging and environmental destruction by a foreign company in a Convention State A and subsequent sale to foreign company in a Convention State B and purported mediated settlement payment to be collected in Convention State B – will be good for enforcement in a Convention State B. All forms of offences as well money laundering activities will go unnoticed if no party objects. The convention may easily facilitate such a transaction. This will not happen in arbitration or litigation or even in a mediated settlement through court process via a respected seat.

To the extent that a country takes a similar view, a measure that might minimise the misuse of the Singapore Convention for criminal purposes would be to restrict the class of agreements that can be enforced under it to settlement agreements signed by mediators on the panel of recognised international mediation centres or by mediators who have achieved a statutorily defined level of competence and experience. The country in question can (1) gazette the relevant internationally recognised mediation centres or (2) compile an official list of mediators who have attained the designated level of competence or experience. Mediators could then apply to be listed on the panels of the gazetted mediation centres or to be placed on the country's official list of mediators.[36] The mediation centres to be gazetted and the mediators to be officially listed would not be confined to those in the given country. The gazette or list would be international in nature, so as to cater for the situations where a mediated settlement agreement executed in the relevant country is to be enforced elsewhere and vice versa. The measure could be put into effect through implementing legislation enacting the Singapore Convention into a country's domestic law. It is submitted that such a measure would not contravene a country's international obligations under the Singapore Convention because the instrument does not define who are to be regarded as 'mediators' for its purposes.[37] A suitable definition is consequently left for each contracting state to decide and implement through domestic legislation. A contracting state should thus be free in its implementing law to define which class of

---

[36] The system proposed here would be akin to the system in the 1961 Hague Convention Abolishing the Requirement of Legalisation for Foreign Public Documents (popularly known as the Hague Apostille Convention) for the recognition of notarial acts and deeds certifying the authenticity of private documents. See art 1(d) of the Hague Apostille Convention.

[37] Art 3(3) of the Singapore Convention merely refers to a 'mediator' as a 'third person ... lacking the authority to impose a solution upon the parties to the dispute'.

persons it will treat as 'mediators' for the purposes of the Singapore Convention. Restricting the class of mediators in this way will not eliminate the problems identified by Justice Hamid Sultan. But the measure will go a long way to mitigating the risks presaged.

In short, this chapter endorses what has been said in the other chapters of this book about the benefit to be reaped from accession to the Singapore Convention in terms of enhancing the enforceability across borders of mediated settlement agreements. Nonetheless, it must be accepted that there are legitimate concerns as to how the instrument should be implemented. Those concerns are not insurmountable. But allaying them will require concerted efforts among states in order to come up with protocols and safeguards that can apply uniformly among the parties to the Singapore Convention.

18.6 Conclusion

This final chapter has focused on what might be regarded as the most problematic form of hybrid dispute resolution. It has argued that med-arb can work in a way that (1) will allow ample flexibility and informality in its mediation stage but (2) will not jeopardise any award produced in its arbitration stage by reason of the mediation stage having been conducted too loosely. The proposals here can be generalised to apply to all forms of hybrid dispute resolution where the same neutral first acts as mediator and then as decision-maker in a dispute. Obviously, at the end of the day, no matter what safeguards have been put in place, the success of any hybrid dispute resolution process will depend on the person or persons engaged to act as mediator and decision-maker. But it is hoped that the proposals summarised here will generate renewed interest in the use of the same neutral in the capacities of mediator and decision-maker, as a means of international commercial dispute resolution.

Mediation comes into its own as a mode of dispute resolution in the post COVID-19 era, where cash flow will be tight and lockdowns and quarantine restrictions may periodically disrupt daily life and business. In such atmosphere, in contrast to what has been the norm in the past, protracted and costly arbitrations will not be a sustainable way of resolving commercial disputes, whether of a simple or a complex nature. Nevertheless, mediation by itself may not be a complete solution. It may not be sufficient for finally resolving all differences between commercial parties in the way that arbitration can do. For this reason, parties should take a closer look at med-arb and analogous hybrid dispute resolution clauses as enabling the best of both worlds, especially within the constraints imposed by COVID-19.

If the mediation stage (conducted as recommended in Section 18.4) succeeds, then all will be well and good. If the mediation fails, there is at least a chance, depending on the skills of the neutral engaged, that the mediation will have resolved some of the issues separating the parties. In any event, the mediator can straightaway assume the role of decision-maker and as such seek to resolve all remaining disputes with whatever degree of informality or formality the parties jointly desire. This inherent flexibility is a key advantage. At one end of the spectrum, the mediator turned decision-maker can proceed *ex aequo et bono* and make a determination as to what is just and fair on the basis (among other matters) of the informal concerns raised during the mediation stage and the formal merits of the parties' respective positions. At the other end of the continuum, the mediator turned decision-maker can rule definitively on the strict merits of the remaining issues, setting aside from his or her mind as irrelevant any informal representations made during the mediation and considering only salient facts in accordance with formal legal principles. Judges and tribunals routinely do this when parties raise irrelevant facts and matters in the course of court or arbitral proceedings. There is everything to gain in terms of significant savings in time and cost by using the same person as mediator and decision-maker in a dispute as espoused in this chapter. When wondering whether to opt for such a mode of hybrid dispute resolution, the question ultimately comes down to: what is there to lose?

BIBLIOGRAPHY

'10 Reasons to Mediate' (*US Equal Employment Opportunity Commission*) <www.eeoc.gov/10-reasons-mediate> accessed 1 September 2020

'2011 Population Census' (*Census and Statistics Department, the Government of the Hong Kong Special Administrative Region*, 25 February 2020) <www.censtatd.gov.hk/hkstat/sub/so170.jsp> accessed 7 September 2020

'2019 Annual Report' (*Financial Ombudsman Institution* 2020) <www.foi.org.tw/Article.aspx?Lang=2&Arti=1358&Role=1> accessed 20 September 2020

'2019 ICC Dispute Resolution Statistics' (*International Chamber of Commerce*) <https://iccwbo.org/publication/icc-dispute-resolution-statistics> accessed 24 February 2021

'2019 Statistics' (*Hong Kong International Arbitration Centre*) <www.hkiac.org/about-us/statistics> accessed 26 February 2020

'About the Office of Human Rights Proceedings' (*Office of Human Rights Proceedings*) <www.hrc.co.nz/ohrp/about/> accessed 1 September 2020

'About Us' (*Chinese Arbitration Association, Taipei*) <http://en.arbitration.org.tw/about.aspx> accessed 23 September 2020

'ADR *xunxi gonggao*' [ADR Bulletin] (*Judicial Yuan*) <www.judicial.gov.tw/tw/lp-1493-1.html> accessed 23 September 2020

'ADRIC Arbitration Rules' (*ADR Institute of Canada*) <https://adric.ca/rules-codes/arbrules> accessed 10 September 2020

'ADRIC Med-Arb Rules' (*ADR Institute of Canada*) <https://adric.ca/rules-codes/adric-med-arb-rules> accessed 10 September 2020

'Alberta Provincial Court Civil Claims Mediation' (*Canadian Forum on Civil Justice*, 24 October 2013) <https://cfcj-fcjc.org/inventory-of-reforms/alberta-provincial-court-civil-claims-mediation/> accessed 10 September 2020

'Alphabetical Index of the Political Entities and Corresponding Legal Systems' (*University of Ottawa*) <www.juriglobe.ca/eng/sys-juri/index-alpha.php> accessed 14 August 2020

'APEC's Collaborative Framework for Online Dispute Resolution of Cross-Border Business-to-Business Disputes – Endorsed' (*Asia-Pacific Economic Cooperation*) <http://mddb.apec.org/Documents/2019/EC/EC2/19_ec2_022.pdf> accessed 7 September 2020

'Arrangement between the Mainland and the Macau Special Administrative Region on Reciprocal Recognition and Enforcement of Arbitration Awards' (*Região Administrativa Especial De Macau Gabinete Do Chefe Do Executivo*) <https://bo.io.gov.mo/bo/ii/2007/50/aviso22_cn.asp> accessed 24 February 2021

'Arrangement Concerning Mutual Enforcement of Arbitral Awards between the Mainland and the Hong Kong Special Administrative Region' <www.doj.gov.hk/eng/topical/pdf/mainlandmutual2e.pdf> accessed 1 March 2020

'Belt and Road Portal' <https://eng.yidaiyilu.gov.cn> accessed 26 February 2020

'Chusaiho to no Kaisei ni Kansuru Chukan Shian' [Interim Draft Report on Reform of the Arbitration Act etc] <www.moj.go.jp/> accessed 17 May 2021

'Commercial Arbitration Rules (2019)' (*Japan Commercial Arbitration Association*) <www.jcaa.or.jp/en/arbitration/rules.html> accessed 14 November 2020

'Commercial Mediation Rules (2020)' (*Japan Commercial Arbitration Association*) <www.jcaa.or.jp/en/arbitration/rules.html> accessed 14 November 2020

'Commission Guidelines for the Exercise of the Amicus Curiae Function under the Australian Human Rights Commission Act (*Australia Human Rights Commission*, 18 September 2009) <https://humanrights.gov.au/our-work/legal/amicus-guidelines> accessed 1 September 2020

'Complaints about Banks' (*Hong Kong Monetary Authority*, 28 August 2020) <www.hkma.gov.hk/eng/key-functions/banking-stability/complaints-about-banks.shtml> accessed 7 September 2020

'COVID-19 and Duties of Good Faith under English Law' (*Dechert*, 25 June 2020) <www.dechert.com/knowledge/onpoint/2020/6/covid-19-and-duties-of-good-faith-under-english-law.html> accessed 14 November 2020

'Dazao guoji shangshi faying sifa baozhang "yidaiyilu" jianshe' [Creating the International Commercial Court, Legal Protection for the Belt and Road Construction] (*China International Commercial Court*, 19 March 2018) <http://cicc.court.gov.cn/html/1/218/149/156/571.html> accessed 17 August 2020

'Directive 2013/11/EU (Directive on Consumer ADR) – Issues Emerging from the Meetings of the ADR Expert Group' <http://ec.europa.eu/transparency/regexpert/index.cfm?do=groupDetail.groupDetailDoc&id=18896&no=3> accessed 7 September 2020

'Discrimination: Your Rights' (*gov.uk*) <www.gov.uk/discrimination-your-rights/what-you-can-do> accessed 1 September 2020

'Dispute Resolution Process' (*Financial Dispute Resolution Centre*) <www.fdrc.org.hk/en/html/resolvingdisputes/resolvingdisputes_fdrsprocess.php> accessed 7 September 2020

'Domestic Commercial Arbitration Rules of Procedure' (*British Columbia International Commercial Arbitration Centre*) <https://vaniac.org/arbitration/rules-of-procedure/previous-domestic-commercial-arbitration-rules-of-procedure/> accessed 9 October 2020

'Domestic Commercial Arbitration Rules of Procedure' (*Vancouver International Arbitration Centre*) <https://vaniac.org/arbitration/rules-of-procedure/domestic-arbitration-rules/> accessed 9 October 2020

'Expert Directory' (*China International Commercial Court*) <http://cicc.court.gov.cn/html/1/219/235/237/index.html> accessed 26 February 2020

'Explanatory Notes to Section 64 of the Enterprise and Regulatory Reform Act 2013' <www.legislation.gov.uk/ukpga/2013/24/notes/division/5/4/3/1> accessed 1 September 2020

'FDRC Annual Report' (*Financial Dispute Resolution Centre*) <www.fdrc.org.hk/en/html/publications/annualreport.php> accessed 7 September 2020

'Fees' (*Financial Dispute Resolution Centre*) <www.fdrc.org.hk/en/html/resolvingdisputes/resolvingdisputes_scheduleoffees.pdf> accessed 7 September 2020

'Final Communique of the 45th Session of the Council of Ministers of OHADA' (*OHADA.com*, 25 November 2017) <www.ohada.com/actualite/3856/communique-final-de-la-45e-session-du-conseil-des-ministres-de-l-ohada.html> accessed 18 October 2018

'Financial Dispute Resolution Scheme (FDRS)' (*Financial Dispute Resolution Centre*) <www.fdrc.org.hk/en/html/aboutus/aboutus_fdrs.php> accessed 7 September 2020

'Frequently Asked Questions' (*Office of Human Rights Proceedings*) <www.hrc.co.nz/ohrp/faqs/> accessed 1 September 2020

'General Contract Clauses: Alternative Dispute Resolution (Multi-tiered)' (*Thomson Reuters Practical Law Commercial Transactions*) <https://content.next.westlaw.com/9-555-5330> accessed 1 September 2020

'*Guanyu jianli "yidaiyilu" zhengduan jiejue jizhi he jigou de yijian*' [Opinion on Constructing 'Belt and Road Initiative' Dispute Resolution Mechanism and Institutions] [2018] Zhong Ban Fa 19 <www.gov.cn/zhengce/2018-06/27/content_5301657.htm> accessed 17 August 2020.

'Guidance on Responsible Contractual Behaviour in the Performance and Enforcement of Contracts Impacted by the COVID-19 Emergency (Published 7 May 2020): Update, 30 June 2020' (30 June 2020) <https://assets.publishing.service.gov.uk/government/uploads/system/uploads/attachment_data/file/899175/__Update_-_Covid-19_and_Responsible_Contractual_Behaviour_-_30_June__final_for_web_.pdf> accessed 14 November 2020

'Guide to Judiciary Policy' (*United States Courts*) <www.uscourts.gov/sites/default/files/vol02a-ch02_0.pdf> accessed 20 August 2018

'Home' (*Center for Effective Dispute Resolution*) <www.cedr.com> accessed 14 November 2020

'Home' (*Chinese Arbitration Association, Taipei*) <http://en.arbitration.org.tw> accessed 11 September 2020

'Home' (*Japan Association of Arbitrators*) <https://arbitrators.jp/> accessed 14 November 2020

'Home' (*Japan Commercial Arbitration Association*) <www.jcaa.or.jp/en/> accessed 14 November 2020

'Home' (*Japan International Dispute Resolution Centre*) <https://idrc.jp/en> accessed 14 November 2020

'Home' (*Japan International Mediation Center*) <www.jimc-kyoto.jp/> accessed 14 November 2020

'Home' (*London Chamber of Arbitration and Mediation*) <https://lcam.org.uk> accessed 14 November 2020

'Home' (*United Nations Commission on International Trade Law*) <https://uncitral.un.org> accessed 17 May 2021

'*Huanan guozhong tiaojie zhongxin jieshao*' [Introduction to the SCIA Mediation Centre] (*Yicaiwang*, 10 July 2014) <///www.cnarb.com/Item/1245.aspx> accessed 17 August 2020

'Information for Advocates and Lawyers Participating in Conciliation' (*Australian Human Rights Commission*) <www.humanrights.gov.au/sites/default/files/conciliation_-_information_for_advocates_lawyers_-_april_2017.pdf> accessed 1 September 2020

'International Commercial Arbitration Rules of Procedure' (*Vancouver International Arbitration Centre*) <https://vaniac.org/arbitration/rules-of-procedure/international-commercial-arbitration-rules-of-procedure/> accessed 9 October 2020

'Intervention in Court Proceedings: The Australian Human Rights Commission Guidelines' (*Australia Human Rights Commission*, 18 September 2009) <https://humanrights.gov.au/our-work/legal/intervention-court-proceedings-australian-human-rights-commission-guidelines> accessed 1 September 2020

'Investment Agreement under the Framework of the Mainland and Hong Kong Closer Economic Partnership Arrangement Mediation Rules for Investment Disputes' <www.tid.gov.hk/english/cepa/investment/files/HKMediationRule.pdf> accessed 26 February 2020

'Item for Financial Committee' (*Legislative Council*) <www.legco.gov.hk/yr10-11/english/fc/fc/papers/f11-23e.pdf> accessed 7 September 2020

'LCQ20: Mediation Service' (*info.gov.hk*, 23 February 2011) <www.info.gov.hk/gia/general/201102/23/P201102220246.htm> accessed 7 September 2020

'LCQ5 Annex' (*info.gov.hk*, 10 June 2020) <https://gia.info.gov.hk/general/202006/10/P2020061000538_343171_1_1591784369710.pdf> accessed 1 September 2020

'List of Mediators of Hong Kong Mediation Council' <www.tid.gov.hk/english/cepa/investment/files/mediators_hkiac.pdf> accessed 26 February 2020

'Mainland and Hong Kong Closer Economic Partnership Arrangement (CEPA)' (*Trade and Industry Department of the Government of the Hong Kong Special Administrative Region*) <www.tid.gov.hk/english/cepa/investment/mediation.html> accessed 26 February 2020

'Mandatory Claim Dispute Resolution Procedure (by Goltsblat BLP)' (*SPS 'Konsul'tantPlyus'* – *Consultant Plus Reference Legal System*)

'Mediation Figures and Statistics' (*Hong Kong Judiciary*) <http://mediation.judiciary/hk/en/figures_and_statistics.html> accessed 7 September 2020

'Notice of the General Office of the CPC Central Committee and the General Office of the State Council on Issuing the "Opinions Concerning Establishing BRI's International Commercial Dispute Resolution Mechanisms and Bodies"' (*People's Republic of China Central Government*, 27 June 2018) <www.gov.cn/zhengce/2018-06/27/content_5301657.htm> accessed 25 August 2020

'Opposing the Enforcement of PRC Arbitral Award on Public Policy Ground? Not as Easy as You Think!' (*ONC Lawyers*) <www.onc.hk/en_US/opposing-the-enforcement-of-prc-arbitral-award-on-public-policy-ground-not-as-easy-as-you-think/> accessed 7 September 2020

'PRIME Finance' (*Norton Rose Fulbright*) <www.nortonrosefulbright.com/en/knowledge/publications/11ad2a93/prime-finance> accessed 7 September 2020

'Principles, Criteria, Protocol and Competencies Required for the Designation Chartered Mediator-Arbitrator (C. Med-Arb)' (*ADR Institute of Canada*) <https://adric.ca/wp-content/uploads/2020/05/ADRIC_CMed-ARB_Criteria-1.pdf> accessed 10 September 2020

'Public Information Notice – Ontario Mandatory Mediation Program' (*Government of Ontario, Ministry of the Attorney General*, 9 September 2019) <www.attorneygeneral.jus.gov.on.ca/english/courts/manmed/notice.php> accessed 10 September 2020

'Publicação do Acordo sobre a Confirmação e Execução Recíprocas de Decisões Arbitrais entre o Interior da China e a Região Administrativa Especial de Macau' (*Região Administrativa Especial De Macau Gabinete Do Chefe Do Executivo*) <https://bo.io.gov.mo/bo/ii/2007/50/aviso22.asp> accessed 1 March 2020

'Questions and Answers – 2020 ADR Pilot' (*US Equal Employment Opportunity Commission*) <www.eeoc.gov/questions-and-answers-2020-adr-pilot> accessed 1 September 2020

'Questions and Answers Universal Agreements to Mediate (UAMS)' (*US Equal Employment Opportunity Commission*) <www.eeoc.gov/questions-and-answers-universal-agreements-mediate-uams> accessed 1 September 2020

'Reglement d'Arbitrage, de Mediation et de Conciliation du Centre d'Arbitrage de la CCIAD' [The Arbitration, Mediation, and Conciliation Rules of the CCIAD] <https://docplayer.fr/66350819-Reglement-d-arbitrage-de-mediation-et-de-conciliation-du-centre-d-arbitrage-de-la-cciad.html> accessed 2 April 2021

'Report of the Working Group on the Uniform Act on International Commercial Mediation' (2005)

'Rules on the Efficient Conduct of Proceedings in International Arbitration (Prague Rules)' (*Prague Rules* 2018) <https://praguerules.com/prague_rules/> accessed 1 March 2020

'Scope' (*Financial Dispute Resolution Centre*) <www.fdrc.org.hk/en/html/resolvingdisputes/resolvingdisputes_jurisdiction.php> accessed 7 September 2020

'*Shenxuhui xiangguan tongji ziliao*' [Relevant Statistical Information of the Complaints Commission] (*Public Construction Commission, Executive Yuan*) <www.pcc.gov.tw/cp.aspx?n=F34923ABE419ADE0> accessed 20 September 2020

'Statistics' (*China International Economic and Trade Arbitration Commission*) <http://cietac.org/index.php?m=Page&a=index&id=40&l=en> accessed 17 August 2020

'Status: United Nations Convention on International Settlement Agreements Resulting from Mediation' (*United Nations Commission on International Trade Law*) <https://treaties.un.org/pages/ViewDetails.aspx?src=TREATY&mtdsg_no=XXII-4&chapter=22&clang=_en> accessed 23 September 2020

'Submission to Court as Intervener and Amicus Curiae' (*Australia Human Rights Commission*) <https://humanrights.gov.au/our-work/legal/submissions/submission-court-intervener-and-amicus-curiae> accessed 1 September 2020

'Terms of Reference' (*Financial Dispute Resolution Centre*) <www.fdrc.org.hk/en/html/aboutus/aboutus_tor.php> accessed 7 September 2020

'The Arbitration Rules of Procedure of the CACI' (*Court of Arbitration of Côte d'Ivoire (CACI)*) <www.courarbitrage.ci/download/2/reglements/840/Arbitrage.pdf> accessed 11 October 2018

'The Court of Appeal: Judicial Mediation Program' (*The Courts of Nova Scotia*) <https://courts.ns.ca/Appeal_Court/NSCA_mediation_program.htm> accessed 10 September 2020

'The Mediation Rules of Procedure of the CACI' (*Court of Arbitration of Côte d'Ivoire (CACI)*) <www.courarbitrage.ci/download/47/reglements/838/Reglement%20Mediation%20CACI.pdf> accessed 11 October 2018

'The Rules of Arbitration of the CAC' (*Centre d'Arbitrage du Congo*) <http://cac-rdc.org/reglement-darbitrage/> accessed 12 October 2018

'The Rules of Arbitration of the GICAM' (*Groupement Inter-Patronal du Cameroun*) <www.legicam.cm/media/upload/2019049/reglement-darbitrage-cmag-1.pdf> accessed 2 April 2021

'Uniform Mediation Act' (*National Conference of Commissioners on Uniform State Laws*) <www.uniformlaws.org/shared/docs/mediation/uma_final_03.pdf> accessed 20 August 2018

'United States: EEOC Expands Voluntary Resolution Efforts with Temporary Mediation and Conciliation Pilot Programs' (*Mondaq.com*, 5 August 2020) <www.mondaq.com/unitedstates/employee-rights-labour-relations/972302/eeoc-expands-voluntary-resolution-efforts-with-temporary-mediation-and-conciliation-pilot-programs> accessed 1 September 2020

'Vision and Actions on Jointly Building Silk Road Economic Belt and 21st-Century Maritime Silk Road' (*Belt and Road Initiative – Hong Kong*) <www.beltandroad.gov.hk/visionandactions.html> accessed 26 February 2020

'What You Can Expect after a Charge Is Filed' (*US Equal Employment Opportunity Commission*) <www.eeoc.gov/employers/what-you-can-expect-after-charge-filed> accessed 1 September 2020

'Zuigao fayuan guoji shangshi fating yi shouli yipi guoji shangshi jiufen anjian' [The China International Commercial Court of the Supreme People's Court Have Accepted to Hear a Batch of Cases on International Commercial Disputes] (*China International Commercial Court*, 29 December 2018) <http://cicc.court.gov.cn/html/1/218/149/192/1150.html> accessed 26 February 2020

Abarchi D, 'La Supranationalité OHADA' (2000) 37 Revue burkinabé de droit 7

Abramson HI, 'Protocols for International Arbitrators Who Dare to Settle Cases' (1999) 10 American Review of International Arbitration 1

ADR Institute of Alberta Mediation Advocacy Task Force, 'White Paper 2016' (*ADR Institute of Alberta*, 15 March 2016) <https://adralberta.com/resources/Documents/White%20Paper%202016/WP%20May%2010,%202016.pdf> accessed 10 September 2020

Alberta Law Reform Institute, 'Uniform International Commercial Arbitration, Final Report 114' (6 March 2019)<www.alri.ualberta.ca/2019/03/uniform-international-commercial-arbitration-final-report-114/> accessed 14 August 2020

Alexander N, 'The Mediation Metamodel: Understanding Practice' (2008) 26 Conflict Resolution Quarterly 97

Alexander N, *International and Comparative Mediation: Legal Perspectives* (Wolters Kluwer 2009)

Alexander N, 'The Mediation Meta-model: The Realities of Mediation Practice' (2011) 12(6) ADR Bulletin: The Monthly Newsletter on Dispute Resolution 126

—— and Chong Shouyu (eds), *The Singapore Convention on Mediation: A Commentary* (Global Trends in Dispute Resolution, vol 8) (Kluwer Law International 2019)

Alfini JJ, 'Evaluative versus Facilitative Mediation: A Discussion' (1996) 24 Florida State University Law Review 919

Ali S, 'International Arbitration and Mediation in East Asia: Examining the Role of Domestic Legal Culture and Globalization on Shaping East Asian Arbitration' (PhD thesis, University of California at Berkeley 2007)

Ali SF and Da Roza A, 'Alternative Dispute Resolution Design in Financial Markets – Some More Equal Than Others: Hong Kong's Proposed Financial Dispute Resolution Center in the Context of the Experience in the United Kingdom, United States, Australia, and Singapore' (2012) 21(3) Pacific Rim Law & Policy Journal 486

—— and Kwok JKW, 'After Lehman: International Response to Financial Disputes – A Focus on Hong Kong' (2009) 152 Richmond Journal of Global Law & Business 102

Allemeersch B, 'Een geactualiseerde inleiding tot de bemiddelingswet' in R Van Ransbeeck (ed), *Bemiddeling* (Die Keure 2008)

Allen D, 'Strategic Enforcement of Anti-discrimination Law: A New Role for Australia's Equality Commissions' (2010) 36(3) Monash University Law Review 103

American Arbitration Association, *Commercial Arbitration Rules and Mediation Procedures* <www.adr.org/sites/default/files/CommercialRules_Web.pdf> accessed 29 August 2020

——*Drafting Dispute Resolution Clauses: A Practical Guide* <www.adr.org/sites/default/files/document_repository/Drafting%20Dispute%20Resolution%20Clauses%20A%20Practical%20Guide.pdf> accessed 29 August 2020

Angyal R, 'Med-arb – Past, Present and Future' <www.bar.asn.au> accessed 16 August 2020

Antaki NN, 'Muslims' and Arabs' Practice of ADR' [2009] 2 NYSBA New York Dispute Resolution Lawyer 113

Australian Human Rights Commission, 'Federal Discrimination Law' (*Australian Human Rights Commission* 2016) <https://humanrights.gov.au/sites/default/files/document/publication/AHRC_Federal%20Discrimination%20Law_2016.pdf> accessed 1 September 2020

Bamba A, 'La procédure d'arbitrage devant la Cour Commune de Justice et d'Arbitrage' (2000) Revue Penant numéro spécial no 833

Bang JP, 'South Korea' in FA Acomb and others (eds), *Multi-tiered Dispute Resolution Clauses* (IBA Litigation Committee 2015)

——Yu JJ and Umaer K, 'The Current State of ADR in Korea' (2017) 72 Dispute Resolution Journal 27

Barsky A, '"Med-arb": Behind the Closed Doors of a Hybrid Process' (2013) 51 Family Court Review 637

Baum H, 'Mediation in Japan: Development, Forms, Regulation and Practice of Out-of-Court Dispute Resolution' in KJ Hopt and F Steffek (eds), *Mediation: Principles and Regulation in Comparative Perspectives* (Oxford University Press 2012)

Beijing Arbitration Commission, 'Beijing Arbitration Commission Arbitration Rules' (2015) <http://bjac.org.cn/english/page/ckzl/sz2015.html> accessed 17 August 2020

Benzidi S, 'Med-arb: How to Mitigate the Risk of Setting Aside or Refusal of Recognition and Enforcement of a Med-arb Award' (2017) 10 American Journal of Mediation 1

Berger KP, 'Integration of Mediation Elements into Arbitration: "Hybrid" Procedures and "Intuitive" Mediation by International Arbitrators' (2003) 19 Arbitration International 387

——'Law and Practice of Escalation Clauses' (2006) 22 Arbitration International 1

——*Private Dispute Resolution in International Business* (Wolters Kluwer 2006)

Bergin PA, 'Mediation in Hong Kong: The Way Forward: Perspectives from Australia', paper delivered at the Hong Kong International Arbitration Centre (*Hong Kong International Arbitration Centre*, 30 November 2007) <www.supremecourt.justice.nsw.gov.au/Documents/Publications/Speeches/Pre-2015%20Speeches/Bergin/bergin301107.pdf> accessed 1 October 2020

Bienvenu P and Valasek M, 'Canada: Arbitration Guide: IBA Arbitration Committee' (*International Bar Association* 2018) <www.ibanet.org/Document/Default.aspx?DocumentUid=5A3BA1C8-73A9-4EBD-A160-69D43D25A8FA> accessed 10 September 2020

Bingham LB, 'Mandatory Arbitration: Control Over Dispute-System Design and Mandatory Commercial Arbitration' [2004] Law & Contemporary Problems 221

Blair W, Lein E, Gullifer L and Fu J, 'Breathing Space, Concept Note 2 on the Effect of the 2020 Pandemic on Commercial Contracts, September 2020 Update' (*British Institute of International and Comparative Law*) <www.biicl.org/breathing-space> accessed 14 November 2020

Blanke G, 'The Mediation Directive: What Will It Mean for Us?' (2008) 74 Arbitration 441

Blankley KM, 'Keeping a Secret from Yourself? Confidentiality When the Same Neutral Serves Both as Mediator and as Arbitrator in the Same Case' (2011) 63 Baylor Law Review 317

Bogdan M, 'The New EU Regulation on Online Resolution for Consumer Disputes' (2015) 9 Masaryk University Journal of Law & Technology 155

Boog C, 'The New SIAC/SIMC AMA-Protocol: A Seamless Multi-tiered Dispute Resolution Process Tailored to the User's Needs' (*Singapore International Mediation Centre*, 14 April 2015) <http://simc.com.sg/the-new-siacsimc-ama-protocol-a-seamless-multi-tiered-dispute-resolution-process-tailored-to-the-users-needs/> accessed 25 October 2018

Born G, *International Commercial Arbitration* (2nd edn, Wolters Kluwer 2014)

—— and Šćekić M, 'Pre-arbitration Procedural Requirements: "A Dismal Swamp"' in DD Caron and others (eds), *Practising Virtue: Inside International Arbitration* (Oxford University Press 2015)

Bourdin R, 'Le Règlement d'arbitrage de la Cour Commune de Justice et d'Arbitrage' (1999) 5 Revue Camerounaise de l'Arbitrage 10

Brazil WD, 'Judicial Mediation of Cases Assigned to the Judge for Trial' (2011) 17 Dispute Resolution Magazine 24

Bridge C, 'Med-arb and Other Hybrid Processes: One Man's Meat Is Another Man's Poison' (2014) 1(4) Australian Alternative Dispute Resolution Law Bulletin 76

Brown HJ and Marriot AL, *ADR Principles and Practice* (2nd edn, Sweet & Maxwell 1999)

Bühring-Uhle C, Kirchhoff L and Scherer G, *Arbitration and Mediation in International Business* (2nd edn, Kluwer Law International 2006)

Bush RAB, 'Handling Workplace Conflict: Why Transformative Mediation' (2001) 18 Hofstra Labor and Employment Law Journal 367

—— and Folger JP, *Promise of Mediation: The Transformative Approach to Conflict* (Jossey-Bass 2004)

Cabinet Office, 'Guidance on Responsible Contractual Behaviour in the Performance and Enforcement of Contracts Impacted by the COVID-19 Emergency' (7 May

2020) <https://assets.publishing.service.gov.uk/government/uploads/system/uploads/attachment_data/file/883737/_Covid-19_and_Responsible_Contractual_Behaviour__web_final___7_May_.pdf> accessed 14 November 2020

—— 'Guidance on Responsible Contractual Behaviour in the Performance and Enforcement of Contracts Impacted by the COVID-19 Emergency (published 7 May 2020): Update, 30 June 2020' (30 June 2020) <https://assets.publishing.service.gov.uk/government/uploads/system/uploads/attachment_data/file/899175/__Update_-_Covid-19_and_Responsible_Contractual_Behaviour_-_30_June__final_for_web_.pdf> accessed 14 November 2020

Cairns DJA, 'Mediating International Commercial Disputes: Differences in US and European Approaches' (2005) 60 Dispute Resolution Journal 3

Campbell D, 'International Dispute Resolution' (2010) 31A Comparative Law Yearbook of International Business 59

Canadian Forum on Civil Justice, 'Ontario Mandatory Mediation Program (Rules 24.1 and 75.1)' (*Canadian Forum on Civil Justice*, 21 November 2013) <https://cfcj-fcjc.org/inventory-of-reforms/ontario-mandatory-mediation-program-rules-24-1-and-75-1> accessed 10 September 2020

Carducci G, 'The New EU Regulation 1215/2012 of 12 December 2012 on Jurisdiction and International Arbitration: With Notes on Parallel Arbitration, Court Proceedings and the EU Commission's Proposal' (2013) 29 Arbitration International 467

Carter JH, 'Part 1 – Issues Arising from Integrated Dispute Resolution Clauses' in AJ van den Berg (ed), *New Horizons in International Commercial Arbitration and Beyond* (ICCA Congress Series No 12, Kluwer Law International 2005)

Catala P and Terré F, *Procédure civile et voies d'exécution* (2nd edn, Presses universitaires de France 1976)

CEDR Commission on Settlement in International Arbitration, *Final Report* (2009) <www.imimediation.org/download/102/public-libraries/31875/cedr-arbitration_commission_doc_final-nov-2009.pdf> accessed 15 April 2021

CEDR Model ADR Clauses for Commercial Contracts, Version 2020 <www.cedr.com/wp-content/uploads/2020/02/Model-ADR-Clauses-for-Commercial-Contracts-2020.docx> accessed 19 November 2020

Cha E, 'Enforcement of International Mediated Settlement Agreements in Asia: A Path towards Convergence' (2019) 15(1) Asian International Arbitration Journal 11

Chaisse J and Górski J (eds), *The Belt and Road Initiative: Law, Economics, and Politics* (Brill 2018)

Chan N, 'eBRAM Centre: The Law Tech Deal-Making & Dispute Resolution Platform to Facilitate Cross-Border Trade' <www.lscm.hk/sites/summit2018/eng/wp-content/uploads/2018/10/Nick-Chan_eBRAM-Centre-3Oct2018_.pdf> accessed 7 September 2020

Chapman S, 'Multi-tiered Dispute Resolution Clauses: Enforcing Obligations to Negotiate in Good Faith' (2010) 27 Journal of International Arbitration 89

Chen Ai'e and Wu Congzhou, '*Yi qiangzhi zhongcai tujing jiejue gonggong gongcheng caigou qiyue lvyue zhengyi zhi yanjiu*' [Research on Resolving Public Construction Procurement Contract Performance Disputes through Mandatory Arbitration] (2010) <www.ndc.gov.tw/News_Content.aspx?n=E4F9C91CF6EA4EC4&sms=4506D295372B40FB&s=D96F97CBFFF7BF8F> accessed 23 September 2020

Chen AHY, 'Confucian Legal Culture and Its Modern Fate' in R Wacks (ed), *The New Legal Order in Hong Kong* (Hong Kong University Press 1999)

Chen S and Chua E, 'Singapore Civil Procedure' in P Taleman (ed), *International Encyclopedia of Laws* (3rd edn, Kluwer Law and Business International 2018)

Chen Y, '*Gongcheng caigou lvyue zhengyi yu xin zhongcai jizhi zhi tantao*' [A Discussion on Construction Procurement Contract Performance Disputes within the New Arbitration Framework] (2018) 13(2) Gaoda faxue luncong 7

Cheng T-H, 'Reflections on Culture in Med-arb' in AW Rovine (ed), *Contemporary Issues in International Arbitration and Mediation: The Fordham Papers (2009)* (Brill 2010)

Cheng T, 'COVID-19 Online Dispute Resolution (ODR) Scheme' (*Department of Justice, the Government of the Hong Kong Special Administrative Region*, 13 April 2020) <www.doj.gov.hk/eng/public/blog/20200413_blog1.html> accessed 7 September 2020

——'Stand in Solidarity Against COVID-19' (*Department of Justice, the Government of the Hong Kong Special Administrative Region*, 11 April 2020) <www.doj.gov.hk/eng/public/blog/20200411_blog1.html> accessed 7 September 2020

——and Liu J, 'Enforcement of Foreign Awards in Mainland China: Current Practices and Future Trends' (2014) 31(5) Journal of International Arbitration 651

China International Commercial Court, *Procedural Rules for the China International Commercial Court of the Supreme People's Court (For Trial Implementation)* <http://cicc.court.gov.cn/html/1/219/208/210/1183.html> accessed 26 February 2020

China International Economic and Trade Arbitration Commission, 'China International Economic and Trade Arbitration Commission Arbitration Rules' (2015) <http://cietac.org/index.php?m=Page&a=index&id=106&l=en> accessed 17 August 2020

——*Zhongguo guoji shangshi zhongcai niandu baogao (2016)* [Annual Report on International Commercial Arbitration in China (2016)] <www.cietac.org/Uploads/201710/59df3824b2849.pdf> accessed 17 August 2020

——'China International Economic and Trade Arbitration Commission International Investment Arbitration Rules (For Trial Implementation)' (2017) <http://cietac.org/index.php?m=Page&a=index&id=390&l=en> accessed 17 August 2020

Chiou L-G, *The Theory of Procedural Choice* (Sanmin 2000)

Chiu H-J, 'New Constructions of Family Dispute Proceedings' [2002] Taiwan Law Journal 18

Choi J-S, 'Mediation Cases: Corporation-Related Disputes' (2019) 1 Asian Pacific Mediation Journal 99

Chong A (ed), *Recognition and Enforcement of Foreign Judgments in Asia* (Asian Business Law Institute 2017)

Chua E, 'Enforcement of Mediated Settlement Agreements in Asia – A Path towards Convergence' (2019) 15(1) Asian International Arbitration Journal 1

Coben JR and Thompson PN, 'Disputing Irony: A Systematic Look at Litigation about Mediation' (2006) 11 Harvard Negotiation Law Review 43

Collins L and Harris J (eds), *Dicey, Morris & Collins on the Conflict of Laws* (15th edn, Sweet & Maxwell 2012)

Comeau M, 'In Defense of Tiered Dispute Resolution Clauses' (*ADR Perspectives*, 17 December 2019) <http://adric.ca/adr-perspectives/in-defence-of-tiered-dispute-resolution-clauses/> accessed 10 September 2020

Corréa J-L, 'La médiation et la conciliation n droit sénégalais: libres propos sur un texte réglementaire' (2017) Bulletin de droit économique 1

Cortes P, *Online Dispute Resolution for Consumers in the European Union* (Routledge 2010)

Couchez G, *Procédure civile* (12th edn, Armand Colin 2002)

Court of Queen's Bench of Alberta, 'Notice to the Profession & Public – Enforcement of Mandatory Alternative Dispute Resolution Rules 8.4(3)(A) and 8.5(1)(A)' (*Alberta Courts*, 2 July 2019) <https://albertacourts.ca/qb/resources/announcements/notice-to-the-profession-public–enforcement-of-mandatory-alternative-dispute-resolution-rules-8.4(3)(a)-and-8.5(1)(a)> accessed 10 September 2020

Court of Queen's Bench of Alberta, 'Notice to the Profession: Mandatory Dispute Resolution Requirement Before Entry for Trial' (*Alberta Courts*, 12 February 2013) <https://albertacourts.ca/docs/default-source/qb/npp/notice-to-the-profession-public–mandatory-dispute-resolution-requirement-before-entry-for-trial–2013–01.pdf?sfvrsn=5664ac80_4> accessed 10 September 2020

Creutzfeldt N, 'Implementation of the Consumer ADR Directive' (2016) 5(4) Journal of European Consumer and Market Law 169

Croft C, 'Alternative Dispute Resolution in Arbitration: Is Arb-med Really an Option?' (November 2014) <www.supremecourt.vic.gov.au/about-the-court/speeches/alternative-dispute-resolution-in-arbitration-is-arb-med-really-an-option> accessed 16 August 2020

Deason EE, 'Combinations of Mediation and Arbitration with the Same Neutral: A Framework for Judicial Review' (2013) 5 Yearbook on Arbitration and Mediation 219

——'Beyond "Managerial Judges": Appropriate Roles in Settlement' (2017) 78(1) Ohio State Law Journal 105

Dedov D and Molotnikov A (eds), *Dispute Resolution in Russia: The Essentials* (Statut 2019)

DeGroote J, 'The Multi-step Dispute Resolution Clause: A Few Reasons Clients Like Them' (*Mediate.com*, April 2010) <www.mediate.com/articles/DeGrooteJbl20100405.cfm> accessed 29 August 2020

Delabrière A and Fenon A, 'La constitution du tribunal arbitral et le statut de l'arbitre dans l'Acte uniforme OHADA' (2000) Revue Penant numéro spécial no 833

De Loisy N, *Transportation and the Belt and Road Initiative: A Paradigm Shift* (SCMO Research 2019)

Dendorfer R and Lack J, 'The Interaction between Arbitration and Mediation: Vision vs. Reality' (2007) 1 Dispute Resolution International 1

De Palo G and Trevor MB, *Arbitration and Mediation in the Southern Mediterranean Countries* (Kluwer 2007)

——Feasley A and Orecchini F, 'Quantifying the Cost of Not Using Mediation – A Data Analysis' (April 2011) <www.europarl.europa.eu/document/activities/cont/201105/20110518ATT19592/20110518ATT19592EN.pdf> accessed 7 September 2020

——and others, '"Rebooting" the Mediation Directive: Assessing the Limited Impact of Its Implementation and Proposing Measures to Increase the Number of Mediations in the EU' (January 2014) <www.europarl.europa.eu/RegData/etudes/etudes/join/2014/493042/IPOL-JURI_ET(2014)493042_EN.pdf> accessed 7 September 2020

Department of Justice, '2018 Policy Initiatives of the Department of Justice' (CB(4) 20/18–19(01)), paper prepared for a discussion of the Legislative Council Panel on Administration of Justice and Legal Services on 29 October 2018 (*Legislative Council of the HKSAR*, October 2018) <www.legco.gov.hk/yr18-19/english/panels/ajls/papers/ajlscb4-20-1-e.pdf> accessed 1 October 2020

De Roo AJ and Jagtenberg RW, 'ADR in the European Union: Provisional Assessment of Comparative Research in Progress' in L Cadiet and others (eds), *Médiation et Arbitrage: Alternative Dispute Resolution: Alternative à la Justice ou Justice Alternative? Perspectives Comparatives* (LexisNexis 2005)

Dickerson CM, 'Harmonizing Business Law in Africa: OHADA Calls the Tune' (2005) 44 Columbia Journal of Transnational Law 17

Dogauchi M, '*Nihon Shoji Chusai Kyokai (JCAA) no atarashii ugoki – 3tsu no Shin Chusai Kisoku no Seko to* [New Movements of the Japan Commercial Arbitration Association – Putting into Force of Three New Arbitration Rules]' [2020] New Business Law 1141

Donahey MS, 'Seeking Harmony: Is the Asian Concept of the Conciliator/Arbitrator Applicable in the West?' (1995) 50 Dispute Resolution Journal 74

Douajni GK, 'Bilan et perspectives de l'arbitrage OHADA 20 ans après la création de l'OHADA' (2014) 48 Rev Burkinabède droit 158

Douajni K, 'Les mesures provisoires et conservatoires dans l'arbitrage OHADA' (2000) 8 Revue Camerounaise de l'Arbitrage 3

Duguid B, 'Multi-tiered Dispute Resolution: Stepping Carefully' (*Mondaq*, 20 August 2008) <www.mondaq.com/canada/x/65050/Arbitration+Dispute+Resolution/MultiTiered+Dispute+Resolution+Stepping+Carefully> accessed 10 September 2020

Edwards L and Wilson C, 'Redress and Alternative Dispute Resolution in EU Cross-Border E-commerce Transactions' (2007) 21 International Review of Law, Computers & Technology 3

Ehle B, 'The Arbitrator as Settlement Facilitator' in O Caprasse (ed), *Walking a Thin Line – What an Arbitrator Can Do, Must Do or Must Not Do: Recent Developments and Trends* (Bruylant 2010)

Equal Opportunities Commission, 'Report on Review of the Equal Opportunities Commission Governance, Management Structure and Complaint Handling Process' (*Equal Opportunities Commission*, 13 December 2019) <www.eoc.org.hk/EOC/Upload/UserFiles/File/Process_Review/EOCs_Review_Report_E.pdf> accessed 1 September 2020

Esplugues C, 'Access to Justice or Access to States Courts' Justice in Europe? The Directive 2008/52/EC on Civil and Commercial Mediation' (2013) 38 Revista de Processo (RePro) 304

——'Mediation in the EU after the Transposition of the Directive 2008/52/EC on Mediation in Civil and Commercial Matters' in C Esplugues (ed), *Civil and Commercial Mediation in Europe (Volume II: Cross-Border Mediation)* (Intersentia 2014)

——'General Report: New Developments in Civil and Commercial Mediation – Global Comparative Perspectives' in C Esplugues and L Marquis (eds), *New Developments in Civil and Commercial Mediation* (Springer 2015)

Fan K, 'Mediation and Civil Justice Reform in Hong Kong' (2011) 27 International Litigation Quarterly 2

——'The New Arbitration Ordinance in Hong Kong' (2012) 29 Journal of International Arbitration 719

——'An Empirical Study of Arbitrators Acting as Mediators in China' (2014) 15(3) Cardozo Journal of Conflict Resolution 777

Farmer D and Kley S, 'Med-arbs – Practical Considerations for Getting the Best of Both' (*ADR Institute of Canada*, May 2018) <https://adric.ca/adr-perspectives/med-arbs-practical-considerations-for-getting-the-best-of-both> accessed 10 September 2020

Fauteux P, 'Online Dispute Settlement: Quebec on a Promising Path' (2019) 28(1) Canadian Arbitration and Mediation Journal 19

Feasley A, 'Regulating Mediator Qualifications in the 2008 EU Mediation Directive: The Need for a Supranational Standard' [2011] Journal of Dispute Resolution 333

Fèviliyé I, 'La Révision du Traité de l'OHADA' (2009) Revue Congolaise de Droit et des Affaires 1

Fiechter EW, 'Mediation – Casting Issues: Can or Should the Same Person Be Mediator, or Conciliator and Arbitrator?' (2008) 15 Croatian Arbitration Year Book 255

Financial Dispute Resolution Centre, 'FDRC Annual Report 2013' <www.fdrc.org.hk/en/annualreport/2013/files/download/FDRC_annual_report.pdf> accessed 7 September 2020

——'Proposals to Enhance the Financial Dispute Resolution Scheme: Consultation Paper' (October 2016) <www.fdrc.org.hk/en/doc/Consultation_Document_ToR_EN.pdf> accessed 7 September 2020

——'FDRC Annual Report 2017' <www.fdrc.org.hk/en/annualreport/2017/files/download/FDRC_annual_report.pdf> accessed 7 September 2020

——'Consumer Fact Sheets 2018' <www.fdrc.org.hk/en/html/publications/publications_factsheetleaflet.php> accessed 7 September 2020

——'FDRC Annual Report 2018' <www.fdrc.org.hk/en/annualreport/2018/files/download/FDRC_annual_report.pdf> accessed 7 September 2020

——'FDRC Mediation and Arbitration Rules 2018' <www.fdrc.org.hk/en/doc/FDRS_Mediation_and_Arbitration_Rules_2018_en.pdf> accessed 2 April 2021

Flannery L and Merkin R, '*Emirates Trading*, Good Faith and Pre-arbitral ADR Clauses: A Jurisdictional Precondition' (2015) 31 Arbitration International 63

Friedland PD, *Arbitration Clauses for International Contracts* (2nd edn, JurisNet 2007)

Friel S and Toms C, 'The European Mediation Directive – Legal and Political Support for Alternative Dispute Resolution in Europe' (2011) 2 Bloomberg Law Reports – Alternative Dispute Resolution 3

Fu H and Cullen R, 'From Mediatory to Adjudicatory Justice: The Limits of Civil Justice Reform in China', in MYK Woo and ME Gallagher (eds), *Chinese Justice: Civil Dispute Resolution in Contemporary China* (Cambridge University Press 2011)

Garimella SR and Siddiqui NA, 'The Enforceability of Multi-tiered Dispute Resolution Clauses: Contemporary Judicial Opinion' (2016) 24(1) IIUM Law Journal 166

Garnett R, 'Australia's International and Domestic Arbitration Framework' in G Moens and P Evans (eds), *Arbitration and Dispute Resolution in the Resources Sector: An Australian Perspective* (Springer 2015)

Golann D, 'Is Legal Mediation a Process of Repair – Or Separation? An Empirical Study, and Its Implications' (2002) 7 Harvard Negotiation Law Review 301

Goldberg SB, 'The Mediation of Grievances under a Collective Bargaining Contract: An Alternative to Arbitration' (1982) 77 Northwestern University Law Review 270

Golvan G, 'What Do Clients Really Want – Hybrid Procedures, the New Frontier of Alternative Dispute Resolution' (2014) 1(4) Australian Alternative Dispute Resolution Law Bulletin 80

Goodrich M, 'Arb-med: Ideal Solution or Dangerous Heresy?' (2016) Construction Law Journal 370

Gorla G, 'Standard Conditions and Form Contracts in Italian Law' (1962) 11 American Journal of Comparative Law 1

Grimmer S, 'Distinction and Connection: Hong Kong and Mainland China, a View from the HKIAC' (*Global Arbitration Review*, 24 May 2019) <https://globalarbitrationreview.com/insight/the-asia-pacific-arbitration-review-2020/1193369/distinction-and-connection-hong-kong-and-mainland-china-a-view-from-the-hkiac> accessed 25 August 2020

—— and Charemi C, 'Dispute Resolution along the Belt and Road' (*Global Arbitration Review*, 22 May 2017) <https://globalarbitrationreview.com/chapter/1141929/dispute-resolution-along-the-belt-and-read> accessed 25 August 2020

Gross JI, 'Justice Scalia's Hat Trick and the Supreme Court's Flawed Understanding of Twenty-First Century Arbitration' (2015) 81 Brook Law Review 111

Grutters L and Barr BS, *FIDIC Red, Yellow and Silver Books: A Practical Guide to the 2017 Editions* (Sweet & Maxwell 2018)

Gu W, *Arbitration in China: Regulation of Arbitration Agreements and Practical Issues* (Sweet & Maxwell 2012)

—— 'The Delicate Art of Med-Arb and Its Future Institutionalization in China' (2014) 31 UCLA Pacific Basin Law Journal 97

—— 'When Local Meets International: Mediation Combined with Arbitration in China and Its Prospective Reform in a Comparative Context' (2016) 10(2) Journal of Comparative Law 84

—— 'China's Belt and Road Development and a New International Commercial Arbitration Initiative in Asia' (2018) 51(5) Vanderbilt Journal of Transnational Law 1305

—— 'Looking at Arbitration through a Comparative Lens' (2018) 13(2) Journal of Comparative Law 164

—— 'Hybrid Dispute Resolution Beyond the Belt and Road: Toward a New Design of Chinese Arb-med(-arb) and Its Global Implications' (2019) 29(1) Washington International Law Journal 117

—— 'Multi-tier Approaches and Global Dispute Resolution' (2020) 63 Japanese Yearbook of International Law 127

—— and Zhang X, 'The Keeneye Case: Rethinking the Content of Public Policy in Cross-Border Arbitration between Hong Kong and Mainland China' (2012) 42(3) Hong Kong Law Journal 1006

Guyon Y, 'Conclusion' (2004) 205 Les petites affiches 59

Hahm P-C, *The Korean Political Tradition and Law* (Royal Asiatic Society Korea Branch 1967)

——*Korean Jurisprudence, Politics, and Culture* (Yonsei University Press 1986)
Hamada Y, 'Minkan no Chotei ni yotteha Funso ga Kaiketsu sarenai toki ni Saibansho ni okeru Hoteki Shudan wo Kaishi suru Mune no Goi ga aru Baai ni oite, Togai Minkan no Chotei no Tetsuzuki wo hezuni Teiki sareta Sosho ga, Sosho Yoken ni kakeru mono deha nai to sareta Jirei [A Lawsuit Brought to the Courts without Prior Reference to Mediation Was Held to Fulfil Procedural Requirements, Although the Parties Had Agreed to Commence Litigation only When a Private Mediation Failed to Resolve Their Disputes]' (2012) Shiho Hanrei Remarks 45
Hamid Sultan bin Abu Backer Haji, 'Singapore Mediation Convention: Is the Rule of Law Intact?' (*CIArb Features*, 6 September 2019) <www.ciarb.org/resources/features/singapore-mediation-convention-is-the-rule-of-law-intact/> accessed 1 October 2020
Hann RG and others, 'Evaluation of Ontario Mandatory Mediation Program (Rule 24.1)' (*Legislative Assembly of Ontario*, 12 March 2001) <www.ontla.on.ca/library/repository/mon/1000/10294958.pdf> accessed 10 September 2020
Harpole SA, 'The Combination of Conciliation with Arbitration in the People's Republic of China' (2007) 24(6) Journal of International Arbitration 623
Harrison D, 'Singapore Convention a Big Boost for International Mediation' (*The Lawyer's Daily*, 17 December 2019) <www.thelawyersdaily.ca/articles/17194> accessed 10 September 2020
Hart S, 'England' in FA Acomb and others (eds), *Multi-tiered Dispute Resolution Clauses* (IBA Litigation Committee, 1 October 2015) <www.ibanet.org/Document/Default.aspx?DocumentUid=9C6E21DE-043C-44C9-BE75-94CADECCF470> accessed 14 November 2020
Hay P, 'Notes on the European Union's Brussels-I "Recast" Regulation' (2013) 1 European Legal Forum 1
Henderson A and Chua E, 'Singapore International Mediation Centre Is Launched, Offering Parties an "Arb-med-arb" Process in Partnership with SIAC' (*Herbert Smith Freehills*, 11 December 2014) <https://hsfnotes.com/arbitration/tag/ama-protocol/> accessed 25 October 2018
Herbert Smith Freehills and PricewaterhouseCoopers, *Global Pound Conference Series: Global Data Trends and Regional Differences* (2018) <www.imimediation.org/download/909/reports/35507/global-data-trends-and-regional-differences.pdf> accessed 2 April 2021
Herisi AA and Trachte-Huber W, 'Aftermath of the Singapore Convention: A Comparative Analysis between the Singapore Convention and the New York Convention' (2019) 12 American Journal of Mediation 154
Hetzel OJ and Gonzales S (eds), *Alternative Dispute Resolution in State and Local Governments: Analysis and Case Studies* (ABA Book Publishing 2015)
Hioureas C and Tewarie S, 'A New Legal Framework for the Enforcement of Settlement Agreements Reached through International Mediation:

UNCITRAL Concludes Negotiations on Convention and Draft Model Law' (*EJIL: Talk!*, 26 March 2018) <www.ejiltalk.org/a-new-legal-framework/for-the-enforcement-of-settlement-agreements-reached-through-international-mediation-uncitral-concludes-negotiations-on-convention-and-draft-model-law/> accessed 7 September 2020

HM Treasury, 'Standardisation of PF2 Contracts' <https://assets.publishing.service.gov.uk/government/uploads/system/uploads/attachment_data/file/207383/infrastructure_standardisation_of_contracts_051212.pdf> accessed 7 September 2020

Hollander-Blumoff R, 'Just Negotiation' (2010) 88 Washington University Law Review 381

Hong Kong Institute of Arbitrators, *Draft Report of the Committee of the Hong Kong Arbitration Law* (June 2002) <www.hkiac.org/sites/default/files/ck_filebrowser/PDF/services/95.pdf> accessed 2 April 2021

Hong Kong International Arbitration Centre, *2018 Administered Arbitration Rules* <www.hkiac.org/arbitration/rules-practice-notes/hkiac-administered-2018> accessed 26 February 2020

Hugo V, *Discours d'ouverture du Congrès littéraire international de 1878* (Calmann Lévy 1878)

Hussin A, Kück C and Alexander N, 'SIAC-SIMC's Arb-Med-Arb Protocol' (2018) 11 New York Dispute Resolution Lawyer 85

Hwang S and Inkook K, *Hangukhyeong daechejeok bunjaeng haegyeol (ADR) jedo ui baljeon banghyange gwanhan yeongu* [A Study for the Development of Korean-Style ADR Systems] Research Monograph 2016–04, Publication Registration No 32–9741568–000851–01 (Judicial Policy Research Institute 2016)

International Bar Association Litigation Committee, 'Multi-tiered Dispute Resolution Clauses' (October 2015) <www.ibanet.org/Document/Default.aspx?DocumentUid=9C6E21DE-043C-44C9-BE75-94CADECCF470> accessed 7 September 2020

Issa-Sayegh J, 'Quelques Aspects Techniques de l'Intégration Juridique: l'Exemple des Actes Uniformes de l'OHADA' [1999] Uniform Law Review 5

——'La portée abrogatoire des Actes Uniformes de l'OHADA sur le droit interne des Etats-Parties' (2001) 40 Revue Burkinabè de Droit 51

——and Lohoues-Oble J, *Harmonisation du droit des affaires* (Collection Droit uniforme africain) (Bruxelles 2002)

——Pougoué P-G and Sawadogo FM, *OHADA: Traité et Actes Uniformes commentés et annotés* (Juriscopte 2014)

James R and Morris P, 'The New Financial Ombudsman Service in the United Kingdom: Has the Second Generation Got It Right?' in CEF Rickett and TGW Telfer (eds), *International Perspectives on Consumers' Access to Justice* (Cambridge University Press 2003)

JAMS, *JAMS Clause Workbook: A Guide to Drafting Clauses for International and Cross-Border Commercial Contracts* (2018) <www.jamsadr.com/files/Uploads/Documents/JAMS-Rules/JAMS-International-Clause-Workbook.pdf> accessed 2 April 2021

Jeong SJ, 'Singapore Convention on Mediation and Recognition and Enforcement of Settlement Agreement' (2020) 24 Civil Procedure 1

Jolles A, 'Consequences of Multi-tier Arbitration Clauses: Issues of Enforcement' (2006) 72(4) Arbitration 329

Jones D, *Commercial Arbitration in Australia* (2nd edn, Thomson Reuters 2013)

Kajkowska E, *Enforceability of Multi-tiered Dispute Resolution Clauses* (Hart 2017)

Kaneko H and others (eds), *Jokai Minji Soshoho* [Commentary of the Code of Civil Procedure] (2nd edn, Kobundo 2011)

Kantor E and Parrott P, '"Gaps" Can End in Tears' (*Herbert Smith Freehills*, August/September 2016) <http://hsfnotes.com/arbitration/wp-content/uploads/sites/4/2016/08/GapsCanEndInTears.pdf> accessed 7 September 2020

Kapai P, 'The Hong Kong Equal Opportunities Commission: Calling for a New Avatar' (2009) 39 Hong Kong Law Journal 339

Karton J, 'Beyond the "Harmonious Confucian": International Commercial Arbitration and the Impact of Chinese Cultural Values' in C-f Lo, NNT Li and T-y Lin (eds), *Legal Thoughts between the East and the West in the Multilevel Legal Order* (Springer 2016)

Kaufmann-Kohler G, 'When Arbitrators Facilitate Settlement: Towards a Transnational Standard' (*Clayton UTZ* 2007) <www.claytonutz.com/internal/archive/ialecture/content/previous/2007/speech_2007> accessed 14 January 2018

——'When Arbitrators Facilitate Settlement: Towards a Transnational Standard' (2009) 25(2) Arbitration International 198

——and Bonnin V, *Arbitrators as Conciliators: A Statistical Study of the Relation between an Arbitrator's Role and Legal Background* (*International Council for Commercial Arbitration*) <https://cdn.arbitration-icca.org/s3fs-public/document/media_document/media012319144605970000950003.pdf> accessed 14 January 2018

——and Fan K, 'Integrating Mediation into Arbitration: Why It Works in China' (2008) 4 Journal of International Arbitration 479

Kayali D, 'Enforceability of Multi-tiered Dispute Resolution Clauses' (2010) 27(6) Journal of International Arbitration 551

Kemfouet É-D, 'Droit des libertés publiques comparé: une nouvelle: avant sa disparition annoncée, la Cour Africaine des Droits de l'Homme et des peuples rend son premier arrêt (Affaire Michelot Yogogombaye c. République du Sénégal)' (2011) 45(1) Revue juridique Thémis 151

Kikui T and Muramatsu T, *Konmentaru Minji Soshoho* [Commentary of the Code of Civil Procedure], vol 3 (2nd edn, Nihon Hyoronsha 2019)

Kim D, 'Sosong jeungganeun gyesok doel geosinga? jesoyulkwa kyeongje yoin bunseok' [Will the Increase of Litigation Continue? An Analysis of the Relationships between the Litigation Rate and Economic Factors] (2015) 48 *Beop gwa sahoe* [Korean Journal of Law and Society] 249

—— and Lee C, 'Dispute Resolution in South Korea' in M Palmer, M Roberts and M Moscati (eds), *Comparative Dispute Resolution* (Edward Elgar 2020)

Kim J, *International Arbitration in Korea* (Oxford University Press 2017)

Kim NH and others, 'Community and Industrial Mediation in South Korea' (1993) 37 Journal of Conflict Resolution 361

Kim S and Kim Y, 'Management of Overseas Construction Claims in Preparation for International Arbitration' (2013) 22 Korean Forum on International Trade and Business Law 103

Kiser R, *How Leading Lawyers Think: Expert Insights into Judgment and Advocacy* (Springer 2011)

Kokusai Chusai Seido Kenkyukai [Working Group on International Arbitration], '*Wagakuni ni okeru Kokusai Chusai no Hatten ni mukete – Nihon Chusai no Kasseika wo Jitsugen suru 7tsu no Teigen*' [Towards Developments of International Arbitration in Japan – 7 Proposals for Enhancing Arbitration in Japan] [2018] New Business Law 1125

Krauss O, 'The Enforceability of Escalation Clauses Providing for Negotiations in Good Faith under English Law' [2015–2016] (2) McGill Journal of Dispute Resolution 142

Krennbauer S, 'Enforceability of Multi-tiered Dispute Resolution Clauses in International Business Contracts' (2010) 1 Yearbook on International Arbitration 199

Kryvoi Y, 'Enforcement of Settlement Agreements Reached in Arbitration and Mediation' (*Kluwer Arbitration Blog*, 25 November 2015) <http://arbitration blog.kluwerarbitration.com/2015/11/25/enforcement-of-settlement-agree ments-reached-in-arbitration-and-mediation/> accessed 25 October 2018

—— and Yokomizo D, 'Improving Arbitration Climate in Japan – Report and Recommendations' (*SSRN*, 9 November 2016) <https://papers.ssrn.com /sol3/papers.cfm?abstract_id=2865717> accessed 14 November 2020

Lande J, 'Failing Faith in Litigation? A Survey of Business Lawyers' and Executives' Opinions' (1998) 3 Harvard Negotiation Law Review 1

Landry S, 'Med-arb: Mediation with a Bite and an Effective ADR Model' (1996) 63 Defense Counsel Journal 263

Lawrence A, Nugent J and Scarfone C, 'The Effectiveness of Using Mediation in Selected Civil Law Disputes: A Meta-analysis' (*Department of Justice*, 7 January 2015) <www.justice.gc.ca/eng/rp-pr/csj-sjc/jsp-sjp/rr07_3/index .html> accessed 10 September 2020

Lee J, 'Agreements to Negotiate in Good Faith' [2013] Singapore Journal of Legal Studies 212

Legislative Council Panel on Administration of Justice and Legal Services, 'Review of the Implementation of Civil Justice Reform' (18 May 2015) <www.legco.gov.hk/yr14-15/english/panels/ajls/papers/ajls20150518cb4-964-5-e.pdf> accessed 26 February 2020

Levin LA and Wheeler RR, *The Pound Conference: Perspectives on Justice in the Future* (West Publishing 1979)

Lew JDM, Mistelis LA and Kröll SM, *Comparative International Commercial Arbitration* (Wolters Kluwer 2003)

Li K and Cheung SO, 'The Potential of Bias in Multi-tier Construction Dispute Resolution Processes' in PW Chan and CJ Neilson (eds), *Proceedings of the 32nd Annual ARCOM Conference* (ARCOM 2016)

Lim G and Chua E, 'Development of Mediation in Singapore' in D McFadden and G Lim (eds), *Mediation in Singapore: A Practical Guide* (2nd edn, Sweet & Maxwell 2017)

Limbury A, 'Don't Be Scared, This Is the Future – Avoiding the Pitfalls of Arb-med-arb' (2014) 1(4) Australian Alternative Dispute Resolution Law Bulletin 84

Lipsky DB and Seeber RL, 'In Search of Control: The Corporate Embrace of ADR' (1998) 1 University of Pennsylvania Journal of Labor and Employment Law 133

Liu J and Benlafkih O, 'Resolving Disputes from Belt and Road Projects' in *CDR Essential Intelligence: Belt & Road Initiative* (Global Legal Group Ltd 2020)

Liu X, 'The Latest Innovation for Mediation in China – From the Perspective of SCIA' (*pkulaw.com* 2014) <http://pkulaw.cn/fulltext_form.aspx?Gid=1510155206&Db=eqikan> accessed 17 August 2020

London Court of International Arbitration, '2019 Annual Casework Report' (19 May 2020) <www.lcia.org/media/download.aspx?MediaId=816> accessed 19 November 2020

Loong SO and Koh D, 'Enforceability of Dispute Resolution Clauses in Singapore' [2016] Asian Journal of Mediation 51

Lum A, 'How Hong Kong Plans to Take Arbitration Online with New eBRAM Project' South China Morning Post (Hong Kong, 8 April 2019) <www.scmp.com/news/hong-kong/law-and-crime/article/3005025/how-hong-kong-plans-take-arbitration-online-new-ebram> accessed 7 September 2020

Lurie PM, 'Using the Guided Choice Process to Reduce the Cost of Resolving Disputes' (2014) 9 Construction Law International 18

—— and Lack J, 'Guided Choice Dispute Resolution Processes: Reducing the Time and Expense to Settlement' (2014) 8 Dispute Resolution International 167

Lye KC, 'A Persisting Aberration: The Movement to Enforce Agreements to Mediate' (2008) 20 Singapore Academy of Law Journal 195

Lynch K, 'Private Conciliation of Discrimination Disputes: Confidentiality, Informalism and Power' (paper presented at a conference on *Enforcing Equal Opportunities in Hong Kong: An Evaluation of Conciliation and Other Enforcement Powers of the EOC*, June 2003)

MacFarlane J and Keet M, 'Civil Justice Reform and Mandatory Civil Mediation in Saskatchewan: Lessons from a Maturing Program' (2005) 42(3) Alberta Law Reports 677

Marrie M, 'Alternative Dispute Resolution in Administration Litigation: A Call for Mandatory Mediation' (2010) 37(2) Advocates' Quarterly 149

Mason PE, 'The Arbitrator as Mediator, and Mediator as Arbitrator' (2011) 28(6) Journal of International Arbitration 541

McEwen CA, 'Managing Corporate Disputing: Overcoming Barriers to the Effective Use of Mediation for Reducing the Cost and Time of Litigation' (1998) 14 Ohio State Journal of Dispute Resolution 1

—— and Maiman RJ, 'Small Claims Mediation in Maine: An Empirical Assessment' (1981) 33 Maine Law Review 237

McFadden D, 'Mediation/Arbitration' in D Brock (ed), *Arbitration in Hong Kong* (Sweet & Maxwell 2011)

—— *Mediation in Greater China: The New Frontier for Commercial Mediation* (CCH Hong Kong Ltd 2013)

McIlwrath M, 'UNCITRAL to Consider Proposal for Convention on Enforcement of Mediated Settlements' (*Kluwer Arbitration Blog*, 7 July 2014) <http://arbitrationblog.kluwerarbitration.com/2014/07/07/uncitral-to-consider-proposal-for-convention-on-enforcement-of-mediated-settlements/> accessed 7 September 2020

Menkel-Meadow C, 'Regulation of Dispute Resolution in the United States of America: From the Formal to the Informal to the "Semi-formal"' in F Steffek and others (eds), *Regulating Dispute Resolution: ADR and Access to Justice at the Crossroads* (Hart 2013)

—— 'Alternative and Appropriate Dispute Resolution in Context Formal, Informal, and Semiformal Legal Processes' in PT Coleman, M Deutsch and EC Marcus (eds), *The Handbook of Conflict Resolution: Theory and Practice* (Wiley 2014)

—— *Mediation: Practice, Policy, and Ethics* (Aspen 2018)

Menon S, 'Arbitrator's Blade: International Arbitration and the Rule of Law' (*Supreme Court of Singapore*, 2 September 2020) <www.supremecourt.gov.sg/docs/default-source/default-document-library/siac-virtual-congress-2020-arbitration%27s-blade-international-arbitration-and-the-rule-of-law-(020920-as-delivered).pdf> accessed 1 October 2020

Merkin R and Hjalmarsson J, *Singapore Arbitration Legislation Annotated* (2nd edn, Informa Law 2016)

Minister of Land, Infrastructure and Transportation, Report on Status and Activities of Committees, 31 December 2016

—— Report on Status and Activities of Committees, 30 June 2019

Ministry of Commerce of People's Republic of China, 'Report on Development of China's Outward Investment and Economic Cooperation' (2018) <http://images.mofcom.gov.cn/fec/201901/20190128155348158.pdf> accessed 26 February 2020

Nadar A, 'Construction Arbitration in the Context of China's Belt and Road Projects' in S Brekoulakis and DB Thomas (eds), *The Guide to Construction Arbitration* (Global Arbitration Review 2018)

Nakamura T, 'Brief Empirical Study on Arb-med in the JCAA Arbitration' <www.jcaa.or.jp/e/arbitration/docs/news22.pdf> accessed 24 September 2020 *Chusaiho no Ronten* [Issues on Arbitration Law] (Seibundo 2017)

Nakano S, 'Minkan Chotei de Funso ga Kaiketsu sarenai toki ni Saiban Tetsuzuki wo Kaishisuru Mune no Goi no Koryoku' [Effects of an Agreement to Institute Litigation When Disputes Cannot Be Resolved in Mediation by Private Institutions] [2012] 636 Hanrei Hyoron 171

Nelson N and Stipanowich TJ, *Commercial Mediation in Europe: Better Solutions for Business* (International Institute for Conflict Prevention & Resolution 2004)

Ng P-L and Banaitis A, 'Construction Mediation and Its Hybridization: The Case of the Hong Kong Construction Industry' (2017) 9 Organization, Technology and Management in Construction 1528

Ngwanza A, 'L'essor de l'arbitrage international en Afrique subsaharienne: les apports de la CCJA' (2013) 3 Revue de l'ERSUMA 31

Nigmatullina D, 'The Combined Use of Mediation and Arbitration in Commercial Dispute Resolution: Results from an International Study' (2016) 33(1) Journal of International Arbitration 37

—— *Combining Mediation and Arbitration in International Commercial Dispute Resolution* (Routledge 2018)

—— 'Aligning Dispute Resolution Processes with Global Demands for Change: Enhancing the Use of Mediation and Arbitration in Combination' [2019] Belgian Review of Arbitration 7

Ning F and Liu J, 'Mediation Meets Arbitration – The Experience of Med-arb in Mainland China and Hong Kong' (2014) 1(5) Alternative Dispute Resolution Law 97

Nishitani Y, 'Coordination of Legal Systems by the Recognition of Foreign Judgments – Rethinking Reciprocity in Sino-Japanese Relationships' (2019) 14(2) Frontiers of Law in China 193

Nolan-Haley JM, 'Lawyers, Non-lawyers and Mediation: Rethinking the Professional Monopoly from a Problem-Solving Perspective' (2002) 7 Harvard Negotiation Law Review 235

—— 'Mediation: The "New Arbitration"' (2012) 17 Harvard Negotiation Law Review 6

—— *Alternative Dispute Resolution in a Nutshell* (4th edn, West Academic 2013)

Norton Rose Fulbright, 'The Singapore Mediation Convention: An Update on Developments in Enforcing Mediated Settlement Agreements' (September 2019) <www.nortonrosefulbright.com/en/knowledge/publications/b5906716/the-singapore-mediation-convention> accessed 14 August 2020

Nottage L, 'Arb-med in Australia: The Time Has Come' (2007) 5 ADR Reporter 8

—— 'Arb-med and New International Commercial Mediation Rules in Japan' (*University of Sydney*, 21 July 2009) <https://japaneselaw.sydney.edu.au/2009/07/arb-med-and-new-international-commercial-mediation-rules-in-japan/> accessed 14 November 2020

—— 'Top 20 Things to Change in or around Australia's International Arbitration Act' (2010) 6 Asian International Arbitration Journal 1

—— 'International Commercial Arbitration in Australia: What's New and What's Not' (2013) 30 Journal of International Arbitration 465

—— and Garnett R (eds), *International Arbitration in Australia* (Federation Press 2010)

—— and Garnett R, 'The Top 20 Things to Change in or around Australia's International Arbitration Act' in L Nottage and R Garnett (eds), *International Arbitration in Australia* (The Federation Press 2010)

Oberman S, 'Confidentiality in Mediation: An Application of the Right to Privacy' (2012) 27 Ohio State Journal on Dispute Resolution 539

OECD, 'The Belt and Road Initiative in the Global Trade, Investment and Finance Landscape' in OECD, 'OECD Business and Finance Outlook 2018' (2018) <https://doi.org/10.1787/bus_fin_out-2018-6-en> accessed 23 September 2020

Oghigian H, 'The Mediation/Arbitration Hybrid Concept in Dispute Resolution (Med/arb)' (30 July 2019) <https://journal.arbitration.ru/analytics/the-mediation-arbitration-hybrid-concept-in-dispute-resolution-med-arb-/> accessed 1 October 2020

Onyema E, 'The Use of Med-arb in International Commercial Dispute Resolution' (2001) 12 American Review of International Arbitration 411

Palmer M, 'Formalisation of Alternative Dispute Resolution Processes: Some Socio-legal Thoughts' in J Zekoll, M Bälz and I Amelung (eds), *Formalisation and Flexibilisation in Dispute Resolution* (Brill 2014)

Pappas BA, 'Med-arb and the Legalization of Alternative Dispute Resolution' (2015) 20 Harvard Negotiation Law Review 157

Pappas VFL and Vlavianos GM, 'Multiple Tiers, Multiple Risks – Multi-tier Dispute Resolution Clauses' (2018) 12(1) Dispute Resolution International 5

Parfait D, 'L'article 10 du Traité de l'OHADA: quelle portée abrogatoire et supranationale?' (2007) 12(2) Revue de droit uniforme 265

Park J, *Minsa jojeong jedo ui ipbeopjeok gaeseon bangan* [Legislative Policy for the Improvement of Civil Conciliation] (2017) NARS Issue Report 310, Publication Registration No 31–9735020–000632–14 (National Assembly Research Service 2017)

Park WW, 'Arbitration in Banking and Finance' (1998) 17 Annual Review of Banking Law 213

Pasas G, 'The Arbitrator as Mediator: *Ku-ring-gai Council v Ichor Constructions Pty Ltd* [2018] NSWSC 610' (2019) 29 Australian Dispute Resolution Journal 266

Peter JT, 'Med-arb in International Arbitration' (1997) 8(1) American Review of International Arbitration 83

Petersen CJ, Fong J and Rush G, *Enforcing Equal Opportunities: Investigation and Conciliation of Discrimination Complaints in Hong Kong* (Centre for Comparative and Public Law, University of Hong Kong 2003)

Phang A, 'Mediation and the Courts – The Singapore Experience' [2017] Asian Journal of Mediation 14

Phillips FP, 'The European Directive on Commercial Mediation: What It Provides and What It Doesn't' (*Business Conflict Management*) <www.businessconflictmanagement.com/pdf/BCMpress_EUDirective.pdf> accessed 7 September 2020

Polster DA, 'The Trial Judge as Mediator: A Rejoinder to Judge Cratsley' (*Mediate.com*, March 2007) <www.mediate.com/articles/polsterD1.cfm/#4> accessed 20 August 2018

Prause M, 'A Methodology for the Determination of the MRI (Mediation Receptivity Index)' (2007) 22 Ohio State Journal on Dispute Resolution 610

Province of Saskatchewan Ministry of Justice and Attorney General, 'Annual Report (2007–2008)' <http://publications.gov.sk.ca/documents/9/33067-JAG-07-08.pdf> accessed 10 September 2020

Pryles M, 'Multi-tiered Dispute Resolution Clauses' (2001) 18 Journal of International Arbitration 159

——and Taylor VL, 'The Cultures of Dispute Resolution in Asia', in M Pryles (ed), *Dispute Resolution in Asia* (3rd edn, Kluwer Law International 2006)

Pusceddu P, 'PRIME Finance Arbitration – A Lighthouse Safe Harbour in the Mare Magnum of Financial Dispute Resolution' (2014) 3(1) Indian Journal of Arbitration Law 45

Queen Mary University of London and PricewaterhouseCoopers, 'International Arbitration: Corporate Attitudes and Practices' (2008) <www.pwc.co.uk/assets/pdf/pwc-international-arbitration-2008.pdf> accessed 24 September 2020

Queen Mary University of London and White & Case LLP, '2015 International Arbitration Survey: Improvements and Innovations in International Arbitration' <www.arbitration.qmul.ac.uk/media/arbitration/docs/2015_International_Arbitration_Survey.pdf> accessed 2 April 2021

Queen Mary University of London and White & Case LLP, '2018 International Arbitration Survey: The Evolution of International Arbitration' <www.arbitration.qmul.ac.uk/media/arbitration/docs/2018-International-Arbitration-Survey-report.pdf> accessed 2 February 2020

Queirolo I, Carpaneto L and Dominelli S, 'Italy' in C Esplugues, JLI Buhigues and GP Moreno (eds), *Civil and Commercial Mediation in Europe (Volume I: National Mediation Rules and Procedures)* (Intersentia 2012)

Quek Anderson D, 'Mandatory Mediation: An Oxymoron? Examining the Feasibility of Implementing a Court-Mandated Mediation Program' (2010) 11(2) Cardozo Journal of Conflict Resolution 479

——'Comment: A Coming of Age for Mediation in Singapore? Mediation Act 2016' (2017) 29 Singapore Academy of Law Journal 275

——and Seah CL, 'Finding the Appropriate Mode of Dispute Resolution: Introducing Neutral Evaluation in Subordinate Courts' (2011) Law Gazette 21

Quigley J, Sharp G and Souter J, '"Action" to Justice: Addressing Access to Justice in the Saskatchewan Court of Queen's Bench' (*University of Saskatchewan, College of Law*, February 2016) <https://law.usask.ca/documents/research/deans-forum/13_SuperiorCourtandCourtProcesses_PolicyDiscusion Paper_2016DeansForum.pdf> accessed 10 September 2020

Rajah VK, 'W(h)ither Adversarial Commercial Dispute Resolution?' (2017) 33 Arbitration International 17

Redfern A and Hunter M, *Law and Practice of International Commercial Arbitration* (3rd edn, Sweet & Maxwell 1999)

Reyes A (ed), *Recognition and Enforcement of Judgments in Civil and Commercial Matters* (Hart 2019)

Reyes A, 'Recourse against Awards, Applications to Resist Enforcement and Tactical Considerations: Some Lessons from Singapore and Hong Kong Law' (2020) 63 Japanese Yearbook of International Law 127

Riskin LL, 'Understanding Mediators' Orientations, Strategies, and Techniques: A Grid for the Perplexed' (1996) 1 Harvard Negotiation Law Review 7

Robinson P and others, 'The Emergence of Mediation in Korean Communities' (2015) 15 Pepperdine Dispute Resolution Law Journal 518

Roth M and Gherdane D, 'Mediation in Austria: The European Pioneer in Mediation Law and Practice' in KJ Hopt and F Steffek (eds), *Mediation: Principles and Regulation in Comparative Perspective* (Oxford University Press 2013)

Saint-Martin CC, 'Arb-med-arb Service in Singapore International Mediation Centre: A Hotfix to the Pitfalls of Multi-tiered Clauses' [2015] Asian Journal of Mediation 35

Salehijam M, 'Challenges of Mediation – The Need to Address the English Approach to Agreements to Mediate' (*Courts and Tribunals Judiciary*) <www.judiciary.uk/wp-content/uploads/2018/02/challenges-of-commercial-mediation-maryam-salehijam-cjc-adr.pdf> accessed 14 November 2020

——'Enforceability of ADR Agreements: An Analysis of Selected EU Member States' (2018) 21 International Trade Business Law Review 255

Sander FEA, 'Varieties of Dispute Processing' (1976) 70 Federal Rules Decision 111

——'Developing the MRI (Mediation Receptivity Index)' (2007) 22(3) Ohio State Journal on Dispute Resolution 599

——and Goldberg SB, 'Fitting the Forum to the Fuss: A User-Friendly Guide to Selecting an ADR Procedure' (1994) 10 Negotiation Journal 49

Sanders P, *Quo Vadis Arbitration? Sixty Years of Arbitration Practice: A Comparative Study* (Kluwer Law International 1999)

Sanderson C, 'South Korea Averts Treaty Claim over Island Resort' (*Global Arbitration Review*, 9 July 2020) <https://globalarbitrationreview.com/article/1228592/south-korea-averts-treaty-claim-over-island-resort> accessed 17 August 2020

Sato Y, *Commercial Dispute Processing and Japan* (Kluwer Law International 2001)

Sawadogo FM, 'Les 20 ans de l'Organisation pour l'harmonisation en Afrique du droit des affaires (OHADA): bilan et perspectives' in L Cadiet (ed), *Droit et attractivité économique: le cas de l'OHSADA* (IRJS 2013)

Sawyer DC, 'Revising the UNCITRAL Arbitration Rules: Seeking Procedural Due Process under the 2010 UNCITRAL Rules for Arbitration' (2011) 1 International Commercial Arbitration Brief 24

Scanlon KM, *Drafting Dispute Resolution Clauses: Better Solutions for Business* (International Institute for Conflict Prevention & Resolution 2006)

Scherpe JM and Marten B, 'Mediation in England and Wales: Regulation and Practice' in KJ Hopt and F Steffek (eds), *Mediation: Principles and Regulation in Comparative Perspective* (Oxford University Press 2013)

Schnabel T, 'The Singapore Convention on Mediation: A Framework for the Cross-Border Recognition and Enforcement of Mediated Settlements' (2019) 19 Pepperdine Dispute Resolution Law Journal 1

Schneider ME, 'Combining Arbitration with Conciliation' (1998) 8 ICCA Congress Series 57

Shanghai International Economic and Trade Arbitration Commission, 'Shanghai International Economic and Trade Arbitration Commission Arbitration Rules' (2015) <http://shiac.org/upload/day_141230/SHIAC_ARBITRATION_RULES_2015_141222.pdf> accessed 17 August 2020

Shen K-L, 'Current Situation and Developments of Out-of-Court Dispute Resolution in Taiwan: Focus on Court-Annexed Mediation' in J-R Yeh (ed), *East Asian Courts under Transformation: Changing Judicial Functions in Leading Cases* (National Taiwan University Press 2014)

——'Mediation in Taiwan: Present Situation and Future Development' in C Esplugues and L Marquis (eds), *New Developments in Civil and Commercial Mediation* (Springer 2015)

——and Chen Y-L, 'Arbitration, Procedural Choice, and Rights of Litigation: Issues about Mandatory Arbitration of Government Procurement Act Article 85–1 Paragraph 1' [2008] *Taiwan Law Review* 218

Shenzhen Court of International Arbitration, '*Shenzhen guoji zhongcai yuan zhongcai guize*' [Shenzhen Court of International Arbitration Rules] (2016) <http://sccietac.org/index.php/Home/index/rule/id/798.html> accessed 17 August 2020

Shoji Homu Kenkyukai [Japan Institute of Business Law], '*Chusai Hosei no Minaoshi wo Chushin to shita Kenkyukai Hokokusho*' [Report of the Working Group on Amendments of the Arbitration Act etc] (*Japan Institute of Business Law* 2020) <www.shojihomu.or.jp/> accessed 14 November 2020

Shusuke K, 'Relationship between Family Mediation and Family Litigation' [2010] Jurist 58

Silvestri E, 'Alternative Dispute Resolution in the European Union: An Overview' [2012] Herald of Civil Procedure 166

—— 'The Singapore Convention on Mediated Settlement Agreements: A New String to the Bow of International Mediation' (2019) 2 Access to Justice in Eastern Europe 5

Singapore International Arbitration Centre, 'SIAC Rules 2016' <https://siac.org.sg/our-rules/rules/siac-rules-2016> accessed 16 August 2020

Singapore International Dispute Resolution Academy (SIDRA), 'International Dispute Resolution Survey: 2020 Final Report' (*Singapore International Dispute Resolution Academy*) <https://sidra.smu.edu.sg/sites/sidra.smu.edu.sg/files/survey/index.html> accessed 5 October 2020

Singapore International Mediation Centre, 'Mediation Rules' <http://simc.com.sg/mediation-rules/> accessed 25 October 2018

—— 'SIAC-SIMC Arb-Med-Arb Protocol' <http://simc.com.sg/v2/wp-content/uploads/2019/03/SIAC-SIMC-AMA-Protocol.pdf> accessed 2 February 2020

Singer LR, 'The Quiet Revolution in Dispute Settlement' (1989) 7 Mediation Quarterly 105

Sita NYM, 'Le ntumbu ou le kibaku: vers une théorie formelle du contrôle social' (Thèse de doctorat en criminologie, Université Catholique de Louvain, Brussels 1989)

Sneddon L and Lees A, 'Frequently Asked Questions: Is My Tiered Dispute Resolution Clause Binding?' (*Ashurst*, 1 February 2013) <www.ashurst.com/en/news-and-insights/legal-updates/frequently-asked-questions-is-my-tiered-dispute-resolution-clause-binding/> accessed 14 November 2020

Soo G, Zhao Y and Cai D, 'Better Ways of Resolving Disputes in Hong Kong – Some Insights from the Lehman-Brothers Related Investment Product Dispute Mediation and Arbitration Scheme' (2010) 9(1) Journal of International Business & Law 137

Spencer D and Brogan M, *Mediation Law and Practice* (Cambridge University Press 2007)

Steele BL, 'Enforcing International Commercial Mediation Agreements as Arbitral Awards' (2006–07) 54 ULCA Law Review 1385

Stein P, *Legal Institutions: The Development of Dispute Settlement* (Butterworths 1984)

Stipanowich TJ, 'Of "Procedural Arbitrability": The Effect of Noncompliance with Contract Claims Procedures' (1989) 40 South Carolina Law Review 847

—— 'The Multi-door Contract and Other Possibilities' (1997) 13 Ohio State Journal on Dispute Resolution 303

—— 'The Arbitration Penumbra: Arbitration Law and the Rapidly Changing Landscape of Dispute Resolution' (2007) 8 Nevada Law Journal 427

—— 'Arbitration and Choice: Taking Charge of the "New Litigation"' (2009) 7 DePaul Business and Commercial Law Journal 383
—— 'Arbitration: The "New Litigation"' [2010] University of Illinois Law Review 1
—— 'Managing Construction Conflict: Unfinished Revolution, Continuing Evolution' (2014) 34(4) Construction Law 13
—— 'Reflections on the State and Future of Commercial Arbitration: Challenges, Opportunities, Proposals' (2014) 25 American Review of International Arbitration 297 <http://ssrn.com/abstract=2519084> accessed 1 September 2020
—— 'Beyond Getting to Yes: Using Mediator Insights to Facilitate Long-Term Business Relationships' (2016) 34(7) Alternatives to the High Cost of Litigation 97
—— 'Insights on Mediator Practices and Perceptions' [2016] Dispute Resolution Magazine 4 <http://ssrn.com/abstract=2759982> accessed 1 September 2020
—— 'Living the Dream of ADR: Reflections on Four Decades of the Quiet Revolution in Dispute Resolution' (2017) 18 Cardozo Journal of Conflict Resolution 513 <http://ssrn.com/abstract=2920848> accessed 1 September 2020
—— 'Arbitration, Mediation and Mixed Modes: Seeking Workable Solutions and Common Ground on Med-arb, Arb-med and Settlement-Oriented Activities by Arbitrators' (2021) 26 Harvard Negotiation Law Review (forthcoming) <http://ssrn.com/abstract=3689389> accessed 1 September 2020
—— and Fraser V, 'The International Task Force on Mixed Mode Dispute Resolution: Exploring the Interplay between Mediation, Evaluation and Arbitration in Commercial Cases' (2017) 40(3) Fordham International Law Review 839 <http://ssrn.com/abstract=2920785> accessed 1 September 2020
—— and Kaskell P (eds), *Commercial Arbitration at Its Best: Successful Strategies for Business Users* (ABA Book Publishing 2001) 5–6.
—— and Lamare JR, 'Living with ADR: Evolving Perceptions and Use of Mediation, Arbitration and Conflict Management in Fortune 1,000 Corporations' (2014) 19 Harvard Negotiation Law Review 1 <http://ssrn.com/abstract=2221471> accessed 1 September 2020
—— and others, 'East Meets West: An International Dialogue on Mediation and Med-arb in the United States and China' (2009) 9(2) Pepperdine Dispute Resolution Law Journal 395
—— and Ulrich ZP, 'Arbitration in Evolution: Current Practices and Perspectives of Experienced Commercial Arbitrators' (2014) 25 American Review of International Arbitration 395
—— and Ulrich ZP, 'Commercial Arbitration and Settlement: Empirical Insights into the Roles Arbitrators Play' (2014) 6 Yearbook on Arbitration and Mediation 1 <http://ssrn.com/abstract=2461839> accessed 1 September 2020
Storskrubb E, 'Alternative Dispute Resolution in the EU: Regulatory Challenges' (2016) 24 European Review of Private Law 1

Sun W, 'Singapore Mediation Convention – Harmonization of China's Legal System with the Convention: Suggestions for the Implementation of the Convention in China' (*Kluwer Mediation Blog*, 2 March 2019) <http://mediationblog.kluwerarbitration.com/2019/03/02/singapore-mediation-convention-harmonization-of-chinas-legal-system-with-the-convention-suggestions-for-the-implementation-of-the-convention-in-china/> accessed 26 February 2020

Supreme People's Court, 'Notice on the Determination of the First International Commercial Arbitration and Mediation Agencies Incorporated into the "One-Stop" International Commercial Disputes Diversification Mechanism' <http://cicc.court.gov.cn/html/1/218/149/192/1124.html> accessed 25 August 2020

Sussman E, 'Developing an Effective Med-arb/Arb-med Process [2009] 2(1) New York Dispute Resolution Law 71

——and Kummer VA, 'Drafting the Arbitration Clause: A Primer on the Opportunities and the Pitfalls' (2012) 67(1) Dispute Resolution Journal 30

Sutton DSJ, Gill J and Gearing M (eds), *Russell on Arbitration* (24th edn, Sweet & Maxwell 2015)

Suzuki C, '*Gaikoku no Hishosaiban no Shonin, Torikesi, Henko*' [Recognition, Revocation and Alteration of Foreign Decisions in Non-contentious Matters] (1974) 26(9) Hoso Jiho 1489

Svatos M, 'The UNCITRAL Draft Convention on the Enforcement of Mediated Settlement Agreements: The Dawn of Cross-Border Mediation?' (2017) <http://forarb.com/wp-content/uploads/2017/04/Georgetown-mediation.pdf> accessed 7 September 2020

Swiss Chambers of Commerce Association for Arbitration and Mediation, *Swiss Rules of Mediation* (2019) <www.swissarbitration.org/files/838/Swiss%20Rules%202019/Web%20versions%202019/Mediation%20Web%202019/mediation_2019_webversion_englisch.pdf> accessed 1 March 2020

Tai M, Copeman J and Phillips A, 'Mediating Commercial Disputes: A Call to Action in Hong Kong' [2017] Asian Dispute Review 72

Taiti K and Kazuyuki T (eds), *Family Dispute Procedures* (2nd edn, Yuhikaku Publishing 2007)

Takada H, 'Article 200' in M Suzuki and Y Aoyama (eds), *Chushaku Minji Soshoho* [Commentary of the Code of Civil Procedure], vol 4 (Yuhikaku 1997)

Takeshi K and Takashi I, '*Chusai Tetsuzuki to Wakai & Chotei*' [Arbitration Procedure and Settlement & Mediation] in K Matsuura and Y Aoyama (eds), *Gendai Chusaiho no Ronten* [Issues of Modern Arbitration Law] (Yuhikaku 1998)

Takeshita M, 'Article 200' in Hajime Kaneko and others (eds), *Jokai Minji Soshoho* [Commentary of the Code of Civil Procedure] (2nd edn, Kobundo 2011)

Tan P and Tan K, 'Kinks in the SIAC-SIMC Arb-Med-Arb Protocol' (*Law Gazette*, January 2018) <https://lawgazette.com.sg/feature/kinks-in-the-siac-simc-arb-med-arb-protocol/> accessed 14 August 2020

Tang H and others, 'Supreme People's Court Issues Rules of Procedure for the China International Commercial Courts' (*Herbert Smith Freehills*, 7 December 2018) <https://hsfnotes.com/arbitration/2018/12/07/supreme-peoples-court-issues-rules-of-procedure-for-the-china-international-commercial-courts/> accessed 26 February 2020

Tang H, 'Is There an Expanding Culture that Favors Combining Arbitration with Conciliation or Other ADR Procedures?' (1998) 8 ICCA Congress Series 101

Tchakoua J-M, 'Le statut de la sentence arbitrale d'accord parties: les limites d'un déguisement bien utile' (2002) 7 International Business Law Journal 775

Teh L, 'Singapore' in FA Acomb and others (eds), *Multi-tiered Dispute Resolution Clauses* (IBA Litigation Committee 2015)

Teramura N, *Ex Aequo et Bono as a Response to the 'Over-Judicialisation' of International Commercial Arbitration* (Wolters Kluwer 2020)

Tevendale C, Ambrose H and Naish V, 'Multi-tier Dispute Resolution Clauses and Arbitration' (2015) 1 Turkish Commercial Law Review 31

Thompson PN, 'Good Faith Mediation in the Federal Courts' (2011) 26 Ohio State Journal on Dispute Resolution 363

Titi C and Fach Gómez K, *Mediation in International Commercial and Investment Disputes* (Oxford University Press 2019)

Tomasich L, Morgan E and Firestone S, 'Two Hats, or Not Two Hats?' (*ADR Institute of Canada*, 17 December 2019) <http://adric.ca/adr-perspectives/two-hats-or-not-two-hats> accessed 10 September 2020

Tomic K, 'Multi-tiered Dispute Resolution Clauses: Benefits and Drawbacks' [2017] Journal of Legal and Social Studies in South East Europe 360

Toru K, *Saibangai Funso Kaiketsu Sokushinho* [Act on Promotion of ADR] (Shoji Homu 2005)

Trakman L and Sharma K, 'The Binding Force of Agreements to Negotiate in Good Faith' (2014) 73 Cambridge Law Journal 598

Trenczek T, 'Stand Und Zukunft Der Mediation – Konfliktvermittlung In Australien Und Deutschland' (2008) <https://waage-hannover.de/wp-content/uploads/2015/06/SchiedVZ_Trenczek_Stand_und_Zukunft_Mediation-Mskr2008.pdf> accessed 11 September 2020

Tsiattalou B, 'Understanding FCA's Ban on Speculative Mini-Bonds' Financial Times (London, 5 December 2019) <www.ftadviser.com/investments/2019/12/05/understanding-fca-s-ban-on-speculative-mini-bonds/> accessed 7 September 2020

Uchibori K, *ADR Ho Gaisetsu to Q&A* [Commentary of the ADR Act and Q&A] (Bessatsu NBL No 101) (Shoji Homu 2005)

Ueda T, '*Chotei Zenchi no Goi ha Shokyokuteki Soshoyoken ni naruka*' [Does an Agreement to Mediate Precedent to Litigation Constitute a Negative Procedural Requirement?] (2012) 690 Hogaku Seminar 144

Uniform Law Conference of Canada, 'Uniform Arbitration Act (2016)' (1 December 2016) <www.ulcc.ca/images/stories/2016_pdf_en/2016ulcc0017.pdf> accessed 10 September 2020

United Nations Commission on International Trade Law, *Guide to Enactment and Use of the UNCITRAL Model Law on International Commercial Conciliation* (2002)

United Nations Secretariat Statistical Division, *Standard Country or Area Codes for Statistical Use*, Series M no 49 <https://unstats.un.org/unsd/methodology/m49/> accessed 14 August 2020

Utterback M, Li R and Blackwell H, 'Enforcing Foreign Arbitral Awards in China – A Review of the Past Twenty Years' (*King & Wood Mallesons*, 15 March 2016) <www.kwm.com/en/knowledge/insights/enforcing-foreign-arbitral-awards-in-china-20160915> accessed 26 February 2020

Vlavianos GM and Pappas VFL, 'Multi-tier Dispute Resolution Clauses as Jurisdictional Conditions Precedent to Arbitration' in JW Rowley, D Bishop and G Kaiser (eds), *The Guide to Energy Arbitrations* (2nd edn, Law Business Research 2017)

Wagner GG, 'Sicherung der Vertraulichkeit von Mediationsverfahren durch Vertrag' [2001] Neue Juristische Wochenschrift 1399

Wang G, 'Mediation in the Globalised Business Environment' (2009) 17(2) Asia Pacific Law Review 47

—— *Dispute Resolution Mechanism for the Belt and Road Initiative* (Zhejiang University Press 2017)

Wang T, *See You in Court: Transformation of Taiwanese Conception of Justice During the Japanese Rule* (National Taiwan University Press 2017)

Weisman MC, 'Med-arb: The Best of Both Worlds' (2013) 19 Dispute Resolution Magazine 40

Wellington A, '"Exquisite Examples" of Creative Judicial Dispute Resolution: The Potential of Alternative Dispute Resolution for Intellectual Property Cases' (2011) 23 Intellectual Property Journal 289

Wendland M, *Mediation Und Zivilprozess: Dogmatische Grundlagen einer Allegemeinen Konfliktbehandlungslehre* (Mohr Siebeck 2018)

White A and Kim S, 'Early Resolution of Disputes in Korea: Negotiation, Mediation, and Multi-tiered Dispute Resolution' (2017) 15 Dispute Resolution Journal 16

Winship P, 'Law and Development in West and Central Africa (OHADA)' (2016) SMU Dedman School of Law Legal Studies Research Paper No 272

Wolski B, 'ARB-MED-ARB (and MSAs): A Whole Which Is Less Than, Not Greater Than, the Sum of Its Parts' (2013) 6(2) Contemporary Asia Arbitration Journal 249

—— 'Re-assessment of QCAT's Hybrid Hearing and Arb-med-arb under Section 27D of the Commercial Arbitration Act' (2014) 3 Journal of Civil Litigation and Practice 156

Wright K and others, 'Parental Experiences of Dealing with Disputes in Additional Support Needs in Scotland: Why Are Parents Not Engaging with Mediation?' (2012) 16 International Journal of Inclusive Education 1099

Yamada A, '*Minkan-gata ADR no Riyo to Sosho Tetsuzuki no Kankei*' [Use of Private Mediation and Its Relationship to Litigation] in Y Toyoda and others (eds), *Wakai wa Mirai wo Tsukuru: Kusano Yoshiro Sensei Koki Kinen* [Settlements Make Future: Liber Amicorum Yoshiro Kusano for His 70th Birthday] (Shinzansha 2018)

Yamamoto K, 'Article 118' in T Kikui and T Muramatsu (eds), *Konmentaru Minji Soshoho* [Commentary of the Code of Civil Procedure], vol 2 (2nd edn, Nihon Hyoronsha 2006)

——'*ADR no Igi, Enkaku, Tenbo*' [Significance, History and Perspectives of ADR] in Japan Association of the Law of Arbitration and Alternative Dispute Resolution and Meiji University Law School (eds), *ADR no Jissai to Tenbo* [Practice and Perspectives of ADR] (Journal of Japanese Arbitration and ADR) (Shoji Homu 2014)

——'*ADR Goi no Koryoku – Soken Seigen Goi nit suite no Jakkan no Kento*' [Effects of ADR Agreements – Some Considerations on Agreements Limiting Right of Access to the Courts] in *ADR Hosei no Gendaiteki Kadai* [Legal Framework of ADR and Its Modern Challenges] (Yuhikaku 2018)

——and Yamada A, *ADR Chûsaihô* [Law of ADR and Arbitration] (2nd edn, Nihon Hyôronsha/Yuhikaku 2015)

Yip M, 'The Singapore International Commercial Court: The Future of Litigation?' in X Kramer and J Sorabji (eds), *International Business Courts: A European and Global Perspective* (Eleven International 2019)

Zhang X, 'Rethinking the Mediation Campaign' (2015) 10(2) Journal of Comparative Law 45

Zhu W, 'Some Considerations on the Civil, Commercial and Investment Dispute Settlement Mechanisms between China and the Other Belt and Road Countries' in J Chaisse and J Górski (eds), *The Belt and Road Initiative: Law, Economics, and Politics* (Brill 2018)

INDEX

Page numbers in bold indicate information in tables and those in italics indicate information in figures.

access to justice
   Canada, 316, 329
   Hong Kong, 95
   Singapore, 182
ad hoc arbitration, 403, 408, 410
adjudication-arbitration clauses, 214
administrative mediation, 136
   Hong Kong, 95
   Korea, 169, 172–174, 180
   Taiwan, 110, 114–115
      Financial Consumer Protection Act, 129–130
      Government Procurement Act, 125–129
ADR Institute of Canada (ADRIC)
   Chartered Mediator-Arbitrator, role of, 340
   med-arb rules, 340
adversarial versus non-adversarial dispute resolution, 4–5, 373–375
Africa. *See* Organisation for the Harmonisation of Business Law in Africa (OHADA)
agreements to agree
   Australia
      enforceability, 345, 346, 347, 350–352, 425
      good faith requirement distinguished, 347
      mediation clauses treated as, 425
   United States
      enforceability, 281
AMA Protocol (Singapore), 9–10, 182, 194–195
   advantages, 195

arbitrators and mediators, separate roles, 196
arb-med-arb three-stage process, 195–196
   concerns
      interim measures, 197–199
      jurisdictional objections, 196–197
      party autonomy, 199
      procedural flexibility, 199
      timing of the mediation process, 199
   reforming med-arb/arb-med procedures, 195
   utilisation rate, 200
amicable settlement, 206
   European Union, 19, 370
   Hong Kong, 94–96
   Japan, 11, 155
   OHADA region, 406, 414
   Prague Rules 2018, 210
   Russia, 384
   Singapore, 192, 197
   Singapore Convention, 225
   United Kingdom, 298, 364
amicus curiae
   discrimination-based complaints, 248, 256
apparent bias, 192
   Hong Kong
      discrimination cases, 259
      Keeneye case, 10, 13, 77, 98–99, 422–424
   United Kingdom, 15
arbitration
   discrimination-based complaints arbitration, 250–251

ex aequo et bono arbitration, 434–436
Korea, 168–169
lack of flexibility, 5
Organisation for the Harmonisation
    of Business Law in Africa,
    403–404
United States, 273–274, 286–290
Arbitration Act 2001 (Singapore), 186
  appointment of mediators, 191
  confidentiality, 193
  conflict of interests, 193
  mediation timelines, 191
  same person as mediator and
      arbitrator, 191–193
  settlement agreements, 191
Arbitration Ordinance (HK), 10, 97
  med-arb, 429–430
arbitration-mediation, 6–7, 27, 42–44
  Hong Kong, 429–430
  Japan, 157
  no provision/unclear, 50–51
  Organisation for the Harmonisation
      of Business Law in Africa,
      409–410
  permitted with party consent, 44–45
  permitted without party consent,
      45–47
  prohibited, 49–50
  regulatory regimes, 8
  same neutral arb-med, 31–32
    United States, 292–293
arbitration-mediation-arbitration, 6,
    47–49
  Canada, 335, 338, 342
  English law, 14–15
  failure to produce a settlement, 47–49
  Hong Kong, 429–430
  Japan, 157–158
  Singapore, 195–196
    AMA Protocol, 194–201
    see also AMA Protocol
        (Singapore).
arbitrator attitudes towards med-arb
  Canada, 40, 316, 338, 341
  Mainland China, 71
  Singapore, 9, 21
arbitrators and mediators, conflicting
    roles, 436–437

Canada, 336
Hong Kong, 430–431
Japan, 157
Mainland China, 72–75, 98
  confidentiality concerns, 75–79,
      422–424
Organisation for the Harmonisation
    of Business Law in Africa,
    411–413
see also conflicts of interest.
Asia
  civil law Asia
    Japan, 11–12
    see also Japan.
    Korea. *See* Korea
    Mainland China, 12–14
    see also Mainland China.
    Taiwan. *See* Taiwan
  common law Asia
    Hong Kong, 10–11
    see also Hong Kong.
    Singapore, 9–10
    see also Singapore.
Australia, 17–18, 21, 150
  agreements to agree
    *Computershare Ltd v Perpetual
        Registrars Ltd (No 2)*,
        350–351
    enforceability, 350–352
    Passlow v Butmac, 351
    *WTE Co-Generation v RCR Energy
        Pty Ltd*, 351–352
  arbitrators acting as mediators, 355
    disclosure, 361–362
  arb-med, 353–354
    Commercial Arbitration Act
        section 27D, 355–357
    international commercial
        arbitration, 354–355
    not subject to appeal, 359
    statutory provisions, 355–362
  arb-med clauses, 343
  arb-med-arb, 343
    not subject to appeal, 359–360
  Australian Human Rights
      Commission
    conciliation, 245–247
    lodging complaints, 245

478 INDEX

Australia (cont.)
  (un)certainty of agreements,
    345–346
  consent, 58
    arb-med, 355–357, 362
    arb-med-arb, 360
  discrimination-related complaints
    conciliation, 245–247
    litigation, 247–248
    lodging complaints, 245
    resolution, 247
  enforcement of mediation
    agreements, 345–346
  mediation agreements, 344–346
  mediation termination, 355
  negotiation, 343
  negotiation agreements, 346–350
  severance of the tiers, 352–353
Australian Commercial Disputes
    Centre (ACDC), 345
Australian Human Rights Commission
    (AHRC)
  discrimination-based complaints,
    244–249
Australian Model Commercial
    Arbitration Act 2010
    (Australia), 32
Austria
  mediation law, 41, 50
  same neutral arb-med, 49

bad faith
  Australia, 347
  Canada, 323–324
  enforceability of multi-tier clauses,
    323–324
  EU law, 376
  Japan, 154
  Russia, 387
  United Kingdom, 301
  United States, 282
Beijing Arbitration Commission
    (BAC), 13, 89
  independent mediation, 74–75
Belgium
  Mediation Directive, 374
Belt and Road Initiative (BRI), 13–14,
    84, 86, 219–220, 231

Electronic Business Related
    Arbitration and Mediation, 107
  HKIAC arbitration, 220–222
  med-arb, 88–90
    due process concerns, 90
  Singapore Convention
    exemption, 227
best endeavours requirement, 420,
    425–427
bilateral investment treaties (BITs), 174
  Korea, 175
breach of contract, 283, 285, 286,
    305, 375
breaches of confidentiality, 260, 418
  China, 13, 14
    arbitrators and mediators,
      conflicting roles, 75–79
  European Union, 371
  Hong Kong, 105, 430–431
    discrimination-related
      complaints, 259–260, 266
    labour mediation, 123–124
  Organisation for the Harmonisation
    of Business Law in Africa, 413
  Russia, 396
  Singapore, 193
Brussels I Recast
  Mediation Directive, relationship
    with, 377–379
Bulgaria, 373
burden of proof, 124

Cameroon, 28, 405
Canada
  ambivalence towards ADR, 316,
    341
  arb-med, 56–57
  arb-med-arb, 335, 338, 342
  consent, 58
  deference to arbitrators, 325
    competence-competence,
      326–327
    enforcement proceedings,
      327–328
    setting-aside proceedings,
      327–328
  enforceability of mediation clauses,
    321–322

INDEX 479

futility exception, 323–324
preconditions to litigation or
    arbitration, 324
unconscionability, 317
increasing popularity of ADR,
    315–316, 341
institutional support for med-arb,
    339–341
interpretation of multi-tier dispute
    resolution clauses, 318–321
judicial support for med-arb,
    336–339
limitation periods, 325
mandatory mediation, 330–332
    multi-tier dispute resolution
    agreements, 332–334
med-arb, 335–341
mediation, support for, 328–329
non-mandatory mediation, 334–335
Centre of Dispute Resolution (CEDR)
    (UK), 296, 304, 307, 427
China Arbitration Law (2017), 79
China International Commercial Court
    (CICC), 85, 87, 231
    jurisdiction, 87–88
    med-arb, 88
China International Economic and
    Trade Arbitration Commission
    (CIETAC), 13, 70, 74, 89
    commercial arbitration rules
    (2015), 80
    investment arbitration rules
    (2017), 80
Chinese Arbitration Association (CAA)
    Taiwan
    arbitration to mediation, 131–132
    construction disputes, 132–133
    mediation to arbitration, 130–131
Chinese International Commercial
    Courts (CICC), 13–14, 222–225
civil law jurisdictions, 21–22
    China. *See* Mainland China
    civil litigation, 163, 164, 165,
    166
    continental Europe. *See* European
    Union (EU)
    good faith, 428
    Japan. *See* Japan

Korea. *See* Korea
mediation clauses, 428
mixed civil/customary law
    jurisdictions, 28
mixed civil/Muslim law
    jurisdictions, 28
mixed common law/civil law
    jurisdictions, 28
procedural safeguards, 22
Russia. *See* Russia
Closer Economic Partnership
    Arrangement (CEPA)
    (China/HK)
    Investment Agreement, 229–230,
    231
common law jurisdictions, 21
    arb-med, 56
    Australia. *See* Australia
    Canada. *See* Canada
    good faith, 428
    Hong Kong. *See* Hong Kong
    med-arb, 56
    mediation clauses, 428
    mixed common law/civil law
        jurisdictions, 28
    mixed common/customary law
        jurisdictions, 28
    mixed common/Muslim law
        jurisdictions, 28
    procedural safeguards, 22
    Singapore. *See* Singapore
    Taiwan. *See* Taiwan
    UK. *See* United Kingdom
    USA. *See* United States
Complaint Review Board for
    Government Procurement
    (CRBGP) (Taiwan),
    126–129
conciliation. *See* mediation
conditions precedent, 17, 303, 310,
    317, 375
    Australia
        enforcement of mediation
        clauses, 345
    Canada, 317–318
    Japan
        enforcement of mediation clauses,
        149–150, 154

conditions precedent (cont.)
  Korea
    enforcement of mediation clauses, 179
  United Kingdom
    escalation clauses, 300, 303–305, 310
  United States
    enforcement of mediation clauses, 283–285, 287–290
confidentiality. *See* breaches of confidentiality
conflict of laws, 311–313
conflicts of interest, 418
  China, 12, 14
    arbitrators and mediators, roles of, 72–75
  Hong Kong Equal Opportunities Commission, 258
  Organisation for the Harmonisation of Business Law in Africa
    arbitrators and mediators, roles of, 411–413
Confucian legal culture, 22–23
  China, 71–72, 83–84
  Taiwan, 110
Congo, 405
consent
  arb-med
    party consent, with, 44–45
    party consent, without, 45–47
    common law jurisdictions, 58
    Canada, 337
  med-arb
    ex ante consent, 39
    ex post consent, 39
    Mainland China, 80
    Singapore, 182
construction disputes
  European Union, 363–364
  FIDIC, 178, 364
  Hong Kong, 96
  Taiwan
    Chinese Arbitration Association, 132–133
    government procurement, 127–129
  United States, 275

Consumer ADR Directive, 379
contract performance disputes, 127
contractual liability, 420
coronavirus, 295–296
  Cabinet Office's guidance on 'responsible contractual behaviour' (UK), 310, 313
  COVID-19 online dispute resolution scheme (HK), 107–108
  financial impact of, 419, 441–442
  virtual mediations, 255, 333
cost-effectiveness
  discrimination-related disputes, 249
  med-arb, 71, 97, 109
Côte d'Ivoire, 404, 407
court-annexed mediation. *See* judicial mediation
cross-border arbitration
  China, 69, 74, 79, 84, 85
    Belt and Road Initiative, 88–90
cross-border commercial disputes
  Japan, 153, 159
cross-border disputes, 12
  European Union, 377–379
cross-border enforcement, 92
  European Union, 363, 383
  settlement agreements, 159
cultural diversity and implementation of MDR, 22–23, 53, 173
  Confucian legal culture. *See* Confucian legal culture
  Organisation for the Harmonisation of Business Law in Africa, 414
customary law jurisdictions, 28, 34, 64
Cyprus, 375
Czech Republic, 20, 50, 372

damages, 283
  Japan, 146–148, 149
  United Kingdom, 305, 308, 312
database of national mediation and arbitration laws, 32–33
  arb-med, 42–44
  arb-med-arb, 47–49
  no provision/unclear, 50–51
  permitted with party consent, 44–45

permitted without party consent,
     45–47
   prohibited, 49–50
 excluded countries, 35
 med-arb, 37–38
   no provision, 41–42
   permitted with party consent,
     38–40
   prohibited, 40–41
   representativeness, 33–34
Denmark, 370, 378
Directive 2008/52/EC on Certain
     Aspects of Mediation in Civil
     and Commercial Matter. *See*
     Mediation Directive (EU)
discrimination-related disputes
   Hong Kong. *See* Hong Kong Equal
     Opportunities
     Commission (EOC)
   New Zealand, 249–252
   UK, 252–254
   USA, 254–257
dismissal of actions, 283–285
   European Union, 375
   Japan, 151–152
   United States, 283–285
Diversified Harmonious Dispute
     Resolution (DHDR), 82
Domestic Relations Case Procedure Act
     (DRCPA) (Japan), 153, 154
due process concerns, 13, 14, 22, 23–24,
     69, 84, 90–91, 362, 421
   apparent bias. *See* apparent bias
   arbitrators and mediators,
     conflicting roles, 26, 72–75, 77,
     98–99, 422–424
   confidentiality, 75–79, 156
   party autonomy, 362

Eastern collectivism and harmony,
     22–23, 53–54
Electronic Business Related Arbitration
     and Mediation (eBRAM)
     (HK), 107
   COVID-19 online dispute solution
     scheme, 108
enforcement of arbitration agreements,
     424–425

enforcement of contracts, 162
enforcement of multi-tier clauses/
     agreements
  Australia
    agreements to agree, 350–352
  Canada
    bad faith exception, 323–324
    consensual tiers, 321–322
    deference to arbitrators,
      325–328
    futility exception, 323–324
    intention and clarity, 319–321
    limitation periods, 325
    preconditions to arbitration, 324
    preconditions to litigation, 324
  Japan, 146–148
    Tokyo High Court judgment,
      148–149
  med-arb clauses, difficulties
    agreements to agree, treated
      as, 425
    voluntary nature of process, 425
  United Kingdom, 298
    *Cable & Wireless plc v IBM United
      Kingdom Ltd*, 299–300
    *Emirates Trading Agency LLC
      v Prime Mineral Exports Private
      Ltd*, 303
    good faith negotiations, 308–310
    mandatory procedure, 310
    *Ohpen Operations UK Ltd
      v Invesco Fund Managers Ltd*,
      304–306
    *Petromec Inc v Petroleo Brasileiro
      SA Petrobras*, 301
    precise definition of the escalation
      stages, 307–308
    public interest, 304
    severance of the tiers, 311
    sufficient certainty, 306–307
    Walford v Miles, 298–299
  United States, 280, 281–282
    judicial remedies for non-
      compliance, 283–285
escalation clauses, 208, 294–295,
    303, 311
  condition precedent, 300, 303, 310
Estonia, 19, 372, 376

estoppel, 423, 424
  Canada, 323
European Union (EU), 18–19, 383
  arbitration, 363
  Brussels I Recast. *See* Brussels I Recast
  construction disputes, 363–364
  Consumer ADR Directive, 379
  cultural constraints on implementation of MDR, 22–23
  domestic implementation of EU law, 368
  European Parliament Resolution 2019, 382
  mediation, 363
  Mediation Directive. *See* Mediation Directive (EU)
  multi-tier dispute resolution clauses, 364–365
  Rebooting Study, 379–382
  see also Rebooting Study (EU).
  uneven development of mediation, 19–20
evaluative mediation, 70, 75, 114, 134, 137, 366
ex aequo et bono arbitration, 31, 434–436
expert advisory mediation, 366

facilitative mediation, 130, 133, 135–137, 155, 366
family mediation
  Canada, 338
  Taiwan, 118–120
Federal Arbitration Act (FAA) (USA), 15–16
FIDIC, 178, 364
Financial Consumer Protection Act (Taiwan), 129–130
Financial Dispute Resolution Centre (FDRC) (HK), 99–100
  confidentiality, 105
  establishment, 102
  'mediation first, arbitration next' process, 103–106
  objective, 102–103
  origins, 100–101

Financial Dispute Resolution Scheme (FDRS) (HK), 103
foreign arbitration awards. *See* New York Convention 1958
foreign judgments. *See* Hague Convention on the Recognition and Enforcement of Foreign Judgments in Civil or Commercial Matters 2019
forum conveniens, 223
France, 20, 22, 28, 150, 166, 373
free trade agreements (FTAs), 174
  Korea, 175
frivolous, vexatious, misconceived or lacking in substance claims, 237, 239, 241, 257, 258, 260, 262, 267
futility defence
  Australia
    negotiation agreements, 349–350
  Canada
    mediation clauses, 323–324

Gao Haiyan v Keeneye Holdings Ltd
  apparent bias, 10, 13, 77, 98–99, 422–424
  Hong Kong, 97–99
  Mainland China, 13, 76–77, 89
  public policy, 422–423
  same neutral med-arb, 422–424
Germany, 20, 22, 120, 136, 150, 373
  Mediation Directive, 374
good faith requirement, 5, 26, 143, 184, 281–282, 308–310, 419–421, 425–428
  agreement to agree distinguished, 347
  Australia, 345, 346–351, 352
  Canada, 322, 331–332
  Japan, 147, 148
  Russia, 387, 388, 391
  Singapore, 183–184
  United Kingdom, 297, 298, 301, 303
government procurement
  construction disputes, 127–128
  contractual disputes, 126–127
Government Procurement Act (Taiwan), 125–129

INDEX

habitual residence, 370
Hague Choice of Court Agreements
    Convention 2005, 438
Hague Convention on the Recognition
    and Enforcement of Foreign
    Judgments in Civil or
    Commercial Matters 2019,
  Japan, 160
  Taiwan, 141
harmonisation of hybrid dispute
    resolution. *See* Organisation for
    the Harmonisation of Business
    Law in Africa (OHADA),
    Singapore Convention 2019
HKIAC Administered Arbitration
    Rules 2018, 216–218
HKIAC Lehman Brothers Scheme,
    101–103
Hong Kong, 10–11, 21, 109
  ADR reforms
    promotion of mediation, 94–96
  arb-med, 98–99
  consent, 58
  discrimination-related claims. *See*
      Hong Kong Equal
      Opportunities
      Commission (EOC)
  Keeneye case, 97–99
  med-arb, 97–98, 215, 429–430
  med-arb to resolve financial
      disputes, 94
  mediation
    Hong Kong Mediation
        Accreditation Association
        Limited, 96
    law reform, 94–96
    Model Law 2018
        (Conciliation), 94
  online dispute resolution, 107
    COVID-19 online dispute
        resolution scheme, 107–108
  procedural safeguards, 22, 69, 78, 99
  same neutral hybrid processes,
      57–58, 93, 215
  Singapore Convention, 108–109
Hong Kong Equal Opportunities
    Commission (EOC), 232–233,
    267–268

complaint handling process,
    233–234
Complaint Services Division, 235,
    236–237
conciliation, 236–237
criticisms, 241–244
disclosure, 265
External Report, 241–244
  confidentiality, 259–260, 264,
      266
  conflicts of interest, 258
  early conciliation, 258
  failure of conciliation, 258
  investigations, 260–262
  frivolous or vexatious claims, 260
functions, 234
honest broker role, 263
Internal Operating Procedures
    Manual, 234
legal assistance, 258–259, 260
Legal Services Division, 236, 237–240
  complaints about complaint-
      handling, 241–244
litigation, 237–240
respondents, 263
structure
  board, 235
  chairperson, 235
  management team, 235
victims' privilege, 262–263
Hong Kong International Arbitration
    Centre (HKIAC), 10, 89,
    101, 231
  adj-arb clauses, 214
  HKIAC Administered Arbitration
      Rules 2018. *See* HKIAC
      Administered Arbitration Rules
      2018
  HKIAC Lehman Brothers Scheme.
      See HKIAC Lehman Brothers
      Scheme
  med-arb clauses, 212, 213
  neg-arb clauses, 211–212
  neg-med-arb clauses, 212–213
  same neutral med-arb, 214–216
Hong Kong Mediation Accreditation
    Association Limited
    (HKMAAL), 96

Hong Kong Monetary Authority
  (HKMA), 101–103
 Financial Dispute Resolution
  Scheme, 103, 104
Human Rights Commission (HRC)
  (New Zealand), 249–252
Human Rights Review Tribunal
  (HRRT) (New Zealand),
  251
Hungary, 56
hybrid modes of dispute resolution. *See*
  arbitration-mediation,
  arbitration-mediation-
  arbitration, mediation-
  arbitration

interim measures, 358–359
 Australia, 358–359
 China, 224
 OHADA region, 411
 Russia, 388
 Singapore, 198
International Arbitration Act 2002
  (Singapore), 186
 appointment of mediators,
  191
 confidentiality, 193
 mediation timelines, 191
 same person as mediator and
  arbitrator, 191
 settlement agreements, 191
International Bar Association
  Rules, 210
International Centre for Settlement of
  Investment Disputes (ICSID)
 Canada, 316
 Korea, 175
International Commercial Expert
  Committee (ICEC), 14
International Institute for Conflict
  Prevention and Resolution
  (CPR) (USA), 273
interpretation of multi-tier dispute
  resolution clauses
 Canada
  common law provinces, 318–319
  contractual interpretation,
   318–321

 contractual unfairness, 319
 Québec, 319
 standard of review on appeal, 318
investor-State dispute settlement
  (ISDS)
 Korea, 174, 175–176
Ireland, 370
Italy
 Mediation Directive, 374

Japan, 11–12, 160
 arbitration, 144
 arb-med, 157
 arb-med-arb, 157–158
 cross-border dispute resolution,
  142–143
 med-arb, 155–157
 mediation clauses, 149
  case law, 146–149, 153–154
  enforcement, 146–149, 150–151
  procedural effects, 151–153
 Model Law 2006 (Arbitration),
  145
 Model Law 2018 (Mediation),
  146, 156
 procedural safeguards, 22, 69
 promotion of arbitration and
  mediation, 144–146
Japan Association of Arbitrators
  (JAA), 144
Japan Commercial Arbitration
  Association (JCAA), 12,
  144, 154
 2019 Interactive Arbitration Rules,
  432–434
Japan International Mediation Center
  (JIMC), 144
judicial mediation, 70, 71
 Korea, 169–172
 Russia, 393
 Taiwan, 111–113, 115–117, 140
  civil mediation, 117–118
  family mediation, 118–120
  labour mediation, 120–125, *126*
 United States, 278

Korea, 161–162
 arbitration, 168–169

INDEX 485

free trade agreements, 175
hybrid modes of dispute resolution, 176–177
  domestic disputes, 178–179
  international transactions, 177–178
  international investment agreements, 174
  legal history, 165–167
  litigation, 162–165, 167, 180
    attorneys, number of, 168
    decline, 167
  mediation
    judicial mediation, 170–172
  mediation clauses, 179
  Model Law 2002 (Conciliation), 172
Korean Commercial Arbitration Board (KCAB), 169

labour mediation
  Canada, 338
  Taiwan, 120–121
    Labour Mediation Committee, 121
    resolution without objection of the parties, 122–125
Labour Mediation Committee (Taiwan), 121–125
legal aid, 239
legal assistance, 239–240, 242–243, 258, 262
  Hong Kong Equal Opportunities Commission, 258–259, 260
legal culture, 368
  Confucian legal culture, 22–23, 71–72, 83–84, 110
  Mainland China, 71–72, 83–84
legal traditions, 22–23, 53, 173
  growing importance of hybrid dispute resolution models, 56–58
  Organisation for the Harmonisation of Business Law in Africa, 414
  see also Confucian legal culture; legal culture.
Lehman Brothers-Related Products Dispute Mediation and Arbitration Scheme. *See* HKIAC Lehman Brothers Scheme
litigation
  discrimination-based complaints
    Australia, 247–248
    Hong Kong Equal Opportunities Commission, 237–240
    New Zealand, 252
    UK, 254
    USA, 256–257
  Korea, 162–165, 167, 180
    attorneys, number of, 168
    decline, 167
  Taiwan
    mediation, relationship with, 135–137
  United States
    mediation, relationship with, 134–135, 274
London Chamber of Arbitration and Mediation (LCAM) (UK), 307

Mainland China, 12, 22
  Belt and Road Initiative, 13–14
    HKIAC arbitration, 220–222
    med-arb, 88–90
  Closer Economic Partnership Arrangement (China/HK), 229
  confidentiality, 13, 75–79
    Belt and Road Initiative, 13–14
  conflicts of interest, 12–13, 72–75
    Belt and Road Initiative, 14
  Confucian legal culture, 71–72, 83–84
  cross-border arbitration, 69–70
  cultural constraints on implementation of MDR, 22–23
  domestic arbitration, 69–70
  institutional design, 84–86
  Keeneye case, 13, 76–77, 89
  market-based regulation of med-arb arbitration institutions, 80–82
  med-arb procedure, 214
    mediation stage, 69–71
  popularity of med-arb, 69–72, 82–83, 86, 90–91, 419
    Confucian culture, 83–84

Mainland China (cont.)
    institutional design, 84–86
  procedural concerns, 22, 69, 72
    arbitrators and mediators,
      conflicting roles, 72–75
    confidentiality, 75–79
  regulation of med-arb
    China Arbitration Law, 79
    institutional encouragement of
      med-arb, 82–83
    market-based regulation, 80–82
    sources of law, 79–80
    Supreme People's Court, 79
mandatory arbitration, 126
mandatory mediation, 45
  Australia, 346
  Canada, 328–332
    multi-tier dispute resolution
      agreements, 332–334
  European Union, 381
  HKIAC Administered Arbitration
    Rules 2018, 217
  Japan, 153, 154
  Taiwan, 116
market-based regulation of med-arb
  China International Economic and
    Trade Arbitration Commission
    commercial arbitration rules, 81
Model Law (Arbitration). *See* Model
  Law 2006 (Arbitration)
Model Law (Conciliation). *See* Model
  Law 2002 (Conciliation)
Model Law (Mediation). *See* Model
  Law 2018 (Mediation)
Shenzhen Court of International
  Arbitration, 81–82
mediated settlement agreements, 6–7,
  58, 104, 146, 225–226
  enforcement, 158–160, 437–441
  European Union, 367, 381, 383
  Hong Kong, 108
  Japan, 158–160
  Mainland China, 224, 227–229, 231
  res judicata, 158, 159
  Singapore, 189–190, 195, 201
mediation
  benefits of, 3–4, 294–295
  discrimination-based complaints
    Australia, 245–247
    Hong Kong Equal Opportunities
      Commission, 236–237
    New Zealand, 250
    UK, 254
    USA, 254–256
  European Union, 369–370
    minimum regulatory standards,
      368
    see also Mediation Directive (EU).
  evaluative mediation, 70, 75, 114,
    134, 137, 366
  facilitative mediation, 130, 133–134,
    135–137, 155, 366
  Hong Kong
    Hong Kong Mediation
      Accreditation Association
      Limited, 96
    law reform, 94–96
  litigation, relationship with
    Taiwan, 135–137
    United States, 134–135
  Mainland China
    coercive mediation, 70
    domestic mediation, 70–71
    ex parte communication,
      75–76
  pre-condition to arbitration, as, 4
  Russia, 392–394
  transformative mediation, 134, 366
  USA, 15–16, 277–278
  see also administrative mediation;
    judicial mediation.
Mediation Act 2017 (Singapore),
  187, 189
mediation agreements/clauses,
  149–150, 179
  Australia, 344–346
  breach
    stay of proceedings, 187
  enforcement of
    Japan, 146–149, 150–151
    Korea, 179
    public interest, 303, 350
    public policy interest, 305
    United States, 283–285, 287–290
  procedural effects, 151–153
  Russia, 392–394

INDEX 487

Mediation Directive (EU), 19, 28, 30, 369, 374
  Brussels I Recast, relationship with, 377–379
  Consumer ADR Directive, relationship with, 379
  enforcement, 374, 375
  impact, 370–371
  implementation diversity, 372–373
  implementation nationally, 19–20
  objectives, 369–370
  Rebooting Study, 379
  see also Rebooting Study (EU).
  same neutral med-arb, 42
mediation-arbitration, 6, 27
  alternative approaches
    Japan Commercial Arbitration Association, 432–434
    sealed arbitral awards, 431–432
  arbitration compared, 420
  Belt and Road Initiative, 88–90
  benefits, 155
    cost benefits, 419, 424
    psychological benefits, 419–421
    time efficiency, 419, 424
  Canada
    ADR Institute of Canada, 340
  clauses. *See* mediation-arbitration clauses
  consent
    ex ante consent, 39
    ex post consent, 39
    Mainland China, 80
  different neutral med-arb, 40–41
  drawbacks, 155
  Hong Kong
    financial disputes, 94
  Japan, 155–157
  litigation compared, 420
  Mainland China
    Belt and Road Initiative, 88–90
    Model Law 2018 (Mediation), 8
    Organisation for the Harmonisation of Business Law in Africa, 404–405, 407–409
  regulation. *See* mediation-arbitration regulation

regulatory regimes, 8
same neutral med-arb, 30, 214–216
  alternative approaches, 431–437
  balancing formality and informality, 421
  breaches of confidentiality, 418
  concerns, 418, 422–424
  conflicts of interest, 418
  Keeneye case, 422–424
  Mainland China, 419
  United States, 292–293
  Taiwan, 113, 114, 116, 117–118
  see also Singapore Convention 2019.
mediation-arbitration clauses, 212, 213
  commencement of arbitration proceedings, 429
  enforcement difficulties, 425
  good faith requirement, 425–427
  see also Singapore Convention 2019.
  lack of clarity, 413
  open-endedness, 429
  partial mediation, 429
mediation-arbitration regulation, 8, 37–38, 61
  Mainland China, 79–80
    institutional encouragement of med-arb, 82–83
    market-based regulation, 80–82
  no provision, 41–42
  permitted with party consent, 38–40
  prohibited, 40–41
Model Law 2002 (Conciliation), 30, 42, 56
Model Law 2006 (Arbitration), 8, 28, 31
  procedural safeguards, 78
Model Law 2018 (Mediation), 7, 29, 30, 146, 156
multi-tier dispute resolution
  advantages, 205–206, 294–296, 364
  Chinese International Commercial Courts, 222–225
  Closer Economic Partnership Arrangement (China/HK), 229–230
  concept, 4–6
  definition, 4–6
  disadvantages, 206, 296–298, 365

multi-tier dispute resolution (cont.)
  discrimination-related disputes
    Australia, 244–249
    Hong Kong, 232–244
    New Zealand, 249–252
    United Kingdom, 252–254
    United States, 254–257
  flexibility, 5
  growing popularity, 3–4, 53–54, 205, 206–210
    Mainland China, 69–71, 86
    United Kingdom, 294–298
  Hong Kong International Arbitration Centre
    adj-arb clauses, 214
    Administered Arbitration Rules 2018, 216–218
    Belt and Road Initiative, 220–222
    med-arb clauses, 212, 213
    neg-arb clauses, 211–212
    neg-med-arb clauses, 212–213
    same neutral, 214–216
  Singapore Convention 2019, 225–229
Muslim law jurisdictions, 28

negotiation
  Australia, 343
  Russia
    participation, 394–396
    recording, 394
  Singapore, 186
  United States, 277
negotiation agreements
  Australia
    duty to negotiate, 347–349
    enforceability, 349–350
    futility defence, 349–350
    good faith negotiations, 346
    stay of proceedings, 350
    validity, 347
negotiation-arbitration clauses, 211–212
negotiation-mediation-arbitration clauses, 212–213
Netherlands, 19, 33, 372
neutral evaluation, 4, 310

New York Convention 1958, 7, 10, 32, 225, 438
  European Union, 367
  Japan, 142, 158
  Mainland China, 74, 224, 229, 424
  res judicata for settlement agreements, 158
  Singapore, 189, 195
  Taiwan, 141
New Zealand
  discrimination-based complaints
    arbitration, 250–252
    litigation, 252
    mediation, 250
  Human Rights Commission
    lodging complaints, 249–250
    mediation, 250
  Office of Human Rights Proceedings, 251–252

Office of Human Rights Proceedings (OHRP) (New Zealand), 251–252
online dispute resolution
  Hong Kong, 93, 107
    COVID-19 online dispute resolution scheme, 108
Organisation for the Harmonisation of Business Law in Africa (OHADA), 397–398
  aims and objectives, 398–399
  arbitration
    pre-2017, 403–404
  Arbitration Rules of Procedure of the CCJA, 407
  arb-med, 409–410
  Common Court of Justice and Arbitration, 398, 400–401
    Arbitration Rules of Procedure, 407
  Conference of Heads of State and Government, 398, 399
  Council of Ministers, 398, 399
  dispute resolution post-2017
    arbitration, 406–407
  dispute resolution pre-2017
    arbitration, 403–404
    med-arb, 404–405

interim measures, 411
med-arb, 407–409
  same neutrals, 412–413
Permanent Secretariat, 399
Regional School For Magistrates, 399
Regulations, 402–403
Uniform Act on Arbitration, 407
Uniform Act on Mediation, 407
Uniform Acts, 401–402
Organisation pour l'Harmonisation en Afrique du Droit des Affaires. *See* Organisation for the Harmonisation of Business Law in Africa (OHADA)
out-of-court mediation. *See* administrative mediation

Panel of Recognised International Market Experts in Finance (PRIME Finance), 366
party autonomy, 9, 56, 352, 439
  Australia, 362
  European Union, 371
  Japan, 151
  Mainland China, 70
  prioritisation of, 184, 199
  Singapore, 10, 184, 197, 199, 200
Poland
  Mediation Directive, **374**
Prague Rules 2018, 210
Prague Rules on the Efficient Conduct of Proceedings in International Arbitration. *See* Prague Rules 2018
pre-trial protocols
  Russia, 387–389, 394
procedural fairness
  Australia, 360
  China, 13
  Hong Kong, 243, 257
  Japan, 143, 156
  United Kingdom, 427
procedural safeguards, 22, 69
procurement. *See* government procurement
public inquiries, 248

public interest, 120
  enforcement of mediation clauses, 303, 350
public policy interest
  enforcement of mediation clauses, 305
  Keeneye case, 422–423

qualifications
  mediators, 96

Rebooting Study (EU), 377
mediation
  deterrent sanctions, 381
  education on mediation, 381
  enforcement, 381
  governmental support, 381
  promoting mediation, 381
  regulation, 381
  voluntary versus mandatory, 380
Regional Economic Integration Organisations (REIOs), 376
regulatory regimes, 51–53, 63–65
  arbitration laws, 8
  arb-med regulation, 8
    med-arb regulation compared, 61
    see also arbitration-mediation.
  common law, impact of, 58
  development status, 59–61
  diversity, 7–8
  East Asian influence, 53–54
  lack of coordination and consistency, 62–63
  lack of robust regulation, 61–62
  legal tradition, impact of, 56–58
  med-arb regulation, 8
    arb-med regulation compared, 61
    see also mediation-arbitration regulation.
  mediation laws, 8
remedies for non-compliance
  Australia, 246
  Hong Kong, 94, 256
  United States
    damages, 283
    dismissal of claims, 283–285
    stay of proceedings, 283

res judicata
   settlement agreements, 158, 159
Restatement (Third) of the Law of International Commercial Arbitration (USA), 290
Romania
   Mediation Directive, **374**
rule of law, 116, 162, 439–440
Russia, 20–21
   Civil Procedure Code, 387
   Commercial Procedure Code, 385, 386, 387–388
      compliance, 388–389
   judicial system
      courts, 385–386
      proceedings, 386–387
   mediation, 392
      judicial mediation, 393–394
      pre-judicial mediation, 393
      written mediation agreements, 392–393
   multi-tier resolution for non-regulated disputes, 390–392
   pre-trial protocol
      compliance, 389–390
   procedural legislation, 384–385

same neutral hybrid processes, 7
   arb-med, 31–32
      med-arb compared, 61, 97–99
      United States, 292–293
      see also arbitration-mediation.
   common law, influence of, 58
   development status, influence of, 59–61
   due process concerns, 23
   East Asian culture, influence of, 53–58
   English law, 14–15
   lack of coordination and consistency, 62–63
   lack of robust regulation, 61–62
   legal tradition, influence of, 56–58
   med-arb, 30–31, 214–216
      arb-med compared, 61, 97–99
      Organisation for the Harmonisation of Business Law in Africa, 412–413
      United States, 292–293
      see also mediation-arbitration; mediation-arbitration regulation.
   regulation, 51–53, 63–65
Same Person Model (Singapore), 192, 194, 201, 202
Scotland, 373
Securities and Futures Commission (SFC) (HK), 101
Senegal, 405, 407
setting aside arbitral awards, 26, 82, 90, 98, 138, 139, 140, 327, 421, 422, 424, 431
settlement agreements. *See* mediated settlement agreements
severance of tiers
   Australia, 352–353
   Singapore, 186
   United Kingdom, 311
Shanghai International Arbitration Center (SHIAC), 74
Shenzhen Court of International Arbitration (SCIA), 74, 89
   Diversified Harmonious Dispute Resolution, 82
Singapore, 9–10, 21, 150, 201–202
   Arbitration Act. *See* Arbitration Act 2001 (Singapore)
   consent, 58, 182
   cultural constraints on implementation of MDR, 22–23
   dispute resolution clauses, 183–184
      enforceability, 184–186
      unitary dispute resolution mechanisms, as, 186–187
   International Arbitration Act. *See* International Arbitration Act 2002 (Singapore)
   Lufthansa decision, 185–186
   Mediation Act. *See* Mediation Act 2017 (Singapore)
   popularity of hybrid modes of dispute resolution, 183
   legal history, 188–190
   procedural safeguards, 22, 69
   PT Selecta decision, 186

INDEX

Singapore Convention 2019, 6, 31, 225–229, 437
  Article 5 grounds (refusal to grant relief), 226–227
  Canada, 316
  China, 91
  enforcing mediated settlement agreements internationally, 437–438
  European Union, 367
  Hong Kong, 108–109
  international and domestic commercial disputes, 438–439
  Japan, 146, 157
    settlement agreements, enforcement of, 159
  Korea, 174
  limitations, 227–228
  organised crime concerns, 439–441
  Singapore, 182, 189
  Taiwan, 141
Singapore International Arbitration Centre (SIAC), 9, 89
  AMA Protocol. *See* AMA Protocol (Singapore)
  Investment Arbitration Rules 2017, 182
Singapore International Commercial Court (SICC), 85, 182
Singapore International Mediation Centre (SIMC), 9, 182, 188
  AMA Protocol. *See* AMA Protocol (Singapore)
Singapore International Mediation Institute (SIMI), 182, 188
Slovenia
  Mediation Directive, **374**
Spain, 166, 167
  Mediation Directive, **374**
Sri Lanka, 28
standard form contracts, 319, 329
  construction contracts, 275
  consumer contracts, 96
standard of review on appeal, 318
stay of proceedings
  Australia, 349, 350
  Canada, 324, 326
  Japan, 149, 151–153

Organisation for the Harmonisation of Business Law in Africa, 409
Singapore, 186–187, 194, 199
United Kingdom, 306
United States, 283
Switzerland, 20, 22, 150

Taiwan, 140–141
  arbitration
    pre-arbitration process, 138–139
  civil mediation
    compulsory mediation cases, 117
    consent of both parties, 117–118
    court-proposed mediation resolution, 118
    voluntary mediation cases, 117
  consumer protection, 129–130
  dispute resolution, 110
    Chinese Arbitration Association cases, 112
    mediation, 111
  family mediation, 118–119
    consent of both parties, 119–120
    mediation to ruling by agreement, 119
  government procurement, 125–127
    construction disputes, 127–129
    contractual disputes, 126–127
  hybrid modes of dispute resolution, 114–115
    judicial mediation, 115–117
  judicial mediation, 111–113, 115–117, 140
    civil mediation, 117–118
    family mediation, 118–120
    labour mediation, 120–125, *126*
  labour mediation, 120–121
    consent of both parties, 121
    no objection of the parties, 122–125
  mediation and arbitration, relationship between, 137–139
  mediation and litigation, relationship between, 133–137
  terminology, 5–6
  arb-med, 27
  conciliation and mediation, 27
  med-arb, 27

time limits, 213, 260, 265
  Australia, 343
  Canada, 325
  European Union, 371
tradition-based mediation, 366
transformative mediation, 134, 366
transparency
  European Union, 370
  Hong Kong, 265
  Japan, 145
  Singapore, 193–194
  see also conflicts of interest.
Treaty on the Functioning of the European Union (TFEU)
  Mediation Directive, 369, 379

UNCITRAL Conciliation Rules 1980, 8, 30
  European Union, 367
UNCITRAL Model Law on International Commercial Arbitration 2006. *See* Model Law 2006 (Arbitration)
UNCITRAL Model Law on International Commercial Conciliation 2002. *See* Model Law 2002 (Conciliation)
UNCITRAL Model Law on International Commercial Mediation and International Settlement Agreements Resulting from Mediation 2018. *See* Model Law 2018 (Mediation)
Uniform International Commercial Arbitration Act 1986 (Canada), 57
Uniform International Commercial Arbitration Act 2016 (UAA) (Canada), 32, 47, 336
Uniform International Commercial Mediation Act 2005 (UICMA) (Canada), 30, 41
Uniform Law Conference of Canada (ULCC), 56
Uniform Mediation Act 2001 (UMA) (USA), 30

United Kingdom, 150, 372
  agreements to negotiate/mediate uncertainty and unenforceability, 298–304
  applicable law, 311–313
  arb-med-arb, 15
  (un)certainty of agreements
    Holloway v Chancery Mead Ltd, 300
    Sulamerica CIA Nacional De Seguros SA v Enesa Engenharia SA, 302–303
    Wah (aka Alan Tang) v Grant Thornton International Ltd, 300–301
  discrimination-based complaints, 252–254
    litigation, 254
    mediation, 254
  (un)enforceability of agreements, 298
    Cable & Wireless plc v IBM United Kingdom Ltd, 299–300
    Emirates Trading Agency LLC v Prime Mineral Exports Private Ltd, 303
    Ohpen Operations UK Ltd v Invesco Fund Managers Ltd, 304–306
    Petromec Inc v Petroleo Brasileiro SA Petrobras, 301
    strictness of criteria, 313–314
    Walford v Miles, 298–299
  Equality and Human Rights Commission, 252–254
  escalation clauses, 294–298
    internal escalation, 304–305
    Mediation Directive, **374**
    Ohpen Operations UK Ltd v Invesco Fund Managers Ltd
      internal escalation, 304–305
      jurisdiction, 305
  United Nations Convention on International Settlement Agreements Resulting from Mediation. *See* Singapore Convention 2019

INDEX

United Nations Convention on the Recognition and Enforcement of Foreign Arbitral Awards. *See* New York Convention 1958
United States, 149
  ambivalence towards MDR, 15, 279–280, 290–292
  arbitrability
    BG Group plc v Republic of Argentina, 289
    Chorley Enters v Dickey's Barbecue Restaurants Inc, 289
    John Wiley & Sons Inc v Livingston, 286–287
    Kemiron Atlantic Inc v Aguakem International Inc, 286
    responsibilities of courts and arbitrators, 287–288
  arbitration, 273–274
  cultural constraints on implementation of MDR, 22–23
  discrimination-based complaints
    litigation, 256–257
    mediation, 254–256
  enforcement concerns, 280, 281–282
    judicial remedies for non-compliance, 283–285
    refusal to participate in contractually-mandated mediation, 286–290
  Equal Employment Opportunity Commission, 254–257
  functionality of the multi-tier dispute resolution system, 290–292
  International Institute for Conflict Prevention and Resolution, 273
  med-arb, 276–277
  mediation, 15–16, 273, 277–278
  mediation and litigation relationship between, 134–135, 274
  multi-step 'funneling' mechanism, 275–277
  negotiation, 277
  non-compliance with valid MDR agreements, 17
  Quiet Revolution, 271–274
  tailored dispute resolution, 278–279

vexatious claims. *See* frivolous, vexatious, misconceived or lacking in substance claims
voluntary mediation, 117, 236, 334, 425

Western individualism, 22–23, 53–54
wise counsel mediation, 366